AI IN eHEALTH

The emergence of digital platforms and the new application economy are transforming healthcare and creating new opportunities and risks for all stakeholders in the medical ecosystem. Many of these developments rely heavily on data and AI algorithms to prevent, diagnose, treat, and monitor diseases and other health conditions. A broad range of medical, ethical and legal knowledge is now required to navigate this highly complex and fast-changing space. This collection brings together scholars from medicine and law, but also ethics, management, philosophy and computer science, to examine current and future technological, policy and regulatory issues. In particular, the book addresses the challenge of integrating data protection and privacy concerns into the design of emerging healthcare products and services. With a number of comparative case studies, the book offers a high-level, global and interdisciplinary perspective on the normative and policy dilemmas raised by the proliferation of information technologies in a healthcare context.

MARCELO CORRALES COMPAGNUCCI is Associate Professor of Information Technology Law at the Centre for Advanced Studies in Biomedical Innovation Law, Faculty of Law, University of Copenhagen, Denmark.

MICHAEL LOWERY WILSON is Associate Professor of Injury Epidemiology and Prevention at the Faculty of Medicine, University of Turku, Finland.

MARK FENWICK is Professor of International Business Law at the Graduate School of Law, Kyushu University, Japan.

NIKOLAUS FORGÓ is Professor of IT and IP Law at the Department of Innovation and Digitalisation in Law, Faculty of Law, University of Vienna, Austria.

TILL BÄRNIGHAUSEN is Professor in Epidemiology at the Heidelberg Institute of Global Health, Germany.

CAMBRIDGE BIOETHICS AND LAW

This series of books - formerly called Cambridge Law, Medicine and Ethics - was founded by Cambridge University Press with Alexander McCall Smith as its first editor in 2003. It focuses on the law's complex and troubled relationship with medicine across both the developed and the developing world. In the past twenty years, we have seen in many countries increasing resort to the courts by dissatisfied patients and a growing use of the courts to attempt to resolve intractable ethical dilemmas. At the same time, legislatures across the world have struggled to address the questions posed by both the successes and the failures of modern medicine, while international organisations such as the WHO and UNESCO now regularly address issues of medical law. It follows that we would expect ethical and policy questions to be integral to the analysis of the legal issues discussed in this series. The series responds to the high profile of medical law in universities, in legal and medical practice, as well as in public and political affairs. We seek to reflect the evidence that many major health-related policy and bioethics debates in the UK, Europe and the international community over the past two decades have involved a strong medical law dimension. With that in mind, we seek to address how legal analysis might have a trans-jurisdictional and international relevance. Organ retention, embryonic stem cell research, physician-assisted suicide and the allocation of resources to fund health care are but a few examples among many. The emphasis of this series is thus on matters of public concern and/or practical significance. We look for books that could make a difference to the development of medical law and enhance the role of medico-legal debate in policy circles. That is not to say that we lack interest in the important theoretical dimensions of the subject, but we aim to ensure that theoretical debate is grounded in the realities of how the law does and should interact with medicine and health care.

A list of books in the series can be found at the end of this volume.

AI IN eHEALTH

Human Autonomy, Data Governance and Privacy in Healthcare

Edited by

MARCELO CORRALES COMPAGNUCCI
University of Copenhagen

MICHAEL LOWERY WILSON
University of Turku

MARK FENWICK
Kyushu University

NIKOLAUS FORGÓ
University of Vienna

TILL BÄRNIGHAUSEN
Heidelberg University

CAMBRIDGE
UNIVERSITY PRESS

CAMBRIDGE
UNIVERSITY PRESS

University Printing House, Cambridge CB2 8BS, United Kingdom

One Liberty Plaza, 20th Floor, New York, NY 10006, USA

477 Williamstown Road, Port Melbourne, VIC 3207, Australia

314–321, 3rd Floor, Plot 3, Splendor Forum, Jasola District Centre, New Delhi – 110025, India

103 Penang Road, #05–06/07, Visioncrest Commercial, Singapore 238467

Cambridge University Press is part of the University of Cambridge.

It furthers the University's mission by disseminating knowledge in the pursuit of education, learning, and research at the highest international levels of excellence.

www.cambridge.org
Information on this title: www.cambridge.org/9781108830966
DOI: 10.1017/9781108921923

First published 2022

A catalogue record for this publication is available from the British Library.

Library of Congress Cataloging-in-Publication Data
Names: Corrales Compagnucci, Marcelo, 1978– editor.
Title: AI in eHealth : human autonomy, data governance and privacy in healthcare / Marcelo Corrales Compagnucci, Centre for Advanced Studies in Biomedical Innovation Law (CeBIL), Faculty of Law, University of Copenhagen (Copenhagen, Denmark); Mark Fenwick, Graduate School of Law, Kyushu University (Fukuoka, Japan); Michael Lowery Wilson, Injury Epidemiology and Prevention (IEP), Turku Brain Injury Centre, Division of Clinical Neurosciences, Turku University Hospital and University of Turku (Turku, Finland); Nikolaus Forgó, Department of Innovation and Digitalisation in Law, University of Vienna (Vienna, Austria); Till Bärnighausen, Department of Global Health and Population, Harvard T.H. Chan School of Public Health (Boston, USA), Heidelberg Institute of Global Health, Universitäts Klinikum (Heidelberg, Germany).
Other titles: Artificial intelligence in eHealth
Description: Cambridge, United Kingdom ; New York, NY : Cambridge University Press, 2022. | Series: Cambridge bioethics and law | ECIP acknowledgements. | Includes bibliographical references and index.
Identifiers: LCCN 2021063026 | ISBN 9781108830966 (hardback) | ISBN 9781108921923 (ebook)
Subjects: LCSH: Medical informatics – Law and legislation. | Artificial intelligence – Law and legislation.
Classification: LCC K3611.R43 A75 2022 | DDC 344.03/21–dc23/eng/20220531
LC record available at https://lccn.loc.gov/2021063026

ISBN 978-1-108-83096-6 Hardback

CONTENTS

CONTRIBUTORS

TILL BÄRNIGHAUSEN Department of Global Health and Population, Harvard T. H. Chan School of Public Health (Boston, USA); Heidelberg Institute of Global Health, Heidelberg University (Heidelberg, Germany).

KAREN L. CELEDONIA Injury Epidemiology and Prevention, Turku Brain Injury Centre, Division of Clinical Neurosciences, Turku University Hospital and University of Turku (Turku, Finland).

MARCELO CORRALES COMPAGNUCCI Centre for Advanced Studies in Biomedical Innovation Law, Faculty of Law, University of Copenhagen (Copenhagen, Denmark).

DENA DERVANOVIĆ Gernandt & Danielsson (Stockholm, Sweden).

MARK FENWICK Graduate School of Law, Kyushu University (Fukuoka, Japan).

NIKOLAUS FORGÓ Department of Innovation and Digitalisation in Law, University of Vienna (Vienna, Austria).

HELENA HAAPIO School of Accounting and Finance, Business Law, University of Vaasa (Vaasa, Finland); Faculty of Law, University of Lapland (Rovaniemi, Finland); and Lexpert Ltd (Helsinki, Finland).

SHAWN H. E. HARMON IWK Health Centre and Dalhousie University (Halifax, Canada).

THOMAS HOEREN Faculty of Law, Münster University (Münster, Germany).

ANANT JANI Oxford Martin School, University of Oxford (Oxford, UK); Heidelberg Institute of Global Health, Heidelberg University (Heidelberg, Germany).

YKI KORTESNIEMI Department of Communications and Networking, School of Electrical Engineering, Aalto University (Espoo, Finland).

AUDREY LEBRET Centre for Advanced Studies in Biomedical Innovation Law, Faculty of Law, University of Copenhagen (Copenhagen, Denmark); Paris Human Rights Center, Faculty of Law, University Panthéon-Assas (Paris, France).

MICHAEL LOWERY WILSON Injury Epidemiology and Prevention, Turku Brain Injury Centre, Division of Clinical Neurosciences, Turku University Hospital and University of Turku (Turku, Finland).

JAN D. LÜTTRINGHAUS Faculty of Law, House of Insurance, Leibniz University Hannover (Hannover, Germany).

JANOS MESZAROS Centre for IT & IP Law, Faculty of Law, Katholieke Universiteit Leuven (Leuven, Belgium).

TIMO MINSSEN Centre for Advanced Studies in Biomedical Innovation Law, Faculty of Law, University of Copenhagen (Copenhagen, Denmark).

MAURICE NIEHOFF Faculty of Law, Münster University (Münster, Germany).

PÄIVI PÖYRY-LASSILA Department of Management Studies, School of Business, Aalto University (Espoo, Finland).

MAXIMILIAN SCHUESSLER Heidelberg Institute of Global Health, Medical Faculty of Heidelberg University (Heidelberg, Germany).

MARC STAUCH Institute for Legal Informatics, Leibniz University Hannover (Hannover, Germany).

SHINTO TERAMOTO Graduate School of Law, Kyushu University (Fukuoka, Japan).

EVA THELISSON AI Transparency Institute (Lausanne, Switzerland).

ERIK P. M. VERMEULEN Department of Business Law, Tilburg Law School, Tilburg University; Signify (formerly Philips Lighting) (Eindhoven, The Netherlands).

MARIE-CATHERINE WAGNER Department of Innovation and Digitalisation in Law, University of Vienna (Vienna, Austria).

PREFACE

This edited collection is part of the *Cambridge Bioethics and Law* series with Graeme Laurie and Richard Ashcroft as General Editors (formerly called *Cambridge Law, Medicine and Ethics* and founded by Cambridge University Press with Alexander McCall Smith as its first editor in 2003). The aim of the series is to offer comprehensive analyses in complex areas of law and ethical issues in medicine from a global perspective.

This volume brings together a series of contributions by leading scholars from different disciplines and diverse nationalities to examine the technical features that are driving the development of artificial intelligence (AI) in a medical context, as well as the efficacy of the current regulatory responses. As such, this book offers a high-level, comparative and interdisciplinary view of current debates on AI in eHealth. The book attempts to navigate the contours of the highly complex ethical dilemmas and legal challenges raised by these disruptive technologies with the aim of designing sound and practical proposals for policy reforms.

The unique selling point of this collection is the international and multidisciplinary background of its contributors. The disciplines represented include medicine and law, but also ethics, management, philosophy and computer science. The chapters are tied together by a focus on bringing all these disciplines and their associated policy proposals into better alignment and deepening our understanding of the various regulatory responses to these game-changing technological, economic, legal and social developments.

The book contains several comparative studies emphasizing local, national or regional initiatives (legislation, guidelines, policy initiatives, public or private projects) that connect with the chapter topics. Most notably, some of these approaches examine to what extent the General Data Protection Regulation has exerted a global influence in this field, but also covers other areas of law and ethics.

This volume constitutes the result of a joint co-operative effort drawing on the extensive global network of five academic institutions: the Centre for Advanced Studies in Biomedical Innovation Law, part of the Law Faculty of the University of Copenhagen (Copenhagen, Denmark); the Turku Brain Injury Centre in the Department of Clinical Neurosciences at the University of Turku in Finland (Turku, Finland); the Graduate School of Law of Kyushu University (Fukuoka, Japan); the Department of Innovation and Digitalization of Law at the University of Vienna (Vienna, Austria); and the Heidelberg Institute of Global Health in the Faculty of Medicine at Heidelberg University (Heidelberg, Germany).

The book is designed for anyone interested in an up-to-date analysis of current trends related to AI in the digital health space. It provides a solid foundation for newcomers to the topic and broadens and deepens the understanding of experts in the field. With the rise of new AI technology tools and methods, this book will provide an invaluable resource for a wide audience. Obviously, this is a fast-moving space, and the book considers developments until August 2021.

There are three different target groups. The first group belongs to the international legal community in different jurisdictions in the EU, USA, and Asia – particularly, legal scholars and practitioners in the field of medical law. The second group are researchers of the healthcare sector – particularly professional physicians and biotechnologists who deal with patients' personal and sensitive data on a daily basis within their hospitals and clinical research centres. Finally, the book will also serve as an important reference for computer scientists and software developers who design AI wearables and applications for the healthcare industry.

This book was supported by a Novo Nordisk Foundation grant for a scientifically independent Collaborative Research Program in Biomedical Innovation Law (grant agreement number NNF17SA0027784) and by the Alexander von Humboldt-Stiftung, Bonn, Germany. The editors would like to thank Professor Timo Minssen, Managing Director of CeBIL, for his continued support in this project and Nicolai Stig Hallander Hansen for his invaluable editorial assistance. The editors are also indebted to the authors and co-authors of each chapter for their hard work, patience and cooperation throughout the whole process from initial concept to the final manuscript. Finally, the editors are grateful to Joe C. H. Ng (acquisitions editor) and the Cambridge University Press staff for their support and efforts in ensuring final and timely publication.

ACRONYMS

AI	Artificial Intelligence
AI-RIH	AI Readiness Index for Hospitals
AM	Automated Mathematician
APA	American Psychiatric Association
BDSG-New	Federal Data Protection Act (Germany)
BGH	Federal Supreme Court (Germany)
CAD	Computer Aided Diagnosis
CADRIS	Health Canada's Adverse Drug Reaction Reporting System
CAHAI	Ad Hoc Committee on Artificial Intelligence
CCPA	California Consumer Privacy Act
CDL	Customer Dominant Logic
CDS	Clinical Decision Support
CEDAW	Convention on the Elimination of All Forms of Discrimination against Women
CEO	Chief Executive Officer
CESCR	UN Committee on Economic, Social and Cultural Rights
CFR	Charter of Fundamental Rights
CJEU	Court of Justice of the EU
CSR	Corporate Social Responsibility
DFKI	German Research Centre for Artificial Intelligence
DNA	Deoxyribonucleic Acid
DTC	Direct-to-Consumer
ECG	Electrocardiogram
ECHR	European Convention on Human Rights
ECtHR	European Court of Human Rights
EDPB	European Data Protection Board
EEA	European Economic Area
EHRs	Electronic Health Records
EHS	European Hospital Survey
EMRAM	Electronic Medical Record Adoption Model
EPHI	Electronic Protected Health Information
ESC	European Social Charter
EU	European Union

FAQ	Frequently Asked Questions
FDA	US Food and Drug Administration
FHIR	Fast Healthcare Interoperability Resources
GDPR	General Data Protection Regulation
GP	General Practitioner
GPT	General Purpose Technology
GPAI	Global Partnership on AI
GPD	Gross Domestic Product
HICs	High-Income Counties
HIMSS	Healthcare Information and Management Systems Society
HIPAA	Health Insurance Portability and Accountability Act of 1996
HIT	Health Information Technology
HIV	Human Immunodeficiency Virus
HL7	Health Level 7
IACCM	International Association for Contract and Commercial Management
ICESCR	International Covenant on Economic, Social and Cultural Rights
ICO	Information Commissioner's Office
ICT	Information and Communication Technology
IES	Ingestible Electronic Sensors
IFs	Incidental Findings
IoT	Internet of Things
IPAI	International Panel on Artificial Intelligence
ISO	International Organization for Standardization
IT	Information Technology
IVDR	In Vitro Diagnostic Medical Devices
LIME	Local Interpretable Model-Agnostic Explanations
LMICs	Low- and Middle-Income Countries
LRP	Layer-Wise Relevance Propagation
MIT	Massachusetts Institute of Technology
ML	Machine Learning
NASSS	Non-adoption, Abandonment, Scale-up, Spread, Sustainability
NFC	National Forensic Centre
NGO	Non-Governmental Organization
NHS	UK's National Health Service
NPfIT	National Programme for IT
NSPC	Nova Scotia Privacy Commissioner
NUTS	EU's Nomenclature of Territorial Units for Statistics
O2O	Online-to-Online
OAS	Organization of American States
OECD	Organisation for Economic Co-operation and Development
OHCHR	Office of UN High Commissioner for Human Rights
OLG	Higher Regional Court (Germany)

PHI	Protected Health Information
PHIA	Personal Health Information Act
PHR	Personal Healthcare Records
PI	Personal Information
PIIDPA	Personal Information International Disclosure Protection Act
PIPEDA	Personal Information Protection and Electronic Documents Act (Canada)
PPC	Privacy Commissioner of Canada
PPH	Precision Public Health
R&D	Research and Experimental Development
REB	Research Ethics Board
SAPP	Swedish Authority for Privacy Protection (Sw. *Integritetsskyddsmyndigheten*)
SCCs	Standard Contractual Clauses
SDGs	UN Sustainable Development Goals 2030
SLO	Social Licence to Operate
SMI	Serious Mental Illness
SNPs	Single Nucleotide Polymorphisms
STRs	Short Tandem Repeats
TFEU	Treaty on the Functioning of the European Union
UHC	Universal Health Coverage
UI	User Interface
UN	United Nations
UNESCO	United Nations Educational, Scientific and Cultural Organization
US	United States
USD	United States Dollar
WEF	World Economic Forum
WFO	Watson for Oncology
WHO	World Health Organization
WorldCC	World Commerce & Contracting
WP29	Article 29 Working Party
XaaS	Everything-as-a-Service

1

Mapping the Digital Healthcare Revolution

MARCELO CORRALES COMPAGNUCCI, MARK FENWICK, MICHAEL LOWERY WILSON, NIKOLAUS FORGÓ, AND TILL BÄRNIGHAUSEN

1.1 Introduction

Digital technologies are disrupting healthcare and creating new opportunities and risks for all actors in the medical ecosystem. Moreover, many of these developments rely heavily on data and artificial intelligence (AI) algorithms to prevent, diagnose, treat, and monitor sources of epidemic diseases, such as the ongoing COVID-19 pandemic and other pathogenic outbreaks. However, these opportunities and risks have a complex character involving multiple dimensions (notably legal, ethical, technical, and governance), and any mapping and navigation of this new space requires an appreciation of the complexity of these issues and multidisciplinary dialogue.

This introductory chapter briefly outlines the main theme of this volume, namely, to review the new opportunities and risks of digital healthcare from various disciplinary perspectives – specifically law, public policy, organisational studies, and applied ethics. Based on this interdisciplinary approach, we hope that effective strategies to ensure that the benefits of this ongoing revolution are deployed in a responsible and sustainable way can be developed. Section 1.3 consists of an overview of the four constituent parts and other substantive chapters that comprise this volume.

1.2 Challenges and Strategies of AI in Digital Healthcare

In recent years, there has been an increasing awareness of the vital role that AI plays in various domains of economic and social life to resolve multiple issues. By way of a provisional definition, AI aims at simulating human intelligence (e.g., by planning, strategising, and making advanced decisions).[1] Particularly significant in this regard, AI systems are being developed to analyse the massive amounts of medical and genetic data, understand human conditions, recognise disease patterns, make highly accurate diagnoses, and deliver precision health interventions at scale.[2] There are several kinds of AI tools and techniques currently being utilised across a number of settings including hospitals, clinical laboratories, and research facilities.[3] For this reason, AI is widely predicted to provide the foundations for the 'next Industrial Revolution' and provide the driving force that will disrupt how healthcare is delivered and experienced in the future.[4]

Digital health can be understood as the convergence of digital technologies with health, healthcare, living, and society to enhance the efficiency of healthcare delivery and make medicine more personalised and effective. The broad scope of digital health includes categories such as mobile health, health information technology, wearable devices, telehealth and telemedicine, and personalised medicine. These technologies can empower patient-consumers to make better-informed decisions about their own health and provide new options for facilitating prevention, early diagnosis of life-threatening diseases, and management of chronic conditions outside traditional care settings.[5]

A lot of developments fall within the scope of this definition. From mobile medical apps and software that support the clinical decisions doctors make every day, to AI and machine learning, digital technology is driving a revolution in healthcare. Digital health tools have the potential to improve our ability to accurately diagnose and treat disease and to enhance the delivery of healthcare for the individual. Digital tools are also offering healthcare providers a more holistic view of patient health through access to data and giving patients more control over their health. Digital health offers genuine opportunities to improve medical outcomes and enhance efficiency.

[1] G Yang, 'Office Operating Problem Scoring System Based on AI', in Yang H (ed.), *Artificial Intelligence: Science and Technology*, Proceedings of the 2016 International Conference (AIST 2016) (World Scientific 2017), 21.

[2] A Agah, *Medical Applications of Artificial Intelligence* (CRC Press 2014).

[3] A Panesar, *Machine Learning and AI for Healthcare: Big Data for Improved Health Outcomes* (Apress 2019).

[4] P Jayanthi et al., 'Fourth Industrial Revolution: An Impact on Healthcare Industry', in Ahram T (ed.), *Advances in Artificial Intelligence, Software and Systems Engineering* (Springer 2019), 58.

[5] L Afinito, *Empowering the Connected Physician in the E-Patient Era: How Physicians Empowerment on Digital Health Tools Can Improve Patient Empowerment and Boost Health(Care) Outcomes* (Routledge 2019).

At the level of populations, more granular data and new technologies have driven the growth of what is now called precision public health (PPH), providing governments and private companies with new mechanisms for offering more effective interventions. Again, PPH is intimately connected with developments in AI as it leverages data and predictive analytics to identify health risks, detect diseases more rapidly, and design interventions for subpopulations that reach the appropriate target audience.[6] PPH also holds out the tantalising possibility of more effective prevention and individualised interventions at lower costs and delivering better healthcare to individuals in low-income environments who lack insurance or access to facility-based healthcare.[7] PPH begs the questions how individual-focused care approaches can be reconciled with benefits on a population scale – in a manner that respects the individual, ensures privacy, and increases, rather than decreases, autonomy and choice.[8] As in other domains of healthcare, this requires a combination of ethical principles, multifaceted regulatory framework, and robust governance structures.

While opening a world of new opportunities, however, rapid advances in AI have been compared to a 'black box', potentially unleashing several serious ethical dilemmas and raising uncertainty about the current legal framework on privacy and data protection. It has been argued that AI systems, for example, may run afoul of the consent of data subjects, as such systems often collect, process, and transfer sensitive personal data in unexpected ways without the necessary means of giving adequate notice, choice, and explaining options in a timely manner.[9]

Despite promising results, the application of AI in medical devices must still confront technological, legal, and ethical issues.[10] A serious limitation lies in the lack of interoperability and standardisation among medical IT systems,[11] and healthcare provision often involves complex judgements

6 A Dunn et al., 'Social Media Interventions for Precision Public Health: Promises and Risks' (2018) 1 *NPJ Digital Medicine* 47.

7 S Dolley, 'Big Data's Role in Precision Public Health' March (2018) 6, Article 68 *Frontiers in Public Health.*

8 M Prosperi, 'Big Data Hurdles in Precision Medicine and Precision Public Health' (2018) 18 *BMC Medical Informatics and Decision Making*, 139.

9 W Barfield and U Pagallo (eds.), *Research Handbook on the Law of Artificial Intelligence* (Edward Elgar Publishing 2018), 280–385.

10 S Gerke, S Young, and G Cohen, 'Ethical and Legal Aspects of Ambient Intelligence in Hospitals' (2020) *JAMA* (24 January).

11 G Brindha, 'A New Approach for Changes in Health Care' (2012) 12(12) *Middle-East Journal of Scientific Research*, 1657–1662.

and abilities that AI is currently unable to replicate, such as the ability to read social cues.[12] Since AI medical devices can err, reliability and safety are crucial issues, particularly in the early stages of development when awareness of knowledge of likely problems is much less developed.[13]

As such, these complex technological developments raise several important and difficult questions. What impact will AI systems have on biomedical and automated scientific research, especially on data sharing and confidentiality? What kind of control over personal data should be adjudicated to patients? How can we ensure that AI-based methods and solutions adhere to general legal and ethical principles? And how will these technological advancements in the MedTech industry be affected by different legal frameworks? Which regulatory, ethical, and legal principles should guide the design of precision public health interventions and the implementation of precision medicine?

Regulators and other policymakers are reacting to these technological and professional issues with several important initiatives. The General Data Protection Regulation (GDPR) has tried to adequately respond to some of these challenges, for example by its rule on automated decision-making. A striking feature of the GDPR is its potentially global reach, and this might have prompted legislators to carry out reforms in other jurisdictions outside the European Union (EU). However, many uncertainties and lingering questions still remain regarding the scope, direction, and effects of the impact of AI in digital healthcare systems and personalised medicine. For instance, a serious problem of the GDPR is that the regulation, due to the high level of abstraction it adopts, is not capable of adequately differentiating between different applications of AI in a medical context. Addressing the many challenges generated by AI, therefore, requires going beyond any one disciplinary perspective or frame of reference. This means that we need a more seamlessly integrated or interdisciplinary approach as there are still multiple concerns to be resolved.

It is instructive in this regard to focus on the GDPR as an example. There are several provisions within the GDPR that allow for the processing of

[12] M Louwerse et al., 'Social Cues in Animated Conversational Agents' (2005) 19(6) *Applied Cognitive Psychology: The Official Journal of the Society for Applied Research in Memory and Cognition*, 693–704.

[13] RM Wachter, 'Why Diagnostic Errors Don't Get Any Respect and What Can Be Done about Them' (2017) 29(9) *Health Affairs*, https://doi.org/10.1377/hlthaff.2009.0513, accessed 27 July 2021.

health data for scientific research to, for example, inform population health decision-making. On 21 April 2020, the European Data Protection Board (EDPB) published its Guidelines 03/2020 on the processing of data concerning health for the purpose of scientific research in the context of the COVID-19 outbreak.[14] The EDPB guidelines support research and data-sharing under the appropriate legal framework. For example, data that is transmitted by devices and applications should include both unique and pseudonymous identifiers. These identifiers should be generated by the application and be specific to it. They also have to be renewed on a regular basis at intervals that are compatible with the goals of containing the virus spread. These aspects should also be done in a manner that allows for a reduction in the risk of identification or tracking of individual persons. However, even in these cases, the EDPB states that any data processing must be transparent, and that the data should be processed with sufficient privacy safeguards in place and not shared with third parties without prior authorisation.

Another important strategy pursued by the EU has been the release of guidelines to encourage the development of trustworthy and more ethical AI.[15] The Ethics Guidelines for Trustworthy AI were published on 8 April 2019 by the High-Level Expert Group on AI, and they received more than 500 comments after open consultation.[16] Although not legally binding, they address some of the diffuse problems that AI will bring to society as we integrate it in sectors such as healthcare, education, and consumer technology. The Guidelines focus on how governments, companies, and other organisations need to develop ethical applications of AI. According to the Guidelines, AI systems should be accountable, explainable, and unbiased. To help achieve this goal, the EU recommends using an assessment list of seven fundamental areas that AI systems should meet in order to be deemed trustworthy. Among these requirements, human autonomy, privacy, and data governance are at the core. Personal data collected by AI systems should be lawful, secure, resilient, reliable, robust,

[14] Guidelines 03/2020 on the processing of data concerning health for the purpose of scientific research in the context of COVID-19, https://edpb.europa.eu/our-work-tools/our-documents/ohjeet/guidelines-032020-processing-data-concerning-health-purpose_en, accessed 20 July 2021.

[15] European Commission, Ethics Guidelines for Trustworthy AI, https://ec.europa.eu/digital-single-market/en/news/ethics-guidelines-trustworthy-ai, accessed 27 July 2021.

[16] European Commission, Shaping Europe's Digital Future, Ethics Guidelines for Trustworthy AI, Report Study, https://digital-strategy.ec.europa.eu/en/library/ethics-guidelines-trustworthy-ai, accessed 27 July 2021.

and private. The Guidelines also underscore the importance of 'transparency'. Data and algorithms used to create AI systems should be accessible and traceability should be ensured. Similar guidelines can be found in other jurisdictions, and the use of guidelines is a striking feature of the contemporary regulatory landscape regarding AI.

More traditional legal forms are still relevant. On 21 April 2021, the European Commission released its draft regulation governing the use of AI. The proposed AI regulation follows a risk-based approach, with different categories of AI system uses such as prohibited, high-risk, limited, and minimal risk.[17] Prohibited AI systems are those that contravene union values (e.g., by violating fundamental rights) and are considered unacceptable. The high-risk category will be subject to stricter regulatory requirements before and after releasing the product to the market (e.g., ensuring the quality of data sets used to train the algorithm, applying a level of human agency and oversight, providing relevant information to users, etc.). Nevertheless, makers of limited or minimal risk (e.g., where there is a risk of manipulation, for example via the use of chatbots), will be encouraged to adopt non-legally binding codes of conduct.[18]

The GDPR and the above-mentioned AI draft regulation/guidelines are just a few examples that have, inevitably given the importance of the EU, received a lot of media and academic attention, but policy initiatives are occurring across the globe. Several other international organisations have published guidance on AI such as the Organisation for Economic Co-operation and Development (OECD) Council Recommendation on Artificial Intelligence,[19] which promotes AI that is innovative and trustworthy and that respects human rights and democratic values. The OECD Council Recommendation on AI is the first of such principles signed up to by governments not part of the OECD such as Argentina, Brazil, Costa Rica, Peru, Malta, Romania, and Ukraine. Another example is the recently published World Health Organization (WHO) guidance on the Ethics and Governance of AI for Health.[20] This guidance is based on six principles:

[17] At the time of writing, the EU Member States have not yet adopted the proposed AI Regulations.

[18] Julia Wilson, New Draft Rules on the Use of Artificial Intelligence (14 May 2021), www.bakermckenzie.com/en/insight/publications/2021/05/new-draft-rules-on-the-use-of-ai, accessed 27 July 2021.

[19] OECD Recommendation of the Council on Artificial Intelligence, adopted in May 2019 by the OECD, https://legalinstruments.oecd.org/en/instruments/OECD-LEGAL-0449, accessed 6 December 2021.

[20] Ethics and Governance of Artificial Intelligence for Health, WHO Guidance (28 June 2021), www.who.int/publications/i/item/9789240029200, accessed 27 July 2021.

protecting human autonomy; promoting human well-being and safety and the public interest; ensuring transparency, explainability, and intelligibility; fostering responsibility and accountability; ensuring inclusiveness and equity; promoting AI that is responsive and sustainable. This is clearly a fast-moving space, but the basis for future regulation has already started to emerge, and disseminating information and subjecting these developments to rigorous review seems important, as initiatives taken now seem likely to structure debate and regulatory responses for the foreseeable future.

1.3 Argumentation and Structure

This edited collection brings together a series of contributions by leading scholars from different disciplines and diverse nationalities to examine the technical features that are driving the development of AI in medical contexts, as well as the efficacy of the current regulatory responses. As such, this book offers a high-level, global, and interdisciplinary perspective on current debates on AI in eHealth. The book attempts to navigate the contours of the highly complex ethical dilemmas and legal challenges raised by these disruptive technologies with the aim of designing practical proposals.

The unique selling point of this collection is the international and multidisciplinary background of its contributors. Represented disciplines include medicine and law, but also management, philosophy, and computer science. The chapters are tied together by a focus on bringing all these disciplines and their associated policy proposals into better alignment and deepening our understanding of the various responses to these game-changing technological, economic, legislative, and social developments.

The book comprises fourteen thematic chapters divided into four main parts (Part I 'Platforms, Apps and Digital Health'; Part II 'Trust and Design'; Part III 'Knowledge, Risk and Control'; Part IV 'Balancing Regulation, Innovation and Ethics'). Each part focuses on different technical, legal, and ethical processes and outcomes, providing stimulation for beginners and experts, academia, and business. It is our hope that this collection illustrates the art of emerging possibilities across the many levels and dimensions that lie at the interface between AI and eHealth.

1.3.1 Part I: Platforms, Apps and Digital Health

The three chapters in Part I explore the impact of software applications – often developed by companies with software, rather than medical expertise in the digital healthcare space.

Chapter 2, 'Technology-Driven Disruption of Healthcare & UI Layer Privacy-by-Design' by Marcelo Corrales Compagnucci, Mark Fenwick, Helena Haapio, Timo Minssen and Erik P. M. Vermeulen describes how the use of digital technologies in healthcare is changing how medical treatments are developed by researchers, practised by medical professionals, and experienced by patients. The chapter argues that a defining feature of this disruption is the emergence of new medical 'apps' that leverage algorithm-based AI systems. As the use of such apps and AI wearables goes mainstream and new players – notably 'Super Platforms' with digital rather than a medical expertise – enter the healthcare sector, the traditional means of providing medical services are further disrupted.

These developments pose several challenges for regulators and other policymakers, most obviously, in the areas of privacy and data protection. The chapter describes how the emerging field of Legal Design can provide a more transparent and accessible infrastructure that embeds relevant legal protections in the user interfaces of healthcare products and services. This user interface focused Privacy-by-Design approach offers multiple advantages, most obviously greater transparency, accountability, and choice. The chapter offers several real-world examples of design patterns that illustrate the value of UI focused Privacy-by-Design in protecting individuals' sensitive information, enabling people to make choices and retain control of their personal data. The chapter concludes by reflecting on the challenges specific to implementing Legal Design in an eHealth context.

In Chapter 3, 'Social Media Platforms as Public Health Arbiters: Global Ethical Considerations on Privacy, Legal and Cultural Issues Associated with Suicide Detection Algorithms', by Karen L. Celedonia, Michael Lowery Wilson and Marcelo Corrales Compagnucci, the authors discuss the issue of the responsibility of social media firms for medical issues. The development of Facebook's suicide prevention algorithm has prompted discussion around whether social media platforms have a role to play in public health surveillance. Concerns have been raised about an entity that is not a public interest health authority collecting and acting on the private health information of its users, particularly when it involves personally sensitive data, such as an individual's mental health status. Mental illnesses are still heavily stigmatised, despite continued efforts to normalise these conditions. Depending on a user's geographic location, the ramifications of the suicide detection algorithm generating 'false positives' for suicide risk could have severe repercussions. This chapter seeks to stimulate further debates on this question by examining the ethical implications of Facebook's suicide prevention algorithm from diverse perspectives.

In Chapter 4, 'Promoting the Use of PHR by Citizens and Physicians – Proposed Design for a Token to be Allocated to Citizens', Shinto Teramoto focuses on health records. The digitalised medical and health records of citizens are stored in the Electronic Health Records (EHR) of hospitals or clinics, and in Personal Healthcare Records (PHR). The quality of medical care is improved if physicians have access to the complete past records of patients. A user-friendly service that enables individual citizens to share their health and medical records in PHR with their physicians is, therefore, essential to achieving this objective. To encourage patients and physicians to share medical records utilising PHR, while avoiding conflict with the recent trend demanding that citizens have autonomous control of their own personal information, governments must develop various legal measures to encourage individual citizens to take the initiative to record their medical and health data in their PHR and to give their physicians access to PHR. The chapter proposes mathematical schemes that might be implemented within the framework of the existing regulatory framework.

1.3.2 Part II: Trust and Design

Part II consists of three chapters looking closely at data protection issues with a particular emphasis on questions of consent and trust.

Chapter 5, 'Privacy Management in eHealth Using Contextual Consenting' by Yki Kortesniemi and Päivi Pöyry-Lassila starts from the fact that sharing one's health data with one's doctor can be an important factor in improving one's own health and sharing data for scientific research can help improve the health of everyone. At the same time, health data is highly confidential, so the sharing process must provide sufficient control over one's privacy. Legally, sharing is often based on consent, which theoretically affords extensive individual control, but in practice often requires the processing of complicated information. Therefore, the way the consenting process is implemented plays a significant role in either hindering or helping the individual. This chapter illustrates the potential of AI-based technologies and explores how an individual's ability to make informed consenting decisions can be simplified by utilising AI-based recommendations with the consent intermediary approach and by making the consenting decisions in the context of utilising the health data thus making individuals more aware of the data they are sharing.

In Chapter 6, 'Artificial Intelligence and Data Protection Law', Thomas Hoeren and Maurice Niehoff describe how the increasing automation of medical decision-making is also accompanied by a range of new problems, in particular the maintenance of the relationship of trust between physicians and patients or the verification of decisions. This is where the patient's right to explanation comes into play, which is enshrined in the GDPR. This chapter explains how the right is derived from the GDPR and how it should be established in the context of automated medical decision-making.

Chapter 7, 'AI Technologies and Accountability in Digital Health' by Eva Thelisson focuses on a similar question, namely, how to build an ecosystem of trust in this new arena of digital health? The availability of large amounts of personal data, from multimodal sources, combined with AI and ML capacities, Internet of Things and strong computational platforms have the potential to transform healthcare systems in a disruptive way. The emergence of personalised medicine offers opportunities and raises new legal, ethical, and societal challenges. A silent transformation towards a data-driven preventive and personalised medicine may improve diagnosis and therapies while reducing the cost of public health policy. In order to build an ecosystem of trust, the risks of harm and misuses such as data breaches, privacy issues, discrimination, eugenics must be addressed. This chapter presents the disruptive nature of AI and ML technologies in healthcare and makes specific recommendations to build a trustworthy digital health system. The chapter first identifies some general parameters to advance the field of digital health in a responsible way, and, secondly, proposes possible solutions to shape a sound policy in digital health taking into consideration a rights-based governance framework.

1.3.3 Part III: Knowledge, Risk and Control

Part III, comprising three chapters, explores various risks that arise as a result of the emergence of new forms of knowledge produced by AI-related analysis of medical data.

Chapter 8, 'The Principle of Transparency in Medical Research: Applying Big Data Analytics to Electronic Health Records' by Nikolaus Forgó and Marie-Catherine Wagner describes how in recent years, the amount of data provided by EHRs worldwide has greatly expanded bringing obvious benefits to diverse stakeholders. The more heath data that is collected, the more can be learned from it and better decisions can be made based on Big Data analysis of that data. This can be seen in projects such as the InteropEHRate project, an EU Horizon 2020 project, which tries to provide models on how health data from EHRs can be made interoperable and available for medical research organisations. However, the processing of personal data in this way might interfere with the fundamental right to data protection or privacy. On a European level, the GDPR treats specific forms of data processing differently, if it is to be expected that those are specifically protected by other, potentially conflicting fundamental rights and freedoms. The GDPR provides privileges for scientific research in some respects and allows additional derogations for Member States. In particular, Art 89 (2) GDPR provides exemptions from data subjects' rights. When health data are analysed on the basis of ML, special attention needs to be paid to the transparency principle, which is a fundamental feature in EU law as – evidently – transparency is both needed and challenged when machines, replacing or supporting humans, take decisions. This chapter provides an analysis of the principle of transparency and its compatibility with Big Data analytics in medical research. Apart from an evaluation of the current European legal framework, including the Council of Europe's Convention 108–, the chapter also examines global initiatives, such as the 'Recommendation on the Protection and Use of Health-Related Data', whose final text was presented by the UN Special Rapporteur for Privacy to the UN General Assembly in October 2019.

Chapter 9, 'The Next Challenge for Data Protection Law: AI Revolution in Automated Scientific Research' by Janos Meszaros proceeds from the observation that although an extensive literature has been published on autonomous vehicles, robotics in healthcare, and the disruption of work by automation, there has been relatively little discussion on how AI might change scientific research itself. AI-assisted scientific research is already providing a significant boost in the process of scientific discovery, particularly in a medical context. Not surprisingly, this radical change in scientific research will have significant consequences. Firstly, if the research process becomes automated, it may be conducted by anyone, which puts citizen science in a new context. As developments in hardware and software made personal computers feasible for individual use, automated research may have a similar effect on science in the future. Secondly, unlike researchers, AI and neural networks cannot explain their thinking yet. As fully automated research extends the potential "black box" of AI even further, this makes the oversight and ethical review more problematic in systems that are opaque to outside scrutiny. Automated research raises many further questions about regulation, safety, funding, and patentability. This chapter focuses on the issues connected with privacy and data protection, from the GDPR point of view.

In Chapter 10, 'A Global Human-Rights Approach to Medical Artificial Intelligence', by Audrey Lebret the focus is on the role of algorithms. The use and development of algorithms in health care, including ML, contributes to the discovery of better treatments for patients and offers promising perspectives in the fight against cancer and other diseases. Yet, algorithms are not a neutral health product since they are programmed by humans, with the risk of propagating human rights infringements and discrimination. In the medical area, human rights impact assessments need to be conducted for applications involving AI. Apart from offering a consistent and transversal substantive approach to AI, human rights law, and in particular the UN guiding principles on business and human rights, would allow the targeting of all stakeholders, including the corporations developing health care algorithms. Such an approach would establish a chain of duties and responsibilities bringing more transparency and consistency in the overall AI development process and later uses. Although this approach may not solve all AI challenges, it could offer a frame for discussion with all relevant actors, including vulnerable populations. An increase in human rights education of medical doctors and data scientists, and further collaboration at the initial stages of the development of algorithms would greatly contribute to the creation of a human rights culture in this fast-developing techno-science space.

1.3.4 Part IV: Balancing Regulation, Innovation and Ethics

Part IV, comprising four chapters, examines the challenges of balancing the different concerns that arise in real world settings, most obviously in hospitals and in physician-patient relations.

In Chapter 11, 'Doctors without Borders? The Law Applicable to Cross-Border eHealth Services and AI-based Medicine', Jan D. Lüttringhaus proceeds from the idea that health applications – including telemedicine, AI-based medicine and smart medical devices – are ubiquitous. Such tools may be used by the physician located next door as well as in the most remote locations abroad. Moreover, highly sensitive medical data may flow around the world within a split second. Against this backdrop, eHealth and telemedicine services can be provided from – and the necessary data can be transferred to – virtually every corner of the world. By contrast, the scope of application of regulation relating to AI-driven medicine as well as eHealth- and telemedicine is usually confined to the legislating state.

Moreover, the number and complexity of rules and regulations in this field varies considerably from state to state. Does this mean that international 'MedTech'-businesses may simply set up camp in the jurisdiction most favourable to their business models? For practitioners in telemedicine, the MedTech-industry providing AI applications or digital medical devices such as eHealth-apps as well as for patients, it is essential to know which law governs activities undertaken in cross-border scenarios: This concerns licensing requirements and the level of data protection as well as contract and tort law applicable to eHealth, telemedicine and telesurgery services.

Chapter 12, 'Barriers to Artificial Intelligence in Hospitals and Arguments for Developing a Hospital-Specific AI Readiness Index' by Maximilian Schuessler, Till Bärnighausen and Anant Jani describes how AI has considerable potential to improve diagnosis and therapy, enhance access to healthcare, and promote population health. Although in its infancy, AI-enabled healthcare is increasingly seen as part of the solutions needed to address the growing gap between the supply and demand of hospital care. AI is well placed to help us tackle new challenges, though these novel applications are likely to render technology implementation even more complex. AI technologies are on the cusp of entering hospitals. Yet, many hospitals within the EU are unprepared for this change. Historically, hospitals have faced multiple challenges when implementing new technologies. This chapter discusses the importance of AI readiness and highlights the benefits and limitations of a new policy tool: an AI Readiness Index for Hospitals (AI-RIH). The authors conceptualise AI readiness from an organisational perspective and discuss the dual functionality of the AI-RIH. For hospital managers, such an index could constitute a benchmarking tool. For policy-makers, national and EU-wide, knowledge about AI readiness and changes therein can help customise targeted technology policies and measure their effectiveness. The chapter also discusses conceptual challenges of indices and illustrates why a hospital index might provide more policy insights than an aggregated or national index. Finally, it explains how AI readiness can strengthen hospitals' role as innovators and support the development and deployment of AI.

Marc Stauch in Chapter 13, 'Regulating the Benefits of eHealth – Information Disclosure Duties in the Age of AI', looks at how much of the legal and ethical attention in the fields of eHealth focuses on the risks of health data processing 'going wrong' – a breach of privacy occurs, data is misused in an unauthorised way, or the analysis of data gives a faulty result. However, significant challenges are also posed by such processing where the data processing 'goes to plan' – the analysis gives the correct result in the way intended. Such challenges stem both from the nature of the information generated, and the new contexts in which this occurs. Thus, Big Data analysis may produce ever more information in relation to a person's future health, usually of a probabilistic nature. In what situations should such information be returned to the subject (bearing in mind also that the decision-maker increasingly will be an entity outside the traditional health care context)? This chapter considers key ethical considerations that arise in such cases, and how well the law – through liability rules for harm, caused by failure to disclose, or by unjustified disclosure – is equipped to respond to these complex situations.

Chapter 14, 'Privacy and Direct-to-Consumer Genetic Tests', by Dena Dervanović examines the growing interest of law enforcement authorities' in using DTC genetic test providers' databases for solving crime. The chapter discusses the legal avenues that were used by the Swedish police authority in their use of GEDmatch to resolve a 16-year-old double murder. It discusses the legal prerequisites for genetic test data access and use as well as embarks on a discussion about the possibility of relying on the derogation of special categories of personal data which are made public by the data subject. The chapter also discusses possible amendments to the existing legal landscape around such data.

In Chapter 15 'Health Research, eHealth and Learning Healthcare Systems: Key Approaches, Shortcomings and Design Issues in Data Governance', Shawn Harmon examines how the pressure to collect more health data and use that data more effectively is mounting as healthcare systems face greater challenges. However, the risks of increasing health data collection and making our health data work harder are myriad. Given that 'good outcomes' in relation to health data usage will be context specific and temporally contingent, the emphasis here is on fit-for-purpose instruments and good practice, acknowledging that health data usage is mediated not only through law, but also through governance structures around data resources themselves. This chapter therefore reviews the Canadian health data ecosystem, examining its federal and provincial legislative elements (with an emphasis on Nova Scotia). It then critiques that ecosystem, bearing in mind the needs of learning healthcare systems. In doing so, it highlights four ecosystem shortcomings, which are grounded in no small part on the perceived competition between private and public interests, and the poor alignment between contemporary data uses and traditional protections associated with autonomy (consent) and privacy (anonymisation). Finally, it offers some key considerations for ecosystem design, addressing specifically social licenses to operate and the value foundation of both legislation and repository governance instruments.

Our primary intention in putting together this collection is to stimulate further debate on the various issues raised and to provide a framework for thinking about effective strategies to ensure that the benefits of this on-going health care revolution are developed in a responsible and sustainable way.

Acknowledgements

The research for this chapter was supported by a Novo Nordisk Foundation grant for a scientifically independent Collaborative Research Program in Biomedical Innovation Law (grant agreement number NNF17SA0027784) and by the Alexander von Humboldt-Stiftung, Bonn, Germany.

Bibliography

Afinito, L, *Empowering the Connected Physician in the E-Patient Era: How Physicians Empowerment on Digital Health Tools Can Improve Patient Empowerment and Boost Health(Care) Outcomes* (Routledge 2019).

Agah, A, *Medical Applications of Artificial Intelligence* (CRC Press 2014).

Barfield, W and Pagallo, U (eds.), *Research Handbook on the Law of Artificial Intelligence* (Edward Elgar Publishing 2018).

Brindha, G, 'A New Approach for Changes in Health Care' (2012) 12(12) *Middle East Journal of Scientific Research*, 1657–62.

Chowkwanyn, M, '"Precision" Public Health – Between Novelty and Hype' (2018) 379(15) *New England Journal of Medicine*.

Dolley, S, 'Big Data's Role in Precision Public Health' (2018) 6, Article 68 *Frontiers in Public Health*.

Dunn, A and others, 'Social Media Interventions for Precision Public Health: Promises and Risks' (2018) 1 *NPJ Digital Medicine*, 47.

Gerke, S, Young, S, and Cohen, G, 'Ethical and Legal Aspects of Ambient Intelligence in Hospitals' (2020) *JAMA*.

Guidelines 03/2020 on the processing of data concerning health for the purpose of scientific research in the context of COVID-19, https://edpb.europa.eu/our-work-tools/our-documents/ohjeet/guidelines-032020-processing-data-concerning-health-purpose_en, accessed 20 January 2021.

Jayanthi, P and others, 'Fourth Industrial Revolution: An Impact on Healthcare Industry', in Tareq Ahram (ed.), *Advances in Artificial Intelligence, Software and Systems Engineering* (Springer 2019) 58.

Louwerse, M and others, 'Social Cues in Animated Conversational Agents', (2005) 19(6) *Applied Cognitive Psychology: The Official Journal of the Society for Applied Research in Memory and Cognition*, 693–704.

Panesar, A, *Machine Learning and AI for Healthcare: Big Data for Improved Health Outcomes* (Apress 2019).

Prosperi, M, 'Big Data Hurdles in Precision Medicine and Precision Public Health'(2018) 18 *BMC Medical Informatics and Decision Making*, 139.

Wachter, R, 'Why Diagnostic Errors Don't Get Any Respect and What Can Be Done about Them' (2017) *Health Affairs*.

Yang, G, 'Office Operating Problem Scoring System Based on AI', in Hui Yang (ed.), *Artificial Intelligence: Science and Technology*, Proceedings of the 2016 International Conference (AIST 2016) (World Scientific 2017).

PART I

Platforms, Apps and Digital Health

2

Technology-Driven Disruption of Healthcare and 'UI Layer' Privacy-by-Design

MARCELO CORRALES COMPAGNUCCI, MARK FENWICK, HELENA HAAPIO, TIMO MINSSEN, AND ERIK P. M. VERMEULEN

2.1 Introduction

The use of digital technologies in healthcare – most obviously in hospitals and research facilities – is changing how medical treatments are developed by researchers, delivered by medical professionals and experienced by patients. Central to this disruption is the use of algorithm-based artificial intelligence (AI) systems to analyse massive amounts of medical data, better understand medical conditions and their causes and make more accurate diagnoses. As the use of mobile apps and medical wearables goes mainstream and the capacities of new technologies further develop, this disruption seems certain to continue. The traditional means of providing medical services will be further transformed as new players – notably Super Platforms with a digital, rather than a medical, expertise (Apple or Tencent, for instance) – enter the healthcare space.

These developments are already influencing the work of medical professionals and researchers. Adapting to this new environment is now crucial for all stakeholders, but such adaptation is not always easy. After all, new technologies create an unprecedented combination of ethical dilemmas and technological challenges, and existing 'best practice' offers little assistance in identifying the way forward. But the ongoing disruption of healthcare also creates several complex legal challenges for regulators and other policymakers. Many of these challenges are a result of the processing of highly personal and sensitive data that are crucial to emerging healthcare models. Finding effective and transparent solutions to these regulatory issues is a key challenge in ensuring public confidence in healthcare providers, both old and new. Moreover, given the importance of medical information to individuals, effectively addressing these policy challenges is crucial in ensuring public confidence in the capacity of governments to navigate the Digital Revolution, more generally.

While opening a new world of possibilities, the application of new digital technologies involves complex issues that create serious doubts and uncertainties about current legal arrangements. Most obviously, there are privacy concerns and the suggestion that the use of such technologies can run counter to the consent of individuals. This is because new forms of healthcare involve the collection, processing and transfer of personal data in unanticipated ways and often without adequate opportunities for truly informed consent.

Everyone seems to agree about the general principles for dealing with these regulatory challenges. Respect for human autonomy and dignity is at the core of all discussion. Personal data collected by data systems should also be secure and commentators also underscore the importance of 'transparency'. Data and algorithms used to create digital systems should be accessible and the traceability of data should be guaranteed. In other words, operators should be able to explain all decisions that computer systems make involving private data. There is a broad consensus that data systems should empower human beings, allowing individuals to make informed decisions and, ultimately, retain full control over their personal information.

However, operationalising these principles has proved much more difficult. In part, this reflects reasonable disagreement as to the appropriate level of regulation and the specific formulation of relevant rights. But difficulties in identifying an appropriate regulatory response also reflect the reality that lawyers and the law do not enjoy a good reputation when it comes to transparency, clarity and the empowerment of 'ordinary' people (i.e. those unfamiliar with the law). There is currently an enormous amount of public mistrust of 'the law' – particularly in a privacy context – and recent scandals involving Facebook have merely fed such concerns. Moreover, legal issues are often confounded with organisational and ethical issues. Any regulatory response must overcome legitimacy concerns before being able to establish credibility amongst the public.

In this chapter, we, therefore, make an argument for a Legal Design-based approach to privacy that we present as an example of Privacy-by-Design. Legal Design is an interdisciplinary approach that utilises human-centred design to prevent or solve legal problems.[1] It prioritises

[1] Legal Design Alliance (LeDA), www.legaldesignalliance.org, accessed 9 August 2021. In addition to preventing and addressing legal problems, Legal Design can be and has been applied to provide positive developments and opportunities in the legal sphere, promote

the point of view of ordinary people as the 'end users' of law, that is, citizens, consumers and business people, rather than legal professionals. It builds on the vision of a legal system that is more straightforward, more engaging and more user-friendly. Crucially, this includes how information is presented, as well as how processes are set up and how policies are established. In the broadest sense, Legal Design can be situated in the Access to Justice movement in that it focuses on making the legal system work better for people and opening access to legal protections. In a narrower sense, it aims to bring a design focus to legal information, products and services. The overall goal is to improve how we communicate, deliver services and make rules and policies – all with the aim of enhancing the experience, comprehension and empowerment of the users.[2]

As indicated, privacy represents a broad variety of concerns including autonomy, accountability, transparency and security. The traditional Privacy-by-Design approach focused on anticipating such concerns early in the software development process – that is, the architectural design of the computer software or its 'code layer'.[3] But translating and responding to these concerns to meet the needs of the end users has proven more difficult. Therefore, the approach taken here is to emphasise accessible communication of relevant information and interactive design – and, in particular, to focus on the 'user-interface' (UI) layer. In that respect, the examples provided in this work come mainly from (legal) information design, namely patterns that aim to improve the communication and comprehension of legal information. Such 'design patterns' can provide this approach with a more universal set of tools. For architects, interaction designers and software engineers, design patterns and pattern libraries are a common way to share transferable solutions to commonly occurring problems. In a legal context, design patterns were first applied to contract communications.[4] In recent years, however, the development of prototypes of design patterns and pattern libraries has developed rapidly in different contexts.

innovation and improve access to justice. For examples, see M Corrales Compagnucci and others (eds), *Legal Design: Integrating Business, Design and Legal Thinking with Technology* (Edward Elgar Publishing 2021).

2 Legal Design Alliance (LeDA).

3 See, e.g., the privacy patterns available at https://privacypatterns.org and https://privacy-patterns.eu.

4 See H Haapio and M Hagan, 'Design Patterns for Contracts', in E Schweighofer and others (eds), *Networks: Proceedings of the 19th International Legal Informatics Symposium IRIS 2016* (Österreichische Computer Gesellschaft 2016); H Haapio and others, 'Legal Design Patterns for Privacy', in E Schweighofer and others (eds), *Data Protection/LegalTech Proceedings of the 21st International Legal Informatics Symposium IRIS 2018* (Editions Weblaw 2018).

In a healthcare–privacy context, Legal Design can, therefore, provide a reliable and transparent infrastructure for embedding relevant legal protections in the UIs of healthcare products and services. Such a UI-focused Privacy-by-Design approach offers a number of advantages, most obviously greater transparency, accountability and (consequently) human choice.

The chapter is structured as follows. Section 2.2 introduces the claim that digital technologies are disrupting healthcare. We focus on the emergence of new healthcare apps and the trend for Super Platforms to move into this space, often via the acquisition of start-ups. These developments raise several legal issues, particularly in the context of recent developments in privacy and data protection. Section 2.3 introduces the main argument, namely that the emerging field of Legal Design can play a crucial role in ensuring better privacy protection by providing more open and accessible infrastructures that embed relevant legal requirements in user-friendly interfaces for healthcare products and services. The chapter offers several real-world examples of such 'UI layer' design patterns to illustrate how Privacy-by-Design can be implemented by helping participants better understand their choices, rights and the types and uses of data that are being collected. Section 2.4 provides some of the challenges and examples of implementing Legal Design in the digital healthcare sector. Section 2.5 concludes.

2.2 Technology-Driven Disruption of Healthcare, Super Platforms and Evolving Privacy Law

This section makes three claims. Firstly, in the healthcare sector multiple start-ups, as well as traditional healthcare providers, are developing new and innovative apps – often powered by AI and algorithm solutions – to improve healthcare services (Section 2.2.1). Secondly, what we here refer to as Super Platforms, such as Tencent and Apple, see the healthcare sector as a potentially lucrative market and are now moving into the space, often via the acquisition of the above-mentioned start-ups (Section 2.2.2). Finally, these two developments involve the collection, processing and transfer of personal and highly sensitive data in unanticipated ways and often without adequate opportunities for truly informed consent. Given the sensitivity of the information and public concerns around Super Platforms, this is a worrying trend. Some of the resulting legal challenges are introduced via a discussion of European Union (EU) developments, namely the EU General Data

Protection Regulation (GDPR)[5] and Ethics Guidelines for Trustworthy AI[6] (Section 2.2.3).[7]

2.2.1 *Technology-Driven Disruption of Healthcare*

Digital innovation has impacted all sectors of the economy and society. Some industries, such as retail, travel and entertainment, have experienced fast change, whereas the disruption of other sectors, such as healthcare, has proceeded more slowly. This presents something of a paradox. While life-changing technological breakthroughs can develop at a rapid pace, improvements in the way healthcare is delivered are often deployed more slowly.[8] One of the reasons for this slower adoption of digital technologies in healthcare contexts is the heavily regulated nature of this sector. Stringent rules for safety and quality control often stifle the dissemination of new products and services.[9] Sweeping

[5] Regulation (EU) 2016/679 of the European Parliament and of the Council of 27 April 2016 on the protection of natural persons with regard to the processing of personal data and on the free movement of such data, and repealing Directive 95/46/EC [2016] OJ L119/1 (General Data Protection Regulation, GDPR).

[6] High-Level Expert Group on Artificial Intelligence, 'Ethics Guidelines for Trustworthy AI' European Commission, 8 April 2019, https://digital-strategy.ec.europa.eu/en/library/ethics-guidelines-trustworthy-ai, accessed 17 August 2021.

[7] During the time of writing this chapter there were other initiatives released in the context of AI, data protection and ethics, and the safety and liability implications of AI, such as the European Commission's 'Report on Safety and Liability Implications of AI, the Internet of Things and Robotics' COM (2020) 64 final, https://ec.europa.eu/info/sites/info/files/report-safety-liability-artificial-intelligence-feb2020_en_1.pdf, accessed 17 August 2021; the European Commission's 'White Paper on Artificial Intelligence: A European Approach to Excellence and Trust' COM (2020) 65 finalx, https://ec.europa.eu/info/sites/info/files/commission-white-paper-artificial-intelligence-feb2020_en.pdf, accessed 17 August 2021; and the European Commission draft regulation governing the use of AI. The proposed AI regulation follows a risk-based approach with different categories of AI system uses such as prohibited, high-risk, limited and minimal risk. See European Commission, 'Proposal for a Regulation of the European Parliament and of the Council Laying Down Harmonised Rules on Artificial Intelligence (Artificial Intelligence Act) and Amending Certain Union Legislative Acts' COM (2021) 206 final, https://digital-strategy.ec.europa.eu/en/library/proposal-regulation-european-approach-artificial-intelligence, accessed 17 August 2021.

[8] K Murphy and N Jain, 'Riding the Disruption Wave in Healthcare' *Forbes*, 1 May 2018, www.forbes.com/sites/baininsights/2018/05/01/riding-the-disruption-wave-in-healthcare/#184a33652846, accessed 17 August 2021.

[9] M Herrmann and others, 'Digital Transformation and Disruption of the Health Care Sector: Internet-Based Observational Study' (2018) 20(3) *Journal of Medical Internet Research* e104, https://doi.org/10.2196/jmir.9498, accessed 17 August 2021.

technological advances are posing challenging legal questions and the pre-eminent question is always how to balance the protection of consumers/patients and at the same time foster innovation and economic growth.[10]

Nevertheless, despite this structural obstacle, different types of technological enablers, business models and value networks seem to have facilitated a digital transformation. A recent systematic study by Hermann and others surveyed the 2017 Forbes 2000 data from an annual ranking of the top 2,000 companies in the world. A search query of the terms 'digital health', 'digital medicine', 'eHealth', 'health care', 'mHealth', 'outcomes-based reimbursement' and 'value-based care' was used to identify the 100 leading companies. Furthermore, the 100 most successful technology, life science and start-ups active in the healthcare sector were scrutinised based on the amount of funding they received according to the CB Insights database.[11]

A further analysis revealed more than 400 projects and collaborations, identifying emerging patterns that differentiate corporations within the healthcare sector with respect to their strategies in the context of the digital transformation in healthcare. The results of the study revealed that established companies show strengths in improving the traditional business model they have been pursuing before. In contrast, start-ups seem to be more agile and flexible in exploring new market segments and moving towards new forms of collaboration and disruptive innovations. Since the healthcare sector is heavily regulated, established companies with a more developed understanding of its regulatory framework appear to have clear advantages. However, start-ups seem to be getting better at meeting this challenge.[12]

Start-ups with their agile corporate culture and innovative technology and life science companies with their regulatory experience should partner to drive the digital transformation of the healthcare sector. By engaging in collaborative projects, large companies can lower their costs, while addressing all patient needs. This will also allow them to innovate in new products and services and to quickly adapt when a disruptive business model emerges.[13]

[10] WD Eggers, M Turley and P Kishnani, 'The Future of Regulation: Principles for Regulating Emerging Technologies' *Deloitte Insights*, 19 June 2018, www2.deloitte.com/insights/us/en/industry/public-sector/future-of-regulation/regulating-emerging-technology.html, accessed 17 August 2021.

[11] Herrmann and others, 'Digital Transformation and Disruption of the Health Care Sector'.

[12] Ibid.

[13] Ibid.

Against this backdrop, the new digitally driven healthcare sector will crucially disrupt healthcare services by providing consumers and providers (patients, researchers and physicians) with more choice, access, transparency, curation of medical information and discovery, and information will be more focused and analytic-driven.[14] This is largely due to the democratisation of healthcare, which has opened up the opportunity for start-ups to disrupt the industry.[15]

According to the Stanford Medicine 2018 Health Trends Report,[16] the democratisation of healthcare is characterised by two major components: (1) the distribution of data and (2) the ability to generate and scale-up insights. Data are growing exponentially – and flowing more freely – across our healthcare system faster than ever before. Historically, the healthcare system has operated as a closed ecosystem, having the hospital or research institution as the main hub and primary gatekeepers of medical information. Information flow was hierarchical and linear, *from* the expert physician *to* the patient. But now – again, largely due to digitisation – information flow has become much more ubiquitous and 'flatter'. Data are constantly generated, and patients are now experiencing a much more diverse healthcare system and more complex forms of information-sharing relationships.[17]

This transformation is challenging the healthcare sector to adapt. New tools are now available that can interpret data more accurately and patients are now experiencing a new digital healthcare system. A growing number of healthcare providers and other firms – often tech-driven start-ups – are leveraging the above-mentioned developments to create different kinds of apps to provide better services to patients. They use AI solutions and algorithms to improve personalised medicine, genetic research, clinical trials, mental health, drug discovery, data analytics, medical records, communication with

[14] H Landi, 'Disruption and the Future of Healthcare: Industry Leaders Parse the Challenges, and Strategic Opportunities' *Healthcare Innovation*, 4 April 2018, www.hcinnovationgroup.com/population-health-management/article/13030041/disruption-and-the-future-of-healthcare-industry-leaders-parse-the-challenges-and-strategic-opportunities, accessed 17 August 2021.

[15] See J Paine, 'How These 3 Technologies Are Disrupting the Health Care Industry' *Inc.*, 28 November 2017, www.inc.com/james-paine/3-disruptive-technologies-shaping-future-of-healthcare.html, accessed 17 August 2021.

[16] Stanford Medicine, 'Stanford Medicine 2018 Health Trends Report: The Democratization of Health Care', December 2018, https://med.stanford.edu/content/dam/sm/school/documents/Health-Trends-Report/Stanford-Medicine-Health-Trends-Report-2018.pdf, accessed 17 August 2021.

[17] Ibid.

patients and so forth.[18] The availability of large amounts of data from multiple modes of information, combined with AI, machine learning (ML) and other expert systems, has the potential to transform the healthcare system.

Patient-oriented medical 'chatbots' and conversational AI technology are good examples of these solutions. Chatbots are computer programs designed to simulate human conversations and learn directly from such communication. These chatbots interact with potential patients visiting the website online, helping them to schedule appointments, find a doctor and even receive a first consultation based on the symptoms. For instance, Florence is a chatbot designed for older patients that reminds them to take their pills on a regular basis,[19] and Super Izzy helps women better track their menstrual cycle and can also work as a reminder for the birth control pill.[20] Efficient diagnosis assistant systems such as Your.MD and CitizenDoc are other examples of chatbots based on such expert systems.[21] They were developed to help patients find a solution to the most common symptoms through AI.[22]

The market for AI wearable devices (smartwatches, fitness trackers, connected headsets, smart glasses, wrist bands and other forms of smart wearable devices) is also increasing steadily.[23] Among the wide range of wearable devices now available, wrist wearables such as smartwatches and wrist bands – commonly used in fitness and sports activities – seem to have become mainstream. Such wearable devices include a number of sensors providing continuous real-time valuable data about users' vital signs (e.g. heart rate, skin temperature) and environmental variables (e.g. movements) that can be used for many different purposes.[24]

[18] See, e.g., C Rijcken, 'Sequoias of Artificial Intelligence', in C Rijcken (ed.), *Pharmaceutical Care in Digital Revolution: Insights towards Circular Innovation* (Academic Press/Elsevier 2019) 127–28.

[19] See 'Florence – Your Health Assistant', https://florence.chat, accessed 17 August 2021.

[20] See 'Super Izzy', www.superizzy.ai/, accessed 17 August 2021; also B Peyrou, J-J Vignaux and A André, 'Artificial Intelligence and Healthcare', in A André (ed.), *Digital Medicine* (Springer 2019) 30–31.

[21] Your.MD is a free service that uses AI to help patients find health-related information and improve their choices. See Your.MD, www.your.md, accessed 17 August 2021 and CitizenDoc, https://app.citizendoc.fr, accessed 9 March 2021.

[22] Peyrou, Vignaux and André, 'Artificial Intelligence and Healthcare', 30–31.

[23] DD Luxton and others, 'Intelligent Mobile, Wearable, and Ambient Technologies for Behavioral Health Care', in DD Luxton (ed.), *Artificial Intelligence in Behavioral and Mental Healthcare* (Academic Press 2016) 139.

[24] F De Arriba-Pérez, M Caeiro-Rodríguez and JM Santos-Gago, 'Collection and Processing of Data from Wrist Wearable Devices in Heterogeneous and Multiple-User Scenarios' (2016) 16(9) *Sensors* 1538, https://doi.org/10.3390/s16091538, accessed 17 August 2021.

What is particularly significant, however, is that these new healthcare products and services have attracted the attention of some of the largest companies in the world, and these companies are now starting to expand their healthcare operations. A disruptive challenge for both the start-ups and life science companies is the strong focus of Big Tech companies to establish the emerging platform business model and assume the necessary negotiating power to appropriate the value created, as will be explained in the following section.[25]

2.2.2 *Super Platforms*

A major development in the global economy over the last two decades has been the emergence of businesses that organise and define themselves as 'platforms'.[26] By platform, we refer to any organisation that uses digital and other emerging technologies to create value by facilitating connections between two or more groups of users. Obvious examples of such companies are Amazon, Facebook and Uber.[27] The type of connection facilitated by different platforms varies according to the platform. Some platforms facilitate connections between the buyer and seller of goods (e.g. Amazon); some facilitate connections between those wanting a service and those willing to provide it (e.g. Airbnb and Uber); and others simply facilitate connections (information exchange) between friends (e.g. Facebook).[28] What is common to all platforms, however, is that they make connections between 'creators' and 'extractors' of value and the platform generates a profit from making these connections, either by taking a commission or through advertising.[29] What is interesting, however, is the speed with which these platform-oriented businesses have evolved into what is sometimes referred to as 'Big Tech' or what we would call here Super Platforms. Here, we first

[25] Herrmann and others, 'Digital Transformation and Disruption of the Health Care Sector'.

[26] See, e.g., generally, C Codagnonce, A Karatzogianni and J Matthews, *Platform Economics: Rhetoric and Reality in the 'Sharing Economy'* (Emerald Publishing 2019).

[27] M Corrales Compagnucci, T Kono and S Teramoto, 'Legal Aspects of Decentralized and Platform-Driven Economies', in M Corrales Compagnucci and others (eds), *Legal Tech and the New Sharing Economy* (Springer 2020).

[28] See M Fenwick and EPM Vermeulen, 'The New Firm' (2015) 16(4) *European Business Organization Law Review* 595, https://doi.org/10.1007/s40804-016-0040-4, accessed 17 August 2021; M Fenwick, JA McCahery and EPM Vermeulen, 'The End of "Corporate" Governance: Hello "Platform" Governance' (2019) 20 *European Business Organization Law Review* 171, https://doi.org/10.1007/s40804-019-00137-z, accessed 17 August 2021.

[29] GG Parker, MW Van Alsyne and SP Choudary, *Platform Revolution: How Networked Markets Are Transforming the Economy and How to Make Them Work for You* (W. W. Norton 2016).

describe Super Platforms and then show how they are moving into the healthcare space.

2.2.2.1 Super Platforms Have a Huge Global User-Base and Enormous Market Power and Cultural Influence

A cursory look at any list of the world's largest companies illustrates the speed of growth of platforms such as Amazon, Facebook and Uber. In the 2000s, none of the biggest companies in the world was a platform. Today, you could make the argument that over half of the world's ten largest companies are organised as platforms or, at least derive a significant slice of their income from platform operations. The emergence and growth of Super Platforms is a significant event, not least because such platforms have become a routinised feature of everyday life within such a short period.[30] To illustrate this rise, consider that it took the radio thirty-eight years to reach 50 million users. It took television thirteen years to achieve the same degree of market penetration. Facebook, however, 'only' needed two years to gain the same number of users. Now it has an active user base of over 2 billion. As such, Super Platforms enjoy enormous economic and cultural influence. They can influence and shape nearly every aspect of everyday life, from consumers' shopping behaviour to voting choices (consider the 2016 US presidential election or Brexit referendum).[31] It is this power that has triggered regulators into action, and regulating 'Big Tech' is now one of the main political challenges of the Digital Age.[32]

2.2.2.2 Super Platforms Have Disrupted Incumbents across All Sectors of the Economy

In the same way that industrial companies transformed how business was conducted in the context of the Industrial Revolution, technology-driven Super Platforms have completely changed the contemporary business landscape. In a business context, technologies have offered new opportunities for entrepreneurs and consumers to develop and enjoy previously unimagined products and services. The rapid growth of Super Platforms has compelled incumbents to revisit their business models. Traditional

[30] Ibid.

[31] C Corning, 'The Rise of Super Platform' *Cars.com*, 17 October 2018, https://growwithcars.com/blog/2018/10/17/the-rise-of-the-super-platform, accessed 17 August 2021.

[32] See S Galloway, *The Four: The Hidden DNA of Amazon, Apple, Facebook, and Google* (Random House 2017).

retailers, for example, have been forced to shift their distribution channels for their products from 'stores' to online platforms. For example, big industrial giants, such as General Electric, are attempting to transform themselves from industrial manufacturers into data science companies that utilise platforms, software, applications and Big Data.[33] Also, as new Fintech firms are moving into the financial services space, many banks are thinking about how to add platform services to their operations.[34] In fact, every organisation – including healthcare providers – are obliged to integrate platform ideas and experience into their operations.

2.2.2.3 Super Platforms Are Algorithm- and AI-Driven

The use of platforms has obviously been made possible by the development and proliferation of digital technologies – most obviously, PCs and smartphones, the Internet, algorithms and cloud computing. In particular, they leverage a combination of global networks, massive amounts of data and AI/algorithms analytics. ML and expert systems, such as the abovementioned medical chatbots that simulate human conversation, are obvious examples that illustrate this phenomenon. ML and other related expert systems are based on a relatively new subfield of computer science. This is seen as a subset of AI and refers to the scientific study of algorithms and statistical models that computer systems utilise to effectively perform certain tasks without employing explicit instructions.[35]

2.2.2.4 Super-Platforms Have Evolved into Global 'Ecosystems' and Are Moving into the Healthcare Space

The above features have allowed Super Platforms to leverage their platform operations to support the development of a global business 'ecosystem'.[36] An ecosystem is defined in biology as a community of living organisms

[33] See GE Digital, 'IIoT Platform – Predix Platform', www.ge.com/digital/iiot-platform, accessed 17 August 2021.

[34] Ernst & Young, 'A Vision for Platform Based Banking', 2018, https://assets.ey.com/content/dam/ey-sites/ey-com/en_us/topics/financial-services/ey-a-vision-for-platform-based-banking.pdf, accessed 17 August 2021; I Gulamhuseinwala, 'How Banks Could Join the Platform Economy' *EY Financial Services*, 2017, www.ey.com/gl/en/industries/financial-services/fso-insights-how-banks-could-join-the-platform-economy, accessed 25 May 2020; I Pollari, 'The Rise of Digital Platforms in Financial Services' KPMG 2018, https://assets.kpmg.com/content/dam/kpmg/xx/pdf/2018/02/kpmg-rise-of-digital-platforms.pdf, accessed 17 August 2021.

[35] See, e.g., E Alpaydin, *Machine Learning: The New AI* (MIT Press 2016).

[36] See Fenwick, McCahery and Vermeulen, 'The End of "Corporate" Governance: Hello "Platform" Governance'.

existing in conjunction with the non-living components of their environment, interacting as a system. In a business context, we might think of an ecosystem as a combination of business entities co-existing and working in close partnership. They constitute an online-to-online (O2O) infrastructure, which spans a vast audience including different sectors of economic activity. Super Platforms provide different types of tools, resources, products and services to both businesses and consumers. They operate in a uniform, standardised and highly interconnected fashion.[37] Apple is a good example of such a technology-driven ecosystem comprising connected, interoperable and seamlessly interacting products/devices (iMac, iPad, iPhone, Apple Watch, AirPods, iPod devices).[38] As mentioned, a key challenge today facing regulators – and governments more generally – is to find the necessary mechanisms to promote innovative *and* socially responsible global ecosystems. All too often, such ecosystems become mired in controversy over their business practices.

In particular, there are concerns around the business model that such Super-Platforms have developed. At first, these firms promised a decentralised, efficient and less formal economy and society. However, as these tech businesses scaled into some of the largest businesses in history (Super Platforms), they have become shrouded in controversy and are now widely seen as hugely problematic. A specific concern involves how such firms collect data, analyse that data and then sell targeted advertising to anyone willing to pay. Critics of this model suggest that it represents a new form of 'surveillance capitalism' that needs to be urgently addressed.[39] Understanding these difficulties and finding an appropriate regulatory response is particularly pressing, especially as Super Platforms expand their operations into new and socially sensitive sectors, such as healthcare.

Given that the healthcare market has become a highly dynamic sector of the economy, Super Platforms see healthcare as a potentially lucrative market and are moving into the space often via the acquisition of healthcare-focused start-ups. Tencent and Apple, for example, have already started to invest in the automation of healthcare and scientific research.

One of the best examples of this is Chinese tech giant Tencent, which has become the largest e-health platform in China. Before penetrating the

[37] Corning, 'The Rise of Super Platform'.

[38] iMac, iPad, iPhone, Apple Watch, AirPods and iPod are trademarks of Apple Inc., registered in the US and other countries.

[39] S Zuboff, *The Age of Surveillance Capitalism: The Fight for a Human Future at the New Frontier of Power* (Public Affairs 2019).

healthcare sector, Tencent was already the owner of WeChat, an app used for 'Everything-as-a-Service' (XaaS).[40] WeChat could be basically compared to a combination of WhatsApp, Facebook, PayPal, Uber and more, including services such as text messaging, shopping, ride-hailing, food delivery, money transfers and payments for all kinds of consumers services.[41] Tencent was already considered to be a Super Platform in its own right. In 2014, Tencent started to provide healthcare services and became one of the most important Super Platforms in the healthcare industry. Tencent provides services such as online consultations, medical appointments with doctors, payments for medicine and services at hospitals and so on. Today, there are over 38,000 medical institutions able to deliver integrated healthcare services using Tencent's open platform and applications through a wide range of channels.[42] Tencent recently partnered with Babylon Health, a British start-up developing online healthcare assistant apps. This new cooperation enables users to get immediate access to online medical consultation by just messaging their symptoms. Tencent also entered into a recent collaboration with iCarbonX, a Chinese AI-driven healthcare unicorn that attempts to create a complete digital representation of one's biological self by using genetic data, epigenetics and other factors, allowing for a truly personalised medicine to emerge.[43]

Another example of this trend for Super Platforms to move into healthcare is offered by Apple. Its Health app consolidates data from different devices (iPhone, Apple Watch and third-party apps), enabling individuals to view a wide range of their health and 'wellness' metrics (such as daily step counts, weight, calories use, heart rate, etc.) in one place and follow their daily details, progress and long-term trends.[44] In November 2019, Apple launched its Research app with three health studies, using information from the iPhone and Apple Watch.[45] Apple's 'Kits' offer app

[40] Everything-as-a-Service (XaaS) refers to a variety of services, including platforms, IT infrastructure, software, databases and other IT resources. See I Nanos, V Manthou and E Androutsou, 'Cloud Computing Adoption Decision in E-Government', in A Sifaleras and K Petridis (eds), *Operational Research in the Digital Era – ICT Challenges* (Springer 2019) 129.

[41] A Buvailo, 'Get Ready for "Super-platforms" in Healthcare and Pharmaceutical Research' *BiopharmaTrend.com*, 27 September 2018, www.biopharmatrend.com/post/71-get-ready-for-super-platforms-in-healthcare-and-pharmaceutical-research, accessed 17 August 2021.

[42] See Tencent, 'Tencent Open Platform', http://open.qq.com/eng/, accessed 17 August 2021; Buvailo, 'Get Ready for "Super-platforms"'.

[43] Buvailo 'Get Ready for "Super-platforms"'.

[44] See Apple, 'iOS – Health', www.apple.com/uk/ios/health/, accessed 17 August 2021.

[45] See Apple, 'iOS – Research', www.apple.com/ios/research-app, accessed 17 August 2021.

developers frameworks they can use to develop apps. HealthKit is a repository for health and fitness data that allows developers and researchers to feed information to and from the health app, allowing apps to work with Apple Health and each other.[46] CareKit and ResearchKit are open-source software frameworks for building apps: ResearchKit for researchers and CareKit for helping people to manage their medical conditions, track their symptoms and medications and share the information with their care team.[47] Since the frameworks work seamlessly together, researchers can get access to even more robust data for their studies.[48]

2.2.3 New Legal Risk: The EU GDPR and Guidelines

Healthcare apps, often powered by AI and algorithm solutions, record and process granular sensitive data in real-time. These developments have sparked a debate on the many risks posed to the privacy and data protection of individuals. Not surprisingly, these changes in the traditional way of providing health care services and treatment have significant consequences. While harnessing many benefits, this use of private information raises multiple legal challenges and these developments have been one factor pushing policy makers into a re-evaluation of privacy laws.

Here we take the EU as an illustration of a more general regulatory trend to introduce new and stricter requirements that impact on any business or organisation that handles personal and sensitive data. The new compliance challenge is how to operationalise these requirements and to embed them effectively in the design of products and services in a way that affords meaningful protection of the relevant interests. To give some sense of the complexity of the legal challenge, we consider two recent developments, the GDPR and the EU Ethics Guidelines for Trustworthy AI.

The GDPR was adopted on 27 April 2016 and after a two-year transition period, it came into force on 25 May 2018. The GDPR replaced

[46] See Apple, 'Health and Fitness', *Apple Developer*, https://developer.apple.com/healthkit/, accessed 17 August 021.

[47] See Apple, 'CareKit' *Apple ResearchKit & CareKit*, www.researchandcare.org/carekit/, accessed 17 August 2021; Apple, 'CareKit' *Apple Developer*, https://developer.apple.com/carekit/ accessed 17 August 2021; also Apple, 'Introducing ResearchKit' *ResearchKit*, http://researchkit.org, accessed 17 August 2021. CareKit, HealthKit and ResearchKit are trademarks of Apple Inc., registered in the US and other countries.

[48] R Mehmood, MA Faisal and S Altowaijri, 'Future Networked Healthcare Systems: A Review and Case Study' in M Boucadair and C Jackenet (eds), *Handbook of Research on Redesigning the Future of Internet Architectures* (IGI Global 2015) 535.

the previous European Data Protection Directive[49] and was designed to strengthen and unify data protection and privacy for all EU citizens and to empower individuals by granting them more control and certainty over their data when using Internet services.[50] The GDPR has been generally welcomed for updating some of the rules of the previous data protection regime and has triggered regulatory action around the world. However, it has clearly created a new degree of legal risk for all firms and healthcare providers. The most significant changes can be briefly summarised as follows:[51]

- *International Data Transfers*: The GDPR imposes more stringent rules for the transfer of personal data to third countries and international organisations outside the EU. This change was designed to ensure an adequate level of protection in a globally connected world.[52]

49 Directive 95/46/EC of the European Parliament and of the Council of 24 October 1995 on the protection of individuals with regard to the processing of personal data and on the free movement of such data [1995] OJ L281/31.

50 See, e.g., J McNealy and A Flowers, 'Privacy Law and Regulation: Technologies, Implications and Solutions' in S Zeadally and M Badra (eds), *Privacy in a Digital, Networked World: Technologies, Implications and Solutions* (Springer 2015) 199; H Gjermundrød, I Dionysiou and K Costa, 'PrivacyTracker: A Privacy-by-Design GDPR-Compliant Framework with Verifiable Data Traceability Controls' in S Casteleyn, P Dolog and C Pautasso (eds), *Current Trends in Web Engineering. ICWE 2016* (Lecture Notes in Computer Science, vol 9881, Springer 2016) 4.

51 M Corrales, P Jurčys and G Kousiouris, 'Smart Contracts and Smart Disclosure: Coding a GDPR Compliance Framework' in M Corrales, M Fenwick and H Haapio (eds), *Legal Tech, Smart Contracts and Blockchain* (Springer 2019) 192–93.

52 GDPR, art. 46; M Corrales Compagnucci and others, 'Lost on the High Seas without a Safe Harbour or a Schield? Navigating Cross-Border Data Transfers in the Pharmaceutical Sector After Schrems II Invalidation of the EU-US Privacy Shield' (2020) 4(3) *European Pharmaceutical Law Review* 153. At the time of writing, the European Data Protection Board (EDPB) released its final recommendations for making transfers of personal data to third countries. See European Data Protection Board, 'Recommendations 01/2020 on Measures that Supplement Transfer Tools to Ensure Compliance with the EU Level of Protection of Personal Data' (version 2.0, adopted on 18 June 2021), https://edpb.europa.eu/system/files/2021-06/edpb_recommendations_202001vo.2.0_supplementarymeasurestransferstools_en.pdf, accessed 14 August 2021. In addition, on 4 June 2021, the Commission issued modernised standard contractual clauses (SCCs) under the GDPR for the transfer of personal data to third countries. These modernised SCCs will replace the three sets of SCCs that were adopted under the previous Data Protection Directive 95/46, see European Commission, 'Standard Contractual Clauses for International Transfers' (Directorate-General for Justice and Consumers, 4 June 2021), https://ec.europa.eu/info/law/law-topic/data-protection/international-dimension-data-protection/standard-contractual-clauses-scc/standard-contractual-clauses-international-transfers_en, accessed 14 August 2021.

- *Extra-Territorial Scope*: The GDPR expands its territorial scope of protection (extra-territorial applicability) to data controllers and processors established in the EU and *outside* of the EU territory with regard to the processing of personal data of European citizens.[53]
- *Consent*: The GDPR strengthened the definition of consent as follows: 'consent should be given by a clear affirmative act establishing a freely given, specific, informed and unambiguous indication of the data subject's agreement to the processing of personal data'.[54] It is no longer acceptable for companies to hide crucial privacy information somewhere in the middle of long terms and conditions full of legalese.[55]
- *Transparency*: The GDPR highlights transparency as one of its fundamental requirements, noting that the principle of transparency requires 'that any information addressed to the public or to the data subject be concise, easily accessible and easy to understand, and that clear and plain language and, additionally, where appropriate, visualisation be used'.[56]
- *Breach Notification*: Data breach notifications are mandatory. Data controllers must report the breach immediately (within seventy-two hours) to their supervisory authority, whereas data processors must report the breach to the controllers.[57]
- *Access Rights*: Data subjects have more rights to get access and control regarding their data. This allows them the right to ask the data controller whether personal data concerning them is being processed, where and for what purpose.[58]

[53] GDPR, art. 3; D Svantesson, *Extraterritoriality in Data Privacy Law* (Ex Tuto Publishing 2013) 89; H Hijmans, *The European Union as Guardian of Internet Privacy: The Story of Art. 16 TFEU* (Springer 2016) 497.

[54] GDPR, art. 32.

[55] GDPR, art. 7(4); THA Wisman, 'Privacy, Data Protection and E-Commerce' in AR Lodder and AD Murray (eds), *EU Regulation of E-Commerce. A Commentary* (Edward Elgar Publishing 2017) 357.

[56] GDPR, recital 58. According to the Article 29 Data Protection Working Party, 'Guidelines on Transparency under Regulation 2016/679' (17/EN, WP260 rev.01, 11 April 2018) 5, https://ec.europa.eu/newsroom/document.cfm?doc_id=51025, accessed 17 August 2021, '[t]he concept of transparency in the GDPR is user-centric rather than legalistic'. This highlights the central role of the comprehensibility and presentation of the information.

[57] GDPR, art. 33.

[58] GDPR, arts 12–14; C Quelle, 'Not Just User Control in the General Data Protection Regulation: On the Problems with Choice and Paternalism, and on the Point of Data Protection' in A Lehmann and others (eds), *Privacy and Identity Management: Facing Up to Next Steps* (Springer 2016) 143.

- *Right to be Forgotten (data erasure)*: This right allows data subjects to have the controller delete their personal data and stop further processing and dissemination of data from third parties.[59]
- *Data Portability*: The GDPR creates a new right to data portability. This right allows data subjects to receive personal data concerning them – which they have previously submitted to the data controller – in a 'structured, commonly used and machine-readable format' and to send those data to another controller.[60]
- *Privacy-by-Design and by-Default*: The Privacy-by-Design and by-Default approach[61] entails the notion of embedding privacy and data protection requirements directly into the architecture design of information technologies and related systems. Data controllers and processors must adopt this approach by default, making an explicit reference to 'data minimisation'[62] and the possible use of 'pseudonymisation'.[63]

Even a cursory review of the main features of the GDPR highlights the legal risk confronting any firm handling personal medical information.

Such risk is compounded by a second development worth mentioning, namely the new legal and ethical requirements relating to AI. In this context, the European Commission released a new set of guidelines[64] to

[59] GDPR, art. 17; B Sobkow, 'Forget Me, Forget Me Not – Redefining the Boundaries of the Right to Be Forgotten to Address Current Problems and Areas of Criticism' in E Schweighofer and others (eds), *Privacy Technologies and Policy. APF 2017* (Lecture Notes in Computer Science, vol. 10518, Springer 2016) 36.

[60] GDPR, art. 20; see also Article 29 Data Protection Working Party, 'Guidelines on the Right to Data Portability' (16/EN WP 242 rev.01, 5 April 2017), https://ec.europa.eu/newsroom/document.cfm?doc_id=44099, accessed 17 August 2021.

[61] The Privacy by Design approach was first introduced by the Information and Privacy Commissioner of Ontario and has existed as a general concept ever since. However, the GDPR introduced, for the first time, Privacy by Design (and Privacy by Default) as a legal obligation.

[62] GDPR, art. 5(1)(c); O Lynskey, *The Foundations of EU Data Protection Law* (Oxford University Press 2015) 206; F Thouvenin, 'Big Data of Complex Networks and Data Protection Law: An Introduction to an Area of Mutual Conflict' in M Dehmer and others (eds), *Big Data of Complex Networks* (CRC Press 2017) 218.

[63] GDPR, art. 25(1); see also G D'Acquisto and others, *Privacy by Design in Big Data: An Overview of Privacy Enchanting Technologies in the Era of Big Data Analytics* (European Union Agency for Network and Information Security ENISA 2015), www.enisa.europa.eu/publications/big-data-protection/at_download/fullReport, DOI: 10.2824/641480, accessed 17 August 2021; P Voigt and A von dem Bussche, *The EU General Data Protection Regulation (GDPR): A Practical Guide* (Springer 2017) 62.

[64] See High-Level Expert Group on Artificial Intelligence, 'Ethics Guidelines for Trustworthy AI'.

encourage the development of trustworthy and ethical AI. The guidelines – although they are 'soft law' and not yet legally binding – address some of the diffuse problems that AI will bring to society as we integrate it in sectors such as healthcare, education and consumer technology. The guidelines focus on how governments, companies and other organisations should develop ethical applications of AI. According to the guidelines, AI systems should be accountable, explainable and unbiased. To help achieve this goal, the EU recommends using an assessment list of seven fundamental areas that AI systems should meet in order to be deemed trustworthy.[65] Again, this has clear implications for any firm that uses AI systems to analyse personal information it collects and compiles.

In summary, the expansion of Super Platforms into the healthcare sector is triggering growth of new products and services. As a result, the healthcare sector is offering various kinds of apps for medical treatment, patient's control and research. This sector is growing exponentially ranging from large-scale systems to more moderate micro-services including apps of different kinds. Researchers are increasingly developing apps and other tools that process personal and sensitive data, often powered by AI and algorithm solutions. This complexity at the level of technology is matched by a parallel complexity in regulatory schemes. Anyone handling personal and sensitive data is obliged to manage a high degree of legal risk, particularly if that information is affected by AI.

2.3 'UI Layer' Privacy-By-Design

As noted previously, the emergence of new healthcare products and services, as well as the intervention of Super Platforms in a healthcare context, pose obvious challenges concerning the processing of personal and sensitive data. Here we introduce the claim that the emerging field of Legal Design can play a crucial role in ensuring better privacy protection by providing more open and accessible infrastructures that embed relevant legal requirements in user-friendly interfaces for healthcare products and services (Section 2.3.1). To substantiate this claim, we offer several real-world examples of design patterns to illustrate the centrality of UI-focused Privacy-by-Design in protecting the most sensitive information of individuals who provide their data (Section 2.3.2).

[65] Ibid.

2.3.1 Legal Design

Legal Design is an emerging inter-disciplinary approach to apply human-centred design in order to prevent or solve legal problems.[66] It prioritises the point of view of the 'users' of law, that is, citizens, consumers and business people, rather than legal professionals, and builds on a vision of a legal system that is more straightforward, more engaging and more user-friendly.[67] Design thinking seems particularly timely in the context of the Digital Revolution. As was the case during the Industrial Revolution, business, governments and other organisations are scrambling to take advantage of these technological advancements, but they are also concerned about the direction and speed of change. The Digital Revolution will certainly benefit people in myriad ways, but it can also create a lot of harm if we do not think ahead to potential problems that we may have.

The healthcare industry is one of the sectors that will benefit the most. It will inevitably become more digital and 'smart'. It will also become more efficient and more accurate. And like all 'Revolutions' this coming benefit is welcome, but we have to be aware of the potential problems that these new technologies can bring. AI will reorganise the way we live, work and interact socially due to the sudden amount of data available in the things we use. Therefore, in this section, we argue that we need to improve the design of new products and services in the healthcare sector. Moreover, we also need to improve processes and experiences to address the needs of all users, including patients, healthcare professionals and medical researchers.

To understand how to design better AI apps, we should first understand the essence of design thinking. The first principle of design is simplicity. John Maeda, in his book *The Laws of Simplicity*, explains that the world is full of complex technologies and products. It is, however, a simple design that allows a particular product or service to differentiate itself from rivals. It is, therefore, crucial for all companies to understand how to balance complex technologies with simple design if they want to develop innovative and successful products.[68]

But how to achieve simplicity in a world full of complex technology? According to John Maeda, simplicity is all about 'subtracting the obvious,

[66] M Doherty and others, 'A New Attitude to Law's Empire: The Potentialities of Legal Design' in M Corrales Compagnucci and others (eds) *Legal Design: Integrating Business, Design and Legal Thinking with Technology* (Edward Elgar Publishing 2021).

[67] Legal Design Alliance (LeDA).

[68] J Maeda, *The Laws of Simplicity: Design, Technology, Business and Life* (MIT Press 2006).

and adding the meaningful'. Think of Apple products such as the iPod player. The reason why they became so widely popular is because they were simple to use, and their design was appealing to consumers. There is no functional difference between an iPod player and an MP3 player. But the iPod player took all the obvious complex design functions away, such as the various buttons for every function which were found in other MP3 players, and added the round control pad which was much easier to use.[69]

In addition, the iPod player was the first product to be connected to an online music store such as iTunes which let customers quickly find, purchase and download music without subscription fees. The simplicity, usefulness and user-friendly design of the software and hardware of both the iPod player and the iTunes store together is what led these products to disrupt the market.[70]

David Rose has similarly explained the important role design plays in the development of personal technology.[71] According to Rose, it is time for us to move away from screen-based devices towards a world of more intuitive, useful and efficient devices, designed for a specific purpose, or as he ably puts it, through 'enlightened design'. Rose asked himself the following question: 'what will technology look like in the future?' One idea that could shape our future lives is 'enchanted objects',[72] that is, technology that is not there to distract us but to offer information at a glance. The problem with screen-based devices such as smartphones is that they require your full attention as you read and respond to messages.[73]

The same holds true with regard to reading the terms and conditions of those apps. The clauses of user agreements are usually too long and difficult to be understood by the layperson. When we use our smartphones, the text is even too small to be read properly, and a considerable amount of mental effort is required. The problem with user agreements is that they are too difficult to understand even for lawyers.[74] The importance of this

[69] Ibid.

[70] C Breen, *Secrets of the iPod and iTunes* (5th edn, Peachpit Press 2004). iPod and iTunes are trademarks of Apple Inc., registered in the US and other countries.

[71] D Rose, *Enchanted Objects: Innovation, Design, and the Future of Technology* (Simon and Schuster Inc 2015).

[72] Ibid.

[73] M Raisinghani and others, 'Cloud Computing in the 21st Century: A Managerial Perspective for Policies and Practices' in S Aljawarneh (ed.), *Advanced Research on Cloud Computing Design and Applications* (Idea Group 2015) 188.

[74] H Haapio, TD Barton and M Corrales Compagnucci, 'Legal Design for the Common Good: Proactive Legal Care by Design' in M Corrales Compagnucci and others (eds) *Legal Design: Integrating Business, Design and Legal Thinking with Technology* (Edward Elgar Publishing 2021).

has been examined by the House of Commons Science and Technology Committee in the United Kingdom. They found out that consumers usually just sign up without really reading and knowing what they are signing up to. They were particularly critical of the complexities surrounding terms and conditions, describing them as 'more complex than Shakespeare'.[75]

To demonstrate what reading those terms entails, the Norwegian Consumer Council downloaded and read aloud, word by word, all thirty-three app terms and conditions on an average Norwegian's mobile phone. This 'read-a-thon', which took more than thirty hours, was streamed live online. It revealed that the current state of terms and conditions for digital services is 'bordering on the absurd. Their scope, length and complexity mean it is virtually impossible to make good and informed decisions'.[76]

According to Gillian Hadfield, the 'avalanche' of 'click to agree' boxes, in response to the GDPR, is an example of the low and poor impact regulatory tools have on user privacy and control because people still don't know what they are agreeing to. It will be difficult for consumers to monitor what these companies are doing with their data.[77]

As discussed, it is clearly overwhelming and unrealistic for patients and participants to read and understand the terms and conditions of their medical apps and to fully understand what they are asked to consent to with regard to the processing of their personal data. Legal designers can help to change this by developing better interfaces to empower both medical professionals and patients.

Designers know that if people do not read the information, find what they need or understand what they find, inadvertent non-compliance will occur, and readers' (and non-readers') problems easily become writers' problems. In short, complexity causes unnecessary and avoidable risks. So, designers seek to simplify the user experience. As illustrated in Figure 2.1, there are three main building blocks to simpler communication: (1) empathise with the users' needs and expectations; (2) distil the communication, boil it down to its essence and (3) clarify.

[75] D Anderson, *A Question of Trust* (Williams Lea Group 2015) 159; see also Corrales, Jurčys and Kousiouris, 'Smart Contracts and Smart Disclosure', 195.

[76] E Schumacher, 'Norway Consumer Council Completes 32-hour App Terms Read-a-thon' (*DW.com*, 25 May 2016), www.dw.com/en/norway-consumer-council-completes-32-hour-app-terms-read-a-thon/a-19283288, accessed 17 August 2021, citing Council Digital Policy Director Finn Myrstad.

[77] G Hadfield, 'Governments Can't Handle Tech Regulation. It Is Time for Companies to Take Over' (*Quartz*, 2 July 2018, updated 31 July 2018) https://qz.com/1316426/weve-disrupted-technology-now-its-time-to-disrupt-its-regulation/, accessed 17 August 2021.

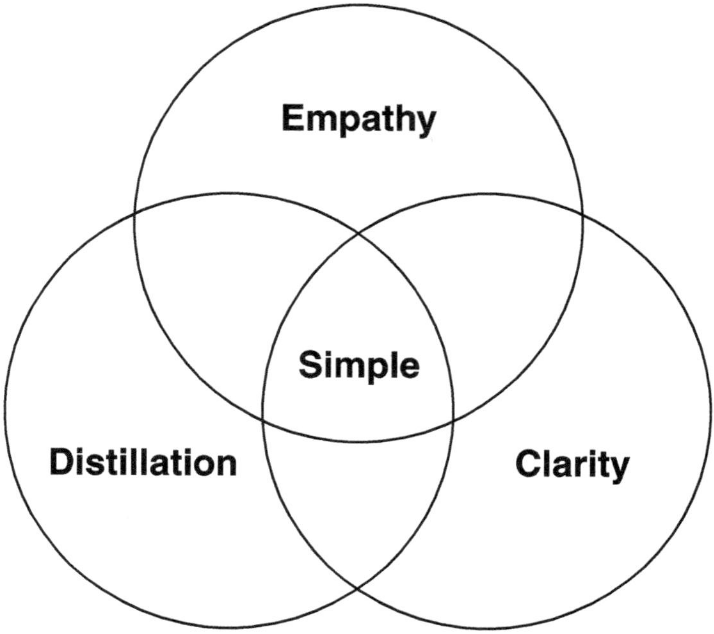

Figure 2.1 The three building blocks of simpler communication
Source: Image by Helena Haapio. Used with permission. The image originally appeared in Spanish in H Haapio, G Siedel and M Bernal Fandiño, 'Aplicación del Derecho Proactivo como una Ventaja Competitiva' (2016) (31) *Revista de Derecho Privado* 265. The three building blocks and the idea of the image are adapted from A Siegel and I Etzkorn, *Simple: Conquering the Crisis of Complexity* (Twelve 2013).

When the goal is clear communication, it is important not to overwhelm the audience with too much information. Instead, readers should be guided through the text, making sure they can skim through and find content and explanations when needed. Procedures can be shown in a step-by-step fashion, with the help of charts and explanatory diagrams. Clear and visible headings can be shown to answer typical questions, and so on. These information design techniques need not be reinvented – they can be identified, shared and reused as *design patterns.*

2.3.2 Design Patterns: From Architecture to Contracts, Privacy and Beyond

Design patterns offer a systematic way to identify, collect and share good practices. In essence, design patterns are reusable solutions to a commonly occurring problem – something that practitioners can develop, collect and share. The original idea stems from Christopher Alexander and others,[78] who collected reusable architectural and design solutions. The idea was later applied to the digital world and gained widespread acceptance with Erich Gamma and others.[79] Since then, design patterns have been extensively used in many other fields, including computer science and interface and UX design. Over the last few years, they have even made their way to contract design,[80] privacy design[81] and Legal Design.[82]

Even before the emergence of Legal Design,[83] early pioneers promoted better and simpler presentation of legal information with user-centred design, simplification and visualisation. Several projects investigated the simplification of online terms and conditions, end-user licences and privacy policies, for example using icons.[84] EU-wide and country-specific guidance was developed to help organisations incorporate GDPR and other

[78] C Alexander and others, *A Pattern Language – Towns, Buildings, Construction* (Oxford University Press 1977).

[79] E Gamma and others, *Design Patterns: Elements of Reusable Object-Oriented Software* (Addison-Wesley 1995).

[80] Haapio and Hagan, 'Design Patterns for Contracts'; H Haapio and S Passera, 'Contracts as Interfaces: Visual Representation Patterns in Contract Design' in DM Katz, R Dolin and MJ Bommarito (eds), *Legal Informatics* (Cambridge University Press 2021); M Corrales Compagnucci, H Haapio and M Fenwick (eds), *The Research Handbook on Contract Design* (Edward Elgar Publishing 2022).

[81] Haapio and others, 'Legal Design Patterns for Privacy'; A Rossi, 'Legal Design for the General Data Protection Regulation. A Methodology for the Visualization and Communication of Legal Concepts' (Dottorato di Ricerca in Law, Science and Technology, Alma Mater Studiorum Università di Bologna 2019); A Rossi and G Lenzini, 'Transparency by Design in Data-Informed Research: A Collection of Information Design Patterns' (2020) 37:105402 *Computer Law & Security Review* https://doi.org/10.1016/j.clsr.2020.105402, accessed 17 August 2021; A Rossi and H Haapio, 'Proactive Legal Design for Health Data Sharing Based on Smart Contracts' in M Corrales Compagnucci, M Fenwick and S Wrbka (eds), *Smart Contracts: Technological, Business and Legal Perspectives* (Hart-Bloomsbury 2021).

[82] For an overview of legal design patterns, see, e.g., A Rossi and others, 'Legal Design Patterns: Towards A New Language for Legal Information Design' in E Schweighofer, F Kummer and A Saarenpää (eds), *Internet of Things. Proceedings of the 22nd International Legal Informatics Symposium IRIS 2019* (Editions Weblaw 2019), and the resources mentioned in notes 80–81.

[83] M Hagan, 'Making Legal Design a Thing – and an Academic Discipline' (*Legal Design and Innovation Blog/Medium*, 14 December 2018), https://medium.com/legal-design-and-innovation/making-legal-design-a-thing-and-an-academic-discipline-5a7e57fa43e8, accessed 17 August 2021.

[84] For a summary, see H Haapio, *Next Generation Contracts: A Paradigm Shift* (Lexpert Ltd 2013), with references; P Lannerö, 'Fighting the Biggest Lie on the Internet: Common Terms Beta Proposal' (Metamatrix 2013), http://commonterms.org/commonterms_beta_proposal.pdf, accessed 17 August 2021. See also Rossi, 'Legal Design for the General Data Protection Regulation'.

requirements within their consent processes. For example, in the United Kingdom, the Information Commissioner's Office (ICO) shared examples of good (and bad) privacy notices and provided guidance on how to make privacy notices more engaging and effective for individuals while emphasising the importance of greater choice and control over what is done with their data.[85] Despite all the guidance, making Privacy-by-Design a reality proved difficult. Lawyers and developers alike were wondering how to best convert 'lawyer speak' into 'engineering speak' and how to anticipate and prevent problems early in the development process.[86]

By collecting, naming and describing *design patterns* and showing examples it is possible to systematise and share knowledge and create a common language for experts and novices alike, irrespective of their discipline or professional background. To enable users to interact with the information, the selection of patterns needs to be based on what is suited to express the information to the particular user group in a particular context. For those in charge of producing information, the focus changes from clear and concise *writing* or *drafting* to *designing communication* with and for multiple user groups. This also involves responding to and balancing different needs and requirements.[87] Our contention is that such design patterns are particularly relevant and have enormous potential in a healthcare context.

In recent years, *pattern libraries* – collections or catalogues of design patterns – have been launched that help those in charge of preparing information engage and empower its targeted users. After the development of prototype collections,[88] several pattern libraries now exist. As regards contracts, the World Commerce & Contracting (WorldCC; formerly International Association for Contract and Commercial Management IACCM) offers a collection of design patterns that help organise and communicate contracts and terms and conditions more clearly so that they are read, understood and acted upon.[89] Research organisations and

[85] See, e.g., Information Commissioner's Office (ICO), 'Privacy Notices, Transparency and Control. A Code of Practice on Communicating Privacy Information to Individuals' (7 October 2016), www.pdpjournals.com/docs/88625.pdf, accessed 17 August 2021. The ICO is the UK's independent body set up to uphold information rights.

[86] Privacypatterns.org, 'About', https://privacypatterns.org/about/, accessed 17 August 2021

[87] A Rossi and H Haapio, 'Proactive Legal Design for Health Data Sharing Based on Smart Contracts'.

[88] See Contract Design Pattern Library, Privacy Design Pattern Library and Know Your Rights Pattern Library at www.legaltechdesign.com/communication-design/?s=pattern. For pioneering Privacy Pattern Libraries, see also https://privacypatterns.eu and https://privacypatterns.org.

[89] World Commerce and Contracting (WorldCC), S Passera and H Haapio, 'WorldCC Contract Design Pattern Library', https://contract-design.worldcc.com, accessed 17 August 2021.

technology studios, too, have opened access to their privacy toolkits, data permissions catalogues and pattern libraries for others to use and be inspired by. For example, Sage Bionetworks has developed a multi-media approach to addressing transparency and comprehension within electronic informed consent (eConsent) for app-mediated research studies.[90] They offer an open-access toolkit of design tools and patterns with accompanying use cases to assist researchers in using the appropriate patterns in their applications.[91] Another valuable resource is offered by IF: a curated catalogue of patterns for sharing data.[92] These resources can help developers and researchers make decisions about how and when to collect and use data about people and effectively communicate their related messages.

2.3.3 Examples of 'UI Layer' Design Patterns for Privacy Communication

To show how design patterns can transform the communication of complex privacy-related messages, let us take some examples. There is compelling evidence that people typically just click 'Accept' when confronted with a privacy policy – telling what is known as 'the biggest lie on the Internet'.[93] Most people using platforms or consuming Internet services just want fast access to whatever service or product they are looking for. As regards policies and terms, anything goes. People feel overwhelmed by the resulting 'wall of text'.

Such a 'wall of text' is a well-known and widely acknowledged issue in the field of contracts, privacy policies and legal documents.[94] The result is that

[90] M Doerr, C Suver and J Wilbanks, 'Developing a Transparent, Participant-Navigated Electronic Informed Consent for Mobile-Mediated Research' (SageBionetworks, Paper 22 April 2016), https://ssrn.com/abstract_id=2769129, accessed 17 August 2021.

[91] For Sage Bionetworks' Privacy Toolkit, see Sage Bionetworks, 'Informed Consent' (*Privacy Toolkit*), https://designmanual.sagebionetworks.org/informed-consent.html, accessed 17 August 2021 and Sage Bionetworks, 'Privacy Toolkit for Mobile Health Research Studies', https://sagebionetworks.org/tools_resources/privacy-toolkit-for-mobile-health-research-studies, accessed 17 August 2021; S Moore and M Doerr, 'The Elements of Informed Consent. A Toolkit. Sage Bionetworks Governance Consent Toolkit' (Megan Doerr ed., v3.0, Sage Bionetworks 2020), https://sagebionetworks.org/wp-content/uploads/2020/01/SageBio_EIC-Toolkit_V3_21Jan20_final.pdf, accessed 17 August 2021.

[92] For IF's Data Patterns Catalogue, see IF, 'Data Patterns Catalogue', https://catalogue.projectsbyif.com, accessed 17 August 2021.

[93] JA Obar and A Oeldorf-Hirsch, 'The Biggest Lie on the Internet: Ignoring the Privacy Policies and Terms of Service Policies of Social Networking Services' (2020) 23(1) *Information, Communication & Society* 128.

[94] For contracts, see S Passera, *Beyond the Wall of Contract Text – Visualizing Contracts to Foster Understanding and Collaboration within and across Organizations* (Doctoral Dissertation, Aalto University 2017). For privacy policies, see Rossi and others, 'Legal Design

finding information is hard due to the opaque and undifferentiated text that provides no highlights or navigational aids. All the information is presented in the same monochromatic, text-only manner, making it difficult to search and find or read key information. It is impossible to skim-read the text to find answers to specific questions or concerns. And when the text seems too long or complex, very few people will take the trouble of reading it. They just give up.

In the following sections, we introduce some examples of UI-layer design patterns and pattern families that have been effectively used in overcoming the 'wall of text' challenge. The following examples illustrate how this can be and has been done in the context of privacy communication and health data sharing. The patterns complement each other, and their goal is to foster the clarity, findability, transparency and comprehensibility of the information.

2.3.3.1 Privacy FAQs and FAQ-Style Heading Patterns

Privacy-related 'frequently asked questions' (FAQs) can be used to provide easy-to-read explanations about the most frequently asked privacy-related questions and the most relevant data practices. In addition to the problem of 'wall of text', they can be used to respond to a number of other communication challenges, including the complexity of language, excessive length, and public lack of familiarity with key concepts and terms. Many organisations present Privacy FAQs on their website.[95] Users can click on each question and a box opens with a short paragraph explaining key privacy and data protection policies. The FAQs make it easier for users to find answers to specific personal data-related questions they might have.

FAQ-style headings, in turn, is a design pattern where headings are shown as questions that readers frequently ask the experts. The example in Figure 2.2 shows how Juro uses FAQ-style headings in their privacy policy as a way to present the topics from the point of view of the reader and to pre-emptively anticipate questions with regard to their data security and data retention policies.

Patterns'; A Rossi and others, 'When Design Met Law: Design Patterns for Information Transparency' (2019) (122–123) *Droit de la Consommation – Consumentenrecht DCCR* 79; Rossi and Lenzini, 'Transparency by Design in Data-Informed Research' 5, where the authors list the 'wall of text' among eight main problems that preclude effective legal-technical communication, leading to impenetrable text where 'details are lost in a sea of text'.

95 See, e.g., 'Health Data Coalition Privacy FAQs' at https://hdcbc.ca/privacy-faqs/; 'Privacy for Your AncestryDNA Test' at www.ancestry.com/cs/legal/PrivacyForAncestryDNA-Testing; 'Aetna Health Care Privacy FAQs' at www.aetna.com/faqs-health-insurance/about-us-privacy-faqs.html; 'Privacy FAQs' at Sony UK Privacy Centre, www.sony.co.uk/eu/pages/privacy/en_GB/privacy_faq.html.

How secure is the data we collect?

We have physical, electronic, and managerial procedures to safeguard and secure the information we collect.

And please remember:

- You provide personal data at your own risk: unfortunately, no data transmission is guaranteed to be 100% secure
- You are responsible of your username and password: keep them secret and safe!
- If you believe your privacy has been breached, please contact us immediately on support@juro.com

Where do we store the data?

The personal data we collect is processed at our offices in London and Riga and in any data processing facilities operated by the third parties identified below.

By submitting your personal data, you agree to this transfer, storing or processing by us. If we transfer or store your information outside the EEA in this way, we will take steps to ensure that your privacy rights continue to be protected as outlined in this Privacy Policy.

How long do we store your data?

We will archive and stop actively using any personal identifiable information about you within 6 months from the last time you used Juro. We will delete your personal data from our archives no later than 6 years from the last time you used Juro or as agreed with you in a separate contract.

Figure 2.2 FAQ-style headings used in the Juro Privacy Policy
Note: The FAQ-style headings pattern can also be used in contracts and terms and conditions. For examples, see World Commerce and Contracting (WorldCC), S Passera and H Haapio, 'FAQ-Style Headings' (*WorldCC Contract Design Pattern Library*), https://contract-design.worldcc.com/FAQ-headings? accessed 17 August 2021. For research consents, see Moore and Doerr, 'The Elements of Informed Consent' 36.
Source: Juro, 'The Juro Privacy Policy' <https://juro.com/policy.html> accessed 17 August 2021.

FAQ-based patterns are useful because users often skim-read to find answers to specific questions or to assess if the text is relevant and worth their time. They may stop to read details only when they think that they are relevant. Questions help reframe the topics from the point of view of the readers, increasing the chances that they will recognise the content as relevant and stop to read it.

2.3.3.2 Organisation and Navigation Patterns

Organisation and navigation patterns help readers find their way through the information and find what they need. They help structure the content so that it is logical, meaningful and relevant to the readers. Used together, the patterns help present information in a way that maximises its clarity and understandability. They facilitate skim-reading and ease of use. Ideally, they offer a visual and logical access structure, with visible and well-organised headings, sections, pages, cross-references, as well as indexes, tables of contents and menus.[96]

A table pattern can be used when there is a need to structure information so that readers can skim and process a lot of information at a glance: tables can be read very rapidly. They can also be used to facilitate comparison and choice between different elements. Tables offer a systematic way to arrange information in rows and columns. This allows readers to search and read the information more easily and break down the 'wall of text'. The example in Figure 2.3 explains the reasons why and how a person's data may be shared with third parties. The information is broken down in order to depict it in a clear and consistent manner.

Third parties who process your data

Tech businesses often use third parties to help them host their application, communicate with customers, power their emails etc. We partner with third parties who we believe are the best in their field at what they do.

When we do this, sometimes it is necessary for us to share your data with them in order to get these services to work well. Your data is shared only when strictly necessary and according to the safeguards and good practices detailed in this Privacy Policy. Where personal data is transferred to a third party in the United States we take steps to ensure we agree the standard contractual clauses with them. We continually monitor this transfer mechanism. Any data transfers to the US are encrypted and generally consist of insensitive personal data.

Here are the details of our main third-party service providers, and what data they collect or we share with them, where they store the data and why they need it:

Infrastructure

Service provider	**Data collected or shared**	**Purpose**	**Place of processing**
Amazon Web Services, Inc. (Privacy policy)	• Contact details • Data from your contracts • Data that identifies you	This is a web hosting provider: we use it to store contracts and other data you generate by using the service securely in the cloud.	EU (or US if you ask us to)
MongoDB, Inc. (Privacy policy)	• Contact details • Data from your contracts • Data that identifies you • Data on how you use Juro	This is a hosted database provider: we use it to store data generated through your use of Juro.	EU

Figure 2.3 Table pattern used in the Juro Privacy Policy
Source: Juro, 'The Juro Privacy Policy'.

[96] See WorldCC, S Passera and H Haapio, 'Navigation' (*WorldCC Contract Design Pattern Library*), https://contract-design.worldcc.com/library/navigation, accessed 17 August 2021; WorldCC, S Passera and H Haapio, 'Organizing' (*WorldCC Contract Design Pattern Library*), https://contract-design.worldcc.com/library/organizing, accessed 17 August 2021.

It is not always practical to use words only. Most readers are busy and need the information to be presented in a simple and straightforward fashion. Timeline patterns may allow them to contextualise and understand at a glance the information according to their own experience.[97] Timelines represent time or duration, a series of steps, tasks or processes taking place within a given time frame, or a sequence of events.[98] Timeline patterns may help to explain the course of actions and requirements that need to be taken in a chronological order. Figure 2.4 illustrates an example of a privacy timeline showing the data collection process. The graphic shows the exact moments when data are collected, making the process more tangible and transparent.

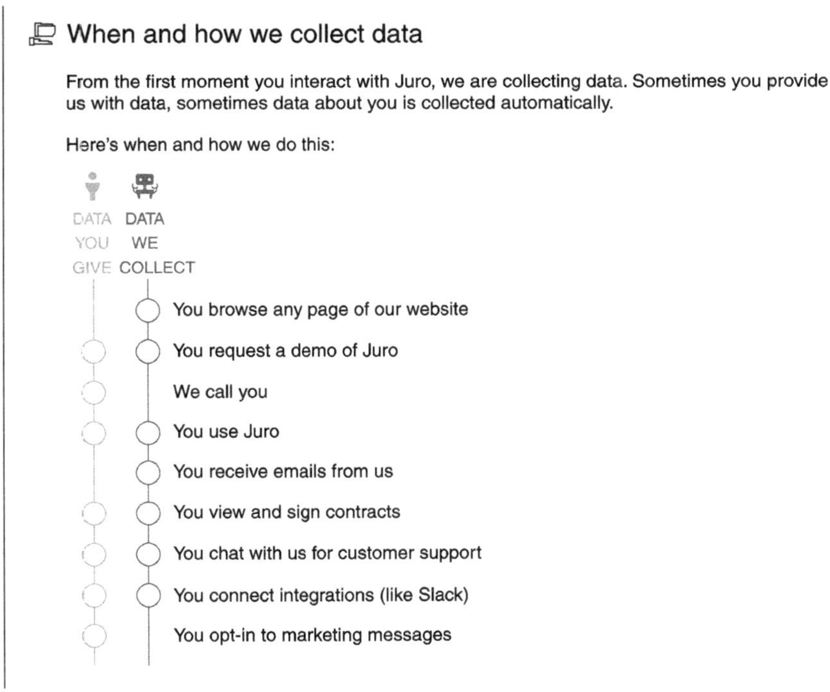

Figure 2.4 Timeline pattern showing the data collection process in the Juro Privacy Policy
Source: Juro, 'The Juro Privacy Policy'.

[97] Haapio and Passera, 'Contracts as Interfaces' 226–28.

[98] See WorldCC, S Passera and H Haapio, 'Timeline' (*WorldCC Contract Design Pattern Library*), https://contract-design.worldcc.com/timeline?, accessed 17 August 2021.

Different outcomes are set out, and different colours indicate the data collection process from both the user and the company experience.[99]

In addition to helping organise the content of complex communication in a way that is meaningful for the reader, navigation patterns can also be used to show information at the time when it matters. By using design patterns at the appropriate time, participants are helped to understand the types of data that are being collected and other aspects, for example how they have the ability to change their data sharing permission.[100]

Consider a person who has heard about a study from recruitment materials and is looking for additional information on the purpose of the study, eligibility criteria and requirements of participation.[101] Different information matters at different stages of the person's journey. Before being able to make her data available for the study, she is required to provide informed consent via a dedicated mobile application. She needs to prove that she has understood the reason why and by whom her data will be analysed, the benefits and risks and her rights as a participant and a data owner. This process can be long and the related information, if everything is presented at one time, can be overwhelming.

Providing the information at stages and turning the process into an easy-to-navigate experience helps guide the participant to a choice that can be genuinely described as informed. The example in Figure 2.5 helps break down the consent process, gives an overview of the various steps and combines simple text with images. Videos, comics or other visual means can be added to support comprehension in each phase. Navigation is supported through the different stages until the person lands on the options for data use authorisation. A quiz and an assessment of her understanding can be made a precondition before activating the possibility to grant consent.[102]

[99] Haapio and Passera, 'Contracts as Interfaces'.

[100] V Barone and others, 'The Privacy Toolkit for Mobile Health Research Studies – Providing Biomedical Researchers with a Catalog of Privacy Design Patterns for Their Digital Studies' (*Privacy Forecast 2019*), https://privacy.shorensteincenter.org/mobilehealth, accessed 17 August 2021.

[101] The following two examples and pattern descriptions are adapted from Rossi and Haapio, 'Proactive Legal Design for Health Data Sharing Based on Smart Contracts', exploring design patterns as a means to bring proactive Legal Design to practice and to promote transparency and trust in health data sharing.

[102] Rossi and Haapio, 'Proactive Legal Design for Health Data Sharing Based on Smart Contracts'. For quizzes and assessments, see Moore and Doerr, 'The Elements of Informed Consent' 27–28. For comics, see WM Botes, 'Visual Communication as a Legal-Ethical Tool for Informed Consent in Genome Research Involving the San Community of South Africa' (Doctoral thesis, University of South Africa 2017); see a portion in Rossi and Lenzini, 'Transparency by Design in Data-Informed Research' 12–13.

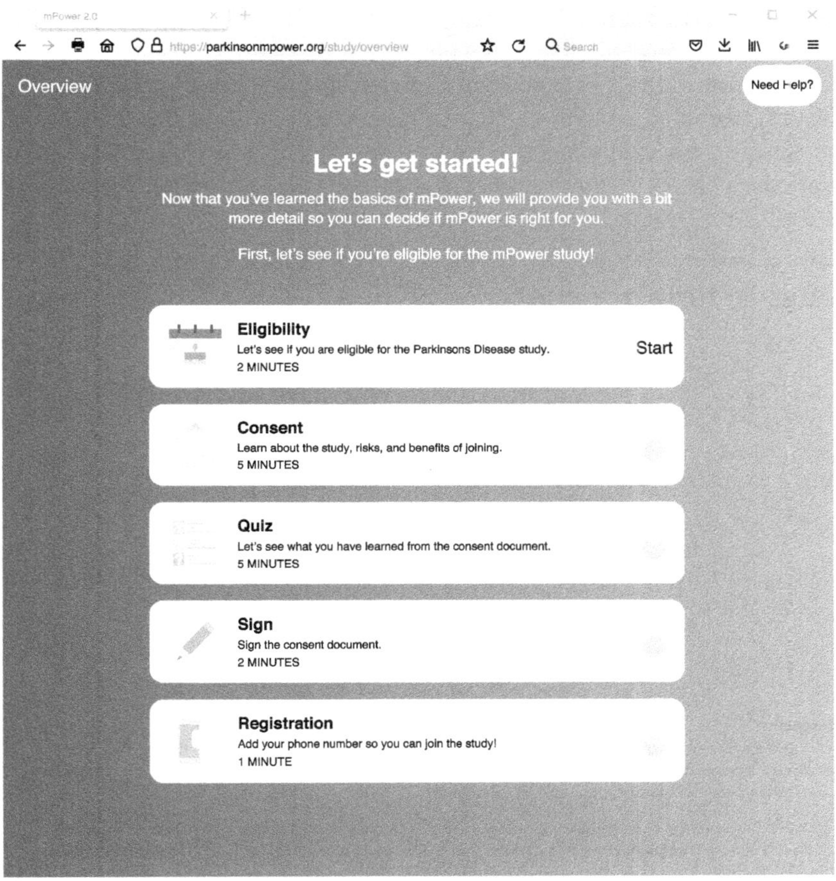

Figure 2.5 Navigable eConsent process: steps for participation in a research study on Parkinson's disease
Source: Sage Bionetworks, 'Overview' (*mPower 2.0*), https://parkinsonmpower.org/study/overview accessed 17 August 2021. Image used with permission.

In conventional consent and permission models, information about possible data uses is provided at a single point in time, often at registration or when installing an app. At that time, participants may not understand the options or may not have time to consider the implications of what they are agreeing to. Permission options that are not relevant for the task at hand may alienate people from participation or nudge them to refuse permission.[103] The example in Figure 2.6 illustrates a dynamic, just-in-time consent pattern that helps provide participants with relevant information at the moment when they need to authorise or refuse the collection of data. It enables participants to receive notifications, engages in the provision of granular authorisations for specific research activities and updates their preferences about data access by certain organisations.[104]

GIVING AND REMOVING CONSENT

Just-in-time consent

Tweet

Description

Ask for a specific permission at the point in time when someone needs to complete a task. This is also known as 'incremental authorisation'. If someone wants to tag a photo with their location, they're asked for permission to access location data as they add the tag.

IF thinks this pattern makes it easier for people to understand why data is being collected. They can weigh up their options at the point when it is needed. Using this pattern too frequently can mean that people ignore it, though.

Figure 2.6 Just-in-time consent pattern shown in IF's Data Patterns Catalogue
Source: IF, 'Just-in-Time Consent' (*Data Patterns Catalogue*), https://catalogue.projectsbyif.com/patterns/just-in-time-consent, accessed 17 August 2021. Licensed under CC BY 4.0.

[103] Rossi and Haapio, 'Proactive Legal Design for Health Data Sharing Based on Smart Contracts'; Sage Bionetworks, 'Just-in-Time Permission' (*Privacy Toolkit*), https://designmanual.sagebionetworks.org/just-in-time-permission.html, accessed 17 August 2021.

[104] Rossi and Haapio, 'Proactive Legal Design for Health Data Sharing Based on Smart Contracts'; I Budin-Ljøsne and others, 'Dynamic Consent: A Potential Solution to Some of the Challenges of Modern Biomedical Research' (2017) 18 *BMC Medical Ethics* art. 4, 3, https://doi.org/10.1186/s12910-016-0162-9, accessed 17 August 2021. For dynamic-informed consent in the context of population genomics, see also FK Dankar and others, 'Dynamic-Informed Consent: A Potential Solution for Ethical Dilemmas in Population Sequencing Initiatives' (2020) 18 *Computational and Structural Biotechnology Journal* 913, https://doi.org/10.1016/j.csbj.2020.03.027, accessed 17 August 2021.

2.3.3.3 Layering Patterns: Overview First, Details on Demand

Full privacy notices are often very long and complex. Readers must scroll down, which can be tedious, particularly in mobile apps. Summarising and layering refer to pattern families which seek to help users get an overview and find the most relevant information easily, without being overwhelmed with details they do not need.[105] Easy-to-read summaries can be placed next to the original text throughout the document or at the beginning of the document to help accommodate the needs of both those who only want to get the main idea and those who want to be informed in-depth.

The example in Figure 2.7 shows the first layer of Juro's Privacy Policy, your-privacy-at-a-glance summary, shown when a user lands on the main page. Users can click through to the full policy if they want to read more. Further information is made available in manageable bits using a design pattern known as accordion: key information is presented at the top which, when clicked, displays further details inside expandable panels. This example also shows the use of further design patterns, such as companion icons.[106]

The examples given earlier indicate that a number of solutions already exist that help break down the wall of text. There are many other challenges in legal communication, of course – and many design patterns to respond to them. As practitioners and researchers collect and share more design patterns, we envision new and better ways to promote transparency and informed consent and to translate regulatory requirements and abstract Privacy-by-Design principles into applicable solutions.[107]

[105] WorldCC, S Passera and H Haapio, 'Layering' (*WorldCC Contract Design Pattern Library*), https://contract-design.worldcc.com/library/layering, accessed 17 August 2021; WorldCC, S Passera and H Haapio, 'Pattern Families' (*WorldCC Contract Design Pattern Library*), https://contract-design.worldcc.com/families-overview, accessed 17 August 2021; WorldCC, S Passera and H Haapio, 'Summarizing' (*WorldCC Contract Design Pattern Library*), https://contract-design.worldcc.com/library/summarizing, accessed 17 August 2021. For examples of using a layered approach in the context of research consents, see Moore and Doerr, 'The Elements of Informed Consent' 33–34.

[106] For a more detailed description of the patterns used and of the project, see S Passera, 'Juro Privacy Policy', https://stefaniapassera.com/portfolio/juro/, accessed 17 August 2021. In the spring of 2021, Juro and Stefania Passera made the privacy design patterns – a 'privacy summary' modal and the full layered privacy notice – and the code base on GitHub openly accessible for those who want to deploy them in their own privacy notice. See design-first privacy notice template at GitHub, 'juro-privacy/free-privacy-notice', https://github.com/juro-privacy/free-privacy-notice, accessed 9 August 2021.

[107] For further examples see, e.g., Rossi and others, 'Legal Design Patterns'; Rossi and others, 'When Design Met Law'; Rossi and Lenzini, 'Transparency by Design in Data-Informed Research'. For contract design patterns, see also WorldCC, Passera and Haapio, 'WorldCC Contract Design Pattern Library'. For informed consent for research, see Moore and Doerr, 'The Elements of Informed Consent', with references.

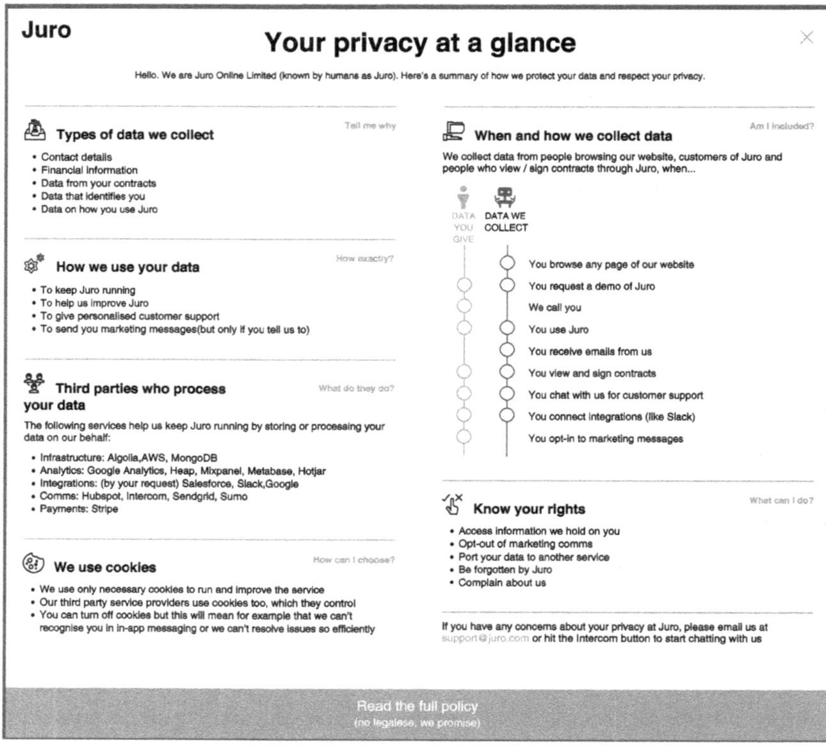

Figure 2.7 The first layer of the Juro Privacy Policy: overview first, details on demand

Source: Juro, 'The Juro Privacy Policy'.

2.4 Legal Design in Digital Health: Examples and Challenges

Sharing data and keeping privacy may seem like conflicting goals. Medical institutions, developers and technology companies around the world have started to look for ways to respond to the needs of individuals and to the challenges faced by healthcare professionals and medical researchers. Solutions already exist that allow individuals to share their health data with the apps of their choice while keeping control over their data and choosing how they want it to be shared, and open access tools are available for researchers and developers to create such apps.[108] For example, the ResearchKit, an open-source framework introduced by Apple, allows researchers and developers to create apps for medical research, offering tools to create visual consent flows, real-time dynamic active tasks and surveys using customisable modules to build on and share.[109]

We envision platforms that provide a user-friendly interface for everyone, both healthcare professionals and the people who want to manage and maintain their health. In addition, we envision open access *toolkits of toolkits*: resources that include design patterns and other tools helping developers and researchers create apps that enable users to better understand and manage their health and their data. Such platforms and toolkits can be built on existing technology, with the goal of being smart at the back, but seeming simple, intuitive and clear at the front.[110]

However, the uniqueness of the healthcare sector brings about specific challenges of implementing Legal Design in the digital health context. Preventive and therapeutic care will soon be driven by disruptive technologies such as AI, ML, wearable devices, Internet of Things (IoT), cloud computing and Big Data predictive analytics. Besides collecting medical data at the point of care, the technology behind Super Platforms will allow engineers and scientists to work with large amounts of data from mobile and wearable devices in unprecedented ways.[111]

[108] See, e.g., Apple, 'CareKit' (*Apple ResearchKit & CareKit*); Apple, 'CareKit' (*Apple Developer*). According to the accompanying Human Interface Guidelines (Apple, 'Data and Privacy. Human Interface Guidelines/CareKit' (*Apple Developer*), https://developer.apple.com/design/human-interface-guidelines/carekit/overview/data-and-privacy/, accessed 17 August 2021), '[n]othing is more important than protecting people's privacy and safeguarding the extremely sensitive data your CareKit app collects and stores'.

[109] See Apple, 'Introducing ResearchKit'. See also Apple, 'Resources' (*Apple ResearchKit & CareKit*), www.researchandcare.org/resources, accessed 17 August 2021: 'We've put together all the content, code, and support you need to get started on your ResearchKit or CareKit app.' Both Kits come with Human Interface Guidelines and other UI resources.

[110] 'Be simple on the front, and smart at the back' is principle 5 in M Hagan, '6 Core Principles for Good Legal Design' (*Legal Design and Innovation Blog/Medium*, 7 November 2016), https://medium.com/legal-design-and-innovation/6-core-principles-for-good-legal-design-1cde6aba866, accessed 17 August 2021; we are indebted to Margaret Hagan for this phrase.

[111] A Ananthan, 'The Imminent Digital Health Revolution' (*Electronic Design*, 4 October 2017), www.electronicdesign.com/embedded-revolution/imminent-digital-health-revolution, accessed 17 August 2021.

To better illustrate this challenge, one may think of it from two different layer perspectives: (1) the underlying infrastructure enabling technology (such as cloud computing and IoT) and (2) the data-analytics framework (such as AI and ML), which focuses on the smart algorithms that help doctors and patients make more data-driven and informed decisions.[112]

The first-layer framework is usually composed of three main elements, namely edge node(s), a cloud aggregator and a back-end data-analytics engine.[113]

Edge nodes collect all kinds of raw physiological health data through various sensors. Most of the wearable devices developed by Big Tech companies described in the Super Platforms context are good examples of such edge nodes. These include some proprietary FDA-regulated devices such as blood-glucose sensors (inserted under the patient's skin to measure glucose levels) and electrocardiogram (ECG) monitors (used to scan and analyse the heart's rhythm and detect cardiac issues).[114]

A *cloud aggregator* is a gateway that can stream data from the edge nodes and take advantage of cloud-based computational resources. With the right signal or image-processing technologies, it is possible to collect signal features and transfer them to the cloud. The cloud infrastructure makes it possible to reduce bandwidth requirements and improve the computational power of these wearable devices.[115]

A *back-end data-analytics engine* allows the data collected to be processed and analysed to extract meaningful information from the aggregated data (for analysing patterns, trends, anomaly detection, etc.).[116]

The second-layer framework which helps us to understand this landscape is the data-analytics framework, including AI and ML algorithms that add intelligence into this entire operating system. This helps physicians and patients to transform data into actionable insights. These smart algorithms allow healthcare professionals to analyse large amounts of data to amplify and accelerate diagnostic capabilities.[117]

112 Ibid.
113 Ibid.
114 Ibid.
115 Ibid.
116 Ibid.
117 Ibid.

This second layer involves the communication between physicians and patients which is crucial for the informed consent and decision-making process. In this phase, doctors need to translate and explain the accrued information back to the patient. One example of this is the integration into electronic health records (EMR) and patient guidance. EMR is a digital version of the conventional paper-based medical record for a patient. Implementing EMR solutions has been known to improve medical practices' productivity as well as the quality of care provided to patients.[118]

One example that illustrates all the phases of this challenging landscape very well is so-called 'ingestible electronic sensors' (IES), also known as 'smart pills'. IES are small electronic devices – roughly the size of a medicine tablet – composed of biocompatible and non-invasive materials, which have the ability to telecommunicate relevant information for the monitoring and diagnosis of disease in the healthcare sector.[119]

IES is a disruptive technology that works through wearable sensors and microprocessors. Once the smart pill is ingested into the human body – either with medicine or as an embedded part of a drug – the sensors and microprocessors are capable of storing and collecting all sorts of valuable data such as medication intake or behavioural and physiological metrics. The wearable sensors and microprocessors then transfer the collected data to a connected computing device such as a smartphone or a tablet, which then displays the information to a user interface.[120]

IES have already entered the mainstream market in the United States and Europe, and it is expected that more products will be launched soon. Examples include Proteus Discover, Abilify MyCite, Atmo Gas-Sensing Capsule and an ingestible bacterial-electronic sensor designed by MIT School of Engineering, which can communicate with

118 For a more detailed description of the infographics used in electronic health records (EHR), see www.capterra.com/infographics/top-emr-software.

119 S Gerke and others, 'Ethical and Legal Issues of Ingestible Electronic Sensors' (2019) 2(8) *Nature Electronics* 329, https://doi.org/10.1038/s41928-019-0290-6, accessed 17 August 2021.

120 E Fernandez, 'That Pill Is Watching You – Privacy and Hackability of Ingestible Electronic Sensors' (*Forbes*, 3 September 2019), www.forbes.com/sites/fernandezelizabeth/2019/09/03/that-pill-is-watching-youprivacy-and-hackability-of-ingestible-electronic-sensors/#24420a08405e, accessed 17 August 2021; Gerke and others, 'Ethical and Legal Issues of Ingestible Electronic Sensors' 329–30.

your gastrointestinal tract, and the wireless transmitters can send and share the information outside the body through the patient's mobile phone.[121]

IES are a promising technology for improving health outcomes and making healthcare more effective, since they make it possible to monitor the interaction of drugs with the human body and to control drug administration. Yet IES also raise a great variety of ethical and legal challenges. On the ethical side, there are key challenges for IES relating to patients, physicians and society more generally, and in particular with regard to autonomy and informed consent, as well as ownership rights of data collected by IES products, including the question of the doctor–patient privilege and the related issue of medical confidentiality.[122]

On the legal side, it is important to consider the regulatory frameworks for the approval of such devices; furthermore, intellectual property rights, privacy protection, international data transfer regimes, cybersecurity, accountability, transparency, explainability, fairness and robustness are of crucial importance.[123] However, regulatory frameworks often face the challenge of keeping apace of technology and the regulatory landscape is always changing.

This is where UI-focused Privacy-by-Design can contribute to the new Super Platforms ecosystem emerging in the healthcare sector. If the goal is that digital health apps should be broadly accepted and trusted by society, patients and markets, it is of vital importance for developers to address and consider such issues at the earliest stages of the product development process.

The UI-layer Privacy-by-Design applied to the digital health context can guide the patients/end users through all the phases of this process where challenges seem to be more acute due to (1) the sensitivity, richness and uncertain limits of the information collected by the 'edge nodes'; (2) the complexity of the processes by which that information is acquired and (3) the need for an interface to translate and explain the informed consent process and accrued information back to the patient.

When preparing a platform or a solution, designers and builders need a common language so they can convey their messages among the team members, for example from subject matter experts to lawyers to coders and vice versa – and then ensure that the output makes sense for the users,

[121] Gerke and others, 'Ethical and Legal Issues of Ingestible Electronic Sensors' 329.
[122] Ibid 332–33.
[123] Ibid 333.

patients and professionals alike. As regards the output, whether displayed on a screen or printed documents, design patterns can help them do so: graphic elements such as tables, bullet lists or diagrams can be used to make the content clearer and easier to navigate. The use of timelines, swim lanes or other visual design patterns can help the reader and make the information easier to find.

We hope that our vision and examples can contribute to digital health platforms and apps adopting new and more transparent ways of conveying complex legal messages, including privacy communication, in the near future. A user-friendly interface can hide the complexity, simplifying and improving the user experience of the platform and apps. The toolkit for developers, as we envision it, would include 'UI layer' design patterns.[124]

2.5 Conclusion

The Digital Revolution has triggered the emergence of new business models, new products and new services. As a result, the healthcare sector is radically changing the traditional way of providing medical services and treatment. Hospitals, clinics, pharmaceuticals and medical research centres are all now partnering with start-ups and Big Tech companies, creating new online decentralised structures or ecosystems that we here labelled Super Platforms.

This opens the way for a new data-driven healthcare market and the development of a wide range of specialised software apps powered by historically unprecedented AI and algorithm capabilities. It is clear that Super Platforms will inevitably emerge and benefit the healthcare and

[124] At the time of writing, some promising new tools and resources have become available that can be added to the toolkit we envision. Apart from those mentioned in notes 46–47, 88–92 and 106, offerings by law firms and legal tech companies include AI-powered analytics, review and generation tools for privacy policy and contracts – see, e.g., Maigon AI https://maigon.io, accessed 16 August 2021, offering a set of tools to analyse privacy policies and data processing agreements for compliance with GDPR criteria, for example – 'Get instant compliance report with extracted clauses, concepts, terms, highlighted risks, and compliance recommendations'; and LegalSifter, www.legalsifter.com, accessed 16 August 2021, introducing LegalSifter Review as 'AI software that reads a contract and gives advice before you sign, reducing risk and saving time'. For computable language models and AI-powered tools for contract readers and writers, see M Corrales Compagnucci, M Fenwick and H Haapio, 'Digital Technology, Future Lawyers and the Computable Contract Designer of Tomorrow' in Corrales Compagnucci M, Haapio H and Fenwick M (eds), *The Research Handbook on Contract Design* (Edward Elgar Publishing 2022).

pharmaceutical industry. However, this new trend also brings a number of legal and ethical concerns as these apps and other online tools have important implications for privacy rights in particular.

Here we have taken the view that in a healthcare context, Legal Design can provide a reliable and transparent infrastructure for embedding relevant legal protections in the user interfaces, privacy policies, and terms of use of healthcare products and services. Legal Design is about putting the user in the centre and finding the right balance between simplicity and ease of use on the one hand and compliance with the applicable legal requirements on the other. Such a UI-focused Privacy-by-Design approach offers several advantages, most obviously greater transparency, accountability and (consequently) human choice. For such an approach to be truly effective, however, it requires further efforts to be applied to the practical challenge of developing design patterns that can be deployed in diverse real-world settings.

With the development of design patterns and pattern libraries, it becomes easier for legal technologists, privacy professionals and legal designers to co-create better AI products and provide better legal communications, systems and solutions, resulting in better experiences for all users, including patients, healthcare professionals and medical researchers. Recent research and practice illustrate how UI layer design patterns can help transform dysfunctional disclosures, legal notices and data processing information into useful and usable communication that works for (rather than against) their intended audience.

And, of course, it is important to note that the law is only one factor amongst a myriad of factors that will impact on how much choice users have in this context. There needs to be 'buy-in' from the technology companies developing these apps and from companies using the data and making accessing apps/platforms contingent upon users surrendering their data for other purposes. How much choice users will ultimately have in determining data uses will be as reliant upon the app platform hosts as it is on the legal infrastructure.

Acknowledgements

Two of the authors (Marcelo Corrales Compagnucci and Timo Minssen) were supported by a Novo Nordisk Foundation grant for a scientifically independent Collaborative Research Program in Biomedical Innovation Law (grant agreement number NNF17SA0027784).

Bibliography

Alexander C, Ishikawa S, Silverstein M, Jacobson M, Fiksdahl-King I and Angel S, *A Pattern Language: Towns, Buildings, Construction* (Oxford University Press 1977).

Alpaydin E, *Machine Learning: The New AI* (MIT Press 2016).

Ananthan A, 'The Imminent Digital Health Revolution' (*Electronic Design*, 4 October 2017), www.electronicdesign.com/embedded-revolution/imminent-digital-health-revolution, accessed 17 August 2021.

Anderson D, *A Question of Trust* (Williams Lea Group 2015).

Apple, 'CareKit' (*Apple Developer*), https://developer.apple.com/carekit/, accessed 17 August 2021.

Apple, 'CareKit' (*Apple ResearchKit & CareKit*), www.researchandcare.org/carekit/, accessed 17 August 2021.

Apple, 'Data and Privacy. Human Interface Guidelines/CareKit' (*Apple Developer*), https://developer.apple.com/design/human-interface-guidelines/carekit/overview/data-and-privacy/, accessed 17 August 2021.

Apple, 'Health and Fitness' (*Apple Developer*), https://developer.apple.com/health-kit/, accessed 17 August 2021.

Apple, 'Introducing ResearchKit' (*ResearchKit*), http://researchkit.org, accessed 17 August 2021.

Apple, 'iOS – Health', www.apple.com/uk/ios/health/, accessed 17 August 2021.

Apple, 'iOS – Research', www.apple.com/ios/research-app, accessed 17 August 2021.

Apple, 'Resources' (*Apple ResearchKit & CareKit*), www.researchandcare.org/resources, accessed 17 August 2021.

Article 29 Data Protection Working Party, 'Guidelines on the Right to Data Portability' (16/EN, WP 242 rev.01, 5 April 2017), https://ec.europa.eu/newsroom/document.cfm?doc_id=44099, accessed 17 August 2021.

Article 29 Data Protection Working Party, 'Guidelines on Transparency under Regulation 2016/679' (17/EN, WP260 rev.01, 11 April 2018), https://ec.europa.eu/newsroom/document.cfm?doc_id=51025, accessed 17 August 2021.

Barone V, MacDuffie W, Guan Y and Simon S, 'The Privacy Toolkit for Mobile Health Research Studies – Providing Biomedical Researchers with a Catalog of Privacy Design Patterns for Their Digital Studies' (*Privacy Forecast 2019*), https://privacy.shorensteincenter.org/mobilehealth, accessed 17 August 2021.

Botes WM, 'Visual Communication as a Legal-Ethical Tool for Informed Consent in Genome Research Involving the San Community of South Africa' (Doctoral thesis, University of South Africa 2017).

Breen C, *Secrets of the iPod and iTunes* (5th edn, Peachpit Press 2004).

Budin-Ljøsne I, Teare HJA, Kaye J, et al., 'Dynamic Consent: A Potential Solution to Some of the Challenges of Modern Biomedical Research' (2017) 18 *BMC Medical Ethics* art. 4, https://doi.org/10.1186/s12910-016-0162-9, accessed 17 August 2021.

Buvailo A, 'Get Ready for "Super-platforms" in Healthcare and Pharmaceutical Research' (*BiopharmaTrend.com*, 27 September 2018), www.biopharmatrend.com/post/71-get-ready-for-super-platforms-in-healthcare-and-pharmaceutical-research, accessed 17 August 2021.

CitizenDoc, https://app.citizendoc.fr, accessed 9 March 2021.

Codagnonce C, Karatzogianni A and Matthews J, *Platform Economics: Rhetoric and Reality in the 'Sharing Economy'* (Emerald Publishing 2019).

Corning C, 'The Rise of Super Platform' (*Cars.com*, 17 October 2018), https://growwith-cars.com/blog/2018/10/17/the-rise-of-the-super-platform, accessed 17 August 2021.

Corrales M, Jurčys P and Kousiouris G, 'Smart Contracts and Smart Disclosure: Coding a GDPR Compliance Framework' in Corrales M, Fenwick M and Haapio H (eds), *Legal Tech, Smart Contracts and Blockchain* (Springer 2019).

Corrales Compagnucci M, Fenwick M and Haapio H, 'Digital Technology, Future Lawyers and the Computable Contract Designer of Tomorrow' in Corrales Compagnucci M, Haapio H and Fenwick M (eds), *The Research Handbook on Contract Design* (Edward Elgar Publishing 2022).

Corrales Compagnucci M, Haapio H and Fenwick M (eds), *The Research Handbook on Contract Design* (Edward Elgar Publishing 2022).

Corrales Compagnucci M, Haapio H, Hagan M and Doherty M (eds), *Legal Design: Integrating Business, Design and Legal Thinking with Technology* (Edward Elgar Publishing 2021).

Corrales Compagnucci M, Kono T and Teramoto S, 'Legal Aspects of Decentralized and Platform-Driven Economies' in Corrales Compagnucci M, Forgó N, Kono T, Teramoto S and Vermeulen EPM (eds), *Legal Tech and the New Sharing Economy* (Springer 2020).

Corrales Compagnucci M, Minssen T, Seitz C and Aboy M, 'Lost on the High Seas without a Safe Harbour or a Schield? Navigating Cross-Border Data Transfers in the Pharmaceutical Sector After Schrems II Invalidation of the EU-US Privacy Shield' (2020) 4(3) *European Pharmaceutical Law Review* 153.

D'Acquisto G, Domingo-Ferrer J, Kikiras P, Torra V, de Montjoye Y-A and Bourka A, *Privacy by Design in Big Data: An Overview of Privacy Enchanting Technologies in the Era of Big Data Analytics* (European Union Agency for Network and Information Security ENISA 2015), www.enisa.europa.eu/publications/big-data-protection/at_download/fullReport, DOI: 10.2824/641480, accessed 17 August 2021.

Dankar FK, Gergely M, Malin B, Badji R, Dankar SK and Shuaiba K, 'Dynamic-Informed Consent: A Potential Solution for Ethical Dilemmas in Population Sequencing Initiatives' (2020) 18 *Computational and Structural Biotechnology Journal* 913, https://doi.org/10.1016/j.csbj.2020.03.027, accessed 17 August 2021.

De Arriba-Pérez F, Caeiro-Rodríguez M and Santos-Gago JM, 'Collection and Processing of Data from Wrist Wearable Devices in Heterogeneous and Multiple-User Scenarios' (2016) 16(9) *Sensors* 1538, https://doi.org/10.3390/s16091538, accessed 17 August 2021.

Directive 95/46/EC of the European Parliament and of the Council of 24 October 1995 on the protection of individuals with regard to the processing of personal data and on the free movement of such data [1995] OJ L281/31.

Doerr M, Suver C and Wilbanks J, 'Developing a Transparent, Participant-Navigated Electronic Informed Consent for Mobile-Mediated Research' (SageBionetworks, Paper 22 April 2016), https://ssrn.com/abstract_id=2769129, accessed 17 August 2021.

Doherty M, Corrales Compagnucci M, Haapio H and Hagan M, 'A New Attitude to Law's Empire: The Potentialities of Legal Design' in Corrales Compagnucci M, Haapio H, Hagan M and Doherty M (eds), *Legal Design: Integrating Business, Design and Legal Thinking with Technology* (Edward Elgar Publishing 2021).

Eggers WD, Turley M and Kishnani P, 'The Future of Regulation: Principles for Regulating Emerging Technologies' (*Deloitte Insights*, 19 June 2018), www2.deloitte.com/insights/us/en/industry/public-sector/future-of-regulation/regulating-emerging-technology.html, accessed 17 August 2021.

Ernst & Young, 'A Vision for Platform Based Banking' (2018), https://assets.ey.com/content/dam/ey-sites/ey-com/en_us/topics/financial-services/ey-a-vision-for-platform-based-banking.pdf, accessed 17 August 2021.

European Commission, 'Proposal for a Regulation of the European Parliament and of the Council Laying Down Harmonised Rules on Artificial Intelligence (Artificial Intelligence Act) and Amending Certain Union Legislative Acts' COM (2021) 206 final, https://digital-strategy.ec.europa.eu/en/library/proposal-regulation-european-approach-artificial-intelligence, accessed 17 August 2021.

European Commission, 'Report on Safety and Liability Implications of AI, the Internet of Things and Robotics' COM (2020) 64 final, https://ec.europa.eu/info/sites/info/files/report-safety-liability-artificial-intelligence-feb2020_en_1.pdf, accessed 17 August 2021.

European Commission, 'Standard Contractual Clauses for International Transfers' (Directorate-General for Justice and Consumers, 4 June 2021), https://ec.europa.eu/info/law/law-topic/data-protection/international-dimension-data-protection/standard-contractual-clauses-scc/standard-contractual-clauses-international-transfers_en, accessed 14 August 2021.

European Commission, 'White Paper on Artificial Intelligence: A European Approach to Excellence and Trust' COM (2020) 65 final, https://ec.europa.eu/info/sites/info/files/commission-white-paper-artificial-intelligence-feb2020_en.pdf, accessed 17 August 2021.

European Data Protection Board, 'Recommendations 01/2020 on Measures that Supplement Transfer Tools to Ensure Compliance with the EU Level of Protection of Personal Data' (version 2.0, adopted on 18 June 2021), https://edpb.europa.eu/system/files/2021-06/edpb_recommendations_202001vo.2.0_supplementarymeasurestransferstools_en.pdf, accessed 14 August 2021.

Fenwick M, McCahery JA and Vermeulen EPM, 'The End of "Corporate" Governance: Hello "Platform" Governance' (2019) 20 *European Business Organization Law Review* 171, https://doi.org/10.1007/s40804-019-00137-z, accessed 17 August 2021.

Fenwick M and Vermeulen EPM, 'The New Firm' (2015) 16(4) *European Business Organization Law Review* 595, https://doi.org/10.1007/s40804-016-0040-4, accessed 17 August 2021.

Fernandez E, 'That Pill Is Watching You – Privacy and Hackability of Ingestible Electronic Sensors' (*Forbes*, 3 September 2019), www.forbes.com/sites/fernandezelizabeth/2019/09/03/that-pill-is-watching-youprivacy-and-hackability-of-ingestible-electronic-sensors/#24420a08405e, accessed 17 August 2021.

Galloway S, *The Four: The Hidden DNA of Amazon, Apple, Facebook, and Google* (Random House 2017).

Gamma E, Vlissides J, Johnson R and Helm R, *Design Patterns: Elements of Reusable Object-Oriented Software* (Addison-Wesley 1995).

GE Digital, 'IIoT Platform – Predix Platform', www.ge.com/digital/iiot-platform, accessed 17 August 2021.

Gerke S, Minssen T, Yu H and Cohen IG, 'Ethical and Legal Issues of Ingestible Electronic Sensors' (2019) 2(8) *Nature Electronics* 329, https://doi.org/10.1038/s41928-019-0290-6, accessed 17 August 2021.

GitHub, 'Juro-privacy/free-privacy-notice', https://github.com/juro-privacy/free-privacy-notice, accessed 9 August 2021.

Gjermundrød H, Dionysiou I and Costa K, 'PrivacyTracker: A Privacy-by-Design GDPR-Compliant Framework with Verifiable Data Traceability Controls' in Casteleyn S, Dolog P and Pautasso C (eds), *Current Trends in Web Engineering. ICWE 2016* (Lecture Notes in Computer Science, vol. 9881, Springer 2016).

Gulamhuseinwala I, 'How Banks Could Join the Platform Economy' (*EY Financial Services*, 2017), www.ey.com/gl/en/industries/financial-services/fso-insights-how-banks-could-join-the-platform-economy, accessed 25 May 2020.

Haapio H, *Next Generation Contracts: A Paradigm Shift* (Lexpert Ltd 2013).

Haapio H, Barton TD and Corrales Compagnucci M, 'Legal Design for the Common Good: Proactive Legal Care by Design' in Corrales Compagnucci M, Haapio H, Hagan M and Doherty M (eds), *Legal Design: Integrating Business, Design and Legal Thinking with Technology* (Edward Elgar Publishing 2021).

Haapio H and Hagan M, 'Design Patterns for Contracts' in Schweighofer E, Kummer F, Hötzendorfer W and Borges G (eds), *Networks. Proceedings of the 19th International Legal Informatics Symposium IRIS 2016* (Österreichische Computer Gesellschaft 2016).

Haapio H, Hagan M, Palmirani M and Rossi A, 'Legal Design Patterns for Privacy' in Schweighofer E, Kummer F, Saarenpää A and Schafer B (eds), *Data Protection/ LegalTech. Proceedings of the 21st International Legal Informatics Symposium IRIS 2018* (Editions Weblaw 2018).

Haapio H and Passera S, 'Contracts as Interfaces: Visual Representation Patterns in Contract Design' in Katz DM, Dolin R and Bommarito MJ (eds), *Legal Informatics* (Cambridge University Press 2021).

Haapio H, Siedel G and Bernal Fandiño M, 'Aplicación del Derecho Proactivo como una Ventaja Competitiva' (2016) 31 *Revista de Derecho Privado* 265.

Hadfield G, 'Governments Can't Handle Tech Regulation. It Is Time for Companies to Take Over' (*Quartz*, 2 July 2018, updated 31 July 2018), https://qz.com/1316426/weve-disrupted-technology-now-its-time-to-disrupt-its-regulation/, accessed 17 August 2021.

Hagan M, 'Making Legal Design a Thing – and an Academic Discipline' (*Legal Design and Innovation Blog/Medium*, 14 December 2018), https://medium.com/legal-design-and-innovation/making-legal-design-a-thing-and-an-academic-discipline-5a7e57fa43e8, accessed 17 August 2021.

Hagan M, '6 Core Principles for Good Legal Design' (*Legal Design and Innovation Blog/Medium*, 7 November 2016), https://medium.com/legal-design-and-innovation/6-core-principles-for-good-legal-design-1cde6aba866, accessed 17 August 2021.

Herrmann M, Boehme P, Mondritzki T, Ehlers JP, Kavadias S and Truebel H, 'Digital Transformation and Disruption of the Health Care Sector: Internet-Based Observational Study' (2018) 20(3) *Journal of Medical Internet Research* e104, https://doi.org/10.2196/jmir.9498, accessed 17 August 2021.

High-Level Expert Group on Artificial Intelligence, 'Ethics Guidelines for Trustworthy AI' (European Commission, 8 April 2019), https://digital-strategy.ec.europa.eu/en/library/ethics-guidelines-trustworthy-ai, accessed 17 August 2021.

Hijmans H, *The European Union as Guardian of Internet Privacy: The Story of Art. 16 TFEU* (Springer 2016).

IF, 'Data Patterns Catalogue', https://catalogue.projectsbyif.com, accessed 17 August 2021.

IF, 'Just-in-Time Consent' (*Data Patterns Catalogue*), https://catalogue.projectsbyif.com/patterns/just-in-time-consent, accessed 17 August 2021.

Information Commissioner's Office (ICO), 'Privacy Notices, Transparency and Control. A Code of Practice on Communicating Privacy Information to Individuals' (7 October 2016), www.pdpjournals.com/docs/88625.pdf, accessed 17 August 2021.

Juro, 'The Juro Privacy Policy', https://juro.com/policy.html, accessed 17 August 2021.

Landi H, 'Disruption and the Future of Healthcare: Industry Leaders Parse the Challenges, and Strategic Opportunities' (*Healthcare Innovation*, 4 April 2018), www.hcinnovationgroup.com/population-health-management/article/13030041/disruption-and-the-future-of-healthcare-industry-leaders-parse-the-challenges-and-strategic-opportunities, accessed 17 August 2021.

Lannerö P, 'Fighting the Biggest Lie on the Internet: Common Terms Beta Proposal' (Metamatrix 2013), http://commonterms.org/commonterms_beta_proposal.pdf, accessed 17 August 2021.

Luxton DD, June JD, Sano A and Bickmore T, 'Intelligent Mobile, Wearable, and Ambient Technologies for Behavioral Health Care' in Luxton DD (ed.), *Artificial Intelligence in Behavioral and Mental Healthcare* (Academic Press 2016).

Lynskey O, *The Foundations of EU Data Protection Law* (Oxford University Press 2015).

Maeda J, *The Laws of Simplicity: Design, Technology, Business and Life* (MIT Press 2006).

McNealy J and Flowers A, 'Privacy Law and Regulation: Technologies, Implications and Solutions' in Zeadally S and Badra M (eds), *Privacy in a Digital, Networked World: Technologies, Implications and Solutions* (Springer 2015).

Mehmood R, Faisal MA and Altowaijri S, 'Future Networked Healthcare Systems: A Review and Case Study' in Boucadair M and Jackenet C (eds), *Handbook of Research on Redesigning the Future of Internet Architectures* (IGI Global 2015).

Moore S and Doerr M, 'The Elements of Informed Consent: A Toolkit'. Sage Bionetworks Governance Consent Toolkit (Megan Doerr ed., v3.0, Sage Bionetworks 2020), https://sagebionetworks.org/wp-content/uploads/2020/01/SageBio_EIC-Toolkit_V3_21Jan20_final.pdf, accessed 17 August 2021.

Murphy K and Jain N, 'Riding the Disruption Wave in Healthcare' (*Forbes*, 1 May 2018), www.forbes.com/sites/baininsights/2018/05/01/riding-the-disruption-wave-in-healthcare/#184a33652846, accessed 17 August 2021.

Nanos I, Manthou V and Androutsou E, 'Cloud Computing Adoption Decision in E-Government' in Sifaleras A and Petridis K (eds), *Operational Research in the Digital Era – ICT Challenges* (Springer 2019).

Obar JA and Oeldorf-Hirsch A, 'The Biggest Lie on the Internet: Ignoring the Privacy Policies and Terms of Service Policies of Social Networking Services' (2020) 23(1) *Information, Communication & Society* 128.

Paine J, 'How These 3 Technologies Are Disrupting the Health Care Industry' (*Inc.*, 28 November 2017), www.inc.com/james-paine/3-disruptive-technologies-shaping-future-of-healthcare.html, accessed 17 August 2021.

Parker GG, Van Alsyne MW and Choudary SP, *Platform Revolution: How Networked Markets Are Transforming the Economy and How to Make Them Work for You* (W. W. Norton 2016)

Passera S, Beyond the Wall of Contract Text – Visualizing Contracts to Foster Understanding and Collaboration within and across Organizations (Doctoral Dissertation, Aalto University 2017).

Passera S, 'Juro Privacy Policy', https://stefaniapassera.com/portfolio/juro/, accessed 17 August 2021.

Peyrou B, Vignaux J-J and André A, 'Artificial Intelligence and Healthcare' in André A (ed.), *Digital Medicine* (Springer 2019).

Pollari I, 'The Rise of Digital Platforms in Financial Services' (KPMG 2018), https://assets.kpmg.com/content/dam/kpmg/xx/pdf/2018/02/kpmg-rise-of-digital-platforms.pdf, accessed 17 August 2021.

Privacypatterns.org, 'About', https://privacypatterns.org/about/, accessed 17 August 2021.

Quelle C, 'Not Just User Control in the General Data Protection Regulation: On the Problems with Choice and Paternalism, and on the Point of Data Protection' in Lehmann A, Whitehouse D, Fischer-Hübner S, Fritsch L and Raab C (eds), *Privacy and Identity Management: Facing Up to Next Steps* (Springer 2016).

Raisinghani M, Idemudia EC, Chekuri M, Fisher K and Hanna J, 'Cloud Computing in the 21st Century: A Managerial Perspective for Policies and Practices' in Aljawarneh S (ed.), *Advanced Research on Cloud Computing Design and Applications* (Idea Group 2015).

Rijcken C, 'Sequoias of Artificial Intelligence' in Rijcken C (ed.), *Pharmaceutical Care in Digital Revolution: Insights Towards Circular Innovation* (Academic Press/Elsevier 2019).

Rose D, *Enchanted Objects: Innovation, Design, and the Future of Technology* (Simon and Schuster Inc 2015).

Rossi A, 'Legal Design for the General Data Protection Regulation. A Methodology for the Visualization and Communication of Legal Concepts' (Dottorato di Ricerca in Law, Science and Technology, Alma Mater Studiorum Università di Bologna 2019).

Rossi A, Ducato R, Haapio H and Passera S, 'When Design Met Law: Design Patterns for Information Transparency' (2019) (122–123) *Droit de la Consommation – Consumentenrecht DCCR* 79.

Rossi A, Ducato R, Haapio H, Passera S and Palmirani M, 'Legal Design Patterns: Towards A New Language for Legal Information Design' in Schweighofer E, Kummer F and Saarenpää A (eds), *Internet of Things. Proceedings of the 22nd International Legal Informatics Symposium IRIS 2019* (Editions Weblaw 2019).

Rossi A and Haapio H, 'Proactive Legal Design for Health Data Sharing Based on Smart Contracts' in Corrales Compagnucci M, Fenwick M and Wrbka S (eds), *Smart Contracts: Technological, Business and Legal Perspectives* (Hart-Bloomsbury 2021).

Rossi A and Lenzini G, 'Transparency by Design in Data-Informed Research: A Collection of Information Design Patterns' (2020) 37 *Computer Law & Security Review* 105402, https://doi.org/10.1016/j.clsr.2020.105402, accessed 17 August 2021.

Sage Bionetworks, 'Informed Consent' (*Privacy Toolkit*), https://designmanual.sagebionetworks.org/informed-consent.html, accessed 17 August 2021.

Sage Bionetworks, 'Just-in-Time Permission' (*Privacy Toolkit*), https://designmanual.sagebionetworks.org/just-in-time-permission.html, accessed 17 August 2021.

Sage Bionetworks, 'Overview' (*mPower 2.0*), https://parkinsonmpower.org/study/overview, accessed 17 August 2021.

Sage Bionetworks, 'Privacy Toolkit for Mobile Health Research Studies', https://sagebionetworks.org/tools_resources/privacy-toolkit-for-mobile-health-research-studies, accessed 17 August 2021.

Schumacher E, 'Norway Consumer Council Completes 32-hour App Terms Read-a-thon' (*DW.com*, 25 May 2016), www.dw.com/en/norway-consumer-council-completes-32-hour-app-terms-read-a-thon/a-19283288, accessed 17 August 2021.

Siegel A and Etzkorn I, *Simple: Conquering the Crisis of Complexity* (Twelve 2013).

Sobkow B, 'Forget Me, Forget Me Not – Redefining the Boundaries of the Right to be Forgotten to Address Current Problems and Areas of Criticism' in Schweighofer E, Leitold H, Mitrakas A and Rannenberg K (eds), *Privacy Technologies and Policy. APF 2017* (Lecture Notes in Computer Science, vol. 10518, Springer 2016).

Stanford Medicine, 'Stanford Medicine 2018 Health Trends Report: The Democratization of Health Care' (December 2018), https://med.stanford.edu/content/dam/sm/school/documents/Health-Trends-Report/Stanford-Medicine-Health-Trends-Report-2018.pdf, accessed 17 August 2021.

Svantesson D, *Extraterritoriality in Data Privacy Law* (Ex Tuto Publishing 2013).

Tencent, 'Tencent Open Platform', http://open.qq.com/eng/, accessed 17 August 2021.

Thouvenin F, 'Big Data of Complex Networks and Data Protection Law: An Introduction to an Area of Mutual Conflict' in Dehmer M, Emmert-Streib F, Pickl S and Holzinger A (eds), *Big Data of Complex Networks* (CRC Press 2017).

Voigt P and von dem Bussche A, *The EU General Data Protection Regulation (GDPR): A Practical Guide* (Springer 2017).

Wisman THA, 'Privacy, Data Protection and E-Commerce' in Lodder AR and Murray AD (eds), *EU Regulation of E-Commerce. A Commentary* (Edward Elgar Publishing 2017).

WorldCC (World Commerce and Contracting), Passera S and Haapio H, 'FAQ-Style Headings' (*WorldCC Contract Design Pattern Library*), https://contract-design.worldcc.com/FAQ-headings?, accessed 17 August 2021.

WorldCC (World Commerce and Contracting), Passera S and Haapio H, 'Layering' (*WorldCC Contract Design Pattern Library*), https://contract-design.worldcc.com/library/layering, accessed 17 August 2021.

WorldCC (World Commerce and Contracting), Passera S and Haapio H, 'Navigation' (*WorldCC Contract Design Pattern Library*), https://contract-design.worldcc.com/library/navigation, accessed 17 August 2021.

WorldCC (World Commerce and Contracting), Passera S and Haapio H, 'Organizing' (*WorldCC Contract Design Pattern Library*), https://contract-design.worldcc.com/library/organizing, accessed 17 August 2021.

WorldCC (World Commerce and Contracting), Passera S and Haapio H, 'Pattern Families' (*WorldCC Contract Design Pattern Library*), https://contract-design.worldcc.com/families-overview, accessed 17 August 2021.

WorldCC (World Commerce and Contracting), Passera S and Haapio H, 'Summarizing' (*WorldCC Contract Design Pattern Library*), https://contract-design.worldcc.com/library/summarizing, accessed 17 August 2021.

WorldCC (World Commerce and Contracting), Passera S and Haapio H, 'Timeline' (*WorldCC Contract Design Pattern Library*), https://contract-design.worldcc.com/timeline?, accessed 17 August 2021.

WorldCC (World Commerce and Contracting), Passera S and Haapio H, 'WorldCC Contract Design Pattern Library', https://contract-design.worldcc.com, accessed 17 August 2021.

Your.MD, www.your.md, accessed 17 August 2021.

Zuboff S, *The Age of Surveillance Capitalism: The Fight for a Human Future at the New Frontier of Power* (Public Affairs 2019).

3

Social Media Platforms as Public Health Arbiters

Global Ethical Considerations on Privacy, Legal, and Cultural Issues Associated with Suicide Detection Algorithms

KAREN L. CELEDONIA, MICHAEL LOWERY WILSON, AND MARCELO CORRALES COMPAGNUCCI

3.1 Introduction

3.1.1 Suicide Prevention and the Use of Technology

Suicide is a growing, global public health problem.[1] No corner of the world remains untouched by the increasing incidence and prevalence of suicidal behaviour across the lifespan. Every forty seconds, an individual takes their own life somewhere in the world. Suicide is the second leading cause of death among adolescents and young adults aged 15–26,[2] and the suicide rates among this age group have been on the rise over the past decade.[3] Recently, there has also been an alarming trend of increased suicidal behaviour and suicide among children as young as five years old.[4]

[1] This is an extended version of an article published in the *Journal of Law and the Biosciences* where we argued that Facebook's practices in this area should be subject to well-established protocols such as an ethical review process and the explicit approval of its users in the form of informed consent. We also proposed a fiduciary framework with the assistance of a panel of external impartial experts from various fields and diverse backgrounds. See KL Celedonia and others, 'Legal, Ethical, and Wider Implications of Suicide Risk Detection Systems in Social Media Platforms' (2021) 8(1) *Journal of Law and the Biosciences*, https://doi.org/10.1093/jlb/lsab021, accessed 23 May 2021.

[2] P Rodríguez Herrero, A de la Herrán Gascón and V de Miguel Yubero, 'The Inclusion of Death in the Curriculum of the Spanish Regions' (2020) *Compare: A Journal of Comparative and International Education*, 1–19.

[3] MF Hogan, 'Suicide Prevention: Rising Rates and New Evidence Shape Policy Options' in *The Palgrave Handbook of American Mental Health Policy* (Springer 2020) 229–57.

[4] AH Sheftall and others, 'Suicide in Elementary School-Aged Children and Early Adolescents' (October 2016) 138(4) *Pediatrics* e20160436, https://doi.org/10.1542/peds.2016-0436, accessed 23 May 2021.

Population-based research suggests that suicide rates are highest in high-income counties (HICs), at 11.5 per 100,000 individuals.[5] However, globally available data suggest that low- and middle-income countries (LMICs) may be disproportionately affected by suicide, with most of the world's suicides occurring in these countries. Of the at least 800,000 global deaths by suicide in a given year, 76 per cent were from LMICs.[6] Given these concerning trends in suicide rates, early detection of suicide warning signs paired with appropriate intervention and treatment by mental health professionals is imperative to saving the lives of individuals at risk of suicide.

The mental health field has embraced the use of technology for timely prevention and treatment of mental health disorders like suicidal behaviour. From tele-psychiatry to mobile health applications (apps), more and more mental health providers are turning to technology to assist in the provision of care to those in need. Transportation barriers and lack of childcare are common impediments to individuals with mental illness initially seeking mental health treatment or keeping appointments once treatment is started.[7] Tele-psychiatry and mobile health apps eliminate the need for treatment sessions to be conducted in person, thereby allowing individuals who may not be able to attend in-person sessions due to economic constraints or competing demands to access the treatment they need without having to leave home. Furthermore, given the potentially crippling nature of mental illnesses like depression and anxiety, individuals experiencing acute symptomology of these disorders may be unable to leave their homes to attend treatment sessions. These individuals can benefit from tele-psychiatry and mobile health apps to manage and improve their symptoms until they feel well enough to attend in-person sessions. Technology-based services like tele-psychiatry have allowed mental health care providers to reach clients at risk of suicide who otherwise might not have received treatment due to service access barriers.[8] Tele-psychiatry is an American Psychiatric Association (APA) approved service delivery method that is recognised by insurance companies as a

5 World Health Organization, 'Suicide in the World: Global Health Estimates' (2019) World Health Organization, https://apps.who.int/iris/handle/10665/326948, accessed 23 May 2021.

6 Ibid.

7 KM Shealy and others, 'Delivering an Evidence-Based Mental Health Treatment to Underserved Populations Using Telemedicine: The Case of a Trauma-Affected Adolescent in a Rural Setting' (2015) 22(3) *Cognitive and Behavioral Practice*, 331–44.

8 DM Hilty and others, 'Telepsychiatry' (August 2002) 16(8) *Molecular Diagnosis and Therapy*, 527–48, https://doi.org/10.2165/00023210-200216080-00003, accessed 23 May 2021.

billable service,[9] and it is held to the same rigorous ethical standards of client privacy and health information protection as treatment-as-usual, in-person services. For example, US providers that offer tele-psychiatry are expected to use Health Insurance Portability and Accountability Act (HIPAA)-compliant video conferencing platforms when conducting virtual treatment sessions.[10]

Beyond treatment sessions, mobile health apps can serve to supplement psychiatric services and promote self-monitoring of symptoms among individuals with mental illness. Though research on the effectiveness of mobile apps in treating symptoms of mental illnesses like depression and anxiety is in its infancy, preliminary investigations suggest that mobile apps have the potential to alleviate symptoms of depression and anxiety. Due to their ease of access and seemingly comparable effectiveness, some health professionals have even suggested that mobile health apps could be a solution to the global shortage of psychiatrists. However, experts warn that mobile health apps currently suffer from inadequate regulation of quality and privacy.[11]

In an effort to leverage their ubiquitous global presence to help prevent suicide, search engines and social media platforms have developed algorithms to detect suicide risk among their users. Google, for example, developed an algorithm to detect suicide risk trends in users' search term history.[12] Depending on the level of risk detected, ads for suicide prevention hotlines and mental health treatment may be displayed to those at higher risk. By using key-word matching, Apple, Google Assistant, and Amazon have also taken efforts to guide users of their digital assistant devices (i.e. Siri, Echo, Alexa) who verbally express suicidal thoughts and intentions to suicide prevention resources.[13]

[9] JS Gardner and others, 'Remote Telepsychiatry Workforce: A Solution to Psychiatry's Workforce Issues' (January 2020) 22(2) *Current Psychiatry Reports*, 8–9, https://doi.org/10.1007/s11920-020-1128-7, accessed 23 May 2021.

[10] JH Wright and R Caudill, 'Remote Treatment Delivery in Response to the COVID-19 Pandemic' (2020) 89(3), *Psychotherapy and Psychosomatics*, 1, https://doi.org/10.1159/000507376, accessed 23 May 2021.

[11] P Chandrashekar, 'Do Mental Health Mobile Apps Work: Evidence and Recommendations for Designing High-Efficacy Mental Health Mobile Apps' (2018) 4 *mHealth*, 6, https://doi.org/10.21037/mhealth.2018.03.02, accessed 23 May 2021.

[12] P Solano and others, 'A Google-Based Approach for Monitoring Suicide Risk' (2016) 246 *Psychiatry Research*, 581–86, www.sciencedirect.com/science/article/pii/S0165178116301949, accessed 23 May 2021.

[13] TW Bickmore and others, 'Patient and Consumer Safety Risks When Using Conversational Assistants for Medical Information: An Observational Study of Siri, Alexa, and Google Assistant' (2018) 20(9) *Journal of Medical Internet Research* e11510.

Perhaps most controversial is Facebook's suicide detection algorithm. The algorithm works by scanning every post a Facebook user makes on the platform and scoring the post on a scale of 0–1 for risk of imminent harm. Facebook does not stop at a simple algorithm and displaying ads for suicide prevention hotlines like Google: it takes suicide detection a step further by relaying the risk information to law enforcement, who then intervene in what are called 'wellness checks'. Depending on the assessment and the severity of the risk detected, users may then be transported to psychiatric inpatient units for a thorough psychiatric evaluation by a mental health professional.

While the use of technology to help prevent suicide seems congruous with the changing landscape of the health care industry to include more widespread implementation of eHealth and artificial intelligence to assist with health care delivery, many of these technology-based suicide prevention programmes have not been adequately researched before being made available to the public. A review of 123 mobile health apps for suicide risk detection and support found that none of the apps offered evidence-based intervention for individuals at risk of suicide, with many apps actually containing content potentially harmful to individuals in a vulnerable mental state.[14] In regard to suicide detection algorithms, concerns have been raised about entities like Facebook, which are not health care providers, conducting health surveillance, providing health advice and intervention without being held to the same ethical standards as legitimate health care providers.[15]

Though mental health concerns like suicide are common on a global scale, stigma persists surrounding individuals with mental health concerns despite concerted efforts over the decades to normalise these common health conditions. In many LMICs, stigma around mental health conditions has not improved,[16] and the disclosure of mental illness can have severe social consequences.[17] Even in countries where mental

[14] ME Larsen, J Nicholas and H Christensen, 'A Systematic Assessment of Smartphone Tools for Suicide Prevention' (2016) 11(4) *PLOS ONE* e0152285.

[15] A Pourmand and others, 'Social Media and Suicide: A Review of Technology-Based Epidemiology and Risk Assessment' (October 2019) 25(10) *Telemedicine and eHealth*, 880–88, https://doi.org/10.1089/tmj.2018.0203, accessed 23 May 2021.

[16] E Heim and others, 'Reducing Mental Health Related Stigma in Primary Health Care Settings in Low- and Middle-Income Countries: A Systematic Review' (2020) 29 *Epidemiology and Psychiatric Sciences*, https://doi.org/10.1017/S2045796018000458, accessed 23 May 2021.

[17] AC Krendl and BA Pescosolido, 'Countries and Cultural Differences in the Stigma of Mental Illness: The East–West Divide' (February 2020) 51(2) *Journal of Cross-Cultural Psychology*, 149–67, https://doi.org/10.1177/0022022119901297, accessed 23 May 2021.

illnesses are more accepted, stigma still exists, and as such, many individuals with mental illness choose not to voluntarily disclose their disorders. Non-health care entities like social media platforms revealing someone's mental state to public officials could therefore be construed as a violation of an individual's right to disability non-disclosure.

Another layer to the aforementioned issues with stigma and involuntary disclosure of mental illnesses is the possibility of the suicide detection algorithm resulting in false positives for suicide risk. As with the mobile health apps for suicide prevention, these detection algorithms were not (and have not been) properly researched before their implementation. Data on the accuracy of the algorithm are not publicly available, and anecdotal accounts of the algorithms erroneously detecting suicide risk when none was present are starting to surface. In countries where mental illnesses are more accepted, these mistakes may mean little more than extreme inconvenience and unnecessary resource expenditures, but in countries where mental illnesses are still misunderstood and severely stigmatised, such a mistake could ruin an individual's life.

With over 2.6 billion users worldwide and an emerging trend of users live-streaming suicide attempts, one might argue that social media platforms like Facebook have a moral obligation to develop suicide detection algorithms to protect their users. To refrain from doing anything to prevent suicide among its users could itself be viewed as unethical. However, given that research is revealing that mental health issues like depression, which is a risk factor for suicide, are associated with social media use,[18] one may wonder if suicide detection algorithms on social media platforms are nothing more than these platforms trying to fix a problem that they themselves created or had a role in exacerbating. In addition to possibly contributing to mental illnesses that put individuals at risk for suicide, the trend of live-streaming suicide attempts on social media creates the possibility of behavioural contagion in which viewers of these videos may mimic the behaviour they witness.[19] Furthermore, studies show that there is a significant positive, predictive association between social media use and loneliness: the more time an individual spends using social media,

[18] MG Hunt and others, 'No More FOMO: Limiting Social Media Decreases Loneliness and Depression' (December 2018 Guilford Publications Inc), https://guilfordjournals.com/doi/abs/10.1521/jscp.2018.37.10.751, accessed 23 May 2021.

[19] M Westerlund, G Hadlaczky and D Wasserman, 'Case Study of Posts before and after a Suicide on a Swedish Internet Forum' (December 2015) 207(6) *British Journal of Psychiatry*, 476–82, https://doi.org/10.1192/bjp.bp.114.154484, accessed 23 May 2021.

the more lonely they report feeling;[20] loneliness is often associated with suicidal behaviour.[21]

3.1.2 The Ethics of Social Media Platforms Acting As Health Care Providers

Providing any sort of health care to an individual is inherently rife with ethical tension. Childress and Beauchamp developed the four principles of health care ethics to guide the ethical provision of health and medical treatment. These four principles are autonomy, beneficence, non-maleficence, and justice.[22] *Autonomy* refers to the right of the client to retain control of their body; a health care provider may suggest a certain treatment course, but the decision to follow the suggested treatment course is ultimately up to the client and must be made by the client independently according to their personal beliefs and values, without coercion from the health care provider. *Beneficence* dictates that health care providers must do all they can to benefit the client in each situation, with all recommendations being made solely within the best interest of the client. This includes health care providers maintaining a high standard of skill and knowledge as evidenced by being trained in the most up-to-date and best practices in health care provision. Additionally, as part of the beneficence principle, health care providers must take into consideration the unique circumstances of each individual client, recognising that what may be the best treatment course for one client may not be the best for another. *Non-maleficence* states that health care providers should strive to do no harm to their clients, other people, and society at large. *Justice* suggests that fairness should be present in health care provision and all treatment decisions. It also proclaims that health care professionals should uphold any relevant laws and legislation when making treatment decisions.[23]

20 M Savci and F Aysan, 'Relationship between Impulsivity, Social Media Usage and Loneliness' (March 2016) 5(2) *Educational Process: International Journal*, 106–15, https://doi.org/10.12973/edupij.2016.52.2, accessed 23 May 2021.

21 A Stravynski and R Boyer, 'Loneliness in Relation to Suicide Ideation and Parasuicide: A Population-Wide Study' (June 2005 Guilford Publications Inc), https://guilfordjournals.com/doi/abs/10.1521/suli.31.1.32.21312, accessed 23 May 2021.

22 JF Childress and TL Beauchamp, *Principles of Biomedical Ethics* (Oxford University Press 2001).

23 R Rawbone, 'Principles of Biomedical Ethics' (January 2015) 65(1) 7th Edition *Occupational Medicine (Lond)* 88–89, https://doi.org/10.1093/occmed/kqu158, accessed 23 May 2021.

It has been suggested that social media platforms – particularly Facebook with its suicide detection algorithm and corresponding intervention protocol – are behaving as health care providers without being held to the same guiding ethical principles as legitimate health care providers. Like health care providers, Facebook is collecting, analysing, and acting upon personal health care information. However, unlike health care providers, Facebook is not adhering to health information and data protection laws that many countries have in regard to collecting and using patient data. In what little has been described of the algorithm and intervention thus far, it is evident that as a social media platform acting as a health care provider, Facebook's suicide detection algorithm and intervention violates the four principles of health care ethics, not to mention ignoring patients' rights to privacy and knowledge of how their personal health information may be used.

In this chapter, a more in-depth review and critical analysis of the aforementioned ethical considerations inherent in social media platforms interjecting their influence into the public health realm as it pertains to suicide detection will be provided. These ethical considerations are classified into three categories: privacy and patient rights, legal, and cultural. For the purposes of the discussion in this chapter, social media platforms will be hypothetically held to the same ethical standards as legitimate health care entities. In so doing, the four principles of health care ethics will be used to frame the discussion in this chapter, providing guidance on what constitutes an ethical violation.

3.2 Privacy and Patient Rights Considerations

The protection of an individual's health information is not a new concept in the health care field. Even in its nascent state, the medical profession sought to protect the privacy of patients' health information through the practice of confidentiality.[24] However, it was not until recently that the protection of health information was enforced through legislation in the form of HIPAA. Under Title II of HIPAA, the Privacy Rule mandates that all health care providers adhere to a strict set of standards when collecting, storing, and reporting on health information acquired on the individuals in their care. In short, Protected Health Information (PHI)

[24] GL Higgins, 'The History of Confidentiality in Medicine' (April 1989) 35 *Canadian Family Physician*, 921, www.ncbi.nlm.nih.gov/pmc/articles/PMC2280818, accessed 23 May 2021.

associated with an individual in care is not to be shared or made available to unauthorised individuals or entities without the patient's clear written consent. In cases where it is deemed necessary to disclose PHI (e.g. legal proceedings, threat to oneself or others), only the minimum amount of information required to satisfy the request should be shared.

By using algorithms like Facebook's suicide detection algorithm, social media platforms are behaving like health care providers though not being held to the same health information protection standards as health care providers. HIPAA currently has no jurisdiction over the way Facebook collects, stores, and uses the health information it collects on its users. And while individuals receiving care from legitimate health care providers are aware that information is being collected and stored pertaining to their health and that treatment suggestions will be formulated based on this information, Facebook users are generally unaware that this type of information is being collected on them. Furthermore, this health-related information is being analysed and acted upon without the user's consent through the application of the suicide detection algorithm.

In one recent example of Facebook's suicide detection algorithm erroneously identifying a suicide risk, a Facebook user was escorted to a psychiatric hospital by law enforcement for a mental health evaluation despite no previous history of mental illness or suicidal behaviour and her assertion that she was not experiencing suicidal thoughts.[25] Per Facebook's protocol for intervention once a suicide risk is detected, law enforcement was sent to the user's home and was obliged to follow through with taking the woman to a psychiatric hospital for evaluation, despite her assertion that such action was not necessary. As such, the woman's right to choose her own treatment course was precluded. As experts have argued that the use of Facebook's suicide prevention algorithm in conjunction with an intervention that may lead to mandatory psychiatric evaluations constitutes the practice of medicine,[26] in the case of the aforementioned individual in which the algorithm produced a false positive, it can be suggested that the health care ethics principle of autonomy was violated.

Returning to the guidelines delineated in HIPAA, there is also a Security Rule as it pertains to PHI, and more specifically, electronic PHI (EPHI).

[25] N Singer, 'In Screening for Suicide Risk, Facebook Takes On Tricky Public Health Role', *New York Times*, June 2019, www.nytimes.com/2018/12/31/technology/facebook-suicide-screening-algorithm.html, accessed 23 May 2021.

[26] EH Morreim, 'Playing Doctor: Corporate Medical Practice and Medical Malpractice' (1998) 32 *University of Michigan Journal of Law Reform*, 939.

This rule outlines three areas of security standards regarding safeguarding EPHI: administrative, physical, and technical. One particularly relevant point from this rule as it relates to the present chapter is the dictate of restricted access to EPHI to only those who need it to perform their job. As there are currently no laws or regulations in the United States around who has access to information collected by social media platforms like Facebook, and very recently user data were made available to a third party for its own private use,[27] it can almost be certain that entities other than social media platforms like Facebook are gaining access to user data. Furthermore, as monetising information gathered from users is integrated into the business models of social media platforms, it is likely they are selling user data. Therefore, the privacy of individuals who wish to keep their mental health status undisclosed or individuals who are falsely identified as having a mental health concern like suicidal behaviour is being disregarded.

Much as social media platforms like Facebook are acting like health care providers when they collect and act upon individuals' health information, one could also claim that by collecting and analysing the same data they are also engaged in a large-scale research project. Suicide detection algorithms are not unique to social media platforms: a growing interest in machine learning and predictive analytics in the health field has led to a burgeoning corpus of research on predictive algorithms relating to a range of health issues, including suicidal behaviour. But the distinction between suicide detection algorithms developed by medical professionals and Facebook's suicide detection algorithm lies in the nature of the research being conducted. Medical professionals and researchers are transparent in their intentions with the algorithms and make findings publicly available through venues like peer-reviewed journals. Additionally, medical professionals and researchers adhere to an ethical code of conduct when engaging in their research, which includes having study protocols reviewed by an objective institutional review board and obtaining participant consent. No such review was conducted on Facebook's suicide detection algorithm before it was implemented, nor was informed consent obtained by users.

To continue with the research analogy, medical professionals researching a novel pharmaceutical treatment, for example, would not disseminate the drug to the wider public before the requisite clinical trials on its efficacy

[27] CO Schneble, BS Elger and D Shaw, 'The Cambridge Analytica Affair and Internet Mediated Research' (August 2018) 19(8) *EMBO Reports*, https://doi.org/10.15252/embr.201846579, accessed 23 May 2021.

and safety were completed. To do so would be a gross violation of research ethics. By implementing its suicide detection algorithm before extensive research was conducted on its effectiveness, rate of false positives, and adverse consequences associated with false positives, social media platforms like Facebook are in violation of research ethical standards.

Privacy violations which lead to involuntary disclosure of mental health status are unacceptable, and even in countries where mental illness is becoming less stigmatised, judgement and misunderstanding of mental illness still exists. In certain areas of the world, such as the African region and much of the Asian continent, mental illness is heavily stigmatised and disclosing a mental health condition like suicidal thoughts or behaviour could have severe, often irreversible legal and cultural consequences. These considerations will be discussed in the following two sections.

3.3 Legal Considerations

Privacy violations committed by the suicide detection algorithm which lead to involuntary disclosure of mental health status can be distressing to an individual with mental illness and potentially life-altering in many areas of the world. But in certain areas of the world, disclosing suicidal thoughts or behaviour could have legal ramifications. According to a recent global review conducted in which criminal codes from 192 countries were obtained and reviewed to determine legal status of suicide and suicide-related behaviours,[28] attempting suicide is illegal in twenty-five countries and therefore punishable by law. Even in countries where suicide attempts are decriminalised, the law may still be used to punish individuals who attempt suicide. For example, in the US military, there have been instances of military personnel who have attempted suicide being tried and convicted in a court of law and sentenced to jail time.[29]

In the countries where suicide attempts are illegal, it is primarily because suicide is seen as a morally or religiously reprehensible act. By making it illegal to attempt suicide, those who attempt suicide are publicly shamed through court hearings and sentences with the intent of deterring the individual from engaging in future attempts. This approach, however, is

[28] BL Mishara and DN Weisstub, 'The Legal Status of Suicide: A Global Review' (2016) 44 *International Journal of Law and Psychiatry*, 54–74.

[29] A Freilich, 'Fallen Soldier: Military (In)justice and the Criminalization of Attempted Suicide After U.S. v. Caldwell' (September 2014) 19 *Berkeley Journal of Criminal Law*, 74, accessed 8 May 2020.

misguided and speaks to the lack of understanding of mental illness in these countries, as punishments like jail time or other forms of social ostracisation are anathema to individuals with mental illness and suicidal thoughts and behaviour, serving to aggravate and intensify symptomology; social isolation is one of the main contributing factors to suicide attempts.[30] Additionally, after these individuals serve their sentences and are reintegrated back into society, they may be less likely to seek the treatment they need for their illness, assuming that appropriate treatment is available in their community.

If suicidal behaviour is therefore brought to the attention of public officials by a social media suicide detection algorithm, law enforcement will arrest the individual rather than escort them to a psychiatric hospital for the necessary treatment of their symptoms. This outcome will not only harm the individual legally but could also amplify existing mental health problems and actually increase the risk of the individual attempting suicide rather than preventing it. Furthermore, in the instance where the apprehended individual is an adolescent, such an early involvement with the legal system could seriously and permanently alter the course of their life. In this scenario, the principles of beneficence and non-maleficence are violated by the implementation of the suicide detection algorithm.

3.4 Cultural Considerations

Mental illnesses and the individuals who experience them have a long history of being stigmatised. In recent years, HICs have committed to reducing mental illness stigma by using strategies such as targeted anti-stigma campaigns.[31] These large-scale public health interventions have helped to decrease mental illness stigma in HICs, but even with these concerted anti-stigma efforts, stigma still persists in HICs, albeit not as acutely as it once did.[32] Additionally, many employers in HICs include disabilities like

[30] World Health Organization, 'Preventing Suicide: A Global Imperative' (May 2014), www.who.int/mental_health/suicide-prevention/world_report_2014/en, accessed 8 May 2020.

[31] ACH Szeto and KS Dobson, 'Reducing the Stigma of Mental Disorders at Work: A Review of Current Workplace Anti-Stigma Intervention Programs' (June 2010) 14(1–4) *Applied and Preventive Psychology*, 41–56, www.sciencedirect.com/science/article/pii/S0962184911000047, accessed 23 May 2021, https://doi.org/10.1016/j.appsy.2011.11.002, accessed 23 May 2021.

[32] CC Young and SJ Calloway, 'Assessing Mental Health Stigma: Nurse Practitioners' Attitudes Regarding Managing Patients with Mental Health Disorders' (March 2020) *Journal of the American Association of Nurse Practitioners*, https://doi.org/10.1097/JXX.0000000000000351, accessed 23 May 2021.

serious mental illness (SMI) in company anti-discrimination policies, further protecting the rights of an individual with mental illness should they choose to disclose their illness.[33] Even with this societal progress and legal safeguards, an individual with a mental illness living in an HIC may still rather choose not to disclose their diagnosis, for fear of judgement and discrimination, personally and professionally.

The state of mental illness stigma in LMICs, however, remains in much need of improvement. This is in large part due to lack of funding for mental health services as well as general disinterest in mental health and individuals with mental illness.[34] As a result, stigma continues to be a very real, very painful reality for individuals with mental illness in LMICs who either choose to disclose their mental illness or perhaps have it revealed without their consent. In one study investigating the presence of stigma towards individuals with mental illness in India (an LMIC), it was found that the prevalence of stigma was close to 75 per cent.[35] Because of the pervasiveness of stigma in LMICs, anti-stigma campaigns like those implemented in HICs have not occurred.

Qualitative studies investigating the experience of stigma in LMICs have found that individuals with mental illness describe frequent occurrences of perceived stigma. The behavioural manifestations of stigma can range from rejection and derogatory language aimed at the individual with mental illness to discrimination.[36] The harmful effects of mental illness stigma do not remain isolated to the individual: relatives of individuals with mental illness have reported experiencing stigma due to their association with their ill relative and, in one study, more than a third of relatives felt it necessary to conceal their relative's mental illnesses.[37] It is within this context of mental illness stigma in LMICs that Facebook's suicide detection algorithm and accompanying intervention pose a serious

[33] C Heginbotham, 'UK Mental Health Policy Can Alter the Stigma of Mental Illness' (1998) 352(9133) *The Lancet*, 1052–53.

[34] F Mascayano, JE Armijo and LH Yang, 'Addressing Stigma Relating to Mental Illness in Low- and Middle-Income Countries' (March 2015) 6 *Front Psychiatry*, https://doi.org/10.3389/fpsyt.2015.00038, accessed 23 May 2021.

[35] BT Venkatesh and others, 'Perception of Stigma Toward Mental Illness in South India' (2015) 4(3) *Journal of Family Medicine and Primary Care*, 449.

[36] Mascayano, Armijo, and Yang, 'Addressing Stigma Relating to Mental Illness in Low- and Middle-Income Countries'.

[37] T Shibre and others, 'Perception of Stigma among Family Members of Individuals with Schizophrenia and Major Affective Disorders in Rural Ethiopia' (June 2001) 36(6) *Social Psychiatry and Psychiatric Epidemiology*, 299–303, https://doi.org/10.1007/s001270170048, accessed 23 May 2021.

ethical dilemma. Social media use is just as prevalent in LMICs as HICs, and in fact, social media use may be even more prevalent in LMICs than in HICs. Data as recent as October 2020 indicate that nine of the top ten countries with the most Facebook users are LMICs.[38] Depending on whom the results of a positive suicide risk detected by the algorithm are reported to, an individual with mental illness living in such settings could be ostracised from their community and support systems. For example, if a family member is made privy to the information, they may choose to dissociate with their ill family member, perhaps even disowning them. Being disconnected from family is a devastating, stressful situation for any person, but for individuals with mental illness, such isolation and social upheaval may exacerbate symptoms. Especially for individuals experiencing suicidal thoughts, discord in interpersonal relationships can intensify suicidal thoughts and often precipitate suicide attempts.[39]

At the community level in LMICs, for an individual with mental illness to have their illness disclosed could either impede their ability to make a substantial living or result in a total loss of livelihood. In one study of mental illness and income among South Africans, adults living with depression or anxiety experienced a mean estimated lost income of around $5,000 per year.[40] It was suggested by the authors of the study that stigma may contribute to lower earnings for individuals with mental illness.[41] In a qualitative study investigating experiences of stigma in the Philippines, participants discussed the potential for stigma towards their mental illness to economically destroy their entire family.[42] In the same study, participants also described how stigma towards their mental illness reduced their social networks and opportunities, both of which play an important role in procuring and maintaining gainful employment.[43]

[38] Facebook users by country 2020 | Statista (December 2020), www.statista.com/statistics/268136/top-15-countries-based-on-number-of-facebook-users, accessed 31 Dec. 2020.

[39] BL Robustelli and others, 'Marital Discord and Suicidal Outcomes in a National Sample of Married Individuals' (2015) 45(5) *Suicide and Life-Threatening Behavior*, 623–32.

[40] C Lund and others, 'Mental Health Services in South Africa: Taking Stock' (2012) 15(6) *African Journal of Psychiatry*, 402–5.

[41] C Lund and others, 'Mental Illness and Lost Income among Adult South Africans' (2013) 48(5) *Social Psychiatry and Psychiatric Epidemiology*, 845–51.

[42] C Tanaka and others, 'A Qualitative Study on the Stigma Experienced by People with Mental Health Problems and Epilepsy in the Philippines' (October 2018) 18(1) *BMC Psychiatry*, 325–13, https://doi.org/10.1186/s12888-018-1902-9, accessed 23 May 2021.

[43] A Calvó-Armengol and MO Jackson, 'The Effects of Social Networks on Employment and Inequality' (June 2004) 94(3) *American Economic Review*, 426–54, https://doi.org/10.1257/0002828041464542, accessed 23 May 2021.

To further compound the cultural ramifications of positive suicide risk detection with the suicide detection algorithm, it is not understood how well the algorithm performs across various cultures. Though the algorithm is trained to detect key words and phrases related to suicide risk in English, Spanish, Portuguese, and Arabic, experts in the medical field question whether the algorithm works equally when applied to different races, genders, and nationalities.[44] Such unknowns leave room for the possibility of false positives, which in LMICs can be much more detrimental to an individual's life than in an HIC. A false positive in an HIC may certainly cause inconvenience in the form of an unnecessary hospital visit, but in an LMIC, a false positive can also result in some or all of the aforementioned cultural consequences.

The negative cultural consequences of suicidal behaviour being detected by a suicide detection algorithm like that of Facebook – accurate or not – among individuals living in LMICs may be particularly damaging to women in these countries. Suicidal ideation and suicidal behaviour (i.e. attempts) are more prevalent among females compared with males.[45] It is therefore likely that a suicide detection algorithm will identify suicide risk more often in women than in men. In many LMICs, gender equality is lacking, as evidenced by low scores on the Gender Development Index.[46] Gender inequality creates unfavourable living conditions for women as they are rendered powerless in male-dominated societies. Furthermore, in countries where gender inequality exists, women are more likely to be subjected to physical and sexual abuse,[47] both of which are risk factors for suicidal ideation and behaviour.[48] Women in LMICs already contend with subordinate social status due to gender inequality, and if the stigma associated with mental illness is thrown into the mix, women in LMICs with mental illness may find themselves completely

[44] M Thielking, 'Experts Raise Questions about Facebook's Suicide Prevention Tools – STAT' (February 2019), www.statnews.com/2019/02/11/facebook-suicide-prevention-tools-ethics-privacy, accessed 8 May 2020.

[45] EK Mościcki, 'Gender Differences in Completed and Attempted Suicides' (1994) 4(2) *Annals of Epidemiology*, 152–58.

[46] AG Dijkstra and LC Hanmer, 'Measuring Socio-Economic Gender Inequality: Toward an Alternative to the UNDP Gender-Related Development Index' (2000) 6(2) *Feminist Economics*, 41–75.

[47] FT Alloh and others, 'Mental Health in Low and Middle Income Countries (LMICs): Going Beyond the Need for Funding' (2018) 17(1) *Health Prospect*, 12–17.

[48] Y Cohen and others, 'Physical and Sexual Abuse and Their Relation to Psychiatric Disorder and Suicidal Behavior among Adolescents Who Are Psychiatrically Hospitalized' (1996) 37(8) *Journal of Child Psychology and Psychiatry*, 989–93.

disenfranchised citizens if their illness is disclosed. For women not yet married, this could mean an end to any prospects of a decent life, as in many LMICs being married and having children are core aspects of a woman's livelihood.

Given that social media use, in particular use of Facebook, is so high among individuals living in LMICs, it would be prudent to ensure that the aforementioned cultural considerations within many LMICs are taken into account when implementing a suicide detection algorithm among this population of social media users. If we return again to the four principles of health care ethics and treat social media platforms engaging in public health-like activities such as suicide detection and accompanying interventions like health care providers, to ignore the unique cultural context of LMICs as it relates to mental illness and suicide would be violating the principles of beneficence and non-maleficence. In these cultural contexts, a one-size-fits-all approach to suicide detection and intervention is not best practice and does not take into account what is best for the individual living with mental illness in these environments that are at best intolerant of individuals with mental illness, and at worst hostile towards these individuals.

3.5 Conclusion

Suicide detection algorithms implemented on social media platforms have the potential to prevent death by suicide. With billions of individuals across the globe using social media platforms daily, the reach of such a public health intervention is unprecedented. However, the usefulness, and indeed the appropriateness, of suicide detection algorithms on social media platforms needs to be assessed within certain ethical considerations, as well as the cultural context in which the algorithms are deployed. By acting as a health care provider through the collection and use of personal health information via the suicide detection algorithm, social media platforms using this technology should be held to the same ethical standards as legitimate health care providers.

Acknowledgements

The research for this chapter was supported by a Novo Nordisk Foundation grant for a scientifically independent Collaborative Research Program in Biomedical Innovation Law (grant agreement number NNF17SA0027784) and by the Alexander von Humboldt-Stiftung, Bonn, Germany.

Bibliography

Alloh FT and others, 'Mental Health in Low and Middle Income Countries (LMICs): Going Beyond the Need for Funding' (2018) 17(1) *Health Prospect*, 12–17.

Bickmore TW and others, 'Patient and Consumer Safety Risks When Using Conversational Assistants for Medical Information: An Observational Study of Siri, Alexa, and Google Assistant' (2018) 20(9) *Journal of Medical Internet Research*, e11510.

Calvó-Armengol A and Jackson MO, 'The Effects of Social Networks on Employment and Inequality' (June 2004) 94(3) *American Economic Review*, 426–54, https://doi.org/10.1257/0002828041464542.

Celedonia KL and others, 'Legal, Ethical, and Wider Implications of Suicide Risk Detection Systems in Social Media Platforms' (2021) 8(1) *Journal of Law and the Biosciences*, https://doi.org/10.1093/jlb/lsab021.

Chandrashekar P, 'Do Mental Health Mobile Apps Work: Evidence and Recommendations for Designing High-Efficacy Mental Health Mobile Apps' (2018) 4 *mHealth*, 6, https://doi.org/10.21037/mhealth.2018.03. 02.

Childress JF and Beauchamp TL, *Principles of Biomedical Ethics* (Oxford University Press 2001).

Cohen Y and others, 'Physical and Sexual Abuse and Their Relation to Psychiatric Disorder and Suicidal Behaviour among Adolescents Who Are Psychiatrically Hospitalized' (1996) 37(8) *Journal of Child Psychology and Psychiatry*, 989–93.

Dijkstra AG and Hanmer LC, 'Measuring Socio-Economic Gender Inequality: Toward an Alternative to the UNDP Gender-Related Development Index' (2000) 6(2) *Feminist Economics*, 41–75.

Facebook users by country 2020 | Statista (December 2020), www.statista.com/statistics/268136/top-15-countries-based-on-number-of-facebook-users.

Freilich A, 'Fallen Soldier: Military (In)Justice and the Criminalization of Attempted Suicide after U.S. v. Caldwell' (September 2014) 19 *Berkeley Journal of Criminal Law*, 74, www.bjcl.org/assets/files/19.1-Freilich.pdf, accessed 8 May 2020.

Gardner JS and others, 'Remote Telepsychiatry Workforce: A Solution to Psychiatry's Workforce Issues' (January 2020) 22(2) *Current Psychiatry Reports*, 8–9, https://doi.org/10.1007/s11920-020-1128-7.

Heginbotham C, 'UK Mental Health Policy Can Alter the Stigma of Mental Illness' (1998) 352(9133) *The Lancet*, 1052–53.

Heim E and others, 'Reducing Mental Health Related Stigma in Primary Health Care Settings in Low- and Middle-Income Countries: A Systematic Review' (2020) 29 *Epidemiology and Psychiatric Sciences*, https://doi.org/10.1017/S2045796018000458.

Higgins GL, 'The History of Confidentiality in Medicine' (April 1989) 35 *Canadian Family Physician*, 921, www.ncbi.nlm.nih.gov/pmc/articles/PMC2280818.

Hilty DM and others, 'Telepsychiatry' (August 2002) 16(8) *Molecular Diagnosis and Therapy*, 527–48, https://doi.org/10.2165/00023210-200216080-00003.

Hogan MF, 'Suicide Prevention: Rising Rates and New Evidence Shape Policy Options' in Goldman HH, Frank RG, Morrissey JP (eds) *The Palgrave Handbook of American Mental Health Policy* (Springer 2020), 229–57.

Hunt MG and others, 'No More FOMO: Limiting Social Media Decreases Loneliness and Depression' (December 2018) Guilford Publications Inc., https://guilfordjournals.com/doi/abs/10.1521/jscp.2018.37.10.751.

Krendl AC and Pescosolido BA, 'Countries and Cultural Differences in the Stigma of Mental Illness: The East–West Divide' (February 2020) 51(2) *Journal of Cross-Cultural Psychology*, 149–67, https://doi.org/10.1177/0022022119901297.

Larsen ME, Nicholas J and Christensen H, 'A Systematic Assessment of Smartphone Tools for Suicide Prevention' (2016) 11(4) *PLOS One*, e0152285.

Lund C and others, 'Mental Illness and Lost Income among Adult South Africans' (2013) 48(5) *Social Psychiatry and Psychiatric Epidemiology*, 845–51.

Lund C and others, 'Mental Health Services in South Africa: Taking Stock' (2012) 15(6) *African Journal of Psychiatry*, 402–05.

Mascayano F, Armijo JE and Yang LH, 'Addressing Stigma Relating to Mental Illness in Low- and Middle-Income Countries' (March 2015) 6 *Front Psychiatry*, https://doi.org/10.3389/fpsyt.2015.00038.

Mishara BL and Weisstub DN, 'The Legal Status of Suicide: A Global Review' (2016) 44 *International Journal of Law and Psychiatry*, 54–74.

Morreim EH, 'Playing Doctor: Corporate Medical Practice and Medical Malpractice' (1998) 32 *University of Michigan Journal of Law Reform*, 939.

Mościcki EK, 'Gender Differences in Completed and Attempted Suicides' (1994) 4(2) *Annals of Epidemiology*, 152–58.

Pourmand A and others, 'Social Media and Suicide: A Review of Technology-Based Epidemiology and Risk Assessment' (October 2019) 25(10) *Telemedicine and e-Health*, 880–88, https://doi.org/10.1089/tmj.2018.0203.

Rawbone R, 'Principles of Biomedical Ethics' (January 2015) 65(1) 7th Edition *Occupational Medicine (Lond)*, 88–89, https://doi.org/10.1093/occmed/kqu158.

Robustelli BL and others, 'Marital Discord and Suicidal Outcomes in a National Sample of Married Individuals' (2015) 45(5) *Suicide and Life-Threatening Behavior*, 623–32.

Rodríguez Herrero P, de la Herrán Gascón A and de Miguel Yubero V, 'The Inclusion of Death in the Curriculum of the Spanish Regions' (2020) 52(1) *Compare: A Journal of Comparative and International Education*, 1–19.

Savci M and Aysan F, 'Relationship between Impulsivity, Social Media Usage and Loneliness' (March 2016) 5(2) *Educational Process: International Journal*, 106–15, https://doi.org/10.12973/edupij.2016.52.2.

Schneble CO, Elger BS and Shaw D, 'The Cambridge Analytica Affair and Internet Mediated Research' (August 2018) 19(8) *EMBO Reports*, https://doi.org/10.15252/embr.201846579.

Shealy KM and others, 'Delivering an Evidence-Based Mental Health Treatment to Underserved Populations Using Telemedicine: The Case of a Trauma-Affected Adolescent in a Rural Setting' (2015) 22(3) *Cognitive and Behavioral Practice*, 331–44.

Sheftall AH and others, 'Suicide in Elementary School-Aged Children and Early Adolescents' (October 2016) 138(4) *Pediatrics* e20160436, https://doi.org/10.1542/peds.2016-0436.

Shibre T and others, 'Perception of Stigma among Family Members of Individuals with Schizophrenia and Major Affective Disorders in Rural Ethiopia' (June 2001) 36(6) *Social Psychiatry and Psychiatric Epidemiology*, 299–303, https://doi.org/10.1007/s001270170048.

Singer N, 'In Screening for Suicide Risk, Facebook Takes on Tricky Public Health Role', *New York Times*, June 2019, www.nytimes.com/2018/12/31/technology/facebook-suicide -screening-algorithm.html.

Solano P and others, 'A Google-Based Approach for Monitoring Suicide Risk' (2016) 246 *Psychiatry Research*, 581–86, www.sciencedirect.com/science/article/pii/S0165178116301949.

Stravynski A and Boyer R, 'Loneliness in Relation to Suicide Ideation and Parasuicide: A Population-Wide Study' (June 2005) Guilford Publications Inc., https://guilfordjournals.com/doi/abs/10.1521/suli.31.1.32.21312.

Szeto ACH and Dobson KS, 'Reducing the Stigma of Mental Disorders at Work: A Review of Current Workplace Anti-Stigma Intervention Programs' (June 2010) 14(1–4) *Applied and Preventive Psychology*, 41–56, www.sciencedirect.com/science/article/pii/ S0962184911000047.

Tanaka C and others, 'A Qualitative Study on the Stigma Experienced by People with Mental Health Problems and Epilepsy in the Philippines' (October 2018) 18(1) *BMC Psychiatry*, 325–13, https://doi.org/10.1186/s12888-018-1902-9.

Thielking M, 'Experts Raise Questions about Facebook's Suicide Prevention Tools – STAT' (February 2019), www.statnews.com/2019/02/11/facebook-suicide-prevention-tools -ethics-privacy.

Venkatesh BT and others, 'Perception of Stigma Toward Mental Illness in South India' (2015) 4(3) *Journal of Family Medicine and Primary Care*, 449.

Westerlund M, Hadlaczky G and Wasserman D, 'Case Study of Posts before and after a Suicide on a Swedish Internet Forum' (December 2015) 207(6) *British Journal of Psychiatry*, 476–82, https://doi.org/10.1192/bjp.bp.114.154484.

World Health Organization, 'Preventing Suicide: A Global Imperative' (May 2014), www.who.int/mental_health/suicide-prevention/world_report_2014/en.

World Health Organization, 'Suicide in the World: Global Health Estimates' (2019) World Health Organization, https://apps.who.int/iris/handle/10665/326948.

Wright JH and Caudill R, 'Remote Treatment Delivery in Response to the COVID-19 Pandemic' (2020) 89(3) *Psychotherapy and Psychosomatics*, 1, https://doi.org/10.1159/000507376.

Young CC and Calloway SJ, 'Assessing Mental Health Stigma: Nurse Practitioners' Attitudes Regarding Managing Patients with Mental Health Disorders' (March 2020) 33(4) *Journal of the American Association of Nurse Practitioners*, 278–82, https://doi.org/10.1097/JXX.0000000000000351.

4

Promoting the Use of PHR by Citizens and Physicians

Proposed Design for a Token to Be Allocated to Citizens

SHINTO TERAMOTO

4.1 Introduction

This section outlines the background of the study described herein. After this section, this chapter proceeds as follows.[1] Section 4.2 defines the purpose of this study. Section 4.3 describes the requirements to design a token allotted to citizens to promote their use of Personal Health Records (PHRs). Section 4.4 presents the first model of a token whose liquidity increases in a non-linear manner. The second model of a token whose liquidity increases in a non-linear manner is explained in Section 4.5, and Section 4.6 details a model in which a token can be spent while inhibiting a drastic change in the liquidity of the remaining tokens. Section 4.7 examines a model combining two wallets. The chapter concludes with the idea that lawyers are able to propose mathematical schemes that can be implemented in the legal incentives.

4.1.1 Media and Location of Medical and Health Records of Citizens

Conventionally, the medical records of patients are stored at hospitals and clinics in paper form and on photographic film, and the provisions of the relevant medical regulations were drafted accordingly. For example, Article 24 of the Medical Practitioners' Act of Japan (Act No. 201 of 1948, as amended) provides as follows (the English translation was prepared

[1] This chapter is based on 'Designing a Law to Promote the Sharing of Medical and Health Records: Striking a Balance between Protection of Personal Information and Promotion of Healthcare – Using a Token to Encourage Citizens to Utilize PHR', presented by the author at the Ninth International Conference on Health, Wellness & Society, held at the University of California, Berkeley, on 19 and 20 September 2019. The discussion, models, and codes in this article have been updated from those presented at the said conference.

and published by the Ministry of Justice of Japan at www.japaneselawtranslation.go.jp/?re=2):

Article 24 (1) When a medical practitioner has provided medical treatment, he/she shall enter the matters related to that medical treatment in a medical record without delay.

(2) Medical records as set forth in the preceding paragraph shall be stored for a period of five years by the administrator of the hospital or clinic where medical treatment was provided by a medical practitioner [who] works at that hospital or clinic, and by the medical practitioner himself/herself for medical records related to other medical treatment.

However, due to the widespread digitalisation of records, medical records in paper form have become obsolete and have been replaced by Electronic Health Records (EHRs). Moreover, the EHR, which was originally kept at hospitals and clinics, is now stored at data centres by means of housing and/or hosting and is increasingly being moved to cloud computing services. For example, the history of the amendment of the Guidelines for Secure Management of Medical Information Systems (*Iryo Joho System no An-zen Kanri ni Kansuru Guideline*) issued by the Ministry of Health, Labor and Welfare of Japan shown in the guidelines as of May 2017 clearly depicts such a change in the media and location of medical records.[2]

4.1.2 Possible Improvement of Medical Care by Sharing Past Records

It is generally agreed that the quality of medical care could be improved if physicians could access the past medical records and everyday health records of patients. In addition, it would lead to a reduction in redundant medical examinations, which would result in medical cost savings.[3]

[2] See www.mhlw.go.jp/file/05-Shingikai-12601000-Seisakutoukatsukan-Sanjikanshitsu_Shakaihoshoutantou/0000166260.pdf.

[3] For example, see Miriam Reisman, 'EHRs: The Challenge of Making Electronic Data Usable and Interoperable' (2017) 42(9) *Pharmacy and Therapy* 572; American Hospital Association, 'Sharing Data, Saving Lives: The Hospital Agenda for Interoperability' (January 2019), www.aha.org/system/files/2019-01/Report01_18_19-Sharing-Data-Saving-Lives_FINAL.pdf, accessed 10 February 2020; Ministry of Health, Labour and Welfare, '*Chiiki Iryō Renkei no Fukyū ni Muketa Kenkō Jōhō Katsuyō Kiban Jisshō Jigyō*' (Electronic Health Records Infrastructure Program for Diffusion of Regional Medical Cooperation) (March 2015), www.mhlw.go.jp/file/06-Seisakujouhou-10800000-Iseikyoku/0000102029.pdf, accessed 10 February 2020. In addition, such sharing of past medical records would aid in the provision of appropriate medical care to citizens in case of disaster. Also see K Furukawa

4.1.3 *Problems Accompanying the Interconnection of EHRs Belonging to Multiple Institutions*

In light of the current situation in which medical records are digitalised (EHR) and are gradually becoming cloud-based, it would seem that we can facilitate the sharing of medical records among past, current, and future physicians, as well as patients, by interconnecting the EHRs of multiple medical institutions. However, the interconnection of EHRs may not be very practical and could cause problems from the perspective of information security and exposing medical institutions to legal liability.

Many medical institutions have used EHRs for a very long time, and multiple vendors have supplied EHR systems and services. Their standardisation is still ongoing.[4] It may not be easy to establish interoperability between different EHRs already installed at various medical institutions.

Moreover, we will face another problem if EHRs of multiple institutions are interconnected. Suppose, for example, that Alice Memorial Hospital implements very strict security standards. Each of the physicians and paramedics belonging to Alice has to use their own ID, pass code, and biometrics or vocal pattern to be authorised to access individual patients' records. They are not permitted to access the records of a patient unless they belong to the medical team in charge of the patient or have a specific reason to refer to such records for a justifiable purpose. In contrast, suppose that Bob Memorial Hospital's information security

and H Arai, 'Earthquake in Japan' (2011) 377(9778) *The Lancet* 1652; K Kobayashi, 'Role Sharing between DMAT and JMAT' (2013) 56(1) *Japan Medical Association Journal* 25; Japan Medical Association Emergency and Disaster Medicine Management Committee, 'Program of the Activities of the Japan Medical Association Team (JMAT)' (2013) 56(3) *Japan Medical Association Journal* 143; J Starkey and S Maeda, 'Earthquake in Japan' (2011) 377(9778) *The Lancet* 1653; K Matsumoto, 'Mental Health of Disaster Relief Supporters' (2013) 56(2) *Japan Medical Association Journal* 70; S Teramoto and T Fukazu, 'Cloud Computing for Medical Data: A Legal Perspective' (2012) 25 *It Vision* 38; T McGhin and others, 'Blockchain in Healthcare Applications: Research Challenges and Opportunities' 135 *Journal of Network Computer Applications* 62.

[4] See, e.g., R Yamamoto, '*Kokunaigai ni okeru iryō jōhō no hyōjunka no genjō to tenbō: Sōgo un'yōsei no kōjō o mezashite*' (Situation and Prospects of Standardization of Health Information in Japan: for Improvement of Interoperability) (2017) 60(9) *Joho Kanri* 619; '*Iryō jōhō netto no riyō teimei shōhi zōzei, yūkō katsuyō sa rezu*' (Stagnation in Use, Consumption Tax Increase and Ineffective Utilization of Healthcare Information Network) *Nippon Keizai Shinbun* (28 October 2019), www.nikkei.com/article/DGXMZO51505040Y9A021C1CR8000/, accessed 10 February 2020.

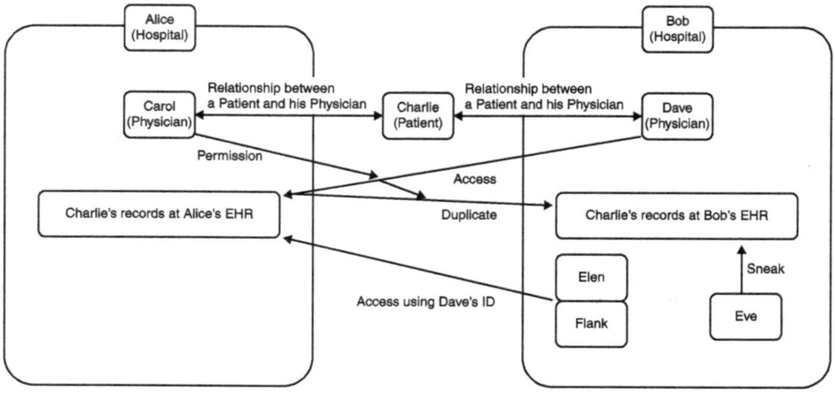

Figure 4.1 Alice's EHR exposed to information security risk

practices are inadequate or are routinely disregarded. The physicians and paramedics belonging to Bob often use the IDs and pass codes of their colleagues or medical team members. Moreover, any physician or paramedic can access the records of every patient. Then, suppose that Carol, a physician belonging to Alice responsible for the care of Charlie, a former patient at Alice and now hospitalised at Bob, within her authority given by Alice, permits Dave, a physician belonging to Bob, to access Charlie's medical records stored in Alice's EHR. Ellen or Frank, colleagues of Dave, may access Charlie's records in conflict with the information security policy of Alice. Furthermore, Eve, who is also a medical employee of Bob, may take a look at Charlie's records that were generated at Alice and duplicated at Bob's EHR. In this way, Alice is unable to protect the information security of its EHR according to its own information security policy. The security standard of Alice will be reduced to that of Bob (Figure 4.1).

Of course, the information security managers of Alice would not want to accept such risk. Those who are responsible for managing and operating medical institutions like Alice are expected to reduce the risk of institutions becoming liable to compensate for the damages of their patients caused by the actions or failure to act of their physicians or paramedics. It is likely to be one of their biggest fears that they could be liable for damages caused by the actions or failure to act of persons who are not controlled by Alice. The only way Alice can control the activities of the physicians and other medical employees of Bob is to reject any and all attempts at sharing Alice's EHR from outside.

4.1.4 PHRs Can Provide a Solution

In light of the previously discussed concerns, we should consider how we can facilitate the sharing of medical records by a patient and her past, present, and future medical providers without the interconnection of EHRs between multiple institutions.

Recently, the market for PHR services has been growing rapidly.[5] PHRs are designed to enable every citizen to record their own everyday health records, diet, and so forth so that they can take control of their own healthcare and also share such records with physicians and healthcare advisors. If we can utilize PHR as a tool to intermediate between physicians, paramedics, medical teams, medical institutions, and patients, the said concerns of medical institutions like Alice will be greatly mitigated.

Suppose that Frank Health Cloud Service Company is providing PHR services by means of cloud computing, and Charlie is subscribing to the PHR service provided by Frank. By using this service, Charlie can save his everyday health records, as well as the records of medical tests and medical imaging, which are duplicated from EHRs in hospitals and clinics.

Suppose also that Carol intends to have Dave access Charlie's past medical records generated at Alice and stored at Alice's EHR. Carol may duplicate Charlie's records from Alice's EHR to Charlie's PHR upon the explicit request by Charlie. Nobody other than Carol can access Alice's EHR. Moreover, Carol is authorised to access and duplicate Charlie's records at Alice's EHR and deliver such duplication to Charlie. Accordingly, this process does not expose Alice's PHR to the information security risk that could have been realised if Alice permitted Dave to access Alice's EHR. Further, since this process is implemented by Charlie's explicit request, Alice does not have to concern herself about the possible infringement of Charlie's right to protect his personal information.

Before accessing Charlie's past medical record stored in his PHR, Dave explains to Charlie the following to obtain his consent:

5 According to the survey by Yano Research Institute Ltd, the size of the PHR service market was 12.5 billion Japanese yen in 2016 (an increase from 2015 of 8.7%) and was estimated to be 14.5 billion Japanese yen in 2017, www.yano.co.jp/press-release/show/press_id/1752. See also Ministry of Internal Affairs and Communication, '*Kenkō Iryō Kaigo no Dēta Kiban no Kōchiku ni Muketa Sōmu-shō no Torikumi (PHR kanren)*' (Ministry of Internal Affairs and Communications (PHR related) Efforts to Build a Database for Health, Health Care and Nursing Care) (2019), www.kantei.go.jp/jp/singi/keizaisaisei/miraitoshikaigi/suishinkaigo2018/health/dai6/siryou2.pdf, accessed 10 February 2020.

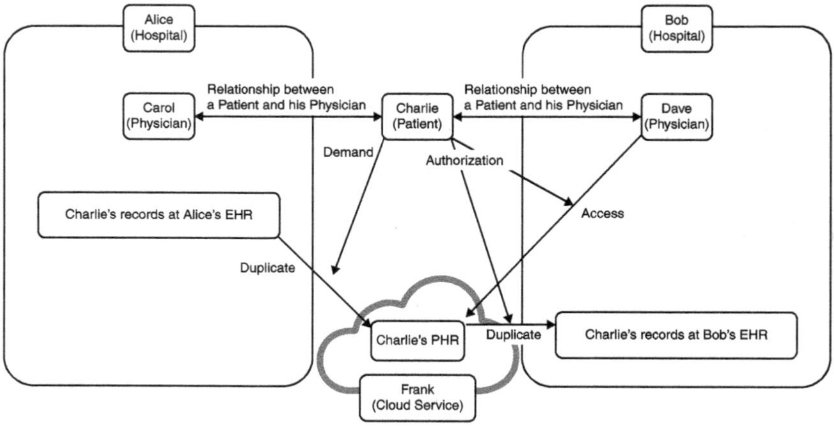

Figure 4.2 PHR intermediates between Alice and *Bob*

- the scope or extension of Charlie's past medical records to which Dave and his colleagues at Bob who are in charge of the medical services provided to Charlie will access and duplicate to Bob's EHR;
- the purpose of such records at Bob, including aiding in the provision of medical services to Charlie, and for the reference and education/learning of medical professionals and augmented intelligence (AI) for the computer aided diagnosis (CAD) belonging to Bob for the purpose of academic research, internal training, and continuous development of their CAD system; and any other necessary or appropriate matters.

Then, upon the explicit authorisation by Charlie or his duly entitled representative (such as his attorney or a family member), Bob accesses Charlie's PHR and retrieves his past medical records. This process is totally out of the control of Alice and completed with the explicit consent of Charlie. Therefore, Alice does not have to be concerned about its possible liability caused by Bob, which may fail to comply with the appropriate information security standard (Figure 4.2).

4.1.5 The Utilisation of PHR by Individual Citizens Is Essential

A user-friendly service that enables individual citizens to share their medical and health records with their physicians through PHR is essential to achieve the aforementioned purpose. The involvement of private businesses is expected to make such service available to most citizens.

However, recently, many citizens have been frustrated with the collection and control of personal data by the giants of Information and Communication Technology (ICT) industries such as so-called GAFA, and, in response, governments are establishing rules to regulate the collecting and handling of personal data. This trend is likely to make medical institutions hesitate to share patients' records with other institutions without the explicit approval of patients themselves. Furthermore, physicians rarely access the everyday health records of their patients without their understanding and approval.

In order to encourage patients and physicians to share medical records utilising PHRs, while avoiding conflict with the recent trend demanding that citizens have autonomous control of their own personal information, governments have to develop legal measures to encourage individual citizens to take the initiative to record their medical and health records to their PHR and to give their physicians access to their PHR. Assuming that a citizen is well informed,[6] her taking the initiative to disclose or share her own personal information, including her medical and health records, to or with her physicians and medical or healthcare providers should not cause any concern about infringing her right to protect her personal data.

4.1.6 Continuous Use of PHRs by Citizens Cannot Be Relied Upon

Another problem is likely to be caused by the typical behaviour of citizens. Some citizens are quick to adopt new products and services but just as quickly lose interest in using them. It is possible that many citizens will stop using their PHR if they are not given a good reason to continue before they obtain any benefit from it.

[6] It must be admitted that it is not easy to ensure that citizens are well informed about medical and healthcare services in advance. However, this issue is not discussed herein. The author has discussed this issue elsewhere, such as in S Teramoto and Y Haga, 'Informed Consent in Building Big Data in Healthcare: The Essential Role of Hubs in Curating and Disseminating Knowledge' (2017) 4(2) *RANGSIT Journal of Social Sciences and Humanities* 69; S Teramoto and K Sugimura, '*Shakai ni Kakusan Sareru Iryō Kenkō Jōhō no Kenzen-sei o Iji Suru Tame ni Obujekushon no Katsuyō*' (The Diffusion of Soundness of Medical Care and Health Information to Society: Objection Application) (2019) 84 *Law & Technology* 66; S Teramoto, '*Iryō, Kenkō Bun'ya ni Okeru Kyurēshon Saito no Yakuwari to Un'yō no Muzukashisa*' (The Role of Curation Sites in The Medical Care and Health Fields and the Difficulty of Operation) (2018) 78 *Law & Technology* 10.

According to a study that surveyed the behaviours and activities of 419,297 citizens whose health data (in this study, irregular pulses) were continuously monitored using a smartwatch, in which 2,161 of them received an irregular pulse notification, more than half of them failed to initiate a first study visit and were excluded from the research.[7] This example suggests that the said concern is understandable.

4.1.7 Necessary Legal Measures

I believe it will be necessary or, at least, appropriate to implement legal measures to encourage individual citizens to take the initiative to record their medical and health records to their PHR and to give their physicians access to it to promote the sharing of medical and health records, while avoiding conflict with the recent legal trend to regulate the collection and handling of personal data including patients' records in EHRs without the explicit approval of each individual citizen.

It would not be practicable to realise such legal measures by giving citizens an incentive to utilise PHRs or to give citizens who rarely utilize PHRs a disincentive. Rather, such legal measures have to be a bundle of multiple incentives and disincentives and also subject to continuous modifications and adjustments, because whether a specific incentive or disincentive will have an impact on the behaviours of citizens is likely to greatly depend on family circumstances, income and resources, health condition and challenges thereto, where they live, and any other life and work conditions of the respective citizens.

Suppose that a citizen who records her weight, diet, or other health records in her PHR every day can obtain additional financial support from the public health insurance budget when she needs a medical or healthcare service. This might work as an incentive to encourage her to utilise her PHR every day. However, suppose also that her income is too low to afford to procure medical or healthcare services when she needs them even if the cost for such services is subsidised by public health insurance. The said tactic is not likely to incentivise her to utilise her PHR every day.

Suppose that a citizen who does not give her physicians access to her PHR can obtain only reduced financial support from public health insurance to procure medical services from her physicians. This might work as

[7] See MV Perez and others, 'Large-Scale Assessment of a Smartwatch to Identify Atrial Fibrillation' (2019) 381 *The New England Journal of Medicine* 1909.

a disincentive against her declining to share her PHR with her physicians. However, this tactic will not work until she needs medical care.

Moreover, the social, economic, health, and other conditions of individual citizens change, and some of these changes cannot be predicted at the time when we design the initial incentives and disincentives. Therefore, it is inevitable that such legal measures will have to be frequently amended, modified, and improved after their initial enactment.

In this study, the author proposes the use of a digital token to be used as a possible incentive or disincentive.

4.2 The Purpose of the Study

The purpose of the study discussed herein is to consider whether we can design a token that can be allotted to citizens upon utilising their respective PHRs – for example:

i) upon recording everyday health data to their respective PHRs;
ii) upon requesting their physicians to duplicate relevant medical data such as records of medical tests and medical images to their respective PHRs; and
iii) upon sharing the medical and health records stored in their respective PHRs with their physicians.

Such allotment of tokens is likely to encourage citizens to make these behaviours everyday practices, if the tokens can be used to pay for the cost (or a part thereof) of procuring medical or healthcare services, and also the tokens are carefully designed, although this is not an exhaustive list of preferred characteristics of the tokens,

- to inhibit an instant draining of cash from the public health insurance budget;
- to prevent citizens from spending tokens too quickly; and
- to encourage citizens to save tokens continuously.

4.3 Designing a Token Allotted to Citizens to Promote Their Use of PHRs

4.3.1 *Requirements of the Tokens*

In order for the tokens to have the said preferred characteristics, several requirements have to be satisfied by the tokens. The following is a list of such requirements, although it is not necessarily exhaustive.

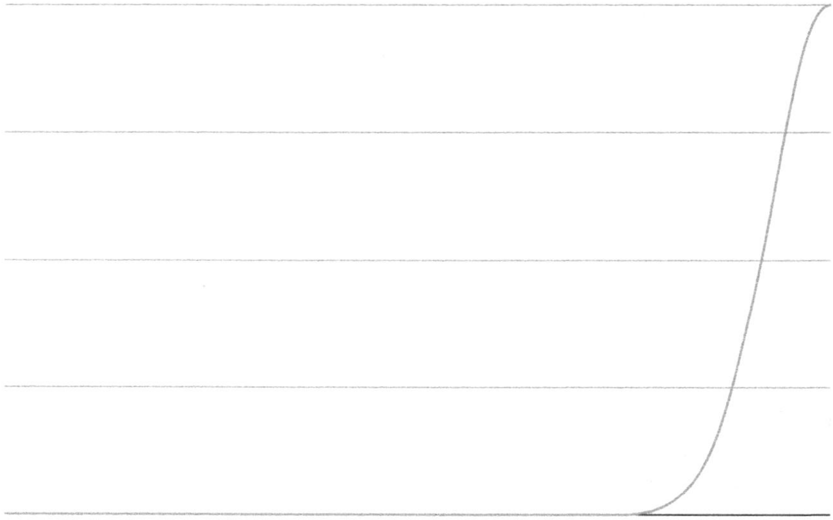

Figure 4.3 Non-linear increase in the liquidity of tokens

4.3.2 Non-linear Increase in the Liquidity of Tokens

Here, the liquidity of a token means the exchange rate of the token against publicly traded cryptocurrency or fiat currency, by which citizens can procure medical or healthcare services. The liquidity should be very low for a certain period after a relevant citizen receives a token and should quickly increase after such period (Figure 4.3).

This requirement has already been satisfied by the invention of Good Luck 3, Inc., Fukuako, Japan as described in its patent application (Japan Patent Application 2019-025726). However, the second (Section 4.3.3, below) and third (Section 4.3.4, below) requirements were not satisfied by this invention. Moreover, the mathematical scheme disclosed in the said patent application as a working example of the invention was not intended to be easily applicable to satisfy the second and third requirements. The author tried to find a method that would satisfy all three requirements described herein by using a common mathematical scheme to define the liquidity of a token.

4.3.3 Spending Tokens While Inhibiting a Change in the Liquidity of the Remaining Tokens

Spending tokens should have a very limited impact on the liquidity of the remaining tokens. If spending tokens significantly decreases the liquidity of the remaining tokens, citizens are likely to hesitate to spend tokens even when they really need medical or healthcare services. In contrast, if spending tokens greatly increases the liquidity of the remaining tokens, citizens are likely to procure too many medical and healthcare services by using tokens, which could threaten the budget of public healthcare insurance.

4.3.4 Increasing the Liquidity of Tokens with Lower Liquidity by Blending Them with Tokens with Much Greater Volume and Higher Liquidity

We can assume that a citizen is likely to have one or more groups of a smaller number of tokens with lower liquidity (that is, the tokens allocated to her recently) and, also, one or more groups of a larger number of tokens with higher liquidity (that is, tokens she has saved for a very long period). Suppose that a citizen needs to procure a very expensive medical procedure or healthcare service. She is likely to want to spend tokens from both kinds of groups simultaneously. In such case, the liquidity of all the tokens spent by the citizen should increase so that the citizen can procure the medical or healthcare services immediately. Otherwise, the citizen is likely to be disappointed by the limited benefit from the tokens allotted to her.

4.3.4.1 Same Mathematical Scheme

In order to simplify the design of tokens, it is preferable to employ the same mathematical scheme to satisfy all the said requirements.

4.3.5 Tools

In order to design tokens, the author employed the tools listed here. Presumably, there are various alternative tools that can be employed to design tokens. For the purpose of convenience, the author employed these tools because he has used these tools in previous works,[8] and these tools are widely used in the context of social network analysis.[9]

[8] See, e.g., S Teramoto and P Jurčys, 'Allocation of Public Resources for Scientific Research: The Role of Governments and the Law' (2018) 85(1) *Hosei Kenkyu* 362; S Teramoto, 'How Industrial Policy Affects the Nurturing of Innovation: From the Perspective of Intellectual Property Rights', in Basedow J and Kono T (eds), *Special Economic Zones: Law and Policy Perspectives* (Mohr Siebeck 2016); Teramoto and Haga 'Informed Consent in Building Big Data in Healthcare'.

[9] See, e.g., J Scott, *Social Networks Analysis* (SAGE 2017); C Prell, *Social Networks Analysis: History, Theory & Methodology* (SAGE 2011).

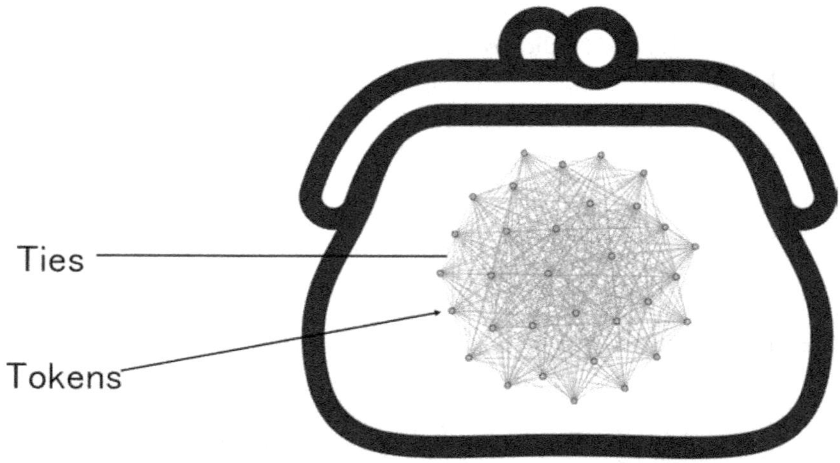

Figure 4.4 A wallet comprised of tokens as vertices

4.3.5.1 A Network

We deem a group of tokens allocated to a citizen (hereinafter, a 'wallet') as an undirected network comprised of tokens as vertices. The relationship between a pair of tokens is represented by the existence or non-existence of an undirected tie connecting them (Figure 4.4).

4.3.5.2 Density of a Network

Suppose that the number of tokens contained in a wallet is n, and the number of ties (here it is assumed that a tie has no direction) connecting such tokens with one another is m. Here, n is a positive integer. In order to enable us to assume that one or more ties connecting tokens possibly exists, $n \geq 2$. Furthermore, m is an integer not less than 0. The possible maximum number of m is ${}_nC_2 = n(n-1)/2$. Accordingly, $0 \leq m \leq n(n-1)/2$. The *density* of the said wallet is defined as $\frac{m}{{}_nC_2} = \frac{m}{n(n-1)/2}$.

The density of a network is non-linearly increased (or decreased) when the vertices in the network gain (or lose) incrementally additional ties with one another (a non-linearly decreasing density of a network is shown in Figure 4.6). This suggests that we will be able to design a non-linearly increasing liquidity of tokens by utilising a wallet with non-linearly increasing or decreasing density.

4.4 The First Model of Tokens Whose Liquidity Increases in a Non-linear Manner

4.4.1 *Expected Change in Liquidity of Tokens*

In order to encourage citizens to utilise PHRs every day, we have to incentivise citizens to continuously save tokens for a considerable length of time. For this purpose, spending tokens quickly after their allotment should be disadvantageous to citizens, while spending tokens after saving and accumulating tokens for a long time should be advantageous to citizens. In other words, the liquidity of the tokens should be very low for a certain period from their allotment to citizens, and the liquidity of the tokens should quickly increase after the end of such period, as shown in Figure 4.3.

4.4.2 *A Network*

It is assumed that a wallet (see Section 4.3.5.1, above) held by a citizen contains the tokens allotted to her on one occasion, unless the wallet is combined with another wallet as described in Section 4.7. For the purpose of simplicity, it is also assumed that the relevant wallet has never been combined with another wallet.

Suppose that the number of tokens in the wallet is n (n is an integer that is 2 or greater), and every token in a wallet is connected with the others by undirected ties when they are allotted to her. The number of ties m is ${}_nC_2 = n(n-1)/2$.

4.4.3 *Density*

The density of the said wallet is $\frac{m}{n(n-1)/2} = 1$. Suppose also that we reduce the density of the network denoting the wallet incrementally by repeating the following steps:

1) to select one vertex (i.e., one token) that is not isolated from other vertices (i.e., other tokens); and
2) to isolate the selected vertex from other vertices by cutting off any ties that connect the selected vertex with other vertices.

Assuming that $n = 256$, the incremental change in the network denoting the wallet is outlined in Figure 4.5.

According to the said changes, the density of the network denoting the wallet decreases in a non-linear manner as shown in Figure 4.6.

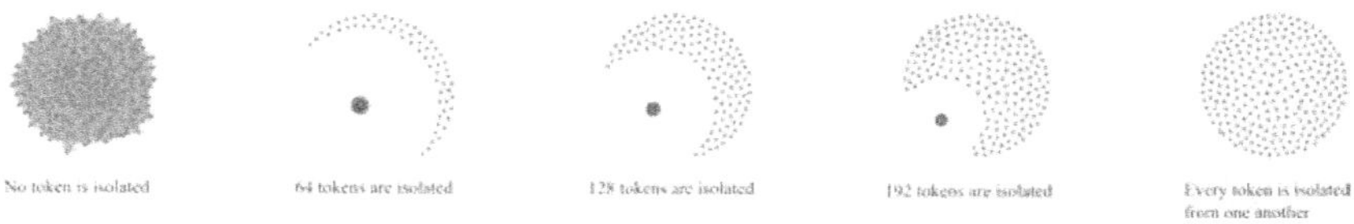

Figure 4.5 The incremental change in the network denoting a wallet

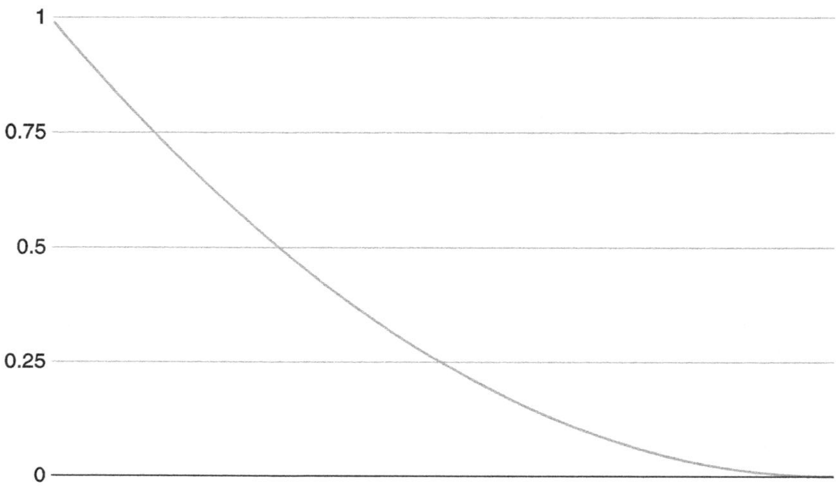

Figure 4.6 The non-linear decrease in the density of the network denoting the wallet

4.4.4 *Liquidity*

Since the density of the wallet is decreasing in a non-linear manner, we can easily devise a formula to produce a non-linear increase in the liquidity of the tokens. For example, the following formula can generate such a non-linear increase in liquidity:

$$liquidity = exp\left(-\frac{density}{\tau}\right)$$

τ is a constant appropriately defined.

The increasing curve of liquidity can be adjusted by adopting a different value for τ. Figure 4.7 shows the non-linear increase in the liquidity of the tokens contained in the said wallet, assuming that $\tau = 0.01$.

In this way, we can design a model of tokens that satisfies the requirement that the liquidity of tokens increases in a non-linear manner.

Figure 4.7 The non-linear increase in the liquidity of tokens

4.4.5 Code

We can implement the said model by using a very short code. The following is an example of such code prepared by using R language:

```
library (igraph)
n<-256
w01adj<-matrix(1,n,n)
for (i in 1:n){
w01adj[i,i]<-0
}
w01<-graph_from_adjacency_matrix(w01adj,
  mode=c("undirected"))
tiff (file="000.tiff")
plot(w01, vertex.size=5, vertex.label=NA)
dev.off()
w01dens<-graph.density(w01)
τ<-0.01
nwd<-w01dens
w01Liquid<-exp(-nwd/τ)
w01cAdj<-w01adj
for (q in 1:n){
file.name<-sprintf("%03d.tiff", q)
for (i in 1:n){
w01cAdj[q, i]<-0
```

```
w01cAdj[i, q]<-0
}
w01c<-graph_from_adjacency_matrix(w01cAdj,
  mode=c("undirected"))
tiff (file.name)
plot(w01c, vertex.size=5, vertex.label=NA)
dev.off()
w01cD<-graph.density(w01c)
cat(w01cD, "\n", file="w01coolingDensity.csv",
  append=TRUE)
nwd<-w01cD
w01cLiquid<-exp(-nwd/τ)
cat(w01cLiquid, "\n", file="w01coolingLiquidity.csv",
  append=TRUE)
}
```

4.5 The Second Model of Tokens Whose Liquidity Increases in a Non-linear Manner

4.5.1 The Problem with the First Model

The first model, described in Section 4.4, assumes that the initial condition of a wallet is a complete graph (that is, in the network representing the wallet, every vertex is directly connected with the others). Furthermore, the first model assumes no combination of multiple wallets.

Accordingly, at any stage of the network, of which density is incrementally reducing, every vertex in the network is totally isolated (that is, the vertex has no tie connecting it with any other vertex or vertices) or connected with every other vertex which is not isolated. This means that, among the vertices connected with one another, every vertex has the same number of ties that connect it with other vertices. Therefore, whichever vertex you select, eliminating the ties held by the vertex results in the same reduction in density. Accordingly, under the said assumptions, the first model employs no specific means to select a vertex whose ties are to be eliminated.

However, if the holder of tokens combines multiple wallets, as described in Section 4.7, the number of ties held by the respective vertices are not likely to be the same. Some vertices may have more ties, while other vertices may have fewer ties or even no ties (that is, they are isolated). In addition, it is probable that the density of the network denoting the wallet is much lower than 1 (and the liquidity of the tokens in the wallet is considerably higher than 0) because considerable time has passed since the tokens were given to the holder.

If you select a vertex having a greater number of ties and eliminate such ties, the reduction in the density of the network is greater. If you select a vertex having a smaller number of ties and eliminate such ties, the reduction in the density of the network is less. In consideration of this issue, we have to employ a rule in which the vertex should be selected so that the ties held by the vertex will be eliminated.

Suppose that the density of the network denoting a wallet is very high, and, accordingly, the liquidity of the tokens contained in the wallet is very low. Assuming that the liquidity of a token is very low for a certain period after a relevant citizen receives a token, and that it quickly increases after such period, as discussed in Section 4.4, such a condition implies that the wallet contains many tokens that have been allotted recently. Therefore, there is little reason to accelerate the reduction in density (and the increase in liquidity). It is a safe option to select a vertex having fewer ties and eliminate such ties.

Suppose that the density of the network denoting a wallet is very low, and, accordingly, the liquidity of the tokens contained in the wallet is very high. Such a condition implies that the number of ties held by each of the vertices denoting tokens contained in the wallet is likely to be limited. Therefore, whichever vertex we select to eliminate the ties held by such vertex, the reduction in the density of the network (and the increase in the liquidity of the tokens in the wallet) is likely to be very slow.

4.5.2 *A Default Network*

Now, we have to prepare the models of networks that have irregular structures. That is, the number of ties held by respective vertices belonging to a network is not the same. Assuming that the holder has held their tokens for a very long time, the structure of the network denoting the wallet containing the tokens will greatly deviate from a complete graph (see the model described in Section 4.4). We cannot definitely predict the structure of such a network because some of the ties therein have been diminished according to the time that has lapsed, and the structure of the network may have become complex due to a combination of multiple wallets.

Having regard for the well-known finding that we can frequently find scale-free networks in the real world,[10] and for the purpose of simplicity

[10] See A Barabási and R Albert, 'Emergence of Scaling in Random Networks' (1999) 286(5439) *Science* 509.

Figure 4.8 Scale-free networks having 256 vertices (Left: a dense network; Right: a sparse network)

and convenience, in the example outlined later the author assumed that the condition of the network denoting a wallet is a scale-free network comprised of 256 vertices. The author generated the network by using the function 'barabasi.game' contained in the 'igraph' library (igraph.org) prepared for R language (see the code shown in Section 4.5.3).[11]

In addition, at least one of the models must have a considerably higher density, while another must have a considerably lower density. Figure 4.8 shows the appearance of such networks (Left: a dense network with higher density; Right: a sparse network with lower density). The density of the left network is approximately 0.438 and the liquidity of the tokens contained in the wallet denoted by such network is approximately 9.28^{e-20}. The density of the right network is approximately 0.015 and the liquidity of the token contained in the wallet denoted by such network is approximately 0.210.

4.5.3 Choice of Vertices and Elimination of Ties

Among the well-known tools used for social network analysis, degree centrality of a vertex corresponds to the number of ties held by such vertex. A vertex with a lower degree of centrality has fewer ties, while a vertex with a higher degree of centrality has a greater number of ties.

In accordance with the discussion in Section 4.5.1, the model described herein repeats the following procedure – to select a vertex having a minimum degree of centrality from among the vertices that are not isolated (that is, having one or more ties connecting with another vertex or vertices) and to isolate it from other vertices by eliminating every tie held by such vertex.

The structure of the network denoting a wallet incrementally changed by isolating vertices denoting tokens one by one in a dense network

[11] See www.rdocumentation.org/packages/igraph/versions/0.1.1/topics/barabasi.game.

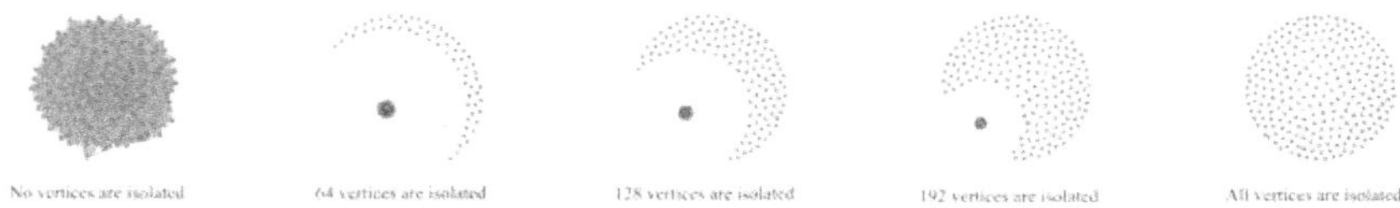

Figure 4.9 The incremental change in a dense network denoting a wallet

Figure 4.10 The change in density (left) and liquidity (right)

Figure 4.11 The incremental change in a sparse network denoting a wallet

Figure 4.12 The change in density (left) and liquidity (right)

according to the said scheme is outlined in Figure 4.9. The changes in density (left) and liquidity (right) are shown in Figure 4.10. Apparently, the increase in the liquidity is very slow in the earlier steps and accelerates in later steps.

The structure of the network denoting a wallet incrementally changed by isolating vertices denoting tokens one by one in a sparse network according to the said scheme is outlined in Figure 4.11. The change in density (left) and liquidity (right) are shown in Figure 4.12. Apparently, the liquidity incrementally increases with the passage of time.

4.5.4 Code

The following is an example of the code prepared by using R language to implement the said model. The number 64 is assigned to e in order to generate the said dense network, while 2 is assigned to e in order to generate the said sparse network.

```
library(igraph)
n<-256
w01<-barabasi.game(n, m=e, directed=FALSE)
tiff (file="000.tiff")
plot(w01, vertex.size=5, vertex.label=NA)
dev.off()
w01D<-graph.density(w01)
cat(w01D, "\n", file="w01timeDensity.csv", append=TRUE)
τ<-0.01
nwd<-w01D
w01Liquid<-exp(-nwd/τ)
cat(w01Liquid, "\n", file="w01timeLiquidity.csv",
  append=TRUE)
for (q in 1:n){
file.name<-sprintf("%03d.tiff", q)
w01Adj<-as_adj(w01)
w01Dg<-degree(w01)
for (i in 1:n){
if (w01Dg[i]==0) w01Dg[i]<-256
}
k<-which.min(w01Dg)
for (j in 1:n){
w01Adj[k, j]<-0
w01Adj[j, k]<-0
}
w01<-graph_from_adjacency_matrix(w01Adj,
  mode=c("undirected"))
tiff (file.name)
plot(w01, vertex.size=5, vertex.label=NA)
dev.off()
w01D<-graph.density(w01)
cat(w01D, "\n", file="w01timeDensity.csv", append=TRUE)
nwd<-w01D
w01Liquid<-exp(-nwd/τ)
cat(w01Liquid, "\n", file="w01timeLiquidity.csv",
  append=TRUE)
if (w01D==0) break
}
```

4.6 A Model in Which Tokens Can Be Spent While Inhibiting a Drastic Change in the Liquidity of the Remaining Tokens

4.6.1 Choice of Tokens to Be Spent

A wallet containing tokens is represented by a network, in which each vertex corresponds to a token. Suppose that the number of tokens in the wallet is n (n is an integer that is not less than 2), and the number of ties connecting tokens is m (m is a positive integer, and $m \le {}_nC_2 = n(n-1)/2$). The density of the network representing the wallet is $\frac{m}{n(n-1)/2}$.

Suppose also that you spend one token, and the vertex corresponding to the token has l ties that connect it with other vertices. Spending a token results in eliminating the vertex corresponding to such token from the network. Accordingly, the ties that connect it with other vertices are also eliminated. Therefore, the density of the network after spending the token is $\frac{m-l}{(n-1)(n-1-1)/2} = \frac{m-l}{(n-1)(n-2)/2}$.

Assuming that $liquidity = exp\left(-\frac{density}{\tau}\right)$, as defined in the first model discussed in Section 4.4, the liquidity of the tokens will change according to the change in the density of the network denoting the wallet containing the tokens. Therefore, if you want to inhibit a change in liquidity, you have to inhibit a change in density.

The most preferable result is $\frac{m}{n(n-1)/2} = \frac{m-l}{(n-1)(n-2)/2}$. This means that the density of the network remains unchanged after the relevant token is spent. If $l = \frac{2m}{n}$, the density of the network is not changed because

$$\frac{m-2m/n}{(n-1)(n-2)/2} = \frac{nm-2m}{n(n-1)(n-2)/2} = \frac{m(n-2)}{n(n-1)(n-2)/2} = \frac{m}{n(n-1)/2}.$$

Of course, there is no guarantee that any specific vertex denoting a token in the wallet precisely has such number of ties. Therefore, in order to minimise a change in the density of the network denoting the wallet, you should count the number of ties held by the respective vertices in the wallet, select a vertex whose number of ties is nearest to $\frac{2m}{n}$, and spend the token that is denoted by such vertex.

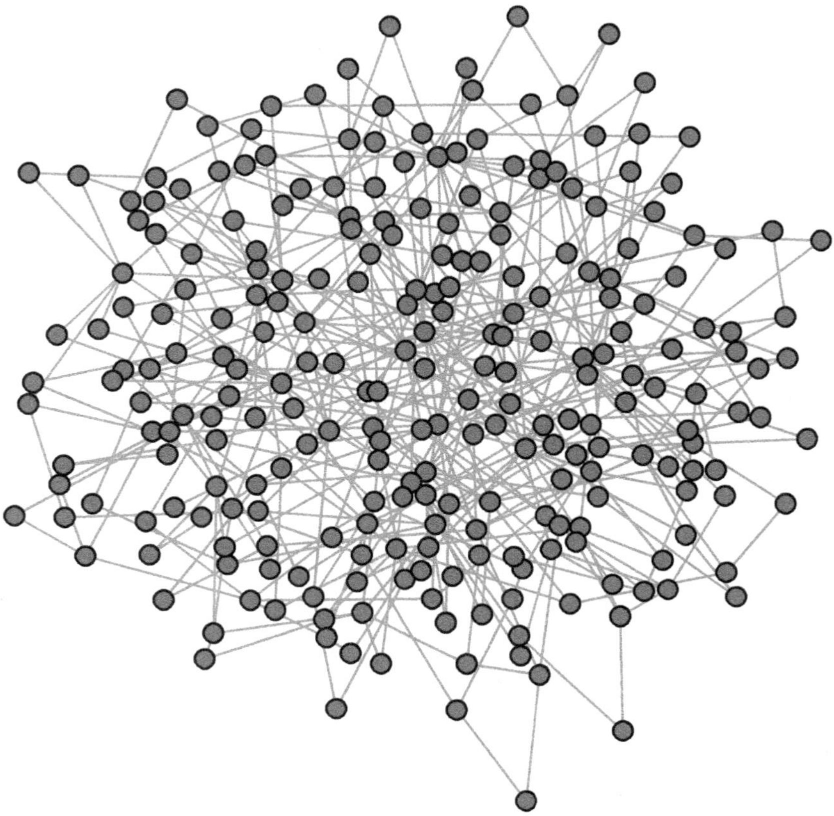

Figure 4.13 A scale-free network having 256 vertices

Figure 4.14 The incremental change in a wallet

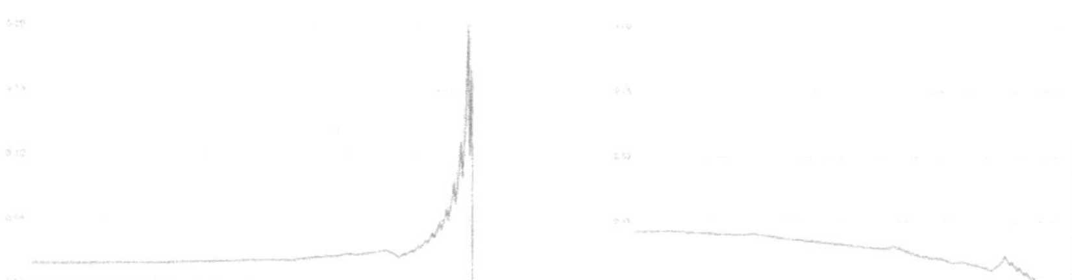

Figure 4.15 The changes in density (left) and liquidity (right)

4.6.2 *Density and Liquidity*

It is difficult to predict the condition of the network corresponding to a wallet held by a citizen, because the density of the network may be decreased and the network may become sparse according to the passage of time after the allotment of the tokens in the wallet to the citizen (see the models described in Sections 4.4 and 4.5). Moreover, the citizen may change the structure of the network in the wallet by combining two or more wallets (see the model described in Section 4.7).

For the purpose of convenience, in the example outlined here, the author assumed that the condition of the network denoting a wallet is a scale-free network comprised of 256 vertices. Figure 4.13 shows the appearance of such network generated by using 'barabasi.game'. Its density is approximately 0.015 and the liquidity of the token contained in the network denoted by such network is approximately 0.210.

The structure of a network denoting a wallet incrementally changed by spending up to 254 tokens one by one according to the said scheme is outlined in Figure 4.14. The changes in density (left) and liquidity (right) are shown in Figure 4.15. It appears that the changes in density and liquidity are restrained until the number of remaining tokens is very small.

4.6.3 *Code*

The following is an example of the code prepared by using R language to implement the said model:

```
library (igraph)
n<-256
w01<-barabasi.game(n, m=2, directed=FALSE)
tiff (file="000.tiff")
plot(w01, vertex.size=5, vertex.label=NA)
dev.off()
w01D<-graph.density(w01)
cat(w01D, "\n", file="w01spentDensity.csv", append=TRUE)
τ<-0.01
nwd<-w01D
w01Liquid<-exp(-nwd/τ)
cat(w01Liquid, "\n", file="w01spentLiquidity.csv",
  append=TRUE)
for (q in 1:(n-2)){
file.name<-sprintf("%03d.tiff", q)
w01Adj<-as_adj(w01)
rt<-n-q+1
m<-ecount(w01)
```

```
l<-2*m/rt
w01Dg<-degree(w01)
for (i in 1:rt){
w01Dg[i]<-(w01Dg[i]-l)^2
}
k<-which.min(w01Dg)
w01Adj<-w01Adj[, -k]
w01Adj<-w01Adj[-k, ]
w01<-graph_from_adjacency_matrix(w01Adj,
  mode=c("undirected"))
tiff (file.name)
plot(w01, vertex.size=5, vertex.label=NA)
dev.off()
w01D<-graph.density(w01)
cat(w01D, "\n", file="w01spentDensity.csv", append=TRUE)
nwd<-w01D
w01Liquid<-exp(-nwd/τ)
cat(w01Liquid, "\n", file="w01spentLiquidity.csv",
  append=TRUE)
}
```

4.7 A Model of a Combination of Two Wallets

4.7.1 A Use Case of a Combination of Multiple Wallets and Accompanying Concerns

Suppose that a citizen has saved tokens for a very long time because she has been using her PHR every day and, accordingly, tokens have been allotted to her continuously, but she has not suffered a medical condition that is sufficiently serious to require her to spend many tokens to procure expensive medical or healthcare services.

As a result of her everyday habit of using PHR, she is likely to have multiple wallets, each of which contains tokens. Further, many of the saved tokens are likely to be highly liquid because they have been saved for a long period.

Suppose also that the citizen needs to procure medical or healthcare services due to a sudden severe illness or accidental injury. She is likely to consider spending the tokens in order to cover all or part of the expenses of such services. Spending tokens with higher liquidity is advantageous to her, while spending tokens with lower liquidity is disadvantageous to her. If her tokens with higher liquidity are insufficient to cover such expenses, she will be obliged to spend tokens with lower liquidity. Such a disadvantageous experience is likely to disappoint her and be a disincentive to her habit of using her PHR every day.

4.7.2 A Possible Solution to Mitigate This Concern

How can we mitigate such a problematic situation, which is likely to disappoint the citizen who is obliged to spend tokens with lower liquidity in combination with tokens with higher liquidity?

A possible idea is to automatically adjust the liquidity of the tokens with lower liquidity when the citizen spends such tokens in combination with the tokens with higher liquidity. For example, we may deem that the liquidity of the former tokens is identical to that of the latter tokens. However, providing a citizen with a benefit automatically is likely to deprive the citizen of the opportunity to observe and recognise the relationship between her own habit of using her PHR and the benefits given to her.

In order to address such concerns, we can enable each citizen to increase the liquidity of their tokens, which were recently allotted to them and have lower liquidity, at their own initiative. The capability and motivation of a person to make diligent decisions is likely to deteriorate when they face illness or injury. In light of this concern, it would be better to enable citizens to make such adjustments to the liquidity of their tokens in advance at any time.

4.7.3 Allowing Qualified Citizens the Benefit of Adjusting the Liquidity of Their Tokens

A citizen who has continuously saved tokens by using their PHR every day should be allowed to increase the liquidity of the tokens with lower liquidity. In contrast, such a benefit should not be given to a citizen who rarely uses their PHR.

A citizen of the former type is likely to have a considerably larger number of tokens with higher liquidity unless she spent a large number of tokens to pay for medical or healthcare services recently, and, also, a smaller number of tokens with lower liquidity. In contrast, the number of tokens held by a citizen of the latter type is likely to be small, either with higher liquidity or with lower liquidity.

Suppose that the combination of tokens with higher liquidity and tokens with lower liquidity barely increases the liquidity of the latter tokens, unless the volume of the former tokens is much larger than the volume of the latter tokens. Such a scheme is likely to benefit citizens of the former type, while citizens of the latter type are not likely to be able to enjoy the same benefit.

4.7.4 Assumptions

In order to design a scheme whereby the liquidity of tokens increases by using the other tokens whose liquidity has become sufficiently low, the author has made the following assumptions.

For the purpose of simplicity and convenience, the author assumed that there is one group of tokens with higher liquidity and another group of tokens with lower liquidity. If we can design a mathematical scheme of combining two groups of tokens, three or more groups of tokens are easily combined by repeating the process of combining two groups of tokens in sequence. Accordingly, we do not have to consider a specific scheme in order to combine three or more groups of tokens at once.

A wallet '$w01$', containing $n01$ tokens ($n01$ is an integer, and $n01 \geq 2$) held by a citizen and having $m01$ undirected ties ($m01$ is an integer, and $0 \leq m01 \leq n01(n01-1)/2$) connecting tokens therein with one another, denotes a group of tokens with higher liquidity.

A wallet '$w02$', containing $n02$ tokens ($n02$ is an integer, and $n02 \geq 2$) held by the same citizen and having $m02$ undirected ties ($m02$ is an integer, and $0 \leq m02 \leq n02(n02-1)/2$) connecting tokens therein, denotes a group of tokens with lower liquidity. If $n02 = 1$, no ties connecting tokens exist in $w02$. So, the author assumes that $n02 \geq 2$.

The citizen combines $w01$ and $w02$ and makes them into one wallet, '$w03$'.

4.7.5 Requirements for the Scheme to Generate w03

First of all, every token contained in $w03$ should have the same liquidity. In addition, the liquidity of the tokens contained in $w03$ calculated in accordance with the mathematical scheme used in Section 4.4 to Section 4.6, should be kept very high.

Moreover, the holder of $w03$ should be able to spend the tokens contained in $w03$ in accordance with the mathematical scheme implemented in the model described in Section 4.6.

Therefore, we have to be able to represent $w03$ by one network comprised of vertices, each of which corresponds to each of the tokens contained in $w03$, and the existence or non-existence of the ties connecting them with one another.

4.7.6 A Possible Scheme

Suppose that we put the network denoting $w01$ and the network denoting $w02$ in a box and deem the inside of the box as constituting the network

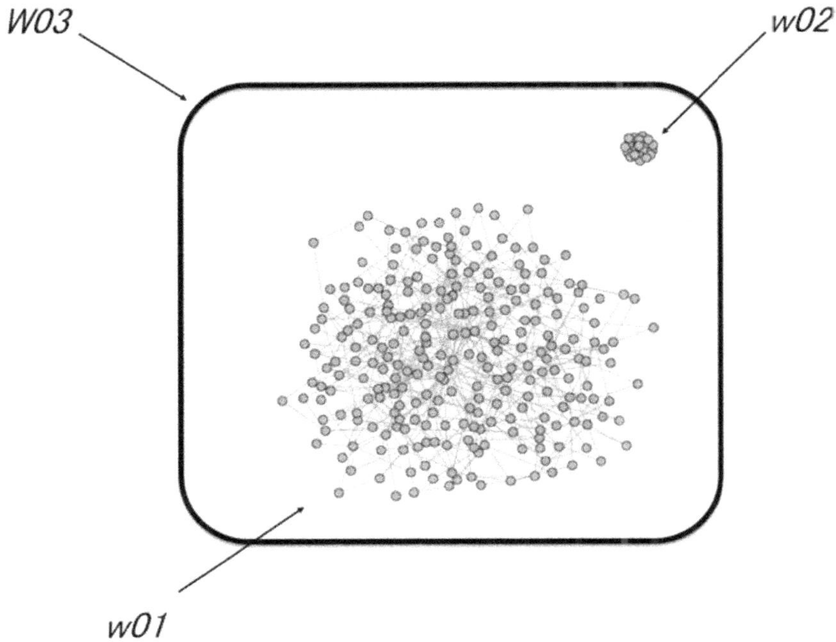

Figure 4.16 The relationship between *w*01, *w*02, and *w*03

corresponding to *w*03 (Figure 4.16). The number of vertices contained in the network will be *n*01 + *n*02.

In order to give the citizen holding *w*01 and *w*02 a benefit, the liquidity of the tokens contained in *w*03 should be very high. Therefore, the density of the network denoting *w*03 should be very low. Because a network is comprised of vertices and ties connecting vertices, a change that we can give to a network is either or both of the increase or decrease in the number of vertices, and the establishment of new ties or the elimination of existing ties. The number of vertices belonging to *w*03 is fixed as *n*01 + *n*02. Accordingly, in order to change the network, we need to establish new ties or eliminate existing ties.

Suppose that we intend to give the highest possible liquidity to the tokens contained in *w*03. The density of the network denoting *w*03 must be as low as possible. This means that we should introduce no new ties when we generate *w*03 by combining *w*01 and *w*02. Diminishing existing ties will make the density of the network lower. However, we have to decide which tie or ties should be diminished and by which standard.

Such a decision is likely to make the mathematical scheme to implement the combination of the two wallets very complex. Simply establishing no new ties and making the number of ties in the network $m01 + m02$ seems very simple and convenient.

4.7.7 *Justification of Said Scheme*

The density of $w03$ is $\frac{m01+m02}{{}_{n01+n02}C_2} = \frac{m01+m02}{(n01+n02)(n01+n02-1)/2}$. The liquidity of the tokens contained in $w03$ is $exp\left(-\frac{Density\ of\ w03}{\tau}\right)$. In order to maximise the said liquidity, we have to minimise the density of $w03$.

Suppose that the values of $n01$ and $m01$ are fixed. Suppose also that the density of $w02$ is fixed as 1 (and, accordingly, the liquidity of the tokens in $w02$ is nearly equal to 0), which is the maximum possible density. This assumption is reasonable in this context because we have assumed that the tokens in $w02$ were allotted to the relevant citizen very recently, and it represents the most unfavourable conditions for the holder of the tokens in $w01$ and $w02$.

Because $the\ density\ of\ w02 = \frac{m02}{{}_{n02}C_2} = 1$, $m02 = {}_{n02}C_2$. Accordingly, $the\ density\ of\ w03 = \frac{m01+m02}{{}_{n01+n02}C_2} = \frac{m01+{}_{n02}C_2}{{}_{n01+n02}C_2}$. Because $n02$ is variable, while $n01$ and $m01$ are constants, it is convenient to read as $f(n02) = \frac{m01+{}_{n02}C_2}{{}_{n01+n02}C_2}$. Then,

$$
\begin{aligned}
& f(n02+1) - f(n02) \\
&= \frac{m01+{}_{n02+1}C_2}{{}_{n01+n02+1}C_2} - \frac{m01+{}_{n02}C_2}{{}_{n01+n02}C_2} \\
&= \frac{2n01n02 - 4m01}{(n01+n02)(n01+n02-1)(n01+n02+1)} \\
&= \frac{2n01(n02 - 2m01/n01)}{(n01+n02)(n01+n02-1)(n01+n02+1)}
\end{aligned}
$$

Because both $n01$ and $n02$ are greater than 2, the denominator of the said formula is always greater than 0. Accordingly, while $n02 < \frac{2m01}{n01}$, $f(n02+1) - f(n02) < 0$. Namely, when $n02$ increases from 2 to $\frac{2m01}{n01}$, the density of $w03$ reduces incrementally. While $n02 > \frac{2m01}{n01}$, $f(n02+1) - f(n02) > 0$. Namely, when $n02$ increases from $\frac{2m01}{n01}$, the density of $w03$ increases incrementally.

Assuming that $w01$ is held for a very long time, and its density has become low (that is, the liquidity of the tokens in $w01$ has become very high), $n01$ is likely to be a very large number, and $m01$ is likely to be a very small number. Accordingly, $\frac{2m01}{n01}$ is likely to be a very small number. Therefore, assuming that the density of $w02$ is very close to 1, $n02$ should be a very small number in order to make the liquidity of the tokens in $w03$ very high.

4.7.8 *Examples*

4.7.8.1 Models of $w01$

The author has prepared several examples to demonstrate how said scheme works.

It is assumed that $w01$ contains a very large number of tokens. For the purpose of convenience, the author assumed that $n01 = 256$.

For the purpose of simplicity and convenience, the author assumed that the first example of the network denoting $w01$ is a scale-free network. The author generated the network by using the 'barabasi.game' function (see the code shown in Section 4.7.10).

Figure 4.17 shows the appearance of such network. Its density is approximately *0.015* and the liquidity of the token contained in $w01$ is approximately *0.210*.

In addition, the author incrementally reduced the density of the said network to denote $w01$ (and, in turn, increased the liquidity of the tokens contained therein) and generated networks having *256* vertices with various densities. Each of these networks was used to denote $w01$.

4.7.8.2 Models of $w02$

The author assumed that the tokens in $w02$ were allotted to the holder of tokens very recently. To represent this assumption in a very simple way,

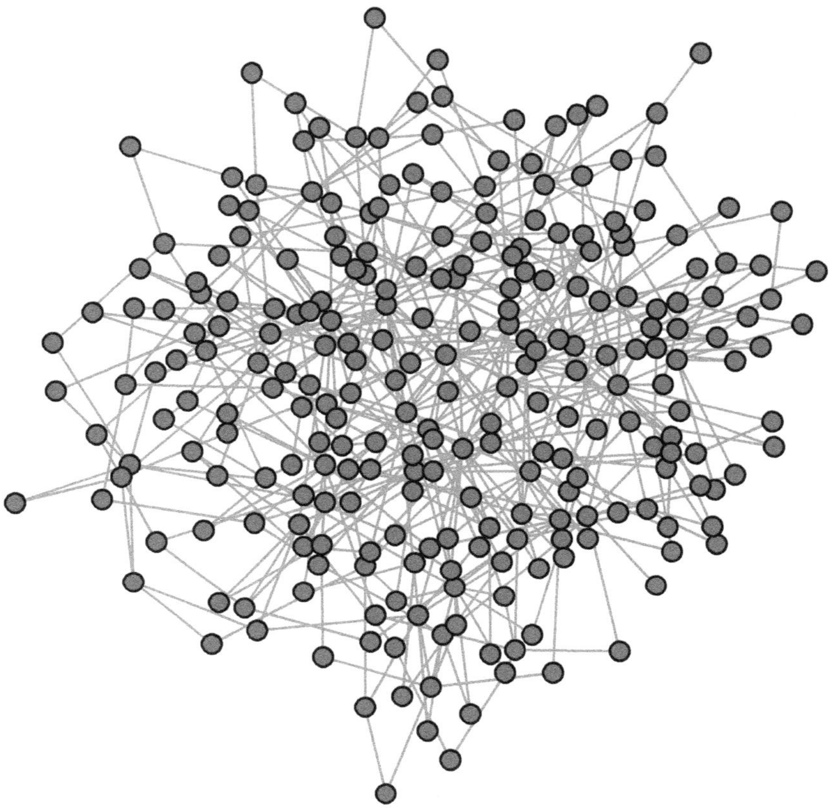

Figure 4.17 An example of a network denoting $w01$

$w02$ is represented by a network of which the density is 1, and the liquidity of the tokens contained in $w02$ is approximately 0. In the examples, the number of tokens contained in $w02$ is 4, 8, 12, 16, 20, 24, 28, 32, 36, 40, 44, 48, 52, 56, 60, or 64.

4.7.8.3 Results

Table 4.1 shows the combination of $w01$ and $w02$. Both are defined by their respective number of nodes, density, and the liquidity of tokens contained therein.

Moreover, Figures 4.18, 4.19, and 4.20 show the density and liquidity of $w03$, which change according to the number of tokens contained in $w02$ ($n02$) in the said first, seventh, and thirteenth examples.

Table 4.1 *The combination of* w01 *and* w02

	*w*01			*w*02
	*n*01	density	liquidity	*n*02
Examples-1		0.01559436	0.2102546	
Examples-2		0.01421569	0.2413352	
Examples-3		0.01372549	0.2534601	
Examples-4		0.01314338	0.268652	
Examples-5		0.01262255	0.2830151	
Examples-6		0.01228554	0.2927156	
Examples-7	256	0.01188725	0.3046092	4, 8, 12, 16, 20, 24, 28, 32, 36, 40, 44, 48, 52, 56, 60, or 64
Examples-8		0.01148897	0.3169862	
Examples-9		0.01121324	0.3258482	
Examples-10		0.01090686	0.3359858	
Examples-11		0.01060049	0.3464388	
Examples-12		0.01026348	0.3583131	
Examples-13		0.009987745	0.3683306	

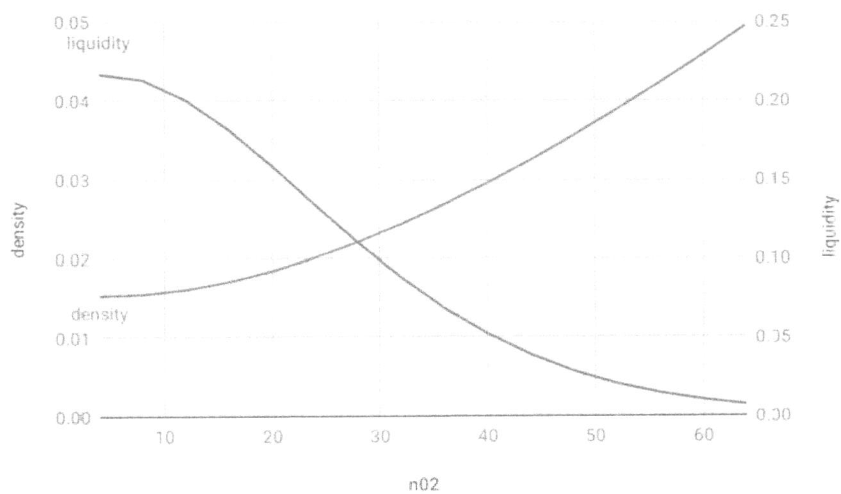

Figure 4.18 The density and liquidity of *w*03 in example – 1

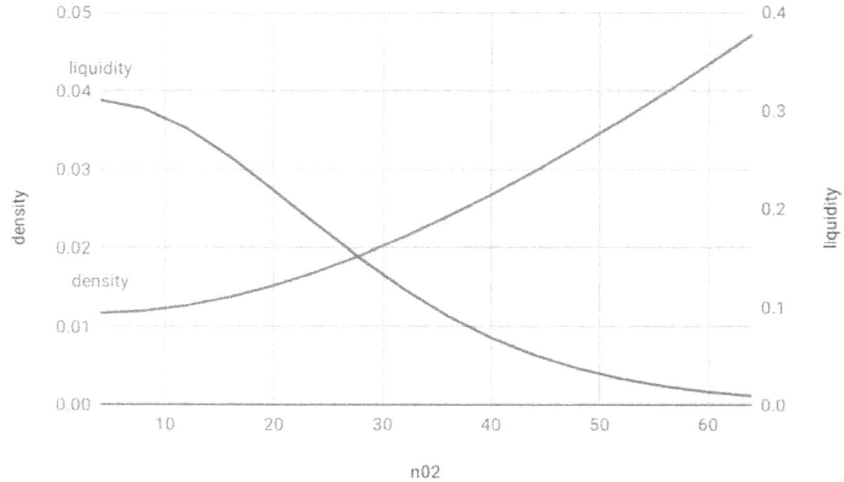

Figure 4.19 The density and liquidity of $w03$ in example – 7

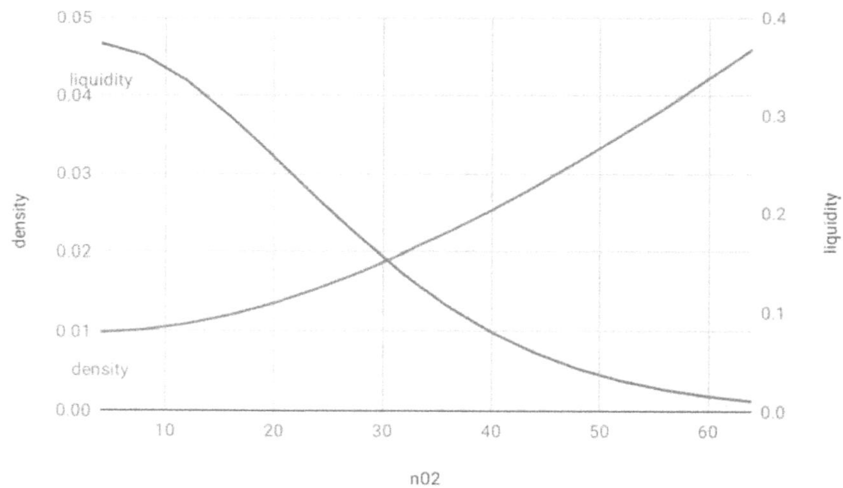

Figure 4.20 The density and liquidity of $w03$ in example – 13

4.7.9 *Outcome*

Basically, the outcome of the examples satisfies the requirements described in Section 4.6.3. If $n01$ is significantly greater than $n02$, the liquidity of the tokens contained in $w03$ is very close to that in $w01$, and much higher than that in *w*02. Such an outcome is beneficial to the holder of tokens who has saved their tokens for a very long time and contemplates combining *w*01 and *w*02.

4.7.10 Code

We can implement the said model by using a very short code. The following shows an example of such code prepared by using R language:

```
library(igraph)
τ<-0.01
n<-256
w01<-barabasi.game(n, m=2, directed=FALSE)
for (q in 0:n){
file1.name<-sprintf("%03d.tiff", q)
w01adj<-as_adj(w01)
if (q>0){
for (i in 1:n){
w01adj[w01evcentMax, i]<-0
w01adj[i, w01evcentMax]<-0
}
w01<-graph_from_adjacency_matrix(w01adj,
  mode=c("undirected"))
}
w01evcent<-evcent(w01)$vector
tiff (file1.name)
plot(w01, vertex.size=5, vertex.lable=NA)
dev.off()
w01dens<-graph.density(w01)
cat(w01dens, "\n", file="w01density.csv", append=TRUE)
nwd<-w01dens
w01Liquid<-exp(-nwd/τ)
cat(w01Liquid, "\n", file="w01liquidity.csv",
  append=TRUE)
w01evcent<-evcent(w01)$vector
nn<-16
for (kk in 1:nn){
k<-kk*4
file3.name<-sprintf("%06d.tiff", q*1000+k)
w02adj<-matrix(1, k, k)
for (i in 1:k){
w02adj[i,i]<-0
}
p<-n+k
w03adj<-matrix(0, p, p)
```

```
for (i in 1:n){
for (j in 1:n){
w03adj[i,j]<-w01adj[i,j]}}
nn<-n+1
for (i in nn:p){
for (j in nn:p){
w03adj[i,j]<-w02adj[i-n, j-n]
}}
w03<-graph_from_adjacency_matrix(w03adj,
  mode=c("undirected"))
tiff (file3.name)
plot(w03, vertex.size=5, vertex.lable=NA)
dev.off()
w03dens<-graph.density(w03)
cat(w03dens, "\n", file="w03density.csv", append=TRUE)
nwd<-w03dens
w03Liquid<-exp(-nwd/τ)
cat(w03Liquid, "\n", file="w03liquidity.csv",
  append=TRUE)
kk<-k+1
}
if (w01dens < 0.01) break
}
```

4.8 Tentative Conclusion and Prospects

The models described in Sections 4.6 and 4.7 are disclosed in Japan Patent Application 2019-168443 filed by Good Luck 3, Inc., Fukuako, Japan (Inventors: Kazuhisa INOUE, Masaaki HATAMURA, and Shinto TERAMOTO) on 17 September 2019.

It is the role of lawyers to design incentives and disincentives to be implemented in a law to incentivise or disincentivise citizens to employ or avoid specific behaviours. However, conventional laws, which are represented by natural language, are not capable of defining the details of such incentives and disincentives. Accordingly, lawyers are obliged to draft appropriate laws using computer code to design and define such incentives and disincentives.

The foregoing models suggest that we can design a token that can substantially satisfy the initially intended requirements. However, it should also be pointed out that the examples shown here still need several adjustments and improvements before carrying out a social experiment. For example, the combination of two wallets described in Section 4.6 does not guarantee a result that is always advantageous to the holder of the tokens. Governments and healthcare insurance organisations that are operating public insurance, as well as citizens, might prefer to employ safeguards that can automatically prevent citizens from combining wallets when such a combination is disadvantageous to them.

Furthermore, the example codes contain a matrix calculation that could possibly prevent efficient and quick calculation by a CPU. Employing a quicker and more efficient scheme would be desirable.

Acknowledgement

This work was supported by GoodLuck3, Inc., Fukuoka, Japan.

Bibliography

American Hospital Association, 'Sharing Data, Saving Lives: The Hospital Agenda for Interoperability' (2019), www.aha.org/system/files/2019-01/Report01_18_19-Sharing-Data-Saving-Lives_FINAL.pdf, accessed 10 February 2020.

Barabási AL and Albert R, 'Emergence of Scaling in Random Networks' (1999) 286(5439) *Science* 509.

Furukawa K and Arai H, 'Earthquake in Japan' (2011) 377(9778) *The Lancet* 1652.

'*Iryō Jōhō Netto no Riyō Teimei Shōhi Zōzei, Yūkō Katsuyō sarezu*' (Stagnation in Use, Consumption Tax Increase and Ineffective Utilization of Healthcare Information Network) *Nippon Keizai Shinbun* (28 October 2019), www.nikkei.com/article/DGXMZO51505040Y9A021C1CR8000/, accessed 10 February 2020.

Japan Medical Association Emergency and Disaster Medicine Management Committee, 'Program of the Activities of the Japan Medical Association Team (JMAT)' (2013) 56(3) *Japan Medical Association Journal* 143.

Kobayashi K, 'Role Sharing between DMAT and JMAT' (2013) 56(1) *Japan Medical Association Journal* 25.

Matsumoto K, 'Mental Health of Disaster Relief Supporters' (2013) 56(2) *Japan Medical Association Journal* 70.

McGhin T and others, 'Blockchain in Healthcare Application: Research Challenges and Opportunities' (2019) 135 *Journal of Network Computer Applications* 62.

Ministry of Health, Labour and Welfare, '*Chiiki Iryō Renkei no Fukyū ni Muketa Kenkō Jōhō Katsuyō Kiban Jisshō Jigyō*' (Electronic Health Records Infrastructure Program for diffusion of regional medical cooperation) (2015), www.mhlw.go.jp/file/06-Seisakujouhou-10800000-Iseikyoku/0000102029.pdf, accessed 10 February 2020.

Ministry of Health, Labour and Welfare, 'PHR *ni Kansuru Kore Made no keii to Kentō no Susumekata Nitsuite*' (The History of PHR and How to Proceed with the Studies) (2019), www.mhlw.go.jp/content/10904750/000546635.pdf, accessed 10 February 2020.

Ministry of Internal Affairs and Communication, '*Kenkō Iryō Kaigo no Dēta Kiban no Kōchiku ni Muketa Sōmu-shō no Torikumi (PHR Kanren)*' (Ministry of Internal Affairs and Communications (PHR Related) Efforts to Build a Database for Health, Health Care and Nursing Care) (2019), www.kantei.go.jp/jp/singi/keizaisaisei/miraitoshikaigi/suishinkaigo2018/health/dai6/siryou2.pdf, accessed 10 February 2020.

Perez and others, 'Large-Scale Assessment of a Smartwatch to Identify Atrial Fibrillation' (2019) 381 *The New England Journal of Medicine* 1909.

Prell C, *Social Networks Analysis: History, Theory and Methodology* (SAGE 2011).

Reisman M, 'EHRs: The Challenge of Making Electronic Data Usable and Interoperable' (2017) 42(9) *Pharmacy and Therapeutics* 572.

Scott J, *Social Networks Analysis* (4th ed. SAGE 2017).

Starkey J and Maeda S, 'Earthquake in Japan' (2011) 377(9778) *The Lancet* 1653.

Teramoto S, 'How Industrial Policy Affects the Nurturing of Innovation: From the Perspective of Intellectual Property Rights' in Basedow J and Kono T (eds), *Special Economic Zones: Law and Policy Perspectives* (Mohr Siebeck 2016).

Teramoto S, '*Iryō, Kenkō Bun'ya ni Okeru Kyurēshon Saito no Yakuwari to Un'yō no Muzukashisa (The Role of Curation Sites in the Medical Care and Health Fields and the Difficulty of Operation)* (2018) 78 *Law and Technology* 10.

Teramoto S and Fukazu T, 'Cloud Computing for Medical Data: A Legal Perspective' (2012) 25 *It Vision* 38.

Teramoto S and Haga Y, 'Informed Consent in Building Big Data in Healthcare: The Essential Role of Hubs in Curating and Disseminating Knowledge' (2017) 4(2) *RANGSIT Journal of Social Sciences and Humanities* 69.

Teramoto S and Jurčys P, 'Allocation of Public Resources for Scientific Research: The Role of Governments and the Law' (2018) 85(1) *Hosei Kenkyu* 362.

Teramoto S and Sugimura K, '*Shakai ni Kakusan Sareru Iryō Kenkō Jōhō no Kenzensei o Iji Suru Tame ni Obujekushon no Katsuyō*' (The Diffusion of Soundness of Medical Care and Health Information to Society: Objection Application) (2019) 84 *Law and Technology* 66.

Yamamoto R, '*Kokunaigai Ni Okeru Iryō Jōhō no Hyōjunka no Genjō to Tenbō: Sōgo Un'yōsei no Kōjō o Mezashite*' (Situation and Prospects of Standardization of Health Information in Japan: For Improvement of Interoperability) (2017) 60(9) *Joho Kanri* 619.

PART II

Trust and Design

5

Privacy Management in eHealth Using Contextual Consenting

YKI KORTESNIEMI AND PÄIVI PÖYRY-LASSILA

5.1 Introduction

We are all increasingly using smart devices to collect data about our health, and sharing this data with healthcare professionals to be combined with official measurements opens up possibilities for healthcare professionals to have a more complete picture of our health and how it can be further improved. In addition, sharing the same data to scientific research opens up possibilities to improve the health of us all. However, sharing health data also raises major privacy issues due to the highly sensitive nature of the information.

Legally, data sharing is often based on individuals' consent, which requires the individuals to study the provided information to be able to make an informed decision about what they are consenting to – and the sheer scale of consenting decisions alone is daunting: as an example, in 2008 McDonald and Cranor estimate that it would take 80–300 hours for the average individual just to read the privacy policies of the websites they visit in a year,[1] let alone all the other services used in everyday life. Thus, the way the consenting process is implemented plays a major role in how informed the individuals can be and how empowered they feel about their privacy.

This chapter approaches the question of privacy management in health data sharing by building on the concept of *consent intermediary*,[2] a trusted third party that offers tools for managing consents of multiple data using services from a unified view, and by developing the *contextual consenting* approach, where data sharing is coupled within an app that already

[1] Aleecia McDonald and Lorrie Faith Cranor, 'The Cost of Reading Privacy Policies' (2008) *I/S: A Journal of Law and Policy for the Information Society*.

[2] Tuukka Lehtiniemi and Yki Kortesniemi, 'Can the Obstacles to Privacy Self-Management Be Overcome? Exploring the Consent Intermediary Approach' (2017) *Big Data & Society*.

utilises the data with the aim of making the individuals better aware of what they are sharing. Another aspect is utilising AI (machine learning) based recommendations to ease the cognitive burden of decision making. These approaches are then user tested with a prototype health app to gauge user attitudes toward both contextual consenting and AI-based recommendations. The prototype app development process utilised service design process and methods to create an app that addresses some real user needs, fits into their contexts of use, and thus creates value-in-use.

The results show that users found the approaches clear and would prefer to use such apps in the future. However, the users were also quite careful about sharing their data and often wanted to make it available only to specific health care professionals, but not the healthcare organisations at large.

The rest of the chapter is organised as follows: Section 5.2 provides background to the challenges of informed consent and how the consent intermediary approach has previously been utilised to overcome them. Section 5.3 presents the service innovation and design methodologies utilised in the prototype development process, and Section 5.4 introduces the developed app. Section 5.5 then presents the results of the user tests, and Section 5.6 discusses the findings and points out potential future work in this area.

5.2 Towards an Informed Consent

In EU legislation, privacy has long been considered a fundamental right of the individual,[3] and strict limits guard the processing of personal data. In theory, people are expected to manage their privacy by weighing the subjective costs and benefits of data processing in each case,[4] but in practice many are neither well informed on the uses of their personal data nor feel in control of it.[5, 6]

3 Sandra Wachter, 'Privacy: Primus Inter Pares – Privacy as a Precondition for Self-Development, Personal Fulfilment and the Free Enjoyment of Fundamental Human Rights', https://ssrn.com/abstract=2903514, accessed 30 April 2020.

4 Daniel J. Solove, 'Privacy Self-Management and the Consent Dilemma' (2013) 126(7) *Harvard Law Review* 1880–1903.

5 European Commission, *Data Protection. Special Eurobarometer (431)* (2015).

6 Joseph Turow, Michael Hennessy and Nora Draper, *The Tradeoff Fallacy. How Marketers Are Misrepresenting American Consumers and Opening Them Up to Exploitation*, A Report from the Annenberg School for Communication, University of Pennsylvania (2015).

Though personal data can be processed can rely on a number of legal bases, of particular importance in this context is the consent with which the individuals can authorise and revoke the processing of their personal data for many purposes. The consent process, however, has historically been misused by the parties asking for consent, for example by being intentionally vague and misleading about what the individual is consenting to. The General Data Protection Regulation (GDPR)[7] has therefore significantly tightened the requirements for legal consent – it now has to be freely given, specific, informed, and unambiguous. This chapter focuses on the implementation of the consenting process, how well it informs the individual, and what demands it places on the individual's ability to make informed decisions.

The difficulty of consenting stems from eight obstacles:[8] *timing and duration* refers to the fact that consent to the use of data is given when processing begins, while the harms and benefits of processing accumulate over time. *Non-negotiability* describes the fact that individuals are often not free to negotiate the consent details but have to accept the terms of the service as defined by the controller or not use the service at all. The third obstacle, *scale*, refers to the large number of decisions and the amount of effort behind each decision. The fourth obstacle, *aggregation*, refers to the difficulty for a data subject to assess the effects of data processing operations, including what additional information can be revealed by combining data from multiple sources. The fifth obstacle, *downstream uses* of data, refers to the effect that the consented processing of data expands without further consent, when, for example, the authorised data processor transfers information to third parties. Data subjects would not know or foresee all such downstream uses and can therefore not consider them when giving consent to processing. The sixth obstacle, *cognitive demands*, refers to conceptual problems of humans as rational decision makers: we are only boundedly rational,[9] showing the fallacies of consent and choice theories. The seventh obstacle of *social norms* refers to social conventions that force people to behave differently than they otherwise would, for example sometimes revealing more of themselves because social networking services are now regarded as an integral part of modern life.[10] Finally,

7 European Union, 'Regulation (EU) 2016/679 of the European Parliament and of the Council' (2016) L119 *Official Journal of the European Union* 1–88.

8 Lehtiniemi and Kortesniemi, 'Can the Obstacles to Privacy Self-Management Be Overcome?'

9 Gerd Gigerenzer and Reinhard Selten, *Bounded Rationality: The Adaptive Toolbox* (MIT Press 2001).

10 Shoshana Zuboff, 'Big Other: Surveillance Capitalism and the Prospects of an Information Civilization' (2015) *Journal of Information Technology*.

the *social nature* of personal data refers to the fact that some personal data reveals information about other people, for example when cooperation with others also reveals information about the other parties. Hence, revealing information about oneself can reveal information about others, which can have a harmful effect on them – and vice versa. Of the eight obstacles, the first three are *solvable* because they are not fundamentally insurmountable but rather the result of how consenting has been implemented. The next three obstacles are classified as challenging: they can be partially solved with better tools, but they also contain elements that are insurmountable. The final group of obstacles relate to the social aspects of humans: they are considered insuperable because an individual-focused privacy self-management model simply cannot fully cope with them.[11]

To address these problems, the *consent intermediary approach* tries to empower users to better manage their privacy by collecting the management of all service-related consents (and, through them, user's privacy) into a single service. Just having all consents in one place makes it easier to compare them, but the true potential of the approach is that it facilitates the building of new tools that help people make better-informed decisions, help to simplify the consent management process, and potentially shift the balance of power between the services and users towards the benefit of the users.[12] Examples of such intermediaries include commercial service developers such as the personal cloud server Cozy Cloud[13] and the personal information control services digi.me[14] and Meeco,[15] as well as research-originated initiatives such as the networked personal data indexing device Databox,[16] personal data stores Hub of All Things[17] and OpenPDS,[18] and the personal data management model MyData.[19]

11 Lehtiniemi and Kortesniemi, 'Can the Obstacles to Privacy Self-Management Be Overcome?'

12 Ibid.

13 Cozy Cloud, Cozy cloud website, https://cozy.io/en/, accessed 30 April 2020.

14 Digi.me, Digi.me website, https://digi.me, accessed 30 April 2020.

15 Meeco, Meeco website, https://meeco.me, accessed 30 April 2020.

16 Amir Chaudhry and others, 'Personal Data: Thinking Inside the Box' (2015) 1(1) *Aarhus Series on Human Centered Computing*, https://doi.org/10.7146/aahcc.v1i1.21312, accessed 12 March 2021.

17 Hub of All Things, Hub of All Things GitHub page, https://github.com/Hub-of-all-Things, accessed 30 April 2020.

18 Yves-Alexandre de Montjoyeya and others, 'OpenPDS: Protecting the Privacy of Metadata through SafeAnswers' (2014) 9(7) *PloS One*.

19 Antti Poikola, Kai Kuikkaniemi and Harri Honko, 'MyData – A Nordic Model for Human-Centered Personal Data Management and Processing' (Finnish Ministry of Transport and Communications 2015).

A user study ($n = 23$)[20] explored the consent intermediary approach in the context of health data with a prototype app designed to manage the sharing of different types of data and found that ~80 per cent of participants, none of whom had previous experience of the consent intermediary approach, felt that a similar tool would be valuable in controlling their personal data and that the participants would like to control all data sharing from the same place. So, the consent intermediary approach appears to address some real user needs. A question raised by the study, however, is how well the user actually understands what they are sharing if the same app is used to manage the sharing of a large number of different data types.

Another way of helping the users reduce the effort of consenting is to provide the users' recommendations from experts or artificial intelligence (AI). This approach potentially makes it easier for the users to understand the benefits of each option, but depending on the implementation, it may still require significant effort to utilise the recommended choices by manually choosing the suggested options in the user interface. Having user interfaces that simplify the utilisation of the recommendations by automatically making them available as a pre-filled option can further reduce the effort required. The challenge is that making pre-filled options easy to choose runs the risk of nudging the user towards the proposed choices,[21] which may run against the GDPR. Furthermore, the choice of the source of recommendations and their ulterior motivations and impartiality are also significant factors affecting the users' ability to control their privacy: the party making the recommendations has the potential to influence the individuals beyond what is allowed by the GDPR.

The questions of how far the automation and even full delegation of consenting decisions can be taken under the GDPR were addressed through four progressively more automated scenarios: 1) user selects all details based on own knowledge, 2) user manually selects all details using recommendations from trusted third party, 3) trusted third party provides a simplified selection, and 4) user selects what services to use and automation takes care of all consenting details. The paper then points out that '[r]ecommendation and automation which influence data subjects' decisions require ensuring that they truly represent the genuine will and expression of such data

[20] Yki Kortesniemi, Tuomas Lappalainen and Fayez Salka, 'User Attitudes towards Consent Intermediaries', Paper presented at Legal Design as Academic Discipline: Foundations, Methodology, Applications (Groningen, Netherlands 2018).

[21] Richard H. Thaler and Cass R. Sunstein, *Nudge: Improving Decisions about Health, Wealth, and Happiness* (Penguin Books 2009).

subject. In this light, scenario 4's fully automated consenting system where the data subject does not participate in the consenting process at all is a step too far under GDPR'.[22] So, utilising AI for making personalised consenting recommendations is technically and legally possible under the GDPR, but care has to be taken as to how far the automation can be taken.

5.3 Tools for Designing a Health Data App

When dealing with such a complex topic as management of health-related data, it is important to take the customer's perspective carefully into account in order to design an understandable and easy-to-use service that is at the same time highly useful. The literature of service innovation and design offers concepts, processes, and tools for developing and designing services in a customer-centric way, thus ensuring that the customer's needs and requirements are well met and that value is created for the customer. In particular, understanding the customers and their *living worlds* should be the starting point for designing the service. In this study, the process and the specific methods of service design were utilised to produce the consenting prototype in a user-centric way.

The focus of *service innovation* research is on new service development and the customer (or user) needs,[23, 24] and especially the customers' active role in the service process and value creation.[25, 26] The *service-dominant logic* approach emphasises the central role of the customer in co-creating value through the service,[27, 28, 29] and *value co-creation* is a central notion in the field of service research. Value is fundamentally derived

[22] Yki Kortesniemi and Jens Kremer, 'Recommendations and Automation in the Consenting Process: Designing GDPR Compliant Consents', Paper presented at Legal Design as Academic Discipline: Foundations, Methodology, Applications (Groningen, Netherlands 2018).

[23] Lance Bettencourt, 'Service Innovation: How to Go from Customer Needs to Breakthrough Services' (McGraw-Hill 2010).

[24] Jon Sundbo and Marja Toivonen, 'User-Based Innovation in Services' (Edward Elgar 2011).

[25] Per Carlborg, Daniel Kindström and Christian Kowalkowski, 'The Evolution of Service Innovation Research: A Critical Review and Synthesis' (2014) 34(5) *The Service Industries Journal* 373–98.

[26] Robert F. Lusch and Stephen L. Vargo, *Service-Dominant Logic: Premises, Perspectives, Possibilities* (Cambridge University Press 2014).

[27] Stephen L. Vargo and Robert F. Lusch, 'Evolving to a New Dominant Logic for Marketing' (January 2014) 68 *Journal of Marketing* 1–17.

[28] Stephen L. Vargo and Robert F. Lusch, 'Service-Dominant Logic: Continuing the Evolution' (2008) 36 *Journal of the Academy of Marketing Science* 1–10.

[29] CK Prahalad and Venkat Ramaswamy, 'Co-creation Experiences: The Next Practice in Value Creation' (2004) 18(3) *Journal of Interactive Marketing* 5–14.

and determined in the customer's use of a particular service through the 'integration and application of resources' related to that service 'in a specific context'.[30] As value is co-created in the interaction between the customer and the organisation (providing the service), the focus of service development should be on this interaction and its quality.[31] Furthermore, the *experience* of the interaction should be in focus because the co-creation experiences of individuals become the new basis of value.[32]

The value creation process involves three different spheres, namely, the provider, the customer, and the joint sphere.[33] The most important one is the *joint sphere*, a platform where value is co-created through interaction between the customer and the organisation.[34, 35] Further, it is not enough to analyse the interaction process between the customer and the organisation; instead, according to *customer dominant logic* (CDL), the focus should be shifted from the organisation-centric view to a customer-centric view.[36, 37] In order to design and provide valuable services to the customer, the organisation should understand the customer's world, their everyday activities, and how the customer integrates the service in their activities and systems, including the customer's prior experiences, current goals, and other's opinions. But not only the visible customer actions but also the invisible and mental life of the customer should be better understood.[38] This is because value is formed in 'the highly dynamic and multi-contextual reality and life of the customer'. Further, the organisations should pay more attention on how to become involved in the customer's world (and not vice versa) to produce *value-in-use*.[39, 40] To sum up, the

30 Stephen L. Vargo, Paul P. Maglio and Melissa Archpru Akaka, 'On Value and Value Co-creation: A Service Systems and Service Logic Perspective' (2008) 26(3) *European Management Journal* 145–52.

31 Prahalad and Ramaswamy, 'Co-creation Experiences'.

32 Venkat Ramaswamy, 'It's about Human Experiences … and Beyond, to Co-creation' (2011) 40 *Industrial Marketing Management* 195–96.

33 Christian Grönroos and Päivi Voima, 'Critical Service Logic: Making Sense of Value Creations and Co-creation' (2013) 41 *Journal of the Academy of Marketing Science* 133–50.

34 Ibid.

35 Christian Grönroos, 'Value Co-creation in Service Logic: A Critical Analysis' 2011) 11(3) *Marketing Theory* 279–301.

36 Kristiina Heinonen and others, 'A Customer-Dominant Logic of Service' (2010) 21(4) *Journal of Service Management* 531–48.

37 Kristiina Heinonen, Tore Strandvik and Päivi Voima, 'Customer Dominant Value Formation in Service' (2013) 252 *European Business Review* 104–23.

38 Ibid.

39 Kristiina Heinonen and Tore Strandvik, 'Customer-Dominant Logic: Foundations and Implications' (2015) 29(6/7) *Journal of Services Marketing* 472–84.

40 Kristiina Heinonen and Tore Strandvik, 'Reflections on Customers' Primary Role in Markets' (2018) 36(1) *European Management Journal* 1–11.

customers and their needs and worlds must be thoroughly analysed and understood in order to design services that fit into the customers' contexts.

However, co-creation may also refer to a co-creation process of the service innovation in which the customers may be involved.[41] Research on *service design* has produced an understanding on how to involve customers and other stakeholders in different phases of the design process.[42,43] Service design has been introduced and implemented as a distinct methodology and a process for enabling customer-centric development and co-creation.[44, 45, 46, 47] The idea of service design is to enable collaborative development based on deep customer insight, and on collaboration and interaction between various stakeholders.

The British Design Council has introduced a widely utilised service design process model called *Double Diamond*,[48] which is summarised in Figure 5.1. The model can be divided into two main spaces: the *problem* and the *solution* space. Both spaces include the processes of *divergence*, that is, finding or creating plenty of new information or ideas, and *convergence*, referring to information condensation or idea selection for further development. Following this model, the service design work consists of four phases, namely, discover, define, develop, and deliver. First, as a part of the *discover* phase, existing knowledge is reviewed, and new

[41] Anders Gustafsson, Per Kristensson and Lars Witell, 'Customer Co-creation in Service Innovation: A Matter of Communication?' (2012) 23(3) *Journal of Service Management* 311–27, https://doi.org/10.1108/09564231211248426, accessed 12 March 2021.

[42] Turkka Keinonen, Kirsikka Vaajakallio and Janos Honkonen (eds), *Designing for Wellbeing* (Aalto University, School of Arts, Design and Architecture 2013).

[43] Kirsikka Vaajakallio and Tuuli Mattelmäki, 'Yhteissuunnittelu avaa uusia näkymiä julkiselle sektorille', in Keinonen T, Vaajakallio K and Honkonen J (eds), *Hyvinvoinnin muotoilu, Helsinki: Aalto-yliopiston taiteiden ja suunnittelun korkeakoulu* (Aalto Arts Books 2013).

[44] Marc Stickdorn and others, '*This Is Service Design Doing: Applying Service Design Thinking in the Real World: A Practitioner's Handbook*' (O'Reilly Media 2018).

[45] Eun Yu and Daniela Sangiorgi, 'Service Design As an Approach to Implement the Value Cocreation Perspective in New Service Development' (2018) 21(1) *Journal of Service Research* 40–58.

[46] Tor Andreassen and others, 'Linking Service Design to Value Creation and Service Research' (2016) 27(1) *Journal of Service Management* 21–9.

[47] Satu Miettinen, 'Designing Services with Innovative Methods', in Miettinen S and Koivisto M (eds), *Designing Services with Innovative Methods*. University of Art and Design & Kuopio Academy of Design. Taideteollisen korkeakoulun julkaisusarja, B. Taitemia. Keuruu: (Otava Book Printing 2009).

[48] Design Council, 'What Is the Framework for Innovation? Design Council's Evolved Double Diamond' (2015), www.designcouncil.org.uk/news-opinion/what-framework-innovation-design-councils-evolved-double-diamond, accessed 30 April 2020.

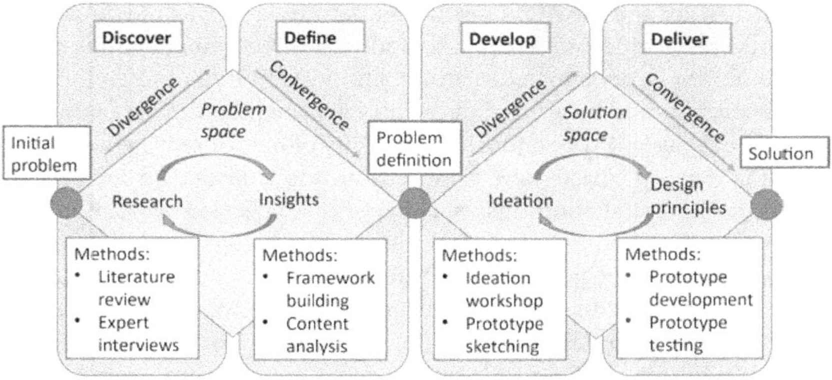

Figure 5.1 The research and development process of the study

information or data is collected covering the problem field from several perspectives. Next, as a part of the *define* phase, this information is analysed and condensed. At this point the problem field can be understood thoroughly enough so that the initial problem can be redefined. Next, in the solution space during the *develop* phase, again new information will be collected in a diverging process for creating the potential solutions to the problem, and in the *deliver* phase, the potential solutions will be narrowed down into a solution that can be implemented or at least tested in practice.[49]

The Double Diamond model was chosen for this study for two reasons: firstly, the model was seen as consistent with the constructive research approach aiming at creating a testable solution to the identified challenge,[50] and secondly, through following the phases of the model, it was possible to redefine the initial problem during the research process. The methods utilised in this study are included in Figure 5.1.

During the *discover* phase, information was collected by reviewing the literature and by interviewing experts ($N = 5$) in the field of consenting, privacy, and MyData (used as an example of the consent intermediary approach in this study) in health care services. During the *define* phase, the literature framework was constructed, and the interview data was

[49] Ibid.

[50] Liisa Lehtiranta and others, 'The Constructive Research Approach: Problem Solving for Complex Projects', in Pasian B (ed.), *Designs, Methods and Practices for Research of Project Management* (Gower Applied Business Research 2015).

analysed. After these two phases the initial problem was redefined: the interview results indicated that automation and recommendations could be utilised for supporting consenting, and visualisation and layering of information should be utilised to clarify the presentation. The main goal should be the usability and understandability of the consenting solution.

In the *develop* phase, new information was collected to ideate and create the potential solutions. A collaborative ideation workshop was arranged with the potential users of the solution being developed, resulting in concrete user needs and requirements as well as solution ideas. Use cases and the functionalities of the prototype were defined as well as the design principles of the solution. In addition, based on reviewing other solutions in the field and the already collected information, several potential solutions were sketched and iterated. Next, in the *deliver* phase, the solution was created in the form of a prototype app that was tested with the users.

Based on the information collected and analysed during the four phases of the process, the concept of *contextual consenting* was defined. The basic idea of contextual consenting is to *combine the utilisation of data and the data sharing and consenting processes.* Data collected from various sources is to be presented in a visual form so that the users understand what information is collected from them. The mirror metaphor supports the utilisation of the data through giving the users feedback on their health. In addition, the data flows are to be visualised to help the users understand how their data is shared and utilised. The possibility to utilise one's personal data together with visualisation aims to facilitate the consenting process through concretising it. Recommendations based on users' preferences are then utilised to simplify the users' consenting decisions. To sum up, the idea of consenting in context is that combining consenting with the actual use of data facilitates the consenting process and makes it more understandable for the users, as the use of data concretises the process through making the data and its usage visible for the users.

5.4 A Contextual Consenting App

To evaluate user attitudes towards the contextual consenting approach and AI-based recommendations, a prototype app was designed, built, and tested with end users. The app was designed for the general public at large, and the example data types were chosen as they are the most commonly used health predictors in public health care. The contextual consenting approach was implemented so that with the help of the app the user was able to view and utilise the data from the various apps and devices and also manage the data sharing requests and control the consents from a single place.

The prototype was built for a tablet device as a partly functional app consisting of two main views: *My Health Dashboard* and *My Data Sharing Permissions*. The app is protected with a login page due to the sensitive nature of the information. When using the app for the first time, the users then answer a questionnaire related to their personal preferences related to data protection, data sharing, and consenting. The information collected with these questions is utilised by the app for giving the users AI-based recommendations related to the consenting decisions. For example, if the user wants to support scientific research at universities, the app would recommend that the user give the consent more easily for this kind of a data sharing request than for commercial purposes of a private company. For the purposes of user testing, no AI recommendation system was implemented, and some of this functionality of the app was simulated by the tester.

As the first main view of the app, the user sees a collage of their health data. As shown in Figure 5.2, this view is called *My Health Dashboard* and it utilises the *mirroring metaphor* to provide the user with a simple analysis of their data as an overview of their personal health situation. At the top, the user sees the traffic lights giving feedback based on *combined data analysis* and telling how the user is doing regarding their health. Then, under the traffic lights, the user can see measurements and analyses from four data types (each an aggregate from all available sources for that type of data, that is, measurements collected by various apps and devices about blood pressure, physical activity, body weight, and blood sugar). The original data sources for the data can be seen as icons in the bottom right corner of each data type, and by clicking the icons the user can see the data from that source separately. For each of these data types, the user is again given some feedback with the help of colours and traffic lights. The red colour signals something worrying, and the green colour means there is nothing to worry about. The yellow colour means that the user should pay attention to avoid future challenges related to the data type's measurements.

After viewing the measurements and the analysis results, the user is able to see the pending data sharing requests in two places of this view: firstly, as a blue banner at the top of the view, and secondly, at the bottom of the view as a red dot with a number in the *Permissions* tab. By clicking either of these two, the user can access the data sharing side of the app, called *My Data Sharing Permissions* view, shown in Figure 5.3.

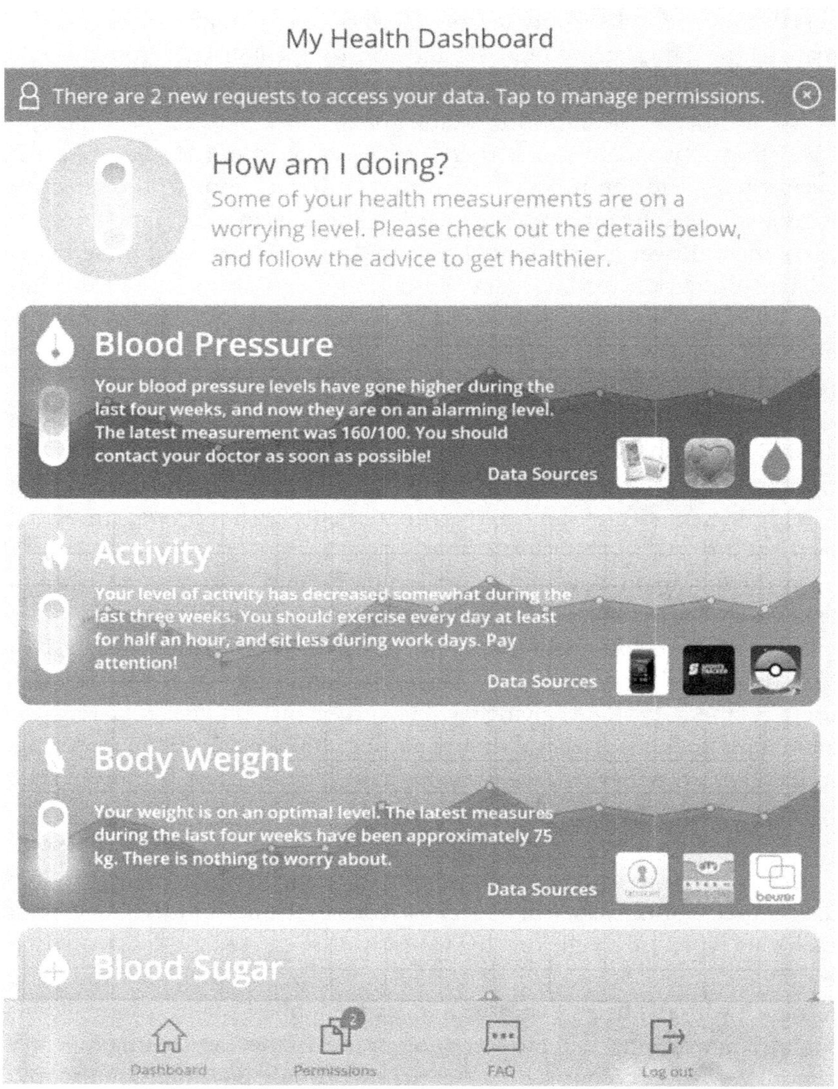

Figure 5.2 My Health Dashboard view of the app

In this view, the user can see in red colour and with a question mark all the pending data sharing requests by data type. The previously given consents can be seen through clicking the icons in each data type field, for example the doctor icon for seeing what kind of consent has been given to their own doctor. Any consent can be revoked at will, and the refused

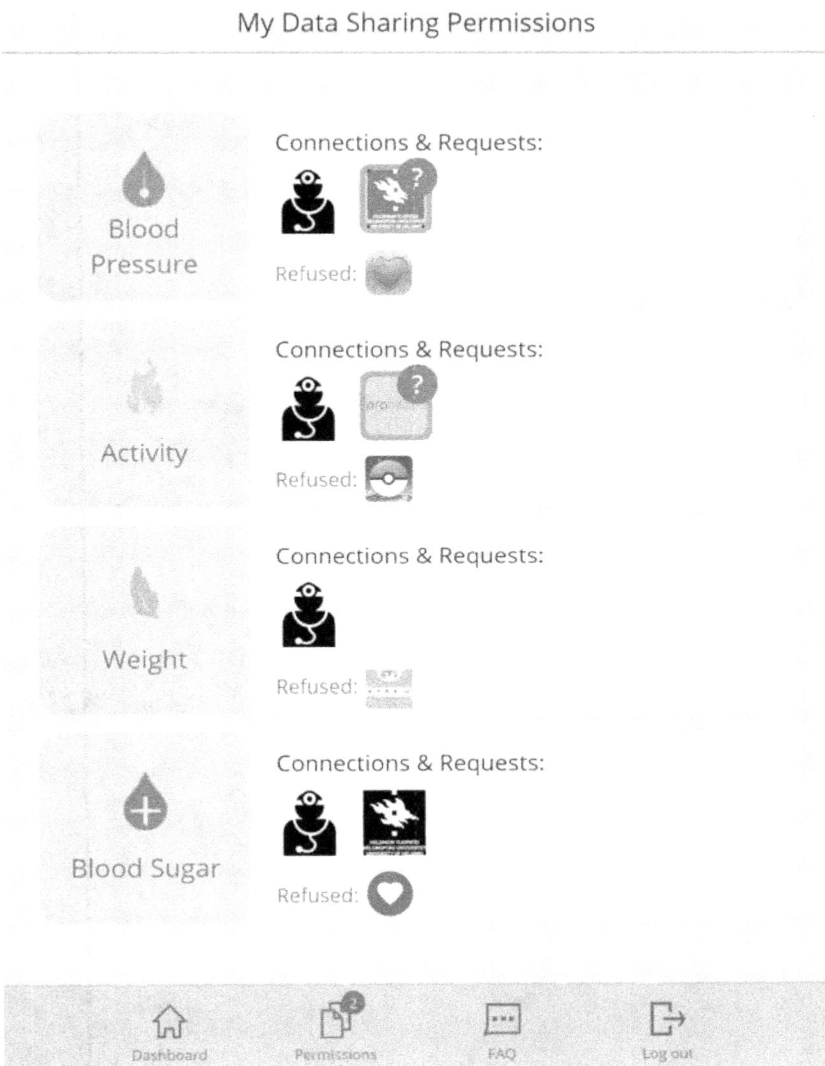

Figure 5.3 My Data Sharing Permission view of the app

and revoked data sharing requests are visible at the bottom of each data type as icons of the requesting service or organisation. Again, icons are utilised to visualise and simplify the presentation of information, and the idea of layering information is implemented so that the details of each data sharing request or decision are always available by clicking the icon.

Figure 5.4 Data sharing request with AI-based recommendation

The details of the data sharing and the AI's recommendation for making the consenting decision for the pending data sharing request are shown in Figure 5.4. In this example, the user is given a recommendation to accept a university's data sharing request for scientific research, and the recommendation is based on the user's data sharing preferences and previous behaviour in similar situations.

In addition to the two main views, the app also includes the Frequently Asked Questions (FAQ) and the logout page. The idea of the FAQ is to give the user information about the most typical questions, and the logout function is to give the user the ability to lock the app so that others cannot access the information or the app.

The designed prototype app tackles the obstacles of consenting in multiple ways: it provides a unified format for all consent requests to simplify the comparisons between different data requests, and it utilises AI-based recommendations to provide personalised advice on how to decide in each consenting situation and a reason for that particular recommendation. If the individual chooses to follow the recommendation, they can do so with a simple click, but equally easily they can make the alternative decision. The context of using the same data and showing example uses for the data also makes the individual better aware of the possible consequences of sharing the data. The proposed solution also follows the guidelines to not automate the solution too far.[51]

5.5 Results from the User Tests

The user tests had two main goals: to find out how the targeted users feel about the contextual consenting approach and the AI-based consenting recommendations. In addition, the users' overall experiences of the app and its user interface and usefulness were collected. The prototype app was tested with users ($N = 10$) representing the targeted user groups. In addition, the users participated in an interview after the test tasks. Both situations were voice-recorded and transcribed to enable content analysis of the discussions.

The test consisted of eleven pre-defined tasks that all test users were able to complete. The test began with logging in (task 1), followed by a short interview focusing on the user's preferences about health-related data sharing and protection (task 2). As the app was not implemented with full functionality, the aim of the interview was to simulate the filling in of a questionnaire to be done when using the app for the first time, which would then be used to seed the AI-based recommendations. In the test situation, the users were specifically told that their answers would be

[51] Kortesniemi and Kremer, 'Recommendations and Automation in the Consenting Process'.

utilised as the basis for AI's consenting recommendations. According to the interviews, the users had a suspicious or doubtful attitude towards the idea of sharing their health-related data. Two of the test users did not want to share their data at all and were very mistrustful. The other eight test users were willing to share their data only cautiously and with restrictions, and only for enabling or improving their own health care services. For example, they were willing to share their data only with their personal doctors or nurses but not with their health care organisation in general. More precisely, all of them were against the idea of sharing their data 'with unspecified health care professionals in general'. Further, the test users did not want to share their data with, for example, employers or commercial organisations or make it public in any way.

The test continued with the users viewing the collage of their health data (task 3, Figure 5.2) then being asked how they understood this health data overview. All test users responded that the view was clear and understandable. The users also experienced positively the possibility to actually view their own data and that the data was collected in one place. Two of the test users even wondered whether there could be even more data that the users could add themselves, for example related to their diets and medications to be shared with their doctors. When viewing the traffic light feedback based on analysed data (task 4), the test users were asked how they understood the feedback given by the app and how they liked the traffic lights and the graphs. Again, all test users felt that the traffic lights and the colours helped them to understand the feedback given by the app and that the graphs were clear and helpful.

Next, the users were asked to proceed to the data sharing side of the app (task 5, Figure 5.3). After having an overall look at the data sharing view (task 6), the test users were asked how they understood where their data was and where it would go or had gone through sharing. Again, all users reported that the view of data sharing was clear and understandable. The users continued that all relevant and needed information was there, and being able to see the given consents and denied requests was experienced as useful and beneficial so that the users could remember what kinds of decisions they had made and what kinds of requests they had received earlier. Each test user also reported that the data sharing requests and the refused requests were understandable. The users were unanimous that they could easily see who could view their data and with whom it was shared or not. Thus, it can be said that the app supported transparency in data sharing.

Task 7 was about making a consenting decision based on an AI recommendation offered by the app. After accomplishing this, the test users were asked whether they understood how consenting worked through the recommendations. All test users were able to make the consenting decision, and they also experienced it to be easy. Further, the recommendations were experienced as clear and helpful. As for task 8, the users were asked to view how their data had been shared, and after this they were asked questions about sharing and utilising their data. All test users reported that they were able to see well how their data had been viewed or utilised and by whom. Moreover, they experienced this opportunity as a good thing as they would be able to ensure that their data would not be misused or accessed without permission. However, seven of the test users were worried that the data management service provider (the test claimed it was the public Social Insurance Institution of Finland) would be able to view their data without permission after all. Moreover, in this task the users felt that the app supported transparency.

Task 9 dealt with revoking a previously given consent, after which the users were asked about what they thought happened to their data after revoking the permission. None of the test users were able to tell what would happen to their data, and they wondered about it and wished that the data would be deleted. However, almost all of them doubted that this would happen.

Tasks 10 and 11 were related to the FAQ and logging out. The test users were unanimous that the information contained in the FAQ section was understandable and useful. As for logging out from the app, all test users wanted to do this. They said that they wanted to close the app because it contained confidential and delicate information about their health, and they did not want any other users of the device to view that.

After accomplishing all the eleven test tasks, the test users were interviewed about their overall experiences on the prototype app. All test users experienced the app as a clear and useful tool for collecting and controlling their own data through a single interface. The app was seen as either useful or potentially useful, and the majority of test users might use this kind of an app in the future, especially if they had challenges related to their health. The concept of collecting the data in one place was seen as generally useful. Further, the users experienced the information offered by the app as sufficient, useful, and easy to understand. As for data protection, each test user felt that their data was protected and handled in a safe way. The experience on transparency and feeling of control were also supported by the app from the test users' perspective.

Both the contextual consenting approach and the idea of supporting consenting with an AI-based recommendation were well understood and positively experienced. The test users felt that they understood the consequences of the consenting decisions well enough based on the offered information. However, when it comes to the use of machine learning, or AI, the test users had little to say. None of them commented on the use of AI directly, but they experienced the AI-based recommendations as useful. This is an interesting finding for the future development of the concept if the users do not yet fully understand the use of AI in this context.

5.6 Discussion

Based on our findings, the contextual consenting approach of combining the utilisation and sharing of data seems like a promising solution for the privacy management challenge. According to the user test of the prototype app, the possibility to view and utilise personal health-related data facilitates the user's understanding of data management, sharing, and protection, resulting in a better understood consenting decision by the user. Further, the visualised user interface of both data utilisation and data management seems to support the user's data usage and consenting processes.

The idea of utilising AI-based recommendations for supporting the user's consenting decisions was also tested. As a result, the recommendations were welcomed by the test users, and they seemed to make the consenting decision easier and simpler for the user. In the future, the role of utilising AI in consenting necessitates further research into the technologies for providing the AI-based recommendations, which is possible, for example, using a machine learning and clustering-based approach.[52] However, such a solution requires large amounts of data to train the system, and finding suitable training data is not trivial due to the highly sensitive nature of the data. In addition, the solution must find a suitable balance in automation to meet the requirements of the GDPR.

Another finding is that the use of CDL and service design seems to support the development of an understandable and valuable consenting solution from the user's perspective. As CDL argues, the starting point of the service innovation and design process must be the thorough understanding of the customer's world. Based on this study, it can be concluded that knowing the customer's world is essential for creating solutions for such a complex service as personal data sharing and consenting. Moreover, this study confirmed the view that including the customers in the

[52] Bin Liu and others, 'Follow My Recommendations: A Personalized Privacy Assistant for Mobile App Permissions', in *Proceedings of the 12th symposium on usable privacy and security, Denver, USA, 22–24 June* (USENIX 2016).

co-design process of the service[53] ensures that the customer's needs and requirements are met as well as possible, resulting in a service that enables value creation (value in use) for the customer.[54] The developed prototype app for utilising and managing health data can be seen as a joint sphere,[55] a digital platform where value is co-created in interaction between the user and the service provider.

In the field of digital behavioural design,[56] the concept of *nudging* would be an interesting direction for further research. The aim of nudging is to make some decisions easy for the customer in order to affect the customer's behaviour. For example, in the context of consenting, the idea of nudging could be utilised to enable the customer to make 'better' decisions with regard to personal data protection. However, here the role of ethics[57] and law[58] become crucial. In which ways is it ethically and legally acceptable to steer the customer's privacy-related decisions? How should the customer be made aware of the nudging? How to support the customer's autonomy and avoid paternalism and even manipulation?

Acknowledgements

The authors would like to thank Fayez Salka for his work in designing and implementing the prototype app.

Bibliography

Andreassen T and others, 'Linking Service Design to Value Creation and Service Research' (2016) 27(1) *Journal of Service Management* 21–29.

Bettencourt L, *Service Innovation: How to Go from Customer Needs to Breakthrough Services* (McGraw-Hill 2010).

Carlborg P, Kindström D and Kowalkowski C, 'The Evolution of Service Innovation Research: A Critical Review and Synthesis' (2014) 34(5) *The Service Industries Journal* 373–98.

53 Vaajakallio and Mattelmäki, 'Yhteissuunnittelu avaa uusia näkymiä julkiselle sektorille'.

54 Heinonen, Strandvik and Voima, 'Customer Dominant Value Formation in Service'.

55 Grönroos and Voima, 'Critical Service Logic'.

56 Tobias Mirsch, Christiane Lehrer and Reinhard Jung, 'Digital Nudging: Altering User Behavior in Digital Environments', in *Proceedings of 13. Internationale Tagung Wirtschaftsinformatik* (WI, St. Gallen, Switzerland 2017).

57 Cass R. Sunstein, 'The Ethics of Nudging' (2015) 32 *Yale Journal on Regulation* 413–50.

58 Anne van Aaken, 'Judge the Nudge: In Search of the Legal Limits of Paternalistic Nudging in the EU', in Alemanno A and Sibony AL (eds), *Nudge and the Law: A European Perspective* (Hart Publishing 2015).

Chaudhry A and others, 'Personal Data: Thinking Inside the Box' (2015) 1(1) *Aarhus Series on Human Centered Computing*, https://doi.org/10.7146/aahcc.v1i1.21312, accessed 12 March 2021.

Cozy Cloud, Cozy cloud website, https://cozy.io/en/, accessed 30 April 2020.

de Montjoyeya Y-A and others, 'OpenPDS: Protecting the Privacy of Netadata through SafeAnswers' (2014) 9(7) *PloS One* e98790, https://doi.org/10.1371/journal.pone.0098790.

Design Council, 'What Is the Framework for Innovation? Design Council's Evolved Double Diamond' (2015), www.designcouncil.org.uk/news-opinion/what-framework-innovation-design-councils-evolved-double-diamond, accessed 30 April 2020.

Digi.me, Digi.me website, https://digi.me, accessed 30 April 2020.

European Commission, *Data Protection. Special Eurobarometer (431)* (2015).

European Union, 'Regulation (EU) 2016/679 of the European Parliament and of the Council' (2016) L119 *Official Journal of the European Union* 1–88.

Gigerenzer G and Selten R, *Bounded Rationality: The Adaptive Toolbox* (MIT Press 2001).

Grönroos C, 'Value Co-creation in Service Logic: A Critical Analysis' (2011) 11(3) *Marketing Theory* 279–301.

Grönroos C and Voima P, 'Critical Service Logic: Making Sense of Value Creations and Co-creation' (2013) 41(2) *Journal of the Academy of Marketing Science* 133–50.

Gustafsson A, Kristensson P and Witell L, 'Customer Co-creation in Service Innovation: A Matter of Communication?' (2012) 23(3) *Journal of Service Management* 311–27, https://doi.org/10.1108/09564231211248426, accessed 12 March 2021.

Heinonen K and others, 'A Customer-Dominant Logic of Service' (2010) 21(4) *Journal of Service Management* 531–48.

Heinonen K and Strandvik T, 'Customer-Dominant Logic: Foundations and Implications' (2015) 29(6/7) *Journal of Services Marketing* 472–84.

Heinonen K and Strandvik T, 'Reflections on Customers' Primary Role in Markets' (2018) 36(1) *European Management Journal* 1–11.

Heinonen K, Strandvik T and Voima P, 'Customer Dominant Value Formation in Service' (2013) 25(2) *European Business Review* 104–23.

Hub of All Things, Hub of All Things GitHub page, https://github.com/Hub-of-all-Things, accessed 30 April 2020.

Keinonen T, Vaajakallio K and Honkonen J (eds), *Designing for Wellbeing* (Aalto University, School of Arts, Design and Architecture 2013).

Kortesniemi Y and Kremer J, 'Recommendations and Automation in the Consenting Process: Designing GDPR compliant consents', Paper presented at Legal Design as Academic Discipline: Foundations, Methodology, Applications (Groningen, Netherlands 2018).

Kortesniemi Y, Lappalainen T and Salka F, 'User Attitudes towards Consent Intermediaries', Paper presented at Legal Design as Academic Discipline: Foundations, Methodology, Applications (Groningen, Netherlands 2018).

Lehtiranta L, Junnonen J, Kärnä S and Pekuri L and others, 'The Constructive Research Approach: Problem Solving for Complex Projects' in Pasian B (ed), *Designs, Methods and Practices for Research of Project Management* (Gower Applied Business Research 2015).

Lehtiniemi T and Kortesniemi Y, 'Can the Obstacles to Privacy Self-Management Be Overcome? Exploring the Consent Intermediary Approach' (2017) 4(2) *Big Data and Society* 1–11.

Liu B and others, 'Follow My Recommendations: A Personalized Privacy Assistant for Mobile App Permissions' in *Proceedings of the 12th Symposium on Usable Privacy and Security, Denver, USA, 22–24 June* (USENIX 2016).

Lusch RF and Vargo SL, *Service-Dominant Logic: Premises, Perspectives, Possibilities* (Cambridge University Press 2014).

McDonald A and Cranor LF, 'The Cost of Reading Privacy Policies' (2008) *I/S: A Journal of Law and Policy for the Information Society*.

Meeco, Meeco website, https://meeco.me, accessed 30 April 2020.

Miettinen S, 'Designing Services with Innovative Methods' in Miettinen S and Koivisto M (eds), *Designing Services with Innovative Methods*. University of Art and Design & Kuopio Academy of Design. Taideteollisen korkeakoulun julkaisusarja, B. Taitemia (Otava Book Printing 2009).

Mirsch T, Lehrer C and Jung R, 'Digital Nudging: Altering User Behavior in Digital Environments' in *Proceedings of 13. Internationale Tagung Wirtschaftsinformatik* (WI, St Gallen, Switzerland 2017).

Poikola A, Kuikkaniemi K and Honko H, 'MyData – A Nordic Model for Human-Centered Personal Data Management and Processing' (Finnish Ministry of Transport and Communications 2015).

Prahalad CK and Ramaswamy V, 'Co-creation Experiences: The Next Practice in Value Creation' (2004) 18(3) *Journal of Interactive Marketing* 5–14.

Ramaswamy V, 'It's about Human Experiences … and Beyond, to Co-creation' (2011) 40, *Industrial Marketing Management* 195–96.

Solove DJ, 'Privacy Self-Management and the Consent Dilemma' (2013) 126(7) *Harvard Law Review* 1880–1903.

Stickdorn M and others, *This Is Service Design Doing: Applying Service Design Thinking in the Real World: A Practitioner's Handbook*' (O'Reilly Media 2018).

Sundbo J and Toivonen M, *User-Based Innovation in Services* (Edward Elgar 2011).

Sunstein CR, 'The Ethics of Nudging' (2015) 32 *Yale Journal on Regulation* 413–50.

Thaler RH and Sunstein CR, *Nudge: Improving Decisions about Health, Wealth, and Happiness* (Penguin Books 2009).

Turow J, Hennessy M and Draper N, *The Tradeoff Fallacy. How Marketers Are Misrepresenting American Consumers and Opening Them Up to Exploitation*. A Report from the Annenberg School for Communication, University of Pennsylvania (2015).

Vaajakallio K and Mattelmäki T, 'Yhteissuunnittelu avaa uusia näkymiä julkiselle sektorille' in Keinonen T, Vaajakallio K and Honkonen J (eds), *Hyvinvoinnin muotoilu, Helsinki: Aalto-yliopiston taiteiden ja suunnittelun korkeakoulu* (Aalto Arts Books 2013).

van Aaken A, 'Judge the Nudge: In Search of the Legal Limits of Paternalistic Nudging in the EU' in Alemanno A and Sibony AL (eds), *Nudge and the Law: A European Perspective* (Hart Publishing 2015).

Vargo SL and Lusch RF, 'Evolving to a New Dominant Logic for Marketing' (January 2014) 68 *Journal of Marketing* 1–17.

Vargo SL and Lusch RF, 'Service-Dominant Logic: Continuing the Evolution' (2008) 36 *Journal of the Academy of Marketing Science* 1–10.

Vargo SL, Maglio PP and Akaka MA, 'On Value and Value Co-creation: A Service Systems and Service Logic Perspective' (2008) 26(3) *European Management Journal* 145–52.

Wachter S, 'Privacy: Primus Inter Pares – Privacy as a Precondition for Self-Development, Personal Fulfilment and the Free Enjoyment of Fundamental Human Rights', https://ssrn.com/abstract=2903514, accessed 30 April 2020.

Yu E and Sangiorgi D, 'Service Design As an Approach to Implement the Value Cocreation Perspective in New Service Development' (2018) 21(1) *Journal of Service Research* 40–58.

Zuboff S, 'Big Other: Surveillance Capitalism and the Prospects of an Information Civilization' (2015) 30(1) *Journal of Information Technology* 75–89.

6

Artificial Intelligence and Data Protection Law

THOMAS HOEREN AND MAURICE NIEHOFF

6.1 Introduction

Initial scientific research on artificial intelligence (AI) dates back to the 1940s.[1] Since then, technical development has made rapid progress. AI has become more and more important in recent years due to the rapidly increasing computing power of computers and the emergence of huge amounts of data, referred to as 'Big Data'.[2] The German Research Centre for Artificial Intelligence (DFKI) and the Fraunhofer Institute are conducting intensive research in this area.

This debate is being revived by the introduction of the General Data Protection Regulation (GDPR). Bitkom, the digital association of Germany, recently published a position paper[3] in which the topic was examined from an interdisciplinary perspective. The German Federal Government is also aware of the importance of the topic; for example, it organised Safer Internet Day 2018, the flagship event under the title of artificial intelligence.[4] In this context, the focus is increasingly on how technical progress can be made accessible in terms of data protection law. The GDPR, which aims to ensure that the data protection level for those affected is as uniform as possible, now joins this list. Among other things, this should be achieved by banning automated decisions and the associated information rights and obligations.

1 Christian Honey, 'Künstliche Intelligenz – Die Suche nach dem Babelfisch' (2016) Zeit Online, www.zeit.de/digital/internet/2016-08/kuenstliche-intelligenz-geschichte-neuronale-netze-deep-learning, accessed 24 April 2019.

2 Wolfgang Hoffman-Riem, 'Verhaltenssteuerung durch Algorithmen – Eine Herausforderung für das Recht' (2017) 142 *Archiv des Öffentlichen Rechts* 6.

3 DFK, Bitkom e.V., 'Künstliche Intelligenz – Wirtschaftliche Bedeutung, gesellschaftliche Herausforderungen, menschliche Verantwortung' (2017), www.bitkom.org/sites/default/files/file/import/171012-KI-Gipfelpapier-online.pdf, accessed 25 April 2019.

4 See www.saferinternetday.org/, accessed 3 March 2019.

This chapter focuses on these automated decisions using algorithms and artificial intelligence uncovers their legal difficulties and offers solutions.

6.1.1 *Algorithms*

Algorithms are used to systematically solve a problem. They work with the help of (usually) deterministic, stringently followed, unambiguous and finite rules of action. The input of a certain value is followed by the output of a result, whereby the same result is always obtained due to the determinism with the same input values.[5] Classical examples in the analogue world are cooking recipes, for example, where a clear sequence of actions (recipe) is always followed by the same result (finished dish), that is, 'if …, then … processes'.[6] In the digital world, the rules of action are represented and processed by computer programs.

6.1.2 *Artificial Intelligence*

Artificial intelligence is also based on the algorithms described previously.[7]

Artificially intelligent applications also make use of rules of action, but they go far beyond that. The term 'artificial intelligence' generally refers to algorithms that are able to simulate human action.[8] In order to achieve the most human-like action possible, so-called artificial 'neural networks' are created. These correspond to the structure of the human brain.

A neural network consists of input and output neurons and intermediate layers, the so-called hidden layers.[9]

This construction is particularly capable for 'machine learning' and its sub-area of 'deep learning'. In addition to the linear 'if …, then … process', it includes the possibility of self-learning.[10]

Where pure machine learning is based on the ability to learn through human influence, the system learns contexts in deep learning without any

5 Thomas Cormen et al., *Algorithmen – Eine Einführung* (4th ed. de Gruyter 2017), 5.

6 Armin Barth, *Algorithmik für Einsteiger* (2nd ed. Springer Spektrum 2013), 2.

7 Christian Ernst, 'Algorithmische Entscheidungsfindung und Personenbezogene Daten' (2017) 72(21) *Juristen Zeitung* 1027.

8 There is still no scientific consensus on a definition; see DFK, Bitkom 'Künstliche Intelligenz', 28–31; Wolfgang Ertel, *Grundkurs künstliche Intelligenz* (4th ed. Springer Vieweg 2016), 1.

9 Yann LeCun et al., 'Deep Learning' (2017) 521 *Nature Deep Review* 437.

10 Jürgen Schmidhuber, 'Deep Learning in Neural Networks: An Overview' (2015) 61 *Neural Networks* 86.

human intervention. The system is trained using Big Data components, that is, large amounts of data. Based on the training data entered, the system recognises correlations and structures, questions the initial result and improves itself.[11]

This learning process leads to an increase in the layers between the input and output neurons, enabling increasingly complex decisions.

As a result, however, it is no longer possible to understand how the result is generated from an external point of view – we know that it works without knowing how it works.[12] The decision basis, the original algorithm, is also subject to constant change. The decision becomes a 'black box' for the person concerned.

In order to protect the rights of those affected, the GDPR contains various regulations, in particular the articles on automated decisions that are important for algorithms and AI. Automated decisions concern Arts 22 and 13–15 of the GDPR. These open up obligations to provide information or rights. There is a broad discussion on the content of this topic. Those affected are interested in receiving as much information as possible, and those responsible must be protected within the framework of trade secrets. For those affected, effective protection must be provided against automated decisions. You must not be left helplessly at the mercy of the AI's decisions.

In a first step, the chapter explains the applicability of the prohibition standard of Art. 22 GDPR in the case of automated decisions. On this basis, the rights of information and obligations according to Arts 13–15 of the GDPR will be discussed. In this context, the question arises: what specific requirements have to be placed on the information duty of those responsible? For this purpose, the present legal situation on the issue of dispute will be explained – whether a disclosure of the algorithm formula is required in the context of the information, or whether the mere principle behind it is sufficient.

Based on this, specific requirements for the type and scope of the information are developed: what does this mean in practice for those responsible? What standards are necessary for this? How does a company explain itself today if it decides against an applicant or a supplier?

[11] Ibid.

[12] Oliver Stiemerling, 'Künstliche Intelligenz – Automatisierung geistiger Arbeit, Big Data und das Internet der Dinge' (2015) 12 *Computer & Recht* 764; Ertel, *Grundkurs künstliche Intelligenz*, 308–10.

In a further step, the question is raised as to how the requirements for the justification of an automated decision will develop in the future.

This is where the peculiarities of AI-based decisions come into play. The differences to linear algorithms are worked out and the problem is raised that, due to the deep learning process, the responsible persons themselves may not be able to understand or represent either the algorithm or the principle behind it. How can the uncertainty be represented in enterprise applications when machine learning techniques only give probability indications? How can you make them understandable to the user? What is required by law?

Accordingly, the relationship between GDPR and the national law of the new Federal Data Protection Act (BDSG-New) will be examined in particular. It deals explicitly with the relationship of Section 31 BDSG-New to Art. 22 GDPR. To what extent does GDPR include scoring in the BDSG-New? Is there a priority of the GDPR or does the BDSG-New substantiate the GDPR?

Finally, aspects related to the topic are dealt with, such as the obligation to carry out a data protection impact assessment in accordance with Art. 35 (3) (a) GDPR, the right of objection according to Art. 21 GDPR, the obligation to appoint a data protection officer (Art. 37 GDPR) and the possibility of imposing a fine under Art. 83 GDPR.

The chapter ends with a view on the challenge that the legal system faces with the development of artificial intelligence.

6.2 Lion's Share

Artificially intelligent applications are also finding more and more applications in automated decisions. Since they are particularly suitable for large amounts of data, the application areas of image and speech recognition can be mentioned above all; for example, most citizens are familiar with Google image search or the speech assistant Siri.

Even in the banking, insurance and government sectors, algorithm-based decisions are increasingly being used.

Article 22 of the GDPR wants to take this into account by banning automated decisions.

6.2.1 Article 22 (1) GDPR

The model for Art. 22 GDPR is Art. 15 (1) of the Data Protection Directive. According to the Directive, every person has been granted the right not to be subject to a decision which is detrimental to him or her and which is based solely on automated processing of personal data for the purpose of assessing individual aspects of this person. Article 22 GDPR goes beyond Art. 15 of the Directive, which only concerned disadvantageous or weighty measures.

Article 22 (1) of the GDPR prohibits the persons concerned from excluding a 'decision based solely on automated processing'. This means a procedure that is carried out without human intervention from the data acquisition up to the decision making.[13] Thus the question arises when a decision is considered to be exclusively automated.[14]

This is clearly the case when decision-making processes are carried out from beginning to end without any human influence.

It is unclear whether Art. 22 GDPR also includes those processing operations where the algorithm completely prepares a decision, but where a person ultimately implements the decision without wanting to influence the decision content. This is the case, for example, with a mere confirmation of the result.[15] In this respect, the mere decision making (pressing the 'OK' button) of the human being is not to be taken into consideration. This would ultimately render the standard useless. Further, human intervention in the neural network to improve decisions, such as supervised learning,[16] does not constitute sufficient human action. It has no influence on the content but is comparable to maintenance. It must therefore be based on whether the person who is involved in the decision-making process also deals with the content of the decision. This argument goes beyond mere consent.[17]

This can be derived from the purpose of Art. 22 of the GDPR. The purpose of the prohibition regulation of Art. 22 (1) GDPR is to protect the parties concerned from an exclusively computer-based decision. At the end of every decision there must be a human being.[18] The background is the fundamental rights protected under Art. 2 (1) of the Basic Law and Art. 2 (1) in conjunction with Art. 1 of the Basic Law, the general freedom

13 GDPR, Recital 71 explicitly states so.

14 Mario Martini 'Art. 22 Automatisierte Entscheidungen im Einzelfall einschließlich Profiling' in Boris Paal and Daniel Pauly (eds), *Datenschutz-Grundverordnung, Bundesdatenschutzgesetz* (2nd ed. C. H. Beck 2018), DS-GVO Art. 22 ref. 16–18.

15 Wolfgang Hoffman-Riem, 'Verhaltenssteuerung durch Algorithmen – Eine Herausforderung für das Recht' (2017) 142 *Archiv des Öffentlichen Rechts* 36.

16 Hereto Jürgen Schmidhuber, 'Deep Learning in Neural Networks: An Overview' (2015) 61 *Neural Networks* 89–91; Stiemerling, 'Künstliche Intelligenz', 763.

17 Martini DS-GVO Art. 22 ref. 16–18.

18 Mario Martini, 'Algorithmen als Herausforderung für die Rechtsordnung' (2017) 72(21) *Juristische Zeitung* 1019.

of action and the right to informational self-determination. For those affected, it must remain transparent whether they have been the target of a fully automated decision; otherwise, a 'feeling of helplessness'[19] arises. Furthermore, an exclusively algorithm-based decision concerns the identity and right of self-determination of each person concerned. The algorithm processes the acquired personal data on the basis of predefined criteria and weightings, draws conclusions and correlations and comes to a result. The affected person is nothing more than a collection of input data; the individual personality of the person is not taken into account.[20]

Ultimately, however, the prohibition in Art. 22 (1) GDPR turns out to be isolated and a blunt sword. Due to its paragraph 2, there are numerous exceptional possibilities, which will probably become the norm in practice.

In this respect, the legal focus does not lie on the prohibition in accordance to Art. 22 (1) GDPR. Consideration should be given to the rights and obligations which result from the references in Arts 13–15 of the GDPR to Art. 22 of the GDPR. Indeed, if the door is already open for the application of automated decisions, there must in any case be rules that guarantee the effective exercise of the rights of those concerned.

6.2.2 Rights and Obligations under Articles 13–15 GDPR

Articles 13–15 of the GDPR are therefore relevant due to the prohibition of automated decisions.

6.2.2.1 Description

Articles 13–15 GDPR are preventive means of protection.

Article 13 (2) (f) and Art. 14 (2) (g) of the GDPR establish a duty of information for those responsible as soon as persons are affected by automated decisions according to Art. 22 of the GDPR. At the same time the data subjects shall also be granted a right to information pursuant to Art. 15 (1) (h) of the GDPR.

6.2.2.2 The Purpose of the Provisions

Following the purpose of the prohibition standard of Art. 22 of the GDPR, Arts 13–15 of the GDPR are intended to enable those affected to take

[19] Christian Ernst, 'Algorithmische Entscheidungsfindung und Personenbezogene Daten' (2017) 72(21) *Juristen Zeitung* 1030.

[20] Ibid.

effective measures against decisions that are exclusively automated. This is already explained in Recital 63, p. 1, which gives the person concerned the right to 'verify the legality'. The person concerned must be given a fair and transparent insight as far as possible. This includes, in addition to the information on the existence of a processing operation of personal data, its circumstances and purpose.[21] An 'effective enforcement' is only possible if the person concerned has a comprehensive insight into the decision. Only then can he or she raise specific concerns about the processing process and effectively raise his or her own objections.

6.2.2.3 Requirements for Article 13 (2) (f), Article 14 (2) (g) and Article 15 (1) (h) GDPR

However, the precise scope of the disclosure obligation is controversial.

Article 12 (1) of the GDPR confirms the requirements for the greatest possible disclosure obligation of those responsible towards the persons concerned.

This places the following requirements on the disclosure obligations of the responsible persons according to Arts 13–15 of the GDPR: 'Precise, transparent, comprehensible and easily accessible form in a clear and simple language'.

For this purpose, in Recital 58, p. 3, it is clear that 'the complexity of the technology required for this purpose makes it difficult for the data subject to recognise and understand whether, by whom and for what purpose personal data concerning him/her are collected'. The EU therefore recognised the conflict threatening those affected and tried to counteract it with the aforementioned obligations.

The Union also recognised that automated decisions have a special feature, namely their lack of transparency. For this reason, Arts 13–15 of the GDPR respectively impose the following requirements in their second paragraphs f) and g) and h) on the duty of the responsible persons to provide information: significant information on the logic involved must be provided.

Which leads to the question: what is behind the concept of the involved logic? What exactly do those responsible for automated decisions have to communicate?

[21] Boris Paal and Moritz Hennemann 'Art. 13 Informationspflicht bei Erhebung von personenbezogenen Daten bei der betroffenen Person' in Boris Paal and Daniel Pauly (eds), *Datenschutz-Grundverordnung, Bundesdatenschutzgesetz* (2nd ed. C. H. Beck 2018) Art. 13 ref. 4.

6.2.3 *The Scope of the Information Obligations in Terms of Content*

The algorithm may need to be disclosed in a second step, taking into account the peculiarities of AI-based decisions.

6.2.3.1 Disclosure Algorithm

One possibility would be to have to disclose the operating algorithm behind the processing. This would fulfil the requirements for a disclosure obligation that is as comprehensive as possible and would also get to the bottom of the 'involved logic'.

This contradicts the prevailing opinion of literature. According to the latter, it is only the principle behind the decision, not the algorithmic formula itself, that should be explained.

On the one hand, this would result from the interpretation of Recital 63, p. 3, to Art. 15 of the GDPR. In its German version it is still not very productive. It merely repeats the wording of the standard by declaring: 'Every person concerned should therefore be entitled to know ... the logic underlying the automatic processing of personal data'.

However, the French language version explicitly states that only the basis of the logic is revealed. This is also the case for the Dutch language version.

On the other hand, Recital 63, p. 5, should also be used. Accordingly, the disclosure is explicitly intended not to impair the business secrets of other persons. Sentence 6 restricts this to the extent that the person concerned may not be denied access to all information due to the protection of trade secrets. This entails weighing the interests of the parties responsible for business secrets against the interests of the parties concerned in providing the information.

Exactly this consideration had to be decided by the Federal Supreme Court (BGH) in its judgement of 28 January 2014,[22] in the so-called SCHUFA judgement. In this, the plaintiff brought an action against SCHUFA for disclosure of the score formula that was used. This score formula is exactly such an algorithm that uses personal data to determine whether a person is creditworthy or not.

At that time the BGH ruled, still on the basis of Section 34 BDSG-Old, that the plaintiff was not entitled to this claim. The reason for this was that SCHUFA's trade secrecy prevailed over the plaintiff's right to

[22] Federal Supreme Court (BGH), judgement of 28 January 2014 – VI ZR 156/13.

transparency of the decision. This takes up the prevailing opinion in the literature and transfers it to the application of the GDPR.

As an interim result, it can be stated on the basis of this argumentation that the disclosure obligation does not have to include the algorithm formula.[23] The Higher Regional Court of Nuremberg, as a preliminary instance of the Federal Supreme Court, explained in its decision of 2012 that 'comprehensible' does not mean 'recalculable for the person concerned'.[24]

Recital 63, p. 6, may be used to disclose the algorithmic formula. The latter explicitly states that the protection of trade secrets in accordance to Recital 63, p. 5, should not lead to a refusal of information to the person concerned. The responsible persons must not hide behind their secrecy because otherwise there would be no effective information. It must always be weighed on a case-by-case basis. In individual cases, this can also lead to the publication of the algorithm. In this respect, it is questionable to what extent the definition of the algorithm affects the trade secret at all. It is important to note that the disclosure of the algorithm does not represent a factual threat to the business secrets of the responsible person. This does not mean that the data subject or third parties can exploit or misuse this information just because the relevant regulations and program procedures are explained to the data subject with the appropriate weightings. In order to do this, the source code has to be released, which translates the algorithm into working, usable software.

While the prevailing opinion may have now spoken out against the publication of the algorithmic formula,[25] the question of AI-based decisions must be completely reiterated. Following this controversy, the special feature of AI-based decisions has to come into play.

6.2.3.2 Special Features of the Right to Information in the Case of AI

In contrast to 'normal' algorithm-based decisions, the problem with AI-based decisions is that AI decisions are based on the deep learning process. AI systems correspond to neural networks; they are not programmed according to a linear model of a line of code but continue to program themselves. This means that the algorithm is self-developed – it learns by itself.

23 Paal and Hennemann, DS-GVO, Art. 13 ref. 31.
24 Higher Regional Court (OLG) Nuremberg, judgement of 30 October 2012 – 3 U 2362/11.
25 Paal and Hennemann, DS-GVO, Art. 13 ref. 31.

Therefore, it is not possible to perform an ordinary linear control. Usually, the developers themselves do not know how the AI system works and how it is decided.[26] The developers only know that it works.[27] The algorithm could not be published at all, as it is constantly evolving.

Looking at the GDPR, it quickly becomes clear that the authors did not consider this. The GDPR is far too one-dimensional: it does not take into account the possibility of non-transparent, self-learning processes. All too superficially, the regulation speaks of automated decisions, logic and a fair and transparent procedure, without considering the complexity of self-learning AI processes.

For this reason, GDPR must be specially designed with regard to AI decisions. When interpreting the requirements of Arts 12 and 13–15 GDPR, it is important to observe the constant leitmotif of the information rights. The person concerned must receive the necessary transparency so that he or she can raise objections effectively and decisively against automated decision-making. The requirement of Art. 12 of the GDPR is to be considered thereby. The information must therefore be provided in a 'concise, transparent, intelligible and easily accessible form, using clear and plain language'.[28]

How should this be done with AI, even if the developers do not know how the AI system works and the algorithm is not transparent?[29] The impending 'black box character' must therefore be dissolved. This is done in a way that allows the person concerned to understand the outcome of the decision:

> 'Every far-reaching decision should be verifiable by a human being'.[30] This does not necessarily require an explanation of how the neural network works, it is sufficient to understand how the decision was made.[31]

[26] Joshua Kroll et al., 'Accountable Algorithms' (2017) 165(3) *University of Pennsylvania Law Review* 638; W. Nicholson Price II, 'Black-Box Medicine' (2015) 28(2) *Harvard Journal of Law & Technology* 432–33.

[27] Stiemerling, 'Künstliche Intelligenz', 764; Ertel, *Grundkurs künstliche Intelligenz*, 308–10.

[28] See Art. 12 (1) GDPR.

[29] Kroll et al., 'Accountable Algorithms'.

[30] Gianclaudio Malgieri and Giovanni Comandé, 'Why a Right to Legibility of Automated Decision-Making Exists in the General Data Protection Regulation' (2017) 7(4) *International Data Privacy* 246; Finale Doshi-Velez and Mason Kortz, 'Accountability of AI under the Law: The Role of Explanation' (2017) 18-07 Harvard Public Law Working Paper, 1–2.

[31] Sandra Wachter et al., 'Counterfactual Explanations without Opening the Black Box: Automated Decisions and the GDPR' (2018) 31(2) *Harvard Journal of Law & Technology* 850–51; Doshi-Velez and Kortz, 'Accountability of AI under the Law', 2–3.

One possibility would be to publish the output algorithm, the basic construct of the neural network. This could at least provide an indication of how the automated decision came about. In this case, the objection of the prevailing opinion that the trade secret is contrary to this should have far less weight. After all, it is not the working algorithm in the status quo that is issued, but a 'predecessor version'. However, depending on the developmental progress of the neural network, the output algorithm may not have much in common with the algorithm at the time the decision is made. In this respect, this will not help the person concerned to effectively assert her or his rights as an affected person. The requirements of Recitals 63 and 71 and the meaning and purpose of the right to information would not be respected. The logic behind the decision would no longer have been revealed. The algorithm in the predecessor version most likely has significantly different weightings, criteria and structures than the decisive AI algorithm. Thus, it does not help the affected person to find out possible decision criteria of the output algorithm if the later algorithm has created new criteria for itself through the self-learning process.

Another possibility would be to provide the person concerned with information about the training data. The input neurons, that is, the input data of the system, are known to the responsible persons. However, this leads to the same problem: the hidden layers, which are relevant for decision making, are not easily visible and develop independently from the original training data. Again, it would not be possible to provide information that meets the requirements.

One way to make these hidden layers visible is the so-called Layer-Wise Relevance Propagation (LRP). Here, the decision-making process of a neural network is played backwards through a complicated mathematical procedure. It is visualised for the human eye using a heatmap. On this heatmap, positive and negative decisions of the hidden layers are made visible with the help of different colours and thus the decision is explained. Until now, this method has been particularly successful with image recognition software. This variant solves the problem by not releasing the algorithm. Nevertheless, the reason for the decision is worked out. It is questionable to what extent this is technically applicable to non-visual decisions.

A similar solution is to make artificial intelligence explainable.[32] By means of so-called Local Interpretable Model-Agnostic Explanations

[32] Joshua A. Kroll et al., 'Accountable Algorithms' (2017) 165 *University of Pennsylvania Law Review*, 650–52; Christin Seifert et al., 'Visualisations of Deep Neural Networks in Computer Vision: A Survey' in Tania Cerquitelli, Daniele Quercia and Frank Pasquale (eds), *Transparent Data Mining for Big and Small Data* (Springer 2017), 123–25.

(LIME), predictions of a neuronal network are made comprehensible for the affected persons. Using a technical procedure, the relevant word fields around the decision are recognised. This may not encompass the complete decision of the neural network as given as only the local, neuronal activities around the decision are recognised. In the event of a refused creditworthiness check, the criteria 'unemployed', 'debt' and 'SCHUFA entry' might be identified as relevant for the result.[33] These results are therefore verifiable and comprehensible for the affected person. Each interested party may use this information to assess whether the decision is based on criteria that are correct and appropriate or not.

However, this is only an approximate value, albeit a very reliable one. The possibility that in the depths of the neural network other criteria – which may possibly be factual and discriminating – may have led to the decision cannot be completely ruled out. In order to understand the logic behind the decision, it is necessary for the person concerned to be informed about this imponderability. Automated decisions remain statements of probability.

This should also be kept in mind while contemplating the disclosure obligations of users. In practice, users must ensure that they present the automated decision to the affected parties in such a way that it can be explained in a verifiable and comprehensible manner. The fact that from a technical point of view (as of today) there is no way to fully implement decisions of neural networks must be taken into account. In this respect, technical innovations must not be blocked by data protection legislation. There is a need for an appropriate balance between promoting innovation and safeguarding the rights of those affected. This line of thought should also lead the interpretation and application of the GDPR. The illustrated possibility to explain automated decisions by means of an approximation test which complies with the technical standards and which is as close as possible to reality is sufficient.

6.2.4 *Scoring According to BDSG and GDPR*

Another fragment for standardisation in the area of AI is Section 28b BDSG-Old and Section 31 (1) BDSG-New with their regulations on scoring. There is a new criterion for the evaluation of information gathering

[33] See Marco Tulio Ribeiro et al., 'Why Should I Trust You? Explaining the Predictions of Any Classifier' (2016) 2 ff, https://arxiv.org/abs/1602.04938, accessed 27 June 2018.

methods, namely the basis of a 'scientifically recognized mathematical-statistical method' for calculating the probability value (No. 2).[34]

This classification has far-reaching consequences for the Big Data scene. In accordance with Section 31 (1) No. 2 BDSG-New, the mathematic standards must be 'verifiable' for calculating probability. The reference to 'verifiability' shifts the burden of presentation and proof to the users and allows the data protection supervision to keep informed about the parameters for verifiability in the case of the use of personal data within the framework of Section 40 (4) sentence 1 BDSG-New.

To this end, it must be explained to what extent the BDSG-New will be used in addition to the GDPR.

6.2.4.1 Definition Scoring

Section 31 BDSG-New defines scoring as 'the probability value of a certain future behaviour of a natural person for the purpose of deciding on the establishment, execution or termination of a contractual relationship with that person'.[35]

This means that a forecast for the future is created on the basis of collected data of a person.

6.2.4.2 Applicability of Section 31 BDSG-New Compared with Article 22 GDPR

The GDPR does not mention scoring in any way. Nevertheless, the application of scoring under Art. 22 of this regulation can be argued for.

For this purpose, the ranges of the respective standards must be determined and compared with each other.

The scope of Section 31 BDSG-New is unclear. It can be interpreted in such a way that it is also applicable to automated decisions in accordance with Art. 22 of the DS Regulation, in addition to the narrow scope of financial scoring. This is supported by the explanatory statement of the Federal Government's bill: 'Scoring is a mathematical-statistical procedure that allows the probability of a certain person showing a certain behaviour to be calculated'. There is no evidence anywhere that the scoring procedure must be limited to credit checks. The only limitation contained in the provision is the indication that scoring should be used to 'decide on the establishment, performance or termination of a contractual relationship

[34] See Section 31 (1) No. 2 BDSG-New.

[35] See Section 31 (1) BDSG-New.

with the party concerned'. The term used to describe the collection of probabilities goes far beyond the usual methods of credit scoring. For all business transactions, therefore, the decision to conclude a transaction will inevitably be influenced by forecast assessments. Similarly, many AI processes are based on scoring, which is incorporated into the design of differentiated business models.

In this respect, the wording is consistent with Recital 71 to Art. 22 of the DS Regulation, which inter alia reads as follows: in sentence 1, 'automatic rejection of an online credit application'; in sentence 2, 'analysis or forecasting of aspects relating to ... economic situation'; and in paragraph 2, 'appropriate mathematical or statistical methods'.

With regard to Art. 22 GDPR, a differentiation must be made as to whether the scoring method is directly related to the final automated decision or whether scoring is merely an upstream method by external credit agencies. This differentiation can also be seen in the wording of Section 31 BDSG-New. Paragraph 1 refers to 'probability values ... for the purpose of the decision', and paragraph 2 explicitly mentions the 'use of a probability value determined by credit agencies'. The criterion here, as in the interpretation of exclusivity, is whether a human decision has been made in the meantime.

Article 22 GDPR therefore covers internal scoring. The collection of probability values is immediately followed by an automated decision without human intervention. In this respect, the term scoring meets the requirements of a 'decision based exclusively on automated processing'. It is subject to the requirements of Art. 22 GDPR.

The GDPR is regarded as a European ordinance in accordance with Art. 288 (2) sentence 1 Treaty on the Functioning of the European Union (TFEU), which comes into force immediately and bindingly for all member states. It takes precedence over contradicting national regulations. However, priority is limited by the extent of contradiction through national law. Interpretations and concretions by national law are possible. An example of concretion can be found in Section 31 (1) BDSG-New, substantiating the term 'involved logic' of the GDPR for the benefit of the concerned parties as a 'scientifically recognized mathematical-statistical procedure'. The added value of concretion compared with the wording in Recital 71, p. 2, lies in the aforementioned shift in the burden of proof. In accordance with Section 31 (1) BDSG-New, suitable mathematical and statistical methods must be demonstrated.

However, external scoring, which also includes classic credit scoring, cannot be covered by Art. 22 of the DS Regulation. The upstream collection of probability values, which does not yet lead directly to a decision, constitutes an upstream measure and merely prepares a decision. This remains unchanged by Recital 71, which sees 'online credit applications' of Art. 22 of the DS Regulation specifically covered. In relation to Art. 22 GDPR, the purpose of the standard, as outlined earlier, must be taken into account. Article 22 GDPR protects the persons concerned from a completely mechanical decision without regard to human individuality. It does not protect against being affected by surveys of probability values. Their legality is thus judged according to the general requirements of the GDPR. Therefore, the GDPR requires an opening clause for external scoring to open up the possibility for the national legislature to create specific, supplementary or deviating regulations from the GDPR.

The relevant opening clause can be seen in the summary from Art. 6 (4), 23 (1) lit. e) GDPR. Here, the national legislature is granted derogations to the 'protection of other important objectives of the general public interest of a member state, in particular an important economic or financial interest'.[36]

This goal was set in the legal justification of the Bundestag. In this, the Federal Government declares that it wants to adopt the 'material protection standard of Sections 28a and 28b BDSG-Old'.[37] This results out of efforts to protect the economy. Among other things, economic transactions are based on protecting consumers from excessive indebtedness by means of credit checks. Scoring is therefore 'the foundation of the German banking system and thus of the functioning of the economy'. Hence, the German Federal Government remains true to its policy of adhering to national scoring regulations. The German government already presented this justification in the DSAnpUG-EU draft.[38] The objection of it being merely a private-sector purpose which does not serve the public interest of the member state and leads to an undervaluation of the GDPR system does not apply. On the one hand, the functioning of the economy is indeed a public interest of the state. On the other hand, the GDPR as a system with innumerable opening clauses is intended to be put into practice in this manner by the member states.

Scoring, being directly related to the automated decision, is thus covered by the provision of Art. 22 of the DS Regulation. The GDPR is made

[36] See Art. 23 (1) lit. e) GDPR.

[37] See Deutscher Bundestag: 18. Wahlperiode (2017) Drucksache 18/11325, 101, http://dipbt.bundestag.de/doc/btd/18/113/1811325.pdf, accessed 24 June 2021.

[38] Ibid.

more specific for the benefit of those affected by Section 31 BDSG-New such that the verifiability of the mathematical-statistical methods of probability calculations is imposed on the users.

6.2.5 Follow-up Aspects of Automated Decisions

Automated decisions in accordance with Art. 22 GDPR are accompanied by further rights and obligations.

6.2.5.1 Data Protection Impact Assessment, Article 35 (3) lit. a GDPR

Article 35 (3) lit. a GDPR subjects the processor to a data protection impact assessment with systematic and comprehensive evaluation of personal aspects of natural persons. In accordance with paragraph 1, it is necessary to assess the consequences of the processing operations envisaged for the protection of personal data. In analogy to the previous remarks, this is particularly problematic for AI-based decisions, since the extent of the self-learning process of neural networks is hardly or not at all predictable for those responsible.

6.2.5.2 Right of Objection, Article 21 GDPR

In addition to the right of information under Art. 15 GDPR, the data subject is entitled to a right of objection in accordance with Art. 21 (1) GDPR.

6.2.5.3 Obligation for Data Protection Officer, Article 37 GDPR

If authorities should carry out automated decisions, a data protection officer shall be appointed in accordance with Art. 37 (1) lit. a GDPR. The same applies to private individuals in accordance with lit. b) for extensive, regular and systematic monitoring of persons affected.

6.2.5.4 Fines, Article 83 GDPR

Violations of the prohibition standard of Art. 22 GDPR as well as the information rights and obligations under Arts 13–15 GDPR are sanctioned with fines of up to €20,000 or up to 4 per cent of the total annual turnover achieved worldwide (Art. 83 (5) GDPR).

6.3 Conclusion

Algorithm-based, and above all AI-based, decisions continue to pose major problems for the legal system. These problems will not be solved by the introduction of the GDPR. On the contrary, further questions arise. Particularly in view of the increasing social significance of such decisions, a review of the legal assessment is required.

The justification requirements of the rights and obligations under Arts 13–15 GDPR must be fulfilled by users to the extent that the parties concerned must be given the opportunity to effectively defend themselves against an automated decision. This is achieved by explaining the decision to the person concerned in a way that is as coherent and comprehensible as possible. To this end, the criteria leading to each decision must be disclosed to the parties concerned.

This is put into practice by means of a state-of-the-art procedure which determines the criteria for finding results with the highest possible validity. However, errors in the deep, (still) impenetrable neural networks cannot be entirely eliminated. The person affected must also be informed about this.

Since automated decisions are increasingly making important social decisions, it remains to be seen whether further regulatory measures are appropriate in addition to disclosure obligations. Martini proposes these at various levels for preventive as well as supportive self-regulation and *ex post* regulation while warning about the dangers of over-regulation.[39]

In addition, Section 31 BDSG-New, which constitutes a legally binding specification for Art. 22 GDPR in the context of automated decisions, imposes the burden of explanation and proof for the verifiability of the mathematical standards on the users.

Attention must also be paid to the side effects, which should not be underestimated. Data sequence estimation, for example, presents the user with problems that he or she already has in relation to the obligation to provide information: he or she needs to assess the range of his or her AI-based system.

There is probably also the obligation of a data protection officer.[40] Otherwise, there is a risk of substantial fines for violations.[41]

The introduction of the GDPR will in practice require users of automated AI-based decisions to replace them comprehensively with their systems. In order to comply with the disclosure obligations and the data impact assessment, it is de facto assumed that users of AI can trace the basis of their decision – at least to the core criteria. This must be verifiable on the part of the users. The application of the law must always take place

39 Martini, 'Algorithmen als Herausforderung für die Rechtsordnung'.

40 See Art. 37 (1) GDPR.

41 See Art. 83 GDPR.

in step with technical development. In no way must technical innovation be blocked by excessive regulation.[42] At the same time, the rights of those affected must be protected. The goal must be to dissolve the black box character of AI without hindering its development.

This is a major task for the future.

Bibliography

Arel I, Rose D and Karnowski T, 'Deep Machine Learning – A New Frontier in Artificial Intelligence Research' (2010) 5(6) *November IEEE Computational Intelligence Magazine* 13–18.

Barth A, *Algorithmik für Einsteiger* (2nd ed. Springer Spektrum 2013).

Cormen TH, Leiserson CE, Rivest R and Stein C, *Algorithmen – Eine Einführung* (4th ed. de Gruyter 2017).

DFK, Bitkom (eds), 'Künstliche Intelligenz – Wirtschaftliche Bedeutung, gesellschaftliche Herausforderungen, menschliche Verantwortung' (2017), www.bitkom.org/sites/default/files/file/import/171012-KI-Gipfelpapier-online.pdf, accessed 25 April 2019.

Doshi-Velez F and Kortz M, 'Accountability of AI under the Law: The Role of Explanation' (2017) 18-07 Harvard Public Law Working Paper.

Ernst C, 'Algorithmische Entscheidungsfindung und Personenbezogene Daten' (2017) 72(21) *Juristen Zeitung* 1026–36.

Ertel W, *Grundkurs künstliche Intelligenz* (4th ed. Springer Vieweg 2016).

Hall P, Phan W and Ambati S, 'Ideas on Interpreting Machine Learning' (2017), www.oreilly.com/ideas/ideas-on-interpreting-machine-learning, accessed 15 March 2017.

Hoffman-Riem W, 'Verhaltenssteuerung durch Algorithmen – Eine Herausforderung für das Recht' (2017) 142 *Archiv des Öffentlichen Rechts* 6–36.

Honey C, 'Künstliche Intelligenz – Die Suche nach dem Babelfisch' (2016) Zeit Online, www.zeit.de/digital/internet/2016-08/kuenstliche-intelligenz-geschichte-neuronale-netze-deep-learning, accessed 24 April 2019.

Kroll JA, Huey J and Barocas S et al., 'Accountable Algorithms' (2017) 165(3) *University of Pennsylvania Law Review* 633–705.

LeCun Y, Bengio Y and Hinton G, 'Deep Learning' (2017) 521 *Nature Deep Review* 436–44.

Malgieri G and Comandé G, 'Why a Right to Legibility of Automated Decision-Making Exists in the General Data Protection Regulation' (2017) 7(4) *International Data Privacy* 243–65.

[42] Martini, 'Algorithmen als Herausforderung für die Rechtsordnung'.

Martini M 'Algorithmen als Herausforderung für die Rechtsordnung' (2017) 72(21) *Juristische Zeitung* 1017–25.

Paal B and Pauly D (eds), *Datenschutz-Grundverordnung, Bundesdatenschutzgesetz* (2nd ed. C. H. Beck 2018).

Price II N, 'Black-Box Medicine' (2015) 28(2) *Harvard Journal of Law & Technology* 419–67.

Ribeiro M, Singh S and Guestrin C, 'Why Should I Trust You? Explaining the Predictions of Any Classifier' (2016), https://arxiv.org/abs/1602.04938, accessed 27 June 2018.

Schmidhuber J, 'Deep Learning in Neural Networks: An Overview' (2015) 61 *Neural Networks* 85.

Seifert C et al., 'Visualizations of Deep Neural Networks in Computer Vision: A Survey' in Cerquitelli T, Quercia D and Pasquale F (eds), *Transparent Data Mining for Big and Small Data* (Springer 2017), 123–25.

Stiemerling O, 'Künstliche Intelligenz – Automatisierung geistiger Arbeit, Big Data und das Internet der Dinge' (2015) 12 *Computer & Recht* 762.

Sydow G, *Europäische Datenschutzgrundverordnung* (2nd ed. Nomos 2018).

Wachter S, Mittelstadt B and Russell C, 'Counterfactual Explanations without Opening the Black Box: Automated Decisions and the GDPR' (2018) 31(2) *Harvard Journal of Law & Technology* 841–87.

Wolff H and Brink S, '*Beck'scher Online-Kommentar Datenschutzrecht*' (27th ed. C.H. Beck 2019).

7

AI Technologies and Accountability in Digital Health

EVA THELISSON

7.1 Introduction

In the Preamble to the Constitution of the World Health Organisation (WHO), health is defined as 'a state of complete physical, mental and social well-being'. The right to health is considered as a human right and is now well recognised in international law, particularly in the 1946 Constitution of the WHO and the 1948 Universal Declaration of Human Rights.[1] The COVID-19 pandemic, nevertheless, has challenged its effective implementation, straining health systems, creating suffering, upending international institutions and slowing down economic growth. The pandemic also created moral dilemmas particularly for medical professionals and policy makers facing a scarcity of resources available in particular respiratory devices and adequate data on the consequences of the pandemic. It precisely raised the question of the value of human life in a context of resources scarcity. In sum, the COVID-19 pandemic demonstrated that health systems must be resilient to outbreaks and be better prepared to predict and react to such a human and economic tragedy.

In such a context, the question is whether a large amount of personal data, from multi-modal sources, combined with artificial intelligence (AI) and machine learning (ML) algorithms, has the potential to improve the access and quality of healthcare services for the end-users in a cost-benefit perspective. In the race for a vaccine, Moderna, for instance, managed to use AI systems in an effective way. Indeed, the company used structured data to design more efficient algorithms to support decision making in the clinical space where they provide predictions that humans wouldn't be able to make

[1] As per the 1966 International Covenant on Economic, Social, and Cultural Rights (ICESCR), it includes 'access to health facilities, goods, and services'.

in a reasonable time frame.[2] Moderna is certainly not the only company that has benefited from new technologies. The global digital health market is expected to reach a valuation of more than $234 billion by 2023, up from 2019's estimated $147 billion, according to the Frost & Sullivan report.[3]

Frost & Sullivan define digital health as the 'application of data to the delivery of healthcare, using computational and telecommunications technologies, to support business process workflow, clinical workflow, and patient data management'. The goal of digital health is to achieve better patient outcomes while improving efficiency and containing costs. Digital health is multidisciplinary but primarily focuses on three domains: health process automation, patient engagement and mobility.[4]

Expectations of regulations and market access to digital health are set high at a time when more than one billion people cannot obtain the health services they need, since these services are either inaccessible, unavailable, unaffordable or of poor quality.[5] On the one hand, in order to meet these expectations, recent initiatives to scale up digitalisation of healthcare services should assist national institutions in providing a resilient, effective and human-centred health system. A new paradigm of personalised medicine is founded on data access, data analytics and computation. It is reinforced by the convergence between the internet of things, computational platforms, data sharing and biology (in particular, genomics and Crispr-Cas 9 technology). In addition, 5G networks should enhance access to remote digital health services whose importance the COVID-19 pandemic has made obvious.

On the other hand, the current state of the art raises some significant challenges that need to be addressed before AI systems enjoy the widespread use that is necessary for them to have a meaningful impact on people's lives. These challenges concern mainly privacy, security, accuracy and the transparency of AI systems, as well as some ethical questions. In this chapter, design recommendations are given and relevant security, privacy and ethical considerations specific to the use of digital technologies in healthcare are discussed.

2 Moderna CEO Stéphane Bancel stated that 'we relied on digitization early on, not for the sake of digitization but for generating data. Today, we have a lot of structured data, for instance in research and pre-clinical production'.

3 Global Digital Health Outlook (2019), Frost & Sullivan, https://store.frost.com/global-digital-health-outlook-2020.html, accessed 7 April 2021.

4 Ibid.

5 World Health Organisation, Presentation of health systems, www.who.int/healthsystems/about/en/, accessed 19 February 2021.

The Organisation for Economic Co-operation and Development (OECD) and the EU Commission, as well as China, have published key AI principles to frame the development of AI technologies[6] However, these soft law mechanisms are not legally binding and shape rather moral obligations for AI developers, without offering an effective quality process being defined to mitigate the risk of misuse or harm for patients. In the specific context of digital health, since the accuracy of data plays a central role, the relevance and effective enforcement mechanisms of data protection regulation are essential,[7] in particular for sensitive health data and vulnerable individuals like patients and children. Another important issue is the transparency of government procurement, as the COVID-19 pandemic has demonstrated. Transparency implies a need to explain why particular suppliers are chosen over others and how governments identify and manage potential conflicts of interest. Finally, a delegation of sensitive data processing to private actors in digital health would raise the risk of undermining core values of the health system, as well as patient trust.

This chapter aims to raise questions and present solutions which are yet to be tested, with the hope that it will lead to business models for beneficial and responsible use of digital technologies in healthcare. To this end, we identify the key parameters for a more comprehensible, personalised and sustainable medicine and propose possible solutions to shape a sound policy that, while taking into account the ethically and legally compliant governance[8] framework, also aims at developing an effective liability regime. We explore three intersections of digital technologies and accountability in digital healthcare. We first define health in a digital era (Section 7.2). We then focus on the impact of data-driven systems on healthcare (Section 7.3). Finally, we analyse key ethical issues in digital health, particularly accountability for decisions made by AI systems (Section 7.4). Section 7.5 concludes.

[6] OECD Principles on AI, www.oecd.org/going-digital/ai/principles/, accessed 14 March 2021, High-Level Expert Group on AI presented Ethics Guidelines for Trustworthy Artificial Intelligence, https://ec.europa.eu/digital-single-market/en/news/ethics-guidelines-trustworthy-ai, accessed 14 March 2021. Beijing AI Principles. Datenschutz Datensich 43, 656 (2019), https://doi.org/10.1007/s11623-019-1183-6, accessed 14 March 2021.

[7] Paolo Guarda, '"Ok Google, Am I Sick?": Artificial Intelligence, e-Health, and Data Protection Regulation' (2019) 15(1) *BioLaw Journal-Rivista di BioDiritto* 359–75.

[8] Alan FT Winfield and Marina Jirotka, 'Ethical Governance Is Essential to Building Trust in Robotics and Artificial Intelligence Systems' (2018) 376(2133) *Philosophical Transactions of the Royal Society A: Mathematical, Physical and Engineering Sciences* 20180085.

7.2 Health in a Digital Era

7.2.1 The Right to Health

The right to health is a fundamental right, one of the most pressing UN Sustainable Development Goals 2030 (SDGs), and a condition for economic growth and wellbeing.[9] Indeed, health is both a cause and a consequence of economic growth and thus helps us get closer to different SDGs, end poverty, fight hunger, reduce inequalities and build peace. The effective implementation of the right to health incrementally depends mainly on a global strategy and policy on digital health, as well as on innovative digital technologies.

Digital health can be defined as 'a broad umbrella term encompassing digital healthcare, as well as emerging areas, such as the use of advanced computing sciences in "Big Data", genomics and artificial intelligence'.[10] This is 'an emerging field in the intersection of medical informatics, public health and business, referring to health services and information delivered or enhanced through the Internet and related technologies. In a broader sense, the term characterizes not only a technical development but also a state-of-mind, a way of thinking, an attitude, and a commitment for networked, global thinking, to improve healthcare locally, regionally, and worldwide by using information and communication technology'.[11]

Digital health can assist medical doctors in managing the volume of patients while improving the quality of diagnosis, fostering its statistical accuracy and helping the user in monitoring his/her chronic diseases[12] more closely.

One of the recent innovations which could have a significant impact on access to digital health technologies while revolutionizing the way healthcare providers monitor their patients' health is the project Starlink, launched by SpaceX in the United States. Starlink promises to offer

[9] In 2013, United Nations Deputy Secretary-General Jan Eliasson launched a call for urgent action to end the crisis of 2.5 billion people without basic sanitation, and to change a situation in which more people worldwide have mobile phones than toilets.

[10] WHO Guidelines: 'Recommendations on Digital Interventions for Health System Strengthening' (2018), www.who.int/reproductivehealth/publications/digital-interventions-health-system-strengthening/en/, accessed 14 March 2021.

[11] Gunther Eysenbach, 'What Is Digital Health?' (2001) 3(2) *Journal of Medical Internet Research* e20.

[12] Paul Wicks and others, 'Scaling PatientsLikeMe via a "Generalized Platform" for Members with Chronic Illness: Web-Based Survey Study of Benefits Arising' (2018) 20(5) *Journal of Medical Internet Research* e175.

high-speed broadband internet, using cutting-edge satellite systems.[13] As of now, the company states that it 'is targeting service in the Northern U.S. and Canada in 2020, rapidly expanding to near global coverage of the populated world by 2021'.[14] This innovation has the potential to enhance the implementation of the right to health across the globe, facilitating access-to-care in underserved and remote areas and accelerating telemedicine. Indeed, Starlink will use a global network of 42,000 low Earth orbit satellites to facilitate 'access in places where Internet access is unreliable, expensive, or completely unavailable'.[15]

Combined with technological innovations, policy choices also play a central role in fostering the effective implementation of the right to health. Decision-makers can focus on improving hygiene, education and medical research, or they can create economic incentives to foster innovation. Developing healthcare AI systems is a political priority for many African countries that face numerous challenges in delivering care to a fast-growing population and in dealing with epidemiological crises that threaten not only local populations but also the other countries on the African continent and beyond. Rwanda, for example, is a regional leader in technology and innovation, and a proof-of-concept hub. The country hosts the Centre for the Fourth Industrial Revolution,[16] a partnership with the World Economic Forum (WEF), to promote emerging technologies such as AI, ML, blockchain and the internet of things. Further, in a humanitarian context, the effective implementation of the right to health depends on policy choices, which impacts timely delivery of healthcare services.[17]

Since data is the raw material of digital health and of the economy, policy choices play a central role in building trust. Policy choices reveal the values of a nation in making trade-offs that are sometimes complex, for example between open data and data protection, low-cost equipment and security, innovation and the precaution principle or ethical use of data.

This reasonable balance will enable a sustainable development of digital healthcare, aligning the interests of all actors. Educated stakeholders give priority to qualitative tools both from a technical and an ethical perspective. This leads to more responsible technologies particularly facilitating

[13] Starlink website, www.starlink.com, accessed 14 March 2021.

[14] Ibid.

[15] Ibid.

[16] Klaus Schwab, *The Fourth Industrial Revolution* (Penguin Books 2016).

[17] The health sector has particularly benefited from adoption of new technology and innovation, for example, Telehealth with Babyl, and unmanned aerial vehicles/drone-delivery of blood products, as well as other essential medical products (with Zipline and Charis UAS).

the access and process of personalised health data in low/middle income countries.[18]

The World Health Assembly Resolution on digital health unanimously approved by WHO Member States in May 2018 recognised the value of digital technologies to contribute to advancing universal health coverage (UHC) and other health aims of the SDGs.[19] This resolution urged ministries of health 'to assess their use of digital technologies for health … and to prioritize, as appropriate, the development, evaluation, implementation, scale-up and greater use of digital technologies'.[20]

In practice, however, the pace of technology development does not fit with the pace of development of a regulatory framework. For example, the General Data Protection Regulation (GDPR) required six years of negotiations prior its implementation. The new EU Regulation proposal on AI as well as the Digital Services Act Proposal of the EU Commission will take at least two years to be implemented and to enter into force. There is a sense of urgency in tackling these problems as technology is already in the market and patient protection can't wait.

This was highlighted by Christine Fox at a TED conference: 'we have a toxic brew' where advanced technologies are 'available to anyone who wants to buy them with few if any constraints over their development and accessibility'.[21]

Therefore, we advocate specific standards as well as a sound regulatory[22] and ethical framework both allowing for the protection of patients' right to health and encouraging innovation to tackle this problem.[23] Such

18 Deborah Lupton, 'The Internet of Things: Social Dimensions' (2020) 14 *Sociology Compass*, https://onlinelibrary.wiley.com/doi/abs/10.1111/soc4.12770, accessed 14 March 2021; see also Deborah Lupton, 'Teaching and Learning Guide – The Internet of Things: Social Dimensions' (2020) 14 *Sociology Compass*, https://onlinelibrary.wiley.com/doi/10.1111/soc4.12777, accessed 14 March 2021.

19 WHO News Release, 'May 2018', www.who.int/news/item/25-05-2018-seventy-first-world-health-assembly-update-25-may, accessed 14 March 2021.

20 WHO guidelines, 'Recommendations on Digital Interventions for Health System Strengthening' (2018), www.who.int/reproductivehealth/publications/digital-interventions-health-system-strengthening/en/, accessed 14 March 2021.

21 Christine Fox, 'The Ethical Dilemma We Face on AI and Autonomous Tech' (New Rules, TEDxMidAtlantic Event, Washington DC, 21 October 2016).

22 Jess Whittlestone and others, 'The Role and Limits of Principles in AI Ethics: Towards a Focus on Tensions', *Proceedings of the 2019 AAAI/ACM Conference on AI, Ethics, and Society* (2019) 195–200.

23 White Paper for the ITU/WHO Focus Group on Artificial Intelligence for Health, Thomas Wiegand (Fraunhofer HHI, Germany), Naomi Lee (The Lancet, UK), Sameer Pujari (WHO), Manjula Singh (ICMR, India), Shan Xu (CAICT, China), Monique Kuglitsch

a framework can improve the legal certainty and reinforce the obligations regarding data protection and digital platforms used in clinical studies and operations. In order to contribute to this end-goal, the ITU/WHO Focus Group on artificial intelligence for health (FG-AI4H) was established by ITU-T Study Group at its meeting in Ljubljana, Slovenia, 9–20 July 2018. This group is committed to establish a standardised assessment framework for the evaluation of AI-based methods for health, diagnosis, triage or treatment decisions.[24] It will develop 'a basic framework for a standardised methodology of artificial intelligence for health, including generalized consideration on ethics, regulatory, requirement, data processing, model training, model evaluation, adoption and scale-up, etc. It will also develop use cases in specific domains with corresponding AI/ML tasks'.[25] This is an important initiative because any technical fault within an AI system can adversely affect people's health, privacy and consequently their entire lives. International standards are required for thoroughly validating AI solutions for health to build trust in AI solutions which are provably accurate, fair, effective and reliable.[26] It is also important to tackle the challenge of interoperability. Since AI systems are mainly designed and deployed by private companies, it is essential that businesses introduce these standards as part of a sound corporate social responsibility framework.

7.2.2 Corporate Social Responsibility and Transparency

Since businesses designing digital healthcare services and products[27] know the vulnerabilities and benefits of their products and services, the corporate social responsibility (CSR) model is an effective solution to mitigate the risks of these products and services and build trust and social acceptance for them. Indeed, before putting their products and services

(Fraunhofer HHI, Germany), Marc Lecoultre (MLLab.AI, Switzerland), Ana Riviere-Cinnamond (PAHO/WHO), Eva Weicken (Fraunhofer HHI, Germany), Markus Wenzel (Fraunhofer HHI, Germany), Alixandro Werneck Leite (University of Brasilia, Brazil), Simão Campos (ITU), and Bastiaan Quast (ITU), ITU.

24 ITU/WHO Focus Group on Digital Health, www.itu.int/en/ITU-T/focusgroups/ai4h/Pages/default.aspx, accessed 7 April 2021.

25 Ibid.

26 Ibid.

27 Kaira Sekiguchiand Koichi Hori, 'Organic and Dynamic Tool for Use with Knowledge Base of AI Ethics for Promoting Engineers' Practice of Ethical AI Design' 35(1) (2018) 51 *AI & SOCIETY*, https://doi.org/10.1007/s00146-018-0867-z, accessed 14 March 2021.

on the market, businesses should be capable of identifying whether security, privacy, ethical and safety standards are met. They particularly ensure that interactions between patients and AI systems used in the healthcare industry[28] should be clear, meaningful, realistic, and supply the required functionality.

To be effective, this model requires that these actors be motivated in promoting the values of AI social benefits and be willing to reduce risks of harm. As some actors won't have intrinsic motivation to act for good in the interest of all stakeholders, they might be motivated by a competitive advantage. This strategy can be incentivised by the brand or international reputation which will result in economic growth. This leadership role is formalised by internal codes of conduct and national AI strategy and should be controlled by supervisory authorities.

In the global effort to create a successful CSR program for AI technologies, the AI Transparency Institute developed standardised indices to assist businesses, research centres and laboratories to identify means of improvement. They enable patients to question companies, to get a scoring system and a radar chart.[29] This methodology is based on specific laws (GDPR, ISO Norms) and policies (EU HLEG Recommendations). This is a first step towards a dedicated audit.[30]

After an analysis of the data life cycle, data management, ML models and corporate governance, an AI certification on digital health can be delivered. Such a procedure would permit businesses designing AI technologies in digital health to have self-assessment tools provided for by an

[28] Knud Thomasen, 'Ethics for Artificial Intelligence, Ethics for All' (2019) 10(1) *Paladyn, Journal of Behavioral Robotics* 359–363, https://doi.org/10.1515/pjbr-2019-0029, accessed 14 March 2021.

[29] AI Transparency Institute, www.aitransparencyinstitute.com, accessed 14 March 2021.

[30] Roger Clarke, 'Principles and Business Processes for Responsible AI' (2019) 35(4) *Computer Law & Security Review* 410–22; see also Inioluwa Deborah Raji and others, 'Closing the AI Accountability Gap: Defining An End-to-End Framework for Internal Algorithmic Auditing' in *Proceedings of the 2020 Conference on Fairness, Accountability, and Transparency* (Association for Computing Machinery 2020); see also Petros Terzis, 'Onward for the Freedom of Others: Marching Beyond the AI Ethics' (in *Proceedings of the 2020 Conference on Fairness, Accountability, and Transparency* (Association for Computing Machinery 2020); Christian Sandvig and others, 'Auditing Algorithms: Research Methods for Detecting Discrimination on Internet Platforms' (Preconference 'Data and Discrimination: Converting Critical Concerns into Productive Inquiry' at the 64th Annual Conference of the International Communication Association, Seattle WA, 22 May 2014), http://social.cs.uiuc.edu/papers/pdfs/ICA2014-Sandvig.pdf, accessed 1 March 2022; Pedro Saleiro, 'Aequitas: A Bias and Fairness Audit Toolkit' (v2, 29 April 2019), https://arxiv.org/abs/1811.05577, accessed 1 March 2022.

independent body. This can also be valuable for hospitals willing to evaluate the quality of AI-based equipment prior to any purchase.

These exploratory steps towards evaluation standards for AI technologies and its organisations offer substantial potential for synergies, because many national regulatory institutions, public health institutes, physicians, patients, developers, health insurance companies, licensees, hospitals and other decision-makers around the globe can profit from a common, standardised benchmarking framework for AI and ML solutions for health. In order to establish a sound governance structure and policy, businesses could also set up a Centre of AI Excellence, capable of providing multidisciplinary expertise in data, ML models and ethics. These centres (like Red Teams)[31] could be assisted by independent organisations when it comes to assessing whether the AI trustworthiness and responsible AI standards are met from a multi-stakeholder perspective. Before the medical systems based on AI technologies are deployed on the market, such centres could identify the legal and ethical risks related to AI systems, particularly taking into account the risk of misuse, the risk of harm, unfairness, inaccuracy, lack of explainability and so forth. This way of anticipating problems would permit centres to:

- take necessary measures to mitigate the level of risk and decide whether to put its AI system into circulation;
- improve the quality of AI-based products and services, which in turn would lead to more social acceptance and new market share for businesses;
- contribute to (more) meaningful digital health solutions, particularly for vulnerable patients;
- present 'stress tests' for digital health products or services to test their security resilience;
- increase the chance to receive market approval from a supervisory authority (e.g., for medical devices).

Having said that, not all problems arising out of the use of AI systems can be anticipated by CSR principles. The protection of persons using digital health services or products requires safety standards and transparency in the information communicated to patients regarding the risks related to the use of AI systems. We also believe that the public should be informed

[31] David Levin, 'Lessons Learned in Using Live Red Teams in IA Experiments' (2003), in *Proceedings DARPA Information Survivability Conference and Exposition* 110–19.

about the normative features of a model (algorithmic transparency, also called 'design publicity') as a safety standard.[32]

Safety standards for AI-based medical devices are indeed keystones because of the risks for the patients: inaccuracy and data bias require external mechanisms to verify that the risks are not endangering people's lives. Information sharing on the functioning of AI systems and the use of data are at the core of a patient-centric perspective, since this can facilitate the exercise of the right to self-determination and mitigate the risk of discrimination.

In addition to the principle of transparency and fairness, accountability principles should become a pillar for ensuring that AI-based systems used in medicine as well as automated individual decisions can be legally challenged and that the parties in the chain of responsibility take all reasonable steps to avoid harm. Finally, the principle of explainability should ensure that all stakeholders impacted by an AI system can understand the logic involved in the reasoning of the system. We advocate transparent and accountable algorithms,[33] machine learning fairness principles and methodologies, and secure digital transaction systems.[34]

7.3 Towards an Ecosystem of Trust

7.3.1 New Actors, Approaches and Challenges

Several private actors are simultaneously involved in digital health applications. Cloud services providers, telecommunications companies, research laboratories in cryptography, privacy-enhancing technologies partnering with medical professionals and blockchain[35] companies not only enable financial and insurance services in healthcare but also provide digital infrastructure. Some equipment is designed directly for end-users, while others, like telemedicine services[36] (tele-radiology,

32 Michele Loi, Andrea Ferrario and Eleonora Viganò, Transparency As Design Publicity: Explaining and Justifying Inscrutable Algorithms' (2020) *Ethics and Information Technology* 1–11.

33 Joshua Kroll and others, 'Accountable Algorithms' (2017) 165(3) *University of Pennsylvania Law Review* 633.

34 Alex Pentland, 'Healthwear: Medical Technology Becomes Wearable' (2004) 37(5) *Computer* 42–49.

35 Xiao Yue and others, 'Healthcare Data Gateways: Found Healthcare Intelligence on Blockchain with Novel Privacy Risk Control' (2016) 40(10) *Journal of Medical Systems* 218.

36 Paul Webster, 'Virtual Health Care in the Era of COVID-19' (2020) 395(10231) *The Lancet* 1180–81.

tele-consultation, tele-nursing and tele-surgery), are delivered to clinics and hospitals. Particularly microrobots that can be used in surgery reduce the side effects of pharmaceuticals and avoid unnecessary interventions.[37] Platform companies enable online appointments for patients with the right doctor to suit their specific needs. They can also offer scoring systems related to the quality of the service that help patients to make an informed decision. Smartphone providers facilitate access to mobile health applications[38] which, via a real-time monitoring of patient behaviour,[39] permit a tailor-made treatment specific to the personal context. In addition to digital clinics,[40] online-only pharmacies and physical pharmacies with an online presence are also becoming part of the data-driven preventive systems.[41]

The digitisation of patient health records[42] should also be mentioned here, as such activities carried out by service providers are gaining more and more acceptance. On the one hand, improving access to relevant information (via federated learning), digitisation of clinical and genomic information provides great opportunities for reducing the risks of medical errors and improving targeted therapies as well as preventive medicine. On the other hand, digital management of health records raises security concerns and new challenges related to privacy. Indeed, such an activity enables any doctor to access the medical history of the patient, even if they haven't met before. Blockchain technologies offer an interesting

[37] David J Cappelleri, Chenghao Bi and Maria Guix, 'Tumbling Microrobots for Future Medicine: Robots Smaller Than a Grain of Sand Could Move Through the Body by Tumbling End Over End, Opening Up the Possibility of Intriguing Biomedical Applications' (2018) 106(4) *American Scientist* 210–14.

[38] Anja Thieme and Danielle Belgrave, 'Data-Driven Insights for More Effective, Personalized Care in Online Mental Health Interventions' (*Microsoft Research Blog*, 24 March 2020); Prerna Chikersal and others, 'Understanding Client Support Strategies to Improve Clinical Outcomes in an Online Mental Health Intervention' (2020) *Proceedings of the 2020 CHI Conference on Human Factors in Computing Systems* 1–16; see also John Torous and others, 'Creating a Digital Health Smartphone App and Digital Phenotyping Platform for Mental Health and Diverse Healthcare Needs: An Interdisciplinary and Collaborative Approach' (2019) 4(2) *Journal of Technology in Behavioral Science* 73–85.

[39] Dimiter V Dimitrov, 'Medical Internet of Things and Big Data in Healthcare' (2016) 22(3) *Healthcare Informatics Research* 156.

[40] Daniel SW Ting and others, 'Artificial Intelligence, the Internet of Things, and Virtual Clinics: Ophthalmology at the Digital Translation Forefront' (2020) 2(1) *The Lancet Digital Health* e8–e9.

[41] Luís Velez Lapao and others, 'Implementing an Online Pharmaceutical Service Using Design Science Research' (2017) 17(1) *BMC Medical Informatics and Decision Making* 1–14.

[42] Alex Roehrs and others, 'Personal Health Records: A Systematic Literature Review' (2017) 19(1) *Journal of Medical Internet Research* e13.

architecture to tackle this issues,[43] though they also create new challenges,[44] like the energy consumption, the right to be forgotten, mining incentives, mining attacks and key management.

Medical data protection is, therefore, a central concern, and such data needs elevated protection. In the next section, we first focus on the key benefits of the integration of digital technologies such as mobile applications, AI-based diagnosis and surgery robotics as well as on the advantages of other digital solutions used particularly for telemedicine services.

7.3.2 Key Benefits of a Data-Driven Preventive System

7.3.2.1 Improving Efficiency

AI systems have the potential to improve public health policy in enabling state-level real-time surveillance of diseases like COVID-19 or influenza.[45] Thus, a benefit of such technology is that it makes it possible to assist public health regulators in enabling a geographic visualisation of virus transmission. In addition, AI allows scientists to better understand the infection and its modes of transmission as well as virus mutations.[46] It helps to identify gene variants associated with the disease of interest. However, the scope of application of AI technologies is not limited to the efficient management of pandemic crises.

The pandemic revealed the limitations of a face-to-face model of healthcare. Data-driven systems have filled the gap during lockdown and greatly improved human resources allocation, avoiding unnecessary

43 Peng Zhang and others, 'Blockchain Technology Use Cases in Healthcare' in Raj P and Delka GC (eds) *Advances in Computers*, vol. 111: *Blockchain Technology: Platforms, Tools and Use Cases* (Academic Press 2018) 1–41; see also Yue and others, 'Healthcare Data Gateways; Guy Zyskind, Oz Nathan and Alex Pentland 'Enigma: Decentralized Computation Platform with Guaranteed Privacy (2015) arXiv preprint arXiv:1506.03471.

44 Thomas McGhin and others, 'Blockchain in Healthcare Applications: Research Challenges and Opportunities' (2019) 135 *Journal of Network and Computer Applications* 62–75.

45 Jennifer M Radin and others, 'Harnessing Wearable Device Data to Improve State-Level Real-Time Surveillance of Influenza-Like Illness in the USA: A Population-Based Study' (16 January 2020), https://doi.org/10.1016/S2589-7500(19)30222-5, accessed 16 March 2021.

46 Yurim Park and others, 'Emergence of New Disease: How Can Artificial Intelligence Help?' (2020) 26(7) *Trends in Molecular Medicine* 627–29; see also Mostafa A Salama, Aboul Ella Hassanien and Ahmad Mostafa, 'The Prediction of Virus Mutation Using Neural Networks and Rough Set Techniques' (2016) 2016(1) *EURASIP Journal on Bioinformatics and Systems Biology* 1–11; Aya Sedky Adly, Afnan Sedky Adly and Mahmoud Sedky Adly, 'Approaches Based on Artificial Intelligence and the Internet of Intelligent Things to Prevent the Spread of COVID-19 Scoping Review' (2020) 22(8) *Journal of Medical Internet Research* e19104.

surcharge of hospitals and providing new remote service options that have contributed to efficiency gains.[47] New AI-based technologies incrementally assist medical doctors in the diagnosis of diseases[48] while saving time for the interaction with the patient. AI systems are capable of revealing currently unknown patterns in disease, treatment and care. Moreover, AI brings agility and a better service to patients; those located in an isolated place, with limited healthcare infrastructure available, can be remotely informed about their health with a mobile application or device and act accordingly without need for new appointments with medical professionals. When it comes to chronic diseases like diabetes,[49] personalised and timely data collection fosters decision-making processes in medical diagnosis as well as treatment and enables hospitals and medical professionals to treat priority patients who present with high risk for their health conditions. Finally, AI systems enable remote assistance for surgical procedures in real time, providing better accessibility of healthcare for remote populations.[50]

Digital health can empower patients with a device that will assist them in answering their questions, constantly monitoring[51] their health status and receiving personalised treatment. Deep learning plays a crucial role in this context. Indeed, it outperforms classical techniques in natural language processing, image, speech and motion recognition.[52] The benefits of deep learning are noticeable particularly in medical image processing when it comes to the diagnostics of skin cancer as well as diabetic retinopathy, glaucoma, age-related macular degeneration and cataract in ophthalmology.[53]

[47] Phillipp Pointer, 'The Rise of Telemedicine: How to Mitigate Potential Fraud' (2020) 2020(6) *Computer Fraud & Security* 6–8.

[48] Giovanni Briganti and Olivier Le Moine, 'Artificial Intelligence in Medicine: Today and Tomorrow' (2020) 7 *Frontiers in Medicine* 27.

[49] José Tomás Arenas-Cavalli and others, 'Clinical Validation of an Artificial Intelligence-Based Diabetic Retinopathy Screening Tool for a National Health System' (2022) 36 (1) *Eye* 78; see also Kelvin Tsoi and others, 'Applications of Artificial Intelligence for Hypertension Management' (2021) 23 (3), *The Journal of Clinical Hypertension*; Kristina F Simacek and others, 'Patient Engagement in Type 2 Diabetes Mellitus Research: What Patients Want' (2018) 12 *Patient Preference and Adherence* 595.

[50] Jacques Marescaux and others, 'Transatlantic Robot-Assisted Telesurgery' (2001) 413(6854) *Nature* 379–80.

[51] Michael Sung, Carl Marci and Alex Pentland, 'Wearable Feedback Systems for Rehabilitation' (2005) 2(1) *Journal of Neuroengineering and Rehabilitation* 1–12.

[52] Yann LeCun, Yoshua Bengio and Geoffrey Hinton, 'Deep Learning' (2005) 521 *Nature* 436–44.

[53] Daniel SW Ting and others, 'Deep Learning in Ophthalmology: The Technical and Clinical Considerations' (2019) 72 *Progress in Retinal and Eye Research* 100759

In order to achieve true progress in digital healthcare, the new data-driven technologies should foster positive and meaningful interactions with the users in order to improve their quality of life and contribute to a flourishing life.[54]

7.3.2.2 Personalised Contents and Services

One of the benefits of AI is that it enables the emergence of personalised health and precision medicine. Personalised health can be defined as the 'ability to provide contents and services tailored to individuals based on knowledge about their needs, expectations, preferences, constraints and behaviours'.[55] Precision medicine encompasses a broad remit, including genomics, epigenetics, gene editing technologies[56] and the development of targeted therapies.[57]

Data-driven personalised preventive care and therapy requires the analysis of large health data sets with genetic profiles and disease status, as well as medical imaging data in order to develop ML algorithms. These methods can detect disease-associated patient features in large-scale data sets, with potentially millions of features for many patients. Machine learning methods have the potential to increase the understanding of the factors involved in diseases and to facilitate phenotype predictions, in particular disease risks, from their features. Machine learning can also facilitate health data mining and modelling for improved medical decision support. The associated methods can analyse, model and predict the disease progression and therapy potential for each individual. Improving efficiency must be combined with quality.

Building trust in large-scale healthcare analytics is key for the safe and beneficial use of precision medicine.

54 SM Skevington, M Lotfy and K O'Connell, 'The World Health Organization's WHOQOL-BREF Quality of Life Assessment: Psychometric Properties and Results of the International Field Trial. A Report from the WHOQOL Group' (2004) 13 (2), *Quality of Life Research* 299–310, https://doi.org/10.1023/B:QURE.0000018486.91360.00, accessed 18 March 2021; see also Deborah Lupton, 'A More-Than-Human Approach to Bioethics: The Example of Digital Health' (2020) 34(9) *Bioethics* 969–76.

55 Thibaut Vallee and others, 'On Personalization in IoT' (2016) 2016 International Conference on Computational Science and Computational Intelligence (CSCI), IEEE 186–91.

56 Gavin J Knott and Jennifer A Doudna, 'CRISPR-Cas Guides the Future of Genetic Engineering' (2018) 361(6405) *Science* 866–69.

57 For instance, the companies 23andMe and AncestryDNA# propose precision medicine services.

This is especially important due to the advances in genome sequencing and the associated field of genomics which promise to offer a better understanding of how diseases affect different individuals, leading to better predictions and treatments. Genomic testing promises to enable personalised treatment, especially in rare diseases or in cancer patients, promising improved outcomes and fewer side effects. The visualisation of a unique set of genetic information, set of mutations and genetic alterations facilitates the identification of the genes that are important and the targeting of them directly to develop new treatments, tailored to patient needs.[58] With the genetic profile of a person's disease, and knowledge of his or her response to treatment, it is indeed possible to find out more about the likely effectiveness of medical interventions such as prescribing drugs to treat a disease (pharmacogenomics).

However, gene-driven medicine should also take into consideration the research on epigenetics, which studies the impact of way of life, quality of food and stress level on gene expression. Joel de Rosnay's research is a must in this field,[59] as well as the activities of the Association for Responsible Research and Innovation in Genome Editing (ARRIGE) association.

In some countries like Denmark, Sweden, Finland, Austria, the United Kingdom, Switzerland and Spain, the nationwide implementation of digital health is strongly promoted by the government.

Genetic disease can be viewed as a potential resource of economic opportunity for biotechnology companies through privatised funding for research practices and the patenting of inventions like diagnostic testing methods and sequencing machines. Furthermore, bodily processes generate economic value through data analytics.

In order to be true progress for the common good, investment in digital health should also be made in education to raise the level of awareness of the challenges. Education has a central role to play in enriching the academic curriculum of computer scientists in both humanities and computational biology including healthcare. Humanities would improve the understanding of the societal, legal and ethical challenges raised by this silent transformation in healthcare. Data science could also become a part

[58] J Fellay, 'Le Champ des Possibles: Recherche Translationnelle et Médecine de Précision' (La Rencontre entre la Science et le Droit dans le Numérique 2. Les Défis Juridiques de l'Intelligence Artificielle: Regards Croisés entre Santé et Justice, Lausanne, 13 February 2020).

[59] V Urman and others, *La révolution épigénétique* (Albin Michel 2019).

of the curriculum of lawyers and ethicists as a compulsory requirement. This would create bridges as well as a better understanding among future professionals.

From the point of view of patients, on the one hand, digital health enables the rise of 'technology of the self'[60] 'via personalised dashboards and mobile applications, increasing the users' understanding of their own genes and the impact of the way of life on health'.[61] On the other hand, it also raise the question of the use of health data, privacy, security and governance mechanisms around those data-driven services to build trust in associated business models and social acceptance of digital health innovations and balance the interests of all stakeholders.[62]

7.3.3 *Key AI Challenges to Build an Ecosystem of Trust*

How to build an AI ecosystem of trust? An ecosystem that is both robust from a technical perspective while taking into account its social environment? How to build an AI ecosystem that is also lawful, that is, that respects all applicable laws and regulations, and ethical, that is, that respects ethical principles and values? AI-based systems in healthcare should indeed comply with the rights set out by the European Convention on Human Rights (ECHR), its Protocols and the European Social Charter (ESC). Trustworthiness of AI systems should be met throughout the system's entire life cycle, paying specific attention to these three elements: robustness, lawfulness and ethics.

7.3.3.1 From a Technical Standpoint

Despite all the advantages presented earlier for both patients and professionals, AI systems in healthcare present several technical challenges. The first risk deals with the robustness of AI systems in digital healthcare: they should be technically robust and reproducible, and able to deal with and inform users about possible failures, inaccuracies and errors, proportionate to the assessed risk posed by the AI-based system or technique. To be reproducible, data sets should be made public, which raises the questions

60 Deborah Lupton, 'Data Mattering and Self-Tracking: What Can Personal Data Do?' (2020) 34(1) *Continuum* 1–13.

61 Cinnamon S Bloss and others, 'Direct-to-Consumer Personalized Genomic Testing' (2011) 20(R2) *Human Molecular Genetics* R132–41.

62 Deborah Lupton, 'Thinking with Care about Personal Data Profiling: A More-Than-Human Approach' (2020) 14 *International Journal of Communication* 3165–83, https://ijoc.org/index.php/ijoc/article/view/13540, accessed 19 March 2021.

of the robustness of anonymisation techniques. Moreover, an AI system should be able to provide a suitable explanation of its decision-making process (whenever an AI-based system can have a significant impact on people's lives). AI systems should also be socially robust, in that they duly consider the context and environment in which they operate, that is, the sensitivity of the data used and the vulnerability of patients.

The second risk deals with the accuracy rate of AI systems and its consequences for the patient. This accuracy is measured in drawing a comparison between the performance of AI systems and that of medical professionals. An AI system should be reliable and function as intended.

Here are some examples illustrating the problem:

- A model diagnoses childhood diseases with 90 per cent accuracy, recognising symptoms more accurately than many human doctors, resulting in redundancies amongst junior medical doctors. Ten per cent of the children are not diagnosed correctly.
- A model predicts the probability with 80 per cent accuracy of the mortality of a smoker, within six months, based on X-ray images (image classification). However, the patient loses his job because the employer was informed of this probability.
- A model calculates the dosage of wireless infusion pumps with 95 per cent accuracy but resulting in the death of the patient in the 5 per cent of cases when it is poorly dosed. Healthcare providers rely on network-connected devices, such as wireless infusion pumps, to treat patients more safely and efficiently. This last case raises ethical and legal concerns because the poor quality of the model can expose the patients to significant risk. In addition, this network of wireless devices increases cybersecurity vulnerabilities.[63]

An independent external validation of AI models ought to be deemed essential before deployment can even be considered. It would not be appropriate to fully rely on decisions taken by an AI-based system, since these decisions are based on statistical probabilities. This is confirmed by a research project led by Regina Barzilay, a computer scientist at the Massachusetts Institute of Technology (MIT). She carried out research[64]

[63] NIST and NCCoE, Guide NIST Cybersecurity Practice Guide, 'Securing Wireless Infusion Pumps in Healthcare Delivery' (2018), NIST SP 1800-8.

[64] A Yala and others, A Deep Learning Mammography-Based Model for Improved Breast Cancer Risk Prediction (July 2019) 292(1) *Radiology* 60–66, http://doi.org/10.1148/radiol.2019182716.

on machine learning model accuracy in the context of analysing a person's risk of developing breast cancer. She collected almost 89,000 mammograms from nearly 40,000 women who had been screened over a four-year period and checked the images against a national tumour registry to determine which women were eventually diagnosed with breast cancer. She then trained a machine-learning algorithm with a subset of those images and outcomes, before testing the system to see how well it predicted cancer risk. The computer put 31 per cent of the women who eventually developed breast cancer into the highest risk group. But the standard Tyrer–Cuzick model that physicians use to estimate risk placed only 18 per cent in that group.[65] How to improve the system accuracy? With more training data and improved algorithms. It is also important to validate the medical AI system against populations other than the ones they were trained on; a system that seems to work on tests on a particular population might fail when applied to a different group of people.[66]

Article 22(1) of the GDPR states that 'the data subject shall have the right not to be subject to a decision based solely on automated processing, including profiling, which produces legal effects concerning him or her or similarly significantly affects him or her'.

'The data controller shall implement suitable measures to safeguard the data subject's rights and freedoms and legitimate interests, at least the right to obtain human intervention on the part of the controller, to express his or her point of view and to contest the decision' (Art. 22(3) GDPR).

Accordingly, in practice, any recommendation made by an AI system should be critically assessed by a professional.

The third risk deals with the robustness to cyberattacks.[67] Digital health technologies and healthcare institutions are increasingly digitalised and connected but often unprotected and therefore particularly vulnerable to cyberattacks, cybercrime, cybersabotage and cyberterrorism, leading to patient harm and data misuse. The COVID-19 pandemic in 2020 demonstrated the dangers of such attacks. Hospitals around the world were victims of ransomware attacks, locking their networks and

[65] Neil Savage, 'How AI Is Improving Cancer Diagnostics' (2020) *Nature Outlook*, https://doi.org/10.1038/d41586-020-00847-2, accessed 1 March 2022

[66] Ibid.

[67] Daniel Minoli, Kazem Sohraby and Jacob Kouns, 'IoT Security (IoTSec) Considerations, Requirements, and Architectures' (2017), 14th IEEE Annual Consumer Communications & Networking Conference (CCNC), IEEE 1006-7.

endangering the lives of patients until they agreed to pay a ransom to the criminals. The World Economic Forum Global Risks Report 2021 reported that 'cybersecurity failure' is the fourth largest danger facing the world, behind infectious diseases, livelihood crises and extreme weather events.

For instance, ANSSI reported that during the pandemic in France, twenty-seven hospitals were attacked in 2020, and one hospital per week since 2021. The number of attacks was multiplied by four between 2019 and 2020. On 9 February 2021, Dax Hospital[68] was the victim of a security threat. RYUK ransomware encrypted the full network of the hospital in fifteen seconds, blocking all machines and requesting a ransom to get data access back. This endangers human life because an increasing number of patients are receiving healthcare via digital equipment, in particular in intensive care and reanimation units. In this scenario, isolating the machines being blocked by ransomware is a priority to prevent the spread of the attack to the rest of the network and to its external partners. Paying the ransom doesn't guarantee that the hospital will get the network in the same state as before the attack, nor is it a guarantee that the network won't be attacked by another group after the attack. Paying a ransom is also a way to support the ransomware market and to promote further cyberattacks. However, this is sometimes a reasonable choice; for example, if a hospital loses USD 1 million per day, a ransom of EUR 500,000 may be perceived as reasonable.

We advocate federative learning to protect privacy and security. Privacy and ownership of data became very salient in digital health, and decentralised systems for privacy-conscious statistical analysis on distributed datasets like Drynx[69] offer a promising solution to ensure data confidentiality and the privacy of the data providers using homomorphic encryption,[70] zero-knowledge proofs of correctness and differential privacy. In the specific context of contact tracing, a decentralised approach better protects the personal sphere of citizens and affords multiple benefits: it allows for detailed information gathering for infected people in a privacy-preserving fashion, and this in turn enables both contact tracing and the early

[68] ANSSI, Dossier de presse, 'Cybersécurité, faire face à la menace: la stratégie française' (18 February 2021), www.ssi.gouv.fr/, accessed 1 March 2021.

[69] Christian Mouchet and others, 'Multiparty Homomorphic Encryption from Ring-Learning-With-Errors' (2020) Report 2020/304, Cryptology ePrint Archive, https://eprint.iacr.org/2020/304, accessed 1 March 2021

[70] Ibid.

detection of outbreak hotspots on a more finely granulated geographic scale.[71] The decentralised approach is also scalable to large populations, in that only the data of positive patients need be handled at a central level.[72]

7.3.3.2 From a Legal and Ethical Standpoint

Digital health technologies must be lawful[73] and aligned with moral values.[74]

7.3.3.2.1 Legal Challenges The Council of Europe published its Feasibility Study[75] in December 2020. This document evaluates the project of an international Convention on Artificial Intelligence as a legally binding instrument. In this study, AI systems are qualified as 'socio-technical systems', in the sense that the impact of an AI system – whatever its underlying technology – 'depends not only on the system's design, but also on the way in which the system is developed and used within a broader environment, including the data used, its intended purpose, functionality and accuracy, the scale of deployment, and the broader organisational, societal and legal context in which it is used'.[76] The Council of Europe further underlines the role of the values and behaviour of the human beings that develop and deploy AI systems, which requires ensuring human responsibility.[77]

In Europe, the ECHR and its interpretation by the Court are also of central importance in the discussion on digital health. Article 8 of the Convention has assumed particular prominence in the Court's case law on 'the right to health'. The Court has interpreted the notion of private life as covering the right to the protection of one's physical, moral and psychological integrity, as well as the right to choose or to exercise one's personal autonomy. Respecting the autonomy of others requires a few requirements to be met:

71 Mirco Nanni and others, 'Give More Data, Awareness and Control to Individual Citizens, and They Will Help COVID-19 Containment' (2021) *Ethics and Information Technology*, https://doi.org/10.1007/s10676-020-09572-w, accessed 19 March 2021.

72 Ibid.

73 European Commission's High Level Expert Group on Artificial Intelligence, 'Ethics Guidelines for Trustworthy AI' (8 April 2019) 5.

74 Iyad Rahwan, 'Society-in-the-Loop: Programming the Algorithmic Social Contract' (2018) 20(1) *Ethics and Information Technology* 5–14.

75 Council of Europe, Ad Hoc Committee on Artificial Intelligence (CAHAI) (17 December 2020), Feasibility Study, CAHAI (2020) 23, 1–56.

76 Ibid., 12.

77 Ibid.

- all the information necessary for an informed decision must be given;
- it is verified that this information has been understood;
- it is verified that the sick person is capable of making a decision;
- the decision taken is consistent with the previous conditions.[78]

The Council of Europe reiterates the importance of AI systems complying with the ECHR, its Protocols and the ESC. In particular, AI systems should respect the right to liberty and security (Art. 5, 6 ECHR) and the right to privacy of Art. 8 ECHR, that is, a person's privacy, a person's physical, psychological and moral integrity, and a person's identity and autonomy.[79]

This applies to invasive AI applications (tracking the faces with facial recognition, collecting biometrical data such as heart rate, temperature data) or to AI systems used to assess, predict and influence patient behaviours in a healthcare context. The Council of Europe puts the stress on the prohibition of discrimination and right of equal treatment (Art. 12 ECHR and Protocol 12), which could be endangered due to AI systems. Regarding social and economic rights, the Council of Europe refers to Articles 11 and 13 of the ESC, highlighting the risk that automated decisions 'regarding the provision of healthcare and medical assistances, can impact the rights enshrined in the Charter, which respectively state that everyone has the right to benefit from measures that enable the enjoyment of the highest possible standard of health attainable, and that anyone without adequate resources has the right to social and medical assistance'. The use of AI to access to healthcare services by analysing patients' personal data (healthcare records, lifestyle data, etc.) raises some concerns regarding the right to privacy and personal data protection, but also with all the social rights laid down in the ESC.

This study is complementary to the public consultation results received by the EU regarding the White Paper on AI (2020), which also identified legal concerns related to AI: breach of fundamental rights (like privacy), discriminatory outcomes, safety, lack of explainability and accuracy, and difficult reparation in the event of damage.

The context of healthcare is very specific. Behind the legal basis of data processing, what is at stake is finding the right balance between privacy and open data for social and economic benefit. Public policy plays a key role in

[78] JD Roy and others, *La Bioéthique, ses fondements et ses controverses* (Renouveau pédagogique 1995).

[79] Ibid.

shaping an effective data protection framework while building incentives to encourage open data and data sharing in specific circumstances. The public health response to COVID-19 highlighted this dilemma between data protection and data sharing. The serious lack of consensus on privacy protecting proximity tracing using digital apps resulted in a trust deficit between users on the one hand and governments and/or private companies on the other, leading and to low adoption rates in the EU.[80]

The GDPR increases the obligations on data controllers and data processors in the EU. In particular, a privacy policy shall be put in place and wording used must be in clear and plain language adapted to the concerned person. The more identifiable the data or the higher the risk, the greater the control needed by the data controller and data processors. For fully aggregated anonymised data, with absolutely no potential of re-identifying,[81] the same level of control is not necessary. This is indeed essential for putting the data in the public domain.[82]

Particularly as far as the genome is concerned, as Jean Louis Raisaro has pointed out:

> (i) the genome can be used to re-identify individuals, (ii) it can reveal information about their genetic diseases such as cystic fibrosis, and their predispositions to severe medical conditions such as Alzheimer's, cancer, or schizophrenia, (iii) it contains information about ancestors, siblings, and progeny, and sharing it could unveil telling insights into a whole family's health issues (possibly against the family's will), (iv) the genome does not (almost) change over time, hence revoking or replacing it (as with other forms of identification) is impossible, and (vi) it is already being used both in law enforcement and healthcare, thus prompting also numerous ethical issues.[83]

For high-risk data processing, a data protection impact assessment shall be carried out prior to data processing. Furthermore, the data controller must be able to document that the data processing took place in a lawful, fair and transparent manner, while minimising data collection. Data

[80] Alejandro de la Garza, 'Contact Tracing Apps Were Big Tech's Best Idea for Fighting COVID-19. Why Haven't They Helped?' *Time*, 10 November 2020.

[81] L Rocher, JM Hendrickx and YA de Montjoye, 'Estimating the Success of Re-identifications in Incomplete Datasets Using Generative Models' (2019) 10(1) *Nature Communications* 3069.

[82] The United Kingdom published a specific statement in 2019 to guide approaches to Public Involvement and Engagement with Data-Intensive Health Research.

[83] Jean Louis Raisaro, 'Privacy-Enhancing Technologies for Medical and Genomic Data: From Theory to Practice' (PhD thesis, École Polytechnique Fédérale de Lausanne 2018).

controllers must be able to document the purpose limitation, the data accuracy, the storage limitation, and the respect of the integrity and confidentiality of the data processed.

The GDPR requires specific technical and organisational measures to be implemented by data controllers and data processors. Only a control a posteriori is put in place. In order to mitigate the risks of abuse, a right of contestation shall be effectively implemented in national law.

The obligation to inform the patients regarding the use of personal data and the finalities of the data processing aim at bringing control back to the user over his/her personal data. In practice, however, the patients are more concerned by their health and are not often aware of the risk of misuse. They can also consider that sharing the data will enhance medical research, which can benefit other patients, which is also true.

The regulation of biobanks, in particular the question of informed consent, should command more attention. Some projects are based on biobanks and aim at proposing personalised diagnosis and treatment, which means that an identification of the person is foreseen. Inferences play a central role in this outcome.

The data controller remains responsible if anonymised data can be re-identified. He/she must provide safeguards that anonymised data cannot be re-identified. The GDPR takes the position that all pseudonymised data is considered personal data, regardless of whether it is, or ever will be, in the hands of a person who holds the key needed for re-identification.

7.3.3.2.2 Ethical Challenges Since 2016, more than eighty AI ethics documents – including codes, principles, frameworks and policy strategies – have been produced by corporations, governments and non-governmental organisations (NGOs).[84] However, the ethical aspects regarding the use of sensitive data and AI in the healthcare context are already well studied in the literature. While Mittelstaadt highlight the risk of stigmatisation,[85] Horvitz and Mulligan[86] assess the risk of inference of sensitive information from data

[84] Daniel Schiff and others, 'What's Next for AI Ethics, Policy, and Governance? A Global Overview' in *Proceedings of the AAAI/ACM Conference on AI, Ethics, and Society* (2020) 153–58.

[85] Brent Mittelstaadt and others, 'Principles Alone Cannot Guarantee Ethical AI' (2019) 1(11) *Nature Machine Intelligence* 501–07; see also Brent Mittelstaadt and others, 'The Ethics of Algorithms: Mapping the Debate' (2016) 3(2) *Big Data & Society* 2053951716679679.

[86] Eric Horvitz and Deirdre Mulligan, 'Data, Privacy, and the Greater Good' (2015) 349 (6245) *Science* 253–55.

sets, and Vayena[87] puts the stress on the ethical risks of digital disease detection and the aspects of fairness.[88]

The real-time monitoring of the health status of a patient via a connected device can indeed violate the right to privacy of the patient[89] and reduce his/her autonomy. However, depending on the case and on the context, the real-time monitoring of one's health status can also be perceived as an increase of autonomy. This can be the case if a patient is spared a medical service delivered by a hospital or a medical doctor and can stay at home while medical parameters are safely monitored. Safeguards are essential due to the rise of wearable,[90] symbiotic and ubiquitous technologies[91], which should be reconciled with the right to patient autonomy.

In its feasibility study published in December 2020, the working group on AI from the Council of Europe raises a concern regarding the concept of 'autonomy': how to respect the right to autonomy while at the same time ensuring a quality service that is safe and requires regular or real-time health status monitoring or even an invasive treatment like an intervention. The literature also addresses these concerns in an extensive way.[92]

Another issue is the delegation of responsibility.[93] Connected devices can indeed assist the patient or his/her family taking care of him/her. Who will supervise the treatment of the patient and provide him/her with information about it while answering his/her questions? Interface design will play a key role in sharing information with the patient and interacting with him/her. Research in human–computer interaction is becoming a crucial aspect of social acceptance of digital health technologies.

[87] Effy Vayena and others, 'Ethical Challenges of Big Data in Public Health' (2015) 11(2) *PLoS Computational Biology* e1003904.

[88] Effy Vayena and others, 'Digital Health: Meeting the Ethical and Policy Challenges' (2018) 148 *Swiss Medical Weekly* w14571; see also Camille Nebeker, John Torous and Rebecca J. Bartlett Ellis, 'Building the Case for Actionable Ethics in Digital Health Research Supported by Artificial Intelligence' (2019) 17(1) *BMC Medicine* 1–7.

[89] Horvitz and Mulligan, 'Data, Privacy, and the Greater Good', 253–55; see also Jianying Hu, Adam Perer and Fei Wang, 'Data Driven Analytics for Personalized Healthcare', in Weaver CA and others (eds), *Healthcare Information Management Systems* (Springer 2016) 529–54.

[90] Pentland, 'Healthwear'.

[91] Mark Weiser, 'The Computer for the 21st Century' (July 1999) 3(3) *SIGMOBILE Mobile Computing and Communications Review* 3–11, https://doi.org/10.1145/329124.329127, accessed 7 April 2021; see also Mark Weiser, 'Some Computer Science Issues in Ubiquitous Computing' (July 1999) 3(3) *SIGMOBILE Mobile Computing and Communications Review* 12, https://doi.org/10.1145/329124.329127, accessed 7 April 2021.

[92] Colleen R Bennett and others, 'Visitors and Resident Autonomy: Spoken and Unspoken Rules in Assisted Living' (2017) 57(2) *The Gerontologist* 252–60.

[93] Luciano Floridi and Andrew Strait, 'Ethical Foresight Analysis: What It Is and Why It Is Needed?' (2020), 30(1) *Minds and Machines* 77.

The ethical use of digital health technologies requires ensuring that people are aware they are interacting with an AI system and are informed about its abilities, limitations, risks and benefits. Furthermore, the use of AI in healthcare should not limit the human rights and freedoms of patients. For instance, AI should not be designed in a way that may lead to objectification, dehumanisation, subordination, discrimination, stereotyping, coercion, manipulation of people or creation of attachment or addiction by design. AI designers have the positive responsibility to design AI systems in a way to avoid bias in both input data and algorithm design. They should also anticipate the potential impact of the AI system on the individual, society or the environment. Digital health technologies should contribute to the wellbeing and safety of the patients. It should be developed in a way that enables human oversight, traceability and auditability.

This becomes all the more complex with public–private partnerships.

7.3.3.2.3 Public–Private Partnership Challenges Public–private partnerships are a central concern in digital health. Patient data is indeed increasingly collected by proprietary software owned by private organisations.

The appointment of Palantir to manage NHS Health data in the UK raises specific concerns. Palantir Technologies is a public listed company initially funded by the CIA's venture capital fund (In-Q-Tel). Data collection by Palantir results in the privatisation of data assets by a security firm into the health service. This raises the question of the legal safeguards the legislator has to put in place to bring legal certainty and the security of the personal data that is processed and prevent the risk of misuse and harm for British patients.

Palantir Technologies develops software designed to analyse data from thousands of different sources. It does not publish its codes and is subject to the Cloud Act.

Its service in the COVID-19 context entails monitoring the epidemic and predicting scenarios for exiting containment. It remains unclear whether patient data is being used to train other products provided by the company. Palantir is carrying out a modelling of behaviour based on mobile data via a dedicated platform, namely Foundry. It compiles big data and uses it to make decisions. It makes these available to health authorities for crisis management.

This platform will receive data from Google, Facebook, Microsoft, Facebook, McKinsey & Company, the Gates Foundation, the University of Cambridge and Swiss Re in the context of the Trinity Challenge.[94] This

[94] The Trinity Challenge, https://thetrinitychallenge.org, accessed 20 March 2021.

platform 'provides the basis for new modelling, ground-breaking analyses and actionable solutions'.[95] It also raises concerns about future use of the data and its security. How to make sure that these measures do not outlive the pandemic when the state of emergency is over? Which legal safeguards are in place?

The GDPR, in its Art. 36, states that 'Member States *may* require controllers to consult with, and *obtain prior authorisation from*, the supervisory authority in relation to processing by a controller for the performance of a task carried out by the controller in the public interest, including processing in relation to social protection and public health'.

It appears consistent to engage independent supervisory authorities in a constructive dialogue in this context.

7.4 Accountability

7.4.1 A Sustainable Governance Framework

Building an ecosystem of trust for AI technologies and data use is becoming a priority at an international level. This requires embedding key values into the design of digital health technologies and auditing the system *ex ante* or *ex post* to make sure that these values are effectively implemented. As digital health includes many technologies, there is no consensus on the most appropriate governance.[96] Several options exist, including corporate self-regulation or collective industry regulation.[97] It is often argued that premature regulation would stifle innovation and competitiveness[98] and that governments lack the flexibility or understanding to regulate effectively. Others believe that sector-specific laws or general AI regulation should be pursued.[99] What is a stake is patient safety, security and privacy. We propose an overview of the initiatives on AI governance at global scale.[100]

[95] 'Swiss Re and Palantir Technologies Put Pioneering Data and Analytics Platform at the Service of Global Health and Joins The Trinity Challenge' (*The Trinity Challenge*, 28 October 2020, updated 3 June 2021), https://thetrinitychallenge.org/news-and-stories/swiss-re-and-palantir-technologies-join-the-trinity-challenge/, accessed 7 March 2022.

[96] James Butcheret Irakli Beridze, 'What Is the State of Artificial Intelligence Governance Globally?' (2019) 164(5–6) *The RUSI Journal* 88–96; see also Margarita Robles Carrillo, 'Artificial Intelligence: From Ethics to Law' (2020) 44(6) *Telecommunications Policy* 101937; Corinne Cath, 'Governing Artificial Intelligence: Ethical, Legal and Technical Opportunities and Challenges' (2018) 44(6) *Telecommunications Policy* 101937.

[97] Schiff and others, 'What's Next for AI Ethics, Policy, and Governance?

[98] Ibid.

[99] Ibid.

[100] Ibid.

The EU Commission aims at becoming a global leader on AI ethics and prepares draft legislative proposals following the publication in 2020 of its White Paper on AI[101] and in 2019 of its Ethics Guidelines for Trustworthy AI. The EU Commission launched its AI Strategy in 2018, with the appointment of a group of fifty-two experts. The group members comprised representatives from academia, civil society and industry. The High-Level Expert Group of the European Commission worked on Ethics Guidelines for Trustworthy AI and Policy and Investment Recommendations for Trustworthy AI. The Group published recommendations as well as a questionnaire that translates the ethics guidelines into a self-assessment checklist. It also published sectorial considerations in the public sector, healthcare and manufacturing, and the internet of things.

The OECD is a also pioneer in AI governance. It fosters global AI policy coordination. It adopted its first AI principles in 2019. Endorsed by the G20, the OECD AI principles are the first intergovernmental standard on AI. This instrument is not legally binding and belongs to soft law mechanisms. However, the political component of this mechanism and the peer-review process that could be developed around it makes it an important instrument. In February 2020, the OECD established a new AI Policy Observatory (OECD.AI). This is a platform for public policy on AI. It promotes international dialogue and collaboration between governments, international regulators, the private sector, academia and civil society. It focuses on evidence-based policy analysis.

In 2019, the G20 welcomed the G20 AI Principles drawn from the OECD Recommendation on AI. These principles seek to foster public trust and confidence in AI technologies and realise their potential through promoting principles such as inclusiveness, human-centricity, transparency, robustness and accountability. Under the Italian presidency, the G20 will focus on 'People, Planet and Prosperity' in order to take care of people and our planet, while ensuring a strong, inclusive and sustainable economic recovery. This means tackling the health and economic crisis in the short run while eradicating poverty (SDG1), tackling inequality, protecting the most vulnerable, promoting women's empowerment and ensuring universal access to education.

In November 2019, UNESCO launched a two-year programme to draft the first global standards on AI ethics. Like the OECD, UNESCO adopts a multi-stakeholder approach. It also contributes to achieving the SDGs adopted by the UN General Assembly in 2015.

[101] European Commission, 'On Artificial Intelligence – A European Approach to Excellence and Trust' (19 February 2020) COM(2020) 65 final.

On 11 September 2019, the Committee of Ministers of the Council of Europe set up an Ad Hoc Committee on Artificial Intelligence – CAHAI. The mandate of the Committee is to examine the feasibility and potential elements, on the basis of broad multi-stakeholder consultations, of a legal framework for the development, design and application of AI based on the Council of Europe's standards on human rights, democracy and the rule of law. After in-depth discussions with all participating members and observers, the feasibility study was adopted by the CAHAI in December 2020 and was presented in 2021 to the Committee of Ministers of the Council of Europe. This is an important milestone as it recommends human oversight mechanisms that safeguard human autonomy, and it puts an emphasis on the need to protect the physical and mental integrity of human beings and the obligation for AI deployers to strive to avoid the use of 'attention economy' models that can limit human autonomy. The feasibility study also states that Member States should ensure that developers and deployers of AI systems take adequate measures to minimise any physical or mental harm to individuals, society and the environment.

In June 2018, France and Canada launched the International Panel on Artificial Intelligence (IPAI), which became the Global Partnership on AI (GPAI). This organisation aims at promoting best practices on beneficial AI which is inclusive and human-centred, respects human rights and fosters innovation and economic growth.

The AI Transparency Institute launched the first AI Governance Forum in 2019 in Geneva, sponsored by the Swiss Confederation. This neutral forum fosters dialogue on AI governance. Its 2020 event was focused on digital health and climate change. This independent NGO has observer status at the European Committee for Standardization (CEN), Council of Europe and OECD working groups on AI and offers live testimony to Member States on a market-driven approach to regulate AI technologies, engaging private actors in effective, sustainable and eco-responsible AI business models, able to align the interests of all stakeholders for the interest of future generations with a certification and audit mechanism of AI systems. The OECD is now moving towards building a classification system of AI based on a similar methodology, as are KPMG Global, IBM, Deloitte, Ernst & Young and Pricewaterhouse Coopers. This demonstrates that independent NGOs can influence the private- and public-sector entities arguably responsible for most AI development, implementation and governance decisions.

Due to the imperative to set up an inclusive and democratically legitimate decision-making body, nation states must play a key role in the enactment of an AI governance framework. We value the work of the Council of Europe due to the potential for a legally binding instrument on AI similar to the Convention 108. We similarly value the work of the OECD due to its political impact.

What about the EU Commission? Formally announced on 21 April 2021, the draft proposals for the regulation of AI were leaked on 14 April 2021.[102] These proposals are based on a European Commission White Paper dated 2020.

The proposals follow the same logic as the GDPR: they have an extra-territorial effect and fines are up to 4 per cent of annual global turnover. Data protection impact assessments must also be carried out in some cases. In a similar way as the GDPR, which enacted the European Data Protection Board (EDPB), a European Artificial Intelligence Board will be in charge of ensuring a harmonised application of the regulation in the EU while cooperating with the EDPB.

Member States may create AI authorities with the power to issue fines up to €20 million or 4 per cent of global turnover, whichever is higher. Why not mutualise the competences of the data protection authorities with the AI authorities to foster synergies, exchange relevant information and reduce costs?

The proposals mainly focus on three categories of AI systems: some AI systems are prohibited, some are considered 'high-risk' and some are specifically addressing human interaction. These proposals target the developers of AI ('providers') as well as the organisations which procure and make use of these systems ('users'), the importers and distributors of AI systems.

First, some AI practices are prohibited: AI systems must not be used to manipulate human behaviour via a specific design or user interface nor to exploit information known about an individual to target vulnerabilities. AI systems also must not be used to implement general surveillance of a population (e.g. the indiscriminate, large-scale monitoring or tracking of individuals in a public hospital must be prohibited). Finally, large-scale evaluation or classification of people's trustworthiness is also prohibited.

[102] Tech Monitor, 'The EU's Leaked AI Regulation Is Ambitious but Disappointingly Vague' (Laurie Clark), https://techmonitor.ai/policy/eu-ai-regulation-machine-learning-european-union, accessed 15 April 2021; see also Hogan Lovells, 'AI & Algorithms (Part 2): The EU Releases Its New Regulation on Artificial Intelligence', www.engage.hoganlovells.com/knowledgeservices/news/ai-algorithms-part-2-the-eu-releases-its-new-regulation-on-artificial-intelligence, accessed 15 April 2021.

Second, the proposals also deal with high-risk AI systems and call for specific obligations for providers and users. The providers must verify the quality of training and testing data, documentation and record-keeping, transparency, human oversight, product safety, accuracy of outputs and security, alongside the need to register each AI system on a Commission-managed database.

Providers must implement a quality management system (ISO Norms) and ensure ongoing monitoring of the performance of AI systems. This governance framework is perfectly aligned with the self-assessment tools developed by the AI Transparency Institute, which assist companies in verifying adherence and compliance to the regulation (policy, safeguards to manage high-risk AI systems and for allocating responsibilities).

In the context of healthcare, AI systems can interact with patients. The patient must be informed that he/she is interacting with an AI system. Transparency and disclosure are also required for AI systems able to identify emotions.

A public consultation took place after 21 April 2021, and was followed by trilateral negotiations with the EU Council and EU Parliament.

Hard Law is necessary and should be complemented in conjunction with economic incentives to engage private actors in business models that are effective, eco-responsible and sustainable. Market-driven mechanisms like scoring systems may be an efficient solution to assist companies in building an ecosystem of trust in AI for the full value chain. Many initiatives are currently developing ethical requirements for AI systems, including IEEE, ISO, IETF, WEF, UNESCO, governments (e.g., Singapore, New York City, California, Australia, Denmark) and industry (FATML, XAI, CertNexus, Google, Microsoft, IBM). They can contribute to aligning the interests of all stakeholders depending on the methodology used and on corporate governance.

To be meaningful and trustworthy, ethics-based audits of AI systems should be carried out by an independent organisation with no conflict of interest resulting from its business models or legal structure. Any potential conflicting values will impact the certification process, from the choice of the methodology used to the choice of relevant use cases. The end-user's trust in the certification of AI-based systems and services deployed in the market will depend on the independence of the certification bodies. A due diligence approach (so-called ethics-by-design) should be incorporated into any design methodology and choice of use cases.

What will be the liability scheme in the event of damage caused by an AI system?

7.4.2 *Which Liability and Insurance Schemes?*

In the event of damage caused by a high-risk AI system in digital health, the EU plans to put in place a strict liability regime. Defining a liability scheme for AI actors is indeed crucial to identify whether developers have responsibility for their algorithms when in use, what those firms are responsible for and the normative grounding for that responsibility.[103] This is also important to repair the harm resulting from damage caused by an AI system. It is worth noting that AI systems won't be qualified as having legal personhood in the EU project.[104]

On 20 October 2020, the European Parliament adopted a Resolution governing particularly the liability for AI.[105] This Resolution proposes a Directive without replacing existing regimes in terms of product liability, consumer protection and the protection against discrimination as well as in matters of contractual liability (Art. 2 par. 3).

The strict liability regime is limited to the operators of high-risk AI systems for any damage caused by such systems. The operators will be held liable even if they can demonstrate that they acted with due diligence or that the high-risk AI system was acting in an autonomous manner. *Force majeure* is the only motive of exoneration of liability (Art. 4 par. 3). This Resolution brings legal certainty: fault-based liability schemes, product liability or contractual liability were indeed not protective enough for patients. The operators will be held liable if the victim can demonstrate that damage occurred, that a decision was made by the system and that there is a causal link between the damage and the decision.

The Resolution adopts a risk-based approach. The higher the risk, the higher the protection of the patients (objective liability regime). As AI-based systems are probabilistic systems, they intrinsically present high risks of harm for patients. 'High risk' means a significant potential in an autonomously operating AI system to cause harm or damage to one or more persons in a manner that is random and goes beyond what can reasonably be expected; the significance of the potential depends on the interplay between the severity of possible harm or damage, the degree of

103 Kirsten Martin 'Ethical Implications and Accountability of Algorithms' (2019) 160(4) *Journal of Business Ethics* 835–50.

104 European Parliament Resolution of 20 October 2020 with recommendations to the Commission on a civil liability regime for artificial intelligence (2020/2014(INL)), 20 October 2020, P9_TA(2020)0276, www.europarl.europa.eu/doceo/document/TA-9-2020-0276_EN.html, accessed 20 March 2021.

105 Ibid.

autonomy of decision making, the likelihood that the risk materialises and the manner and the context in which the AI system is being used (Art. 3 let. C).

The EU Parliament proposes holding liable the various persons who create, maintain or control the risk associated with the AI system, for any damage – both material and immaterial. However, immaterial damages must result in a verifiable economic loss (Art. 2). This liability scheme channels liability exclusively to the operators of an AI system.

In addition, the EU Medical Device Regulation entered into force on 26 May 2021.[106] As AI-based technologies are software medical devices, we can't exclude that its provisions apply to AI designers, as well as other stakeholders engaged in decision making related to patients. A specific concern is the liability of stakeholders engaged in the design and use of data and AI models for digital health applications.

Compensation for immaterial harm (e.g., pure economic damage) doesn't require fault under a strict liability regime (Art. 2 par. 1). In the context of digital health, if an AI system takes a decision which probably causes harm, the operator will be held liable for the damage on the basis of the risk of the use of the AI system. The EU Resolution recognises the loss of opportunity as a recoverable damage. We recommend medical doctors investigate additional insurance appropriate to this new risk of strict liability.

Which liability framework will apply to AI software remains unclear. Historically case law didn't recognise software as a 'product' subject to product liability law, but this might change for the specific context of healthcare AI software. AI can indeed assist medical doctors in diagnosis and decision making. IBM Watson used in oncology, DeepMind Health and Microsoft are some examples where AI software is used in healthcare powered by ML algorithms.

Supervisory authorities like the US Food and Drug Administration could regulate AI software as a 'medical device' if the software is intended to be used for medical purposes (i.e., for the diagnosis, cure, mitigation, prevention or treatment of a disease or condition). National supervisory authority in healthcare could regulate ML, that is, self-learning agents which require stricter safety standards.

106 Regulation (EU) 2017/745 of the European Parliament and of the Council of 5 April 2017 on medical devices, amending Directive 2001/83/EC, Regulation (EC) No 178/2002 and Regulation (EC) No 1223/2009 and repealing Council Directives 90/385/EEC and 93/42/EEC.

Software could enter into the scope of the Products Liability Directive and be considered as part of medical malpractice standards.

We believe that the EU should harmonise the liability framework applicable to AI software in healthcare in order to bring legal certainty in the Single Digital Market and increase patient protection. Safeguards should indeed be in place to ensure that AI-based systems are safe and efficient, and training data are accurate and reliable.

As AI technologies are a human artefact, it is reasonable to believe that a collective decision-making process should result in a diagnosis or treatment plan. For instance, only a team of physicians should review recommendations of AI systems and decide to stop a treatment. Instead of replacing a medical judgement, AI should be perceived as a tool to complement a human judgement. This approach will benefit patients and mitigate the risks for companies to enter into product litigation related to such a contextual use in healthcare.

7.4.3 The Specific Governance of Digital Platforms: The Digital Services Act

AI platforms are increasingly used in healthcare[107] and are the subject of European regulatory interventions. Directive 2161/1019 intervened by modifying the regulations for consumer protection, Regulation 1150/2019 applies to the relationship between platform and 'business user' and Directive 770/2019 introduced additional provisions applicable to digital contents and digital services. The European Commission initiated a legislative reform contained in the so-called 'Digital Service Act'.

The European Commission published in December 2020 the Digital Services Act. The Digital Services Act aspires 'to set a robust and durable governance structure for the effective supervision of providers of intermediary services'. It increased the protection of fundamental rights of the users of platforms in clarifying its due diligence obligations. This initiative aims at reinforcing the liability for very large online platforms (Art. 25) and their obligations. One of the obligations will be to conduct risk assessments on the systemic risks brought about by or relating to the functioning and use of their services (Art. 26) and to take reasonable and effective measures aimed at mitigating those risks (Art. 27). They will also be

[107] Jacob McPadden and others, 'Health Care and Precision Medicine Research: Analysis of a Scalable Data Science Platform' (2019) 21(4) *Journal of Medical Internet Research* e13043.

obliged to submit themselves to external and independent audits (Art. 28) and to comply with transparency reporting obligations (Art. 33). It obliges online platforms to engage with certified out-of-court dispute settlement bodies to resolve any dispute with users of their services (Art. 18). The Digital Services Act plans to set up a European Board for Digital Services (Art. 47). Fines will be effective, dissuasive and proportionate, having regard, in particular, to the nature, gravity, recurrence and duration of the infringement or suspected infringement to which those measures relate, as well as the economic, technical and operational capacity of the provider of the intermediary services concerned where relevant.

The Digital Services Act aims at implementing the saying 'what is allowed offline must be online, what is forbidden offline must be online'. Anything that is prohibited in the public space will also be prohibited in the online space. According to Thierry Breton, European Commissioner for the Internal Market, '[i]n many cases, the digital space is a lawless zone. It is a question for Europe to regain control over the structuring platforms'.

This proposal aims at bringing better protection to consumers and fundamental rights online, establishing a powerful transparency and accountability framework for online platforms and leading to fairer and more open digital markets.

7.5 Conclusion: What Will the Future Hold?

This chapter shows how digital healthcare can improve the quality of life of millions of people around the world. This raises legal and ethical challenges, several initiatives at global, regional and national level are building an ecosystem of trust for AI technologies in healthcare. States have the positive obligation to protect patients and are responsible for ensuring that provably beneficial AI-based systems are deployed on the market. Specific standards, ethics-based and rights-based audit and certification methods will play a crucial role in the future.

Given the tremendous flow of data generated by digital technologies and given the role of platforms that induce a phenomenon of detachment from national territory, Professor Bergé proposes to shift the model with the notion of the 'Datasphere'.[108] The total circulation of data is a

[108] Jean-Sylvestre Bergé, Stephane Grumbach et Vincenzo Zeno-Zencovich, 'The "Datasphere", Data Flows beyond Control, and the Challenges for Law and Governance' (2018), vol. 5, no 2, *European Journal of Comparative Law and Governance* 144–78.

phenomenon of great seriousness that requires policy makers to be focused on its impact for the common good. What is central is a legally conferred right to collect, process and use the data, as well as effective remedies to prevent any abuse in the exercise of this right.[109] Effective remedies as well as market-driven incentives like certification mechanisms can play a key role in engaging private actors in business models that are performant, provably beneficial, sustainable and based on values like human dignity, self-determination and autonomy. This requires cooperation at a global scale to deal with this silent transformation, which can be both a force for good and an instrument of power.

Bibliography

Adly AS and others, 'Approaches Based on Artificial Intelligence and the Internet of Intelligent Things to Prevent the Spread of COVID-19 Scoping Review' (2020) 22(8), *Journal of Medical Internet Research* e19104.

ANSSI, Dossier de presse, 'Cybersécurité, faire face à la menace: la stratégie française' (2021), 18 February 2021, www.ssi.gouv.fr/, accessed 1 March 2021.

Arenas-Cavalli JT and others, 'Clinical Validation of an Artificial Intelligence-Based Diabetic Retinopathy Screening Tool for a National Health System' (2022) *Eye* 78.

Beijing AI Principles. Datenschutz Datensich 43, 656 (2019), https://doi.org/10.1007/s11623-019-1183-6, accessed 14 March 2021.

Belgrave D and others, 'Understanding Client Support Strategies to Improve Clinical Outcomes in An Online Mental Health Intervention' (2020), *Proceedings of the 2020 CHI Conference on Human Factors in Computing Systems*, 1–16.

Bennett CR and others, 'Visitors and Resident Autonomy: Spoken and Unspoken Rules in Assisted Living' (2017) 57(2) *The Gerontologist* 252–60.

Bergé J-S, Grumbach S and Zeno-Zencovich V, 'The "Datasphere", Data Flows beyond Control, and the Challenges for Law and Governance' (2018) 5(2) *European Journal of Comparative Law and Governance* 144–78.

Bloss CS and others, 'Direct-to-Consumer Personalized Genomic Testing' (2011) 20(R2) *Human Molecular Genetics* R132–41.

Briganti G and Le Moine O, 'Artificial Intelligence in Medicine: Today and Tomorrow' (2020) 7 *Frontiers in Medicine* 27.

Butcher J and Beridze I, 'What Is the State of Artificial Intelligence Governance Globally?' (2019) 164(5–6) *The RUSI Journal* 88–96.

109 Ibid.

Cappelleri DJ, Bi C and Guix M, 'Tumbling Microrobots for Future Medicine: Robots Smaller than a Grain of Sand Could Move through the Body by Tumbling End Over End, Opening up the Possibility of Intriguing Biomedical Applications' (2018) 106(4) *American Scientist* 210–14.

Carrillo MR, 'Artificial Intelligence: From Ethics to Law' (2020) 44(6) *Telecommunications Policy* 101937.

Cath C, 'Governing Artificial Intelligence: Ethical, Legal and Technical Opportunities and Challenges' (2018) 44(6) *Telecommunications Policy* 101937.

Clarke R, 'Principles and Business Processes for Responsible AI' (2019) 35(4) *Computer Law and Security Review* 410–22.

De la Garza A, 'Contact Tracing Apps Were Big Tech's Best Idea for Fighting COVID-19. Why Haven't They Helped?' *Time*, 10 November 2020.

Dimitrov DV, 'Medical Internet of Things and Big Data in Healthcare' (2016) 22(3) *Healthcare Informatics Research* 156.

European Commission's High Level Expert Group on Artificial Intelligence, "Ethics Guidelines for Trustworthy AI", 8 April 2019, 5.

European Parliament Resolution of 20 October 2020 with recommendations to the Commission on a civil liability regime for artificial intelligence (2020/2014(INL)), 20 October 2020, P9_TA(2020)0276, www.europarl.europa.eu/doceo/document/TA-9-2020-0276_EN.html, accessed 20 March.

Eysenbach G, 'What Is Digital Health?' (2001) 3(2) *Journal of Medical Internet Research* e20.

Fellay J, 'Le Champ des Possibles: Recherche Translationnelle et Médecine de Précision' (La Rencontre entre la Science et le Droit dans le Numérique 2. Les Défis Juridiques de l'Intelligence Artificielle: Regards Croisés entre Santé et Justice, Lausanne, 13 February 2020).

Floridi L and Strait A, 'Ethical Foresight Analysis: What It Is and Why It Is Needed?' (2020) 30(1) *Minds and Machines* 77.

Fox C, 'The Ethical Dilemma We Face on AI and Autonomous Tech' (New Rules, TEDxMidAtlantic Event, Washington DC, 21 October 2016).

Global Digital Health Outlook, 2020 (2019), 23 August 2019, Frost & Sullivan.

Guarda P, 'Ok Google, Am I Sick?": Artificial Intelligence, e-Health, and Data Protection Regulation' (2019) 15(1) *BioLaw Journal-Rivista di BioDiritto* 359–75.

High-Level Expert Group on AI presented Ethics Guidelines for Trustworthy Artificial Intelligence, https://ec.europa.eu/digital-single-market/en/news/ethics-guidelines-trustworthy-ai, accessed 14 March 2021.

Hu J, Perer A and Wang F, 'Data Driven Analytics for Personalized Healthcare' in Weaver CA and others (eds), *Healthcare Information Management Systems: Cases, Strategies, and Solutions* (Springer 2016).

ITU/WHO Focus Group on Digital Health, www.itu.int/en/ITU-T/focusgroups/ai4h/Pages/default.aspx, accessed 14 March 2021.

Knott GJ and Doudna JA, 'CRISPR-Cas Guides the Future of Genetic Engineering' (2018) 361(6405) *Science* 866–69.

Koene A and others, 'Governance Framework for Algorithmic Accountability and Transparency', Publications Office, https://data.europa.eu/doi/10.2861/59990, accessed 14 March 2021.

Kroll JA and others, 'Accountable Algorithms' (2017) 165(3) *University of Pennsylvania Law Review* 633.

Lapao LV and others, 'Implementing an Online Pharmaceutical Service Using Design Science Research' (2017) 17(1) *BMC Medical Informatics and Decision Making* 1–14.

Levin D, 'Lessons Learned in Using Live Red Teams in IA Experiments' in *Proceedings DARPA Information Survivability Conference and Exposition* (IEEE Computer Society 2003), 110–19.

Lupton D, 'Data Mattering and Self-Tracking: What Can Personal Data Do?' (2020) 34(1) *Continuum* 1–13.

Lupton D, 'The Internet of Things: Social Dimensions' (2020) 14(4) *Sociology Compass* e12770, https://onlinelibrary.wiley.com/doi/abs/10.1111/soc4.12770, accessed 14 March 2021.

Lupton D, 'A More-Than-Human Approach to Bioethics: The Example of Digital Health' (2020) 34(9) *Bioethics* 969–76.

Lupton D, 'Teaching and Learning Guide – The Internet of Things: Social Dimensions' (2020) 14(4) *Sociology Compass* e12777, https://onlinelibrary.wiley.com/doi/10.1111/soc4.12777, accessed 14 March 2021.

Lupton D, 'Thinking with Care about Personal Data Profiling: A More-Than-Human Approach' (2020) 14 *International Journal of Communication* 3165–83, https://ijoc.org/index.php/ijoc/article/view/13540, accessed 19 March 2021.

Marescaux J and others, 'Transatlantic Robot-Assisted Telesurgery' (2001) 413(6854) *Nature* 379–80.

Martin K, 'Ethical Implications and Accountability of Algorithms' (2019) 160(4) *Journal of Business Ethics* 835–50.

McDowell JC, 'The Low Earth Orbit Satellite Population and Impacts of the SpaceX Starlink Constellation' (2020) 892(2) *The Astrophysical Journal Letters* L36.

McGhin T and others, 'Blockchain in Healthcare Applications: Research Challenges and Opportunities' (2019) 135 *Journal of Network and Computer Applications* 62–75.

McPadden J and others, 'Health Care and Precision Medicine Research: Analysis of a Scalable Data Science Platform' (2019) 21(4) *Journal of Medical Internet Research* e13043.

Minoli D, Sohraby K and Kouns J, 'IoT Security (IoTSec) Considerations, Requirements, and Architectures' (2017) 14th IEEE Annual Consumer Communications & Networking Conference (CCNC), IEEE 1006–7.

Mittelstaadt B, 'Principles Alone Cannot Guarantee Ethical AI' (2019) 1(11) *Nature Machine Intelligence* 501–07.

Mittelstaadt BD and others, 'The Ethics of Algorithms: Mapping the Debate' (2016) 3(2) *Big Data and Society* 2053951716679679.

Mouchet C and others, 'Multiparty Homomorphic Encryption from Ring-Learning-With-Errors' (2020), Report 2020/304, Cryptology ePrint Archive, https://eprint.iacr.org/2020/304, accessed 1 March 2021.

Nanni M and others, 'Give More Data, Awareness and Control to Individual Citizens, and They Will Help COVID-19 Containment' (2021) 23(1) *Ethics and Information Technology* 1–6, https://doi.org/10.1007/s10676-020-09572-w, accessed 19 March 2021.

Nebeker C, Torous J and Ellis RJB, 'Building the Case for Actionable Ethics in Digital Health Research Supported by Artificial Intelligence' (2019) 17(1) *BMC Medicine* 1–7.

OECD Principles on AI, www.oecd.org/going-digital/ai/principles/, accessed 14 March 2021.

Park Y and others, 'Emergence of New Disease: How Can Artificial Intelligence Help?' (2020) 26(7) *Trends in Molecular Medicine* 627–29.

Pentland A, 'Healthwear: Medical Technology Becomes Wearable' (2004) 37(5) *Computer* 42–49.

Pointer P, 'The Rise of Telemedicine: How to Mitigate Potential Fraud' (2020) 2020(6) *Computer Fraud and Security* 6–8.

Radin JM and others, 'Harnessing Wearable Device Data to Improve State-Level Real-Time Surveillance of Influenza-Like Illness in the USA: A Population-Based Study' (16 January 2020), https://doi.org/10.1016/S2589-7500(19)30222-5, accessed 16 March 2021.

Rahwan I, 'Society-in-the-Loop: Programming the Algorithmic Social Contract' (2018) 20(1) *Ethics and Information Technology* 5–14.

Raisaro JL, 'Privacy-Enhancing Technologies for Medical and Genomic Data: From Theory to Practice' (PhD thesis, École Polytechnique Fédérale de Lausanne 2018).

Raji ID and others, 'Closing the AI Accountability Gap: Defining an End-to-End Framework for Internal Algorithmic Auditing' (2020) *Proceedings of the 2020 Conference on Fairness, Accountability, and Transparency* (Association for Computing Machinery 2020).

Regulation (EU) 2017/745 of the European Parliament and of the Council of 5 April 2017 on medical devices, amending Directive 2001/83/EC, Regulation (EC) No 178/2002 and Regulation (EC) No 1223/2009 and repealing Council Directives 90/385/EEC and 93/42/EEC.

Rocher L, Hendrickx JM and de Montjoye YA, 'Estimating the Success of Re-identifications in Incomplete Datasets Using Generative Models' (2019) 10(1) *Nature Communications* 3069.

Roehrs A and others, 'Personal Health Records: A Systematic Literature Review' (2017) 19(1) *Journal of Medical Internet Research* e13.

Roy JD and others, *La Bioéthique, ses fondements et ses controverses* (Renouveau pédagogique 1995).

Salama MA, Hassanien AE and Mostafa A, 'The Prediction of Virus Mutation Using Neural Networks and Rough Set Techniques' (2016) 2016(1) *EURASIP Journal on Bioinformatics and Systems Biology* 1–11.

Salathé M, Wiegand T and Wenzeland M, 'Focus Group on Artificial Intelligence for Health' (13 September 2018), https://arxiv.org/abs/1809.04797, accessed 1 March 2022.

Saleiro P and others, 'Aequitas: A Bias and Fairness Audit Toolkit' (v2, 29 April 2019), https://arxiv.org/abs/1811.05577, accessed 1 March 2022.

Sandvig C and others, 'Auditing Algorithms: Research Methods for Detecting Discrimination on Internet Platforms' (Preconference 'Data and Discrimination: Converting Critical Concerns into Productive Inquiry' at the 64th Annual Conference of the International Communication Association, Seattle WA, 22 May 2014), http://social.cs.uiuc.edu/papers/pdfs/ICA2014-Sandvig.pdf, accessed 1 March 2022.

Savage N, 'How AI Is Improving Cancer Diagnostics' (2020) *Nature Outlook*, https://doi.org/10.1038/d41586-020-00847-2, accessed 1 March 2022

Scheibner J and others, 'Data Protection and Ethics Requirements for Multisite Research with Health Data: A Comparative Examination of Legislative Governance Frameworks and the Role of Data Protection Technologies' (2020) 7(1) *Journal of Law and the Biosciences* 1.

Schiff D and others, 'What's Next for AI Ethics, Policy, and Governance? A Global Overview' (2020) *Proceedings of the AAAI/ACM Conference on AI, Ethics, and Society* 153–58.

Schwab K, *The Fourth Industrial Revolution* (Penguin Books 2016).

Sekiguchi K and Hori K, 'Organic and Dynamic Tool for Use with Knowledge Base of AI Ethics for Promoting Engineers' Practice of Ethical AI Design' (2018) 35(1) *AI & SOCIETY* 51, https://doi.org/10.1007/s00146-018-0867-z, accessed 14 March 2021.

Simacek KF and others, 'Patient Engagement in Type 2 Diabetes Mellitus Research: What Patients Want' (2018) 12 *Patient Preference and Adherence* 595.

Skevington SM, Lofty M and O'Connell KA, 'The World Health Organization's WHOQOL-BREF Quality of Life Assessment: Psychometric Properties and Results of the International Field Trial. A Report from the WHOQOL Group' (2004) 13(2) *Quality of Life Research* 299–310, https://doi.org/10.1023/B:QURE.0000018486.91360.00, accessed 18 March 2021.

Sung M, Marci C and Pentland A, 'Wearable Feedback Systems for Rehabilitation' (2005) 2(1) *Journal of Neuroengineering and Rehabilitation* 1–12.

'Swiss Re and Palantir Technologies Put Pioneering Data and Analytics Platform at the Service of Global Health and Joins The Trinity Challenge' (*The Trinity Challenge*, 28 October 2020, updated 3 June 2021), https://thetrinitychallenge.org/news-and-stories/swiss-re-and-palantir-technologies-join-the-trinity-challenge/, accessed 7 March 2022.

Terzis P 'Onward for the Freedom of Others: Marching Beyond the AI Ethics' in *Proceedings of the 2020 Conference on Fairness, Accountability, and Transparency* (Association for Computing Machinery 2020).

Thieme A and Belgrave D, 'Data-Driven Insights for More Effective, Personalized Care in Online Mental Health Interventions' (*Microsoft Research Blog*, 24 March 2020).

Thomasen, K, 'Ethics for Artificial Intelligence, Ethics for All' (2019) 10(1) *Paladyn, Journal of Behavioral Robotics* 359–363, https://doi.org/10.1515/pjbr-2019-0029, accessed 14 March 2021.

Ting DSW and others, 'Artificial Intelligence, the Internet of Things, and Virtual Clinics: Ophthalmology at the Digital Translation Forefront' (2020)2(1) *The Lancet Digital Health* e8–e9.

Ting DSW and others, 'Deep Learning in Ophthalmology: The Technical and Clinical Considerations' (2019) 72 *Progress in Retinal and Eye Research* 100759

Tsoi K and others, 'Applications of Artificial Intelligence for Hypertension Management' (2021) 23(3) *The Journal of Clinical Hypertension*.

Urman V and others, *La revolution épigénétique* (Albin Michel 2019).

Vallee T and others, 'On Personalization in IoT' (2016), 2016 International Conference on Computational Science and Computational Intelligence (CSCI), IEEE 186–91.

Vayana E and others, 'Ethical Challenges of Big Data in Public Health' (2015) 11(2) *PLOS Computational Biology* e1003904.

Vayena E and others, 'Digital Health: Meeting the Ethical and Policy Challenges' (2018) 148 *Swiss Medical Weekly* w14571.

Webster P, 'Virtual Health Care in the era of COVID-19' (2020) 395(10231) *The Lancet* 1180–1.

Whittlestone J and others, 'The role and limits of principles in AI ethics: towards a focus on tensions' Proceedings of the 2019 AAAI/ACM Conference on AI, Ethics, and Society (2019) 195–200.

Wicks P and others, 'Scaling Patients LikeMe via a "Generalized Platform" for Members with Chronic Illness: Web-Based Survey Study of Benefits Arising' (2018) 20(5) *Journal of Medical Internet Research*, e175.

Winfield AFT and Jirotka M, 'Ethical Governance is Essential to Building Trust in Robotics and Artificial Intelligence Systems' (2018) 376(2133) *Philosophical Transactions of the Royal Society A: Mathematical, Physical and Engineering Sciences* 20180085.

WHO (World Health Organisation), Guidelines: 'recommendations on digital interventions for health system strengthening' (2018), www.who.int/reproductivehealth/publications/digital-interventions-health-system-strengthening/en/, accessed 14 March 2021.

WHO (World Health Organisation), Presentation of Health Systems, www.who.int/healthsystems/about/en/, accessed 19 February 2021.

Yala A and others, A Deep Learning Mammography-Based Model for Improved Breast Cancer Risk Prediction (July 2019) 292(1) *Radiology* 60–66, http://doi.org/10.1148/radiol.2019182716, accessed 1 March 2022.

Yue X, and others, 'Healthcare Data Gateways: Found Healthcare Intelligence on Blockchain with Novel Privacy Risk Control' (2016) 40(10) *Journal of Medical Systems* 218.

Zhang P and others, 'Blockchain Technology Use Cases in Healthcare' in Raj P and Deka GC (eds), *Advances in Computers*, vol. 111: *Blockchain Technology: Platforms, Tools and Use Cases* (Academic Press 2018) 1–41.

Zyskind G, Nathan O and Pentland A, 'Enigma: Decentralized Computation Platform with Guaranteed Privacy (10 June 2015), https://arxiv.org/abs/1506.03471, accessed 1 March 2022.

PART III

Knowledge, Risk and Control

8

The Principle of Transparency in Medical Research

Applying Big Data Analytics to Electronic Health Records

NIKOLAUS FORGÓ AND MARIE-CATHERINE WAGNER

8.1 Introduction

> All that may come to my knowledge in the exercise of my profession or in daily commerce with men, which ought not to be spread abroad, I will keep secret and will never reveal.[1]

In our digital age, with phenomena such as Big Data, artificial intelligence (AI), Internet of 'Everything', and so forth, this commitment that has been globally accepted in the medical field for thousands of years seems to be seriously challenged. However, secrecy is fundamental for a trustful doctor–patient relationship. A comprehensive legal framework is therefore necessary in order to further protect the patients' privacy and provide them with rights that support their trust in this spirit.

The use of patients' Electronic Health Records (EHRs) data for medical research, employing Big Data technologies, appears to have almost endless opportunities to develop treatments that might revolutionise the health sector so that there is a considerable public interest in secondary data use. Responsible research should therefore consider both aspects and find the right, lawful balance between innovation and data protection.

Many principles of good research go in parallel with the data protection principle: transparency is a highly relevant feature of quality research. Methods and processes have to be exactly planned and documented, and the research question must be precisely defined. The data used come from samples, which are carefully selected from relevant populations by means of approved scientific sampling methods in order to minimise bias and produce reliable results. As these research principles are universally true,

[1] Dorland, *Dorland's Illustrated Medical Dictionary*, 28th ed (WB Saunders 1994) 768.

they must also be applied to Big Data in medical research. The more, the better does not mean that all heterogeneous data from EHRs can be used randomly without any pre-selection considering the research purpose. As soon as the samples have been chosen, the life cycle of this relevant data has to be planned in detail so that all process steps can be anticipated and retraced.

The core processes of top-quality research build the foundation for fulfilling some requirements of the General Data Protection Regulation (GDPR): a well-defined research question is closely related to 'purpose', the principles of data minimisation and accuracy are also fundamental in scientific research. If we go into detail, however, the situation is of course more complex. Understanding even a concise description of a deep-learning algorithm might demand too much from some data subjects. The right to erasure, which must be guaranteed according to the GDPR, can mean the end of a whole project. GDPR provides a framework where such aspects are considered by frequently providing exceptions and restrictions to some regulations. Scientific research holds a privileged position in the GDPR, avoiding overly restrictive measures that might impede the increase of knowledge.[2]

Starting with an evaluation of Big Data from EHRs and a brief presentation of the logic behind deep learning, this chapter will analyse how the principle of transparency, enshrined by GDPR, might affect medical research making use of Big Data analytics. Finally, international regulations and recommendations will be briefly evaluated as far as transparency of Big Data analytics in medical research is concerned.

8.2 Towards New Frontiers in Medical Research

> Digitising health records, and creating systems that enable them to be securely accessed by citizens and securely shared within and between the different actors in the health system is an important step.[3]

Data from health records has been of great interest for medical research for a long time. Prior to the existence of EHRs, such data had to be manually abstracted from clinical paper documentation in order to make secondary

[2] V Chico, 'The impact of the General Data Protection Regulation on health research' (2018) 128(1) *British Medical Bulletin* 109–18.

[3] Commission Recommendation on a European Electronic Health Record Exchange Format (C(2019)800) of 6 February 2019, Recital 8.

use possible.[4] The digitalisation of medical records was a game changer in this field. Providing information on diseases, previous consultations and exam results, EHRs allow patients and healthcare professionals to store, process and share medical data for the coordination of care electronically.[5] However, in particular, the sharing has been an ongoing challenge for technological ('data silos') and legal reasons.

A primary goal of precision medicine is to develop quantitative models for patients that can be used to predict health status, as well as to help prevent disease or disability. In this context, EHRs offer great promise for accelerating clinical research and predictive analysis,[6] because they include the data that is needed for these predictions.

Today the amount of EHR data is huge and therefore has high statistical power if access to the data is available.[7] The mining of EHRs therefore has the potential for establishing new patient-stratification principles and for revealing unknown disease correlations,[8] considering both the individual patient's standpoint and the collective effects.[9]

Over the years, EHR data have been used with the intent to improve care, increase patient engagement, perform quality improvement, build shared models and standardisation across institutions, create new knowledge, conduct research in 'real-world' settings instead of in controlled trials, enable public health surveillance and intervention, and facilitate personalised care and decision-making. It has been suggested that, in the United States alone, there will soon be one billion patient visits documented per year in EHR systems.[10] The main challenges include limitations of processing ability, interoperability and lack of standardisation, accuracy and completeness of records, cost, security and privacy concerns, and inability to extract the needed information.[11] It must be noted

4 MN Zozus and others, 'Factors Affecting Accuracy of Data Abstracted from Medical Records' (2015) 10(10) *Plos One*.

5 F Khennou and others, 'Improving the Use of Big Data Analytics within Electronic Health Records: A Case Study based OpenEHR' (2018) 127(1) *Procedia Computer Science* 60–68.

6 R Miotto and others, 'Deep Patient: An Unsupervised Representation to Predict the Future of Patients from the Electronic Health Records' (2016) 6(26094) *Scientific Reports* 1.

7 DR Schlegel and G Ficheur, 'Secondary Use of Patient Data: Review of the Literature Published in 2016' (2017) 26(1) *Yearbook of Medical Informatics* 68–71.

8 PB Jensen and others, 'Mining Electronic Health Records: Towards Better Research Applications and Clinical Care' (2012) 13(6) *Nature Reviews Genetics* 395–405.

9 D Dahlem and others, 'Predictability Bounds of Electronic Health Records' (2015) 5(1) *Scientific Reports*.

10 MK Ross and others, '"Big Data" and the Electronic Health Record' (2014) 9(1) *Yearbook of Medical Informatics*.

11 Ibid.

that risk minimisation and accuracy are relevant aspects to ensure transparency in the light of GDPR:

> In order to ensure fair and transparent processing in respect of the data subject, the controller should use appropriate mathematical or statistical procedures for the profiling, implement technical and organisational measures appropriate to ensure ... that factors which result in inaccuracies in personal data are corrected and the risk of errors is minimised.[12]

From the individual patient's standpoint, lawful processing of personal data also has to consider aspects related to profiling, which Article 4(4) GDPR defines as

> any form of automated processing of personal data consisting of the use of personal data to evaluate certain personal aspects relating to a natural person, in particular to analyse or predict aspects concerning that natural person's ... health.

Secondary use of EHRs (the use of data for a purpose other than the one for which it was originally collected) promises to advance clinical research and improve clinical decision-making.[13] There are a wide variety of research studies all over the world where predictive analysis of Big Data from EHRs has contributed to innovation and improvement in healthcare and treatment, disclosed dependencies as well as interrelations, and provided support for decisions.

Many of the formats and standards of information systems currently used for recording, retrieving and managing EHRs across the European Union are incompatible.[14] In order to improve this situation in Europe, the EU is sponsoring (inter alia) an interoperability project called 'InteropEHRate' with two main goals: First, that patients can use their medical records in each European country and second, that European researchers can rely on a standardised quality.[15] The InteropEHRate project aims at developing a model for international healthcare data exchange at Fast Healthcare Interoperability Resources FHIR standard. In order to achieve cross-border interoperability among EHRs, a Smart EHR App and an interoperability platform are being prototyped. Automatic conversion

[12] Regulation (EU) 2016/679, Recital 71.

[13] Miotto and others, 'Deep Patient'.

[14] Commission Recommendation on a European Electronic Health Record exchange format (C(2019)800) of 6 February 2019, Recital 8.

[15] InteropEHRate, 'InteropEHRate in a Nutshell', www.interopehrate.eu/interopehrate-in-a-nutshell/, accessed 10 November 2019.

of legacy systems data shall provide the universal integration of all relevant information. A specific remote protocol for research will be defined to support the health data exchange among the Smart Electronic Health Records (S-EHRs) of citizens and research centres.[16]

The InteropEHRate S-EHR App provides more than that: whereas in general the data being reused for research have often been stored by hospitals and health systems – large databases containing administrative, claims and patient health data –[17] the InteropEHRate project is designing an application where EHRs do not have to be centrally stored.

8.3 From Big Data to Information and Knowledge – A Traceable Transformation Path

> Big Data is not merely taking us to bigger traditional places. Rather, it's taking us to very new places, unimaginable only a short time ago. [...]It is emerging as a major interdisciplinary triumph.[18] More data usually [even] beats better algorithms.[19]

In order to be able to assess the legal consequences of Big Data generation, processing and analysis, it is necessary to define the current use of the term Big Data and understand the basic elements of the related state-of-the-art technology. In this context, traceability of the data lifecycle plays an important role. Not only do data protection laws require transparency here but also scientific quality standards.

> Research [...] is a transparent, interactive process by which societal actors and innovators become mutually responsive to each other with a view on the (ethical) acceptability, sustainability and societal desirability of the innovation process and its marketable products (in order to allow a proper embedding of scientific and technological advances in our society).[20]

Top-quality research has always been based on precise planning, careful documentation and critical evaluation of methodology, data sources and

[16] Ibid.

[17] Schlegel and Ficheur, 'Secondary Use of Patient Data'.

[18] FX Diebold, 'On the Origin(s) and Development of the Term "Big Data"' (2012) 12(037) PIER Working Paper.

[19] A Rajaraman, 'More Data Usually Beats Better Algorithms' *Datawocky*, 24 March 2008, https://anand.typepad.com/datawocky/2008/03/more-data-usual.html, accessed 8 November 2019.

[20] RV Schomberg, *Towards Responsible Research and Innovation in the Information and Communication Technologies and Security Technologies Fields* (Publications Office of the European Union, 2011) 3.

assumptions. Without transparency, the results would not be regarded as reliable and would mean very little. In medical research, making use of Big Data analytics, basically, two major interrelated parallel processes need to be made transparent: the research process itself (samples, methods, models, etc.) and the life cycle of the data. The communication of all these details lays a profound fundamental basis for legal compliance. However, it is unfortunate that some of the most powerful analytic tools also seem to be the most opaque.[21]

8.3.1 Big Data from EHRs: Greater than the Sum of Its Parts

The information explosion of the last decades coined the term Big Data, whose meaning has always corresponded to the technological development of the respective time. Today Big Data means datasets which exceed the processing capacity of conventional database systems and, due to their volume, speed, and complexity, cannot be stored, managed and analysed by standard data management tools. 'The data is too big, moves too fast, and does not fit the structures of traditional database architectures'[22] and so it requires new technologies and techniques to capture, store, and analyse it.[23] However, Big Data is greater than the sum of its parts.[24]

A key to deriving value from Big Data is the use of analytics.[25] In order to unlock information,[26] efficient analysis and processing of Big Data within a given time frame are essential.[27] Sophisticated analytics can substantially improve decision-making, minimise risks and unearth valuable insights that would otherwise remain hidden.[28]

Health data can be an excellent use case for Big Data analytics due to their relevance, size and complexity, provided that they are available in sufficient quantity and quality. Within the emerging context of the

[21] European Commission – European Group on Ethics in Science and New Technologies, 'Statement on Artificial Intelligence, Robotics and "Autonomous" Systems' (2018) 6.

[22] A Banik and SK Bandyopadhyay, 'Big Data – A Review on Analysing 3Vs' (2016) 3(1) *Journal of Scientific and Engineering Research* 21–24.

[23] TechAmerica Foundation, 'Demystifying Big Data' (2012).

[24] Diebold, 'On the Origin(s) and Development of the Term "Big Data"'.

[25] H Watson, 'Tutorial: Big Data Analytics: Concepts, Technologies, and Applications' (2014) 34(1) *Communications of the Association for Information Systems* 65.

[26] Diebold, 'On the Origin(s) and Development of the Term "Big Data"'.

[27] M Chandrika and others, 'Impact of Big Data and Emerging Research Trends' (2015) *International Journal of Innovative Technology and Research*.

[28] MY Ambur and others, 'Big Data Analytics and Machine Intelligence Capability Development at NASA Langley Research Center: Strategy, Roadmap, and Progress' (2015).

digitisation of health care, EHRs constitute a significant technological advance in the way medical information is stored, communicated, and processed by the multiple parties involved in medical research. However, in spite of the anticipated potential of this technology, there is widespread concern that consumer privacy issues may impede its diffusion and therefore hinder the development of socially desirable Big Data use cases.[29] The challenge is to develop legally and ethically compliant solutions that enforce the data subjects' fundamental rights and support technological development at the same time.

Transparency, especially, has become an important issue for patients, as they feel unable to trace the processing of their data, and new technologies are often described as 'black boxes'. This concern of patients is also supported by the GDPR, which names transparency as a principle for processing personal data. Recital 63 of the GDPR states that

> every data subject should therefore have the right to know and obtain communication in particular with regard to the purposes for which the personal data are processed, where possible the period for which the personal data are processed, the recipients of the personal data, the logic involved in any automatic personal data processing and, at least when based on profiling, the consequences of such processing.

8.3.2 Transparency in the Blackbox: The Logic Behind Deep Learning and Big Data Analytics

Big Data analytics examines large amounts of data to uncover hidden patterns, correlations and other insights. A frequently employed technology for this purpose is machine learning (ML). The emphasis of ML is on automatic methods. In other words, the goal is to devise learning algorithms that do the learning automatically, without human intervention or assistance. In general, ML is about learning to do better in the future, based on what was experienced in the past.[30] The patterns relate to the relationships between (past) behaviours and outcomes, thus enabling predictions of future behaviour.[31] Lots of input examples (Big Data) and

[29] C Angst and R Agarwal, 'Adoption of Electronic Health Records in the Presence of Privacy Concerns: The Elaboration Likelihood Model and Individual Persuasion' (2009) 33(2) *Management Information Systems Quarterly* 339–70.

[30] G Nguyen and others, 'Machine Learning and Deep Learning Frameworks and Libraries for Large-Scale Data Mining: A Survey' (2019), 52 *Artificial Intelligence Review* 77–124.

[31] L Edwards and M Veale, 'Slave to the Algorithm? Why a "Right to an Explanation" is Probably Not the Remedy You are Looking for' (2017), 16 *Duke Law and Technology Review* 18–84.

trial-and-error guesses are necessary to identify key features and create a predictive system which is based on adjusting parameters and checking them against outcomes.[32]

Such a system learns from examples and generalises them after the learning phase. In order to achieve this, algorithms build up a stochastic model, based on training data. As ML is related to prediction, these algorithms are designed to anticipate outcomes.[33]

An often used algorithm for ML is the multilayer perceptron, which was designed in analogy to the biological system.[34]

> Perceptrons make decisions – determine whether or not an event fits a certain 'pattern' – by adding up evidence obtained from many small experiments.[35]

A perceptron is a mathematical function mapping some set of input values to output values.[36] The basic element of such a network is the artificial neuron: it receives signals which are separately weighted and then summed up. A transfer function is applied to this sum of weighted signals in order to get the output signal of the neuron. A multilayer perceptron consists of several layers of neurons. Consecutive layers are connected through mappings, while there are no connections within the layers. The layers between the input and output layers are called hidden layers, because their values are not given in the data; instead the model must determine which concepts are useful for explaining the relationships in the observed data.[37] Every hidden layer increases the complexity of the learned image features.[38] The goal is to map a certain number of inputs to a desired output value.[39]

> [The] recognition of any stimulus involves the matching or systematic comparison of the contents of storage with incoming sensory patterns, in order to determine whether the current stimulus has been seen before.[40]

32 J Schmidt and others, 'Recent Advances and Applications of Machine Learning in Solid-State Materials Science' (2019), 5 *npj Computational Materials* 83.

33 Edwards and Veale, 'Slave to the algorithm?'.

34 F Rosenblatt, 'The Perceptron: A Probabilistic Model for Information Storage and Organization in the Brain' (1958), 65(6) *Psychological Review* 386–408.

35 M Minsky and S Papert, *Perceptrons: An Introduction to Computational Geometry* (MIT Press 1969).

36 I Goodfellow and others, *Deep Learning* (MIT Press, 2016).

37 Ibid.

38 Mathworks, 'Deep Learning Examples: Training a Model from Scratch', www.mathworks.com/solutions/deep-learning/examples/training-a-model-from-scratch.html, accessed 10 October 2019.

39 R Männer and R Lange, 'Rechnen mit Neuronalen Netzen: Wie funktionieren Neuronale Netze und wie werden sie trainiert?' (1994), 50(5) *Physikalische Blätter* 445–49.

40 Rosenblatt, 'The Perceptron'.

Weights and the bias, the parameters in this structural system of cascading layers of neurons, are varied to see if a better outcome can be obtained. This is repeated until the net classifies the data as correctly as possible.[41] In order to find proper weights and the bias in a training algorithm, generally based on iteration processes and back propagation – the backward calculation of weights from the output to the input layer – is applied.[42] Back propagation is an optimisation method used to calculate the error contribution of each neuron after a patch of data is processed.[43] Neural networks typically have millions of parameters and require large amounts of data to tune these parameters in order to achieve a goal.[44] In a basic ML algorithm, training is done by manual selection of features, data points with particular predictive power or analytic utility. Choosing features usually requires some human intuition.[45] In a deep-learning process, however, human intervention is not necessary anymore. There is no human influence on the results of the learning process, which – due to automatic parameter weighting and continuous optimisation – cannot be traced back completely in some respects. With the deep learning feature, extraction and modelling steps are automatic.[46] So it may remain unclear on the basis of which patterns the computer has made decisions and drawn conclusions.

The success of predictive algorithms largely depends on feature selection and data representation. A common approach with EHRs is to have a domain expert designate the patterns to look for (ie, the learning task and the targets) and to specify clinical variables in an ad-hoc manner. This does not generalise well and sometimes misses opportunities to discover novel patterns and features.

To address these shortcomings, data-driven approaches for feature selection in EHRs can automatically identify patterns and dependencies in the data and make it easier to automatically extract useful information when building classifiers or other predictors. These deep-learning techniques have not been used broadly with EHR data, but their popularity is

41 MA Nielsen, *Neural Networks and Deep Learning* (Determination Press 2015) 7.

42 Männer and Lange, 'Rechnen mit Neuronalen Netzen'.

43 D Rumelhart and others, 'Learning Representations by Back-Propagating Errors' (1986) 323 *Nature* 533–36.

44 V Hedge and S Usmani, 'Parallel and Distributed Deep Learning' (2016).

45 L Hardesty, 'Crowdsourcing Big-Data Analysis' *MIT News*, 30 October 2017, https://news.mit.edu/2017/crowdsourcing-big-data-analysis-1030, accessed 9 November 2019.

46 Mathworks, 'Deep Learning Examples'.

rising, because they significantly improve predictive clinical models for a diverse array of clinical conditions.[47]

8.4 Transparency – An Overarching Obligation

> The principle of transparency requires that any information addressed to the public or to the data subject be concise, easily accessible and easy to understand, and that clear and plain language and, additionally, where appropriate, visualisation be used.[48]

Transparency is a long-established principle in the EU legal framework, even though it has only recently been explicitly incorporated in the legal text as a principle. It is an expression of the fairness principle stated in Article 8 of the Charter of Fundamental Rights of the European Union.[49] In the context of artificial intelligence, it is an essential characteristic of fairness that data subjects get the opportunity to challenge decisions made by AI systems and to seek redress against the humans operating them. In order to do so, the entity accountable for the decision must be identifiable, and the decision-making processes should be explicable.[50] Transparency may have several different meanings, such as a disclosure of the AI applications used, a description of their logic, or access to the structure of the AI algorithms and – as far as ML is concerned – to the datasets used to train the algorithms.[51] Therefore, it can be challenging to satisfy the transparency principle in the development and use of AI.

Under the GDPR, transparency is named as a fundamental principle in the normative text for the first time. Directive 95/46/EC does not use the term 'transparency', and its Recital 38 describes this principle only vaguely.[52] The key goal of the transparency principle is to engender trust

[47] Miotto and others, 'Deep Patient'.

[48] Regulation (EU) 2016/679, Recital 58.

[49] Article 29 Data Protection Working Party, 'Guidelines on Transparency under Regulation 2016/679' (2018) 28.

[50] Independent High-Level Expert Group on Artificial Intelligence Set Up by the European Commission, 'Ethics Guidelines for Trustworthy AI' (2019).

[51] P Boucher for the European Parliament, 'Artificial Intelligence: How Does It Work, Why Does It Matter; and What Can We Do about It?' (2020) 23.

[52] It must be noted that recitals are not binding, so neither rights nor obligations can derive from them. However, one should not underestimate the value of recitals. First and foremost, a recital sets forth the reasons on which the regulation is based. Further and closely related to this is that courts, in particular the Court of Justice of the EU, use recitals as an interpretation tool.

in the data subject before his/her data is processed. With the concept of transparency, the GDPR follows a rather user-centric approach.[53] The controller must provide enough information to the data subject so that he/she can understand, and if needed, challenge the process.

The GDPR does not only specify what kind of information the controller should provide to the data subject, but it also states some specific practical requirements which are imposed on the data controller and processor. The controller is obliged to take 'appropriate measures' to ensure that the information is communicated to the data subject in a transparent way. The following section will deal with what can be understood as 'appropriate measures' in this context and will examine the requirements expressed in Article 12 of the GDPR.

8.4.1 *How to Provide Information to the Data Subject*

Article 12 sets out some general rules on how information should be provided to the data subject:[54] The controller should, in particular, communicate the required information available in a concise, transparent, intelligible, easily accessible way and is supposed to use clear and plain language.

Moreover, the information should be provided preferably in writing; other means, however, are permitted. If requested by the data subject, the information may also be orally communicated. The GDPR does not prescribe any specific formats or modalities by which the required information must be presented to the data subject, but states clearly that the controller must take 'appropriate measures'.

The following sections will deal in more detail with each of the rules mentioned above.

8.4.1.1 Concise, Transparent and Intelligible

It is a key aspect of the principle of transparency that any surprises for the data subject must be avoided. The data subject should know the scope and consequences of the processing in advance. This is only possible if the information is presented in a concise, transparent and intelligible way.

In this context, 'concise and transparent' means that all information and communication should be efficient and succinct. The controller

[53] Article 29 Data Protection Working Party, 'Guidelines on Transparency' 4.
[54] Ibid., 7.

should try to avoid a confusing overflow of information and must ensure that the data subjects can immediately and easily get the information they are looking for. Closely related to this is the requirement to make information 'easily accessible', which means that data subjects must not be required to search intensively for the information they are interested in. It should be immediately clear how to access the information, which should never be more than 'two taps away'.[55]

'Intelligible' means that an average member of the intended audience should be able to understand the information provided. The controller is supposed to have knowledge about the level of intelligibility of his audience. The vocabulary, tone and style of the language used should be chosen in an appropriate manner for the addressee.

The controller is expected to take into consideration that some people may have more difficulties when accessing information.

Article 29 Working Party (WP29) states clearly that transparency is generally a free-standing right, which applies to the same extent to children as to adults. In accordance with Article 13 of the UN Convention on the Rights of the Child, WP29 states explicitly that even though consent is generally given by parents, the child has the right to freedom of expression. This includes the right to seek, receive and impart information and ideas of all kinds. It is important that children recognise when they are addressed directly. Nevertheless, WP29 recognises that in most cases when young pre-literate children are involved, this requirement may not be fulfilled because they are most likely not able to understand the message. Therefore, in this case, it is sufficient to provide the relevant information to the parents.[56]

In case the controller is uncertain, he/she is supposed to consider testing the texts through mechanisms such as user panels, readability testing and dialogue with industry groups.[57] Especially in the context of AI applications, the features of data processing systems must make it possible for data subjects to really understand what is happening with their data, regardless of the legal ground of processing.[58]

In its guidelines on transparency, WP29 also clearly states that the controller should – in addition to the information under Articles 13 and 14 – 'spell out in unambiguous language' the most important consequences of

[55] Ibid., 8–9.
[56] Ibid., 11.
[57] Ibid., 7.
[58] L Mitrou, 'AI and GDPR study' (2019) 42.

the processing. If it is likely that the process will represent a risk to the rights and freedoms of natural persons, the impacts on data protection must also be assessed before personal information is processed. In the case of using new technology, special consideration must be given to the nature of the processing, its scope and purpose, and the context in which it is performed.[59] The data subject should be made aware of particular risks coming along with the processing.

8.4.1.2 Clear and Plain Language

The requirement that all information should be provided in 'clear and plain language' has already been used by the EU legislature.[60] Both semantics and syntax must be clear, easily understandable and to the point. The controller must provide the required information in as simple a manner as possible, trying to avoid complex sentence and language structures. No abstract or ambivalent terms are to be used. The language should not leave any room for different interpretations. In order to fulfil this requirement, no language qualifiers such as 'may', 'might', 'some', 'often' or 'possible' should be inserted. Furthermore, the usage of the active instead of the passive form and the avoidance of too many nouns may facilitate reading. Not only are the terms crucial, but the structure of the text in the written statements should also help to ease reading. Therefore, the use of bullets and/or indents to signal hierarchical relationships should be considered.[61]

8.4.1.3 In Writing or by Other Means or if Requested Orally

According to Article 12(1) the information should by default be provided in writing or by other means. Only if the data subject requests it and the identity of the data subject is proven the information may be provided orally. According to WP29, the requirement to verify a data subject's identity before providing information orally only applies to information relating to the exercise of a right under Articles 15 to 22 and 34.[62] This approach is to follow because all information laid down in Articles 13 and 14 must also be available for future users. Oral information does not mean that there must be person-to-person communication. An automated oral information tool, which would allow the data subject to re-listen to the

59 Datatilsynet – The Norwegian Data Protection Authority, 'Artificial Intelligence and Privacy' (2018) 25.

60 See Council Directive 93/13 EEC.

61 Article 29 Data Protection Working Party, 'Guidelines on Transparency' 35.

62 Ibid., 20.

messages, may be provided in addition to written means. This could be of particular interest for persons with visual impairments.[63]

8.4.1.4 Appropriate Measures

The legal text neither particularly specifies what measures a controller must take nor which are considered appropriate. However, in its guidelines on transparency, WP29 released some possible 'means' helping the controller to fulfil the requirement of transparency.

The controller must take active steps to provide the information so that the data subject does not have to search for the information required by the GDPR. As already mentioned above, the data subject should not be overwhelmed by information. The information should be edited in a well-structured way and presented in one place at the same time. WP29, therefore, recommends using layered privacy notices in a digital context. This would give the data subjects a clear overview of the information available and enable them to directly click on the information they are looking for. The controller must ensure that all information provided is consistent.[64]

Moreover, WP29 recommends the employment of additional transparency tools such as 'privacy dashboards' or 'just-in-time notices' in order to increase the level of transparency. A privacy dashboard gives the data subject a general overview of their data and the opportunity to manage their privacy settings. This could be of particular interest if the controller offers various services. A privacy dashboard would then allow data subjects to edit their preference for each service separately. A 'just-in-time notice' gives users precisely the information they need in order to make a decision about their data. An often used tool in this context is a pop-up information box.[65]

Regardless of the measure chosen, the manner in which the information is provided must be appropriate to the way the controller interacts with the data subject and how data is being collected. Particular circumstances with regard to processing shall always be considered.

8.4.2 When to Provide Information to the Data Subject

Efficient data management along the whole data life cycle is very important. A very relevant part is the planning phase, in which the research

[63] Ibid.
[64] Ibid., 39.
[65] Ibid.

team provides a detailed description of data that will be used and how they will be managed and made accessible throughout their lifecycles. Planning also requires decision-making on aspects related to data lifetime, data security, data archiving, etc. in order to define a data management plan for the cycle.[66] This stage is essential for compliance with the transparency principle, as information must be provided to the data subject at the commencement phase of the processing cycle.[67] This is in line with the principle of fairness and purpose limitation: The purpose of the processing should always be specified at or before the time of collection.

Article 13 applies when data are directly collected from the data subject, whereas Article 14 deals with the scenario where the data is not obtained directly from the data subject, as is often the case in research scenarios where the controller gets the data from other sources such as a third-party data controller, publicly available sources or other data subjects.

Article 13 clearly states that information must be provided 'at the time when personal data are obtained'. The scenario of Article 14 is more complicated. Article 14(3)(a) requires the controller to provide the information 'within a reasonable period after obtaining the personal data, but at the latest within one month'. However, if personal data is used for communication with the data subject, the controller must inform the data subject at the latest at the time of the first communication (Article 14(3)(b)). WP29 follows the opinion that Article 14(3)(b) only describes a specific case of processing. Nevertheless, Article 14(3)(a) continues to apply. This means that if the first communication with a data subject occurred more than one month after collecting the personal data, the 'one-month rule' would still apply, and the controller would have been obliged to provide the required information to the data subject within one month after obtaining the data. Similarly to the position of Article 14(3)(b), the general one-month time limit can also be curtailed under Article 14(3)(c). In case disclosure to another recipient is envisaged, the controller must inform the data subject at the latest when the personal data are first disclosed. However, if this scenario occurred later than one month, Article 14(3)(a) must be considered, and the data subject must be provided with the relevant information within one month of obtaining the data.

[66] M El Arass and N Souissi, 'Data Lifecycle: From Big Data to SmartData' IEEE 5th International Congress on Information Science and Technology 2018, 80–87.

[67] Article 29 Data Protection Working Party, 'Guidelines on Transparency' 16.

In accordance with the principle of accountability, controllers must demonstrate the rationale for their decisions and justify the timing of when the information was provided to the data subject. Moreover, controllers should consider the principle of fairness, which is closely related to the principle of transparency, and make all required information well available in advance of the stipulated time limits.

It is also important to note that transparency is not a one-time requirement which is fulfilled by providing all required information before collecting personal data. Articles 12 to 14 should be considered throughout the processing lifecycle. This means that if any changes occur to the information mentioned in Articles 13 or 14, such as a change in privacy policy, the data subject must be informed. However, WP29 clarifies that only substantive or material changes must be communicated. Correction of misspellings or grammatical flaws are not subject to the obligation to notify the data subject. The GDPR does not state anything on the timing of notifying the data subject about a change.

The controller must especially consider the principles of fairness and accountability. If any fundamental change occurs, the controller should inform the data subject well in advance of the change so he/she has the chance to assess the nature and impact of the change and, if relevant, exercise a right granted by the GDPR. However, a controller needs to evaluate every situation individually and must be able to explain the process of informing the data subject.

8.5 Information to Be Provided to the Data Subject

The information provided to a data subject must be tailored in terms of structure, complexity and content with a particular aim in mind.[68]

Data collection is generally the first step in every data lifecycle. This phase consists of receiving the raw data of different natures and making the conversions and modifications necessary to organise them.[69] There is a fundamental difference between data collected retrospectively from EHRs and data collected prospectively for a specific study. When data are collected according to a protocol for a research study, the protocol defines the context of the data processing. The circumstances around data

[68] S Wachter and others, 'Counterfactual Explanations without Opening the Black Box: Automated Decisions and the GDPR' (2018) 31(2) *Harvard Journal of Law and Technology* 862.

[69] Arass and Souissi, 'Data Lifecycle'.

collection, including procedures for taking samples and making observations as well as recording data, are defined in the protocol, as are other contextual items such as patient positioning, timing, and anatomical location. In designing studies, a top-down approach is usually taken, starting with the research question, and working down to the required data. By contrast, data captured in an EHR in routine-care settings stem from different contexts. These data are the result of an individual patient's circumstances and reflect standard procedures at the patient's healthcare facility.[70] These data most often do not come directly from the patients to the researchers, and they are the outcome of a bottom-down approach (starting with disease-related processing and leading up to an overarching research question).

This differentiation is also important when transparency must be considered in the light of GDPR. As already mentioned above, a controller must evaluate whether or not the data is directly collected from the data subject (Articles 13 and 14). Articles 13 and 14 outline a long list of information the controller needs to provide to data subjects before processing their data. Some of this information, such as the identity and contact details of the controller, is very straightforward. Other aspects, such as content, will need some more consideration. The following sections will deal with information requirements which may be more challenging when processing health data by means of Big Data analytics.

8.5.1 *The Purpose*

Purpose limitation is one of the cornerstones of the EU's data protection regime.[71] Personal data shall be processed for specified and legitimate purposes and not used in a way incompatible with those purposes. Personal data should not be further processed in a way that the data subject might consider unexpected, inappropriate or otherwise objectionable. Exposure of data subjects to different risks or greater risks than those contemplated

[70] R Richesson and others, 'Using Electronic Health Record Data in Pragmatic Clinical Trials' in *Rethinking Clinical Trials: A Living Textbook of Pragmatic Clinical Trials* (NIH Health Care Systems Research Collaboratory, 2021), https://rethinkingclinicaltrials.org/chapters/design/using-electronic-health-record-data-pragmatic-clinical-trials-top/using-electronic-health-record-data-in-pragmatic-clinical-trials-introduction/, accessed 10 March 2021.

[71] T Zarsky, 'Incompatible: The GDPR in the Age of Big Data' (2017) 47(4) *Seton Hall Law Review* 995–1020.

by the initial purposes could be considered a case of further processing of data in an unexpected manner.[72]

> To comply with the purpose specification rule, entities striving to engage in Big Data analysis will need to inform their data subjects of the future forms of processing they will engage in (which must still be legitimate by nature) and closely monitor their practices to assure they did not exceed the permitted realm of analyses.[73]

Purpose builds the fundamental basis for any processing of personal data. Without specifying the purpose, it is not possible to examine whether the processing is legally covered from a data protection point of view. Therefore, the controller is required to inform the data subject about the purpose before the processing. This might be challenging, as in the context of medical research it may not be possible to specify the purpose of the processing before starting the research itself. Moreover, when using data from existing EHRs, the purpose might not be considered compatible with the initial one anymore. GDPR acknowledges this practical issue and therefore provides some privileges with regard to purpose and legal basis for scientific research.

WP29 states two components of the purpose limitation principle: the data controller must only collect data for specified, explicit and legitimate purposes. Once data are collected, they must not be further processed in a way incompatible with those purposes.

8.5.1.1 Specified, Explicit and Legitimate Purpose

The purpose must either be specified prior to collection or at the latest at the time when the collection of personal data occurs.[74]

The first building block of purpose limitation is specifying the purpose. All personal data should only be collected for a specific, explicit and legitimate purpose. When the specific purpose is defined, the usage of vague and very general descriptions should be avoided. If the controller pursues more than one purpose, this must be made clear to the data subject by communicating all different purposes of the envisioned activities.[75]

72 Council of Europe, 'Guidelines on the Protection of Individuals with Regard to the Processing of Personal Data in a World of Big Data' (2017).

73 Zarsky, ' Incompatible'.

74 Article 29 Data Protection Working Party, 'Opinion 03/2013 on purpose limitation' (2013) 15.

75 Ibid., 51.

In accordance with the principle of transparency, the purpose must be explicit. This means that the purpose must be clearly disclosed and explained to the data subject.

In order for a purpose to be considered legitimate, it must not only be in accordance with all applicable law but also with customs, codes of conduct, codes of ethics and contractual arrangements.[76]

8.5.1.2 Further Processing for Scientific Research Purposes

In principle, the processing of personal data for scientific research purposes is subject to the same standards as for all other purposes, but the GDPR provides some important privileges in favour of scientific research.

In order to understand the legal aspects of scientific research in the context of data protection law, it is necessary to become familiar with this key term, which is used repeatedly in the GDPR. The term 'scientific research' itself is not defined in the regulation. However, Recital 159 states that scientific research purposes should be interpreted in a broad manner. This includes applied research and privately funded research, as well as technological developments and demonstrations. The source of funding does not matter. Article 179(1) Treaty on the Functioning of the European Union should be taken into consideration as well.[77] This provision reflects the objective of the Union that scientific research and technological bases should be strengthened. It is explicitly expressed that health studies carried out in the public interest are covered by the concept of scientific research. The GDPR does not provide any additional restrictions concerning university research or research content.

In principle, Articles 13 and 14 require the data controller to inform the data subjects if they intend to further process the personal data for a purpose other than the one for which it was originally collected.

The regulation establishes a presumption that further processing of personal data for scientific research purposes will be compatible with the purpose for which they were originally collected (Article 5(1)(b) and Recital 50). The presumption of compatibility for secondary processing of data for scientific research purposes is a significant relaxation of the restrictions on repurposing personal data for scientific research.[78] In this context, Article 5 refers to Article 89(1) GDPR, which only specifies the

[76] N Forgó and others, 'The Principle of Purpose Limitation and Big Data', in Corrales M and others (eds), 'New Technology, Big Data and the Law' (Springer Nature Singapore 2017) 28.

[77] Regulation (EU) 2016/679, Recital 159.

[78] Chico, 'The impact of the General Data Protection Regulation'.

circumstances of the processing, but not the lawfulness.[79] Firstly, every controller needs to examine whether he/she is allowed to process the data. Depending on the data to be processed, this requires an assessment of Articles 6, 9 and 10.[80] Such an evaluation applies to both the initial data collection and any further processing of data which has been collected in other contexts and is now to be used for purposes in accordance with Article 89 of the GDPR.

The highest possible standards for security and data protection are central to developing and exchanging EHRs. The GDPR requires patient data to be protected and properly secured so that their confidentiality, integrity and availability are ensured,[81] and the data subjects' rights are observed when their medical data are processed. Therefore, secondly, the controller must make sure that all processing for scientific research purposes is in accordance with Article 89(1) of the GDPR. This means that all processing is subject to appropriate safeguards and technical as well as organisational measures, which should ensure the rights and freedoms of the data subject. Article 89(1) refers in particular to the principle of data minimisation. This means that more data than necessary should not be processed.

In principle, the data controller should assess whether the purpose of the processing may also be achieved using anonymised data. If anonymisation would thwart the aim of processing, Article 89 specifically names pseudonymisation as a possible measure one can take to comply with the principle of data minimisation. It should be noted that pseudonymised data are still considered personal data, and therefore GDPR applies to them in its entirety. However, the provision states clearly that pseudonymisation is only one of many possibilities to fulfil this requirement. A controller should assess which measure he/she must take in order to pursue the purpose and should not process more data than necessary.

Although ML necessarily requires large datasets in the training phase, it is important to adopt a design paradigm that critically assesses the nature and amount of data used, reducing redundant or marginal data and only gradually increasing the size of the training dataset. Minimisation may

[79] B Buchner and M-T Tinnefeld, Art 89, 'Datenschutz-Grundverordnung', in Kühling J and Buchner B (eds), *Datenschutz-Grundverordnung, Bundesdatenschutzgesetz* (C.H. Beck 2018) 1–31.

[80] Article 29 Data Protection Working Party, 'Opinion 03/2013' 33.

[81] Commission Recommendation on a European Electronic Health Record Exchange Format (C(2019)800) of 6 February 2019, Recital 12.

also be achieved in training algorithms by using synthetic data originating from a subset of personal data, which were subsequently anonymised.[82]

8.5.2 A Legal Basis for Processing EHR Data in Scientific Research

In general, the processing of personal data is prohibited unless there is a legal basis. The processing of personal data is lawful if at least one of the six conditions set out in Article 6 of the GDPR is met. GDPR defines processing as any operation which is performed on personal data, whether or not by automated means. GDPR grants stronger protection to certain types of personal data, such as data concerning health, genetic data and biometric data.

As an EHR mainly contains health data, controllers must consider Article 9 in order to process it. As a rule, Article 9(1) of the GDPR prohibits any processing of special categories of personal data. However, paragraph 2 sets out ten conditions for the lawful processing of such data. All exceptions are of the same value, which means that only one of the exceptions must be fulfilled. Furthermore, additional measures could be taken by the Member States under Article 9(4) of the GDPR, through which the scope of Article 9(2) of the GDPR may be implicitly expanded, allowing further conditions for processing health and genetic data, or constraining it.[83] Recital 53 clarifies that this opening clause should not hamper the free flow of personal data within the Union when those conditions apply to cross-border processing of such data. However, it has remained unclear how this requirement can be fulfilled if each Member State implements its own rules.

Articles 6 and 9 of the GDPR also apply when personal data or a special category of personal data are processed for scientific research purposes.[84] The controller is required to specify the applicable provision of Article 6 or Article 9 and, where relevant, the applicable Union or Member State law under which the personal data is processed. A general reference to Article 6 or Article 9 is not sufficient.

Once a lawful basis for data processing has been established, any further processing of (sensitive) personal data, which goes beyond the initial

[82] Council of Europe, 'Report on Artificial Intelligence' (2019) 8.

[83] C Stauton and others, 'The GDPR and the Research Exemption: Considerations on the Necessary Safeguards for Research Biobanks' (2019) 27(1) *European Journal of Human Genetics* 1159–67.

[84] B Raum, Art 89, in Ehrmann E and Selmayr M (eds), *Datenschutz-Grundverordnung* (CH Beck 2017).

purpose, will need to be accompanied by a new legal basis for processing. This is relevant for both primary and secondary use of data. This section will therefore outline the potential legal basis for the primary and secondary processing of sensitive data in a scientific context.

8.5.2.1 (Broad) Consent

For primary use of (sensitive) personal data, consent is often considered as an obvious legal basis. Articles 6 and 9 both name consent as the first potential legal basis for processing (sensitive) personal data. Article 4 of the GDPR defines consent as a

> freely given, specific, informed and unambiguous indication of the data subject's wishes by which he or she, by a statement or by a clear affirmative action, signifies agreement to the processing of personal data relating to him or her.

Article 9 makes clear that consent must also be 'explicit'. The best way to comply with the spirit of the law is to seek written consent, although GDPR does not require it. The European Data Protection Board states examples, such as

> in the digital or online context, how a data subject may be able to issue the required statement: eg by filling in an electronic form, by sending an email, by uploading a scanned document carrying the signature of the data subject, or by using an electronic signature.[85]

Orally given consent can also be valid, but in case of dispute, it can be difficult for the controller to prove that the consent was actually given and with what content. In the context of scientific research, the European Data Protection Board clearly states that the previously mentioned Recital 33 must be read in a stricter way and requires a higher degree of scrutiny while processing sensitive data.[86]

The term 'informed' is also an important element of consent. This means that a data subject needs to be informed before giving his/her consent: inter alia to the purposes of the processing, the processing activities and his/her ability to withdraw this consent at any time. In the context of Big Data, a data subject's informed consent may become unrealistic and less meaningful due to the mutable character of the data processed and the unpredictability of processing outcomes. The complexity and the

[85] European Data Protection Board, 'Guidelines 05/2020 on consent under Regulation 2016/679' (2020) 21.

[86] Ibid., 30.

transformative use of Big Data do not offer a real chance to data subjects to understand potential future uses so as to make a conscious choice.[87]

Given the transformative nature of the use of Big Data and in order to comply with the requirement of free, specific, informed and unambiguous consent, and the principles of purpose limitation, fairness and transparency, controllers should identify the potential impact of the different uses of data on individuals and inform data subjects about this impact.[88]

Big Data processing, based on ML, often results in repurposing, which questions the adequacy of the information originally provided.[89] This requirement is therefore closely related to the principle of purpose limitation. This could be a problem for processing Big Data for research purposes, since the purpose of the research might not be defined yet. The GDPR acknowledges the challenge for researchers and states in its Recital 33 that

> [i]t is often not possible to fully identify the purpose of personal data processing for scientific research purposes at the time of data collection. Therefore, data subjects should be allowed to give their consent to certain areas of scientific research when in keeping with recognised ethical standards for scientific research.

This concept is often considered 'broad consent', meaning that consent can be formulated in a broader range of research, not only for a specific research question.[90]

8.5.2.2 Scientific Research Purpose (Article 9(2)(j) GDPR)

Article 9(2)(j) provides a legal basis for processing a special category of personal data for scientific research purposes. In order to avoid the scope of this provision becoming overly broad, there must be an EU or Member State law which allows processing in this regard. GDPR sets forth certain requirements of such a law: The law shall be proportionate to the aim pursued, respect the essence of the right to data protection, and provide suitable and specific measures to safeguard the fundamental rights and the interests of the data subject. Furthermore, Member States should consider Article 89(1) of the GDPR while drafting the provisions. As already mentioned in Section 8.4.1.2 of this chapter, Article 89(1) of the GDPR states

[87] Mitrou, 'AI and GDPR study' 39.
[88] Council of Europe, 'Guidelines on the Protection of Individuals'.
[89] Mitrou 'AI and GDPR study' 39.
[90] Forgó and others, 'The Principle of Purpose Limitation and Big Data' 28.

that all processing shall be subject to appropriate safeguards, technical and organisational measures, which should ensure the rights and freedoms of the data subject.

8.5.3 *Data Subject's Rights*

All data subjects must be informed about their rights granted by the GDPR. This should include a summary of what the right involves and how the data subjects can exercise it. Moreover, the controller must explain any limitations or restrictions on their rights.

These include the rights to:

- Access
- Rectification
- Erasure
- Restriction on Processing
- Objection to Processing and
- Portability

8.5.3.1 Exercise of Data Subject's Rights

In order to be compliant with the transparency principle, the GDPR does not only require the controller to provide information to data subjects on their rights and communicate it in a concise, transparent, intelligible, easily accessible manner, using a clear and plain language, but also to facilitate the exercise of data subjects' rights under Articles 15 to 22.

The controller must give data subjects all the necessary tools so that they can exercise their rights. The modality should be appropriate to the situation and interaction between the controller and the data subject. The controller should consider offering more than one modality, although this is not required by law.

8.5.3.2 Restriction of Data Subject's Rights for Scientific Research

The privileges regarding data processing in scientific research are shown by the fact that the GDPR limits the obligations of the controller as well as the rights of the data subject in several areas. On the one hand, the GDPR directly restricts the obligations and rights, while on the other hand, it allows – in opening clauses – the legislative bodies of the Union and Member States to enact laws that derogate the data subject's rights.

In principle, Article 17 of the GDPR guarantees data subjects the right to obtain the erasure of their personal data without undue delay from the controller. Article 17(3) lays down some exceptions to the right to be forgotten. In the context of scientific research, subparagraph (d) the 'right to be forgotten' does not apply, as this right is likely to render impossible or seriously impair the achievement of the objectives of the processing. Article 17(3) refers to Article 89(1), which means that a controller may only refer to this exception if he/she implements appropriate measures in accordance with Article 89(1).[91]

Another restriction of the data subject's rights may be found in Article 21(6). This article states that the data subject, on grounds relating to his/her particular situation, has the right to object to the processing of his/her personal data, unless the processing is necessary for the performance of a task carried out for reasons of public interest. Since the data subject may only object to the processing on grounds relating to his/her particular situation, the hurdle for a successful objection is high.[92] This means that data subjects must find themselves in a situation which is considered especially worthy of protection.[93] If so, the data subject may be successful with his/her objection unless the controller can show credibly that the processing is necessary for reasons of public interest.[94]

Article 89(2) includes an opening clause which allows Member States to derogate data subjects' rights in specific situations. The right of access, rectification, restriction and objection may be subject to such derogation, if these rights make scientific research impossible or seriously impair the fulfilment of the purpose. Moreover, the derogations are subject to the conditions and safeguards set out by Article 89(1) of the GDPR (discussed earlier in this chapter). This means that if a Member State makes use of such derogation, it must at the same time introduce additional safeguards to ensure the rights and freedoms of the data subject.

8.5.4 Automated Decision-Making

According to Article 14, data subjects must be informed if automated decision-making is used for the processing of their personal data. If so, the controller should provide meaningful information about the logic

[91] T Herbst, 'Recht auf Löschung', in Kühling J and Buchner B (eds), 'Datenschutz-Grundverordnung', Bundesdatenschutzgesetz (C.H. Beck 2018) 459.

[92] C Roth, 'Recht für F&E; Open Innovation' in Felten and others (eds), *Digitale Transformation im Wirtschafts- & Steuerrecht* (Lindeverlag 2018), Chapter 11, Section 21.

[93] Ibid.

[94] M Martini, Art 21 Widerspruchsrecht, in Paal BP and Pauly DA (eds), *Datenschutz-Grundverordnung* (Beck'sche Kompakt-Kommentare 2017) 60.

involved as well as the significance and the envisaged consequences of such processing for the data subject. Giving information about the type of input data and the expected output, explaining the variables and their weight, or shining a light on the analytics architecture are various forms of transparency concerning the logic of AI algorithms.[95]

However, all this can become very difficult as far as Big Data analytics is concerned. The principle of the algorithms of deep learning can be explained in a simple way, but the details are complicated to describe as they depend on many parameters and iterations. The description of such a complicated design might confuse data subjects, which would cause a conflict with a simple presentation and explanation required by the GDPR. Although AI is complex, and difficult to understand and explain, the principle of transparent processing of personal data nevertheless applies in the development and use of artificial intelligence.[96]

It should be noted that GDPR focusses more on the individual rather than the societal impacts of algorithms. Even if some form of compensation could be provided to individuals who are unjustly harmed by an algorithm, this would only solve the individual problem of the person who was willing to complain. This approach would not reduce wider societal impacts that may result from adverse algorithmic decisions.[97]

8.5.4.1 General Prohibition of Usage of Automated Decision-Making and Its Exceptions

Article 22(1), which deals with automated individual decision-making, including profiling, reads as follows:

> The data subject shall have the right not to be subject to a decision based solely on automated processing, including profiling, which produces legal effects concerning him or her or similarly significantly affects him or her.

Contrary to the wording used, in particular the term 'right', this article lays down a general prohibition for decision-making based solely on automated processing. The data subject should not be required to take an action to avoid this kind of processing. This interpretation of this article is also supported by Recital 71, which sets out cases where decision-making

[95] Council of Europe, 'Report on Artificial Intelligence' 12.

[96] Datatilsynet, 'Artificial Intelligence and Privacy' 19.

[97] J Shkabatur, 'The Global Commons of Data' (2018) 22 *Stanford Technology Law Review*.

based on such processing should be allowed. By implication, all other decision-making based solely on automated processing is forbidden.[98]

'Based solely' means that there is no human involvement in the decision process.[99] As already mentioned in Section 8.2.2, in a deep-learning process, human intervention is not necessary. There is no human influence on the results of the learning process, which – due to automatic parameter weighting and continuous optimisation- cannot be traced back completely in some respects. In order to qualify as 'human involvement' in the light of the GDPR, a potential actual influence by a human is required. This means that an individual who has the authority and competence to change the decision must be involved. The controller must keep records of the degree of any human involvement in the decision-making process at all stages.

Article 22(2) of the GDPR states cases in which automated decision-making is allowed. This might be the case if the decision is:

(a) necessary for the performance of or entering into a contract;
(b) authorised by Union or Member State law to which the controller is subject and which also lays down suitable measures to safeguard the data subject's rights and freedoms and legitimate interests; or
(c) based on the data subject's explicit consent.

In addition to the requirements mentioned above, it can be said that if special categories of personal data are involved, the controller must also consider Article 22(4) of the GDPR. This Article states that decisions based on sensible data are not allowed, unless the legal basis for processing is Article 9(2)(a) or (g) of the GDPR and suitable measures are in place to safeguard the data subject's rights and freedoms and legitimate interests. In other words, either the data subject gives his/her explicit consent for the processing of his/her sensible data or the processing is necessary for reasons of substantial public interest on the basis of Union or Member State law. If one of the two legal bases apply, the controller must additionally ensure the implementation of appropriate measures to safeguard the data subject's rights and freedoms.

As Article 22 directly impacts Big Data practices, it is possible that companies and researchers might be required to substantially change their technological architectures and even business models, opting for less efficient practices, which comply with this rule.[100]

98 Article 29 Data Protection Working Party, 'Guidelines on Automatic Individual Decision-Making and Profiling for the Purposes of Regulation 2016/679' (2018) 20.
99 Ibid.
100 Zarsky, 'Incompatible'.

8.5.4.2 Meaningful Information about the Logic Involved, and the Significance and Envisaged Consequences

Healthcare organisations are investing heavily in technologies to advance Big Data analytics and precision medicine.[101] As global business multinationals are involved in the processing of EHR data, it must always be considered that transparency 'should not adversely affect the rights or freedoms of others, including trade secrets or intellectual property and in particular the copyright, which protects the software'.[102]

> What would seem to matter ... is the capacity to understand the general logic underpinning the way the algorithm works. It should be possible for everyone to understand this logic, which must therefore be explained in words rather than in lines of code.[103]

The complexity of ML systems can make it challenging for the controller to explain the logic involved to the data subject.

As discussed above, the GDPR states clearly in Article 12 that the controller should provide all information in a concise, transparent, intelligible and easily accessible form to the data subject. Nevertheless, the controller should, at the same time, by any means try to avoid any information fatigue for the data subject.[104] This can be very challenging in the context of Big Data analytics and ML. Moreover, the controller might not want to disclose any business secrets.

The information regarding the model's logic might cover aspects such as whether decision trees are to be used, and how the data is to be weighted and correlated. However, as the information must be understandable to the data subject, it is not always necessary to provide a thorough explanation of the algorithm, or even to include the algorithm.[105] The data subject must be able to understand the reasons for the decision and assess the trade-offs which are at stake. This means that the controller must explain the rationale or criteria which he/she relied on in order to reach

101 J Kent, 'Big Data Analytics, Precision Medicine Top Priorities in 2020' *Health IT Analytics*, 25 November 2019, https://healthitanalytics.com/news/big-data-analytics-precision-medicine-top-priorities-in-2020?eid=CXTEL000000519439&elqCampaignId=12525&utm_source=nl&utm_medium=email&utm_campaign=newsletter&elqTrackId=4e968b96b27c420ab1fff6c2e4a654f5&elq=c801b7efe6444ef394d45338b78dc755&elqaid=13156&elqat=1&elqCampaignId=12525, accessed 30 November 2019.

102 Regulation (EU) 2016/679, Recital 63.

103 Commission Nationale Informatique & Libertés, 'Comment Permettre À L'homme de Garder la Main?' (2017) 51.

104 Article 29 Data Protection Working Party, 'Guidelines on Transparency' 8.

105 Datatilsynet, 'Artificial Intelligence and Privacy' 16.

the decision.[106] The controller must provide clarity about the causal connections and the interference processes of the system.[107] The right to an explanation does not necessarily mean that the black box must be opened, but the explanation has to enable the data subject to understand why a particular decision was reached or what needs to be changed in order to reach a different decision.[108]

Moreover, the data subject should be informed about the possible effects of the processing. In order to make this information meaningful and understandable, the controller is supposed to give examples and consider using tools in order to illustrate such effects.[109] This does not mean that the controller should predict any results, but he/she should inform the data subject about the possible span and scope of the decision.[110]

8.5.4.3 Safeguards

Article 22(3) of the GDPR requires the controller to implement suitable measures to safeguard the data subject's rights and freedoms and legitimate interests. As a minimum requirement, this article states that the data subject should have the right to obtain human intervention. This ensures that the data subject has the chance to express his/her point of view and contest the decision. Therefore, human intervention is a central element in this context. Article 22(3) does not refer to Article 22(2)b because the law which authorises the controller to use automated decision-making tools must foresee suitable measures. In order to check for any bias, controllers should carry out assessments on a regular basis.

> In order to ensure fair and transparent processing in respect of the data subject, taking into account the specific circumstances and context in which the personal data are processed, the controller should use appropriate mathematical or statistical procedures for the profiling, implement technical and organisational measures appropriate to ensure, in particular, that factors which result in inaccuracies in personal data are corrected and the risk of errors is minimised, secure personal data in a manner that takes account of the potential risks involved for the interests and rights of

106 Article 29 Data Protection Working Party, 'Guidelines on Automatic Individual Decision-Making' 25.

107 Ibid., 27.

108 S Wachter and others, 'Counterfactual Explanations Without Opening The Black Box' 862.

109 Article 29 Data Protection Working Party, 'Guidelines on Automatic Individual Decision-Making' 26.

110 Ibid., 28.

> the data subject, and prevent, inter alia, discriminatory effects on natural persons on the basis of racial or ethnic origin, political opinion, religion or beliefs, trade union membership, genetic or health status or sexual orientation, or processing that results in measures having such an effect.[111]

Although accurate AI systems can reduce or eliminate human bias in decision-making, it is also possible that data-intensive applications are affected by potential bias, as both deterministic and machine-learning AI use data input to extract further information (analytics) or create and train ML models. The bias may concern the data scientists' methods, the object of their investigation, their data sources (selection bias) or the person responsible for the analysis. If data subjects got the opportunity to access an algorithms' structure, they might be able to detect potential biases. However, time and special skills are required to perform such an analysis.[112]

8.6 Limits of Transparency

As mentioned above, when data is collected from EHRs and not directly from the data subject, Article 14 of the GDPR, with its information obligations, applies. Article 14(4) sets out the limits of the information obligation when data is not collected directly from the data subject. According to WP29, these exceptions must be interpreted and applied narrowly.[113]

Like in Article 13(4), when data is collected directly from the data subjects, the controller is not required to provide the information to the data subjects if they already have it. In accordance with the principle of accountability, it must be noted that the controller is required to set forth what information the data subject already has. Moreover, it must be clearly stated how and when the data subject received the information.[114]

Article 14(4)(b) includes several separate situations where the controller is not required to provide information to the data subject set out in Articles 14(1) to 14(3). Firstly, the obligation may be lifted if such information 'proves impossible'. The controller must demonstrate the factors that actually prevent him/her from providing the information in question to the data subject. As soon as the factor which caused the impossibility no longer exists, the controller is obliged to provide all information required

[111] Regulation (EU) 2016/679, Recital 71.
[112] Council of Europe, 'Report on Artificial Intelligence' 12.
[113] Article 29 Data Protection Working Party, 'Guidelines on Transparency' 57.
[114] Ibid., 56.

by Article 14(1) of the GDPR. Practically speaking, it is very unlikely that a controller will be able to prove that it was actually impossible to provide the information.[115] Secondly, the controller is not required to provide the information where this would involve a disproportionate effort. Recital 62 clearly states that the number of data subjects, the age of the data and appropriate safeguards adopted must be taken into consideration. Both these exceptions to the information obligation are particularly relevant for scientific research. In the context of Big Data analytics, these exceptions may be pertinent, as a large number of samples processed, and the data may have been collected years. Lastly, Article 14(4)(b) also refers to the situation where the obligation to provide information, set forth in Article 14(1), would lead to a serious impairment of objectives. However, in order to rely on this exception, the controller is required to demonstrate that the provision of the information would nullify the objectives of the processing.[116]

In the context of medicine, a very important exception is the situation where the personal data must remain confidential, subject to an obligation of professional secrecy regulated by Union or Member State law, including a statutory obligation of secrecy. In order to rely on this exception, the controller must have identified professional secrecy as a reason for not informing the data subject and he/she must be able to show that he/she is subject to this obligation. For example, a healthcare professional is under a professional obligation of secrecy in relation to his patients' medical information. In case the patient discloses personal data of other persons, such as relatives who have similar conditions, the healthcare professional (controller) is not required to provide Article 14 information to the relatives.[117]

8.7 Council of Europe: The Modernised Convention 108

In 1981, Convention 108 was the first legally binding international instrument in the data protection field. Under this convention, the parties are required to take the necessary steps in their domestic legislation to apply the principles it lays down. The goal was to ensure respect in their territory for the fundamental human rights of all individuals with regard to the processing of personal data. The convention has recently undergone a process

115 Ibid., 59.
116 Ibid., 65.
117 Ibid., 66.

of modernisation in order to deal with challenges resulting from the use of new information and communication technologies.[118] The Modernised Convention 'Convention 108+', which has not entered into force yet, maintains the neutral nature of the original convention. Coherence and compatibility with other relevant legal frameworks, such as GDPR, have also been preserved. Regulators at the Council of Europe and EU level were very careful to secure consistency and compatibility between the two legal frameworks.[119]

The Modernised Convention reaffirms important principles but also integrates new principles, such as transparency and proportionality. Like GDPR, Convention 108+ requires data processing to be done in a transparent manner in relation to the data subject:[120] 'Personal data should be processed lawfully, fairly and in a transparent manner'.[121] Council of Europe law also specifies that certain essential information has to be compulsorily provided to the data subject in a proactive manner by the controller.[122] Article 8 sets forth a list of information which must be provided to the data subject. The list of required information is not as long as in the GDPR. However, it covers the same key aspects. Moreover, it states that any necessary additional information to ensure fair and transparent processing should also be communicated. This leaves room for interpretation. Nevertheless, Convention 108 and GDPR go hand in hand in this regard, and do not contradict each other. Like the GDPR, Articles 8(2) and 8(3) of the convention foresee some exceptions to this obligation, such as when the data subject already has the information, where the processing is expressly prescribed by law or where the provision of information is impossible or involves disproportionate efforts. The Modernised Convention also loosens regulations in research contexts: Restrictions on the provisions specified in Articles 8 and 9 may be provided by law. The principle of transparency and data subjects' rights may only be restricted for scientific research, where there is no recognisable risk of infringement of the rights and fundamental freedoms of data subjects.[123]

As far as lawfulness of data processing is concerned, the Modernised Convention also uses the same language as GDPR: The purpose must be

[118] European Union Agency for Fundamental Rights and Council of Europe, *Handbook on European Data Protection Law* (2018) 24–7.

[119] Council of Europe, 'Explanatory Report Modernised Convention' (2018) 3.

[120] Modernised Convention (2018), articles 5(4)(a) and 8.

[121] Ibid., Article 5(4)(a).

[122] Explanatory Memorandum of the Modernised Convention (2018), No. 68.

[123] Modernised Convention (2018), Article 11(1).

'explicit, specified and legitimate'. Moreover, Article 5(4)(b) also states that no personal data should be processed in a way which may be considered incompatible with the initial purpose. The further processing of personal data for scientific research purposes is a priori considered compatible, provided that appropriate safeguards exist in both the original and intended further processing operations.[124] The explanatory memorandum lists some examples of what may be considered appropriate safeguards, for instance, anonymisation of data or data pseudonymisation, as well as other technical and organisational data security measures.[125]

In order to give data subjects greater control over their data in the digital age, the Modernised Convention provides new rights such as the right not to be subject to a decision significantly affecting him or her, which is solely based on automated processing of data, without having his/her views taken into consideration. As mentioned above, in the scientific area this right might be restricted by law.[126]

Finally, it may be noted that the Modernised Convention does not provide any new data protection aspects, which have not been already covered by the GDPR. However, as the Council of Europe has a larger audience, Convention 108+ is an important instrument to increase the level of data protection and harmonise this field beyond the European borders. On an even larger scale, the United Nations Special Rapporteur on the Right to Privacy and experts on health data protection from all over the world developed a recommendation, intended to set a common minimum standard for the protection of health-related data.

8.8 The New UN Recommendation on Health Data Protection

An international approach to the regulation of privacy aspects concerning health data is being provided by the UN. The United Nations Special Rapporteur on the Right to Privacy and experts on health data protection from all over the world developed a 'recommendation on the protection and use of health-related data', the first draft of which was published in February 2019. Two rounds of written public consultations were to follow. Stakeholders from all different sections of society

124 Explanatory Memorandum of the Modernised Convention (2018), No. 49.
125 Ibid., 59.
126 Modernised Convention (2018), Article 11(1).

and international organisations worldwide assessed privacy aspects of health data and shared their opinions with respect to the development of a global legal recommendation. Then a task force analysed and discussed the several hundred comments and contributions. An oral presentation took place in June 2019 at a joint event with the Council of Europe in Strasbourg, and the final text was presented to the UN General Assembly in October 2019. The recommendation builds on the existing international consensus in the field of privacy and data protection for health-related data and aims to provide further guidance. This recommendation is intended to set a common minimum standard for the protection of health-related data, which should be implemented at the domestic level. Together with other human rights, it should also serve as a guideline for the protection of privacy in the processing of health-related data. This recommendation does not limit or affect any laws that grant data subjects better rights or protections, or that impose stricter obligations on the processor.

Like European laws, the recommendation enshrines the right to fair and transparent processing. It requires information to be made available to the data subject which must be intelligible, easily accessible, in plain language and suited to the circumstances to enable a full understanding. This information has to be provided before processing and it must contain – among other details – the source and categories of the health-related data being processed and the purpose and legal basis of the processing as well as the length of storage period.

8.8.1 Scientific Research

The recommendation dedicates a whole section (21) to scientific research. This not only shows the importance of this area but also expresses the specific needs of the field.

It is a research-friendly recommendation, illustrating that it is indeed feasible to offer a best practice level of data protection while promoting research and innovation.

Unlike the GDPR and the convention, the recommendation defines scientific research. Even though the definition is very long and seems to be very specific, the recommendation uses a wide approach to what qualifies as scientific research.

> Scientific research means creative and systematic work undertaken in order to increase the stock of knowledge and/or to devise new application

> of available knowledge.[127] The activity must be novel, creative, uncertain, systematic, and transferable and/or reproducible. Factors for determining whether an activity is scientific research include the role of the legal entity where the activity is carried out; the role of the natural person(s) carrying out the activity; quality standards including use of scientific methodology and scientific publication; and adherence to research ethical norms. Research within any discipline that may process health-related data, including medical and health sciences, natural sciences, engineering and technology, social sciences, humanities and fine arts, is scientific research. The scientific research may be basic research, applied research or experimental development, and policy analysis, health services and epidemiology are all examples of scientific research. Scientific research can be both publicly and privately funded and conducted, and may in some cases be conducted for profit.[128]

The need to process health-related data for scientific research must – among other features – be evaluated in light of the research purposes, the state-of-the-art of scientific knowledge, respect for ethical rules, the purported benefits, the constraints placed on the processing of the data and the risks to the data subject.

The recommendation requires that the processing of health-related data for scientific research purposes complies with the provisions of this recommendation and with any other rights and fundamental freedoms of the data subject, and is carried out for a legitimate purpose.

All processing for research purposes must find its legal basis either in seeking consent from the data subject or in a legal provision. The recommendation clearly states that consent to research participation may not be considered as consent for processing health data. However, the recommendation follows a broad approach regarding the purpose a data subject may consent to. If it is not possible to determine the specific purpose at the time of collection, data subjects may consent to certain areas of scientific research or parts of scientific research projects. Nevertheless, as soon as the purpose may be specified any further, the data subject should be informed.

The recommendation provides guidelines for legislators on what a law, used as a legal basis for processing health data for research purposes, should look like. Such a law must be necessary for and proportionate to the aim pursued, respect the right to data protection, and provide suitable

[127] OECD, *Frascati Manual 2015: Guidelines for Collecting and Reporting Data on Research and Experimental Development* (OECD Publishing 2015).

[128] UN Recommendation on the Protection and Use of Health-Related Data (2019), Section 24.

and specific safeguards in order to protect the rights and freedoms of the data subject. This provision is similar to GDPR Articles 89(1) and 89(2). This shows again that this recommendation builds on an already existing consensus and is not in contradiction to existing data protection rules.

In accordance with European laws, health data should – where possible – be anonymised. However, the recommendation acknowledges that sometimes it is technically not feasible and/or not practicable to anonymise the data. In such situations, the controller should implement pseudonymisation in order to comply with the principle of data minimisation.

In the context of scientific research, paragraph 21.7 states that the data subject must be additionally provided with transparent, comprehensible and reasonably precise information such as the nature of the envisaged scientific research, the aims, methods, sources of funding, any possible conflicts of interest, post-study provisions, institutional affiliations of the researcher, the anticipated benefits and potential risks of the study, and the discomfort it may entail, as well as any other relevant aspects of the study. Furthermore, it must be clearly communicated that the data subject has the right to refuse to consent to data processing for scientific research and to withdraw consent.

8.8.2 Electronic Health Records

In its section on EHRs, the recommendation guarantees all individuals a right to privacy and the confidentiality and protection of their health-related data in EHR systems, which must be rigorously managed with respect to data protection as well as ethical, professional, legal and all other applicable requirements. An EHR system must include an electronic protocol of who had access to the data in it, the duration of that access, as well as logs of modifications and protocols in order to prevent unauthorised access. If health workers or authorised personnel of healthcare institutions who are not treating the data subject want to process health-related data of an EHR, they must have the data subject's consent prior to processing.

Evidence of patients' consent to access their EHR data is necessary. Electronic means to give and withdraw consent have to be used wherever technically feasible. A data subject must have access to his/her health-related data in an EHR without undue delay or expense. Health-related data should not be stored in an EHR beyond the time required for the purposes for which it was collected.

Processing of health-related data in EHR systems for scientific or statistical purposes is allowed where necessary, if the specific purpose was previously determined and there is a necessary and proportionate law that protects the data subject's rights. Health-related data from EHR systems used for research purposes must be in an anonymised form wherever possible.

8.8.3 *Big Data, Algorithmic Processing and Automated Decisions*

The recommendation also provides guiding principles for the regulation of health-related algorithms.

In accordance with GDPR principles, a data subject shall have the right not to be subject to a health-related decision based solely on automated processing, including profiling, which relates to prognosis, diagnosis or treatment. Moreover, data subjects can require that the original decision resulting from automated processing is reviewed and finally taken by a human being and that any automated decision is explained in an easily understandable manner by a competent person. The explanation must at least include how the automated decision-making technology works as well as describe the factors that lead to the decision.[129]

The recommendation presents three scenarios when the data subject's rights are lifted. As far the GDPR is concerned, this is when the decision is either authorised by law, the data subject consented to the processing by automated means, or if the decision is necessary for entering into or the performance of a contract between the data subject and the controller.

Nevertheless, data subjects should be made aware of the fact that a health-related algorithm is used and that risks are associated. Being transparent, fair and predictable, these algorithms should meet a high and specified standard of quality and safety. Monitoring of any adverse effects of health-related or ML algorithms, as well as of all forms of AI should be undertaken in accordance with this recommendation and other relevant laws. Processes and systems must be designed and implemented to identify any potential implicit algorithmic bias. Where a bias is identified, steps must be taken to address it. Any bias must be disclosed to data subjects who may be unfairly assessed by the health-related algorithm. If a health-related algorithm is not sufficiently explainable, it can only be used in support of a decision, unless it is being used in pre-clinical trials or research.

[129] Ibid., Section 33.1.

8.9 Conclusion

Big Data analytics in health research and treatment has considerable potential for good and bad. On the one hand, it may significantly increase the quality of treatment and research. On the otherhand, it may lead to unwanted consequences such as algorithmic bias and loss of patients' autonomy and freedom. It is no wonder, therefore, that the law and lawyers try to regulate the upcoming threats and possibilities intensely. These regulatory approaches have several challenges in common: first, the technical development in AI is fast and unpredictable. Second, different legal regimes are linked to diverse legal frameworks that differ both in the details and the fundamentals, and it is difficult to obtain an appropriate overview. Third, regulatory approaches tend to be late and 'lost in translation' between computer science, economics, different cultural backgrounds and the law.

However, for these reasons, it is specifically important to identify basic regulatory principles in the domain. Transparency is one of these principles. Transparency as an instrument for better data protection is common in all the regulatory frameworks analysed here.

GDPR and Convention 108+ are important instruments to foster European regulatory approaches to transparency in data protection. Due to their European foundation, their applicability and also their legal interpretation are limited to Europe. For this reason, attempts to broaden and discuss their scope and principles in a global context are important for further development. The UN recommendation on health data protection is such an instrument, and it deserves further analysis and discussion.

Bibliography

Ambur MY and others, 'Big Data Analytics and Machine Intelligence Capability Development at NASA Langley Research Center: Strategy, Roadmap, and Progress' (2015), https://ntrs.nasa.gov/citations/20170000676.

Angst C and Agarwal R, 'Adoption of Electronic Health Records in the Presence of Privacy Concerns: The Elaboration Likelihood Model and Individual Persuasion' (2009) 33(2) *Management Information Systems Quarterly* 339–70.

Article 29 Data Protection Working Party, 'Guidelines on Automatic Individual Decision-Making and Profiling for the Purposes of Regulation 2016/679' 17/EN, WP251rev.01 (2018), https://ec.europa.eu/newsroom/article29/items/612053.

Article 29 Data Protection Working Party, 'Guidelines on Transparency Under Regulation 2016/679' 17/EN, WP260 rev.01 (2018), https://ec.europa.eu/newsroom/article29/items/612053.

Article 29 Data Protection Working Party, 'Opinion 03/2013 on Purpose Limitation' 00569/13/EN, WP203 (2013), https://ec.europa.eu/newsroom/article29/items/612053.

Banik A and Bandyopadhyay SK, 'Big Data-A Review on Analysing 3Vs' (2016) 3(1) *Journal of Scientific and Engineering Research* 21–24.

Boucher P for the European Parliament, 'Artificial Intelligence: How Does It Work, Why Does It Matter; and What Can We Do about It?' (2020).

Buchner B and Tinnefeld M-T, Art 89. 'Datenschutz-Grundverordnung' in Kühling J and Buchner B (eds), *Bundesdatenschutzgesetz* (C.H.Beck 2018) 1–31.

Chandrika M and others, 'Impact of Big Data and Emerging Research Trends' (2015) *International Journal of Innovative Technology and Research*. International Conference on Computational Systems for Health & Sustainability (CSFHS) 17–18 April 2015 14–17.

Chico V, 'The Impact of the General Data Protection Regulation on Health Research' (2018) 128(1) *British Medical Bulletin* 109–18.

Commission Nationale Informatique & Libertés, 'Comment Permettre À L'homme de Garder la Main ?' (2017), www.cnil.fr/sites/default/files/atoms/files/cnil_rapport_garder_la_main_web.pdf.

Commission Recommendation on a European Electronic Health Record Exchange Format (C(2019)800) of 6 February 2019, https://eur-lex.europa.eu/legal-content/EN/TXT/PDF/?uri=CELEX:32019H0243&from=EN.

Council Directive 93/13 EEC of 5 April 1993 on Unfair Terms in Consumer Contracts, https://eur-lex.europa.eu/legal-content/EN/TXT/PDF/?uri=CELEX:31993L0013&from=EN.

Council of Europe, Convention 108 +, Convention for the protection of individuals with regard to the processing of personal data (2018), www.europarl.europa.eu/meetdocs/2014_2019/plmrep/COMMITTEES/LIBE/DV/2018/09-10/Convention_108_EN.pdf.

Council of Europe, 'Explanatory Report Modernised Convention' (2018), https://rm.coe.int/cets-223-explanatory-report-to-the-protocol-amending-the-convention-fo/16808ac91a.

Council of Europe, 'Guidelines on the Protection of Individuals with Regard to the Processing of Personal Data in a World of Big Data' (2017), https://rm.coe.int/16806ebe7a.

Council of Europe, 'Report on Artificial Intelligence', T-PD(2018)09Rev (2019), https://rm.coe.int/artificial-intelligence-and-data-protection-challenges-and-possible-re/168091f8a6.

Dahlem D and others, 'Predictability Bounds of Electronic Health Records' (2015) 5(1) *Scientific Reports* 1–9.

Datatilsynet (The Norwegian Data Protection Authority), 'Artificial Intelligence and Privacy' (2018), www.datatilsynet.no/globalassets/global/english/ai-and-privacy.pdf.

Diebold FX, 'On the Origin(s) and Development of the Term "Big Data"' (2012), 12(037) PIER Working Paper. Dorland, WA Newman, *Dorland's Illustrated Medical Dictionary* (28th ed., WB Saunders 1994).

Edwards L and Veale M, 'Slave to the Algorithm? Why a "Right to an Explanation" Is Probably Not the Remedy You Are Looking for' (2017) 16(1) *Duke Law and Technology Review* 18–84.

El Arass M and Souissi N, 'Data Lifecycle: From Big Data to SmartData' IEEE 5th International Congress on Information Science and Technology, 208, 80–7. doi: 10.1109/CIST.2018.8596547.

European Commission – European Group on Ethics in Science and New Technologies, 'Statement on Artificial Intelligence, Robotics and "Autonomous" Systems' (2018), https://op.europa.eu/en/publication-detail/-/publication/dfebe62e-4ce9-11e8-be1d-01aa75ed71a1.

European Data Protection Board, 'Guidelines 05/2020 on Consent under Regulation 2016/679' (2020), https://edpb.europa.eu/sites/default/files/files/file1/edpb_guidelines_202005_consent_en.pdf.

European Union Agency for Fundamental Rights and Council of Europe, *Handbook on European Data Protection Law* (Publications Office of the European Union, 2018) 24–27, https://fra.europa.eu/sites/default/files/fra_uploads/fra-coe-edps-2018-handbook-data-protection_en.pdf.

Explanatory Memorandum of the Modernised Convention (2018), https://eur-lex.europa.eu/legal-content/EN/TXT/PDF/?uri=CELEX:52018PC0449&from=HU

Forgó N and others, 'The Principle of Purpose Limitation and Big Data' in Corrales M and others (eds), *New Technology, Big Data and the Law* (Springer Nature Singapore 2017) 17–42.

Goodfellow I and others, *Deep Learning* (MIT Press 2016).

Hardesty L, 'Crowdsourcing Big-Data Analysis', *MIT News*, 30 October 2017, https://news.mit.edu/2017/crowdsourcing-big-data-analysis-1030, accessed 9 November 2019.

Hedge V and Usmani S, 'Parallel and Distributed Deep Learning' (2016), https://web.stanford.edu/~rezab/classes/cme323/S16/projects_reports/hedge_usmani.pdf.

Herbst T, 'Recht auf Löschung' in Kühling J and Buchner B (eds), *'Datenschutz-Grundverordnung', Bundesdatenschutzgesetz* (General Data Protection Regulation, Federal Data Protection Act) (C.H. Beck 2018) 459.

Independent High-Level Expert Group on Artificial Intelligence set up by the European Commission, 'Ethics Guidelines for Trustworthy AI' (2019), www.aepd.es/sites/default/files/2019-12/ai-ethics-guidelines.pdf.

InteropEHRate, 'InteropEHRate in a Nutshell' *InteropEHRate* (2019), www.interopehrate.eu/interopehrate-in-a-nutshell/, accessed 10 November 2019.

Jensen PB and others, 'Mining Electronic Health Records: Towards Better Research Applications and Clinical Care' (2012) 13(6) *Nature Reviews Genetics* 395–405.

Kent J, 'Big Data Analytics, Precision Medicine Top Priorities in 2020' *Health IT Analytics*, 25 November 2019, https://healthitanalytics.com/news/big-data-analytics-precision-medicine-top-priorities-in-2020?eid=CXTEL000000519439&elqCampaignId=12525&utm_source=nl&utm_medium=email&utm_campaign=newsletter&elqTrackId=4e968b96b27c420ab1fff6c2e4a654f5&elq=c801b7efe6444ef394d45338b78dc755&elqaid=13156&elqat=1&elqCampaignId=12525, accessed 30 November 2019.

Khennou F and others, 'Improving the Use of Big Data Analytics within Electronic Health Records: A Case Study based OpenEHR' (2018) 127(1) *Procedia Computer Science* 60–68.

Männer R and Lange R, 'Rechnen mit Neuronalen Netzen: Wie funktionieren Neuronale Netze und wie werden sie trainiert?' (Computing with neural networks: How neural networks work and how are they trained?) (1994) 50(5) *Physikalische Blätter* 445–49.

Martini M, 'Art 21 Widerspruchsrecht' in Paal BP and Pauly DA (eds), *Datenschutz-Grundverordnung* (General Data Protection Regulation) (Beck'sche Kompakt-Kommentare 2017) 60.

Mathworks, 'Deep Learning Examples: Training a Model from Scratch', www.mathworks.com/solutions/deep-learning/examples/training-a-model-from-scratch.html, accessed 10 October 2019.

Minsky M and Papert S, *Perceptrons: An Introduction to Computational Geometry* (MIT Press 1969).

Miotto R and others, 'Deep Patient: An Unsupervised Representation to Predict the Future of Patients from the Electronic Health Records' (2016) 6(26094) *Scientific Reports* 1–10.

Mitrou L, 'AI and GDPR Study' (2019).

Nguyen G and others, 'Machine Learning and Deep Learning Frameworks and Libraries for Large-Scale Data Mining: A Survey' (2019) 52 *Artificial Intelligence Review* 77–124.

Nielsen MA, *Neural Networks and Deep Learning* (Determination Press 2015).

Rajaraman A, 'More Data Usually Beats Better Algorithms' *Datawocky*, 24 March 2008, https://anand.typepad.com/datawocky/2008/03/more-data-usual.html, accessed 8 November 2019.

Regulation (EU) 2016/679 of the European Parliament and of the Council of 27 April 2016 on the Protection of Natural Persons with Regard to the Processing of Personal Data and on the Free Movement of Such Data, and Repealing Directive 95/46/EC (General Data Protection Regulation), https://eur-lex.europa.eu/legal-content/EN/TXT/PDF/?uri=CELEX:32016R0679&from=EN.

Richesson R and others, 'Using Electronic Health Record Data in Pragmatic Clinical Trials' in *Rethinking Clinical Trials: A Living Textbook of Pragmatic Clinical Trials* (NIH Health Care Systems Research Collaboratory 2021), https://rethinkingclinicaltrials.org/chapters/design/using-electronic-health-record-data-pragmatic-clinical-trials-top/using-electronic-health-record-data-in-pragmatic-clinical-trials-introduction/, accessed 10 March 2021.

Rosenblatt F, 'The Perceptron: A Probabilistic Model For Information Storage and Organization in the Brain' (1958) 65(6) *Psychological Review* 386–408.

Ross MK and others, '"Big Data" and the Electronic Health Record' (2014) 9(1) *Yearbook of Medical Informatics* 97–104.

Roth C, 'Recht für F&E; Open Innovation' in Felten E and others (eds), *Digitale Transformation im Wirtschafts- & Steuerrecht* (Digital Transformation in Business and Tax Law) (Lindeverlag 2018) 11/21.

Rumelhart D and others, 'Learning Representations by Back-Propagating Errors' (1986) 323 *Nature* 533–36.

Schlegel DR and Ficheur G, 'Secondary Use of Patient Data: Review of the Literature Published in 2016' (2017) 26(1) *Yearbook of Medical Informatics* 68–71.

Schmidt J and others, 'Recent Advances and Applications of Machine Learning in Solid-State Materials Science' (2019) 5(83) *npj Computational Materials*, www.nature.com/articles/s41524-019-0221-0.pdf.

Shkabatur J, 'The Global Commons of Data' (2018) 22(2) *Stanford Technology Law Review* 1–46.

Stauton C and others, 'The GDPR and the Research Exemption: Considerations on the Necessary Safeguards for Research Biobanks' (2019) 27(1) *European Journal of Human Genetics* 1159–67.

TechAmerica Foundation, 'Demystifying Big Data' (2012), https://bigdatawg.nist.gov/_uploadfiles/M0068_v1_3903747095.pdf.

UN Recommendation on the Protection and Use of Health-Related Data (2019), https://undocs.org/A/74/277.

Von Schomberg R, *Towards Responsible Research and Innovation in the Information and Communication Technologies and Security Technologies Fields* (Publications Office of the European Union 2011).

Wachter S and others, 'Counterfactual Explanations Without Opening The Black Box: Automated Decisions and the GDPR' (2018) 31(2) *Harvard Journal of Law and Technology* 841–87.

Watson H, 'Tutorial: Big Data Analytics: Concepts, Technologies, and Applications' (2014) 34(1) *Communications of the Association for Information Systems* 65.

Zarsky T, 'Incompatible: The GDPR in the Age of Big Data' (2017) 47(4) *Seton Hall Law Review* 995–1020.

Zozus MN and others, 'Factors Affecting Accuracy of Data Abstracted from Medical Records' (2015) 10(10) *Plos One* e0138649.

9

The Next Challenge for Data Protection Law

AI Revolution in Automated Scientific Research

JANOS MESZAROS

9.1 Introduction

Scientific discovery is one of the main driving forces of our civilisation. However, the process of discovery as we know it today might be considered unpredictable and inefficient, since discoveries take a long time or a great moment of serendipity.[1] Artificial Intelligence (AI) and digital technology might aid the process of research by supporting scientists. This support is possible through the analysis of previous experiments and research results and testing previous hypotheses. Furthermore, the application of AI might provide a novel perspective for scientists. For instance, to make potent drug molecules, researchers might start with a known molecule and make structural changes that increase potency. However, an AI research tool might suggest that they instead experiment on less effective molecules if their 'failures' might reveal key insights about the underlying mechanism of the drug to reach the desired goal in another way.[2]

With the improvement of technology, scientists no longer need to conduct physical experiments in several fields. Instead, they can use simulation or data mining to discover new knowledge from existing datasets.[3] Automation of scientific research might also allow scientists to conduct dangerous or previously impractical experiments, such as those that need frequent measurements over a long period of time or that deal with dangerous chemicals.

1 H Kitano 'Artificial Intelligence to Win the Nobel Prize and Beyond: Creating the Engine for Scientific Discovery' (2016) 37(1) *AI Magazine*, 45.

2 Royal Society of Chemistry, 'Digital Futures, A New Frontier for Science Exploration and Invention', 2020, 34, www.rsc.org/globalassets/22-new-perspectives/discovery/digital-futures/rsc-digital-futures-report---digital.pdf, accessed 17 May 2021.

3 A Szalay and J Gray, '2020 Computing: Science in an Exponential World' (2006) 440(7083) *Nature* 413–14.

There are several human cognitive limitations that pose a hurdle for accelerated scientific discovery. AI systems can 'out-compute all possible hypotheses' and redefine scientific research. One of the aims of the pioneering researchers in this field is to make AI earn the Nobel Prize in physiology or medicine by 2050.[4] The main benefits of partially or fully automating scientific research are: 1) Freeing up researcher time; 2) accelerating output and productivity; 3) accuracy (automated systems are more precisely controlled); 4) reproducibility (automated experiments are highly repeatable within the same setup); 5) safety (researchers can be isolated from potentially hazardous substances).[5]

Computers have been applied for decades to automate some parts of the process of scientific discovery.[6] DENDRAL was the first AI project in the 1960s, created with the goal of studying hypothesis formation and discovery. It was developed at Stanford University to help automate the decision-making process and problem-solving behaviour of organic chemists.[7] Automated Mathematician (AM) was a heuristic AI programme that modelled mathematical discovery in the 1970s. This system later evolved into EURISKO, which was made for multiple purposes, such as designing integrated circuits for microchips.[8] EURISKO also became part of pop culture, appearing on TV shows such as *The X-Files*.[9] However, to fully automate the process of scientific research, AI applications need to be able to create a hypothesis to design the experiment and then be capable of learning from the results of the research.[10] This process can be called 'closed-loop learning'. The advantages of computational closed-loop learning systems over human scientists are clear: they can incorporate large volumes of explicit

[4] Kitano, 'Artificial Intelligence to Win the Nobel Prize', 39–49.

[5] Royal Society of Chemistry, 'Digital Futures', 40.

[6] U Pagallo and others, 'The Rise of Robotics & AI: Technological Advances & Normative Dilemmas' in Corrales M and others (eds) *Robotics, AI and the Future of Law* (Springer, 2018), 1–13.

[7] RK Lindsay and others, 'DENDRAL: A Case Study of the First Expert System for Scientific Hypothesis Formation' (1993) 61(2) *Artificial Intelligence* 209–61.

[8] DB Lenat and JS Brown, 'Why AM and EURISKO Appear to Work' (1984) 23(3) *Artificial Intelligence* 269–94.

[9] IMDB, 'Ghost in the Machine', www.imdb.com/title/tt0751131/, accessed 15 December 2020.

[10] P Flach and others, 'Abduction, Induction, and the Logic of Scientific Knowledge Development' ECAI '06 workshop on Abduction and Induction in AI and Scientific Modelling, 2006, www.cs.bris.ac.uk/Publications/pub_master.jsp?id=2000630, accessed 17 May 2021.

background knowledge, analyse data much faster, and do not need to rest.

The first real 'robot scientist' was built with a combination of AI, closed-loop learning, and advanced laboratory robotic systems. The first such system was 'Adam', and the second was 'Eve'.[11] Both robots were designed to carry out biomedical research. They resembled a big box, about the size of an office cubicle. They were equipped with robotic arms, incubators, a freezer, cameras and other essential parts to conduct research. 'The idea of using a robot is not new, but what's different about ours is the robot was also involved in developing hypotheses and experiments on its own', said King, the builder of the machine.[12] 'Eve' was searching for drugs against neglected tropical diseases.

One of the main concerns with AI systems in research is the ability to make a hypothesis: would an AI scientist be able to ask the right questions? As Kitano highlighted, the necessity of asking the right question (finding a good hypothesis) is due to resource constraints, since scientists usually have limited time and budgets. Thus, efficiency is the main reason for needing to ask the right questions. However, as Kitano argues, in the case of AI systems, when the time and resources are available on a different scale, asking the right question might be not as crucial. Another fact is that many major scientific discoveries have been the result of accidents; thus, it is not always the right questions that lead to a discovery. Therefore, AI systems will become a crucial part of the infrastructure for top-level research institutions in the future. Crowd intelligence might also be part of these systems, utilising the contributions of both professional researchers and laypeople, each for different tasks, thereby building a collaborative form of intelligence.[13]

In order to shed light on these issues, Section 9.2 examines citizen science to highlight concerns about the processing of personal data by laypeople. Section 9.3 elucidates the main challenges for AI research in the EU General Data Protection Regulation (GDPR). Section 9.4 tackles the issue of sharing medical data for AI research in the light of data protection law. Section 9.5 elucidates feasible and safe ways to share health data for the research of AI products and services, to balance privacy and innovation. Section 9.6 concludes the chapter.

[11] A Sparkes and others, 'Towards Robot Scientists for Autonomous Scientific Discovery' (2010) 2(1) *Automated Experimentation*.

[12] RD King and others, 'The Automation of Science' (2009) 324(5923) *Science* 85–89.

[13] Kitano, 'Artificial Intelligence to Win the Nobel Prize', 48.

9.2 Citizen Science and Open Science

9.2.1 Citizen Science

The Oxford English Dictionary defines citizen science as 'scientific work undertaken by members of the general public, often in collaboration with or under the direction of professional scientists and scientific institutions'.[14] This definition has been adopted by the European Commission.[15] The dictionary also defines a citizen scientist as someone who is '(a) a scientist whose work is characterised by a sense of responsibility to serve the best interests of the wider community (now rare); (b) a member of the general public who engages in scientific work, often in collaboration with or under the direction of professional scientists and scientific institutions; an amateur scientist'.[16]

In the United States, the Crowdsourcing and Citizen Science Act defined citizen science as 'public participates voluntarily in the scientific process, addressing real-world problems in ways that may include formulating research questions, conducting scientific experiments, collecting and analysing data, interpreting results, making new discoveries, developing technologies and applications, and solving complex problems'.[17]

The origin of the term 'citizen science' can be attributed to two scientists. Irwin used the term to indicate when the research goals were determined by the public and professional scientists in the UK.[18] At the same time, Bonney started to use the term with a similar meaning in avian research in the US.[19] After introducing the roots and the contemporary definition of citizen science in both the EU and the US, it can be summarised as a research activity conducted by people other than professional scientists. Furthermore, citizen science projects can be categorised by their organisational method: they can be organised 'from below' or

[14] 'Citizen Science', *Oxford English Dictionary*, 2020.

[15] European Commission, *Open Innovation, Open Science, Open to the World: A vision for Europe* (Publications Office of the European Union 2016).

[16] 'Citizen Scientist', *Oxford English Dictionary*, 2019.

[17] United States Code, 2012 Edition, Supplement 4, Title 15 – COMMERCE AND TRADE 15 U.S.C. 3724 – Crowdsourcing and citizen science (2016), www.govinfo.gov/app/details/USCODE-2016-title15/USCODE-2016-title15-chap63-sec3724, accessed 24 February 2021.

[18] A Irwin, *Citizen Science: A Study of People, Expertise, and Sustainable Development* (Routledge 1995).

[19] R Bonney, 'Citizen Science: A Lab Tradition' (1996) 15 (4) *Living Birds* 7–15.

'from above'. When the project is organised from below, the participants organise themselves. In the second case, the projects are mostly organised and managed by organisations (which can also be commercial), and the public are asked to join the initiative.[20]

The EU aims to open the innovation process to people with experience in fields other than academia and science. By including more actors in the innovation process, knowledge may spread more freely. The EU believes this knowledge may be used to develop products and services which can create new markets.[21] Furthermore, the EU promotes open science, focusing on spreading knowledge as soon as possible by using digital and collaborative technologies. This is a significant change from the standard practice of publishing results only at the end of the research process, which cannot be reached by everyone since most scientific journals require paid access and publishing results takes longer to ensure their quality through the peer-review process.

9.2.2 Open Science

Open science is a movement to make the output of publicly funded research more widely accessible.[22] Paul A. David is often credited with coining the term 'open science'. He researched the scientific goods created by the public sector and compared them to the private sector's goods, which is protected by intellectual property rights.[23] A widely accepted definition of open science is provided by the Organisation for Economic Cooperation and Development (OECD), which describes it as 'efforts by researchers, governments, research funding agencies or the scientific community itself to make the primary outputs of publicly funded research results – publications and the research data – publicly accessible in a digital format with no or minimal restriction as a means for accelerating

20 AB Suman and R Pierce, 'Challenges for Citizen Science and the EU Open Science Agenda Under the GDPR' (2018) 4(3) *European Data Protection Law Review* 284–95.

21 European Commission, 'Open Innovation, Open Science, Open to the World: A Vision for Europe' White Paper, 2016.

22 One essential requirement for this is 'data access'. This movement is also known as 'open data' in the public sector, 'data commons' in fields such as science, and 'data portability', which is a more restrictive concept to empower consumers. See, for example, M Corrales Compagnucci, *Big Data, Databases and 'Ownership' Rights in the Cloud* (Springer 2020), 94.

23 PA David, 'The Historical Origins of "Open Science": An Essay on Patronage, Reputation and Common Agency Contracting in the Scientific Revolution' (2008) 3(2) *Capitalism and Society* 5.

research'.[24] The OECD highlighted that there are many advantages of open science, since 'access to scientific inputs and outputs can improve the effectiveness and productivity of the whole scientific and research system, by reducing duplication costs in collecting, creating, transferring and reusing data and scientific material; allowing more research from the same data; and multiplying opportunities for domestic and global participation in the research process'.[25]

9.2.3 AI and Ethical Concerns in Citizen Science

AI can be a valuable tool or play the main role in citizen science projects. Ceccaroni and others highlighted the possible contributions of AI in these projects:

1) Assisting or replacing humans in completing tasks;
2) Influencing human behaviour;
3) Improving insights.

In the first use of AI, it might replace citizen scientists, doing tasks instead of them. For instance, in the iNaturalist biodiversity project, AI tools can help to recognise species.[26] In the second case, AI might influence human behaviour. There are projects using social media to engage participants in contributing to their observations.[27] In the third case, citizen science projects can collect and analyse Twitter and Google data about health or the environment.[28]

The ethical concerns of AI systems can be divided into two groups: the moral behaviour of humans as they design, construct and use these tools; and the moral behaviour of AI systems (machine ethics).[29] When citizen science projects are organised from 'above' (e.g., by an IT or

[24] Organisation for Economic Co-operation and Development (OECD), *Making Open Science a Reality* (2015) 7.

[25] Ibid., 10.

[26] LN Joppa, 'The Case for Technology Investments in the Environment' (2017) 552(7685) *Nature* 325–28.

[27] D-P Deng and others, 'Using Social Media for Collaborative Species Identification and Occurrence: Issues, Methods, and Tools' Proceedings of the 1st ACM SIGSPATIAL International Workshop on Crowdsourced and Volunteered Geographic Information, 2012, 22–29.

[28] EA MacDonald, 'Aurorasaurus: A Citizen Science Platform for Viewing and Reporting the Aurora' (2015) 13(9) *Space Weather* 548–59.

[29] The Future of Life Institute, 'Asilomar AI Principles' developed in conjunction with the 2017 Asilomar Conference, 2017.

pharmaceutical company), there is a risk of monetising the collected information via the secondary use of data. Furthermore, monetising the collected information and intellectual property rights might be against the initiatives of large parts of the projects. There is a possibility that AI citizen science start-ups without a long-term funding model might adopt revenue models to monetise their 'value-added' services, that is, algorithmic intellectual property.[30] As Ceccaroni argues, when citizens contribute data for the public good in a project, it should be recommended that an open-data policy be adopted by default.[31]

9.2.4 The Secondary Use of Data in These Projects

Using data for secondary purposes in open science projects without explicit consent may violate the GDPR, since even pseudonymised data is still personal data. Furthermore, this could also violate Member States' laws regulating scientific research.[32] For instance, French law requires explicit consent for processing identifiable data for research.[33] Moreover, a significant issue is that the project may change its purpose and the way of processing, by the community's or new owners' decision, which might not be covered by the original consent.[34] The easiest solution would be to anonymise the data in citizen science projects to protect the participants privacy at the highest level to avoid issues of data protection, since the GDPR does not apply in the case of anonymised data. However, anonymisation is not possible in many cases, and the anonymous data may not be useful for research because of decreased data utility. Pseudonymisation is highly promoted by the GDPR, and it can significantly increase the data protection in these projects. However, many citizen science projects lack the expertise and resources to effectively pseudonymise datasets.[35]

30 R Schüritz and others, 'Capturing Value from Data: Revenue Models for Data-Driven Services' *Proceedings of the 50th Hawaii International Conference on System Sciences*, 2017.

31 L Ceccaroni and others, 'Opportunities and Risks for Citizen Science in the Age of Artificial Intelligence' (2019) 4(1) *Citizen Science: Theory and Practice* 29.

32 J Meszaros and others, 'Nudging Consent & the New Opt-Out System to the Processing of Health Data in England' in Corrales Compagnucci M and others (eds), *Legal Tech and the New Sharing Economy* (Springer 2020), 61–72.

33 Act No. 78-17 of 6 January 1978 on Information Technology, Data Files and Civil Liberties, France, Article 53, 54.

34 Suman and Pierce 'Challenges for Citizen Science', 288.

35 M Corrales Compagnucci and others, 'Homomorphic Encryption: The "Holy Grail" for Big Data Analytics & Legal Compliance in the Pharmaceutical and Healthcare Sector?' (2019) 3(4) *European Pharmaceutical Law Review* 144–55.

Another issue is that the GDPR requires responsible data controller(s) for all processing. However, citizen science projects are often decentralised, organised 'from below', thus they do not have one data controller, since they are managed by the community. In these cases, it can be a burden to identify the person or organisation who is responsible for following the requirements of the GDPR.

9.2.5 *The Influence of Big Data on Open Science and Citizen Science*

The availability of digital technology broadened the possibilities to share and reuse information for a wide range of users, not just professionals. AI, user-friendly applications and cheaper technology provide the next step in this process, by allowing the secondary use of scientific data for laypeople. However, this new 'power' creates unseen dangers, especially from the point of view of data protection law.

The GDPR provides several special rules to support scientific research. Thus, a crucial question is whether citizen science can be qualified as scientific research. Justifying citizen science as scientific research is challenging since citizen scientists usually lack the expertise of professional researchers. They may have tools such as devices and software, which are becoming better and more user-friendly with the advancement of technology. However, these tools are not substitutes for the expertise of professional scientists, who follow strict ethical guidelines and are responsible to their employers, such as universities and companies. Furthermore, professional data controllers, such as academic institutions or companies, need to be aware of the data protection rules and other requirements of research, and these organisations have the financial background to hire or consult with data protection lawyers and IT and other professionals to comply with the rules. If the activity of citizen scientists were classified as scientific research, then the research exemptions of the GDPR would apply to their activity. This means they could use the data with fewer restrictions since the GDPR provides several privileges for researchers.[36] However, the language of the GDPR suggests that the scientific research exemption is provided for professional researchers, following scientific regulations and guidelines.

Firstly, the GDPR always operates with the term 'scientific' research, so the activity is expected to be scientific. The question is whether the

[36] J Meszaros and C-H Ho, 'Big Data and Scientific Research: The Secondary Use of Personal Data Under the Research Exemption in the GDPR' (2018) *Acta Juridica Hungarica* 403–19.

amateur or nonprofessional person's activity can qualify as 'scientific'. However, we will not find an answer to this question in the GDPR. I contacted the EU data protection authorities and ministries of science, but the definition and scope of scientific research vary among the EU Member States. Article 159 of the GDPR states that the definition of scientific research must be interpreted in a broad manner, and the recital only provides examples, such as fundamental and applied research, including privately funded research.[37] However, it is not clear if a citizen scientist' activity could qualify as privately funded research. After defining scientific research, Recital 159 of the GDPR requires that specific conditions should apply to the publication or other disclosure of personal data in the context of scientific research purposes. Furthermore, the GDPR poses numerous requirements for data controllers, which cannot be fulfilled by a layperson. Appropriate safeguards are also mandatory for the research activity, which should ensure that technical and organisational safeguards are in place. For instance, the GDPR promotes pseudonymisation for scientific research as a safeguard,[38] which is the de-identification of personal data in a reversible way.[39] Furthermore, the GDPR does not just encourage but requires the application of the highest level of de-identification for processing (principle of data minimisation).[40] However, applying such methods would require professional knowledge of programming and data management tools.

37 EU GDPR, 'Regulation (EU) 2016/679 of the European Parliament and of the Council of 27 April 2016 on the Protection of Natural Persons with Regard to the Processing of Personal Data and on the Free Movement of Such Data, and Repealing Directive 95/46/EC (General Data Protection Regulation)', OJ 2016 L 119/1. Recital 159 says that the processing of personal data for scientific research purposes should be interpreted in a broad manner, including, for example, technological development and demonstration, fundamental research, applied research and privately funded research.

38 GDPR Article 89 (1) 1. Processing for archiving purposes in the public interest, scientific or historical research purposes or statistical purposes, shall be subject to appropriate safeguards, in accordance with this regulation, for the rights and freedoms of the data subject. Those measures may include pseudonymisation provided that those purposes can be fulfilled in that manner.

39 GDPR Article 4 (5) 'pseudonymisation' means the processing of personal data in such a manner that the personal data can no longer be attributed to a specific data subject without the use of additional information, provided that such additional information is kept separately and is subject to technical and organisational measures to ensure that the personal data are not attributed to an identified or identifiable natural person.

40 GDPR Article 11 (1). If the purposes for which a controller processes personal data do not or do no longer require the identification of a data subject by the controller, the controller shall not be obliged to maintain, acquire or process additional information in order to identify the data subject for the sole purpose of complying with this regulation.

It is crucial to define the limits of citizen science, because the GDPR does not just impose duties on the researchers, but it also provides 'rewards' for scientific research. The GDPR encourages innovation and technological developments; thus, scientific research has a privileged role in the regulation with several broad exemptions.[41] Qualifying an activity as scientific research might come with the 'reward' for the researchers that they do not need to comply with the right of access (Article 15), rectification (Article 16), erasure (Article 17), restriction of such processing (Article 18), notification obligations (Article 19) data portability (Article 20) and the right to object (Article 21).[42] The next section elucidates the issues around these special rules for scientific research in the GDPR.

9.3 The Main Challenges for AI Research in the GDPR

9.3.1 Research Exemption in the GDPR

Scientific research is a distinguished type of data processing in the GDPR. This activity has several exemptions and constitutes a legal basis for the secondary processing of health data.[43] Even sensitive data (e.g., health data) can be processed for scientific research with fewer restrictions and appropriate safeguards, based on EU or Member State law.[44] Recital 50 of the GDPR discusses the secondary use of personal data for new purposes. The recital states that the processing of personal data for purposes other than those for which they were initially collected should be allowed only where the processing is compatible with those purposes, and further processing for scientific research should be considered as a compatible lawful processing operation.[45] One of the data processing principles in the GDPR is the

[41] GDPR Recital 157 also highlights that 'By coupling information from registries, researchers can obtain new knowledge of great value with regard to widespread medical conditions such as cardiovascular disease, cancer and depression'.

[42] GDPR Article 89 (2). Where personal data are processed for scientific or historical research purposes or statistical purposes, EU or Member State law may provide for derogations from the rights referred to in articles 15, 16, 18 and 21, subject to the conditions and safeguards referred to in paragraph 1 of this article insofar as such rights are likely to render impossible or seriously impair the achievement of the specific purposes, and such derogations are necessary for the fulfilment of those purposes.

[43] GDPR Article 9 (2) (j).

[44] GDPR Recital 52 in the case of sensitive data.

[45] GDPR Recital 50.

purpose limitation, which requires that personal data cannot be further processed in a way that is incompatible with the original purposes. For instance, personal data collected for direct care purposes cannot be used for marketing. However, the GDPR provides an exemption for scientific research tied to this principle: further processing for scientific research purposes shall be compatible with the initial purposes, if safeguards are satisfied.[46] Furthermore, the GDPR highlights that by coupling information from registries, researchers can obtain new knowledge, and research results obtained through registries may provide solid, high-quality knowledge.[47]

However, it is an important issue that the definition of scientific research in the GDPR is legally not binding since it is in the recital part. Therefore, several governments follow the OECD's guidance on scientific research. The OECD's *Frascati Manual* is an essential tool for statisticians, scientists and innovation policymakers worldwide; thus, several governments follow this guideline.[48] It includes definitions of basic concepts, data collection guidelines and classifications for compiling research and development statistics. It defines research and experimental development as a creative and systematic work undertaken in order to increase the stock of knowledge – including knowledge of humankind, culture and society – and to devise new applications of available knowledge. The research activity is also expected to be novel, creative, uncertain, systematic and reproducible. The *Frascati Manual* describes researchers as professionals engaged in the conception or creation of new knowledge. They conduct research and improve or develop concepts, theories, models, techniques, instrumentation, software or operational methods.[49] However, the *Frascati Manual* never defines 'scientific research' as such, even though it makes use of the term in a number of instances throughout the text. The broad definitions of research in the OECD guidelines and the GDPR permit commercial scientific researchers and companies to rely on the research exceptions under the GDPR. However, researchers at commercial entities may not comply with or have in place the same ethical and institutional safeguards as publicly funded academic researchers.[50]

46 GDPR Article 5 (1) (b).

47 GDPR Recital 157.

48 OECD, *Frascati Manual 2015: Guidelines for Collecting and Reporting Data on Research and Experimental Development*.

49 OECD, *Frascati Manual 2015*, 162.

50 European Parliamentary Research Service, 'How the General Data Protection Regulation Changes the Rules for Scientific Research' 2019, www.europarl.europa.eu/RegData/etudes/STUD/2019/634447/EPRS_STU(2019)634447_EN.pdf, accessed 17 May 2021.

9.3.2 *Profiling and Automated Decision-Making*

The rules of the GDPR on profiling and automated decision-making might have crucial impacts on scientific research since the research itself, or the result of it (e.g., product or service), will process personal data at some point. AI medical devices and services have the potential to seriously impact citizens' health by making decisions – for instance, a medical imaging software which decides which image shows signs of cancer.[51] The GDPR defines profiling as 'any form of automated processing of personal data consisting of the use of personal data to evaluate certain personal aspects relating to a natural person, in particular to analyse or predict aspects concerning that natural person's performance at work, economic situation, health, personal preferences, interests, reliability, behaviour, location or movements'.[52]

The most important elements of the definition are the 'automated processing' and 'evaluating personal aspects' about a natural person. It is crucial that the automated processing does not have to be solely automated; thus, this type of processing can also be done with human involvement, compared to 'automated individual decision-making' in the GDPR, which is solely automated. Using the word 'evaluating' indicates that profiling may involve assessment or judgement about a person. A simple classification of the data subjects does not constitute profiling. For instance, if a health insurance company sorts its customers by age and gender, without predictions and further assessment,[53] it is not profiling. Furthermore, the Council of Europe Recommendation requires 'inference' for profiling.[54] The recommendation defines three stages of profiling: (1) data collection, (2) automated analysis to identify correlations, (3) identifying characteristics of present or future behaviour.

There are three ways in which profiling may be used (see Figure 9.1):

1. general profiling;
2. decision-making supported by profiling;
3. automated decision-making supported by profiling.

[51] A Esteva and others, 'Deep Learning-Enabled Medical Computer Vision' (2021) 4 *npj Digital Medicine*.

[52] GDPR Article 4(4).

[53] Article 29 Working Party, 'Guidelines on Automated Individual Decision-Making and Profiling for the Purposes of Regulation 2016/679' 2018, 7.

[54] Council of Europe, 'The Protection of Individuals with Regard to Automatic Processing of Personal Data in the Context of Profiling' recommendation CM/Rec (2010)13 and explanatory memorandum, 23 November 2010, https://rm.coe.int/16807096c3, accessed 17 May 2021.

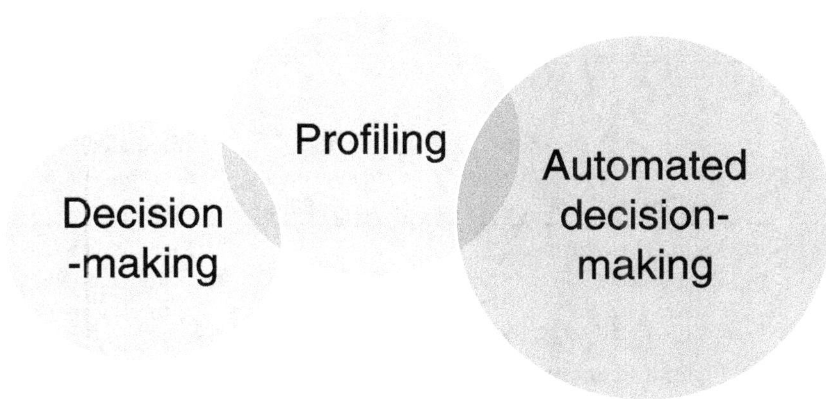

Figure 9.1 Connection among automated decision-making, profiling, and decision-making.

The prohibition on automated decision-making may pose a significant hurdle for the application of medical AI in healthcare settings. However, it is crucial to differentiate between profiling and automated decision-making since profiling has fewer restrictions. AI research without decision-making may constitute profiling only, avoiding several hurdles in the GDPR.

Automated decision-making is different from profiling. However, they may overlap since automated decisions can be made with or without profiling. The GDPR protects individuals from the effects of automated decision-making with the following prohibition: 'The data subject shall have the right not to be subject to a decision based solely on automated processing, including profiling, which produces legal effects concerning him or her or similarly significantly affects him or her'.[55] Profiling can be one of the possible sources of data for decision-making. Other sources might be data from individuals (such as a questionnaire) or directly observed about the data subjects (e.g., their location or preferences). The Article 29 Working Party provides the example of speed tickets. When the government automatically fines drivers based on the traffic camera system, it is automated decision-making based on observed data. On the other hand, when the previous driving history (e.g., fines and offences) of the citizens are evaluated to calculate their fines, then the automated decision is based on profiling.[56]

55 GDPR Article 22 (1).

56 Article 29 Working Party Guidelines on Automated Individual Decision-Making and Profiling for the Purposes of Regulation 2016/679 (2018) 8.

Table 9.1 *The impact of scientific research on the data subjects' rights.*

	Profiling	Decision-making (with profiling)	Automated decision-making (with profiling)	Scientific research (no automated decision-making)
Rights	Right to be informed Data collected directly (Art. 13) and indirectly (Art. 14(3)) Right of access (Art. 15) Right to rectification (Art. 16) Right to erasure (Art. 17) Right to restriction (Art. 18) Right to data portability (Art. 20) Right to object (Art. 21)			Right to information in the case of *directly* collected data (Article 13) Right to data portability (Art. 20)
			General prohibition, additional safeguards Article 22(1)	

As Table 9.1 demonstrates, the data subjects have several rights which might not be applied in the case of scientific research if the Member States follow the GDPR. Where personal data is processed for scientific research purposes, EU or Member State law may provide for derogations from the right of access (Article 15), rectification (Article 16), erasure (Article 17), restriction of such processing (Article 18) and the right to object (Article 21) if these rights are likely to render impossible or seriously impair the achievement of the research purposes, and such derogations are necessary for the fulfilment of those purposes.[57] For the application of these exemptions, several organisational and technical safeguards need to be satisfied. Two rights remain for the data subjects in every case: the right to information and data portability.[58] However, if the personal data is not obtained directly from the individual (e.g., it was sent from a public authority or another company), the data controller does not have to

[57] GDPR Article 89.

[58] GDPR articles 13 and 20.

inform the data subjects if it would be impossible or involve a disproportionate effort, in particular for processing for research purposes.[59] Thus, in the case of profiling for scientific research, even the right to information might be avoided.[60] With these exemptions, the GDPR provides a privileged position for researchers. On the one hand, the rules on profiling and automated decision-making are significant restrictions for data controllers. On the other hand, the regulation attempts to balance privacy and the 'ethical and scientific imperative' to share personal data for scientific research. In the age of AI and Big Data, scientific institutions and data protection authorities need to work together to balance these conflicting rights and interests.

9.3.3 Data Security

Weak security in systems conducting medical research might cause individual harms, which can result in minor or serious damage, ultimately risking patients' lives. The GDPR requires data controllers to process personal data securely. The requirement to take 'appropriate technical and organisational measures' to protect the data against inappropriate use is not new. It replaces and mirrors the previous requirements of the EU Data Protection Directive from 1995. The improvement and the biggest achievement of the GDPR are that these requirements are more standardised and unified among the EU Member States, providing stronger data security in the whole EU. However, the GDPR just states the basic requirements, without going into technical details. On the one hand, this technical neutrality ensures the long applicability of the regulation. On the other hand, there might be a lot of confusion about the level of technical security required to comply with the GDPR, especially in the medical research environment, due to the sensitive data. There is detailed guidance available from national authorities and international organisations, but it may not be immediately clear what kind of security measures the developers and clients need to put in place, what is simply a suggested approach and what is essential.[61]

The GDPR security principle lays down the most important requirements for data security, requiring data controllers and processors to

[59] GDPR Article 14 (5) (b).

[60] GDPR Recital 62.

[61] Information Commissioner's Office, 'Security Outcomes', https://ico.org.uk/for-organisations/security-outcomes/, accessed 11 October 2020.

ensure appropriate security of the personal data, including protection against unauthorised or unlawful processing and accidental loss, and destruction or damage, using appropriate technical and organisational measures. These principles are called 'integrity and confidentiality'.[62] The question is what level of security is necessary to provide an adequate level of protection in the medical and research environment. There is no 'one size fits all' solution to information security; thus, GDPR also provides a risk-based approach. This means that the following circumstances need to be taken into account when the security measures are chosen: (a) state of the art of technology; (b) the costs of implementation; (c) the nature, scope, context and purposes of processing;[63] (d) level of risk of the data processing;[64] (e) the sensitivity of the data (e.g., basic body measurements or genetic information); and, (f) the number of people at the data controller or processor and the extent of their access to personal data (i.e., whether just a few scientists or hundreds of medical doctors can access it; whether they can only read, or also edit or delete the data).

9.4 Data Sharing and the International Transfer of Scientific Data

9.4.1 Data Sharing in Academic and Commercial Research Environments

Data sharing is essential for medical AI, since the results are only as accurate as the data used to train the algorithms. In the case of scientific discovery, sharing failures and negative results are as essential as sharing successful results. Therefore, it is important to publish as much data as possible, rather than just a 'slice' of it, such as a graph in a scientific journal article.[65] It would also be crucial to share algorithms. However, as with data, there are constraints and limitations. Collecting and combining data from different sources can help to draw higher-level insights, but not if this simply creates an unstructured 'data lake'. For instance, in medical AI, there will be many types and sources of data from imaging,

[62] GDPR Article 5 (1)(f).
[63] GDPR Recital 83.
[64] GDPR Article 32.
[65] Royal Society of Chemistry, 'Digital Futures', 49.

pharmacology, toxicology and clinical trials. The international sharing of personal data might also be challenging due to the different data protection regulations.[66]

Researchers and research organisations have different motivations, limitations and constraints about data sharing. Paying attention to these factors is crucial to prevent unintended consequences, such as limited participation of corporate researchers in academic scientific fora if requirements around sharing data or algorithms are incompatible with their companies' policies.

These constraints and disincentives might be:

a) Commercial competition;
b) Competition between individuals, especially in the academic environment;
c) Sharing data between countries, especially in the case of national security;
d) Publicly funded research being shared with and delivering benefit to other countries and private corporations;
e) Proprietary formats and software;
f) Cost implications of systems to enable data sharing.

However, there are several technical and organisational measures to incentivise data sharing, for instance:

a) Private and decentralised algorithms in which no one sees each other's data but can interact with it;
b) Using anonymised or encrypted data, which is already promoted by the GDPR;
c) Collectively annotating public datasets to make it feasible for machine learning;
d) Applying machine learning to automate aspects of data classification.[67]

These constraints and incentives need to be carefully balanced to securely share health data internationally, which is especially crucial during current the COVID-19 pandemic. Developing and improving medical

[66] T Minssen and others, 'The EU-US Privacy Shield Regime for Cross-Border Transfers of Personal Data Under the GDPR: What are the Legal Challenges and How Might These Affect Cloud-Based Technologies, Big Data, and AI in the Medical Sector?' (2020) 4(1) *European Pharmaceutical Law Review* 34–50.

[67] Royal Society of Chemistry, 'Digital Futures', 50.

AI requires as much accurate data as possible to fight against diseases and improve the efficacy of healthcare services.

9.4.2 *International Transfer of Scientific Data*

The GDPR provides uniform protection of personal data across the countries of the European Economic Area (EEA).[68] Thus, personal data can be transmitted freely within this area without restrictions. However, in countries outside the EEA, there are no general rules that provide an equivalent level of data protection. For instance, the Russian and Brazilian data protection rules are different from the European ones. Thus, the GDPR contains several rules that prohibit the transfer of personal data to countries outside the EEA. It is not just sending data directly (e.g., by email or on a flash drive) outside the EEA that triggers this prohibition, but also when a researcher processes personal data that is stored in a cloud service such as Amazon outside the EEA. The transfer of personal data to a third country is when personal data is made available to someone outside the EEA.

The transfer of personal data is permitted to countries outside the EU/EEA, if:

a) There is an 'adequacy decision' from the European Commission that, for example, a certain country outside the EU/EEA ensures an adequate level of protection (e.g., Israel, Japan), or;
b) Adequate safeguards are in place: the data controller has taken appropriate protection measures (e.g., using standard contractual clauses (SCCs) or binding corporate rules to send data), or;
c) Specific derogations and single cases (e.g., consent).[69]

From this outline of the possible means of international transfer of health data (see Table 9.2), it is clear that the transfer might pose a hurdle for researchers since these methods are currently changing. The Court of Justice of the European Union invalidated the EU-US Privacy Shield Framework (*Schrems II* case),[70] which was the most convenient way to transfer data to the United States. Now a case-by-case assessment

[68] The EEA includes EU countries and Iceland, Lichtenstein and Norway.

[69] GDPR Recital 43; articles 4 (3)(b), 5 (1)(c), 7 (4) and 12–14.

[70] C-311/18 *Data Protection Commissioner V Facebook Ireland and Maximillian Schrems* (2020).

Table 9.2 *Assessment of transfer methods for health data.*

Transfer method	Pros	Cons
Explicit consent of the data subject	It can be shaped for the purposes of the processing	It is challenging to reach the data subjects (to provide their consent) Consent can be withdrawn
Adequacy decision by the EU	Smooth data transfer	Few countries have it
Binding corporate rules	Only for companies dealing with the employee data inside the organisation	
Standard data protection clauses	The EU plans to update it, providing a safe and adequate method to transfer health data	

on the application of SCCs is required.[71] On 4 June 2021, the European Commission issued modernised SCCs under the GDPR for the transfer of personal data to third countries. These modernised SCCs will replace the three sets of SCCs that were adopted under the previous Data Protection Directive 95/46.[72]

9.5 Discussion and Recommendations for GDPR-Compliant AI Research Systems

Automated scientific research with AI poses significant risks for the data subjects; thus, organisational and technical safeguards are essential. Supporting research into transparent and privacy-friendly AI products and services by the EU would be an innovative way to protect citizens from the impacts of AI. However, this initiative would need a higher level of cooperation and heavy investment from the EU. Supporting only these types of AI research in the EU could easily fail because of the

[71] M Corrales Compagnucci and others, 'Lost on the High Seas Without a Safe Harbor or a Shield? Navigating Cross-Border Data Transfers in the Pharmaceutical Sector After Schrems II Invalidation of the EU-US Privacy Shield' (2020) 4(3) *European Pharmaceutical Law Review* 153–60.

[72] Modernised standard contractual clauses for the transfer of personal data to third countries can be found at European Commission, 'Standard Contractual Clauses (SCC)', https://ec.europa.eu/info/law/law-topic/data-protection/international-dimension-data-protection/standard-contractual-clauses-scc_en, accessed 17 May 2021.

fragmentation of research and Member State interests. Furthermore, the competitiveness of privacy-friendly and transparent AI products might also be questionable compared to other solutions in the market.[73]

Public interest is an important factor in the government supporting research with funding and data. Developing an emoji, which makes realistic smiley faces in chat programmes with AI, does not serve a public interest, so the case can be made that these kinds of AI products and services should not benefit from the GDPR's special rules and exemptions for scientific research. However, when the AI product is used for medical purposes, such as cancer detection in X-ray pictures, there is at least a general level of public interest, thus this type of research fits into the research exemptions of the GDPR.

Since the GDPR might pose hurdles for automated scientific research with AI, and the EU does not intend to change the current data protection regulation,[74] I think there are means to protect the data subjects without hindering innovation. The first measure would be the flexible application of the GDPR research exemption to AI research, with unified requirements and conditions in the Member States to avoid forum shopping. For realising this goal, new EU laws regulating AI research and ethics would be necessary,[75] based on already existing guidelines laid down by the High-Level Expert Group on Artificial Intelligence.[76]

The following main principles need to be fulfilled during AI research to safeguard both the data subjects whose data is used during research and the citizens who will be the final users of AI products and services.

a) **Technical Robustness and safety:** to prevent and minimise the probability of unintentional harm, AI systems conducting or helping scientific research need to be secure and resilient. This means up-to-date technical (and organisational) safeguards need to be in place. For

[73] M Humerick, 'Taking AI Personally: How the E.U. Must Learn to Balance the Interests of Personal Data Privacy & Artificial Intelligence' (2018) 415–16.

[74] European Parliament Committee on Legal Affairs, 'Report with Recommendations to the Commission on Civil Law Rules on Robotics' 27 January 2017, www.europarl.europa.eu/sides/getDoc.do?pubRef=-//EP//NONSGML+REPORT+A8-2017-0005+0+DOC+PDF+V0//EN, accessed 17 May 2021.

[75] Humerick, 'Taking AI Personally', 415.

[76] Following the launch of its Artificial Intelligence Strategy in 2018, the European Commission appointed a group of 52 experts to advice for its implementation. The group members were selected following an open selection process and comprised representatives from academia, civil society and industry. See European Commission, 'High-Level Expert Group on Artificial Intelligence', https://ec.europa.eu/digital-single-market/en/high-level-expert-group-artificial-intelligence, accessed 12 October 2020.

instance, the data should only be accessed by authorised researchers. In the case of citizen scientists, as highlighted above, providing an adequate level of robustness and safety might be challenging due to the lack of resources and professional knowledge.

b) **Privacy and data governance**: researchers need to comply with data protection rules. The black-box nature of AI devices and automated processes cannot be excuses for failing to comply with the GDPR. As highlighted above, there are several rules in the GDPR whose application in the research environment remains unclear – for instance, the GDPR research exemption, which requires clarification from the EU and Member State authorities. This would be crucial, since this situation might lead to forum shopping, and researchers could choose to conduct automated research projects in countries where the legal environment is less strict.
c) **Resilient and secure AI systems:** to ensure the minimisation of unintentional harm, AI systems need to be safe, ensuring a fallback plan in case something goes wrong, in addition to being accurate, reliable and reproducible. For instance, the system needs to shut down automatically when it is necessary.
d) **Human agency and oversight**: AI systems should empower human beings and foster their fundamental rights. Proper oversight is necessary, and the black-box nature of AI devices should not impede these goals. Even if the hypothesis is made by AI, human researchers should be able to understand the reasoning and take over control, when necessary. Moreover, in the case of AI medical devices, human oversight and review would be crucial for patient safety and the GDPR's restrictions on automated decision-making.
e) **Transparency**: research aided or conducted by AI should still be transparent for reproducibility and for inquiry about bias and safety. Transparency is crucial when the research leads to a product or service which makes decisions about individuals, since the GDPR regulates this field, as elucidated previously in this chapter.
f) **Diversity, non-discrimination and fairness**: the data used to train AI systems need to be diverse to avoid bias. This requirement is of utmost importance in the case of medical products and services since the results of research, such as medicine and medical robots, might cause harm to underrepresented populations.
g) **Societal and environmental well-being**: AI systems have the potential to significantly enhance scientific research, yet this must be done in an environmentally friendly way. AI-assisted research should also take

into account the environmental impact of the possible solutions, aside from profit and other scientific goals.

h) **Accountability**: As the High-Level Expert Group on AI highlighted, mechanisms should be put in place to ensure responsibility and accountability for AI systems and their outcomes.[77] AI research systems might pose risks or cause harm. For these unintended consequences, certain actors need to be responsible, such as the company developing the product or providing special insurance for these services. The liability for the damages caused by autonomous cars is a great example of this issue. However, in the case of citizen science, it is challenging to identify a credible actor behind the possible harms caused by a layperson.

These rules regulating and guiding AI research could only be effective with permission, oversight and enforcement from EU and Member State authorities for the whole lifecycle of AI research. Balancing privacy and innovation is crucial to protect citizens and the efficacy of healthcare services across the EU.

9.6 Conclusion

The application of AI and digital technology is transforming the process of scientific research, especially in the field of medical sciences, due to the growing amount and quality of accessible health data. As developments in hardware and software made personal computers feasible for individual use, AI tools and open data movement might have the same effect on citizen science. However, citizen scientists do not have the funding and professional knowledge to comply with several regulations, especially with data protection and security requirements. Moreover, the openness of citizen science and the data protection requirements are in tension. The chapter highlighted the most important rules of the GDPR affecting both professional and lay researchers, such as regulation on automated decision-making, data security and transferring medical data. These issues pose a challenge for medical researchers in the EU, since their application is not sufficiently harmonised.

[77] High-Level Expert Group on Artificial Intelligence, 'Ethics Guidelines for Trustworthy AI' 2018.

The GDPR has special rules for supporting scientific research. However, the EU and Member State authorities need to clarify these rules to provide the same level of protection and incentives for research. Applying the requirements of ethical and privacy-friendly AI is a good starting point for GDPR-compliant AI research, especially in the case of medical products and services. However, these guidelines on AI need to be implemented in a uniform and consistent way to protect research participants and patients across the EU.

Bibliography

Act No. 78-17 of 6 January 1978 on Information Technology, Data Files and Civil Liberties, France, www.ssi.ens.fr/textes/a78-17-text.html, accessed 24 February 2021.

Article 29 Working Party, 'Guidelines on Automated Individual Decision-Making and Profiling for the Purposes of Regulation 2016/679', 2018 as last Revised and Adopted on 6 February 2018, https://ec.europa.eu/newsroom/article29/items/612053, accessed 24 February 2021.

Bonney R, 'Citizen Science: A Lab Tradition' (1996) 15(4) *Living Birds* 7–15.

C-311/18 *Data Protection Commissioner V Facebook Ireland and Maximillian Schrems* (2020).

Ceccaroni L and others, 'Opportunities and Risks for Citizen Science in the Age of Artificial Intelligence' (2019) 4(1) *Citizen Science: Theory and Practice* 1–14.

'Citizen Science' *Oxford English Dictionary*, 2020.

'Citizen Scientist' *Oxford English Dictionary*, 2019.

Clarke R, 'Regulatory Alternatives for AI' (2019) 35(4) *Computer Law and Security Review*.

Corrales Compagnucci M and others, 'Homomorphic Encryption: The "Holy Grail" for Big Data Analytics & Legal Compliance in the Pharmaceutical and Healthcare Sector?' (2019) 3(4) *European Pharmaceutical Law Review* 144–55.

Corrales Compagnucci M, *Big Data, Databases and 'Ownership' Rights in the Cloud* (Springer 2020).

Corrales Compagnucci M and others, 'Lost on the High Seas Without a Safe Harbor or a Shield? Navigating Cross-Border Data Transfers in the Pharmaceutical Sector After Schrems II Invalidation of the EU-US Privacy Shield' (2020) 4(3) *European Pharmaceutical Law Review* 153–60.

Council of Europe, 'The Protection of Individuals with Regard to Automatic Processing of Personal Data in the Context of Profiling' Recommendation CM/Rec (2010)13 and explanatory memorandum, 23 November 2010, https://rm.coe.int/16807096c3, accessed 17 May 2021.

David PA, 'The Historical Origins of "Open Science": An Essay on Patronage, Reputation and Common Agency Contracting in the Scientific Revolution' (2008) 3(2) *Capitalism and Society* 5–14.

Deng D and others, 'Using Social Media for Collaborative Species Identification and Occurrence: Issues, Methods, and Tools' in Goodchild M, Pfoser D and Sui D (eds), *Proceedings of the 1st ACM SIGSPATIAL International Workshop on Crowdsourced and Volunteered Geographic Information* (2012), https://dl.acm.org/doi/10.1145/2442952.2442957, accessed 24 February 2021.

Esteva A and others, 'Deep Learning-Enabled Medical Computer Vision' (2021) 4 *npj Digital Medicine* 5, https://doi.org/10.1038/s41746-020-00376-2, accessed 24 February 2021.

EU GDPR, 'Regulation (EU) 2016/679 of the European Parliament and of the Council of 27 April 2016 on the Protection of Natural Persons with Regard to the Processing of Personal Data and on the Free Movement of Such Data, and Repealing Directive 95/46/EC' (General Data Protection Regulation), OJ 2016 L 119/1, https://eur-lex.europa.eu/eli/reg/2016/679/oj, accessed 24 February 2021.

European Commission, 'High-Level Expert Group on Artificial Intelligence', https://ec.europa.eu/digital-single-market/en/high-level-expert-group-artificial-intelligence, accessed 12 October 2020.

European Commission, *Open Innovation, Open Science, Open to the World: A vision for Europe* (Publications Office of the European Union 2016).

European Commission, 'Open Innovation, Open Science, Open to the World – A Vision for Europe' White Paper, 2016, https://op.europa.eu/en/publication-detail/-/publication/3213b335-1cbc-11e6-ba9a-01aa75ed71a1, accessed 24 February 2021.

European Commission, 'Standard Contractual Clauses (SCC)', https://ec.europa.eu/info/law/law-topic/data-protection/international-dimension-data-protection/standard-contractual-clauses-scc_en, accessed 17 May 2021.

European Parliament Committee on Legal Affairs, 'Report with Recommendations to the Commission on Civil Law Rules on Robotics' 27 January 2017, www.europarl.europa.eu/sides/getDoc.do?pubRef=-//EP//NONSGML+REPORT+A8-2017-0005+0+DOC+PDF+V0//EN, accessed 17 May 2021.

European Parliamentary Research Service, 'How the General Data Protection Regulation Changes the Rules for Scientific Research' 2019, www.europarl.europa.eu/RegData/etudes/STUD/2019/634447/EPRS_STU(2019)634447_EN.pdf, accessed 17 May 2021.

Flach P and others, 'Abduction, Induction, and the Logic of Scientific Knowledge Development' ECAI '06 workshop on Abduction and Induction in AI and Scientific Modelling, 2006, www.cs.bris.ac.uk/Publications/pub_master.jsp?id=2000630, accessed 17 May 2021.

High-Level Expert Group on Artificial Intelligence, 'Ethics Guidelines for Trustworthy AI' 2018, https://ec.europa.eu/futurium/en/ai-alliance-consultation.1.html, accessed 24 February 2021.

Humerick M, 'Taking AI Personally: How the E.U. Must Learn to Balance the Interests of Personal Data Privacy & Artificial Intelligence' (2018) 34(4) *Santa Clara High Technology Law Journal* 393, https://digitalcommons.law.scu.edu/chtlj/vol34/iss4/3, accessed 24 February 2021.

IMDB, 'Ghost in the Machine', www.imdb.com/title/tt0751131/, accessed 15 December 2020.

Information Commissioner's Office, 'Security Outcomes', https://ico.org.uk/for-organisations/security-outcomes/, accessed 11 October 2020.

Irwin Al, *Citizen Science: A Study of People, Expertise, and Sustainable Development* (Routledge 1995).

Joppa LN, 'The Case for Technology Investments in the Environment' (2017) 552(7685) *Nature* 325–27.

King RD and others, 'The Automation of Science' (2009) 324(5923) *Science* 2–3.

Kitano H, 'Artificial Intelligence to Win the Nobel Prize and Beyond: Creating the Engine for Scientific Discovery' (2016) 37(1) *AI Magazine*, www.rsc.org/globalassets/22-new-perspectives/discovery/digital-futures/rsc-digital-futures-report---digital.pdf, accessed 17 May 2021.

Lenat DB and Brown JS, 'Why AM and EURISKO Appear to Work' (1984) 23(3) *Artificial Intelligence* 236–40.

Lindsay RK and others, 'DENDRAL: A Case Study of the First Expert System for Scientific Hypothesis Formation' (1993) 61(2) *Artificial Intelligence* 209–61.

MacDonald EA, 'Aurorasaurus: A Citizen Science Platform for Viewing and Reporting the Aurora' (2015) 13(9) *Space Weather* 1–12.

Meszaros J and Ho C-H, 'Big Data and Scientific Research: The Secondary Use of Personal Data Under the Research Exemption in the GDPR' (2018) 59(4) *Acta Juridica Hungarica* 403–19.

Meszaros J, Ho C-H and Corrales Compagnucci M, 'Nudging Consent & the New Opt-Out System to the Processing of Health Data in England' in Corrales Compagnucci M and others (eds), *Legal Tech and the New Sharing Economy* (Springer 2020).

Minssen T and others, 'The EU-US Privacy Shield Regime for Cross-Border Transfers of Personal Data Under the GDPR: What are the Legal Challenges and How Might these Affect Cloud-Based Technologies, Big Data, and AI in the Medical Sector?' (2020) 4(1) *European Pharmaceutical Law Review* 34–50.

OECD, *Frascati Manual: Guidelines for Collecting and Reporting Data on Research and Experimental Development* (OECD 2015).

OECD, 'Making Open Science a Reality' Technology and Industry Policy Papers, No. 25, OECD Publishing, Paris (2015), https://doi.org/10.1787/5jrs2f963zs1-en, accessed 24 February 2021.

Pagallo U and others, 'The Rise of Robotics & AI: Technological Advances & Normative Dilemmas' in Corrales M and others (eds), *Robotics, AI and the Future of Law* (Springer 2018) 1–13.

Royal Society of Chemistry, 'Digital futures, a new frontier for science exploration and invention' 2020, www.rsc.org/globalassets/22-new-perspectives/discovery/digital-futures/rsc-digital-futures-report---digital.pdf, accessed 17 May 2021.

Schüritz R and others, 'Capturing Value from Data: Revenue Models for Data-Driven Services' *Proceedings of the 50th Hawaii International Conference on System Sciences* (2017). doi:10.24251/HICSS.2017.648

Sparkes A and others, 'Towards Robot Scientists for Autonomous Scientific Discovery' (2010) 2(1) *Automated Experimentation* 1–11.

Suman AB and Pierce R, 'Challenges for Citizen Science and the EU Open Science Agenda Under the GDPR' (2018) 4(3) *European Data Protection Law Review* 1–12.

Szalay A and Gray J, '2020 Computing: Science in an Exponential World' (2006) 440(7083) *Nature* 413–14.

The Future of Life Institute, 'Asilomar AI principles' developed in conjunction with the 2017 Asilomar Conference (2017), https://futureoflife.org/2017/08/11/ai-principles/, accessed 17 May 2021.

United States Code, 2012 Edition, Supplement 4, Title 15 – COMMERCE AND TRADE 15 U.S.C. 3724 – Crowdsourcing and citizen science (2016), www.govinfo.gov/app/details/USCODE-2016-title15/USCODE-2016-title15-chap63-sec3724, accessed 24 February 2021.

10

A Global Human Rights Approach to Medical Artificial Intelligence

AUDREY LEBRET

10.1 Introduction*

In July 2020, the World Health Organization (WHO) adopted a global strategy on digital health for the period 2020–2025 in order to provide institutional support for the adoption of national digital health strategies. According to WHO, the digital transformation of healthcare 'have proven potential to enhance health outcomes by improving medical diagnosis, data-based treatment decisions, digital therapeutics, clinical trials, self-management of care and person-centred care as well as creating more evidence-based knowledge, skills and competence for professionals to support healthcare',[1] and the organisation aims to 'strengthen health systems'[2] by encouraging collaboration between countries.[3] 'Digital health' encompasses electronic health, advanced computer science (including big data) and artificial intelligence (AI).[4] While the expression AI is widely used, it has a plurality of definitions.[5] Following Frederik Z.

* This chapter is based on a working paper on 'Human Rights Due Diligence for Medical Artificial Intelligence', presented at the 6th Global Business and Human Rights Conference, Monterrey, 3–4 September 2020, and at the Nordic Network of Biomedical and Health Law Conference, Copenhagen, 23 October 2020.

1 WHO, 'Global Strategy on Digital Health 2020–2025', 2021, 8, www.who.int/docs/default-source/documents/gs4dhdaa2a9f352b0445bafbc79ca799dce4d.pdf, accessed 4 February 2022.

2 Ibid., 11.

3 Ibid., 19–20.

4 See WHO, 'What You Need to Know About Digital Health Systems', e-health, 2019, www.euro.who.int/en/health-topics/Health-systems/e-health/news/news/2019/2/what-you-need-to-know-about-digital-health-systems, accessed 24 June 2021; WHO, Regional Office for Europe, 'Future of Digital Health Systems: Report on the WHO Symposium on the Future of Digital Health Systems in the European Region', 6–8 February 2019, https://apps.who.int/iris/bitstream/handle/10665/329032/9789289059992-eng.pdf, accessed 24 June 2021.

5 For a discussion on the definitions of AI and how policy-makers should define the material scope of AI regulations, see J Schuett, 'A Legal Definition of AI', Cornell University, 22 August 2021, https://arxiv.org/abs/1909.01095, accessed 24 June 2021.

Borgesius in his study for the Council of Europe on *Discrimination, AI and Algorithmic Decision-Making*, we adopt a broad definition of AI in this chapter as a 'computer running an algorithm that was fed data by its human operators'.[6] This definition incorporates machine-learning algorithms without being limited to them. '[M]achine learning refers to an automated process of discovering correlations (sometimes alternatively referred to as relationships or patterns) between variables in a dataset, often to make predictions or estimates of some outcome'.[7] AI's capacity to predict and its promises for disease prevention make it a very valuable tool for health, contributing to achieving the UN's Sustainable Development Goals.[8] A plurality of actors work on achieving those goals. In the healthcare sector, private actors play a critical role. More and more companies are entering the medical AI market, especially in the United States and in China. For instance, Google Health and DeepMind used two datasets from the United States and the United Kingdom to create an AI-based solution to identify breast cancer that would outperform human radiologists.[9] Similarly, the health branch of IBM, Watson Health, develops cognitive computing in order to improve medical treatment.[10] In Denmark, a highly digitised country, a programme analyses the voices of patients in emergency calls to detect heart attacks.[11] Examples are numerous.

Although corporations contribute to '*democratize healthcare through artificial intelligence*',[12] studies have shown that seemingly neutral algorithms could generate biases and discrimination with regard to age,

[6] FJZ Borgesius, 'Discrimination, Artificial Intelligence, and Algorithmic Decision-Making', Council of Europe, 2018, https://rm.coe.int/discrimination-artificial-intelligenceand-algorithmic-decision-making/1680925d73, accessed 24 June 2021.

[7] D Lehr and P Ohm, 'Playing with the Data: What Legal Scholars Should Learn About Machine Learning' (2017) 51(653) UCDL Rev. 671.

[8] For a balanced analysis on the interactions between AI and the sustainable development goals, see R Vinuesa and others, 'The role of Artificial Intelligence in Achieving the Sustainable Development Goals' (2020) 11 *Nature Communications*, www.nature.com/articles/s41467-019-14108-y, accessed 24 June 2021.

[9] S Mayer Mckinney and others, 'International Evaluation of an AI System for Breast Cancer Screening' (2020) 577 *Nature*, 89–94.

[10] For a review of some of the main health corporations working on AI medical solutions, see 'Top Artificial Intelligence Companies in Healthcare to Keep an Eye on', 21 January 2020, https://medicalfuturist.com/top-artificial-intelligence-companies-in-healthcare/#, accessed 24 June 2021.

[11] Ibid.

[12] Ibid. Emphasis added.

ethnicity, race or gender.[13] In the health sector, this could lead to inadequate medical treatment. Moreover, the collection of data to train algorithms may raise issues of privacy and protection of sensitive data.

Faced with those risks, several initiatives have emerged nationally and internationally in the past years to provide a framework for AI. For instance, in 2018, the UN published an instructive guidance note on a human rights–based approach to data.[14] The note insists on the application of essential principles for data science: participation of relevant populations, data disaggregation, self-identification of individuals, transparency, privacy and accountability.[15] In 2019, the Office of the UN High Commissioner for Human Rights (OHCHR) launched the B-Tech Project, gathering 'civil society organisations, a national human rights institution, technology companies, academics, multi-stakeholder initiatives, and state representatives'. The project's aim is to provide authoritative guidance and resources for implementing the United Nations Guiding Principles on Business and Human Rights with respect to a selected number of strategic focus areas in the technology space.[16] In the European Union, the High-Level Expert Group on AI adopted the 'Ethics Guidelines on Trustworthy AI' in April 2019.[17] These guidelines led the European Commission to publish a White

[13] See for instance D Cossins, 'Discriminating Algorithms: 5 Times AI Showed Prejudice' *New Scientist*, 27 April 2018, www.newscientist.com/article/2166207-discriminating-algorithms-5-times-ai-showed-prejudice/, accessed 1 May 2021. On skin colour, see A Fefegha, 'Racial Bias and Gender Bias Examples in AI systems' *The Comuzi Journal*, 2 September 2018, https://medium.com/thoughts-and-reflections/racial-bias-and-gender-bias-examples-in-ai-systems-7211e4c166a1, accessed 1 May 2021. On gender bias, see E Short, 'It Turns Out Amazon's AI Hiring Tool Discriminated Against Women' *Silicon Republic*, 11 October 2018, www.siliconrepublic.com/careers/amazon-ai-hiring-tool-women-discrimination, accessed 1 May 2021. See also the recent removal of an MIT database after it was revealed that the dataset taught AI systems to use racist and misogynistic slurs: K Quach, 'MIT Apologises, Permanently Pulls Offline Huge Dataset that Taught AI Systems to Use Misogynistic Slurs' *The Register*, 1 July 2020, www.theregister.com/2020/07/01/mit_dataset_removed/, accessed 1 May 2021.

[14] UN OHCHR, 'A Human Rights-Based Approach to Data: Leaving No One Behind in the 2030 Agenda for Sustainable Development' 2018, www.ohchr.org/Documents/Issues/HRIndicators/GuidanceNoteonApproachtoData.pdf, accessed 24 June 2021.

[15] Ibid.

[16] B-Tech Project, www.ohchr.org/EN/Issues/Business/Pages/B-TechProject.aspx, accessed 1 May 2021.

[17] High-Level Expert Group on AI, 'Ethics Guidelines for Trustworthy AI' 8 April 2019, https://ec.europa.eu/digital-single-market/en/news/ethics-guidelines-trustworthy-ai, accessed 1 May 2021. Other EU initiatives include Expert Group on Liability and New Technologies – New Technologies Formation, 'Liability for Artificial Intelligence and Other Emerging Digital Technologies', 2019, https://ec.europa.eu/newsroom/dae/document.cfm?doc_id=63199, accessed 1 May 2021.

Paper on AI in February 2020 and draft a regulation in April 2021, in order to harmonise certain practices for high-risk AI systems.[18] Although this regulation proposal does not explicitly refer to medical AI as a potential high-risk system, it seems that some healthcare algorithms could be qualified as such when they concern the 'access to and enjoyment of essential private services and public services and benefits'.[19] In parallel to the EU initiatives, several studies were conducted by committees of the Council of Europe.[20] In 2018, the Committee of Ministers of the Council of Europe adopted a Draft recommendation on the impacts of algorithms on human rights.[21] Other initiatives have emanated from civil society and non-governmental organisations. On 16 May 2018, Amnesty International and Access Now gathered to prepare the Toronto Declaration: 'Protecting the right to equality and non-discrimination in machine-learning systems'.[22]

All these studies and recommendations demonstrate the need for a human rights approach to AI. This is also true for medical AI, the focus

[18] European Commission, 'White Paper On Artificial Intelligence – A European Approach to Excellence and Trust', 2020; European Commission, 'Proposal for a Regulation of the European Parliament and of the Council of 21 April 2021 Laying Down Harmonized Rules on Artificial Intelligence (Artificial Intelligence Act) and Amending Certain Union Legislative Acts', 2021. On the regulatory approaches to machine learning–based medical devices in the EU and a comparison with the approach in the United States, see T Minssen and others, 'Regulatory Responses to Medical Machine Learning' (2020) 1 *Journal of Law and the Biosciences*.

[19] European Commission, Proposal of Artificial Intelligence Act, Annex III, § 5.

[20] Borgesius, 'Discrimination, Artificial Intelligence, and Algorithmic Decision-Making'. See also K Yeung, 'Responsibility and AI' Council of Europe study DGI (2019)05, Expert Committee on Human Right Dimensions of Automated Data Processing and Different Forms of Artificial intelligence (MSI-AUT), 2019, https://rm.coe.int/responsability-and-ai-en/168097d9c5, accessed 4 February 2022; Committee of Experts on Internet Intermediaries (MSI-NET), 'Algorithms and Human Rights: Study on the Human Rights Dimensions of Automated Data Processing Techniques and Possible Regulatory Implications', Council of Europe study DGI (2017)12, 2017, https://rm.coe.int/algorithms-and-human-rights-en-rev/16807956b5, accessed 4 February 2022.

[21] Council of Europe, Committee of Experts in Human Rights Dimensions of Automated Data Processing and Different Forms of AI (MSI-AUT), 'Addressing the Impacts of Algorithms on HR', Draft recommendation of the Committee of Ministers to member states on the human rights impacts of algorithmic systems, 2018, https://rm.coe.int/draft-recommendation-of-the-committee-of-ministers-to-states-on-the-hu/168095eecf, accessed 4 February 2022

[22] 'Toronto Declaration: Protecting the Rights to Equality and Non-discrimination in Machine Learning Systems', RightsCon Toronto, 16 May 2018, www.accessnow.org/the-toronto-declaration-protecting-the-rights-to-equality-and-non-discrimination-in-machine-learning-systems/, accessed 1 May 2021. See also Access Now, 'Human Rights in the Age of Artificial Intelligence', November 2018.

of this chapter. Because of the strong involvement of private actors in the development of medical AI and their transnational activities, the UN Guiding Principles on Business and Human Rights would offer a relevant global framework to AI on the international scene. Faced with the 'first truly transformative technology to come of age following the articulation' of the UN Guiding Principles, 'due diligence is the key' to address businesses' responsibility to respect human rights.[23] It is even more relevant because resolution 26/9 of 26 June 2014 established a working group whose mandate is to elaborate 'an internationally legally binding instrument to regulate, in international human rights law, the activities of transnational corporations and other business enterprises'.[24] On 6 August 2020, the working group published the second draft of this instrument.[25] The treaty will apply to business enterprises undertaking business activities of a transnational character,[26] and will offer victims the right to fair access to justice and effective remedy in case of unlawful interference against their privacy and other human rights.[27] States will have to require business enterprises to undertake human rights due diligence, including the identification of actual or potential human rights abuses, the undertaking of 'appropriate measures to prevent and mitigate effectively' such abuses, monitoring and communication to stakeholders.[28] Such a global framework is compatible with the additional adoption of more precise, sector-specific rules in the medical field.[29]

The following sections argue that a human rights approach to medical AI is necessary to protect individual and collective interests from both a substantive and a procedural/organisational perspective. From a substantive

23 FA Raso and others, 'Artificial Intelligence & Human Rights: Opportunities & Risks', Berkman Klein Center research publication no 2018-6, 25 September 2018, p. 53, https://ssrn.com/abstract=3259344, accessed 1 May 2021.

24 UNGA, Human Rights Council, 'Elaboration of an International Legally Binding Instrument on Transnational Corporations and Other Business Enterprises with Respect to Human Rights', A/HRC/RES/26/9, 14 July 2014, https://undocs.org/A/HRC/RES/26/9, accessed 24 June 2021.

25 OEIGWG Chairmanship, 'Legally Binding Instrument to Regulate, in International Human Rights Law, the Activities of Transnational Corporations and Other Business Enterprises' second revised draft, 6 August 2020, www.ohchr.org/Documents/HRBodies/HRCouncil/WGTransCorp/Session6/OEIGWG_Chair-Rapporteur_second_revised_draft_LBI_on_TNCs_and_OBEs_with_respect_to_Human_Rights.pdf, accessed 1 May 2021.

26 Ibid, Art. 3.

27 Ibid, Art. 4 'Rights of Victims'.

28 Ibid, Art. 6. 'Prevention'.

29 Persuasively recommended in Borgesius, 'Discrimination, Artificial Intelligence, and Algorithmic Decision-Making'.

perspective, a human rights framing of medical AI allows the adoption of a transversal and consistent approach to medical AI challenges, in complementarity with the ethical framing, which has received more attention recently (Section 10.2). From an organisational and procedural perspective, it would allow for defining the roles and responsibilities of all stakeholders, and enhancing a human rights culture as part of a methodology for the development of medical AI. In particular, education on human rights should be generalised in the faculties of medicine and data science, and pursued to the extent possible in AI companies (Section 10.3).

10.2 A Substantive Need for a Human Rights Approach to Medical AI

Scholars have expressed several ethical concerns on the use of AI in the medical sector. Despite its contributions to the protection of individual rights, the ethical framework has certain limitations and is not a substitute for a human rights–based approach to AI (Section 10.2.1). Human rights, and especially the right to health in the medical context, provide substantive inputs that help clarify the meaning of 'fair' AI (Section 10.2.2).

10.2.1 The Contributions and Shortcomings of the Ethical Framework to Medical AI

Although algorithms are not, as such, a threat to human rights, the design of such algorithms and the use of digital services give rise to several concerns related to the protection of individual rights. This includes threats to individuals' informed consent when using digital technologies. In the health sector, the ongoing COVID-19 pandemic illustrates how a public health threat can legitimate digital surveillance.[30] Medical AI can also threaten fairness

[30] See, in particular, WHO, 'Contact Tracing in the Context of COVID-19: Interim Guidance', 10 May 2020, https://apps.who.int/iris/handle/10665/332049, accessed 21 May 2020. At the EU level, see European Parliament, 'Covid-19 Tracing Apps: Ensuring Privacy and Use Across Borders', 1 December 2020, www.europarl.europa.eu/news/en/headlines/society/20200429STO78174/covid-19-tracing-apps-ensuring-privacy-and-data-protection, accessed 21 May 2020; N Ram and D Gray, 'Mass Surveillance in the Age of COVID-19', (2020) 7(1) *Journal of Law and the Biosciences*, https://doi.org/10.1093/jlb/lsaa023. See also, among others, F Tréguier, 'The State and Digital Surveillance in Times of the Covid-19 Pandemic' Science Po Center for International Studies, 1 June 2020, www.sciencespo.fr/ceri/en/content/state-and-digital-surveillance-times-covid-19-pandemic, accessed 17 February 2021.

in access to medical resources. In recent years, a wide range of scholarship has focused on making AI more 'fair' and, more broadly, on identifying the ethical concerns of AI.[31] This led to the adoption of declarations and reports by international organisations, including at the United Nations level, the Council of Europe and the EU. In the context of COVID-19, for instance, the WHO adopted ethical guidelines on the use of digital applications.[32] More broadly, as mentioned above, the European Commission's High-Level Expert Group on Artificial Intelligence published 'Ethical Guidelines for Trustworthy AI', which will be soon completed by a United Nations Educational, Scientific and Cultural Organisation (UNESCO) recommendation on the Ethics of AI.[33] Indeed, UNESCO conducted an online consultation on its first draft to collect feedback in the Summer of 2020.[34] The recommendation aims to define shared ethical values from which it derives concrete policy measures. Among those 'not necessarily legal' but inspirational values, the draft recommendation enumerates 'human dignity', human rights, 'leaving no one behind', 'living in harmony', 'trustworthiness', and 'protection of the environment'. It lists principles such as 'fairness', 'privacy', transparency and explainability, and so on. The Director-General of UNESCO, Audrey Azoulay, explained that the recommendation would promote a 'world dialogue' on the Ethics of AI.[35] As a part of an interdisciplinary dialogue on the progress of science, ethics indeed has a major role to play in appreciating the evolution of science and technologies. This project

[31] See, among others, J Morley and others, 'The Ethics of AI in Health Care: A Mapping Review' (2020) 260(1) *Social Science & Medicine*; A Blasimme and E Vayena, 'The Ethics of AI in Biomedical Research, Patient Care, and Public Health', in Dubber MD, Pascuale F and Das S, *The Oxford Handbook of Ethics of AI* (Oxford University Press 2020); S Dalton-Brown, 'The Ethics of Medical AI and the Physician-Patient Relationship' (2020) 29(1) *Cambridge Quarterly of Healthcare Ethics* 115. BD Mittelstadt and others, 'The Ethics of Algorithms: Mapping the Debate' (2016) 3(2) *Big Data & Society*, https://journals.sagepub.com/doi/full/10.1177/2053951716679679, accessed 4 February 2022.

[32] WHO, 'Ethical Considerations to Guide the Use of Digital Proximity Tracking Technologies for COVID-19 Contact Tracing', interim guidance, 28 May 2020, www.who.int/publications/i/item/WHO-2019-nCoV-Ethics_Contact_tracing_apps-2020.1, accessed 17 February 2021. WHO, 'Surveillance Strategies for COVID-19 Human Infection', interim guidance, 10 May 2020, https://apps.who.int/iris/handle/10665/332051, accessed 21 May 2020; WHO, 'WHO Guidelines on Ethical Issues in Public Health Surveillance', 2017, https://apps.who.int/iris/bitstream/handle/10665/255721/9789241512657-eng.pdf?sequence=1, accessed 7 May 2020.

[33] High-Level Expert Group on AI, 'Ethics Guidelines for Trustworthy AI'.

[34] UNESCO, 'Draft Text of a Recommendation on the Ethics of Artificial Intelligence' 25 June 2021, https://en.unesco.org/artificial-intelligence/ethics, accessed 21 May 2020.

[35] ONU, Chronique, Audrey Azoulay, 'Vers une éthique de l'intelligence artificielle', www.un.org/fr/chronicle/article/vers-une-ethique-de-lintelligence-artificielle, accessed 21 May 2020.

complements the Universal Declaration on Bioethics and Human Rights of 2005, a referential soft law instrument adopted by UNESCO and that is applicable to the technology of AI in the context of medicine. 'Bioethics' is the study of the 'ethical issues related to medicine, life sciences and associated technologies as applied to human beings, taking into account their social, legal and environmental dimensions'.[36] This definition of bioethics contrasts with the broader definition given by Van Rensselaer Potter as a 'science of survival' in his influential work of 1970.[37] Bioethics and human rights have common origins. Bioethics was born from the Nuremberg Trials in 1946–1947. It became a real discipline between 1962 and 1972, as a response to the various scandals in the life sciences.[38] As the draft project of UNESCO states, ethics is both a source of law and a tool of interpretation of legal norms.[39] The adoption of ethical guidelines in the context of fast-moving technology certainly appears as a softer (and faster) way to accompany innovation than legal frameworks.

However, ethics is an insufficient framework in itself to address all of AI's challenges to individual rights. Reaching a universal definition of the ethical/non-ethical is virtually impossible, as the difficulties in agreeing on a definition of 'fairness' or on the determination of bias in the literature show.[40] Such ambition is also questionable, especially when the great majority of the issuers of ethical AI guidelines come from the Global North.[41] As a pluralistic forum for debates on human values, ethics aims to think and assess rather than define and prescribe. As the diversity of views

36 UNESCO, 'Universal Declaration on Bioethics and Human Rights' 19 October 2005, Art. 1(1).

37 VR Potter, 'Bioethics: The Science of Survival' (1970) 14 *Perspectives in Biology and Medicine* 127. Although the paternity of the notion of bioethics is regularly ascribed to Potter, the term was first used by F Jahr, 'Bio-Ethik: Eine Umschau über die ethischen Beziehungen des Menschen zu Tier und Pflanze' (1927) 24–1 Kosmos: Handweiser für Naturfreunde 2.

38 For an historical overview of bioethics and an analysis of the Nuremberg Trials, see X Aurey, 'La transformation du corps humain en ressource biomédicale: Etude de droit international et européen' PhD thesis, Université Panthéon-Assas, 2015.

39 Ibid, 34.

40 A Narayanan, '21 Fairness Definitions and Their Politics', tutorial presented at the Conference on Fairness, Accountability, and Transparency, 23 February 2018. On fairness, see also AL Hoffmann, 'Where Fairness Fails: Data, Algorithms and the Limits of Antidiscrimination Discourse' (2019) 22 (7) *Information, Communication & Society* 900; See also K Yeung and others, 'AI Governance by Human-Rights Centered Design, Deliberation, and Oversight: An End to Ethics Washing', in Dubber MD, Pascuale F and Das S (eds), *The Oxford Handbook of Ethics of AI* (Oxford University Press 2020), arguing similarly for a human rights framework to AI.

41 See A Jobin and others, 'The Global Landscape of AI Ethics Guidelines' (2019) 1 *Nature Machine learning* 389.

in Europe on bioethical issues such as organ transplantation or surrogacy show, ethics vary from culture to culture, and country to country. Despite the substantive link between universal human rights and ethics, they are not equivalent. For instance, when the European Court of Human Rights interprets the European Convention in the context of new technologies, it grants its member states a wider margin of appreciation in the application and balancing of fundamental rights when an issue has an important ethical and moral nature.[42]

Beyond the cultural differences, the elaboration process of ethics suffers from a lack of representativeness. Analysing human genetic engineering, John H. Evans rightly observes that although the public is primarily concerned by those debates, it is not sufficiently involved.[43] Similarly, for Daniel Borrillo, bioethical expertise is a 'mechanism for subtracting the democratic deliberation of certain sensitive issues'.[44] In the life sciences, many scholars have underlined the political nature of bioethics. The choice of the language of ethics in the particular field of AI confirms these observations. At the EU level, the goal of the High-Level Expert Group on AI was to act 'as quickly as possible' for 'maximising the benefits and minimising the risks of AI', while acknowledging the place that the EU can have in the AI competition with the United States and China.[45]

Therefore, the ethics discourse needs to be completed by a legal approach to AI, and in particular by human rights law. In a report on freedom of expression and AI, the UN rapporteur David Kaye said:

> [w]hile ethics provide a critical framework for working through particular challenges in the field of artificial intelligence, it is not a replacement for human rights, to which every State is bound by law. Companies and governments should ensure that human rights considerations and responsibilities

42 See, for instance, the Court's case law on abortion (eg, *A, B and C v. Ireland* App. no. 25579/05 (ECHR, 16 December 2010)); or on the 'right to die' (*Pretty v. UK* App. no. 2346/02 (ECHR, 29 April 2002)) . This can result from different socio-technical imaginaries surrounding new technologies; see A Lebret, 'The European Court of Human Rights and the Framing of Reproductive Issues', (2020) *Droits Fondamentaux* 18.

43 JH Evans, *Playing God: Human Genetic Engineering and the Rationalization of Public Bioethical Debate* (University of Chicago Press 2002) 73.

44 « Un mécanisme de soustraction de la délibération démocratique de certaines questions sensibles »: See D Borrillo, 'La République des experts dans la construction des lois: le cas de la bioéthique', (2011)14 *Histoire&Politique. Politique, culture, société* 1.

45 P Ala-Pietilä, 'Towards Trustworthy AI – Ethics & Competitiveness Go Hand-in-Hand' European Commission, 2019, https://ec.europa.eu/digital-single-market/en/blogposts/towards-trustworthy-ai-ethics-competitiveness-go-hand-hand, accessed 21 May 2020.

> are firmly integrated into all aspects of their artificial intelligence operations even as they are developing ethical codes and guidance.[46]

However, scholarship did not give the same attention to the study of the interactions between medical AI and human rights as it did to develop new ethical guidelines for AI.[47] Although AI guidelines usually incorporate the right to privacy, demonstrating a convergence between ethical and legal standards through the right to data protection, the approach to privacy seems generally narrow.[48] Besides, while privacy has received attention,

[46] D Kaye, 'Report of the Special Rapporteur on the Promotion and Protection of the Right to Freedom of Opinion and Expression', A/73/348 (2018).

[47] For recent general scholarship on the interactions of AI and human rights in general, see A Kriebitz and C Lütge, 'Artificial Intelligence and Human Rights: A Business Ethical Assessment' (2020) 5(1) *Business and Human Rights Journal* 84; S Livingston and M Risse, 'The Future Impact of Artificial Intelligence on Human Rights' (2019) 33(2) *Ethics & International Affairs*; K Yeung and others, 'AI Governance by Human-Rights Centered Design'; Raso and others, 'Artificial Intelligence & Human Rights'; EC Schwarz, 'Human vs. Machine: A Framework of Responsibilities and Duties of Transnational Corporations for Respecting Human Rights in the Use of Artificial Intelligence' (2019) 58 *Columbia Journal of Transnational Law* 232, www.jtl.columbia.edu/journal-articles/human-vs-machine-a-framework-of-responsibilities-and-duties-of-transnational-corporations-for-respecting-human-rights-in-the-use-of-artificial-intelligence, accessed 1 May 2021; T Tzimas, 'The Need for an International Treaty for AI from the Perspective of Human Rights' (2019) 4(1) *Scientia Moralitas Journal* 73; L McGregor and others, 'International Human Rights Law as a Framework for Algorithmic Accountability' (2019) 68 *International and Comparative Law Quarterly* 309. On the interactions between AI (in general) and non-discrimination in the EU context, see the recent report by the European network of legal experts in gender equality and non-discrimination, J Gerards and R Xenidis, 'Algorithmic Discrimination in Europe: Challenges and Opportunities for Gender Equality and Non-discrimination Law – A Special Report' 2020, www.equalitylaw.eu/publications, accessed 1 May 2021; S Wachter and others, 'Why Fairness Cannot Be Automated: Bridging the Gap Between EU Non-discrimination Law and AI' 2020, https://ssrn.com/abstract=3547922, accessed 1 May 2021.

[48] Ethical AI acknowledges that privacy is both a value to uphold and a right to protect; Jobin and others, 'The Global Landscape of AI Ethics Guidelines', 395. The right to data protection has been protected as early as in 1981 by Council of Europe Convention 108: Convention for the Protection of Individuals with Regard to Automatic Processing of Personal Data (1981) ETS no. 108. Although this right derives from the right to private life, applied in the context of digital technologies (see Preamble and Art. 1 of Convention 108 (1981), and its explanatory report, § 4 on the necessity to complete the standards of the European Convention on Human Rights), both Convention 108 and EU law recognise the autonomous nature of the right to protection of personal data (Preamble of Convention 108, as amended by its Protocol CETS no 223, recitals 4 and 6; Consolidated versions of the Treaty on the Functioning of the European Union (TFEU) [2016] OJ C202/1 Art. 16 (since the Treaty of Lisbon), EU Charter of Fundamental Rights: Charter of Fundamental Rights of the European Union, OJ 2010 C 83/389, Art. 8, Distinct Right from Right to Private Life, Art. 7; EU General Data Protection Regulation (GDPR): Regulation (EU) 2016/679 of the European Parliament and of the Council of 27 April 2016 on the protection of natural

the interactions between new health technologies and socio-economic rights remain under-explored in the medical area.[49] Yet, such rights are protected by legally binding instruments and provide international standards that concern all stakeholders in medical AI because of the state obligation to effectively protect human rights. In particular, the development of medical AI would benefit from an analysis in the light of the right to health, including non-discrimination in access to health services.

10.2.2 The Material Inputs from the Right to Health to Medical AI

A starting point to assess the design and use of AI in medicine is the right to health. Both the Constitution of the WHO and the International Covenant on Economic, Social and Cultural Rights (ICESCR) protect the 'right to the highest attainable standard of health'.[50] The vast majority of States have ratified the ICESCR. This treaty requires State parties to 'undertake to take steps, individually, and through international assistance and co-operation … to the maximum of its available resources, with a view to achieving progressively the full realisation of the rights [.] by all appropriate means'.[51] The immediate obligation to take steps includes 'the prevention, treatment and control of epidemic, endemic, occupational and other diseases'.[52]

persons with regard to the processing of personal data and on the free movement of such data, and repealing Directive 95/46/EC (General Data Protection Regulation), OJ 2016 L 119/1 (GDPR), Recital 1). The GDPR facilitated data protection and data security by providing clear rules for the processing of personal data. Therefore, it is not surprising that scholarship on ethical AI abundantly refers to data protection as one standard of protection, converging with legal standards. For example, High-Level Expert Group on AI, 'Ethics Guidelines for Trustworthy AI', 17 states that ethical principles are rooted in fundamental rights but refers to privacy essentially as data protection, integrity and access to data. However, data protection is only one of the objects covered by the European Convention on Human Rights, Art. 8 on the right to private (and family) life. The European Court of Human Rights incorporated data protection into the scope of protection on Art. 8 far before the 'autonomisation' of data protection, including for biomedical data (see the Grand Chamber case *S and Marper v UK* App Nos 30562/04 and 30566/04 (ECHR, 4 December 2008), §§ 66 and 103, where the Court interprets the right to private life with regard to the content of Convention 108; see also *L.L. v France* App No 7508/02 (ECHR, 10 October 2006). Hence, a human rights reading of privacy for medical AI is wider than data protection and includes identity, integrity, etc.

49 A Lebret and T Minssen, 'Digital Health, Artificial Intelligence and Accessibility to HealthCare in Denmark' (2021) 1 *European Human Rights Law Review* 40, 41.

50 International Covenant on Economic, Social and Cultural Rights (adopted 16 December 1966, entered into force 3 January 1976) 993 UNTS 3 (ICESCR), Art. 12.

51 ICESCR, Art. 2.

52 ICESCR, Art. 12(c).

General Comment No. 14 of the UN Committee on Economic, Social and Cultural Rights (CESCR) provides substantive elements of the definition of the 'right to health'. It states that all services, goods and facilities must be available, accessible, acceptable and of good quality.[53] Those four essential components provide a relevant grid of analysis for digital technologies in the health sector. Health goods and services must be both physically and economically accessible. Besides, accessibility involves the right to seek and get relevant information. The right to health also requires states to not discriminate and to protect individuals from discrimination by third parties,[54] including by the adoption of a relevant framework.[55] According to the General Comment, non-discrimination and equitable access to healthcare facilities, goods and services are core state obligations.[56]

The design and use of algorithms in the medical sector interact in particular with non-discrimination and acceptability.

First, as a human production, algorithms are not neutral. A broad range of literature has emerged on biases identified in machine-learning algorithms,[57] including in medicine.[58] Although stakeholders converge on the need for justice in AI, they express this requirement in terms of fairness and biases rather than in the legal term of discrimination.[59] Biases can be explicit when they arise from data scientists' own biases, or implicit when they result from a lack of data, underlying

[53] Committee on Economic, Social and Cultural Rights (CESCR), 'The Right to the Highest Attainable Standard of Health', General Comment No. 14, UN Doc. No. E/C.12/2000/4, 11 August 2000, https://digitallibrary.un.org/record/425041, accessed 1 May 2021.

[54] Ibid, § 50 obligation to respect, § 51 on violations of the obligation to protect.

[55] Ibid, § 54.

[56] Ibid, § 19; 43–45.

[57] See among others CNIL and Défenseur des droits (France), 'Algorithmes: prévenir l'automatisation des discriminations' (2020); RH Sloan and R Warner, 'Beyond Bias: Artificial Intelligence and Social Justice' (2020) 24 *Virginia Journal of Law and Technology* 1; N Schmidt and B Stephens, 'An Introduction to Artificial Intelligence and Solutions to the Problems of Algorithmic Discrimination' (2019) 73(2) *Quarterly Report* 130; R Challen and others, 'Artificial Intelligence, Bias and Clinical Safety' (2019) 28 *BMJ Quality & Safety* 231; TB Gillis and JL Spiess, 'Big Data and Discrimination' (2019) 86(2) *The University of Chicago Law Review* 459; KL Booz and A Hamilton, 'Bias Amplification in Artificial Intelligence Systems' paper presented at AAAI FSS-18: Artificial Intelligence in Government and Public Sector, Arlington, VA, 2018; P Hacker, 'Teaching Fairness to Artificial Intelligence: Existing and Novel Strategies Against Algorithmic Discrimination Under EU Law' (2018) 55 *Common Market Law Review*, 1143; S Barocas and AD Selbst, 'Big Data's Disparate Impact' (2016) 104 *California Law Review* 671.

[58] See, among others, RB Parikh and others, 'Addressing Bias in Artificial Intelligence in Health Care' (2019) 322(24) *The Journal of the American Medical Association* 2377.

[59] Jobin and others, 'The Global Landscape of AI Ethics Guidelines', 394.

disparities in diagnosis, and/or when the training sample of an algorithm differs significantly from the population of interest.[60] Biases and discriminatory outputs can occur when data scientists use historical data sets propagating racial or gender biases. The entire development of new algorithms is a costly procedure, which partly explains why algorithms are reused in different contexts, raising issues of socio-cultural and historical compatibility of the used data and the reality of patients. In the US context, for instance, Nicholson Price II observed that various policies encourage the training of medical algorithms on data collected from high-resource contexts, such as medical centres, leading to 'contextual bias'.[61] Because of the difference between populations in such centres and low-resource/rural centres, the algorithms' quality in such settings is lower.[62] The protection of individuals and groups against discrimination is inherent in the right to health and is also guaranteed by international treaties. This includes specific treaties like the Convention on the Elimination of All Forms of Racial Discrimination,[63] or the Convention on the Elimination of All Forms of Discrimination against Women (CEDAW),[64] as well as general human rights treaties like the European Convention on Human Rights, the American Convention on Human Rights, or ICESCR.[65] The ICESCR is part of the Bill of Human Rights that business enterprises must, at a minimum, respect.[66] Interestingly, general instruments, such as the European Convention of Human Rights,[67] the European

[60] Parikh and others, 'Addressing Bias in Artificial Intelligence in Health Care'. For an accessible approach to algorithmic bias in machine learning, see A Jean, *De l'autre côté de la Machine – Voyage d'une scientifique au pays des algorithmes* (L'observatoire 2020).

[61] WN Price II, 'Medical AI and Contextual Bias', (2019) 33 *Harvard Journal Of Law & Technology* 66.

[62] Ibid.

[63] Convention on the Elimination of All Forms of Racial Discrimination (adopted 21 December 1965, entered into force 4 January 1969) 660 UNTS 195.

[64] Convention on the Elimination of All Forms of Discrimination against Women (adopted 18 December 1979, entered into force 3 September 1981)1249 UNTS 13 (CEDAW).

[65] Convention for the Protection of Human Rights and Fundamental Freedoms ((European Convention on Human Rights, adopted 4 November 1950, entered into force 3 September 1953)ETS No 005 (as amended), Article 14; American Convention on Human Rights (Pact of San José adopted 22 November 1969, entered into force 18 July 1978) 1144 OAS Treaty Series 123, Articles 1.1 and 24; ICESCR, Art. 2.2, 3.

[66] UN Guiding Principles A/HRC/17/31, §12 and commentary.

[67] This provision cannot be invoked in combination with the right to health since the convention does not explicitly protect a right to health. However, see the broader protection offered by Protocol No. 12 to the Convention for the Protection of Human Rights and Fundamental Freedoms (adopted 4 November 2000, entered into force 1 April 2005), ETS No 177.

Social Charter,[68] and the Charter of Fundamental Rights,[69] have a non-limiting list of protected characteristics. By contrast, the American Convention on Human Rights enumerates protected characteristics and allows their extension to 'any other *social condition*'.[70] Among the groups requiring special attention, the General Comment on the right to health enumerates women, older people, indigenous peoples, persons with disabilities, children and adolescents.[71]

Concretely, the right to health requires States to be vigilant to the needs of vulnerable populations and to rely on their respective socio-historical contexts to target other marginalised groups by adapting their health policies. In that sense, all stakeholders should determine and target the vulnerabilities associated with specific medical procedures and adapt their policies and their translation into the algorithms,

[68] The European Social Charter prohibits discrimination 'on any ground such as race, colour, sex, language, religion, political or other opinion, national extraction or social origin, health, association with a national minority, birth or other status' in the exercise of 'the rights set forth in the Charter', including the right to health. See European Social Charter (adopted 18 October 1961, entered into force 26 February 1965), 529 UNTS 89, revised in 1996: European Social Charter (revised) (adopted 3 May 1996, entered into force 1 July 1999) ETS No163, Art. E.

[69] EU Charter of Fundamental Rights: Charter of Fundamental Rights of the European Union, OJ 2010 C 83/389, Art. 21. The Charter excludes discrimination in general terms, on 'any ground such as sex, race, colour, ethnic or social origin, genetic features, language, religion or belief, political or any other opinion, membership of a national minority, property, birth, disability, age or sexual orientation'. See also EU Racial Equality Directive: Council Directive 2000/43/EC of 29 June 2000 implementing the principle of equal treatment between persons irrespective of racial or ethnic origin, OJ L 180, 19.7.2000, pp. 22–26; Employment Equality Directive: Council Directive 2000/78/EC of 27 November 2000 establishing a general framework for equal treatment in employment and occupation, OJ L 303, 2.12.2000, pp. 16–22; Recast Gender Equality Directive: Directive 2006/54/EC of the European Parliament and of the Council of 5 July 2006 on the implementation of the principle of equal opportunities and equal treatment of men and women in matters of employment and occupation (recast), OJ L 204, 26.7.2006, pp. 23–36. In *Mangold v. Helm* (22 November 2005, *Mangold*, C-144/04, ECLI:EU:C:2005:709), the European Court of Justice held that non-discrimination on grounds of age was a general principle of EU law that had a horizontal effect. In *Egenberger* (17 April 2018, Case C-414/16, *Vera Egenberger* v *Evangelisches Werk für Diakonie und Entwicklung e. V* (ECLI:EU:C:2018:257)), the court ruled that the right to freedom of religion, protected by the charter of fundamental rights, had a horizontal effect.

[70] American Convention on Human Rights (Pact of San José adopted 22 November 1969, entered into force 18 July 1978) 1144 OAS Treaty Series 123, Art.1 § 1. Emphasis added. The ICESCR's provision on discrimination also applies to 'other situations' than the ones specifically enumerated. See also UN OHCHR, 'Tackling Discrimination Against Lesbian, Gay, Bi, Trans, & Intersex People: Standards of Conduct for Business' 2017, www.unfe.org/standards/, accessed 25 June 2021.

[71] CESCR, 'The Right to the Highest Attainable Standard of Health'.

whether or not they involve machine learning. An example is the use of algorithms for the allocation of human organs for transplantation. In the US context, it has been shown that a purely efficiency-based algorithm targeting the greatest increase in quality-adjusted life expectancy would result in the assignment of lower priorities to African-Americans because of their higher risk of graft failure.[72] While relying on an apparently neutral objective, the algorithm failed to consider a group of people protected by the law, although such a group might require specific measures of protection. Similarly, policies giving priority to transplant candidates with higher chances of long-term graft survival lead algorithms to systematically disadvantage older people. Considering that the elderly belong to a vulnerable and protected category,[73] the outputs of machine-learning algorithms would likely be discriminatory. Thus, the development of medical AI would benefit from a human rights reading.[74]

Besides, non-discrimination law can address the most common risk associated with machine-learning algorithms: their discriminatory effects on a particular group, not just the discriminatory treatment of that group. Indeed, international human rights law prohibits indirect discrimination regardless of the author's intention.[75] This suggests deconstructing all the causes that could lead to discrimination and assessing the potential effects of choices of target and class variables.[76] It is true that the judicial

[72] SA Zenios and others, 'Evidence-Based Organ Allocation' (1999) 107 *The American Journal of Medicine* 52.

[73] See references in n 71, see also CESCR, 'The Right to the Highest Attainable Standard of Health'.

[74] A Lebret, 'Equitable Access to Transplantation: A Human Rights Approach to the Algorithmic Allocation of Organs', Roundtable on Digital Challenges in Health Law: From Telemedicine to AI, Max Planck Institute for Social Law and Social Policy, 17 June 2021.

[75] On the characterisation of discrimination regardless of the author's intent, see ECtHR, *Biao v. Denmark* (2016), App. no 38590/10, § 103: 'difference in treatment may take the form of disproportionately prejudicial effects of a general policy or measure which, though couched in neutral terms, discriminates against a group. Such a situation may amount to "indirect discrimination", which does not necessarily require a discriminatory intent'; See also ECtHR, *Jordan v. UK* (2001), App. no 24746/94, § 154.

[76] Barocas and Selbst have identified five steps in the algorithmic process during which AI can lead to discrimination: the definition of 'class label', the definition of 'target labels', the labelling of training data, collection of data, feature selection and proxies. 'While the target variable defines what data miners are looking for, "class labels" divide all possible values of the target variable into mutually exclusive categories'. Barocas and Selbst, 'Big Data's Disparate Impact', 678.

interpretation of the evidential requirements of non-discrimination does not provide clear and uniform standards to be automated once and for all, and requires case-by-case analysis.[77] European scholars have also highlighted the lack of convergence between European approaches to non-discrimination,[78] and the fact that the development of AI may also challenge the traditional categories of discrimination law.[79] However, the application of interrelated human rights allows (1) the identification of criteria of hard law to prevent discrimination against vulnerable groups and individuals in a given context, even though interpretative work is needed and, arguably, desirable,[80] 2) the distinguishing and ordering of the legal and ethical spheres, overcoming the lack of representativeness of the ethical framework.[81]

Second, the right to health also involves 'acceptability' of health services, which means that they must be respectful of medical ethics and culturally appropriate – that is, respectful of the culture of individuals, minorities, peoples and communities, sensitive to gender and life-cycle requirements, as well as being designed to respect confidentiality and improve the health status of those concerned.[82]

Notwithstanding the universalism of the right to health, 'acceptability' recognises the necessity to integrate the cultural context in reflections on health policies. This conciliation is at the heart of the

[77] Borgesius observes that non-discrimination law (in European law) is 'closer to a 'standard' than to a 'rule'; Borgesius, 'Discrimination, Artificial Intelligence, and Algorithmic Decision-Making', 19. Concerning the study of EU law and statistical evidence of discrimination, see Watcher and others, 'Why Fairness Cannot Be Automated'. For a broader study on the principle of discrimination in EU Law and the Council of Europe, see M Brillat, *Le principe de non-discrimination à l'épreuve des rapports entre les droits européens* (Institut Universitaire Varenne-Collection des Thèses 2016).

[78] See Brillat, *Le principe de non-discrimination*. On the gaps of EU law for algorithmic discrimination in general in EU law, see Wachter and others, 'Why Fairness Cannot be Automated'; Gerards and Xenidis, 'Algorithmic Discrimination in Europe'.

[79] It does so by sometimes blurring the distinction between direct and indirect discrimination. See Gerards and Xenidis, 'Algorithmic Discrimination in Europe'.

[80] For example, Brillat argues persuasively in her thesis for a reading of the principle of non-discrimination in Europe in light of the principle of equality; Brillat, *Le principe de non-discrimination*.

[81] There is broad scholarship on the interactions between international law and democracy, see also S Besson, 'Sovereignty, International Law and Democracy' (2011) 22(2) *European Journal of International Law* 373; K Martin-Chenut, 'Droit international et démocratie' (2007) 4(220) *Diogène* 36, J Crawford, *Democracy in International Law: Inaugural Lecture Delivered 5 March 1993* (Cambridge University Press, 1994).

[82] CESCR, 'The Right to the Highest Attainable Standard of Health', § 12.

human rights approach, relying on balancing between rights and interests. This is a crucial aspect for medical AI, since some authors have denounced data extraction and appropriation by AI corporations as a modern form of colonialism.[83] Corporations have replaced countries in this resource appropriation that, according to Couldry and Mejias, constitutes a form of colonialism since it relies on an ideology and a shift in social relations that matches the features of historical colonialism.[84] Beyond data extraction, a culturally blind approach by transnational corporations' data collectors, and/or the importation/exportation of models between borders and continents raise serious human rights issues. The right to health, and in particular an interpretative work of the notion of 'acceptability' in a given context should work as a method to build responsible algorithms and apply due diligence. The Declaration of Toronto acknowledged this dimension in its guidelines on human rights impacts of algorithmic systems, noting that the level of impact on human rights of algorithms 'will also depend on the broader organisational, thematic, societal and legal context in which they are used, each of which is associated with specific public and ethical values'.[85] One way to include marginalised populations is to facilitate and encourage participation.[86] Concerning data science, in particular, the United Nations listed the participation of individuals and groups as an essential element of a human rights–based approach to data. Alongside participation, data disaggregation is among the six key elements to ensure that data science complies with human rights.[87] Data disaggregation requires the use of as many subcategories as needed to enable countries 'to develop targeted policies to secure the

[83] N Couldry and U Mejias, 'Data Colonialism: Rethinking Big Data's Relation to the Contemporary Subject' (2019) *Television and New Media* 336.

[84] Ibid.

[85] Toronto Declaration', § 8.

[86] This falls within the scope of the right to health as other human rights; CESCR, 'The Right to the Highest Attainable Standard of Health', § 11. See also ICESCR, Art. 13.1 and Art. 15.1; CEDAW, art.7; Convention on the Rights of the Child (adopted 20 November 1989, entered into force 2 September 1990) 1577 UNTS 3 (CRC), Art.12; Convention on the Rights of Persons with Disabilities (adopted 13 December 2006, entered into force 3 May 2008 2515 UNTS 3, Art. 29, among the main relevant treaties. See also UN Declaration on the Rights of Indigenous Peoples (adopted 13 September 2007) UNGARes. 61/295, Art. 5, 18, 19 and 41).

[87] Lebret and Minssen, 'Digital Health, Artificial Intelligence and Accessibility'. The six elements are participation, data disaggregation, self-identification, transparency, privacy and accountability; UN OHCHR, 'A Human Rights-Based Approach to Data'.

realisation of the right to health generally and for discrete groups'.[88] In order to have a more transparent medical AI, states should ensure that public and private actors apply data disaggregation in order to achieve equal access to healthcare.

As a húman right protected by international treaties (and, in addition, by numerous state constitutions), states must respect, protect and fulfil the right to health. In particular, they must ensure information accessibility, and that healthcare resources are allocated in an equitable way, while taking into consideration the needs of vulnerable people. AI contributes in many ways to the realisation of the right to health. However, the involvement of private actors cannot result in a threat to the rights' effectiveness. As for the activities of transnational corporations threatening the environment and human rights, a business and human rights approach to AI allows all stakeholders to share responsibility. Such a transnational framework is needed to detect and remedy potential human rights violations.

10.3 An Organisational and Procedural Need for a Transnational Framework on Human Rights and Medical AI

A business and human rights approach to AI allows for defining the different actors' responsibilities in a transnational context, potentially leading to a more transparent and democratic use of AI, which is a condition to enforce individual rights (Section 10.3.1). The effectiveness of the protection of those rights will not only rely on the adoption of new legal instruments but also on ensuring that medical doctors and data scientists receive adequate education on human rights (Section 10.3.2).

[88] J Tobin, *The Right to Health in International Law* (Oxford University Press 2012) 209. Data disaggregation is required by several human rights bodies, see UN Committee on the Rights of the Child, 'General Comment No. 4: Adolescent Health and Development in the Context of the Convention on the Rights of the Child' (2003), UN Doc. CRC/GC/2003/4§ 9. According to the Convention on the Rights of Persons with Disabilities, 'States Parties undertake to collect appropriate information, including statistical and research data, to enable them to formulate and implement policies to give effect to the present Convention': Convention on the Rights of Persons with Disabilities (adopted 13 December 2006, entered into force 3 May 2008) 2515 UNTS 3, art. 31. UN OHCHR, 'A Human Rights-Based Approach to Data', 8. See also Claire Lougarre's work on data collection and disaggregation as part of the right to health in C Lougarre, 'The Right to Health: Legal Content Through Supranational Monitoring' PhD thesis, University College London, 2016, https://discovery.ucl.ac.uk/id/eprint/1474052/, accessed 1 May 2021.

10.3.1 Defining and Allocating Responsibilities

The development of algorithms can result from 'data colonialism', a combination of 'predatory extractive practices of historical colonialism with the abstract quantification methods of computing'.[89] In this twenty-first–century form of colonialism, the colonial power does not emanate from the Global North against the Global South, but from corporations, crossing borders.[90] When private actors design and use algorithms for the general interest, such as health purposes, state authorities have a direct interest in ensuring that digitalisation and the involvement of private interests are not compromising human rights standards. In particular, states have the responsibility to ensure that the rhetoric of the general interest does not conceal an objective of the commodification of personal data. Data mining should be in line with the needs of the population. More broadly, the digitalisation of health and the design and development of sophisticated algorithms (using machine or deep learning) by private institutions raise the issue of the representativeness of such entities and their policies. The application of the UN principles on business and human rights in the AI context would allow the re-introduction of democratic processes by building bridges between the different stakeholders, public and private, under state scrutiny. Besides, the difficulty in AI is the allocation of responsibilities between the various actors developing and using the algorithms, including software designers, programmers, data scientists, sellers, buyers and so on. A business and human rights approach will allow the adoption of an encapsulating framework by allocating roles and responsibilities to the different actors. Following McGregor and others,[91] we view a business and human approach to AI ('algorithmic accountability') as an organising framework rather than a turnkey solution to all AI challenges for individuals and society. Better than ethics, it allows for the incorporation of all actors in a chain of human rights obligations in a consistent and transparent way. More specific and technical rules, such as professional standards and specific guidelines depending on the medical or biomedical field, will be needed to complete that framework. The Draft Recommendation of the Committee of Ministers of the Council of Europe goes in that direction, aiming to ensure that responsibility and accountability for the protection of human rights are effectively and clearly distributed throughout all stages of the process,

89 Couldry and Mejias, 'Data Colonialism', 336–37.
90 Ibid.
91 McGregor and others, 'International Human Rights Law'.

from the proposal stage through to task identification, data selection, collection and analysis, system modelling and design, ongoing deployment, and review and reporting requirements.[92]

This could involve the de-biasing of data that could lead to indirect discriminatory outcomes. Furthermore, due diligence extends to after the development of the algorithm, when it is sold and used by other parties. When buying, the purchaser will have human rights responsibilities. If the circumstances require a modification of the algorithm, which is likely to be the case in medical AI, the stakeholder will need to carry out an impact assessment.[93]

In this regard, the recent proposal of the Artificial Intelligence Act of the European Commission should strengthen the prevention of harm to rights and interests in the EU territory by imposing obligations on providers, importers, distributors and users of high-risk AI systems placed on the EU market.[94] The regulation proposal requires the prior assessment of the quality of datasets, the training and testing of AI systems on inclusive and appropriate data,[95] and the implementation of a quality management system upon providers.[96] This legislative framework could fit into the scope of a due diligence obligation of AI corporations and other stakeholders operating in the EU.[97] On the international scene, a more global business and human rights–based initiative could also be inspired by the regulation.

Alongside the determination of respective roles and responsibilities, states need to enforce human rights and ensure individuals have access to effective remedies.[98] As recommended by the Committee of Ministers of the Council of Europe, states must develop processes enabling individuals to complain, including 'prompt, transparent, functional and effective' judicial remedies, 'whether stemming from public or private sector actors'.[99]

[92] MSI-AUT, 'Addressing the Impacts of Algorithms on HR', Preamble.

[93] See McGregor and others, 'International Human Rights Law', 334.

[94] European Commission, Proposal of Artificial Intelligence Act. The Regulation would also create a European AI Board, see Art. 56–58.

[95] Ibid., Art. 10.

[96] Ibid., Art. 16(b) and 17.

[97] In parallel, see the ongoing project of EU directive on due diligence; European Parliament resolution of 10 March 2021 with recommendations to the Commission on Corporate Due Diligence and Corporate Accountability (2020/2129(INL)), OJ C 474, 24.11.2021, pp. 11–40. A cross reading of these instruments will certainly be constructive for a responsible medical AI.

[98] UN guiding principles A/HRC/17/31 § 25.

[99] MSI-AUT, 'Addressing the Impacts of Algorithms on HR', 'Obligation of states with respect to the protection and promotion and fundamental freedoms in the context of algorithmic systems', § 4.5.

In the medical area, it will be crucial that human rights bodies effectively protect the right to health. Moreover, in the AI context, one main challenge is to ensure transparency and knowledge in order to ensure that individuals may effectively claim a human rights violation due to the design or use of an algorithm. This will be doable by imposing more transparency in the algorithms' development and monitoring, and the inclusion of civil society.

10.3.2 *Preventing Human Rights Infringements through Education on Human Rights and Consistent Monitoring*

The opacity of algorithms to laypersons makes it difficult to detect a potential human rights violation, and for individuals or groups to know that they have been victims of such a violation. Besides, the analysis *a posteriori* of the algorithms has a certain cost, takes time and may require the development of new human rights–compliant algorithms. Those elements justify a preventive strategy rather than a purely reactive approach by public and private actors. This is in line with the good practices identified by the UN Working Group on the Issue of Human Rights and Transnational Corporations and Other Business Enterprises.[100] A preventive approach to medical AI would require (1) the creation of a human rights culture in the structures that directly develop such algorithms or collaborate on such development; (2) the monitoring of human rights due diligence at each step of the algorithm development and use.

The incorporation of a human rights culture into the medical and data science centres, both public and private, implies cooperation between scientists and human rights experts and, preferably, a stronger place for education on human rights. Awareness of human rights and corporate responsibility remains a challenge, in particular among small and early-stage companies.[101] This applies to the medical sector, too. In 1999, the World Medical Association adopted a resolution on the teaching of medical ethics as well as human rights in medical schools.[102] Yet, a 2008 empirical study showed that the teaching of human rights

100 UNGA, 'Report of the Working Group on the Issue of Human Rights and Transnational Corporations and Other Business Enterprises', 16 July 2018, A/73/163, §25 (d).

101 Raso and others, 'Artificial Intelligence & Human Rights', 54.

102 World Medical Assembly, 'Resolution on the Inclusion of Medical Ethics and Human Rights in the Curriculum of Medical Schools World-wide', adopted by the 51st WMA General Assembly, Tel Aviv, October 1999, revised by the 66th WMA General Assembly, Moscow, October 2015.

was given less importance than ethics in medical faculties in Europe.[103] Therefore, it is not surprising that the abovementioned work showed a tendency to confront medical AI via ethics rather than human rights.[104] In this regard, it is worth noting that the recent UNESCO's recommendation on the ethics of AI follows the UNESCO Declaration on Bioethics by encouraging AI ethics education and awareness, but also includes education on human rights.[105]

The abovementioned 2008 study also revealed that although the teaching of ethics and human rights was generally integrated into the medical curriculum, it was not universal. Besides, even when human rights was taught, there was a certain inadequacy between the course and the reality of medical practice: 'Too often teaching is undertaken by volunteers, and can fail if those volunteers are unable or unavailable to teach, or if that teaching is unduly idiosyncratic or inadequately based upon clinical scenarios'.[106] If interdisciplinary cooperation is needed and encouraged,[107] time constraints usually prevent in-depth thinking on fundamental principles and socio-cultural aspects.[108] Long-term education will reduce misunderstandings and rhetorical confusion during such collaboration.

The same holds true for data scientists. The Toronto Declaration states that in order to mitigate and reduce the harms of discrimination from AI, states should '[e]nsure that public bodies carry out training in human rights and data analysis for officials involved in the procurement,

[103] F Claudot and others, 'Enseignement de l'éthique et des Droits de l'Homme en Europe' 2006 (1)18 *Santé Publique* 85.

[104] See Section 10.2.1.

[105] UNESCO, 'Recommendation on the Ethics of Artificial Intelligence' (adopted 24 November 2021), SHS/BIO/REC-AIETHICS/2021, https://unesdoc.unesco.org/ark:/48223/pf0000380455policy Action 5, §§ 44-45; UNESCO, 'Universal Declaration on Bioethics and Human Rights', Art. 23.

[106] Claudot and others, 'Enseignement de l'éthique'. On the difficulty to make a practical use of human rights, see also JN Erdman, 'Human Rights Education in Patient Care' (2017) 38(14) *Public Health Review* 1. Erdman observes that the broad language of human rights treaties rarely provides clear answers to the real conflicts that health providers are facing. Despite this challenge, healthcare professionals frequently claim that human rights education facilitated their decision-making in practice. For a review, see, R Newham and others, 'Human Rights Education in Patient Care: A Literature Review and Critical Discussion' (2021) 28(2) *Nursing Ethics* 190.

[107] UNESCO, AHEG, 'Draft Text of a Recommendation on the Ethics of Artificial Intelligence', first draft.

[108] For tips on the integration of a human rights culture in medical schools in the US context, see KC McKenzie and others, 'Twelve Tips for Incorporating the Study of Human Rights into Medical Education' (2020) 42(8) *Medical Teacher* 871.

development, use and review of machine learning tools'.[109] Such education can be pursued inside AI corporations. In that sense, the Committee of Ministers of the Council of Europe recommends staff training on human rights among the precautionary measures to be adopted by states,[110] as well as by companies.[111] In order to avoid the propagation of biases, education on human rights must incorporate the protection of marginalised and vulnerable people. This implies the inclusion of such groups and their regular consultation.[112]

A second important aspect for the development of human rights–compliant medical AI is to ensure monitoring by internal as well as external bodies.[113] In the health sector, such ethical committees are frequent and ensure compliance with legal requirements such as respecting privacy (GDPR) and ethical guidelines. However, the composition of such committees needs to be scrutinised. When Google Health created an AI ethics group, a petition was circulated against its composition, leading to the dissolution of the group only one week after its creation.[114] Additionally, even when transparent committees exist, they need to include human rights lawyers and social scientists to engage properly in a human rights assessment. The recent international studies, reports and projects on AI and human rights seem to support such a proposal in the health sector.

10.4 Conclusion

The increasing development and use of AI in healthcare, in particular machine-learning models, contributes to finding better treatments for patients and to optimising the allocation of scarce resources. Yet,

[109] Toronto Declaration', § 33b.

[110] MSI-AUT, 'Addressing the Impacts of Algorithms on HR', pt 5.5.

[111] Ibid., pt 5.2.

[112] On lack of stakeholder engagement, see D Allison-Hope and M Hodge, 'As Artificial Intelligence Progresses, What Does Responsibility Look Like?' *OpenGlobalRights*, www.openglobalrights.org/as-artificial-intelligence-progresses-what-does-real-responsibility-look-like/, accessed 1 May 2021. The UN guiding principles also incorporate 'meaningful consultation with potentially affected groups and relevant stakeholders'; UN Guiding Principles, A/HRC/17/31, § 18 (b).

[113] For a discussion of those committees, see McGregor and others 'International Human Rights Law', 330–33.

[114] K Piper, 'Exclusive: Google Cancels AI Ethics Board in Response to Outcry' *Vox*, 4 April 2019, www.vox.com/future-perfect/2019/4/4/18295933/google-cancels-ai-ethics-board, accessed 1 May 2021.

algorithms are not a neutral health product since they are programmed by humans, with the risk of propagating human rights infringements. Thus, stakeholders should be careful not to be too reliant on the algorithms they use. In order to mitigate the different identified threats to human rights, including in the medical sector, scholars and institutions have prepared several reports and guidelines on ethics for medical AI. Human rights–impact assessments are rarer in the medical area. Yet, a human rights approach to medical AI is both necessary on substance and from an organisational and procedural perspective. On substance, a human right approach allows for an ability to rely on legal standards rather than more vague notions such as 'fairness', for instance, while making room for cultural appropriateness. The interrelation between human rights, especially the right to health and the right to be free from discrimination, allows an endorsement of a broader and more consistent framework for AI. From a procedural perspective, the UN Guiding Principles would allow the targeting of all stakeholders, including corporations developing healthcare algorithms. Such an approach would establish a chain of duties and responsibilities, bringing more transparency and consistency to the overall process. Although this approach would not solve all AI challenges, it would offer a method, a framework for discussion that will include all relevant actors, including vulnerable populations. The creation of a human rights culture in the techno-science space will benefit from the human rights education of medical doctors and data scientists, and from more collaboration at the initial stages of making algorithms. Building human rights–compliant medical AI will not only rely on checking boxes on legal standards but also on education and discussion with all relevant parties and experts.

Bibliography

Access Now, 'Human Rights in the Age of Artificial Intelligence' November 2018, www.accessnow.org/cms/assets/uploads/2018/11/AI-and-Human-Rights.pdf

Ala-Pietilä P, 'Towards Trustworthy AI – Ethics & Competitiveness Go Hand-in-Hand' 2019, European Commission, https://ec.europa.eu/digital-single-market/en/blogposts/towards-trustworthy-ai-ethics-competitiveness-go-hand-hand, accessed 21 May 2020.

Allison-Hope D and Hodge M, 'As Artificial Intelligence Progresses, What Does Responsibility Look Like?' *OpenGlobalRights*, www.openglobalrights.org/as-artificial-intelligence-progresses-what-does-real-responsibility-look-like/, accessed 1 May 2021.

Aurey X, 'La transformation du corps humain en ressource biomédicale. Etude de droit international et européen' PhD thesis, Université Panthéon-Assas, 2015.

Azoulay A, 'Vers une éthique de l'intelligence artificielle' www.un.org/fr/chronicle/article/vers-une-ethique-de-lintelligence-artificielle.

Barocas S and Selbst AD, 'Big Data's Disparate Impact' (2016) 104(3) *California Law Review* 671.

Besson S, 'Sovereignty, International Law and Democracy' (2011) 22(2) *European Journal of International Law* 373.

Blasimme A and Vayena E, 'The Ethics of AI in Biomedical Research, Patient Care, and Public Health' in Dubber MD, Pascuale F and Das S (eds), *The Oxford Handbook of Ethics of AI* (Oxford University Press 2020).

Borgesius FJZ, 'Discrimination, Artificial Intelligence, and Algorithmic Decision-Making' Council of Europe, 2018, https://rm.coe.int/discrimination-artificial-intelligenceand-algorithmic-decision-making/1680925d73, accessed 24 June 2021.

Borrillo D, 'La République des experts dans la construction des lois: le cas de la bioéthique' (2011) 14 *Histoire&Politique. Politique, culture, société.*

Brillat M, *Le principe de non-discrimination à l'épreuve des rapports entre les droits européens* (Institut Universitaire Varenne-Collection des Thèses 2016).

Challen R and others, 'Artificial Intelligence, Bias and Clinical Safety' (2019) 28 *BMJ Quality & Safety* 231. doi:10.1136/bmjqs-2018-008370

Claudot F, Van Baaren-Baudin AJ, Chastonay P, 'Enseignement de l'éthique et des Droits de l'Homme en Europe' (2006) 18(1) *Santé Publique* 85.

Commission Nationale de l'Informatique et des Libertés (CNIL) and Défenseur des droits (France), 'Algorithmes: prévenir l'automatisation des discriminations' (31 May 2020), www.defenseurdesdroits.fr/fr/rapports/2020/05/algorithmes-prevenir-lautomatisation-des-discriminations.

Committee of Experts on Internet Intermediaries (MSI-NET), 'Algorithms and Human Rights: Study on the Human Rights Dimensions of Automated Data Processing Techniques and Possible Regulatory Implications' Council of Europe study DGI (2017) 12, 2017, https://rm.coe.int/algorithms-and-human-rights-en-rev/16807956b5, accessed 4 February 2022.

Committee on Economic, Social and Cultural Rights (CESCR), 'The Right to the Highest Attainable Standard of Health' General Comment No. 14, UN Doc. No. E/C.12/2000/4, 11 August 2000, https://digitallibrary.un.org/record/425041, accessed 1 May 2021.

Cossins D, 'Discriminating Algorithms: 5 Times AI Showed Prejudice' *New Scientist*, 27 April 2018, www.newscientist.com/article/2166207-discriminating-algorithms-5-times-ai-showed-prejudice/, accessed 1 May 2021.

Couldry N and Mejias U, 'Data Colonialism: Rethinking Big Data's Relation to the Contemporary Subject' (2019) 20(4) *Television and New Media* 336–49.

Crawford J, *Democracy in International Law: Inaugural Lecture Delivered 5 March 1993* (Cambridge University Press 1994).

Council of Europe, Committee of Experts in Human Rights Dimensions of Automated Data Processing and Different Forms of AI (MSI-AUT), 'Addressing the Impacts of Algorithms on HR', Draft recommendation of the Committee of Ministers to member states on the human rights impacts of algorithmic systems (2018) https://rm.coe.int/draft-recommendation-of-the-committee-of-ministers-to-states-on-the-hu/168095eecf, accessed 4 February 2022.

Dalton-Brown S, 'The Ethics of Medical AI and the Physician-Patient Relationship' (2020) 29(1) *Cambridge Quarterly of Healthcare Ethics* 115.

Erdman JN, 'Human Rights Education in Patient Care' (2017) 38(14) *Public Health Review* 1.

European Commission, 'Proposal for a Regulation of the European Parliament and of the Council of 21 April 2021 Laying Down Harmonized Rules on Artificial Intelligence (Artificial Intelligence Act) and Amending Certain Union Legislative Acts' 2021 COM/2021/206 final, https://eur-lex.europa.eu/legal-content/EN/TXT/?uri=CELEX%3A52021PC0206

European Commission, 'White Paper on Artificial Intelligence – A European Approach to Excellence and Trust' (Brussels, 19 February 2020) COM(2020) 65 final, https://ec.europa.eu/info/sites/default/files/commission-white-paper-artificial-intelligence-feb2020_en.pdf.

European Parliament, 'Covid-19 Tracing Apps: Ensuring Privacy and Use Across Borders' 1 December 2020, www.europarl.europa.eu/news/en/headlines/society/20200429STO78174/covid-19-tracing-apps-ensuring-privacy-and-data-protection, accessed 21 May 2020.

European Parliament, 'Resolution of 10 March 2021 with Recommendations to the Commission on Corporate Due Diligence and Corporate Accountability' (2020/2129(INL)), OJ C 474, 24.11.2021, pp. 11–40, https://ec.europa.eu/info/sites/default/files/commission-white-paper-artificial-intelligence-feb2020_en.pdf

Evans JH, *Playing God: Human Genetic Engineering and the Rationalization of Public Bioethical Debate* (University of Chicago Press 2002).

Expert Group on Liability and New Technologies – New Technologies Formation, 'Liability for Artificial Intelligence and Other Emerging Digital Technologies' 2019, https://ec.europa.eu/newsroom/dae/document.cfm?doc_id=63199, accessed 1 May 2021.

Fefegha A, 'Racial Bias and Gender Bias Examples in AI systems' *The Comuzi Journal*, 2 September 2018, https://medium.com/thoughts-and-reflections/racial-bias-and-gender-bias-examples-in-ai-systems-7211e4c166a1, accessed 1 May 2021.

Gerards J and Xenidis R, 'Algorithmic Discrimination in Europe: Challenges and Opportunities for Gender Equality and Non-discrimination Law – A Special Report' (2020) www.equalitylaw.eu/publications, accessed 1 May 2021.

Gillis TB and Spiess JL, 'Big Data and Discrimination' (2019) 86(2) *The University of Chicago Law Review* 459.

Hacker P, 'Teaching Fairness to Artificial Intelligence: Existing and Novel Strategies against Algorithmic Discrimination under EU Law' (2018) 55(4) *Common Market Law Review* 1143–85.

High-Level Expert Group on AI, 'Ethics Guidelines for Trustworthy AI', 8 April 2019, https://ec.europa.eu/digital-single-market/en/news/ethics-guidelines-trustworthy-ai, accessed 1 May 2021.

Hoffmann AL, 'Where Fairness Fails: Data, Algorithms and the Limits of Antidiscrimination Discourse' (2019) 22(7) *Information, Communication & Society* 900.

Jean A, *De l'autre côté de la Machine – Voyage d'une scientifique au pays des algorithmes* (L'observatoire 2020).

Jobin A, Lenca M and Vayena E, 'The Global Landscape of AI Ethics Guidelines' (2019) 1 *Nature Machine Learning* 389–99.

Kaye D, 'Report of the Special Rapporteur on the Promotion and Protection of the Right to Freedom of Opinion and Expression' A/73/348 (2018).

Kriebitz A, Lütge C, 'Artificial Intelligence and Human Rights: A Business Ethical Assessment' (2020) 5(1) *Business and Human Rights Journal* 84.

Lebret A, 'The European Court of Human Rights and the Framing of Reproductive Issues' (2020) 18 *Droits Fondamentaux*, www.crdh.fr/revue/n-18-2020/the-european-court-of-human-rights-and-the-framing-of-reproductive-rights/

Lebret A and Minssen T, 'Digital Health, Artificial Intelligence and Accessibility to Health Care in Denmark' (2021) 1 *European Human Rights Law Review* 39.

Lehr D and Ohm P, 'Playing with the Data: What Legal Scholars Should Learn About Machine Learning' (2017) 51(653) *UCDL Rev.*, 653–717.

Livingston S and Risse M, 'The Future Impact of Artificial Intelligence on Human Rights' (2019) 33(2) *Ethics and International Affairs* 141–58.

Lloyd Booz K and Hamilton A, 'Bias Amplification in Artificial Intelligence Systems' paper presented at AAAI FSS-18: Artificial Intelligence in Government and Public Sector, Arlington, VA, 18–20 October 2018, https://arxiv.org/ftp/arxiv/papers/1809/1809.07842.pdf

Lougarre C, 'The Right to Health: Legal Content Through Supranational Monitoring' PhD thesis, University College London, 2016, https://discovery.ucl.ac.uk/id/eprint/1474052/, accessed 1 May 2021.

Martin-Chenut K, 'Droit international et démocratie' (2007) 4(220) *Diogène* 36.

Mayer Mckinney S and others, 'International Evaluation of an AI System for Breast Cancer Screening' (2020) 577(7788) *Nature* 89–94.

McGregor L, Murray D and Ng V, 'International Human Rights Law as a Framework for Algorithmic Accountability' (2019) 68(2) *International and Comparative Law Quarterly* 309.

McKenzie KC, Mishori R and Ferdowsian H, 'Twelve Tips for Incorporating the Study of Human Rights into Medical Education' (2020) 42(8) *Medical Teacher* 871.

Minssen T and others, 'Regulatory Responses to Medical Machine Learning' (2020) 7(1) *Journal of Law and the Biosciences*, https://doi.org/10.1093/jlb/lsaa002

Mittelstadt B and others, 'The Ethics of Algorithms: Mapping the Debate' (2016) 3(2) *Big Data & Society* https://journals.sagepub.com/doi/full/10.1177/2053951716679679, accessed 4 February 2022.

Morley J and others, 'The Ethics of AI in Health Care: A Mapping Review' (2020) 260(1) *Social Science and Medicine* 113172. doi: 10.1016/j.socscimed.2020.113172

Narayanan A, '21 Fairness Definitions and Their Politics' tutorial presented at the Conference on Fairness, Accountability, and Transparency, 23 February 2018. Tutorial at www.youtube.com/watch?v=jIXIuYdnyyk

Newham R and others, 'Human Rights Education in Patient Care: A Literature Review and Critical Discussion' (2021) 28(2) *Nursing Ethics* 190.

OEIGWG Chairmanship, 'Legally Binding Instrument to Regulate, in International Human Rights Law, the Activities of Transnational Corporations and Other Business Enterprises' second revised draft, 6 August 2020, www.ohchr.org/Documents/HRBodies/HRCouncil/WGTransCorp/Session6/OEIGWG_Chair-Rapporteur_second_revised_draft_LBI_on_TNCs_and_OBEs_with_respect_to_Human_Rights.pdf, accessed 1 May 2021.

ONU, Chronique, Audrey Azoulay, 'Vers une éthique de l'intelligence artificielle' www.un.org/fr/chronicle/article/vers-une-ethique-de-lintelligence-artificielle, accessed 21 May 2020.

Parikh RB, Teeple S, Navathe AS, 'Addressing Bias in Artificial Intelligence in Health Care' (2019) 322(24) *The Journal of the American Medical Association* 2377.

Piper K, 'Exclusive: Google Cancels AI Ethics Board in Response to Outcry' *Vox*, 4 April 2019 www.vox.com/future-perfect/2019/4/4/18295933/google-cancels-ai-ethics-board, accessed 1 May 2021.

Potter VR, 'Bioethics: The Science of Survival' (1970) 14(1) *Perspectives in Biology and Medicine* 127–53.

Price II WN, 'Medical AI and Contextual Bias' (2019) 33(1) *Harvard Journal of Law & Technology* 66.

Quach K, 'MIT Apologizes, Permanently Pulls Offline Huge Dataset that Taught AI Systems to Use Misogynistic Slurs' *The Register*, 1 July 2020, www.theregister.com/2020/07/01/mit_dataset_removed/, accessed 1 May 2021.

Ram N and Gray D, 'Mass Surveillance in the Age of COVID-19' (2020) 7(1) *Journal of Law and the Biosciences*, https://doi.org/10.1093/jlb/lsaa023.

Raso FA and others, 'Artificial Intelligence & Human Rights: Opportunities & Risks' Berkman Klein Center research publication no 2018-6, 25 September 2018, https://ssrn.com/abstract=3259344, accessed 1 May 2021.

Schmidt N and Stephens B, 'An Introduction to Artificial Intelligence and Solutions to the Problems of Algorithmic Discrimination' (2019) 73(2) *Quarterly Report* 130.

Schuett J, 'A Legal Definition of AI' Cornell University, 22 August 2021, https://arxiv.org/abs/1909.01095, accessed 24 June 2021.

Schwarz EC, 'Human vs. Machine: A Framework of Responsibilities and Duties of Transnational Corporations for Respecting Human Rights in the Use of Artificial Intelligence' (2019) 58(1) *Columbia Journal of Transnational Law* 232, www.jtl.columbia.edu/journal-articles/human-vs-machine-a-framework-of-responsibilities-and-duties-of-transnational-corporations-for-respecting-human-rights-in-the-use-of-artificial-intelligence, accessed 1 May 2021

Short E, 'It turns out Amazon's AI hiring tool discriminated against women' *Silicon Republic* (11 October 2018) www.siliconrepublic.com/careers/amazon-ai-hiring-tool-women-discrimination.

Sloan RH and Warner R, 'Beyond Bias: Artificial Intelligence and Social Justice' (2020) 24(1) *Virginia Journal of Law and Technology* 1.

Tobin J, *The Right to Health in International Law* (Oxford University Press 2012).

'Top Artificial Intelligence Companies in Healthcare to Keep an Eye on', *The Medical Futurist* (21 January 2020), https://medicalfuturist.com/top-artificial-intelligence-companies-in-healthcare/#

'Toronto Declaration: Protecting the Rights to Equality and Non-discrimination in Machine Learning Systems' RightsCon Toronto, 16 May 2018, www.accessnow.org/the-toronto-declaration-protecting-the-rights-to-equality-and-non-discrimination-in-machine-learning-systems, accessed 1 May 2021.

Tréguier F, 'The State and Digital Surveillance in Times of the Covid-19 Pandemic' Science Po Center for International Studies, 1 June 2020, www.sciencespo.fr/ceri/en/content/state-and-digital-surveillance-times-covid-19-pandemic, accessed 17 February 2021.

Tzimas T, 'The Need for an International Treaty for AI from the Perspective of Human Rights' (2019) 4(1) *Scientia Moralitas Journal* 73.

UNESCO, 'Draft Text of a Recommendation on the Ethics of Artificial Intelligence' 25 June 2021, https://en.unesco.org/artificial-intelligence/ethics, accessed 21 May 2020.

UNESCO, 'Universal Declaration on Bioethics and Human Rights' General Conference of UNESCO, 33rd sess. (adopted19 October 2005), https://en.unesco.org/themes/ethics-science-and-technology/bioethics-and-human-rights.

UNGA, Human Rights Council, 'Elaboration of an International Legally Binding Instrument on Transnational Corporations and Other Business Enterprises with Respect to Human Rights', A/HRC/RES/26/9, 14 July 2014, https://undocs.org/A/HRC/RES/26/9, accessed 24 June 2021.

UNGA, 'Report of the Working Group on the Issue of Human Rights and Transnational Corporations and Other Business Enterprises', A/73/163, 16 July 2018, https://documents-dds-ny.un.org/doc/UNDOC/GEN/N18/224/87/PDF/N1822487.pdf?OpenElement

UN Office of the High Commissioner, *UN Human Rights Business and Human Rights Technology Project (B-Tech): Applying the UN Guiding Principles on Business and Human Rights to digital technologies*, November 2019. Updates on the B-Tech Project may be found at https://www.ohchr.org/EN/Issues/Business/Pages/B-TechProject.aspx.

UN OHCHR, 'Tackling Discrimination Against Lesbian, Gay, Bi, Trans, & Intersex People: Standards of Conduct for Business' 2017, www.unfe.org/standards/, accessed 25 June 2021.

UN OHCHR, 'A Human Rights-Based Approach to Data: Leaving No One Behind in the 2030 Agenda for Sustainable Development' 2018, www.ohchr.org/Documents/Issues/HRIndicators/GuidanceNoteonApproachtoData.pdf, accessed 24 June 2021.

Vinuesa R and others, 'The Role of Artificial Intelligence in Achieving the Sustainable Development Goals' (2020) 11(233) *Nature Communications* www.nature.com/articles/s41467-019-14108-y, accessed 24 June 2021.

Wachter S, Mittelstadt B and Russell C, 'Why Fairness Cannot Be Automated: Bridging the Gap Between EU Non-Discrimination Law and AI' 2020, https://ssrn.com/abstract=3547922, accessed 1 May 2021.

WHO, 'Contact Tracing in the Context of COVID-19: Interim Guidance' 10 May 2020, https://apps.who.int/iris/handle/10665/332049, accessed 21 May 2020.

WHO, 'Ethical Considerations to Guide the Use of Digital Proximity Tracking Technologies for COVID-19 Contact Tracing' interim guidance, 28 May 2020, www.who.int/publications/i/item/WHO-2019-nCoV-Ethics_Contact_tracing_apps-2020.1, accessed 17 February 2021.

WHO, 'Global Strategy on Digital Health 2020–2025' 2021, www.who.int/docs/default-source/documents/gs4dhdaa2a9f352b0445bafbc79ca799dce4d.pdf, accessed 4 February 2022.

WHO, 'Surveillance Strategies for COVID-19 Human Infection' interim guidance, 10 May 2020, https://apps.who.int/iris/handle/10665/332051, accessed 21 May 2020.

WHO, 'What You Need to Know About Digital Health Systems' e-health, 2019, www.euro.who.int/en/health-topics/Health-systems/e-health/news/news/2019/2/what-you-need-to-know-about-digital-health-systems, accessed 24 June 2021.

WHO, 'WHO Guidelines on Ethical Issues in Public Health Surveillance' 2017, https://apps.who.int/iris/bitstream/handle/10665/255721/9789241512657-eng.pdf?sequence=1, accessed 7 May 2020.

WHO Regional Office for Europe, 'Future of Digital Health Systems: Report on the WHO Symposium on the Future of Digital Health Systems in the European Region' 6–8 February 2019, https://apps.who.int/iris/bitstream/handle/10665/329032/9789289059992-eng.pdf, accessed 24 June 2021.

World Medical Assembly, 'Resolution on the Inclusion of Medical Ethics and Human Rights in the Curriculum of Medical Schools World-wide' adopted by the 51st WMA General Assembly, Tel Aviv, Oct 1999, revised by the 66th WMA General Assembly, Moscow, October 2015, www.wma.net/policies-post/wma-resolution-on-the-inclusion-of-medical-ethics-and-human-rights-in-the-curriculum-of-medical-schools-world-wide/#:~:text=The%20WMA%20believes%20that%20medical,graduate%20and%20continuing%20medical%20education accessed 24 June 2021.

Yeung K, 'Responsibility and AI' Council of Europe study DGI (2019) 05, Expert Committee in Human Rights Dimensions of Automated Data Processing and Different Forms of Artificial Intelligence (MSI-AUT), 2019, https://rm.coe.int/responsability-and-ai-en/168097d9c5, accessed 4 February 2022.

Yeung K, Howes A and Pogrebna G, 'AI Governance by Human-Rights Centered Design, Deliberation, and Oversight: An End to Ethics Washing' in Dubber MD, Pascuale F and Das S (eds), *The Oxford Handbook of Ethics of AI* (Oxford University Press 2020).

Zenios SA and others, 'Evidence-Based Organ Allocation' (1999) 107(1) *The American Journal of Medicine* 52.

PART IV

Balancing Regulation, Innovation and Ethics

11

Doctors Without Borders? The Law Applicable to Cross-Border eHealth Services and AI-Based Medicine

JAN D. LÜTTRINGHAUS

11.1 Introduction: Cross-Border eHealth in the Conflict of Laws

As health services are increasingly internationalized, cross-border scenarios are becoming more common. For example, the groundbreaking Lindbergh operation, the forerunner of the now well-established use of robotics in telesurgery, involved a surgeon in New York remotely controlling a 'surgery robot' in Paris.[1] The various eHealth services now available pose new legal challenges even when used in a purely national context, given that the respective applications are subject to various regulatory regimes governing confidentiality, privacy, access and liability.

All of these problems multiply whenever eHealth services are provided across national borders. Here, different – and potentially conflicting – laws in various jurisdictions are concerned. Therefore, the question of which law is applicable has to be answered. Section 11.2 shows that this encompasses, first and foremost, registration and licensing requirements. The Lindbergh case may serve as an illustration: does the US surgeon need a licence in France where his patient is located, or only in the US State of New York, or must he fulfil the licensing requirements in both countries? The question as to the applicable law on medicine and health services also arises with regard to the cross-border provision of teleconsultation and telemonitoring by eHealth apps and medical devices, as well as the use of artificial intelligence (AI), for purposes such as early recognition, diagnosis, treatment and after care. Google, for example, provides AI-driven tools that can detect a condition that causes blindness – it goes without saying that these instruments are used worldwide.[2]

[1] J Marescaux, 'Nom de code: "Opération Lindbergh"' (2002) 127 *Annals of Surgery*: 2 et seq.

[2] See, for example, with regard to India: C Metz, 'India Fights Diabetic Blindness With Help From A.I.' *New York Times*, 10 March 2019, www.nytimes.com/2019/03/10/technology/

Section 11.3 explains that the issue of conflicting laws is particularly acute when it comes to data protection. On the one hand, the ever-growing use of AI, robotics, sensors and IT-driven medicine in general produces vast amounts of data. This data is valuable for all players in the MedTech sphere, including physicians, scientists and manufacturers looking to improve treatments and/or to train AI applications. On the other hand, data protection standards vary considerably around the world, and the use of sensitive medical data often raises concerns, especially when data is collected, aggregated and processed on a global scale, such as for AI applications or in attempts to automate surgery by using robots.[3]

Data protection issues are often strongly linked to contractual relationships between the parties, given that the extent of consent to data processing is often laid down in standard terms and therefore subject to review under legislation to prevent unfair contract terms.[4] Moreover, the specific contractual arrangements and therefore also the – varying – provisions of the applicable national contract laws may serve as a justification for data processing – for example, pursuant to Article 6(1)(a) of the General Data Protection Regulation (EU) 2016/679 (GDPR).[5] In the light of this, it is essential to determine which law governs a contract relating to the provision of cross-border eHealth services. Section 11.4 therefore delves into the details of the conflict of laws in the contractual sphere. Moreover, the violation of data protection rules as well as of local standards relating to eHealth services may trigger liability under national tort laws. Against this backdrop, Section 11.5 examines the conflict of laws pertaining to torts committed in the context of cross-border eHealth services. Section 11.6 points to the impact of overriding mandatory provisions and the public

artificial-intelligence-eye-hospital-india.html, accessed 17 June 2020; C Abrams, 'Google's Effort to Prevent Blindness Shows AI Challenges' *Wall Street Journal*, 26 January 2019, www.wsj.com/articles/googles-effort-to-prevent-blindness-hits-roadblock-11548504004, accessed 19 June 2020.

[3] See K-F Kowalewski and others, 'Kollaborative Automatisierung und Robotik' (2019) 37 *Medizinrecht* 925; Food and Drug Administration, 'Computer-Assisted Surgical Systems' 13 March 2019, www.fda.gov/medical-devices/surgery-devices/computer-assisted-surgical-systems, accessed 9 June 2020.

[4] See Recital (42) GDPR: 'In accordance with Council Directive 93/13/EEC a declaration of consent pre-formulated by the controller should be provided in an intelligible and easily accessible form, using clear and plain language and it should not contain unfair terms'.

[5] Regulation (EU) 2016/679 of the European Parliament and of the Council of 27 April 2016 on the protection of natural persons with regard to the processing of personal data and on the free movement of such data, and repealing Directive 95/46/EC (General Data Protection Regulation) [2016] OJ L 119/1.

policy exception. Finally, Section 11.7 concludes with the main findings and provides an outlook on future challenges posed by conflicts of laws.

11.2 Law Applicable to Licensing and Registration Requirements

The provision of medical services is heavily regulated in almost every jurisdiction. Licensing and registration requirements usually focus on medical education, professional and ethical fitness to practice, as well as sufficient (compulsory) insurance coverage for medical malpractice. Regulations are, of course, not limited to physicians but usually relate to the provision of most health-related services. In the UK, for example, no less than thirty-two professions in the healthcare sector are currently regulated by nine regulators. In the US, medical licensing is usually subject to state legislature and control.[6] In addition, medical devices are also subject to comprehensive regulation, such as under the EU's medical devices regulation, setting forth requirements regarding licensing, certification and, in some countries such as France, compulsory insurance.[7] Similar regulatory frameworks may be found in most countries, although the scope and the approach towards supervision of medical activities and devices may vary. Whenever eHealth services are provided (or medical devices are used) on a cross-border basis, the question arises of whether these services may already fall within the scope of the respective national regulations relating to health professionals and might therefore trigger licensing, certification or registration requirements. The answer will, of course, vary according to the nature of the service – from telemedicine and telesurgery to AI-supported (tele-)diagnosis and eHealth apps.

11.2.1 Telemedicine Services Involving Medical Professionals

Medical professionals providing services across jurisdictions – such as telemedicine, telesurgery or teleconsultation – will undoubtedly trigger registration and other regulatory requirements in at least one of the countries

6 See See Department of Health and Human Services, 'Telemedicine Licensure Report' Office for the Advancement of Telehealth, Centre for Telemedicine, 2003, 1; JK Barnes, 'Telemedicine a Conflict of Laws Problem Waiting to Happen – How Will Interstate and International Claims be Decided?' (2006) 28 *Houston Journal of International Law* 491, 524 et seq; C Ameringer, 'State-Based Licensure of Telemedicine: The Need for Uniformity but Not a National Scheme' (2011) 14 *Journal of Health Care Law and Policy* 55.

7 See Art. L. 252-1 Code des assurances. Moreover, see ECJ Case C-581/18, *RB v TÜV Rheinland LGA Products GmbH and Allianz IARD S.A.*, ECLI:EU:C:2020:453.

involved. In the US, at least at the outset of modern telemedicine, 'most state medical boards have taken the position that the practice of medicine occurs in the state where the patient is located'.[8] Therefore, telemedicine providers will have to comply with the licensing requirements in the place where their patients reside, thus facing fifty different statutory and regulatory regimes in the US alone.[9] In the future, however, given the technical progress and increasing importance of eHealth, a different approach might be mandated.[10] In the EU, the situation is indeed slightly different. If, for example, a surgeon based in France carries out an operation on a patient located in Germany, the surgeon will be subject to all the French rules and regulations. Yet, the question arises of whether he or she also has to satisfy the licensing and registration requirements in Germany (i.e., medical licensing). This has to be answered in the negative. Physicians based in another jurisdiction are, in principle, only subject to their home countries' rules and regulations.[11]

The provision of cross-border telemedicine services inside the EU is guaranteed by the freedom to provide services under Articles 56 and 57 of the Treaty on the Functioning of the European Union (TFEU) and are subject to further regulation under, inter alia, the E-Commerce-Directive 200/31/EC,[12] and Directive 2011/24/EU on patients' rights in cross-border healthcare.[13] Under this set of rules, it will usually be sufficient for the eHealth provider to comply with the requirements for medical professionals in his or her member state of establishment: Article 4(1) of Directive 2011/24/EU on patients' rights in cross-border healthcare requires that cross-border healthcare be provided in accordance with the legislation in the member state of treatment, which Article 4(1)(a) of the directive defines as the telemedicine service provider's member state

[8] See Barnes, 'Telemedicine A Conflict of Laws Problem Waiting to Happen', 524 et seq.

[9] The Office for the Advancement of Telehealth therefore promotes state policies that will reduce statutory and regulatory barriers to the provision of healthcare services through telemedicine technology in the US, cf. Health Resources & Services Administration, 'Office for the Advancement of Telehealth', www.hrsa.gov/rural-health/telehealth/, accessed 24 May 2021.

[10] See Ameringer, 'State-Based Licensure of Telemedicine', 55.

[11] A Spickhoff, 'Rechtsfragen der grenzüberschreitenden Telemedizin', (2018) 36 *Medizinrecht* 535, 539. See C Wendelstein, *Kollisionsrechtliche Probleme der Telemedizin* (Mohr Siebeck 2012), 359 et seq.

[12] Directive 2000/31/EC of the European Parliament and of the Council of 8 June 2000 on Certain Legal Aspects of Information Society Services, in Particular Electronic Commerce, in the Internal Market [2000] OJ L 178/1.

[13] Directive 2011/24/EU of the European Parliament and of the Council of 9 March 2011 on the Application of Patients' Rights in Cross-Border Healthcare [2011] OJ L 88/45.

of establishment.[14] Moreover, the 'country of origin' principle under the E-Commerce-Directive 200/31/EG applies to telemedicine at least as long as the nature of the services does not require the patient's physical presence.[15] In the light of the freedom to provide cross-border services in the EU single market, a physician established in one EU member state is, in principle, only subject to an additional set of rules and regulations relating to licensing to practice medicine in another member state when the physician is also regularly practising on site and therefore physically present in the latter state.[16] However, this does not preclude the state where the patient resides to draw upon the public policy exception and to enforce its overriding mandatory provisions.[17]

The picture is different, however, for the provision of eHealth services across various jurisdictions outside the EU. If, for example, a German physician treats a patient located in the US or in Saudi Arabia, the local US or Saudi rules on medical licensing and registration are likely to apply.[18]

11.2.2 eHealth Services, AI Diagnostics and Medical Devices

By contrast, the vast majority of eHealth services that do not – at least directly – involve a medical professional are less likely to fall within the scope of medical professional regulation. The use of AI or medical devices and other eHealth services for treatment, diagnostics or after care is usually subject to a distinct set of rules: the most relevant legislation ranges from medical device regulation,[19] including device software,[20] to product

[14] See European Commission, 'Staff Working Document on the Applicability of the Existing EU Legal Framework to Telemedicine Services', SWD (2012) 414 final, 6 December 2012, 11. See Art. 3(d) Directive 2011/24/EU on Patients' Rights in Cross-Border Healthcare: 'In the case of telemedicine, healthcare is considered to be provided in the Member State where the healthcare provider is established'.

[15] See Recital 18 of the Directive. See Spickhoff, 'Rechtsfragen der grenzüberschreitenden Telemedizin', 535, 539.

[16] See Wendelstein, *Kollisionsrechtliche Probleme der Telemedizin*, 359 et seq; Spickhoff, 'Rechtsfragen der grenzüberschreitenden Telemedizin', 535, 538 et seq.

[17] See Section 11.6.

[18] See Barnes, 'Telemedicine A Conflict of Laws Problem Waiting to Happen', 525; See Wendelstein, *Kollisionsrechtliche Probleme der Telemedizin*, 359 et seq.

[19] See, for example, Regulation (EU) 2017/745 of the European Parliament and of the Council of 5 April 2017 on medical devices, amending Directive 2001/83/EC, Regulation (EC) No 178/2002 and Regulation (EC) No 1223/2009 and repealing Council Directives 90/385/EEC and 93/42/EEC [2017] OJ L 117/1.

[20] See with regard to the US, for example, Food and Drug Administration, 'Examples of Device Software Functions the FDA Regulates' 26 September 2019, www.fda.gov/medical-devices/device-software-functions-including-mobile-medical-applications/examples-device-software-functions-fda-regulates, accessed 9 June 2020.

safety, product liability,[21] and data protection laws.[22] It is important to note, however, that whenever cross-border eHealth applications, especially AI-driven ones, encompass genuine medical services such as (semi-) autonomous diagnostics, some national laws might consider their activity 'medical practice', which would trigger licensing and registration requirements in the country where the patient or customer is located.

But even with regard to eHealth and AI use cases not requiring a physician for diagnosis, treatment or after care, it should be borne in mind that EU data protection rules may necessitate the intervention of a medical professional: pursuant to Article 22(1) of the GDPR,[23] patients as 'data subjects' have the right to not be subject to a decision based solely on automated processing, including, for example, 'AI-based decisions or profiling, which significantly affects the patient'. Automated decisions regarding diagnosis, treatment or after care will, however, usually significantly affect patients. Moreover, these processes usually involve sensitive health data addressed in articles 22(2) and 9 of the GDPR. If the patient desires, the eHealth provider may therefore be obliged to offer 'human intervention' complementing the automated and/or AI-driven decision-making pursuant to Article 22(3) of the GDPR. In these scenarios, the eHealth provider might have to draw upon the medical expertise of physicians since only they may evaluate the soundness of the automated decision regarding diagnosis and treatment.

In its scope of application, the GDPR may moreover require cross-border eHealth providers to draw upon the carve-out in Article 22(2) and, most prominently, on patients' explicit consent regarding automated and/or AI-based diagnosis and treatments.[24] Given the crucial importance of the territorial reach of data protection laws, the following section will focus on the conflict of laws regarding data protection and product liability.[25]

[21] See with regard to product liability and software in medical devices and eHealth, for example, I Jakobs and F Huber 'Software als Medizinprodukt: Haftungs- und versicherungsrechtliche Aspekte', (2019) *Zeitschrift Medizin Produkte Recht* 1.

[22] See, for example, M Bourassa Forcier and others, 'Integrating Artificial Intelligence into Healthcare Through Data Access: Can the GDPR Act as a Beacon for Policymakers?' (2019) *Journal of Law and the Biosciences* 317.

[23] Regulation (EU) 2016/679 of the European Parliament and of the Council of 27 April 2016 on the Protection of Natural Persons with Regard to the Processing of Personal Data and on the Free Movement of Such Data, and Repealing Directive 95/46/EC (General Data Protection Regulation) [2016] OJ L 119/1.

[24] See Art. 22(2)(c), (4) and Art. 9 GDPR.

[25] See sections 11.3 and 11.5.

11.3 Applicable Data Protection Laws: GDPR and CCPA

The provision of eHealth services often involves the transmission of highly sensitive personal information. In cross-border scenarios, the question of the applicable data protection regime is therefore particularly acute. This chapter focuses on the GDPR as well as on the California Consumer Privacy Act (CCPA),[26] given that many MedTech companies operate from California. Data relating to the eHealth customers' or patients' health as well as genetic and biometric information is considered 'personal data' under both sets of rules.[27] But, at least in principle, neither the CCPA nor the GDPR applies to personal health information that was made publicly available by the data subject themself, such as data relating to heart rate on a training and fitness-tracking website.[28] In the case of sensitive health data, however, the GDPR requires that the data have been 'manifestly' made public by the data subject pursuant to Article 9(2)(e).

11.3.1 GDPR: Territorial Scope and Conflict of Laws

The scope of application of the GDPR has often been described as 'extra-territorial': pursuant to Article 3(1), the regulation applies if the data controller or data processor is established in the EU AND processes personal data 'in the context of the activities' of the establishment, regardless of whether the processing itself takes place in the EU or elsewhere in the world.[29] But even in cases where an eHealth service provider is not established in the EU, its activities may still be governed by the GDPR according to Article 3(2)(a), provided that the company offers its services to customers 'who are in the Union' and processes their personal data.[30] Article 3(1)(b) applies the same rationale to cases where an eHealth business established in a non-EU state (such as the US or China) monitors their patients' or customers' 'behaviour as far as their behaviour takes place within the Union'. In other words, GDPR standards even apply to an

[26] California Civil Code sec. 1789.100 et seq.

[27] See 1798.140(o)(1) CCPA; Art. 4(1), (13) through (15) GDPR.

[28] See 1798.140(o)(1) and (2) CCPA; Art. 9(2)(e) GDPR.

[29] J Lüttringhaus, 'Das internationale Datenprivatrecht: Baustein des Wirtschaftskollisionsrechts des 21. Jahrhunderts – Das IPR der Haftung für Verstöße gegen die EU-Datenschutzgrundverordnung' (2018) 117 *Zeitschrift für Vergleichende Rechtswissenschaft* 50, 60 et seq.; K Pormeister, 'Genetic Research and Applicable Law: The Intra-EU Conflict of Laws as a Regulatory Challenge to Cross-Border Genetic Research' (2018) *Journal of Law and the Biosciences*,706, 715.

[30] Art. 3(2)(a) GDPR also applies if the services are free of charge.

American tourist using eHealth services (eg, a blood sugar monitor) during a three-week vacation in an EU member state, such as France.

Article 44 et seq. of the GDPR also regulates the transfer of personal data to third countries outside the EU, such as the US. The European Court of Justice (ECJ) has recently invalidated the EU-US Privacy Shield framework based on Article 46(2)(a) of the GDPR.[31] It is important to note, however, that the GDPR offers various other grounds for data transfers to third states, such as standard data protection clauses under Articles 46(1) and (2)(c).

The application of the GDPR not only entails a comprehensive set of transparency, information, rectification and erasure rights (Article 12 et seq.), but the eHealth provider as a 'data controller' or 'data processor' may also face important administrative fines (Article 83) and civil action for compensation and liability (Article 82) under the rules on jurisdiction (Article 79(2)) in case of infringements.[32] Given that the GDPR does not specify every detail of the civil action, it is left to conflict of laws and national substantive law to fill the gaps.[33] The EU conflict of law rules for tort in the Rome II Regulation are, however, inapplicable to claims resulting from the violation of privacy or data protection infringements. In the light of this exclusion in articles 1(2)(g) and 30(2) of the Rome II Regulation, courts will have to apply their own national choice of law regimes.[34] It is therefore conceivable that an eHealth business – such as in the case of the American tourist using eHealth services inside the EU – may even face civil damages claims for GDPR infringements under the law of a non-EU state.[35] In the light of this complex and potentially costly litigation risk, it is material for eHealth businesses to thoroughly assess whether or not their activities may fall within the territorial scope of Article 3 of the GDPR.

11.3.2 CCPA and HIPAA: Territorial Scope and Conflict of Laws

The CCPA applies to eHealth companies based in or doing business in California, provided that they either (1) generate gross revenue of more

[31] ECJ Case C-311/18 *Data Protection Commissioner v Facebook Ireland Ltd, Maximillian Schrems*, ECLI:EU:C:2020:559.

[32] See, as to the details, Section 11.5. See with regard to jurisdiction, see C Heinze and C Warmuth, 'Das Sonderprozessrecht der Datenschutz-Grundverordnung' (2016) 21 *Zeitschrift für Zivilprozess International* 175 et seq.

[33] See Lüttringhaus, 'Das internationale Datenprivatrecht', 50, 75 et seq.; see M Brkan, 'Data Protection and Conflict-of-Laws: A Challenging Relationship' (2016) 3 *European Data Protection Law Review* 1, 8 et seq.

[34] See Section 11.5.

[35] See Lüttringhaus, 'Das internationale Datenprivatrecht', 50, 75 et seq.

than $25 million per year, (2) receive or share personal information of more than 50,000 individuals, or (3) earn at least half of their annual revenue by selling the personal information of California residents.[36] 'Doing business' in California is to be understood broadly. Only cases where 'every aspect ... takes place wholly outside of California' shall be excluded from the ambit of the CCPA.[37] In case of a violation of the patients' (i.e., 'consumers') rights under the CCPA by an eHealth provider, the consumer may recover statutory or actual damages as well as injunctive or declaratory relief through a civil action.

Further grounds for civil action may be found in US federal statutes, such as the privacy regulations in the Health Insurance Portability and Accountability Act (HIPAA).[38] These rules may be particularly relevant to cases where a foreign eHealth provider violates the right to privacy of an American patient. US courts have to determine 'whether the contacts and interests of the United States are sufficient to support the exercise of extraterritorial jurisdiction' by taking into account potential conflicts of laws and effects on US commerce as well as the citizenship of the defendant.[39]

11.4 Law Governing Contracts Relating to eHealth Services

The law applicable to contractual obligations is first and foremost determined by the choice of law by the parties.[40] Party autonomy is the guiding principle in all conflict of laws regimes. This holds true, for example, for Article 3 of the Rome I Regulation in the EU,[41] as well as for the principle of choice of law deeply entrenched in all US states.[42] With regard to the

36 See 1798.100 CCPA.

37 See 1798.145(6) CCPA.

38 Barnes, 'Telemedicine A Conflict of Laws Problem Waiting to Happen', 525 et seq.

39 See *American Rice v. Arkansas Rice Growers Coop. Ass'n*, 701 F.2d 408, 414 (5th Cir. 1983) and Civil Rights Act of 1991, Pub. L. NO. 102-166, 105 Stat 1071. See Barnes, 'Telemedicine A Conflict of Laws Problem Waiting to Happen', 525 et seq.

40 See Cheshire, North and Fawcett, *Private International Law* 15th ed (Oxford University Press 2017), 706 et seq.

41 According to Art. 1(1) Rome I Regulation applies 'in situations involving a conflict of laws, to contractual obligations in civil and commercial matters', while Art. 1(2) and (3) exclude certain matters from the ambit of the regulation. See with regard to the regulations' scope of application, for example, J Lüttringhaus, 'Art. 1 Rome I Regulation paras. 1 et seq.', in Ferrari F (ed) *Concise Commentary on the Rome I Regulation*, 2nd ed (Cambridge University Press 2020).

42 See, with regard to cross-border telemedicine, M Cloud, 'Robots Are Coming: A Discussion of Choice-of-Law Issues and Outcomes in Telesurgical Malpractice' (2019) 6 *Texas A&M Law Review* 707, 724.

cross-border provision of eHealth services, two important caveats apply to the general rule that the parties may choose the applicable law as they think fit. First, many national conflict of laws regimes limit the parties' choice for policy reasons, such as consumer and patient protection or public policy exceptions relating to the national healthcare sector. Consumer protection will usually also influence the rules on jurisdiction and provide a forum in the consumers' habitual country of residence. The EU rules on international jurisdiction, found in Article 17 et seq. of the Brussels Ibis Regulation,[43] are a prime example since they also restrict choice of court agreements.[44] Second, not all contracts contain a choice of law clause, and thus the question arises of how the applicable law in the absence of an express or implicit choice of law must be determined. While this section analyses these complex problems primarily in the light of the Rome I Regulation, it will also briefly point to the common law and the US approach to choice of law.

11.4.1 Limits to Freedom of Choice Under Article 3(3), (4) of the Rome I Regulation

Whereas the parties of a contract relating to eHealth services can – explicitly or tacitly – choose the law applicable to their contractual arrangement, their choice of law may be limited by ius cogens.[45] First, where all elements of the case are located in one state, the choice of law shall not prejudice the mandatory provisions of the law of that country according to Article 3(1) of the Rome I Regulation. If all relevant elements are located in France, the parties are free to choose German law only to the extent that they do not derogate from the French ius cogens. Second, Article 3(4) of the Rome I Regulation applies the same rationale to cases where all elements are located inside the European Union and the parties choose the law of a non-EU state. Here, the parties may not derogate from the mandatory provision of EU law contained in its regulations or directives by choosing, for example, the law of a US state such as California. The choice of US state law in general and the law of California, in particular, has been a long-standing practice, especially in agreements relating to 'digital' services such as

[43] Regulation (EU) No 1215/2012 of the European Parliament and of the Council of 12 December 2012 on Jurisdiction and the Recognition and Enforcement of Judgments in Civil and Commercial Matters [2012] OJ L 351/1.

[44] See Art. 19 and 25(4) Brussels Ibis Regulation. On the general rules on jurisdiction, see Dicey, Morris & Collins, *The Conflict of Laws* I, 15th ed (Thomson Reuters 2012) 469 et seq.

[45] See Cheshire, North and Fawcett, *Private International Law* , 743 et seq; Dicey, Morris & Collins, *The Conflict of Laws* II, 15th ed (Thomson Reuters 2012)1827 et seq.

eHealth. In these scenarios, Article 3(4) of the Rome I Regulation prevents the parties from evading the application of provisions of EU law (where appropriate as implemented in the member state of the forum), which cannot be derogated from by agreement. However, Article 3(4) only comes to bear where the parties' choice of law is the only relevant factor pointing to the law of the state chosen by the parties. The situation is therefore quite different if an eHealth service is, in fact, provided on a cross-border basis from a third country, such as the US, to patients in the EU. In the latter scenario, in addition to the rules on licensing,[46] the provisions on consumer protection in international contract law may take effect.

11.4.2 Patient and End User as 'Consumer' According to Article 6 of the Rome I Regulation

Contracts relating to eHealth services may be entered into, on the one hand, by a 'professional', such as a physician or other eHealth provider, and, on the other, by a patient or customer who is usually a natural person receiving eHealth services outside his or her trade or profession. These contracts, therefore, fall within the scope of 'consumer contracts' under Article 6(1) of the Rome I Regulation. In the absence of a choice of law, consumer contracts are governed by the law of the country where the consumer – that is, the patient or customer – has his or her habitual residence, provided that the eHealth service professional either directly pursues his or her activities in that country or 'directs' such activities to the country where the consumer has his or her habitual residence.[47] The latter requirement is fulfilled when the provider of cross-border eHealth services shows explicitly or implicitly that he or she is willing to do business in the country of the patient or customer.[48] Other than mentioning the country by name, evidence of such an intention may stem from, inter alia, the use of a certain top-level domain, language, currency, contact address, phone number or even customer testimonial from that particular country.[49] If, for example, a Swedish eHealth service provider markets his services online by using a French top-level domain ('.fr'), French language and testimonials from French patients, the

[46] See Section 11.2.

[47] See Art. 6(1)(a) and (b) Rome I Regulation. See Cheshire, North & Fawcett, *Private International Law*, 740 et seq.

[48] M Wilderspin, 'Consumer Contracts' in Basedow J and others (eds), *Encyclopedia of Private International Law* I (Edward Elgar 2017), I 464, 467 et seq.

[49] See ECJ Joined Cases C-585/08 and C-144/09 *Pammer v Schlüter and Alpenhof v Heller* (2010) ECR I-12527; ECJ Case C-191/15 *VKI v Amazon* ECLI:EU:C:2016:612.

activity is considered to be 'directed' to France and is therefore governed by French law, pursuant to Article 6(1)(b) of the Rome I Regulation.

The rules on consumer contracts in Article 6(2) of the Rome I Regulation may also impose limits on a choice of law. Although the parties may choose the law applicable to eHealth contracts, this choice of law may not deprive the patient or customer acting as a 'consumer' of the protection afforded to him or her by the mandatory provisions of the law of the country of his or her habitual residence which, in the absence of choice, would have been applicable pursuant to Article 6(1). If the parties in the example given above had chosen Swedish law, this choice of law could therefore not deprive the patient or customer of the protection afforded by the provisions of French law 'which cannot be derogated from by agreement'.[50]

11.4.3 Law Applicable in the Absence of Choice of Law

For non-consumer eHealth contracts, the applicable law is determined pursuant to Article 4 of the Rome I Regulation in the EU if the parties have not chosen the law governing their contract. Contracts falling outside of the scope of Article 6 of the Rome I Regulation may include, for example, activities that do not satisfy the requirements set out in Article 6(1)(a) or (b), or cross-border eHealth services provided to a hospital or other medical professional 'acting in the exercise of his trade or profession' pursuant to Article 6(1).

The provision of eHealth services – including, for example, telemedicine and telesurgery – falls within the meaning of the autonomous concept of 'services' under Art. 4(1)(b) of the Rome I Regulation. Therefore, contracts for the provision of eHealth services will usually be governed by the law of the country where the eHealth service provider has his or her habitual residence. Article 19(1) of the Rome I Regulation defines the 'habitual residence' of companies and other bodies, corporate or non-corporate, as their 'place of central administration' whereas the habitual residence of a natural person acting in the course of his or her business activity – such as a physician or another medical professional providing eHealth services – shall be his or her 'principal place of business'. Against this backdrop, eHealth contracts will usually be governed by the law of the state where the medical professional or the entity providing eHealth

[50] See Art. 6(2) Rome I Regulation. See Wilderspin, 'Consumer Contracts', I 464, 470.

services resides. Another law may only be applied pursuant to Article 4(3) of the Rome I Regulation, where the contract is manifestly more closely connected with another country – for example, because the provision of the entirely digital and therefore 'ubiquitous' eHealth service is deemed to be more strongly linked to the country where the patient resides. A similar outcome may be reached under the varying and complex conflict of laws approaches under US state law, where the general common law method of the 'most significant relationship' is employed.[51]

The application of the law of the country where the eHealth service provider resides may, however, lead to results that are irreconcilable with certain mandatory provisions of the state whose residents are targeted by the individual cross-border eHealth services. In these scenarios, overriding mandatory provisions and the public policy exception may come to bear.

11.5 Applicable Tort Law and Cross-Border eHealth Services: Data Protection Infringements, Medical Malpractice and Product Liability

Just like conventional treatments, neither AI-guided medicine nor eHealth applications are entirely failure-proof. For example, studies of past 'computer-aided' diagnosis attempts suggest that the outcome may at times even be worse than a purely 'human' diagnosis.[52] The increasing use of eHealth tools for diagnosis, treatment and after care is likely to blur the lines between the different sets of civil liability, such as misdiagnosis or medical malpractice: who is liable under contract and/or tort if, for example, a medical practitioner relies on AI-aided tools for diagnosis or on automated surgery by robots? The practitioner himself or herself? The manufacturer or eHealth services provider? All of them jointly? These questions may be relatively easy to answer as long as they are limited to a single jurisdiction. But what if the medical practitioner is based in a different country than the other parties involved, and what if the local approaches – for example to individual, joint and several liability – differ? The following section provides a general outline of the conflict of laws rules for tort, including liability for data protection breaches and product liability.

[51] See Cloud, 'Robots Are Coming', 707, 724.

[52] See e.g. C Lehman and others, 'Diagnostic Accuracy of Digital Screening Mammography With and Without Computer-Aided Detection' (2015) 175(11) *JAMA Internal Medicine*:1828; J Fenton and others, 'Influence of Computer-Aided Detection on Performance of Screening Mammography' (2007) 356 *New England Journal of Medicine* 1399.

11.5.1 Tort Liability and eHealth: Jurisdiction and Applicable Law

As a general principle, most rules on jurisdiction and conflict of laws in matters relating to torts focus on the lex loci commissi, or the law of the place where the tort was committed.[53] The EU Rome II Regulation, however, focuses on the lex loci damni, or the 'law of the country in which the damage occurs irrespective of the country in which the event giving rise to the damage occurred and irrespective of the country or countries in which the indirect consequences of that event occur'.[54] With regard to jurisdiction, the EU Brussels Ibis Regulation combines both approaches. The claim for damages stemming from a non-contractual obligation such as a tort may therefore be brought either before the courts of the country where the tort was committed or before the courts in the country where the damage occurred.[55] In the US, state courts apply a variety of different approaches to choice of law in torts, such as (1) the lex loci delicti rule, (2) interest analysis, (3) a 'better law' approach, (4) the 'most significant relationship test' also employed by Sec. 145 of the Restatement (Second) of Conflict of Laws developed by the American Law Institute.[56]

An important and widely accepted inroad to these approaches and principles on both sides of the Atlantic ocean is the application of the law of the common habitual residence of the tortfeasor and the victim which has been accepted, for example, under New York Law in *Babcock v Jackson*,[57] and also laid down in many codifications, for example, Article 4(2) of the Rome II Regulation and Article 133(1) of the Swiss Private International Law Act.[58] Moreover, many choice of law regimes provide an 'escape clause' for cases in which the tort is manifestly more closely connected with a country other than that indicated by the general conflict of laws rules. In those scenarios, the law of that other country shall apply.[59] A closer connection may,

[53] See with regard to jurisdiction, for example, Art. 7(2) Brussels Ibis Regulation. See, for example, K Graziano 'Torts' in Basedow J and others (eds) *Encyclopedia of Private International Law* II (Edward Elgar 2017), 1709, 1710 et seq.

[54] See Art. 4(1) Rome II Regulation. See Cheshire, North & Fawcett, *Private International Law*, 810 et seq.; Dicey, Morris & Collins, *The Conflict of Laws* II, 2207 et seq.

[55] Art. 7(2) Brussels Ibis Regulation and cf. ECJ Case 21/76 *Bier v. Mines de Potasse d'Alsace* ECR 1978, 1735. With regard to the general rules on jurisdiction, see Dicey, Morris & Collins, *The Conflict of Laws* I, 481 et seq.

[56] For an overview, see P Hay and others, *Conflict of Laws* (West Academic 2018), 713 et seq; see Restatement (Second) of Conflict of Laws (1969 Main Vol.), www.kentlaw.edu/perritt/conflicts/rest145.html.

[57] 191 N.E.2nd 279 (NY 1963).

[58] Graziano, 'Torts', 1709, 1710 et seq.

[59] See Art. 4(3) Rome II Regulation.

in particular, stem from a pre-existing contractual relationship between the parties. In the case of cross-border eHealth services, this means that a tort committed in the course of the provision of such services will be subjected to the same law as the contract between the eHealth provider (eg, a telesurgeon) and his or her patient or customer.[60] Hence, by drawing upon the 'escape clause' in Article 4(3) of the Rome II Regulation, contractual and tortious liability may be aligned. This rule has, however, an exceptional character and it is therefore all but certain that a court will apply it to the case at hand. In order to achieve predictable results, the parties may therefore want to choose the law applicable to torts pursuant to Article 14 Rome II Regulation. Within the limits set forth in Article 14(2), (3) of the Rome II Regulation, parties pursuing a commercial activity (eg, an eHealth provider on the one hand and a medical professional on the other hand) may freely choose the applicable law even before the event giving rise to the damage occurs. Where eHealth services are provided directly to non-commercial parties such as consumers and/or patients, the choice of law may only take place after the event giving rise to the damage occurred.[61]

It is important to note, however, that neither a choice of law pursuant to Article 14 nor the courts' application of the general rules in Article 4 of the Rome II Regulation may preclude the application of local 'rules of safety and conduct' addressed in Article 17. In assessing if, for example, the conduct of an eHealth provider gives rise to his or her liability, account shall be taken 'as a matter of fact and in so far as is appropriate, of the rules of safety and conduct which were in force at the place and time of the event giving rise to the liability'. In other words, Article 17 Rome II Regulation may point to, for example, the standards of care, as to good professional standards in the country where the eHealth provider has acted (lex loci delicti). Thus, Article 17 may act as an important – albeit limited – inroad to the application of the lex loci damni pursuant to Article 4(1) of the Rome II Regulation. For cross-border eHealth providers, Article 17 may therefore offer a strong toehold to draw upon the 'rules of safety and conduct' in place in their respective home countries. This is all the more important, as these standards are still unclear in many jurisdictions. In Germany, for example, the conditions under which eHealth applications, telemedicine, in particular, may be used without prior direct contact with a physician, are still being developed.[62] Still,

[60] See Art. 4(3) Rome II Regulation.

[61] See Art. 14(1)(a) Rome II Regulation.

[62] See M Middendorf and C Wever, 'Telemedicine to the Rescue? Reviewing the Current Liability Picture in Germany' (2020) 4 *Haftpflicht International* 1, 2.

Article 17 of the Rome II Regulation may, of course, not set aside overriding mandatory provisions or public policy considerations of the lex fori.

11.5.2 *Jurisdiction and Liability for Data Protection Breaches*

Whenever data protection breaches occur within the territorial scope of application of the GDPR as defined in its Article 3,[63] the data controller and/or data processor may be liable for civil damages pursuant to Article 82. As already pointed out above, this may even be the case where third-country nationals travelling in the EU (eg, a US citizen in France) are victims of data protection breaches committed outside the EU (eg, by an eHealth services provider operating a digital health-monitoring service from California).[64] In all of these cases, in addition to the general rules on jurisdiction under the Brussels Ibis Regulation, Article 79(2) of the GDPR attributes jurisdiction to the courts of the EU member state where the data controller and/or processor has any type of establishment.[65] Alternatively, proceedings for damages may be brought before the courts of the member state where the data subject has his or her habitual residence.[66] With regard to the law applicable to the civil action for damages following a breach of the GDPR, at least as a starting point, Article 82 provides an autonomous European rule. However, this provision does not apply to important issues, such as the type and calculation of damages, (contributory) negligence and prescription.[67] By consequence, all of these matters are subject to the law designated by the conflict of laws rules of the forum. Given that the Rome II Regulation is inapplicable to tortious claims relating to breaches of privacy and data protection rules pursuant to its Articles 1(2)(g) and 30(2), EU member states' courts have to apply their national conflict of laws rules.[68] These varying national choice of law regimes may point to the lex loci commissi, lex loci damni, the law of the common

[63] See Section 11.3.

[64] See Art. 3(2) GDPR and Section 11.3.

[65] See Recital 147 GDPR. With regard to the complementary function of the Brussels I Regulation, see e.g. Heinze and Warmuth, 'Das Sonderprozessrecht der Datenschutz-Grundverordnung', 175 et seq.

[66] See P De Miguel Asensio, 'Jurisdiction and Applicable Law in the New EU General Data Protection Regulation' (2017) 69 *Revista Española de Derecho Internacional* 75 et seq.

[67] Lüttringhaus, 'Das internationale Datenprivatrecht', 50, 75 et seq.

[68] Brkan, 'Data Protection and Conflict-of-Laws', 1, 8 et seq; C Kohler, 'Conflict of Law Issues in the 2016 Data Protection Regulation of the European Union' (2019) 3 *Rivista di diritto internazionale privato e processuale* 653, 673 et seq; A Dickinson, *The Rome II Regulation* (Oxford University Press 2008), para. 3.228.

habitual residence or the law of the state to which the case presents a manifestly closer connection. In cases of GDPR infringements involving data subjects from non-EU states (eg, American tourists travelling in the EU), national choice of law regimes may even lead to the application of the law of a third country, such as US state law.[69]

11.5.3 Product Liability and eHealth

The rules on product liability may also apply to harm caused by medical products used for the provision of eHealth services. This holds true for conventional as well as 'smart' or software-driven devices.[70] With regard to the EU product liability Directive 85/374/EEC,[71] it is, however, heavily disputed whether the rules on product liability are either limited to damages caused by physical products or they also include immaterial components such as, for example, defective software. In the light of the increasing use of 'smart', 'Internet of Things' (IoT), and other digitally or AI-enhanced devices, legislators are currently moving towards a more comprehensive approach to product liability which might streamline the rules on liability for physical and non-physical components.[72]

The EU conflict of laws rules in matters of product liability aim at 'fairly spreading the risks inherent in a modern high-technology society, protecting consumers' health, stimulating innovation, securing undistorted competition and facilitating trade'.[73] To achieve these objectives, the

[69] For details, see Lüttringhaus, 'Das internationale Datenprivatrecht', 50, 75 et seq.

[70] With regard to product liability in the US, see, for example, D Ferrera and M Woodward, 'Liability Issues Continue to Evolve in Computer-Assisted Surgery" *MDDI Online*, 2020, www.mddionline.com/legal/liability-issues-continue-evolve-computer-assisted-surgery accessed 9 June 2020. See, with regard to EU law, I Bach, 'Medical Apps – wer haftet bei Fehlern?' (2017) 50 *Gynäkologe* 473; Jakobs and Huber 'Software als Medizinprodukt', 1; D Keysers, 'Implantate – (Produkt-)Haftungsrechtliche Fragestellungen unter Berücksichtigung der Medical Device Regulation (Teil 2)', (2020) 1 *Haftpflicht International* 54; R Ortner and F Daubenbüchel, 'Medizinprodukte 4.0 – Haftung, Datenschutz, IT-Sicherheit' (2016) *Neue Juristische Wochenschrift* 2918; M Pfeiffer, 'Europarechtliche Aspekte der Medizinprodukthaftung' (2019) 3 *Haftpflicht International* 116 et seq. See ECJ Case C-503/13 and Case C-504/13, *Boston Scientific Medizintechnik GmbH v AOK Sachsen-Anhalt*.

[71] Council Directive 85/374/EEC of 25 July 1985 on the Approximation of the Laws, Regulations and Administrative Provisions of the Member States Concerning Liability for Defective Products [1985] OJ L 210/9.

[72] See e.g. European Commission, 'Staff Working Document on Liability for Emerging Digital Technologies', SWD(2018) 137 final, 25 April 2018.

[73] See Recital 20 Rome II Regulation.

Rome II Regulation creates a cascade system of connecting factors. The parties may primarily choose the law applicable to product liability only after the event giving rise to the damage occurs.[74] An ex-ante choice of law is limited to scenarios where all parties are pursuing commercial activities.[75] The next connecting factor is the common habitual residence of the parties involved. The cascade system itself is laid down in Article 5(1) of the Rome II Regulation, and each level of the cascade requires the product itself or a product of the same type be marketed in that specific country. Failing that, the next element of the cascade is triggered. On the first level, Article 5(1)(a) of the Rome II Regulation points to the law of the country in which the person sustaining the damage had his or her habitual residence when the damage occurred. The second level draws upon the law of the country in which the product was acquired (Article 5(1)(b)), and the third level points to the law of the country in which the damage occurred. The requirement that the product must be marketed in each of these countries for the respective conflict of laws rule to apply fosters foreseeability for producers and provide a balanced solution with regard to the interests involved.[76] Thus, where an eHealth provider – acting as manufacturer, importer or another entity falling within the scope of Article 5 of the Rome II Regulation – could not reasonably foresee the marketing of the product in the countries referred to in Article 5(1)(a), (b) or (c), the law applicable shall be the law of the country in which the person claimed to be liable is habitually resident.[77] Finally, Article 5(2) of the Rome II Regulation contains an escape clause for scenarios presenting a manifestly closer connection to another country. With regard to the cross-border provision of eHealth services that involve the use of 'products', such a connection may be based, in particular, on a pre-existing contract that is closely connected with the product liability in question.[78]

In the US, the conflict of laws rules for product liability tend to vary from state to state.[79] However, among recent cases, a few common denominators may be identified: (1) the habitual residence of the party

[74] See Art. 14(1)(a) Rome II Regulation. Cheshire, North & Fawcett, *Private International Law*, 820 et seq.

[75] See Art. 14(1)(b) Rome II Regulation.

[76] See Recital 20 Rome II Regulation. See Cheshire, North & Fawcett, *Private International Law*, 822 et seq.

[77] Art. 5(1) Rome II Regulation. See Dicey, Morris & Collins, *The Conflict of Laws* II, 2220 et seq.

[78] See Art. 5(2) Rome II Regulation.

[79] See for example Hay and others, *Conflict of Laws*, 927 et seq.

injured by the product, (2) the place where the injury occurred, (3) the place where the product was marketed, (4) the place where the product was manufactured and/or designed, and (5) the principal place of business of the manufacturer.[80] Although this approach provides more flexibility for the US courts, by comparison, the EU rule in Article 5 of the Rome II Regulation has the advantage of foreseeability for eHealth and medical device providers: the EU regime usually requires in Article 5(1) of the Rome II Regulation that the product be marketed at each of these places in order for the respective conflict of laws rules to operate.

11.6 Overriding Mandatory Provisions and Public Policy

Until recently, some countries, such as Poland and Germany, had generally prohibited the provision of certain health services exclusively by telemedicine. Rather, the relevant national rules require both the physician and patient to be present when the diagnosis or the treatment is made.[81] Although there has been a strong drive towards liberalization, some countries may still oppose the cross-border provision of eHealth services in general and telemedicine and telesurgery in particular. In the US, the operation of choice of law rules is often heavily influenced by policy considerations.[82] With regard to contract and tort law, the EU member states are free to apply so-called overriding mandatory provisions of the forum irrespective of the law otherwise applicable to the eHealth service contract under Article 9 of the Rome I Regulation and Article 16 of the Rome II Regulation. Overriding mandatory rules are provisions 'the respect for which is regarded as crucial by a country for safeguarding its public interests, such as its political, social or economic organisation'. While provisions regulating the medical profession and protecting national health may fall within the ambit of Article 9(1) and (2) of the Rome I Regulation and Article 16 of the Rome II Regulation, it has to be borne in mind that the freedom to provide services as protected under Articles 56 and 57 of the TFEU and explicitly restated in the eCommerce Directive for services rendered by means of electronic or computer-based communications has to be taken into account.[83] In cases of doubt, the ECJ

[80] On the extensive line of case law, see Hay and others, *Conflict of Laws*, 932 et seq.

[81] See the former version of § 7 (Muster-)Berufsordnung für die in Deutschland tätigen Ärztinnen und Ärzte and the Polish Act on the Professions of Physician and Dentist of 5 December 1996, which required the patient to be personally examined by the physician.

[82] See on telesurgery, for example, Cloud, 'Robots Are Coming', 707, 722 et seq.

[83] See Section 11.2.1.

may be summoned to give an authoritative ruling on the interpretation and scope of Article 9(1) and (2) of the Rome I Regulation and Article 16 of the Rome II Regulation.[84] The same holds true for Article 9(3) of the Rome I Regulation which allows for the application of foreign overriding mandatory provisions, or provisions of another country different from the forum state. If the obligations arising out of the contract have to be performed in the foreign state, the overriding mandatory provisions of that state may only be 'given effect' under the substantive law applicable by virtue of the general conflict of laws rules of the Rome I Regulation, 'in so far as those overriding mandatory provisions render the performance of the contract unlawful'.[85] In the case of eHealth services, Article 9(3) of the Rome I Regulation may come to bear where a cross-border eHealth service is, for example, rendered by a provider based in France to a patient in Poland, and the provision of the service is unlawful under Polish law.

Whereas Article 9 of the Rome I Regulation and Article 16 of the Rome II Regulation pave the way for the application of overriding mandatory provisions, the public policy exceptions in Article 21 of the Rome I Regulation and Article 26 of the Rome II Regulation allow the courts to disapply certain foreign provisions deemed incompatible with the public policy ('ordre public') of the forum.[86] This concerns cases where the application of foreign law would lead to a result that is manifestly irreconcilable with public policy and, in particular, the fundamental rights guaranteed by the law of the forum state.

11.7 Conclusion

The idea behind eHealth and telemedicine is all but new. The term 'telemedicine' was coined in the 1960s, and the first 'eHealth' application – a long-distance transfer of electrocardiograms – may be traced back to as early as 1905.[87] Ever since, this discipline has been expected to revolutionize the healthcare market. The ever-rising costs faced by most national healthcare systems as well as the difficulty of offering comprehensive medical services in rural or remote locations may further add to the development of telemedicine and telesurgery. The European Commission had developed a

[84] See ECJ Case C-135/15, *Republik Griechendland v Nikiforidis*, ECLI:EU:C:2016:774.
[85] See ECJ Case C-135/15, *Republik Griechendland v Nikiforidis*, ECLI:EU:C:2016:774.
[86] See Dicey, Morris & Collins, *The Conflict of Laws* II, 1871 et seq.
[87] R Bashshur and G Shannon *History of Telemedicine: Evolution, Context, and Transformation* (Liebert 2009).

'Digital Agenda for Europe' in 2010 that foretold the 'widespread deployment of telemedicine services by 2020' on a cross-border basis.[88] While this goal proved a little too ambitious, the importance and availability of eHealth, telemedicine and telesurgery services are constantly increasing. National borders are – at least from a purely technical point of view – much less of an obstacle for cross-border eHealth services given the availability of high-speed Internet, the widespread use of AI, big-data analytics and IoT technology in medical and surgery equipment, apps and medical devices. It is therefore not surprising that an increasing number of eHealth providers, such as practitioners of telemedicine, and the technology and MedTech industries are offering their services abroad. This chapter has shown that in the light of varying and very complex national eHealth laws and regulations, it is essential to know which law governs activities undertaken in cross-border scenarios. There are different sets of rules on jurisdiction and conflict of laws regarding, inter alia, licensing requirements, data protection, contract, tort and product liability.

Bibliography

Abrams C, 'Google's Effort to Prevent Blindness Shows AI Challenges' *Wall Street Journal*, 26 January 2019, www.wsj.com/articles/googles-effort-to-prevent-blindness-hits-roadblock-11548504004, accessed 19 June 2020.

Ameringer C, 'State-Based Licensure of Telemedicine: The Need for Uniformity but Not a National Scheme' (2011) 14(1) *Journal of Health Care Law and Policy* 55–85.

Bach I, 'Medical Apps – wer haftet bei Fehlern?' (2017) 50(6) *Gynäkologe* 473–78.

Barnes JK, 'Telemedicine A Conflict of Laws Problem Waiting to Happen – How Will Interstate and International Claims be Decided?' (2006) 28(2) *Houston Journal of International Law* 491–529.

Bashshur R and Shannon G, *History of Telemedicine: Evolution, Context, and Transformation* (Liebert 2009).

Bourassa Forcier M and others 'Integrating Artificial Intelligence into Health Care Through Data Access: Can the GDPR Act as a Beacon for Policymakers?' (2019) 6(1) *Journal of Law and the Biosciences* 317–35.

Brkan M, 'Data Protection and Conflict-of-Laws: A Challenging Relationship' (2016) 2(3) *European Data Protection Law Review* 1–18.

Cheshire, North and Fawcett, *Private International Law* 15th ed (Oxford University Press 2017).

[88] A Digital Agenda for Europe, COM(2010)245 final, https://eur-lex.europa.eu/LexUriServ/LexUriServ.do?uri=COM:2010:0245:FIN:EN:PDF, accessed 20 May 2021.

Cloud M, 'Robots Are Coming: A Discussion of Choice-of-Law Issues and Outcomes in Telesurgical Malpractice' (2019) 6(3) *Texas A&M Law Review* 707–30.

Department of Health and Human Services, 'Telemedicine Licensure Report' Office for the Advancement of Telehealth, Centre for Telemedicine, 2003.

Dicey, Morris and Collins, *The Conflict of Laws* I, 15th ed (Thomson Reuters 2012).

Dicey, Morris and Collins, *The Conflict of Laws* II, 15th ed (Thomson Reuters 2012).

Dickinson A, *The Rome II Regulation* (Oxford University Press 2008).

European Commission, 'Staff Working Document on the Applicability of the Existing EU Legal Framework to Telemedicine Services' SWD(2012) 414 final, 6 December 2012, https://eur-lex.europa.eu/LexUriServ/LexUriServ.do?uri=SWD:2012:0414:FIN:EN:PDF

European Commission, 'Staff Working Document on Liability for Emerging Digital Technologies', SWD(2018) 137 final, 25 April 2018, https://eur-lex.europa.eu/legal-content/en/ALL/?uri=CELEX%3A52018SC0137

Fenton J, Taplin S, Carney P and others, 'Influence of Computer-Aided Detection on Performance of Screening Mammography' (2007) 356(14) *New England Journal of Medicine* 1399–1409.

Ferrera D and Woodward M 'Liability Issues Continue to Evolve in Computer-Assisted Surgery' *MDDI Online*, 2020, www.mddionline.com/legal/liability-issues-continue-evolve-computer-assisted-surgery, accessed 9 June 2020.

Food and Drug Administration, 'Computer-Assisted Surgical Systems' 13 March 2019, www.fda.gov/medical-devices/surgery-devices/computer-assisted-surgical-systems, accessed 9 June 2020.

Food and Drug Administration, 'Examples of Device Software Functions the FDA Regulates' 26 September 2019, www.fda.gov/medical-devices/device-software-functions-including-mobile-medical-applications/examples-device-software-functions-fda-regulates, accessed 9 June 2020.

Hay P, Borchers P, Symeonides S and others, *Conflict of Laws* (West Academic 2018).

Health Resources & Services Administration, 'Office for the Advancement of Telehealth', www.hrsa.gov/rural-health/telehealth/, accessed 24 May 2021.

Heinze C and Warmuth C, 'Das Sonderprozessrecht der Datenschutz-Grundverordnung' (2016) 21 *Zeitschrift für Zivilprozess International* 175–98.

Jakobs I and Huber F 'Software als Medizinprodukt: Haftungs-und versicherungsrechtliche Aspekte' (2019) 1 *Zeitschrift Medizin Produkte Recht* 1–6.

Kadner Graziano Th 'Torts' in Basedow J and others (eds), *Encyclopedia of Private International Law* II (Edward Elgar 2017) 1709–17.

Keysers D, 'Implantate – (Produkt-)Haftungsrechtliche Fragestellungen unter Berücksichtigung der Medical Device Regulation (Teil 2)' (2020) 2 *Haftpflicht International* 54–61.

Kohler C, 'Conflict of Law Issues in the 2016 Data Protection Regulation of the European Union' (2019) 3 *Rivista di diritto internazionale privato e processuale* 653–75.

Kowalewski K-F, Kriegmair MC and Michel M-C, 'Kollaborative Automatisierung und Robotik' (2019) 37(12) *Reinprecht* 925–27.

Lehman C and others 'Diagnostic Accuracy of Digital Screening Mammography With and Without Computer-Aided Detection' (2015) 175(11) *JAMA Internal Medicine* 1828.

Lüttringhaus J, 'Art. 1 Rome I Regulation' in Ferrari F (ed), *Concise Commentary on the Rome I Regulation*, 2nd ed (Cambridge University Press 2020).

Lüttringhaus J, 'Das internationale Datenprivatrecht: Baustein des Wirtschaftskollisionsrechts des 21. Jahrhunderts – Das IPR der Haftung für Verstöße gegen die EU-Datenschutzgrundverordnung' (2018) 117(1) *Zeitschrift für Vergleichende Rechtswissenschaft* 50–82.

Marescaux J, 'Nom de code: 'Opération Lindbergh' (2002) 127(1) *Annals of Surgery* 2–4.

Metz C 'India Fights Diabetic Blindness With Help From A.I.' *New York Times*, 10 March 2019, www.nytimes.com/2019/03/10/technology/artificial-intelligence-eye-hospital-india.html, accessed 17 June 2020.

Middendorf M and Wever C, 'Telemedicine to the Rescue? Reviewing the Current Liability Picture in Germany' (2020) 4(2) *Haftpflicht International* 1–4.

De Miguel Asensio P, 'Jurisdiction and Applicable Law in the New EU General Data Protection Regulation' (2017) 69(1) *Revista Española de Derecho Internacional* 75–108.

Ortner R and Daubenbüchel F, 'Medizinprodukte 4.0 – Haftung, Datenschutz, IT-Sicherheit' (2016) 41 *Neue Juristische Wochenschrift* 2918–24.

Pfeiffer M, 'Europarechtliche Aspekte der Medizinprodukthaftung' (2019) 3 *Haftpflicht International* 116.

Pormeister K, 'Genetic Research and Applicable Law: The Intra-EU Conflict of Laws as a Regulatory Challenge to Cross-Border Genetic Research' (2018) 3 *Journal of Law and the Biosciences* 706–23.

Spickhoff A, 'Rechtsfragen der grenzüberschreitenden Telemedizin' (2008) 36(8) *Medizinrecht* 535–43.

Wendelstein C, *Kollisionsrechtliche Probleme der Telemedizin* (Mohr Siebeck 2012).

Wilderspin M, 'Consumer Contracts' in Basedow J, Rühl G, Ferrari F and others (eds), *Encyclopedia of Private International Law* I(Edward Elgar 2017) 464–72.

12

Organisational Readiness for the Adoption of Artificial Intelligence in Hospitals

MAXIMILIAN SCHUESSLER,
TILL BÄRNIGHAUSEN, AND ANANT JANI

12.1 Introduction

Artificial intelligence (AI) harbours the potential to improve diagnosis and therapy, enhance access to healthcare, and promote population health.[1] The European Commission and national governments have recognised the potential of AI to provide more sustainable and better care.[2] Recent policy frameworks by the European Commission aim to bundle national efforts and direct standards of excellence and trustworthiness for AI.[3] New AI applications are on the cusp of entering hospitals and driving a shift to new forms of care.[4] However, current assessments show that the translation gap between new AI technologies and their implementation and health professionals' skills remains particularly large in healthcare. Hospitals have not yet developed comprehensive strategies to bring clinical data into machine-readable formats, devoted time and resources to digital transformation strategies, established expert networks and equipped their workforces with relevant skills for technological transformations sufficiently – all crucial factors to lay the groundwork for successful AI adoption.

Technology implementation in the healthcare sector and hospitals, in particular, is a challenging process.[5] The failure to adopt new technology

[1] This chapter is partly based on work carried out at Oxford Insights and the Blavatnik School of Government, both in partial fulfilment of the requirements of the Master of Public Policy at the University of Oxford.

[2] European Commission, 'White Paper on Artificial Intelligence: a European Approach to Excellence and Trust' 19 February 2020, https://ec.europa.eu/info/sites/default/files/commission-white-paper-artificial-intelligence-feb2020_en.pdf, accessed 5 February 2022.

[3] Ibid.

[4] Eit Health and McKinsey & Company, 'Transforming Healthcare with AI', March 2020.

[5] T Greenhalgh and others, 'Beyond Adoption: A New Framework for Theorizing and Evaluating Nonadoption, Abandonment, and Challenges to the Scale-Up, Spread,

can be attributed to recurring problems that highlight the importance of the development and implementation processes for any technology project.[6] Increasingly complex technologies, scarce evidence for improved clinical outcomes, dependency among multiple stakeholders, delicate patient workflows, regulations and legislation, financial considerations, and the need for garnering support from frontline staff renders sustained technology adoption particularly difficult.[7] With AI, the healthcare sector has witnessed the amplification of old problems and the emergence of new challenges and technology barriers. In addition to an increasing skills gap and data-related issues, technology firms increasingly partner with healthcare providers and transform the sector, while bringing new skills, care concepts and technologies to the forefront of care. At the same time, new technologies are shifting expectations to new care models and require hospitals to embrace their role as innovators.[8] The slow response to these challenges in the healthcare sector has resulted in a translation gap. This raises the question of how hospitals can build more capacity, enabling them to absorb the potential of AI applications.

In this chapter, aimed at policy-makers and hospital managers, we outline steps to prioritise AI capacity-building and discuss the lack of AI readiness at research and speciality hospitals. We propose a new policy tool: an AI Readiness Index for Hospitals (AI-RIH) that could help strengthen organisational readiness and address potential AI barriers that might impede future implementation. In its broader sense, AI readiness has been defined as 'the preparedness of organizations to implement change involving applications and technology related to AI'. For healthcare organisations, we define AI readiness as *the extent to which a care institution has the ability to overcome healthcare-specific barriers in order to absorb and exploit the innovative potential of AI.* While we do not present an actual index, we elucidate hospital-specific AI readiness by proposing six core categories that an index should capture: (i) electronic health records, data quality, and interoperability; (ii) data security, privacy, and regulatory requirements; (iii) patient consultation and safety,

and Sustainability of Health and Care Technologies' (2017) 19 *Journal of Medical Internet Research* e367.

[6] M van Limburg and others, 'Why Business Modeling is Crucial in the Development of eHealth Technologies' (2011) 13 *Journal of Medical Internet Research* e124.

[7] Ibid.; Greenhalgh and others, 'Beyond Adoption'; EJ Topol, 'High-Performance Medicine: The Convergence of Human and Artificial Intelligence' (2019) 25 *Nature Medicine* 44.

[8] T Thunea and A Mina, 'Hospitals as Innovators in the Health-Care System: A Literature Review and Research Agenda' (2016) 45 *Research Policy* 1545.

(iv) AI upskilling, leadership, and change potential; (v) AI innovation and research; and (vi) AI partnerships and procurement.

We argue that the suggested AI-RIH could serve two, audience-dependent functions. For hospital managers, the AI-RIH could serve as a benchmarking tool that helps examine a hospital's individual AI readiness status and develop a locally tailored AI readiness roadmap. For policy-makers, such a readiness index could help distil regional and national trends, tailor AI reforms, and measure reform effectiveness over time. We discuss several advantages that hospital-specific indices might have over a health systems-based index, such as enabling higher resolution, assigning accountability, promoting the visibility of technologically advanced hospitals, and monitoring inter-hospital heterogeneity. We discuss how higher AI readiness across EU hospitals could mitigate emerging AI divides, increase the numbers of hospitals that can partner with the private sector, and drive a shift from technologically possible to need-based AI development.

Finally, we discuss the conceptual challenges of indices, like an AI-RIH, as a policy tool and provide insights into index implementation.

The chapter proceeds in three sections. The first section (12.2) analyses the policy situation and potential for AI in hospitals in the European Union.[9] The third (12.3) conceptualises AI readiness, discusses existing composite indicators for hospitals and presents categories that an AI Readiness Index for Hospitals should capture. The final section (12.4) discusses strengths, limitations, and challenges related to the implementation of indices. Section 12.5 concludes.

12.2 Transformation Gaps and the Lack of Readiness in the EU

12.2.1 Healthcare Systems in the EU Have Reached a Critical Point

Translating medical innovations in prevention, diagnosis, and treatment into better patient outcomes is one of the greatest achievements of public health systems across the EU.[10] Healthcare has become the largest publicly funded sector in the EU, with one in ten of the most skilled workers being

[9] We use the term European Union (EU) to refer to the EU27, but also include examples from the UK.

[10] OECD and European Union, *Health at a Glance: Europe 2020* (OECD Publishing 2020).

employed in national health systems.[11] In many EU countries, universal coverage ensures population-wide access to healthcare as government and compulsory insurance cover over 90 per cent of patient costs.[12]

In recent years, healthcare systems in the EU have reached a critical point because of important shifts on the demand and supply sides. Ageing populations with chronic conditions, increasing disease burdens, and further specialisation have all increased the demand for care.[13] On the supply side, workforce shortages and imbalances extend within EU borders because a scarcity of labour threatens the availability, accessibility, and quality of healthcare.[14]

These shifts in supply and demand have meant that the equity gap between the poor and wealthy remains large: less advantaged citizens are more likely to face access barriers, forego care, and experience higher waiting times.[15] Simultaneously, economic growth has not kept pace with rising healthcare costs.[16] Austerity and supply shortages can have severe consequences for hospitals.[17] In some countries, the lack of resources in hospitals has resulted in declining health performance indicators such as waiting times and increased mortality rates.[18] The COVID-19 pandemic has further laid bare pre-existing structural problems and threatens the financial viability of hospitals and other care structures.[19] This comes with repercussions for medically and financially vulnerable patients, and likely entrenches social gradients.[20]

Strategies to sustain healthcare system performance while curbing rising costs will rely on our ability to transform the factors that increase costs. In the EU, hospitals are the key healthcare providers and account for approximately two-fifths of overall health expenditures. On average, EU countries spent 8.3 per cent of their gross domestic product and €2,572 per capita on

11 Ibid.

12 Ibid.

13 Ibid.; R Atun, 'Transitioning Health Systems for Multimorbidity' (2015) 386 *Lancet* 721.

14 World Health Organisation Regional Office for Europe, 'Core Health Indicators in the WHO European Region 2019. Special focus: Health 2020' 2019.

15 OECD and EU, *Health at a Glance*.

16 Ibid.

17 M Karanikolos and others, 'Financial Crisis, Austerity, and Health in Europe' (2013) 381 *Lancet* 1323.

18 OECD and EU, *Health at a Glance*.

19 L Krishnan and others, 'Historical Insights on Coronavirus Disease 2019 (COVID-19), the 1918 Influenza Pandemic, and Racial Disparities: Illuminating a Path Forward' (2020) 173 *Annals of Internal Medicine* 474.

20 EJ Emanuel and others, 'Fair Allocation of Scarce Medical Resources in the Time of Covid-19' (2020) 382 *New England Journal of Medicine* 2049.

health in 2019.[21] Grouped by provider, 37 per cent of health expenditures were spent on hospitals, followed by ambulatory providers (23 per cent), retailers (e.g., pharmacies selling prescription and over-the-counter medicines, 20 per cent), other institutions (10 per cent), and long-term facilities (8 per cent).[22] Between 2008 and 2018, the unweighted growth rate of health expenditure per capita was 4.4 per cent for long-term care, followed by outpatient care (3.6 per cent), prevention (3.1 per cent), inpatient care (2.7 per cent), administration (2.0 per cent), and pharmaceuticals (1.4 per cent).[23] This indicates that hospital expenditures are likely to remain the most important cost driver in absolute terms.

12.2.2 AI Technologies and Their Promise to Transform Hospital-Based Care

Healthcare planners and policy-makers are increasingly turning their attention to AI technologies to drive the transformation of care.[24] AI is an amorphous umbrella term that spans multiple sub-disciplines with multiple applications and lacks a universal definition.[25]

The European Parliament defines AI as 'the capability of a computer program to perform tasks or reasoning processes that we usually associate with intelligence in a human being'.[26] In this chapter, we focus on *organisational* AI readiness, which we define as the extent to which a healthcare institution has the ability to overcome healthcare-specific implementation barriers in order to absorb and exploit the innovative potential of AI. Organisational readiness for digital innovation has been previously defined as the process and degree of organisational technology fit leading up to implementation and might be summarised as preconditions defining the capacity for change under 'organisation' and 'adopters' in the non-adoption, abandonment, scale-up, spread, sustainability (NASSS) framework of technology implementation.[27] Other models see organisational readiness

[21] OECD and EU, *Health at a Glance*.

[22] Ibid.

[23] Ibid.

[24] T Panch and others, 'Artificial Intelligence, Machine Learning and Health Systems' (2018) 8 *Journal of Global Health* 020303.

[25] S Legg and M Hutter, 'A Collection of Definitions of Intelligence' (2007) 157 *Frontiers in Artificial Intelligence and Applications* 17; J Shaw and others, 'Artificial Intelligence and the Implementation Challenge' (2019) 21 *Journal of Medical Internet Research* e13659.

[26] F Rossi, *Artificial Intelligence: Potential Benefits and Ethical Considerations* (2016).

[27] Greenhalgh and others, 'Beyond Adoption'; S Lokuge and others, 'Organizational Readiness for Digital Innovation: Development and Empirical Calibration of a Construct' (2019) 56

as the capacity to build individual readiness for IT-based change, which subsequently can translate to actual behavioural change in terms of technology adoption.[28]

AI constitutes a general purpose technology (GPT) as it can be applied to serve a wide range of fields, contexts, tasks, and purposes.[29] Below, we illustrate how AI promises to transform prevention, diagnostics, and treatment and to drive structural change in hospitals.

- Prevention: AI is increasingly harnessed to design more targeted disease prevention models, empower patients to lead healthier lifestyles, and overcome geographical boundaries. Current strategies include personalised prevention plans and precision advice based on AI-powered cardiovascular risk scores.[30] Health wearables,[31] smart homes,[32] and AI-powered lifestyle devices are being developed to prevent complications from chronic conditions.[33] Most recently, AI-based data analytics have proven useful in predicting the number of new COVID-19 cases and understanding pathogen spread.[34]
- Diagnostics: Diagnostics constitute the largest group of medical AI tools in the EU.[35] Technology companies increasingly partner with hospitals to outperform traditional strategies and support clinicians in providing more accurate diagnoses. Primary examples include algorithms for early detection and more accurate diagnostics of cancer

Information and Management 445; FC Southon and others, 'Information Technology in Complex Health Services: Organizational Impediments to Successful Technology Transfer and Diffusion' (1997) 4 *Journal of the American Medical Informatics Association* 112; S Yusif and others, 'e-Health Readiness Assessment Factors and Measuring Tools: A Systematic Review' (2017) 107 *International Journal of Medical Informatics* 56.

28 G Paré and others, 'Clinicians' Perceptions of Organizational Readiness for Change in the Context of Clinical Information System Projects: Insights From Two Cross-Sectional Surveys' (2011) 6 *Implementation Science* 15.

29 E Brynjolfsson and A Mcafee, 'The Business of Artificial Intelligence' (2017) 7 *Harvard Business Review* 3; Shaw and others, 'Artificial Intelligence and the Implementation Challenge'.

30 SF Weng and others, 'Can Machine-Learning Improve Cardiovascular Risk Prediction Using Routine Clinical Data?' (2017) 12 *PLoS One* e0174944.

31 L Piwek and others, 'The Rise of Consumer Health Wearables: Promises and Barriers' (2016) 13 *PLoS Medicine* e1001953.

32 ED Muse and others, 'Towards a Smart Medical Home' (2017) 389 *Lancet* 358.

33 D Zeevi and others, 'Personalized Nutrition by Prediction of Glycemic Responses' (2015) 163 *Cell* 1079.

34 B McCall, 'COVID-19 and Artificial Intelligence: Protecting Health-Care Workers and Curbing the Spread' (2020) 2 *Lancet Digital Health* e166.

35 Eit Health and McKinsey, 'Transforming Healthcare with AI'.

to prevent unnecessary surgical excision,[36] automated skin lesion classification systems on par with board-certified dermatologists,[37] and deep-learning solutions for the diagnosis and subsequent referral of retinal disease.[38] During the COVID-19 pandemic, AI tools that automate triaging of COVID-19 infections based on interpretation of chest X-rays were developed.[39]

- Treatment: AI has given rise to new treatment strategies by enabling the processing of large data sets and new sources of data for precision medicine. Recent examples include the AI-based advisory systems to optimise treatment decisions for patients with sepsis,[40] clinical decision support systems emulating tumour boards that match treatment options to molecular patient profiles in metastatic breast cancer,[41] and algorithms that help optimise antibiotic prescription.[42] In practice, these innovations, once validated and implemented, hold promise to address workforce gaps, overcome human limitations in the management of large data, and enable a shift from hospital-based care to patients' homes.

The use of AI in hospitals is not limited to clinical applications. For example, machine-learning models can support the optimisation of scheduling on a range of operational aspects from ancillary to clinical tasks; these include staff planning, timely admission to the operating theatre, and discharge from hospital.[43] A recent study highlighted the use of machine

[36] TA Patel and others, 'Correlating Mammographic and Pathologic Findings in Clinical Decision Support Using Natural Language Processing and Data Mining Methods' (2017) 123 *Cancer* 114.

[37] A Esteva and others, 'Dermatologist-Level Classification of Skin Cancer with Deep Neural Networks' (2017) 542 *Nature* 115.

[38] J De Fauw and others, 'Clinically Applicable Deep Learning for Diagnosis and Referral in Retinal Disease' (2018) 24 *Nature Medicine* 1342.

[39] DSW Ting and others, 'Digital Technology and COVID-19' (2020) 26 *Nature Medicine* 459; SA Harmon and others, 'Artificial Intelligence for the Detection of COVID-19 Pneumonia on Chest CT Using Multinational Datasets' (2020) 11 *Nature Communications* 4080.

[40] M Komorowski and others, 'The Artificial Intelligence Clinician Learns Optimal Treatment Strategies for Sepsis in Intensive Care' (2018) 24 *Nature Medicine* 1716.

[41] SP Somashekhar and others, 'Watson for Oncology and Breast Cancer Treatment Recommendations: Agreement with an Expert Multidisciplinary Tumor Board' (2018) 29 *Annals of Oncology* 418.

[42] TM Rawson and others, 'Artificial Intelligence can Improve Decision-Making in Infection Management' (2019) 3 *Nature Human Behaviour* 543.

[43] S Bacchi and others, 'Machine Learning in the Prediction of Medical Inpatient Length of Stay' (2020) *Journal of Internal Medicine*.

learning in predicting missed attendance of hospital appointments, which could save billions annually in health systems across Europe.[44]

Different AI applications will enter the clinic at varying times. The deployment of AI is likely to proceed sequentially because the varying complexity of technology and implementation barriers require different degrees of AI readiness. Hospital departments with routine, repetitive, and pattern-based tasks will absorb the potential of AI earlier than others. Despite low overall penetration, algorithm-based pattern recognition is already used for diagnostic purposes in radiology, pathology, dermatology, and ophthalmology. The penetration is not homogeneous, however, because in other specialities such AI applications are still far from being deployed for routine use.[45]

Given the large variety of AI applications and methodologies, the implementation of AI is likely to proceed gradually. For example, complex AI applications with daily use on wards could require a consistently high degree of AI readiness. In contrast, AI applications with narrowly scoped, simple tasks might be adopted at earlier stages. This is corroborated by an EIT Health analysis, which projects that hospitals will absorb AI applications in a three step-model: in the short term, fields of low-hanging fruits such as automation of administrative tasks and advances in imaging will gain traction; in the medium term, AI applications will enable more home-based or remote-care models and enter areas like neurology, cardiology, and oncology; and in the long term, hospitals will see the integration of clinical decision support tools that drive precision medicine.[46]

In this chapter, we focus on the most frequently applied subgroup of AI: machine learning. When discussing 'AI devices' in the remainder of this chapter, we are primarily concerned with scalable machine learning (ML)-based clinical decision support (CDS) systems. CDS systems are defined as 'computer systems that generate patient-specific scores, interpretation, advice or risk estimates to support clinical decisions such as diagnosis, treatment or test ordering, and are known to be effective in many settings'.[47] Fully developed and integrated into clinical work, such technologies

[44] A Nelson and others, 'Predicting Scheduled Hospital Attendance with Artificial Intelligence' (2019) 2 *npj Digital Medicine* 26.

[45] Eit Health and McKinsey, 'Transforming Healthcare with AI'.

[46] Ibid.

[47] H Petkus and others, 'What Do Senior Physicians Think About AI and Clinical Decision Support Systems: Quantitative and Qualitative Analysis of Data from Specialty Societies' (2020) 20 *Clinical Medicine* 324.

would *augment* health professionals' capacities in processing multiple sources of data and reaching clinical decisions with higher accuracy, speed, and safety. We discuss AI scenarios in the context of CDS systems because their complexity provides a lens to assess a large spectrum of challenges associated with AI implementation, as opposed to, for example, a software for tumour segmentation on CT scans. In other words, CDS systems illustrate the use of AI as a GPT and highlight issues from the perspective of clinicians, such as black box phenomena, efficiency in clinical workflows, usability, patient safety, validity, and reproducibility.[48]

Many experts estimate that health professionals will remain the primary patient-facing agents in fields with patient contact in the medium term.[49] Put differently, the current generation of AI applications operate at the level of *tasks* and not of entire *jobs*.[50] The former contemplates AI as a solution to augmentation – ie, as technology that enables better prediction and informs decisions that are reached by clinicians. Results from the largest benchmarking study to date on the use of deep learning for interpreting mammography screens corroborate the idea that AI applications, rather than outperforming clinicians, will assist them and enhance human performance.[51] In the medium term, health systems are very unlikely to transform to physician-replacing AI systems with 'autonomous AI algorithms' – such automation scenarios in which decisions are both reached and subsequently executed by AI technologies are conceivable and might gradually develop from *conditional* over *high* to *full* automation.[52] However, autonomous AI algorithms will require years of evidence proving that they enable greater accuracy, consistency, rapidity, and safety than the combination of a human workforce and assistive AI algorithms.[53] The corollary of this vision is that hospitals and policy-makers will need to take measures that prepare for a sequential integration and implementation of AI in clinical workflows. Given this gradual process, AI readiness has become a policy issue with a long-term trajectory.

48 EH Shortliffe and MJ Sepulveda, 'Clinical Decision Support in the Era of Artificial Intelligence' (2018) 320 JAMA 2199.

49 CB Frey and MA Osborne, 'The Future of Employment: How Susceptible are Jobs to Computerisation?' (2017) 114 *Technological Forecasting and Social Change* 254.

50 Shaw and others, 'Artificial Intelligence and the Implementation Challenge'.

51 Shortliffe and Sepulveda, 'Clinical Decision Support in the Era of Artificial Intelligence'.

52 Shaw and others, 'Artificial Intelligence and the Implementation Challenge'; DS Bitterman and others, 'Approaching Autonomy in Medical Artificial Intelligence' (2020) 2 *Lancet Digital Health* e447.

53 Ibid.

12.2.3 *EU Policies and the* Status Quo *of AI Uptake in Hospitals Across the EU*

In the EU, AI is seen as an important means of potentially addressing some of the world's most important healthcare challenges.[54] With the COVID-19 pandemic, hope and expectation vis-à-vis digital technologies and AI-based approaches have gained further traction.[55] Many EU countries have placed AI high on their health policy agenda in national AI strategies.[56] Composed of large public health systems, the EU has the potential to drive the adoption of AI by harmonising regulatory issues, linking multiple member states, and scaling population data. The European Commission and its working groups have established frameworks that aim to orchestrate national efforts. Current initiatives cover broader digital health policies and AI-specific issues, including the regulations of medical devices, reforms of health technology assessment, the design of clinical trials, and investment in innovations and education.[57] In February 2020, the European Commission issued its 'White Paper on Artificial Intelligence', laying out plans to foster collaboration among member states and establish an ecosystem of excellence and trust.[58] This strategy builds on the Commissions' *Ethics Guidelines for Trustworthy AI*, a framework that defines trustworthy AI by drawing on three dimensions: lawful, ethical, and robust.[59]

At an operational level, the European Commission recognises the central role of hospitals to harness the potential of AI and to make the key points in these strategic policies a reality. Strategies, such as those laid out in the 'White Paper on Artificial Intelligence' and the European data strategy, aim to prioritise the development, experimentation, and adoption of AI in hospitals.[60] The 'Adopt AI programme' aims to promote public procurement for AI technologies in hospitals, which can help

[54] Rossi, *Artificial Intelligence*.

[55] Ting and others, 'Digital Technology and COVID-19'; Y Zhou and others, 'Artificial Intelligence in COVID-19 Drug Repurposing' (2020) 2 *Lancet Digital Health* e667; Harmon and others, 'Artificial Intelligence for the detection of COVID-19'.

[56] OECD, 'AI Strategies & Public Sector Components – Observatory of Public Sector Innovation' 2021, https://oecd-opsi.org/projects/ai/strategies/, accessed 3 February 2021.

[57] European Commission, 'Artificial Intelligence' 2021, https://ec.europa.eu/digital-single-market/en/artificial-intelligence, accessed 3 February 2021.

[58] European Commission, 'White Paper on Artificial Intelligence'.

[59] European Commission, *Ethics Guidelines for Trustworthy AI* (Publications Office 2019).

[60] European Commission, 'White Paper on Artificial Intelligence'.

overcome reluctance to AI procurement and streamline this complex process.[61] At the same time, the European Commission wants to address the lack of AI testing in healthcare and promote the process from the proof-of-concept to the validation of technologies, by driving the development of hospital in-facility pilot demonstrators, digital innovation hubs, and special testing centres.[62] Testing sites for AI prototypes will help developers gain a better understanding of how their devices work in clinical environments (as opposed to artificial settings), set reference standards, address issues related to accountability and the trade-offs between black box phenomena and performance, and ultimately increase the chances for technologies to be valued and adopted by physicians and patients.[63]

Despite these strategic and operational initiatives and a growing market, the digital transformation and uptake of AI in healthcare have been slow compared to other sectors. According to a survey by the Healthcare Information and Management Systems Society (HIMSS) in 2018, only 16 per cent of healthcare facilities in Europe used AI tools.[64] Only one in four health facility managers in the EU had specific purchasing plans, and most health facility managers have never been involved in the deployment of AI tools.[65]

The AI gap, the divergence between technological feasibility (and its benefits) and the actual adoption, varies considerably across EU countries, with Nordic countries having higher rates of digitalisation and adoption of AI than Eastern and Southern Europe.[66] With user-friendly digital infrastructure and structured, ontology-based electronic health records being the strongest predictors and technological foundation upon which (real-time) AI applications operate, the gap between available AI innovations and adoption will likely remain wide in healthcare.[67]

[61] Ibid., 8.

[62] Ibid., 5–6.

[63] K Cresswell and A Sheikh, 'Organizational Issues in the Implementation and Adoption of Health Information Technology Innovations: An Interpretative Review' (2013) 82 *International Journal of Medical Informatics* e73.

[64] HIMSS Analytics, 'eHealth Trend Barometer: AI Use in European Healthcare', 2019.

[65] Ibid.

[66] Ibid.; J Bughin and others, *Notes From the AI frontier: Tackling Europe's Gap in Digital and AI* (McKinsey, 2019).

[67] J He and others, 'The Practical Implementation of Artificial Intelligence Technologies in Medicine' (2019) 25 *Nature Medicine* 30.

12.2.4 The Challenges of Technology Implementation in Hospitals

Hospitals are slow adopters of health information technology (HIT) and have often seen large HIT projects fail in the past.[68] The NASSS framework explains this technological conservatism through five sequential problems: *non-adoption* (technology is not used), *abandonment* (people use, then stop), lack of *scale-up* (a small project never mainstreams), problems of distant *spread* (no diffusion to other units or institutions), and lack of long-term *sustainability*.[69]

Hospitals are complex organisations and harbour implementation barriers on multiple levels. Clinical workflows are usually divided into multiple administrative and medically specialised departments (horizontal differentiation), and within the hospital, each department operates on a number of hierarchical levels (vertical differentiation).[70] This is further complicated by the sensitivity of patient data, departmental autonomy, and a high degree of interdependence between hospitals and external stakeholders, such as primary care and social care institutions. The NASSS framework groups factors relating to implementation into seven categories: condition or illness, technology, value proposition, the adopter system, the organisation, the wider context, and embedding and adaptation over time.[71] The interplay of these factors explains why the sustaining and scaling implementation of HIT is highly challenging in hospitals – that is, it is not one but the interaction of many factors that determines implementation success.[72]

Evidence from implementation science highlights that frontline staff's ability and willingness to adopt new technologies is one of the key determinants of implementation.[73] The adoption of machine learning-enabled CDS systems, likewise, will depend on how their users respond to it. Hospital staff are likely to resist the use of HITs technically if they interfere with health professionals' workflows or fail to be compatible with their values, aspirations, and roles.[74] New technologies must demonstrate

68 B Doolin, *Implementing e-Health* (2016); Greenhalgh and others, 'Beyond Adoption'.

69 Ibid.

70 D Mileti and others, 'Size and Structure in Complex Organizations' (1977) 56 *Social Forces* 208.

71 T Greenhalgh and others, 'Adoption, Non-adoption, and Abandonment of a Personal Electronic Health Record: Case Study of HealthSpace' (2010) 341 *BMJ* c5814.

72 Ibid.

73 Ibid.

74 Cresswell and Sheikh, 'Organizational Issues in the Implementation and Adoption of Health Information Technology Innovations'.

ease of use, adaptability, interoperability, and benefits for end users.[75] HITs must align with technology literacy, general user competencies, peer attitudes vis-à-vis technology, professional autonomy, and interprofessional roles.[76] On an organisational level, hospitals are more receptive to HIT when they have large human, organisational and financial capital, strong leadership, strategic consistency, and measures to protect against scope creep – attributes that normally apply to large research and speciality hospitals.[77] The more complex an HIT and the setting in which it is deployed, the less likely adoption, scale-up, spread, and sustainment will be in hospitals.[78]

Surveys on health managers' views on the current status of AI adoption reflect the implementation barriers that are well described in the academic literature. When asked about primary obstacles to AI, hospital managers mention the lack of trust from medical staff, data privacy, interoperability issues, lack of legal approval for AI applications, insufficient user knowledge, and immaturity of the AI tools available.[79] Health managers assign different weights to these factors depending on the health system in which they work: Italian respondents, for example, see legal issues and frontline staff's lack of trust in technology as major concerns; in Nordic countries, with more developed digital infrastructure, immaturity of AI technologies constitutes the major roadblock.[80]

Irrespective of their country of origin, hospital managers find that AI is still at a very early stage and not sufficiently mature for wider use in hospitals, corroborating the need for validating AI applications in real-world settings.[81] The maturity and safety of technologies is a particularly delicate issue in healthcare. Inaccurate decisions or disruption of clinical workflows may cause additional inefficiencies, lead to biased decisions or directly harm patients.

Clinicians are unlikely to embrace AI without evidence from clinical trials that demonstrate benefits for patients and without regulatory clarity on which machine-generated results are considered safe, how to deal with liability issues, and to what extent AI-based devices are reimbursed.

[75] Ibid.
[76] Ibid.
[77] Ibid.
[78] Ibid.
[79] HIMSS Analytics, 'eHealth Trend Barometer'.
[80] Ibid.
[81] Ibid.

Solid evidence on the outcomes associated with HIT is scarce, especially for the comparatively young field of AI.[82] Current expectations regarding AI tend to be overwhelmingly optimistic and risk outpacing the creation of a rigorous evidence base.[83] At the current stage, evidence on the benefits of machine learning in healthcare remains elusive: of the few clinical trials on AI, many are prone to bias, lack transparency, fall short on reporting standards, and do not provide real-world clinical evidence.[84] To establish a solid evidence base, proving the accuracy and efficacy of AI under lab conditions is only a first step.[85] Test conditions in proof-of-concept studies often differ from the clinical environment in hospitals. That is, AI applications that show success under controlled laboratory conditions can easily hit organisational barriers and factors related to data. For example, in testing centres, machine-learning models can be tested for their performance on out-of-distribution or 'new' data on which they have not been previously trained, as well as clinical settings in which they were not previously deployed.[86]

A recent implementation study on the deployment of deep-learning systems for retinal screens highlighted that clinical workflow factors such as lighting conditions, poor data quality and health practitioners' ability to manage technology influenced the effectiveness of AI.[87] Barriers to technology implementation can be unexpected and context-specific, corroborating the need for validation studies in real-world settings.

12.3 AI Readiness and the Use of Indices for Hospitals

12.3.1 Defining AI Readiness for Hospitals

Implementation insights from HITs highlight that building an environment in which AI can be adopted, spread, scaled up, and sustained will

[82] CS Kruse and A Beane, 'Health Information Technology Continues to Show Positive Effect on Medical Outcomes: Systematic Review' (2018) 20 *Journal of Medical Internet Research* e41; MB Buntin and others, 'The Benefits of Health Information Technology: A Review of the Recent Literature Shows Predominantly Positive Results' (2011) 30 *Health Affairs* 464.

[83] M Nagendran and others, 'Artificial Intelligence Versus Clinicians: Systematic Review of Design, Reporting Standards, and Claims of Deep Learning Studies' (2020) 368 *BMJ* m689.

[84] Ibid.

[85] Ibid.

[86] Ibid.; A Esteva and others, 'Deep Learning-Enabled Medical Computer Vision' (2021) 4 *npj Digital Medicine* 5; CR Manz and others, 'Validation of a Machine Learning Algorithm to Predict 180-Day Mortality for Outpatients With Cancer' (2020) *JAMA Oncology*; M Cahan and others, 'Putting the Data Before the Algorithm in Big Data Addressing Personalized Healthcare' (2019) 2 *npj Digital Medicine* 78.

[87] E Beede and others, *A Human-Centered Evaluation of a Deep Learning System Deployed in Clinics for the Detection of Diabetic Retinopathy* (2020).

require readiness on multiple dimensions. We define AI readiness as *the extent to which a hospital has the ability to overcome healthcare-specific implementation barriers in order to absorb and exploit the innovative potential of AI*. Although we acknowledge the importance of each dimension in the NASSS framework, below, we limit our focus to organisational factors specific to hospitals. Organisational readiness has been shown to be associated with individuals' change readiness.[88] Research hospitals, in particular, are primary sites for establishing clinical evidence, validating AI applications in real-world settings, and promoting the innovation and adoption of AI. We propose six distinct organisational dimensions to develop our concept of AI hospital readiness. We argue that these challenges should be addressed when laying the groundwork for implementation and, therefore, be captured by an index that aims to measure AI readiness for hospitals.

12.3.1.1 Electronic Health Records, Data Quality, and Interoperability

Hospitals' potential to absorb and exploit benefits from AI will depend on their technological infrastructure. Machine learning-based CDS systems for the delivery of healthcare are expected to interface with and require the entry of curated and normalised electronic health records (EHR).[89] In addition to turning paper records into machine-readable formats, universal ontologies, high data quality and system interoperability are key to building reliable prediction models. High-quality data is necessary to reach accurate, unbiased decisions, but few hospitals have implemented data quality monitoring so far. Interoperability describes 'the ability of different information systems, devices and applications ("systems") to access, exchange, integrate and cooperatively use data in a coordinated manner, within and across boundaries'.[90] Given the AI-driven shift of care models, the need for interoperability within the hospital, with national and international care facilities (e.g., GPs, pharmacies, specialists laboratories, biobanks, and other hospitals in the EU), and patients themselves (e.g., wearables and smart homes) has increased.[91] Interoperability requires

[88] Paré and others, 'Clinicians' Perceptions of Organizational Readiness'.

[89] A Rajkomar and others, 'Scalable and Accurate Deep Learning with Electronic Health Records' (2018) 1 *npj Digital Medicine* 18.

[90] HIMSS, 'Interoperability in Healthcare' 2020, www.himss.org/resources/interoperability-healthcare, accessed 3 February 2021.

[91] He and others, 'The Practical Implementation of Artificial Intelligence Technologies in Medicine'.

that a data collecting system is able to represent data in a standardised way, for example, when being accessed for research and clinical purposes.[92] However, EHR systems in hospitals are mostly proprietary and have unique data models, each representing clinical data differently. This makes it difficult for clinicians to integrate data from different sources into their clinical decisions or build CDS systems onto EHR systems. The new Health Level 7 (HL7) Fast Healthcare Interoperability Resources (FHIR) standard has become a key player and standard for integrating different models and achieving interoperability for EHRs.[93] The effective deployment of such standards for integrating EHRs will be an important technical element of AI readiness.

12.3.1.2 Data Security, Privacy, and Regulatory Requirements

Cybersecurity, data privacy, and regulatory compliance are increasingly important readiness factors as AI technologies gain traction in clinical decision-making. Following the digitisation of medical equipment at hospitals, the vulnerability to data breaches and hacked medical devices has increased. The 2017 WannaCry attack, a worldwide cyberattack with a cryptoworm, laid bare the deficiency of hospital security standards and caused financial damage, disrupted medical care, and also undermined trust in data-driven technologies.[94] Hacks and malware have the potential to steal, disclose, and alter EHR data, making interfacing CDS systems a high-risk target. Implementing AI applications will likely require prior upfront investments in higher security standards.[95]

The need for data-sharing between hospitals and external partners (e.g., between hospitals and private companies) will also require standards that ensure efficient data de-identification or anonymisation, secure data storage, accountability for data access, safeguards against data misuse, and patient autonomy in deciding how data is used (e.g., via data audits and opt-out mechanisms).[96] In the EU, hospitals' ability

92 ML Braunstein, 'Healthcare in the Age of Interoperability: The Promise of Fast Healthcare Interoperability Resources' (2018) 9 *IEEE Pulse* 24.

93 Ibid.

94 S Ghafur and others, 'A Retrospective Impact Analysis of the WannaCry Cyberattack on the NHS' (2019) 2 *npj Digital Medicine* 98.

95 He and others, 'The Practical Implementation of Artificial Intelligence Technologies in Medicine'.

96 Char and others, 'Implementing Machine Learning in Health Care – Addressing Ethical Challenges' (2018) 378 *New England Journal of Medicine* 981.

to comply with the General Data Protection Regulation (GDPR) and ethics regulations setting out standards for data protection and processing is crucial for deploying ML tools that require data from multiple sources.[97]

12.3.1.3 Patient Consultation and Safety

Hospitals' ability to integrate patients' perspectives in the design and choice of technology employed in their care is a central part of ensuring sustained technology adoption.[98] While AI is on the cusp of entering hospitals in some areas, patients' conceptualisation, knowledge base, preferences, values, and concerns regarding AI have been insufficiently explored.[99] Continuous engagement in patients' perspectives will ensure a high demand-side value of new AI technologies, avoid misperceptions, and promote adoption of new technology by end users.[100] As concepts of data and AI permeate the public sphere, hospitals will also need to engage with their patients and develop strategies that inform the public about the implications, benefits/risks, and safety of AI.

As machine learning-based CDS systems become part of clinicians' decision-making processes, new mechanisms subjecting them to scrutiny and AI-specific safety testing are necessary.[101] Currently, it is still unclear how safety mechanisms for algorithm performance measurement and control might look in practice – particularly for ML algorithms that are not 'locked', but adaptive and, therefore, provide different results when the input changes.[102] To counter variations in system's performance, some have suggested installing AI laboratories that monitor performance metrics and are held to similar standards as clinical laboratories.[103] On a systems level, these laboratories might be complemented by additional safeguards that prevent damage caused by the interaction of scaled, simultaneously working ML technologies.[104]

[97] E Vayena and others, 'Machine Learning in Medicine: Addressing Ethical Challenges' (2018) 15 *PLoS Medicine* e1002689.

[98] Greenhalgh and others, 'Beyond Adoption'.

[99] CL Kovarik, 'Patient Perspectives on the Use of Artificial Intelligence' (2020) 156 *JAMA Dermatology* 493.

[100] Greenhalgh and others, 'Beyond Adoption'.

[101] Char and others, 'Implementing Machine Learning in Health Care'.

[102] S Benjamens and others, 'The State of Artificial Intelligence-Based FDA-Approved Medical Devices and Algorithms: An Online Database' (2020) 3 *npj Digital Medicine* 118.

[103] He and others, 'The Practical Implementation of Artificial Intelligence Technologies in Medicine'.

[104] Shaw and others, 'Artificial Intelligence and the Implementation Challenge'.

12.3.1.4 AI Upskilling, Leadership, and Change Potential

Technology adoption in hospitals requires strong leadership, upskilling, and digital literacy among health professionals.[105] Implementing AI will necessitate preparing 'students for jobs that have not yet been created, technologies that have not yet been invented and problems that we don't yet know will arise'.[106] A recent report on the emerging role of 'Data-Driven Physicians' echoes that AI has widened the transformation gap between technology, hospital innovation, and health professionals' skills.[107] To build confidence and competence in AI, hospitals must invest in upskilling their workforce in statistics, data sciences, genomics, robotic surgery, data analytics, virtual reality, and wider methods of artificial intelligence.[108] AI readiness in this context will require creating new hospital roles, including so-called information specialists (e.g., data scientists, biomedical informaticians, and genomic specialists),[109] orchestrating their integration, and establishing programmes of continuous professional development. Research on organisational readiness culture suggests that the presence of project champions, 'individuals who actively promote their personal vision for using IT, pushing [projects] over or around approval and implementation hurdles'[110] positively influence the implementation success of IT projects.[111] By embracing a strong educational role through revised medical curricula and designing new recruitment strategies, university hospitals can educate and attract digital talents that occupy this role as champions. Upskilling of clinicians and continuous modernisation of learning is likely to drive adaptive change – ie, shift organisational culture and garner support from frontline staff to solve the complexity of sustained technology implementation.[112]

12.3.1.5 AI Innovation and Research

Large speciality hospitals and tertiary-care institutions are not mere adopters of technology, but central actors and brokers in the generation

[105] R Wachter, *Making IT Work: Harnessing the Power of Health Information Technology to Improve Care in England* (2016).

[106] A Schleicher, *The Case for 21st Century Learning*, Vol. 282 (OECD Observer 2011).

[107] L Minor, 'The Rise of the Data-Driven Physician' Stanford Medicine 2020 Health Trends Report, https://med.stanford.edu/dean/healthtrends.html 6 February 2022.

[108] Ibid.

[109] S Jha and E Topol, 'Adapting to Artificial Intelligence: Radiologists and Pathologists as Information Specialists' (2016) 316 *JAMA* 2353.

[110] Paré and others, 'Clinicians' Perceptions of Organizational Readiness'.

[111] EJ Miech and others, 'Inside Help: An Integrative Review of Champions in Healthcare-Related Implementation' (2018) 6 *SAGE Open Medicine* 2050312118773261.

[112] Wachter, *Making IT Work*.

of AI innovations.[113] Hospitals strongly influence the demand side of HIT, provide insights from practising with technology, and have system-level impacts on organisational innovation.[114] Harbouring large amounts of clinical and commercial knowledge, hospitals constitute the loci of education for future innovators, and are centres of theoretical and applied research with the ability to experiment with technology in 'real-world' clinical settings.[115] As major health providers and technology consumers, hospitals are in a unique position to act as innovators and integrate the technology development process from idea generation and testing/validation to implementation and diffusion of AI. The degree to which hospitals are able to embrace this role as innovators is likely to depend on their financial capacities, human capital (e.g., number of AI researchers, data scientists, and spin-out firms) and collaborations with universities, research institutions, and private technology companies. Given the early stage of AI, hospitals' capacity to act as brokers and drive innovation as clinical experimentation sites is a crucial readiness factor for the absorption of AI.

12.3.1.6 AI Partnerships and Procurement

Hospitals play an integrative role in technology innovation, but increasingly depend on companies that drive the development and commercialisation of technologies. With AI, the healthcare sector has witnessed the rise of powerful technology firms that partner with healthcare providers to access large and diverse clinical datasets and, in return, bring new skills and technologies to the forefront of care delivery.[116] Such partnerships are essential to driving progress in AI, but pose additional challenges for hospitals. The more the healthcare sector establishes partnerships with technology corporations, the more hospitals will need to develop expertise in setting up comprehensive contracts, clarifying liability issues, and establishing robust procurement models.[117] New business models will need to provide incentives for technology companies to advance AI development until evidence for the added value of AI can translate into better patient outcomes. Managing hospital–industry partnerships effectively will not only drive progress in AI but also allow hospitals to claim their full role as

113 Thunea and Mina, 'Hospitals as Innovators in the Health-Care System'.
114 Ibid.
115 Ibid.
116 Z Obermeyer and TH Lee, 'Lost in Thought – The Limits of the Human Mind and the Future of Medicine' (2017) 377 *New England Journal of Medicine* 1209.
117 Shaw and others, 'Artificial Intelligence and the Implementation Challenge'.

innovators, counter increasing information asymmetry, and ensure that AI technologies are tailored to local needs.

12.3.2 Lack of AI Readiness: Insights from Early Adopters and Large-Scale Technology Reforms

12.3.2.1 Early Adopters of AI

Examples of early adopters that illustrate the challenges of AI adoption include the hospital–technology company partnerships between IBM Watson and a series of cancer hospitals, as well as the partnership between Google's DeepMind and the Royal Free London NHS Foundation Trust. These partnerships have showcased the challenges for AI implementation in hospitals, highlighted their central role as innovators, and corroborated the need for holistic AI preparedness to prevent implementation failure.

In 2013, IBM Watson started to establish a series of partnerships with the aim of developing a clinical decision tool called Watson for Oncology (WFO).[118] The system uses natural language processing and machine learning, and aims to guide oncologists in matching patients with appropriate clinical trials and improve treatment recommendations. However, some of these initial partnerships ended due to insufficient results, rising costs, and issues related to data quality.[119] The promises of AI did not match clinical expectations, as issues related to real-world medical data had been underestimated.[120] Despite these difficulties, WFO has since made progress and positive results have been reported on its use for breast cancer treatment.[121]

DeepMind and Royal Free joined forces in 2015 to develop Streams, a clinical alert application for the early detection and management of acute kidney injury. The case highlights another pillar of AI readiness: the need to comply with regulatory frameworks. Royal Free shared 1.6 million patient records with DeepMind to build Streams.[122] In 2017,

118 JL Malin, 'Envisioning Watson as a Rapid-Learning System for Oncology' (2013) 9 *Journal of Oncology Practice* 155.

119 C Schmidt, 'MD Anderson Breaks with IBM Watson, Raising Questions About Artificial Intelligence in Oncology' (2017) 109 *JNCI: Journal of the National Cancer Institute*.

120 E Strickland, 'IBM Watson, Heal Thyself: How IBM Overpromised and Underdelivered on AI Health Care' (2019) 56 *IEEE Spectrum* 24.

121 Somashekhar and others, 'Watson for Oncology and Breast Cancer Treatment Recommendations'.

122 G Iacobucci, 'Patient Data were Shared with Google on an "Inappropriate Legal Basis," Says NHS Data Guardian' (2017) 357 *BMJ* j2439.

the Information Commissioner's Office decided that Royal Free had failed to comply with the Data Protection Act – data had been shared without proper legal basis and patient consent.[123] The initial architecture of the partnership was criticised for its omissions in data policy and patient communication.[124] These shortcomings resulted in a backlash against AI and undermined public trust in private–public partnerships that rely on data-sharing agreements.[125]

These case studies illustrate that data-sharing policies, patient communication strategies, and business models are central dimensions of AI readiness. To build effective partnerships and reach informed decisions, hospitals must develop core competencies in areas including AI development, strategic procurement, business models, and regulations.

12.3.2.2 Large-Scale Technology Reforms

Evidence from large-scale technology reforms highlights that top-down technology implementation projects need to be customised to the local realities of each hospital if they want to succeed.[126] Insufficient engagement of frontline clinicians and patients, lack of leadership, over-centralisation, and over-optimistic time frames caused the failure of the National Programme for IT (NPfIT), a reform to establish electronic care records in hospitals of the UK's National Health Service (NHS).[127] Due to implementation failure, the degree of digitisation in the NHS' secondary-care hospitals varies considerably.[128] The digital transformation of hospitals is an organisation-specific process that requires local tailoring rather than the replication of the same reform across hospitals. Sustained technology adoption, therefore, requires local support and preparedness for change.

Technology projects that rely on data-sharing agreements crucially depend on patient buy-in and frontline staff support. In the UK, lack of public trust led to the shutdown of NHS England's *care.data*, a project designed to create a national database that would combine patient records

[123] Information Commissioner's Office, 'Royal Free – Google DeepMind Trial Failed to Comply with Data Protection Law' 2017, https://ico.org.uk/about-the-ico/news-and-events/news-and-blogs/2017/07/royal-free-google-deepmind-trial-failed-to-comply-with-data-protection-law/, accessed 3 February 2021.

[124] J Powles and H Hodson, 'Google DeepMind and Healthcare in an Age of Algorithms' (2017) 7 *Health Technology* 351.

[125] N Hawkes, 'NHS Data Sharing Deal with Google Prompts Concern' (2016) 353 *BMJ* i2573.

[126] Cresswell and Sheikh, 'Organizational Issues in the Implementation and Adoption of Health Information Technology Innovations'.

[127] Wachter, *Making IT Work*.

[128] Ibid.

from acute hospitals and general practitioners.[129] The project was abandoned after the National Data Guardian and the Care Quality Commission had found that more security provisions and patient opt-outs were needed.[130] The campaign around the project had not provided sufficient information on the functioning of the project, data-sharing agreements with commercial organisations, and data opt-outs for patients.[131]

An analysis of the Danish General Practitioners Database and its failure provides similar insights. In 2014, the database, originally designed to enable seamless data extraction and exchange of medical records and improve quality of care through population insights, failed.[132] The case highlights that extended data usage and intensified data sourcing, for new purposes and by new stakeholders, should be counterbalanced by mechanisms of accountability and control.[133]

Another example of the importance of local calibration in technology adoption is Denmark's decision to import the EHR system Epic. Originally developed and deployed in the US, Epic provides generic EHR systems that can be locally customised and, therefore, require strategies to train clinicians to become so-called 'physicians builders' that configure the system based on local needs.[134] The implementation of Epic in Denmark has shown mixed success: tensions between central planning and local autonomy, technical problems such as a lack of interoperability between medical equipment, and delayed preparations for training the health workforce resulted in disruptions of the care process.[135]

Insights from early adopters and projects for large-scale technology implementation highlight that challenges related to getting AI into the clinic are vast and touch upon multiple pillars of institutional readiness and culture. This raises fundamental questions about the current status

129 M Limb, 'Controversial Database of Medical Records is Scrapped Over Security Concerns' (2016) 354 *BMJ* i3804.

130 Ibid.

131 TP van Staa and others, 'Big Health Data: The Need to Earn Public Trust' (2016) 354 *BMJ* i3636.

132 S Wadmann and K Hoeyer, 'Dangers of the Digital Fit: Rethinking Seamlessness and Social Sustainability in Data-Intensive Healthcare' (2018) 5 *Big Data & Society* 2053951717752964.

133 Ibid.

134 M Hertzum and G Ellingsen, 'The Implementation of an Electronic Health Record: Comparing Preparations for Epic in Norway with Experiences from the UK and Denmark' (2019) 129 *International Journal of Medical Informatics* 312.

135 JP Bansler, 'Challenges in User-Driven Optimization of EHR: A Case Study of a Large Epic Implementation in Denmark' (2021) 148 *International Journal of Medical Informatics* 104394; Hertzum and Ellingsen, 'The Implementation of an Electronic Health Record'.

of organisational AI readiness in hospitals across the EU. Moreover, it challenges hospital managers and policy-makers to identify shortcomings in different dimensions of AI readiness, benchmark their progress in building implementation preparedness, and monitor the effectiveness of health technology policies over time.

12.4 A New AI Readiness Index for Hospitals

12.4.1 Indices and Their Use Across Disciplines

Indices, also known as composite indicators, are promising tools to measure AI readiness and develop strategies that lay the foundation for technology implementation. According to the OECD, an index is 'formed when individual indicators are compiled ..., on the basis of an underlying model of the multi-dimensional concept that is being measured'.[136] Indices capture the complexity of multidimensional phenomena (e.g., welfare, innovation, and human development) by aggregating a variety of indicators into a single score or number and, therefore, draw on two defining features: quantification and information condensation.[137] Indices combine multiple sources of evidence, create strong narratives, provide interpretable results, and lend themselves to use as communication tools.[138] Institutions around the world increasingly use indices to provide measurable, comparable, and visualisable outputs. Given the rapid increase of information in recent years (and the need to distil trends from data), indices have gained in popularity across disciplines.[139]

Indices are increasingly used to benchmark development in the fields of digitisation and AI over time. *The Economist's* Intelligence Unit and Oxford Insights created indices that measure national preparedness for the coming wave of AI and automation.[140] Stanford University provides an annual AI Index Report that tracks and combines global data to

[136] OECD, *Handbook on Constructing Composite Indicators: Methodology and User Guide* (OECD Publishing 2008).

[137] Ibid.

[138] Ibid.

[139] S Greco and others, 'On the Methodological Framework of Composite Indices: A Review of the Issues of Weighting, Aggregation, and Robustness' (2019) 141 *Social Indicators Research* 61.

[140] Oxford Insights, 'Government AI Readiness Index 2020' 2020, www.oxfordinsights.com/government-ai-readiness-index-2020, accessed 3 February 2021; Economist Intelligence Unit, *The Automation Readiness Index: Who is Ready for the Coming Wave of Automation?* (Economist Intelligence Unit 2018).

monitor AI trends.[141] In healthcare, the Bertelsmann Foundation presented a sector-specific International Benchmarking and Digital Health Index that assesses advances in digitalisation in national healthcare systems.[142] Moreover, the European Commission recently published the first edition of a sectoral analysis of AI in health with the aim of benchmarking AI development over time.[143]

12.4.2 *Existing Indices that Measure the Degree of Digitisation in Hospitals*

Sector-specific indices have been used to drive the adoption of HIT in hospitals. In 2005, the HIMSS created the Electronic Medical Record Adoption Model (EMRAM).[144] EMRAM encompasses a list of technical indicators that measure the 'adoption and utilisation of electronic medical record (EMR) functions' in seven stages:[145] the higher the grade, the higher the degree of digitisation and paper-free environment within the hospital. Since its development, EMRAM has emerged as a global benchmarking tool and has been used to score hospitals across Europe with respect to EMR adoption and infrastructure.[146]

EMRAM allows hospital managers to track their hospitals' progress in adopting digital health technologies. Aggregated by country, hospital results are useful to identify regional trends and/or monitor national progress in the diffusion of technology across hospitals. In 2018, hospitals in Europe achieved an average score of 3.6, which is behind countries like Turkey (3.8) and the US (5.3).[147] Within Europe, differences are striking: Nordic countries, including Denmark (5.6) and Netherlands (4.8), have higher EMRAM scores than Italy (3.2) and Germany (2.8).[148] Together,

[141] R Perrault and others, *Artificial Intelligence Index Report 2019* (Human-Centered AI Institute, Stanford University 2019).

[142] R Thiel and others, *#SmartHealthSystems – Focus Europe* (Bertelsmann Stiftung 2019).

[143] S De Nigris and others, 'AI Watch: AI Uptake in Health and Healthcare, 2020', EUR 30478, Publications Office of the European Union, 2020, https://doi.org/10.2760/948860.

[144] HIMSS Analytics, 'Enabling Better Health Through Information and Technology', www.lesiss.org/offres/file_inline_src/445/445_mailing_291018_111749_2.pdf, accessed 30 June 2020.

[145] Ibid.

[146] EHR and EMR are used interchangeably in this chapter, as suggested as second definition by HIMSS. For further information, see HIMSS, *HIMSS Dictionary of Health Information Technology Terms, Acronyms, and Organizations* 4th ed (CRC Press 2017); HIMSS Analytics, 'Enabling Better Health Through Information and TECHNOLOGY'.

[147] Ibid.

[148] Ibid.

these scores provide important insights for European policy-makers and hospital managers: many EU hospitals lag behind their international counterparts in adopting EMR.

Another example of the use of indices comes from the EU. Based on hospitals' growing role in the adoption of HIT, the European Commission created the European Hospital Survey (EHS) in 2013. This benchmark survey used two composite indicators – measuring eHealth deployment and eHealth availability and use – to gather data on the deployment of eHealth in a representative sample of acute hospitals in 27 EU member states as well as Iceland, the UK, and Norway (EU27+3).[149] The index covered four dimensions – ICT Infrastructure, ICT Applications, Health Information Exchange, and Security and Privacy – and aimed to identify factors driving the deployment of eHealth services.[150] The survey distinguished between HITs being planned, deployed or used. Distinguishing these three steps helps to clarify the status of digital health technologies in hospitals, because technology deployment is different from its actual use. The survey found that only 57 per cent of all participating hospitals had an IT strategic plan to build eHealth capabilities, 15 per cent of all hospitals did not have clear rules for accessing patients' electronic medical data, and 90 per cent of all hospitals did not allow patients to access electronic patient records.[151]

12.4.3 Limitations of Existing Indices for AI Readiness

EMRAM and EHS are indices that focus on HIT from a technological perspective, ie, they measure the adoption of electronic medical records and digitisation in hospitals. As illustrated by our readiness definition, AI is an emerging field that poses challenges beyond the technological infrastructure of hospitals. A predominantly technocentric approach insufficiently captures the interplay of the social, organizational, and cultural aspects of healthcare.[152] Studies on technology implementation highlight that decision-makers tend to concentrate primarily on the technical capabilities of technology projects, which has negative effects on sustained HIT

149 PwC, *European Hospital Survey: Benchmarking Deployment of eHealth Services (2012–2013)*, final report (JCR Scientific and Policy, 2014).

150 M Deidda and others, 'European Hospital Survey: Benchmarking Deployment of e-Health Services (2012–2013) – Methodological Report' IDEAS Working Paper Series from RePEc, 2013.

151 Ibid.

152 Greenhalgh and others, 'Beyond Adoption'.

implementation.[153] From this perspective, the currently existing hospital indices do not sufficiently account for new, AI-specific implementation challenges.

The shift to new forms of healthcare and the need for data entry into ML technologies has increased the importance of interoperability for patients and external care providers. Although addressed by the EHS, EMRAM captures HIT adoption and interoperability mainly within hospitals. The system-wide adoption of AI, however, will depend on hospitals' ability to establish connections with the outside world, promote seamless data flows, and create an electronic umbilical cord with their patients' homes and wearables.

Another limitation of EMRAM lies in its design, as step-wise models in which hospitals must meet all criteria at one level before they reach the next level – ie, different dimensions to HIT adoption do not stand separately.[154] This impedes identifying key areas in which hospitals are more and less advanced. Hospitals will score poorly if they lag in a single category; conversely, hospitals that perform far above certain requirements will not receive additional credit. From a policy perspective, this yields less analytical power: if hospitals receive multiple sub-scores amenable to aggregation, hospital managers and policy-makers can gain more insight into which types of AI barriers are more difficult to overcome and require sustained effort.

Finally, current indices are contingent on hospitals' willingness to participate in surveys to support the process of benchmarking. This likely results in a self-selection bias (and reduced representativity of the hospital sample for the total hospital landscape). For example, hospital managers who are interested in benchmarking their hospitals against others or want to advance the digital transformation of their hospitals are more likely to participate in a survey than others.

12.4.4 Functions, Strengths and Limitations of an AI-RIH

Hospital managers and policy-makers could take the concept of digital indices for hospitals one step further. A more comprehensive policy

[153] K Garrety and others, 'National Electronic Health Records and the Digital Disruption of Moral Orders' (2014) 101 *Social Science & Medicine* 70.

[154] V Stephani and others, 'Benchmarking der Krankenhaus-IT: Deutschland im internationalen Vergleich' in Klauber J and others (eds), *Krankenhaus-Report 2019: Das digitale Krankenhaus* (Springer Berlin Heidelberg 2019).

approach towards AI readiness benchmarking could help identify transformation gaps and harness the potential of AI in healthcare. Here, we propose an AI Readiness Index for Hospitals (AI-RIH) which is motivated by the increasing potential but also failed implementation of previous AI projects, the need for long-term preparation, and the increasing gap between hospitals HIT status and the private sector. Insufficient preparation for AI could result in technology projects that hinder and disrupt hospital care or undermine trust among staff and patients.

Discussing the potential of an AI readiness index specific to hospitals raises questions about how it should be designed and composed. The technical complexity of constructing, validating, and implementing an index, with each dimension composed of multiple mutually exclusive indicators, is beyond the scope of this chapter. The process of developing an index consists of several steps, including the development of a theoretical framework, data selection, imputation of missing data, multivariate analysis, normalisation, weighting and aggregation, and it requires continuous stakeholder consultation and usability testing.[155] Instead of going into the index development steps, we discuss the functions (i.e., the desirable properties) of an AI-RIH, explore potential limitations, and provide ideas for its implementation and use for benchmarking hospitals' AI readiness.

Here, we limit the discussion of the index to research and speciality hospitals as these hospitals can have more independent oversight, receptive cultures and, oftentimes, incentives to push for higher degrees of digitisation and skilling up their workforce.[156] This gives them distinct advantages in developing individual AI strategies and serving as pioneers or hubs that drive the adoption of AI. In contrast, small district hospitals might rely on regional AI strategies as they are unlikely to have access to sufficient financial and human capital. Third, technology adoption is particularly complex in hospitals with a high degree of specialisation; speciality and research hospitals are, therefore, more likely to embrace the role as innovators (e.g., in terms of education, spin-outs, and partnerships), but equally serve as examples for particularly difficult technology implementation.

A hospital-specific readiness index might bring advantages for two key stakeholders. First, the index might serve hospital managers as a benchmarking tool; second, the index could inform evidence-based

[155] OECD, *Handbook on Constructing Composite Indicators*.

[156] A Boonstra and others, 'Implementing Electronic Health Records in Hospitals: A Systematic Literature Review' (2014) 14 *BMC Health Services Research* 370.

policy-making and reform analysis. Higher AI readiness across hospitals might also diversify the pool of hospitals that contribute to research and learning health systems.

12.4.4.1 AI-RIH Can Serve Hospital Managers as a Benchmarking and Management Tool

At a hospital level, an AI-RIH can help evaluate the current status of AI readiness and become a basis for identifying the strengths and weaknesses of a hospital if indicators are grouped in different categories, as we suggested in Section 12.3.1. An AI-RIH would provide a hospital-specific score that can be monitored over time and benchmarked against other hospitals. This would help hospital managers determine whether they perform well relative to comparable hospitals and in which specific areas (e.g., upskilling of their workforce or improving interoperability) they might need to invest additional resources. In addition to creating awareness about AI readiness, a standardised benchmarking process could provide the basis for a dialogue between different hospitals and incentivise mutual learning. For example, if hospital managers share insights based on this benchmarking process, they might learn from pioneers or help promote best practices.

From a management perspective, an AI-RIH could reduce the perception of arbitrariness of managerial decisions and could foster goal alignment between hospital managers and frontline staff in preparing for AI. As shown in previous studies, good communication, vision clarity (the sentiment that change is necessary) and change appropriateness (the sense that an approach taken to drive change is correct) explain large variations in change-readiness culture for IT implementation across hospitals.[157] Validated indices, with each indicator forming an element of this vision, constitute a transparent and, ideally, evidence-based set of metrics that justifies new leadership directions. If the index reflects goals that align with best practices (e.g., interoperability standards), hospital directors are more likely to ensure change appropriateness and garner support from frontline staff for implementation. In contrast, hospital strategies that are designed without external validation or benchmarking might be prone to a process of trial and error, and to losing support among clinicians.

[157] Paré and others, 'Clinicians' Perceptions of Organizational Readiness'; AA Armenakis and AG Bedeian, 'Organizational Change: A Review of Theory and Research in the 1990s' (1999) 25 *Journal of Management* 293; S Kujala and others, 'The Role of Frontline Leaders in Building Health Professional Support for a New Patient Portal: Survey Study' (2019) 21 *Journal of Medical Internet Research* e11413.

As has been argued for EMRAM, the strength of an individual score lies in its potential to pre-define a path that chief information officers and leading AI experts can follow.[158] Based on their scores in different categories, hospital managers can design an actionable hospital strategy. At the same time, an AI-RIH could provide enough flexibility to tailor the outcome of the readiness analysis to a local hospital AI strategy. For example, a speciality hospital with a focus on oncology might design a medical curriculum that helps educate data-driven physicians, while tailoring these programmes to questions related to cancer medicine. As discussed in Section 12.3.2, technology implementation is not a 'one-size-fits-all solution' that can be applied to each hospital. Implementation success often depends on in-house customisation.[159] High levels of local leadership and ownership among practitioners are necessary to tailor and refine implementation to clinical settings, account for the heterogeneity of social and organisational factors, and promote bottom-up approaches.[160]

An AI-RIH could also provide hospital managers with an AI readiness baseline analysis and justifications to request budgetary assistance.[161] This is crucial because large upfront investments followed by ongoing maintenance costs in technical innovation, security measures, upskilling, and research/development require justification and accountability. An AI-RIH lends itself to follow-up evaluations and target-attainment analysis.

However, it is not clear when returns on investment from AI-enabled care in terms of patient outcomes or higher efficiency will become visible. Nor has it been clarified how AI technologies will be reimbursed – ie, how payment strategies for AI-augmented care ought to be designed. If the evidence of the benefits of AI-enabled care continues to increase, policymakers might need to focus on strategies that incentivise the uptake of AI applications and align with outcomes/value-based payment strategies rather than fee-for-service models.[162]

[158] L Pettit, 'Understanding EMRAM and How It Can be Used by Policy-Makers, Hospital CIOs and Their IT Teams' (2013) 49 *World Hospitals and Health Services* 7.

[159] Cresswell and Sheikh, 'Organizational Issues in the Implementation and Adoption of Health Information Technology Innovations'.

[160] Wachter, *Making IT Work*; Doolin, *Implementing e-Health.*

[161] Pettit, 'Understanding EMRAM'.

[162] He and others, 'The Practical Implementation of Artificial Intelligence Technologies in Medicine'.

12.4.4.2 AI-RIH Could Present a Policy Tool for Diagnosis and Implementation Analysis

On a policy level, AI-RIH could be a valuable screening tool that provides a snapshot of baseline readiness and helps monitor hospital development at local, regional, national, and European levels over time. The analysis on a hospital rather than national level could present three major advantages: (i) enabling universal and more granular policy analysis that can be aggregated for higher-level analysis, (ii) enabling accountability on the level of implementation, and (iii) promoting the visibility of pioneers and monitoring of inter-hospital variation.

A hospital-specific AI index could enable a readiness assessment at the level of implementation. Even if AI strategies are designed on a national level, successful implementation remains primarily contingent upon hospital-specific factors. The extent to which policies and budget for HIT trickle down to hospitals – where AI will ultimately be deployed – is central to informing evidence-based policy-making and to providing concrete implementation insights into hospital-specific AI barriers. This advantage of an index is often diluted when presented in an aggregated manner or combined with factors that are not specific to hospitals. Building AI readiness is likely to require a mix of centralised and locally tailored reforms, incentives for the private sector, and an ongoing exchange of implementation insights among local leaders. A hospital score is amenable to measuring reform effectiveness on multiple levels.

As highlighted by the EHS, hospital indices are also valuable screening tools to detect resistance to reform or blind spots in health systems. If an AI-RIH is composed of indicators that are desirable beyond the use for AI (e.g., data quality and IT security), an AI-RIH can reveal broader structural deficits. Hospital indicators like data security, for example, are often assessed on a voluntary basis and yet constitute the bedrock of safe decision-making in hospital care.

An AI-RIH could also be a powerful tool to analyse regional AI patterns and develop targeted reforms. Measuring performance on a national level, in contrast, often conceals variation.[163] Similar to EMRAM, which provides a snapshot of EHR capabilities across Europe, AI-RIH can trigger policy initiatives and mobilise political will that can drive hospitals towards digitisation and AI readiness.[164] In the EHS, for example, the

[163] JD Singer and HI Braun, 'Testing International Education Assessments' (2018) 360 *Science* 38.

[164] Pettit, 'Understanding EMRAM'.

national analysis was complemented by more regional analyses based on the EU's Nomenclature of Territorial Units for Statistics (NUTS).[165] Such regional analyses lend themselves to targeted reforms and investment in hospitals. In public payer systems, where AI reforms can be designed centrally, the score can elucidate contingencies accounting for regional variation. Aggregated to a national index, an AI-RIH also provides a means for cross-country comparisons. As for EMRAM and the EHS, the advantage of a hospital index lies in its universality for hospitals across EU members. Aggregated results of hospitals are less impacted by country-specific idiosyncrasies and health systems design.

An AI-RIH could provide hospital managers and frontline staff with a mandate and basis for accountability, which is particularly relevant in health systems where policy reforms have limited influence because health providers are highly autonomous or fragmented. National reforms with vague accountability can be prone to collective action problems, blame-shifting on failed projects, and lack of implementation effectiveness. An AI-RIH could place responsibility on hospital management with the potential for performance-based incentives, while ensuring that incentive mechanisms reward hospital managers or that credit is not taken on higher levels or lost due to aggregated analyses.[166]

An AI-RIH is a tool to identify pioneers and highlight variation across hospitals. The common benchmarking process could identify early adopters that have successfully built AI readiness in one or multiple areas, and provides incentives to connect and stimulate learning among hospitals. Promoting a decentralised implementation approach might require the creation of regional AI readiness hubs that promote a bottom-up approach, provide a platform for exchange on implementation, and incentivise peer-to-peer learning. For example, regional hubs could foster relationships between local champions (i.e., hospitals with very high AI readiness) and hospitals struggling to build AI readiness.

From an equity perspective, inter-hospital comparison would also ensure that individual hospitals or regions are not left behind. Scores from hospitals located in the same region can be aggregated to map regional patterns and monitor variation. This information might help mitigate the emergence of an AI technology gap that could create additional equity concerns in national health systems and the EU as a whole. National

[165] PwC, *European Hospital Survey*.

[166] C Hood, *The Blame Game: Spin, Bureaucracy, and Self-Preservation in Government*, Course Book ed (Princeton University Press 2010).

scores, in contrast, present aggregated data, which decreases diagnostic power and cannot be used for intra-country or regional comparisons.

12.4.4.3 AI-RIH Diversifies the Pool of Hospitals for AI Research and Promotes Learning Health Systems

Benchmarking of AI readiness can support research and development in the field of AI and promote more equitable development of AI readiness. Large variations in AI readiness across hospitals could impede the development of AI applications in areas in which they might be most beneficial. If only a small number of hospitals are AI-ready, the development of new AI technologies will not necessarily be guided by the research questions and data sets that are most relevant; instead, technology firms might partner with hospitals that provide the best conditions to access data sets, have a good digital infrastructure, and can deliver rapid outputs on AI projects. In contrast, widespread interoperability and hospital expertise in data-sharing procedures can facilitate the scaling and diversification of AI partnerships. Moreover, if many hospitals (with diverse patient populations) can provide data, this can make training datasets more representative, strengthen validity (e.g., by reducing bias), and promote the scalability of AI tools.[167]

Like EMRAM, an AI-RIH could also support the development of learning health systems. First defined by the Institute of Medicine, learning health systems can enable 'both the seamless and efficient delivery of best care practices and the real-time generation and application of new knowledge'.[168] The AI-RIH would capture key elements that allow for the development and effective implementation of a learning health system through categories including EHR adoption, real-time data collection, support of feedback loops, data integration, and upskilling of health professionals – core elements of any learning health system. For example, an AI-RIH might test the time it takes a hospital's technical infrastructure to complete the data–algorithm–point-of-care loop. Hospital managers being able to track progress in these areas and compare their systems to those of their peers could help to speed up the development of learning health systems across the EU.

167 He and others, 'The Practical Implementation of Artificial Intelligence Technologies in Medicine'.

168 C Grossman and others, *Digital Infrastructure for the Learning Health System: The Foundation for Continuous Improvement in Health and Health Care*, workshop series summary (National Academies Press 2011).

12.4.5 Limitations of an AI-RIH

An AI-RIH has several limitations, including (i) potentially poor or biased index design, (ii) limited scope, ie, lack of applicability to all types of care facilities across the EU, including non-specialist services such as primary care, and (iii) limited ability to predict AI readiness due to the exclusion of readiness factors that are beyond the organisational level of hospitals.

First, the usefulness of indices as policy tools depends on their quality of design. That is, indicators should be unbiased, specific, measurable, acceptable, achievable, realistic, relevant, and timely.[169] The OECD warns against poorly constructed indices as they might yield simplistic or wrong policy inferences, over- or under-emphasise certain elements of multidimensional phenomena, and send erroneous policy messages.[170] To inform the design of indices, the OECD has developed a *Handbook on Constructing Composite Indicators* that recommends ten rigorous steps.[171] Striking a balance between identifying all meaningful indicators (exhaustiveness) that capture AI readiness and creating a practical policy tool that focuses only on the most relevant factors (practicality) – while minimising input bias – is a challenge. The number and detail of potential AI readiness predictors exceed what is practically measurable in an index. The dimensions suggested here to capture AI readiness aim to be a starting point but are not exhaustive or set in stone. For example, one might create additional AI readiness categories for dealing with insurer- and payor-related AI issues. The choice of indicators and their weights have been shown to account for large variations in summary scores and rank positions – which has led to years of discussion about the methodological arbitrariness of composite indicators.[172] The creation of an AI-RIH would, therefore, require a careful selection of indicators followed by the validation of each indicator. This is all the more important as AI and AI readiness are amorphous terms, and many challenges related to AI implementation are still unknown. Research suggests that determinants of organisational change are still insufficiently understood and more studies are needed to confirm the most significant drivers of organisational change in the context of HIT.[173]

169 OECD, *Handbook on Constructing Composite Indicators*.

170 Ibid.

171 Ibid.

172 H Grupp and ME Mogee, 'Indicators for National Science and Technology Policy: How Robust Are Composite Indicators?' (2004) 33 *Research Policy* 1373; A Sharpe, *Literature Review of Frameworks for Macro-indicators* (Centre for the Study of Living Standards 2004).

173 Paré and others, 'Clinicians' Perceptions of Organizational Readiness'.

Second, we suggested some dimensions for an AI-RIH that are specific to research and speciality hospitals. Consequently, an AI-RIH based on the six dimensions that we have suggested may not be applicable to smaller, non-teaching district hospitals. Research and university teaching, for example, go beyond the mandate of many district hospitals. The latter, however, might equally benefit from an AI readiness assessment, especially as they are often less visible and lag in adopting HITs.[174] To address this conflict in methodological design, different types of hospitals might require different index formats, taking into account their roles and specific barriers to AI implementation. Moreover, in an increasingly interdependent health ecosystem, primary, secondary, and tertiary care cannot be seen in isolation but likely depend on each other. Low AI readiness in tertiary care might affect technological progress in primary care and vice versa. As a result, an AI-RIH would capture AI readiness in only one part of the healthcare system.

Third, we described the role of an AI-RIH as a means to advance organisational readiness. However, there are factors such as the wider health system environment that go beyond organisational readiness and influence the implementation success of HITs.[175] These factors are not included in our readiness definition, and yet will impact the adoption of AI technologies by hospitals. For example, public attitudes towards data-sharing, regulatory barriers, shortages of data scientists, broadband networks, funding for AI reforms, and the general innovation potential of a country affects AI readiness.[176] The interdependence between hospital-specific factors and the wider AI ecosystem is particularly relevant for public health systems like the EU's, where central government bodies might set hospital budgets and be mandated to direct hospital policies.

12.4.6 Implementation Challenges for Hospital Indices

The strengths of an index can best be harnessed if it is implemented in many hospitals. To date, the usefulness of hospital benchmarking has shown mixed results and depends on multiple factors.[177] Insights into past

[174] AS Kazley and YA Ozcan, 'Organizational and Environmental Determinants of Hospital EMR Adoption: A National Study' (2007) 31 *Journal of Medical Systems* 375.

[175] Greenhalgh and others, 'Beyond Adoption'.

[176] Kazley and Ozcan, 'Organizational and Environmental Determinants of Hospital EMR Adoption'.

[177] A Wind and WH van Harten, 'Benchmarking Specialty Hospitals, a Scoping Review on Theory and Practice' (2017) 17 *BMC Health Services Research* 245.

implementation raise the question of whether participation in the scoring of hospitals on the basis of an AI readiness index should be voluntary or mandatory, anonymous or published. Moreover, it brings up the question of who should pay for the implementation of an index.

Research suggests that voluntary and anonymous participation increases the success of hospital benchmarking.[178] Moreover, there is evidence that public communication of hospital scores might be beneficial if policy-makers want to use indices to increase the accountability of hospital managers. If indices 'rank hospitals in a way that the public can understand, this generates [reputational] incentives' for hospital managers to improve their scores.[179] In the English NHS, for example, public reporting on hospital performance provided incentives for future improvements.[180] This suggests that the index faces a trade-off: while a more voluntary, self-reporting index design would likely garner more support from hospital management, the function of AI-RIH as a policy tool is contingent on a large and representative sample of hospitals, including those hospitals that are unlikely to participate on a voluntary basis. In addition to legal issues associated with national or even EU-wide mandates, policy-makers might, therefore, need to weigh whether the scoring of hospitals should be mandated or voluntary.

The implementation of an AI-RIH also raises questions about who scores the hospitals and how. To ensure consistency and avoid conflicts of interest or biased reporting, hospitals should receive a structured scoring protocol and oversight by an independent party, as opposed to unsupervised self-reporting. Except for the certification of hospitals with EMRAM grades 6 and 7 – ie, the highest grades of EHR adoption – EMRAM is mainly based on self-selection and self-reporting of hospitals. However, self- and voluntary reporting can impede the quantity of available data on hospitals and reduce representativeness; hospitals that lack readiness are less likely to participate. If participation is voluntary, hospitals might only self-select if they expect themselves to score well in terms of AI readiness. In the 2012/2013 EHS, only a third of all chief information officers at qualified acute hospitals were willing to participate in a phone interview.[181]

178 Ibid.

179 G Bevan, 'If Neither Altruism nor Markets Have Improved NHS Performance, What Might?' (2010) 16 *Eurohealth* 20.

180 Ibid.; G Bevan and D Wilson, 'Does "Naming and Shaming" Work for Schools and Hospitals? Lessons From Natural Experiments Following Devolution in England and Wales' (2013) 33 *Public Money & Management* 245.

181 Deidda and others, 'European Hospital Survey'.

Random selection or inclusion of all eligible hospitals can reduce bias and ensure higher representativeness.

As for technology, the implementation of hospital benchmarking might be more successful if performed in a bottom-up strategy that drives 'adaptive' and people-focused change.[182] Frontline staff should be engaged to lead the adoption of an AI-RIH, promoting a sense of responsibility for score outcomes. Moreover, the implementation would require clear communication of the function and benefits of the index. One misperception might be that such an index would decide whether a hospital should replace its staff with fully automated algorithms. To mitigate these types of problems, the design of the index might also need to involve internal stakeholders. Moreover, members of the hospital should receive feedback about the outcome of the benchmarking process to foster goal alignment and create a sense of ownership.

Hospital scores derived from an AI-RIH will have the most value if they drive continuous improvement. In addition to scoring, the reasons and implementation barriers for each readiness indicator should be investigated. Success factors should be identified to promote peer learning among hospitals. Moreover, policy-makers might develop a policy roadmap with actionable steps to be taken and objectives to be set upon different score outcomes. Without such decision algorithms, index scores might not convey actionable advice and practical implications.

Finally, this chapter has been written under the assumption that healthcare augmented by ML-based CDS systems and other AI technologies will result in improved patient outcomes, higher efficiency and optimal resource utilisation and allocation in the future. Given the early stage of AI, building AI readiness can only be a means but not an aim in itself. Put differently, the creation and implementation of an AI-RIH will only be justified if AI turns its promises into tangible, validated patient and healthcare system benefits. In this regard, this chapter aims to generate new hypotheses about AI implementation; ongoing analysis of patient benefits from AI will need to justify the various solutions that address its implementation in the long term.

12.5 Conclusion

AI applications may offer powerful solutions to address gaps between healthcare supply and demand, and improve the quality of healthcare in

[182] Wachter, *Making IT Work*.

the EU. A lack of readiness for overcoming AI-related challenges, including data security and quality, interoperability, patient and clinician buy-in, skill shortages, and partnership management with technology firms, can prevent hospitals from harnessing the potential of AI-powered healthcare. In this chapter, we invite policy-makers and hospital managers to prioritise AI capacity-building, including workforce training on AI-enabled technologies. We also proposed a new policy tool, an AI-RIH, which can address potential barriers that will impede the future implementation of AI. The AI-RIH could perform two functions: for hospital managers, it would enable diagnosing hospital-specific strengths and weaknesses and could be a negotiation tool for budgetary needs; at a policy level, the AI-RIH would facilitate identification of regional trends, tailoring of AI reforms, and measuring reform effectiveness. Finally, we discussed the conceptual challenges of composite indicators, such as AI-RIH, as a policy tool and provided implementation insights. Increasing degrees of AI readiness among hospitals can increase the number of hospitals ready for AI partnerships, counter AI divides, increase overall interoperability, and shift AI research from what is technologically possible to what drives better patient outcomes. Ultimately, we hope that composite indicators that measure readiness for AI-enabled hospitals will be replaced by performance metrics that track the value of care delivery.

Bibliography

Armenakis AA and Bedeian AG, 'Organizational Change: A Review of Theory and Research in the 1990s' (1999) 25(3) *Journal of Management* 293–315. doi:10.1177/014920639902500303

Atun R, 'Transitioning Health Systems for Multimorbidity' (2015) 386 *Lancet* 721.

Bacchi S and others, 'Machine Learning in the Prediction of Medical Inpatient Length of Stay' (2020) 52(2) *Journal of Internal Medicine* 176–85. doi: 10.1111/imj.14962

Bansler JP, 'Challenges in User-Driven Optimization of EHR: A Case Study of a Large Epic Implementation in Denmark' (2021) 148 *International Journal of Medical Informatics* 104394.

Beede E and others, 'A Human-Centered Evaluation of a Deep Learning System Deployed in Clinics for the Detection of Diabetic Retinopathy' in *Proceedings of the 2020 CHI Conference on Human Factors in Computing Systems* (Association for Computing Machinery 2020) 1–12.

Benjamens S, Dhunnoo P and Mesko B, 'The State of Artificial Intelligence-Based FDA-Approved Medical Devices and Algorithms: An Online Database' (2020) 3 *npj Digital Medicine* 118.

Bevan G, 'If Neither Altruism nor Markets Have Improved NHS Performance, What Might?' (2010) 16 *Eurohealth* 20.

Bevan G and Wilson D, 'Does "Naming and Shaming" Work for Schools and Hospitals? Lessons from Natural Experiments Following Devolution in England and Wales' (2013) 33 *Public Money & Management* 245.

Bitterman DS, Aerts H and Mak RH, 'Approaching Autonomy in Medical Artificial Intelligence' (2020) 2 *Lancet Digital Health* e447.

Boonstra A, Versluis A and Vos JF, 'Implementing Electronic Health Records in Hospitals: A Systematic Literature Review' (2014) 14 *BMC Health Services Research* 370.

Braunstein ML, 'Healthcare in the Age of Interoperability: The Promise of Fast Healthcare Interoperability Resources' (2018) 9 *IEEE Pulse* 24.

Brynjolfsson E and Mcafee A, 'The Business of Artificial Intelligence' (2017) 7 *Harvard Business Review* 3.

Bughin J and others, *Notes from the AI Frontier: Tackling Europe's Gap in Digital and AI* (McKinsey, 2019).

Buntin MB and others, 'The Benefits of Health Information Technology: A Review of the Recent Literature Shows Predominantly Positive Results' (2011) 30 *Health Affairs* 464.

Cahan EM and others, 'Putting the Data Before the Algorithm in Big Data Addressing Personalized Healthcare' (2019) 2 *npj Digital Medicine* 78.

Char DS, Shah NH and Magnus D, 'Implementing Machine Learning in Health Care – Addressing Ethical Challenges' (2018) 378 *New England Journal of Medicine* 981.

Cresswell K and Sheikh A, 'Organizational Issues in the Implementation and Adoption of Health Information Technology Innovations: An Interpretative Review' (2013) 82 *International Journal of Medical Informatics* e73.

De Fauw J and others, 'Clinically Applicable Deep Learning for Diagnosis and Referral in Retinal Disease' (2018) 24 *Nature Medicine* 1342.

Deidda M, Lupiañez F and Maghiros I, 'European Hospital Survey: Benchmarking Deployment of e-Health Services (2012–2013) – Methodological Report' IDEAS Working Paper Series from RePEc, 2013, http://publications.jrc.ec.europa.eu/repository/bitstream/JRC85854/jrc85854.pdf

De Nigris S and others, 'AI Watch AI Uptake in Health and Healthcare, 2020' EUR 30478, Publications Office of the European Union, 2020, https://doi.org/10.2760/948860.

Doolin B, 'Implementing e-Health' in Ferlie E, Montgomery K and Reff Pedersen A (eds) *The Oxford Handbook of Health Care Management* (Oxford University Press 2016).

Economist Intelligence Unit, *The Automation Readiness Index: Who Is Ready for the Coming Wave of Automation?* (Economist Intelligence Unit, 2018).

Eit Health and McKinsey&Company, 'Transforming Healthcare with AI' (March 2020), https://eit.europa.eu/library/eit-health-mckinsey-transforming-healthcare-ai

Emanuel EJ and others, 'Fair Allocation of Scarce Medical Resources in the Time of Covid-19' (2020) 382 *New England Journal of Medicine* 2049.

Esteva A and others, 'Deep Learning-Enabled Medical Computer Vision' (2021) 4 *npj Digital Medicine* 5.

Esteva A and others, 'Dermatologist-Level Classification of Skin Cancer with Deep Neural Networks' (2017) 542 *Nature* 115.

European Commission, 'Artificial Intelligence' 2021, https://ec.europa.eu/digital-single-market/en/artificial-intelligence, accessed 3 February 2021.

European Commission, *Ethics Guidelines for Trustworthy AI* (Publications Office 2019).

European Commission, 'White Paper on Artificial Intelligence: A European Approach to Excellence and Trust' 19 February 2020, https://ec.europa.eu/info/sites/default/files/commission-white-paper-artificial-intelligence-feb2020_en.pdf, accessed 5 February 2022.

Foley TJ and Vale L, 'What Role for Learning Health Systems in Quality Improvement within Healthcare Providers?' (2017) 1 *Learning Health Systems* e10025.

Frey CB and Osborne MA, 'The Future of Employment: How Susceptible Are Jobs to Computerisation?' (2017) 114 *Technological Forecasting and Social Change* 254.

Garrety K and others, 'National Electronic Health Records and the Digital Disruption of Moral Orders' (2014) 101 *Social Science & Medicine* 70.

Ghafur S and others, 'A Retrospective Impact Analysis of the WannaCry Cyberattack on the NHS' (2019) 2 *npj Digital Medicine* 98.

Greco S and others, 'On the Methodological Framework of Composite Indices: A Review of the Issues of Weighting, Aggregation, and Robustness' (2019) 141 *Social Indicators Research* 61.

Greenhalgh T and others, 'Adoption, Non-adoption, and Abandonment of a Personal Electronic Health Record: Case Study of HealthSpace' (2010) 341 *BMJ* c5814.

Greenhalgh T and others, 'Beyond Adoption: A New Framework for Theorizing and Evaluating Nonadoption, Abandonment, and Challenges to the Scale-Up, Spread, and Sustainability of Health and Care Technologies' (2017) 19 *Journal of Medical Internet Research* e367.

Grossman C, Powers B and McGinnis JM, *Digital Infrastructure for the Learning Health System: The Foundation for Continuous Improvement in Health and Health Care*, workshop series summary (National Academies Press 2011).

Grupp H and Mogee ME, 'Indicators for National Science and Technology Policy: How Robust Are Composite Indicators?' (2004) 33 *Research Policy* 1373.

'Health at a Glance: Europe 2018: State of Health in the EU Cycle | en | OECD' (2020).

Harmon SA and others, 'Artificial Intelligence for the Detection of COVID-19 Pneumonia on Chest CT Using Multinational Datasets' (2020) 11 *Nature Communications* 4080.

Hawkes N, 'NHS Data Sharing Deal with Google Prompts Concern' (2016) 353 *BMJ* i2573.

He J and others, 'The Practical Implementation of Artificial Intelligence Technologies in Medicine' (2019) 25 *Nature Medicine* 30.

Hertzum M and Ellingsen G, 'The Implementation of an Electronic Health Record: Comparing Preparations for Epic in Norway with Experiences from the UK and Denmark' (2019) 129 *International Journal of Medical Informatics* 312.

HIMSS, *HIMSS Dictionary of Health Information Technology Terms, Acronyms, and Organizations* 4th ed (CRC Press 2017).

HIMSS, 'Interoperability in Healthcare' 2020, www.himss.org/resources/interoperability-healthcare, accessed 3 February 2021.

HIMSS Analytics, 'eHealth Trend Barometer: AI Use in European Healthcare' 2019, www.himssanalytics.org/europe/ehealth-barometer/ehealth-trend-barometer-ai-use-european-healthcare

HIMSS Analytics, 'Enabling Better Health Through Information and Technology', www.lesiss.org/offres/file_inline_src/445/445_mailing_291018_111749_2.pdf, accessed 30 June 2020.

Hood C, *The Blame Game: Spin, Bureaucracy, and Self-Preservation in Government*, Course Book ed. (Princeton University Press 2010).

Iacobucci G, 'Patient Data Were Shared with Google on an "Inappropriate Legal Basis," Says NHS Data Guardian' (2017) 357 *BMJ* j2439.

Information Commissioner's Office, 'Royal Free – Google DeepMind Trial Failed to Comply with Data Protection Law' 2017, https://ico.org.uk/about-the-ico/news-and-events/news-and-blogs/2017/07/royal-free-google-deepmind-trial-failed-to-comply-with-data-protection-law/, accessed 3 February 2021.

Jha S and Topol E, 'Adapting to Artificial Intelligence: Radiologists and Pathologists as Information Specialists' (2016) 316 *JAMA* 2353.

Karanikolos M and others, 'Financial Crisis, Austerity, and Health in Europe' (2013) 381 *Lancet* 1323.

Kazley AS and Ozcan YA, 'Organizational and Environmental Determinants of Hospital EMR Adoption: A National Study' (2007) 31 *Journal of Medical Systems* 375.

Komorowski M and others, 'The Artificial Intelligence Clinician Learns Optimal Treatment Strategies for Sepsis in Intensive Care' (2018) 24 *Nature Medicine* 1716.

Kovarik CL, 'Patient Perspectives on the Use of Artificial Intelligence' (2020) 156 *JAMA Dermatology* 493.

Krishnan L, Ogunwole SM and Cooper LA, 'Historical Insights on Coronavirus Disease 2019 (COVID-19), the 1918 Influenza Pandemic, and Racial Disparities: Illuminating a Path Forward' (2020) 173 *Annals of Internal Medicine* 474.

Kruse CS and Beane A, 'Health Information Technology Continues to Show Positive Effect on Medical Outcomes: Systematic Review' (2018) 20 *Journal of Medical Internet Research* e41.

Kujala S and others, 'The Role of Frontline Leaders in Building Health Professional Support for a New Patient Portal: Survey Study' (2019) 21 *Journal of Medical Internet Research* e11413.

Legg S and Hutter M, 'A Collection of Definitions of Intelligence' (2007) 157 *Frontiers in Artificial Intelligence and Applications* 17.

Limb M, 'Controversial Database of Medical Records is Scrapped over Security Concerns' (2016) 354 *BMJ* i3804.

Lokuge S and others, 'Organizational Readiness for Digital Innovation: Development and Empirical Calibration of a Construct' (2019) 56 *Information and Management* 445.

Malin JL, 'Envisioning Watson as a Rapid-Learning System for Oncology' (2013) 9 *Journal of Oncology Practice* 155.

Manz CR and others, 'Validation of a Machine Learning Algorithm to Predict 180-Day Mortality for Outpatients with Cancer' (2020) 6(11) *JAMA Oncology* 1723–30.

McCall B, 'COVID-19 and Artificial Intelligence: Protecting Health-Care Workers and Curbing the Spread' (2020) 2 *Lancet Digital Health* e166.

Miech EJ and others, 'Inside Help: An Integrative Review of Champions in Healthcare-Related Implementation' (2018) 6 *SAGE Open Medicine* 2050312118773261.

Mileti D, Gillespie D and Haas J, 'Size and Structure in Complex Organizations' (1977) 56 *Social Forces* 208.

Minor L, 'The Rise of the Data-Driven Physician' Stanford Medicine 2020 Health Trends Report, https://med.stanford.edu/dean/healthtrends.html, accessed 6 February 2022.

Muse ED and others, 'Towards a Smart Medical Home' (2017) 389 *Lancet* 358.

Nagendran M and others, 'Artificial Intelligence Versus Clinicians: Systematic Review of Design, Reporting Standards, and Claims of Deep Learning Studies' (2020) 368 *BMJ* m689.

Nelson A and others, 'Predicting Scheduled Hospital Attendance with Artificial Intelligence' (2019) 2 *npj Digital Medicine* 26.

Obermeyer Z and Lee TH, 'Lost in Thought – The Limits of the Human Mind and the Future of Medicine' (2017) 377 *New England Journal of Medicine* 1209.

OECD, 'AI Strategies & Public Sector Components – Observatory of Public Sector Innovation' 2021, https://oecd-opsi.org/projects/ai/strategies/, accessed 3 February 2021.

OECD, *Handbook on Constructing Composite Indicators: Methodology and User Guide* (OECD Publishing 2008).

OECD, *Health at a Glance: Europe 2016: State of Health in the EU Cycle* (OECD 2016).

OECD and European Union, *Health at a Glance: Europe 2020* (OECD Publishing 2020).

Oxford Insights, 'Government AI Readiness Index 2020' 2020, www.oxfordinsights.com/government-ai-readiness-index-2020, accessed 3 February 2021.

Panch T, Szolovits P and Atun R, 'Artificial Intelligence, Machine Learning and Health Systems' (2018) 8 *Journal of Global Health* 020303.

Paré G and others, 'Clinicians' Perceptions of Organizational Readiness for Change in the Context of Clinical Information System Projects: Insights from Two Cross-Sectional Surveys' (2011) 6 *Implementation Science* 15.

Patel TA and others, 'Correlating Mammographic and Pathologic Findings in Clinical Decision Support Using Natural Language Processing and Data Mining Methods' (2017) 123 *Cancer* 114.

Perrault R and others, *Artificial Intelligence Index Report 2019* (Human-Centered AI Institute, Stanford University 2019).

Petkus H, Hoogewerf J and Wyatt JC, 'What Do Senior Physicians Think about AI and Clinical Decision Support Systems: Quantitative and Qualitative Analysis of Data from Specialty Societies' (2020) 20 *Clinical Medicine* 324.

Pettit L, 'Understanding EMRAM and How It Can be Used by Policy-Makers, Hospital CIOs and Their IT Teams' (2013) 49 *World Hospitals and Health Services* 7.

Piwek L and others, 'The Rise of Consumer Health Wearables: Promises and Barriers' (2016) 13 *PLoS Medicine* e1001953.

Powles J and Hodson H, 'Google DeepMind and Healthcare in an Age of Algorithms' (2017) 7 *Health Technology* 351.

PwC, *European Hospital Survey: Benchmarking Deployment of eHealth Services (2012–2013),* final report (JCR Scientific and Policy, 2014).

Rajkomar A and others, 'Scalable and Accurate Deep Learning with Electronic Health Records' (2018) 1 *npj Digital Medicine* 18.

Rawson TM and others, 'Artificial Intelligence Can Improve Decision-Making in Infection Management' (2019) 3 *Nature Human Behaviour* 543.

Rossi F, Artificial Intelligence: Potential Benefits and Ethical Considerations (2016) Briefing Paper to the European Union Parliament Policy Department C: Citizens' Rights and Constitutional Affairs European Parliament, www.europarl.europa.eu/RegData/etudes/BRIE/2016/571380/IPOL_BRI(2016)571380_EN.pdf

Schleicher A, *The Case for 21st Century Learning*, Vol. 282 (OECD Observer 2011), www.oecd.org/general/thecasefor21st-centurylearning.htm

Schmidt C, 'MD Anderson Breaks with IBM Watson, Raising Questions about Artificial Intelligence in Oncology' (2017) 109 *JNCI: Journal of the National Cancer Institute*, doi: 10.1093/jnci/djx113

Sharpe A, *Literature Review of Frameworks for Macro-Indicators* (Centre for the Study of Living Standards 2004).

Shaw J and others, 'Artificial Intelligence and the Implementation Challenge' (2019) 21 *Journal of Medical Internet Research* e13659.

Shortliffe EH and Sepulveda MJ, 'Clinical Decision Support in the Era of Artificial Intelligence' (2018) 320 *JAMA* 2199.

Singer JD and Braun HI, 'Testing International Education Assessments' (2018) 360 *Science* 38

Somashekhar SP and others, 'Watson for Oncology and Breast Cancer Treatment Recommendations: Agreement with an Expert Multidisciplinary Tumor Board' (2018) 29 *Annals of Oncology* 418.

Southon FC, Sauer C and Grant CN, 'Information Technology in Complex Health Services: Organizational Impediments to Successful Technology Transfer and Diffusion' (1997) 4 *Journal of the American Medical Informatics Association* 112.

Stephani V, Busse R and Geissler A, 'Benchmarking der Krankenhaus-IT: Deutschland im internationalen Vergleich' in Klauber J and others (eds), *Krankenhaus-Report 2019: Das digitale Krankenhaus* (Springer Berlin Heidelberg 2019).

Strickland E, 'IBM Watson, Heal Thyself: How IBM Overpromised and Underdelivered on AI Health Care' (2019) 56 *IEEE Spectrum* 24.

Thiel R and others, *#SmartHealthSystems – Focus Europe* (Bertelsmann Stiftung 2019).

Thunea T and Mina A, 'Hospitals as Innovators in the Health-Care System: A Literature Review and Research Agenda' (2016) 45 *Research Policy* 1545.

Ting DSW and others, 'Digital Technology and COVID-19' (2020) 26 *Nature Medicine* 459.

Topol EJ, 'High-Performance Medicine: The Convergence of Human and Artificial Intelligence' (2019) 25 *Nature Medicine* 44.

van Limburg M and others, 'Why Business Modeling is Crucial in the Development of eHealth Technologies' (2011) 13 *Journal of Medical Internet Research* e124.

van Staa TP and others, 'Big Health Data: The Need to Earn Public Trust' (2016) 354 *BMJ* i3636.

Vayena E, Blasimme A and Cohen IG, 'Machine Learning in Medicine: Addressing Ethical Challenges' (2018) 15 *PLoS Medicine* e1002689.

Wachter R, *Making IT Work: Harnessing the Power of Health Information Technology to Improve Care in England* (Department of Health, 2016).

Wadmann S and Hoeyer K, 'Dangers of the Digital Fit: Rethinking Seamlessness and Social Sustainability in Data-Intensive Healthcare' (2018) 5 *Big Data & Society* 2053951717752964.

Weng SF and others, 'Can Machine-Learning Improve Cardiovascular Risk Prediction Using Routine Clinical Data?' (2017) 12 *PLoS One* e0174944.

Wind A and van Harten WH, 'Benchmarking Specialty Hospitals, A Scoping Review on Theory and Practice' (2017) 17 *BMC Health Services Research* 245.

World Health Organization Regional Office for Europe, 'Core Health Indicators in the WHO European Region 2019. Special focus: Health 2020' 2019, www.euro.who.int/__data/assets/pdf_file/0004/413239/CHI_2019_EN_WEB.pdf

Yusif S, Hafeez-Baig A and Soar J, 'e-Health Readiness Assessment Factors and Measuring Tools: A Systematic Review' (2017) 107 *International Journal of Medical Informatics* 56.

Zeevi D and others, 'Personalized Nutrition by Prediction of Glycemic Responses' (2015) 163 *Cell* 1079.

Zhou Y and others, 'Artificial Intelligence in COVID-19 Drug Repurposing' (2020) 2 *Lancet Digital Health* e667.

13

Regulating the 'Benefits' of eHealth

Information Disclosure Duties in the Age of AI

MARC STAUCH

13.1 Introduction

In health care, as in other spheres of life, complex data-analytical processes, steered by artificial intelligence (AI), are increasingly influencing day-to-day decisions. Moreover, such developments may be regarded as a political and economic necessity: thus, even before the current COVID-19 public health crisis, demographic change in Western countries was rendering the costs of traditional health care systems unsustainable. Equally, the patient's interest in autonomy is enhanced by the ability to distinguish cases where inconvenient medical treatment, including hospitalisation, is required, as opposed to where the condition can be managed with more conservative care in the home environment.[1]

At the same time, as highlighted by other contributors to this volume, there are significant concerns about potential unwanted side-effects to this process of health 'datafication' and analysis, both in terms of the results being inaccurate and/or the risk they may be accessed and misused by third parties. The focus of the present chapter, though, is different: the appropriate management of the new forms of health information, even assuming it is both accurate and secure from misuse. In particular, the discussion will consider ethical and legal rules for deciding when such information should be disclosed to the patient/subject and when it should not.

This new and difficult challenge arises from two new features of health information generation. The first is that health (and other) data collection increasingly takes place outside the traditional health care context of face-to-face interactions between the doctor and patient, and correspondingly is less likely to have been solicited by the patient/subject to whom it

[1] See European Commission, 'Green Paper on Mobile Health ("mHealth")' COM(2014) 219 final, 2014; EU Task Force on eHealth, 'Redesigning Health in Europe for 2020' 2012.

relates. In the second place, the information generated is more often no longer concerned simply with the 'here and now' – the person's present state of health – but assumes increasing predictive power: what conditions is this person likely to develop in the next ten or twenty years?

Traditionally, access to information about their health has been conceived of as something of benefit to persons (or even, indeed, their 'right'). However, it will be questioned how far, given the change of context described, and the advent of ever more accurate predictive algorithms, this conception should still be accepted. Indeed, it is suggested that, without clear ethical or legal rules governing this, there may be a danger of 'over-disclosure' of such information, with negative effects for the concerned subject, or even society at large.[2]

The argument will proceed in three main stages. In Section 13.2, there will be a consideration of the multiple new contexts in which health data may be collected (and information be generated), with little input or influence from the person to whom it relates. In addition, the nature of the information is considered and a broad distinction suggested between that which applies an actual (current) medical diagnosis to the person and that which purports to predict how a person's health condition will change and develop in the future.

Following this, in Section 13.3, there will be an assessment of existing situations in which (in the traditional health care context) unsolicited health information is sometimes disclosed, and the ethical rules that apply to guide the information holder (here doctors or researchers) in doing so. This has been an issue especially in the context of genetic tests on persons that reveal information about the genetic status of their close relatives, and where – as a counterweight to the presumption sometimes in favour of disclosure – a 'right not to know' has also gained traction. There is also consideration of legal requirements that may operate.

In Section 13.4, the chapter then seeks to apply the relevant lessons from Section 13.3 to the increasing number of situations in which AI data mining will now turn up unsolicited health information, so as to outline a framework that may assist information holders (who frequently will no longer be trained health professionals) in thinking about their potential disclosure/non-disclosure duties to subjects. Section 13.5 then concludes by briefly considering how far existing legal liability rules remain sufficient in this area, or if new bespoke legislation is needed.

2 One such danger is the phenomenon of 'cyberchondria', where persons increasingly experience anxiety about possibly suffering from conditions they learn of through the use of ICT and digital media.

13.2 New Forms of Health Information Generation

For the purposes of this chapter, we shall take health information to mean any information, either of an actual (diagnostic) or a predictive (prognostic) nature, relating to the physical or mental state of a given individual. While the information can sometimes be 'read' straight from the data concerning that individual (e.g., a photograph may directly show a given skin disease), those are the obvious cases. In most instances, the information will instead be generated by mining or analysing the data, using some form of algorithmic process.

Computer algorithms, designed to assist in health diagnostics, are developed by using multiple sources of data relating to many past and current patients. Typically, the data scientist will begin with retrospective data sets (where the outcome, in terms of the target value of interest) is also present in the data set itself. Thus, a data set might show a set of medical values plus other variables of interest (e.g., smoker/non-smoker) for past patients presenting with lung diseases (both non-malignant and malignant). Let it be assumed that lung cancer is the target value of interest; the scientists will look for patterns in the variables in the data sets, which show correlations between some combinations of that other data and the target value 'yes/no' for the diagnosis of the cancer.

The patterns identified will then be encoded in an algorithm, which will be trained on further data sets where it is provided just with the other data, omitting the 'yes/no' data point, and asked to calculate what the diagnosis was from the other data; the data researcher who will have the complete set (including the target value) can then check how well the algorithm performs in its calculations. After the algorithm is tweaked as required, it may then be set to work in practice on prospective data sets, where, as yet, the presence of the target value really is unknown, and will assist doctors by offering a diagnosis: how likely is it that this particular new patient has lung cancer? AI-driven algorithms have a further feature in the form of a feedback loop, where they are later provided with further relevant data gathered from the patient, including the ultimate diagnosis, and configured to self-adjust in the light of this, thereby 'learning' from the process, so as to become ever more accurate.[3]

[3] See, on data-analytic processes generally, F Provost and T Fawcett, *Data Science for Business* (O'Reilly Media 2013). On algorithms – including their use in the health context – see H Fry, *Hello World* (Norton 2018).

13.2.1 *Algorithmic Advances in Predictive Information Discovery*

The above algorithm provides diagnostic information concerning a patient's present state (are they suffering from lung cancer?). However, algorithms may equally be developed in order to allow predictions about the future. So, the question or target value may be: will this patient develop lung cancer in ten years' time? In principle, the analytical processes are the same, but far more data is needed (which before now would scarcely have been available) – that is, one needs a detailed data set showing the health and other attributes of a large number of persons at a time ten years before a subgroup of them are diagnosed with lung cancer.

In the past, predicting how any given individual's health would develop was very difficult, given the sheer quantity of imponderable variables. It is true that genetic testing would sometimes turn up highly accurate predictive information, but this was very much an exception. It worked/works in the small number of cases of serious mono-genetic disorders (e.g., Huntington's Disease), where a single factor is so dominant and exclusionary of all other variables that one can indeed say that a person with that particular genetic biomarker will definitely go on in the future to develop the relevant disorder. Much more common is the situation where an illness results from a multiplicity of co-existent conditions, both physical features of the patients – their particular set of genes and proteins – and of the environmental influences (including diet, air-quality, radium-levels, and the millions of other things) that surround them.

Looked at in terms of the classical deterministic causal model of Mill (refined by Mackie),[4] for any given effect in the world, there must be an antecedent causal set made up of multiple necessary conditions that, taken together, are sufficient for the effect. Predictive certainty is generally hampered by incomplete knowledge in a given case as to how far the antecedent conditions are present and/or interact for the outcome of interest. Do the observable conditions represent cumulative – together sufficient – conditions at all? Or do some cancel others out? And how far do they constitute the total set? Are further – as yet unknown – conditions also needed?[5]

An illustration may help at this point: suppose we collect 100 biomarker values from a person in order to predict whether he will later develop lung

[4] JS Mill, *A System of Logic* (John W Parker 1843), Book III, ch. 5; JL Mackie, *The Cement of the Universe: A Study of Causation* (Clarendon Press 1980).

[5] For an illuminating application of this approach to allocating legal responsibility for harmful events, see RW Wright, 'Causation in Tort law' (1985) 73 *California Law Review* 1735.

cancer; we then compare it to a set of biomarkers taken from 2,000 persons, 1,000 of whom later were diagnosed with lung cancer and 1,000 who never developed it. Suppose further that the comparison shows the values are the same in our patient to those for 800 persons in the group which developed the disease, but also to 400 of the group that did not. What are we entitled to infer from this? Most clearly that we possess – in the form of the 100 biomarkers – an incomplete picture of the set(s) of conditions necessary and (together) sufficient for developing the disease.

First, the fact that 200 persons in the disease group had dissimilar biomarkers but also developed lung cancer shows the 100 biomarkers are not in fact necessary for the disease – there must also be an alternative causal mechanism, involving a different, as yet unidentified set of biomarkers. Secondly, there is the fact that 400 persons with the same biomarker values did not develop the disease: this shows the presence of the 100 biomarkers is also insufficient for the disease. Rather, the complete causal set must also contain further, as yet unidentified biomarkers, ones that – while they were present in 800 of the patients who developed the disease, were absent from the 400 patients who did not. The upshot is that we can at most make a probabilistic statement for our person, for example, that he has a 70% likelihood of developing lung cancer.[6]

However, the above picture has now been significantly (albeit not completely) altered by the use of new AI-driven algorithms. Thus, as Mayer-Schönberger and Cukier describe, one of the most striking features of such algorithms is that they are quite indifferent about intricate causal set relationships, as described in the previous paragraphs: a pattern in data generated by co-variables (that simply correlate as opposed to standing in any confirmed causal relationship) is just as serviceable from their perspective. Indeed, they have the uncanny ability to cut through extraneous detail to pinpoint those co-variable patterns of especially striking predictive power.[7]

It remains true that predictive statements based on correlations necessarily retain some probabilistic element, reflecting uncertainties in underlying assumptions made by the relevant algorithm.[8] As we have

[6] See M Stauch, 'Causation, Risk, and Loss of Chance in Medical Negligence' (1997) 17 *Oxford Journal of Legal Studies* 205.

[7] V Mayer-Schönberger and K Cukier, *Big Data* (John Murray 2013), ch. 4.

[8] See JH Chen, 'Machine Learning and Prediction in Medicine – Beyond the Peak of Inflated Expectations' (2017) 376:26 *New England Journal of Medicine* 2507; see also Mayer-Schönberger and Cukier, *Big Data*, 'Afterword'.

seen, the complete (causal) knowledge needed to say what will happen in a specific individual case is not there – indeed, such knowledge would have to extend to the specific future factors in the case, which are inherently unknowable: will the patient still be alive to develop lung cancer, or may he have died in an accident? Or – more prosaically – will he continue to stick to the same diet? Nevertheless, it appears clear that the use of algorithms based on correlations – particularly when enhanced with data-feedback loops and steered by AI – provides a shortcut through causal complexity, allowing predictions of much greater power and probabilistic accuracy than were previously possible.

13.2.2 Greatly Increased Data Collection

As hinted, one reason algorithms are now ever more powerful is the scope for testing them out on far more data than before. Thus, in the health context, in the past, the process of collecting the relevant data usually occurred in the limited context of a doctor–patient interaction in a health care setting. A person (the patient) would, on experiencing symptoms of illness, attend a health practice and allow the doctor to collect data (history of symptoms, measurements of physical attributes and parameters, tissues and samples for further analysis) required for the doctor to reach a considered diagnosis and suggest an appropriate therapy.

Nowadays, of course, doctors and hospitals have at their disposal modern diagnostic devices and equipment, capable of scooping up data from patients in far greater quantities and far more quickly than before; however, the most radical changes in health data collection have occurred outside health care institutions in the everyday world. In particular, there has been an explosion in the market for mobile applications (including 'wearables' with integrated apps) that enable individuals to track their own health and lifestyle activities. Indeed, back in 2014, the European Commission 'Green Paper on Mobile Health' had cited a figure of nearly 100,000 apps on offer in the broad continuum of health/lifestyle, of which some two-thirds were for personal consumer use (both for general fitness monitoring and the self-management of specific conditions).[9] Such apps are powerful data capturers with the ability to monitor the user's health status in real time, and to analyse the data collected in order to offer the user appropriate advice (and reminders) relevant to the daily management of chronic conditions.

[9] European Commission, 'Green Paper on Mobile Health', 7.

Whereas, in the case of mobile apps, the individual may be said to retain a degree of control over the collection of their data and its conversion to health information,[10] there are other recent developments that entirely dispose of such control. This is especially apparent in terms of the growth of networked sensors (as part of the 'Internet of Things') that automatically capture data which potentially can be harvested to produce health information. Thus, as a person goes about their daily business, their movements and bodily features and expressions are more and more likely to be picked up by all manner of sensors; these may be cameras and microphones, but also other sensors incorporated into objects such as smart fridges or self-adjusting car-seats. All of these capture health data (or related 'proxy data') on individuals and store it locally or transmit it to the cloud.

13.2.3 The New Power of 'Proxy Data'

Another resource is provided by the vast amounts of data about themselves that individuals place daily on social networking platforms and other websites, in the form of films, photographs, writing samples, and the like. In the past, most of this data would not have been thought to have much if anything to do with a person's health status, but in the light of the development of intelligent algorithms we are learning to think differently. Thus, in her book *Hello World*, Fry describes the 'Nun Study', which began in the US in 1986.[11] There, a group of some 800 nuns agreed that their brains could be used for post-mortem research into neurodegenerative conditions, including Alzheimer's, as well as making other data about themselves, spanning their entire lives in the convent, available to the researchers. The task of the algorithm the researchers developed was to find correlations between the subgroup of nuns whose brains showed degenerative signs and patterns in the earlier data.

In the event, one of the most accurate predictors in the earlier data of whether a given nun would go on to develop Alzheimer's turned out to be the complexity of the sentence constructions she used in her writing – in some cases, the samples were from application letters they had written to the convent fifty or more years prior to any signs of the disease. Similarly, in their work, *Big Data*, Mayer-Schönberger and Cukier describe recent

[10] An interesting issue to note in passing is the voluntariness of apps whose use is pushed by health insurers (as a condition for offering lower-cost cover); see also Section 4.3.

[11] Fry, *Hello World*, 90–91.

research on 'datafying' seating posture picked up by car-seat sensors, as well as tremor patterns in mobile phone sensors, which may be deciphered to provide highly accurate predictions for health conditions such as Parkinson's.[12]

This ability of intelligent algorithms to find patterns in even the most innocuous data to generate highly sensitive health information poses radical new challenges. As discussed elsewhere in this volume, data protection law currently imposes limits in terms of collecting and storing data. However, given the huge social benefits of data analysis noted at the outset of this chapter, including the help it can offer in the newly important area of public health (in identifying pandemic countermeasures), it should be accepted that the data will be collected and analysed. Indeed, it appears data protection law is already shifting its focus from curtailing data collection or analysis as such to regulating specific (a priori unjustified) data analyses (or, where the analysis as such was justified, subsequent harmful uses of the information generated).[13]

In this regard, as suggested, one potentially harmful informational use for which the law will need to establish rules concerns the disclosure/return of individual health information to the relevant subject (including where the subjects was previously unaware of its existence). To this end, the chapter next considers the traditional rules that have been applied (by doctors in the health care context) for disclosing information to their patients, before seeking to draw out lessons this may provide for guiding health information disclosure in the age of AI.

13.3 Traditional Health Information Disclosure Practices

Typically, in the traditional health care context, the doctor would disclose information relating to the actual diagnosis plus any further information needed by the patient to follow the prescribed therapy. In cases where the current symptoms could be manifestations ('warning signs') of some chronic developing condition, which the patient could influence by lifestyle choices, the doctor might well also draw the patient's attention in a predictive way to the future risk for the patient of developing that condition unless that patient took steps to avoid this (by making lifestyle

[12] Mayer-Schönberger and Cukier, *Big Data*, 76–77, 95.

[13] FH Cate and others, *Data Protection Principles for the 21st Century* (Maurer Faculty Report 2013). This is reflected in part in the more 'risk-based' approach taken in the GDPR (EU regulation 2016/679), as opposed to the earlier Data Protection Directive 95/46 EC.

changes). Generally, the doctor would remain relatively vague about the risks – partly because the vagaries of predictive knowledge about the future foreclosed anything more detailed, but also out of circumspection and respect for the patient's emotional interests. If a particular patient wanted to know more, and asked for specific probabilities, the doctor might then attempt to be more specific.[14]

Admittedly, the advent of predictive genetic testing in the twentieth century changed this situation somewhat. As noted in Section 13.2, this has emerged as a practice in relation to members of families with a history of a given mono-genetic disorder. There, a person may wish to know their status once and for all, rather than living on in uncertainty, and in such cases, where the patient voluntarily seeks the information, then, even if the doctor is highly concerned as to the effect it may have on the patient's well-being, ethically it appears right to disclose – the effect of not doing so would be directly disrespectful of the patient's autonomy, and likely simply to leave them in greater uncertainty.[15] However, such cases also begin to reveal the challenges involved in disclosure: there is an ethical debate, for example, over whether certain categories of people should be allowed to get tested for incurable late-onset conditions such as Huntington's Disease.[16]

More recently, a practice has developed of carrying out predictive testing on unborn children. These too – even where the prospective mother/parents ostensibly wished to be tested – expose the challenges of communicating the resulting information. Indeed, they are often more complex than mono-genetic disorder testing of adults, as typically foetuses are subject to a range of different tests, some providing simple 'yes/no' answers (the presence of the chromosome for Down's Syndrome), but in other cases only probabilistic in form. Here, it may not be possible to guess in advance if the information revealed by the testing will be helpful. Indeed, empirical research suggests a significant proportion of women who state retrospectively that, if they had appreciated the complexity of the information (and of deciding how to act on it), they would have refused testing.[17]

[14] See T Beauchamp and J Childress, *Principles of Biomedical Ethics*, 5th ed. (Oxford University Press 2001) 283ff.

[15] Legally, too, the patient will have a right to access such information (inter alia under data protection law).

[16] RE Duncan, 'Predictive Genetic Testing in Young People: When is It Appropriate?' (2004) 40 *Journal of Paediatrics and Child Health* 593.

[17] BL Gammon and others, 'Decisional Regret in Women Receiving High Risk or Inconclusive Prenatal Cell-Free DNA Screening Results' (2020) 33(8) *Journal of Maternal-Fetal and Neonatal Medicine* 1412.

13.3.1 Disclosure Norms Where Information Is Not Solicited by the Patient/Subject

The above scenarios relate to 'solicited information' – that is, the patient putatively wanted the information. What about situations involving unsolicited information? In such cases, the subject may be aware that information is available, but may prefer not to know it; or they may simply not know of its existence in the first place. Here, it is apparent that both professional medical ethics and the law have been very reluctant to impose disclosure duties on the doctor.

At first sight, this may appear a slightly surprising claim: after all, did not the twentieth century witness the victory of patient autonomy (over old-fashioned medical paternalism) in the form of the courts upholding the right to informed consent, as seen in landmark judgements such as *Canterbury* v. *Spence*, *Rogers* v. *Whitaker*,[18] and now in the UK, *Montgomery* v. *Lanarkshire Health Board*?[19] Though true, it is important to recall the specific context where the duty to impart unsolicited information arises. This is prior to the doctor intervening therapeutically (and invasively) to treat the patient. The content of the required disclosure is the inherent risk that the intervention may lead to additional, 'iatrogenic' injury. In these circumstances, the doctor gains the 'licence' to expose the patient to the risk by ensuring the latter properly understands and accepts it.[20]

A further context in which, at least ethically,[21] a duty of unsolicited health information disclosure has been accepted in principle, is with respect to 'incidental findings' (IFs) that may emerge in medical research when a subject is examined as part of a given clinical study or trial. For example, in an Alzheimer's study, a brain scan might be performed on volunteers who make up the 'control group' (i.e., the healthy comparator group) to the research group of patients exhibiting signs of disease. In some such cases, the scan may show up an unexpected abnormality, such

18 US DC Appeals Court, 464 F 2d 772 (1972); HCA (1993) 4 Med LR 79.

19 (2015) UKSC 11. This authority in fact goes further than the others by imposing a duty to advise of comparative risks of alternative treatments, so as to allow the patient to decide how she wishes her pregnancy to be managed. But the context was still one of entrusting her fate into the hands of the doctors.

20 For a clear judicial exposition and discussion, see *Chester* v. *Afshar* (at the Court of Appeal stage) [2002] EWCA Civ 724.

21 There appear to be no relevant legal authorities.

as a tumour. Here, a significant body of literature has evolved, including empirical studies of the attitudes of the different parties involved, as to when exactly the communications of such findings to the subject may be indicated.

According to this, an important factor is the extent to which the information is liable to be clarifying and empowering for subjects, resulting in the ability to make decisions which are in keeping with their personal values, as opposed to being overwhelming and thus undermining their ability to decide. Here, potential benefits derive from the respect shown to subjects as autonomous agents through the act of disclosure, as well as the fact that the knowledge of an IF may give them the opportunity to prepare themselves psychologically, emotionally, and financially for the future.

At the same time, the researcher, as the information holder, is necessarily in the position of trying to second-guess these matters for the subject, and should remain mindful that their values may differ from those of the subject.[22] Here, it appears that researchers may indeed be more cautious than subjects would wish. Thus, according to one empirical study,[23] participants placed greater emphasis on the ethical right to receive information regardless of the potential consequences. By contrast, researchers appeared more concerned that the return of an IF might cause the subject anxiety and distress. They also adverted to resource implications (of the counselling regarded as an essential accompaniment to the IF feedback), and the broader institutional burden of tracking and storing IFs over time.

Be that as it may, it is apparent that in the above context too, certain special factors (militating in favour of unsolicited disclosure) are at play. These include the heightened duty of care that researchers are regarded generally as owing to subjects (based on the altruistic nature of research participation), as well as the possibility that the subject may rely adversely on the non-communication of a given finding (i.e., they may interpret the non-return of an IF as meaning they are positively in good health). Another significant feature is that the subject will, in any case, be forewarned that they may receive such information. Not only will they have actively undergone the relevant diagnostic procedures, but the informed

[22] RM Epstein and others, 'Withholding Information from Patients – When Less Is More' (2010) 362 (5) *New England Journal of Medicine* 380.

[23] C Cole and others, '"Ethical Responsibility" or "a Whole Can of Worms": Differences in Opinion on Incidental Finding Review and Disclosure in Neuroimaging Research from Focus Group Discussions with Participants, Parents, IRB Members, Investigators, Physicians and Community Members' (2015) 41 *Journal of Medical Ethics* 841.

consent form they signed will make clear the circumstances in which they can expect to receive feedback.[24]

13.3.2 Ethical Concerns about Other Unsolicited Disclosures

Beyond these two contexts (invasive therapy and research studies), the position is much less clear whether and when disclosure may be justified. Thus, there is the well-known dilemma arising from genetic testing for mono-genetic disorders, regarding how far close family relations of the patient should be informed of results that apply to them as well. In the case of serious, incurable conditions, especially, ethical opinion is highly divided, with some commentators taking the view that autonomy requires disclosure, while others reject this on the basis of the non-maleficence principle, given the devastating effect such information may have on the unwitting subject.[25]

More generally, these incurable cases, and also where the results are uncertain (e.g., they reveal a genetic predisposition giving rise to a 10% chance of bowel cancer, which could be reduced to 5% by adopting a spartan diet), where there is no clear path of action for the recipient, most starkly raise the question of whether information per se should always be seen as a human good. In Western philosophy, there is a longstanding tradition, going back to Aristotle, and reaffirmed by Kant, that this should be answered positively.[26] However, as suggested by the previous discussion, other things must arguably also be true: notably, the information must not be too complex, speculative (couched in terms of conditional probabilities), and/or disturbing for an intelligent person to make a meaningful choice.[27]

[24] As a matter of good practice, researchers will be required to have a policy in place to cover the feedback of such findings; A Thorogood and others, 'An Implementation Framework for the Feedback of Individual Research Results and Incidental Findings in Research' (2014) 15 *BMC Medical Ethics* 88.

[25] See R Gilbar, 'Communicating Genetic Information in the Family: The Familial Relationship as the Forgotten Factor' (2007) 33 *Journal of Medical Ethics* 390; B Godard and others, 'Guidelines for Disclosing Genetic Information to Family Members: From Development to Use' (2006) 5 *Familial Cancer* 103.

[26] R Andorno, 'The Right Not to Know – An Autonomy-Based Approach' (2004) 30 *Journal of Medical Ethics* 435.

[27] This ties in, it is suggested, with the conception of autonomy argued for by Gerald Dworkin, in which it is not choice per se that is of value, but an agent's ability to choose in accordance with their second order system of values and aims: G Dworkin, *The Theory and Practice of Autonomy* (Cambridge University Press 1988).

In this regard, an influential academic perspective, which embodies a neutral or even prima facie negative stance to information disclosure is the suggestion by Laurie and others of a basic 'right' (or at least interest) persons have to not receive unsolicited information.[28] This, Laurie argues, exists as an aspect of a person's 'spatial privacy' – that is, their right to be left alone and not imposed upon externally by other persons. It is a free-standing interest that persists – and should be taken account of – independently of other values (autonomy and beneficence) and mandates a default attitude of caution that should guide putative information disclosers.[29]

13.3.3 Legal Issues in Respect of Unsolicited Disclosure

Turning to the law, as suggested already, outside the context of warning of risks from interventional therapy, the courts have largely resisted arguments for imposing a legal duty to disclose. Thus, where the doctor is not the patient's doctor, but discovers health information about them in the course of examining them on behalf of a third party (e.g., their employer), several cases deny that such a duty arises;[30] this may, however, be otherwise in the case of an imminent, and reasonably treatable, dangerous condition.[31]

Similar difficulty surrounds the duty of geneticists to disclose a patient's test findings to relatives who are also implicated by the results; here, as suggested by the recent English authority of *ABC* v. *St George's Hospital*,[32] the courts will be guided by the professional ethical position, and will likely only impose a duty where normative ethics also mandates disclosure.[33] As Yip J. noted in her judgement, 'the legal duty runs parallel to the professional duty to undertake a proper balancing exercise'; and 'non-disclosure

[28] G Laurie, 'In Defence of Ignorance: Genetic Information and the Right Not to Know' (1999) 6 *European Journal of Health Law* 119; Andorno, 'The Right Not to Know'. Such a right is recognised in the 1997 Council of Europe (Oviedo) Convention on Human Rights and Biomedicine (albeit for contexts where the subject could be asked – and express the desire not to know – in advance).

[29] G Laurie, 'Recognizing the Right Not to Know: Conceptual, Professional, and Legal Implications' (2014) 42 *Journal of Law, Medicine and Ethics* 53.

[30] *X (minors)* v. *Bedfordshire CC* [1995] 2 AC 633, per Lord Brown-Wilkinson (*obiter*); *Kapfunde* v. *Abbey National Plc* [1999] Lloyd's Rep Med. 48.

[31] See *Stokes* v. *Guest Keen and Nettlefold Bolts & Nuts Ltd* [1968] 1 WLR 1776; a relevant US case is *James* v. *United States*, 483 F. Supp. 581 (1980).

[32] (2020) EWHC 455 (QB).

[33] Thus, in the case of a *treatable* life-threatening condition, there will be a duty to inform the primary patient that their relatives are at risk of developing the same condition (so the

is the default position'.[34] As this makes apparent, in this area of finely balanced, often speculative and hard to quantify risks, the law will usually be reluctant to second-guess the judgement of an experienced medical professional.

The legal position might up to now be summarised by saying the doctor ordinarily has the discretion (as opposed to duty) to disclose unsolicited information. However, before fully accepting this, we need also to consider the potential legal liability in cases where disclosure *is* made. As discussed, a given piece of information may have a serious impact on the recipient, particularly in terms of mental distress (though other harms may occur).[35] Ethically, as we have seen, the possibility of causing harm engages the principle of non-maleficence, which the doctor should consider when reaching their decision. However, could liability in law also arise for a particular unjustified and harmful disclosure?

In this regard, there are again very few relevant decisions, and these are on the whole against liability. This may also be seen as an aspect of tort law's general reluctance to recognise claims that focus on emotional, as opposed to physical, injury. Indeed, an initial precondition is that the injury must at least amount to a recognised psychiatric condition, which in the circumstances might also have befallen a person of 'reasonable phlegm and fortitude'.[36] Most of the cases do not concern the communication of information, but claimants who were caught up in shocking accidents that led them to fear physical injury or witness physical injury to their loved ones. However, in the medical context, there have been occasional successful claims for psychiatric injury caused by negligently being given distressing information that was false.[37] More generally, English law will compensate for the harm caused if a person deliberately

patient can warn them); in exceptional cases, the doctor may directly inform the relatives. See the US authorities of *Pate* v. *Threlkel*, 661 So2d 278 (1995); and *Safer* v. *Estate of Pack*, 677 A2d 1188 (1996).

34 See (2020) EWHC 455 (QB), at paras 195 and 196. The need to take account of the professional ethical position was also noted by the Court of Appeal in earlier connected proceedings (2017) EWCA Civ 336.

35 For example the patient may suffer a financial loss by having to pay more for health insurance in the future.

36 See *Grieves* v. *F T Everard & Sons* (2007) UKHL 39, which concerned claims for anxiety due to knowledge of a having a latent medical condition associated with heightened health risks. The claimants proceeded not against the discloser of the information, but the creator of the condition.

37 *Allin* v. *City and Hackney HA* (1996) 7 Med LR 167 (mother told falsely that her new-born baby had died); *Farrell* v. *Avon HA* [2001] All ER (D) 17 (father told falsely that his child had been still-born, and given body of another baby to hold).

gives another such information, intending to cause serious distress (or is reckless as to whether it will do so); indeed, compensation will here also lie where the information is true.[38]

By contrast, as regards the (merely) negligent communication of true distressing information, the position remains unclear.[39] A rare case in point is *AB* v. *Tameside & Glossop HA*,[40] in which the health authority sent a letter to around 900 women, informing them that a gynaecologist who had examined them had tested HIV-positive. The defendant conceded it had owed a duty of care to the women in deciding how best to communicate this information, but argued that it had met the required care on the facts (i.e., the decision to send a letter, rather than calling the women in for individual counselling, was not negligent). The Court of Appeal agreed with this assessment and denied liability.[41]

Nonetheless, in that case, it was taken for granted that the disclosure of the health risk itself was justified (on the basis of the authority's responsibility for the source of the risk). And in such cases, as Brooke LJ pointed out, the mode of communicating the news becomes to some extent peripheral, as in practice the claimant will find it very difficult to disentangle the causative impact of this aspect on their mental health from that of the content of the information.[42] By contrast, the decision has nothing to say about the potential liability of a defendant who was under no duty to provide the distressing information, and where its communication per se is found to be unjustified and negligent.

What is clear, at any rate, is that to date, no patient appears to have thought it worth their while to proceed against a doctor for receiving distressing true information. This is unsurprising given that, as discussed, doctors have traditionally been circumspect in disclosing information going beyond the patient's actual diagnosis or other information clearly necessary for the latter's well-being, which they are justified and dutybound to give. By contrast, it would usually not enter their

[38] Under the Rule in *Wilkinson* v. *Downton* (1897) EWHC 1 (QB), as applied by the UK Supreme Court in *Rhodes* v. *OPO* [2015] UKSC 32.

[39] Academically, too, this remains a relatively unexplored area; however, see H Teff, *Causing Psychiatric and Emotional Harm* (Hart 2009), 103 ff.

[40] (1997) PNLR 140.

[41] A relevant fact was the resource implications of proactively organising counselling for the women. The court left open whether the defendant's concession on the anterior duty question (that it had been required to think about the mode of communication) was correct.

[42] See (1997) PNLR 140, at 160: that is, the claim will almost certainly fail (at the latest) at the stage of causation.

heads – unless the patient particularly presses them – to impart detailed predictive information (if they had it) that the patient has a specific chance of developing a specific disease at a specific point in time.

As we saw in Section 13.2, it is the latter kind of information that, given advances in data collection and intelligent algorithms, is now becoming widely available, including beyond the traditional health care context. Section 13.4 considers some further moral conundrums arising from the nature of the new information, and how the law might develop in response, particularly to restrain unjustified and distressing true disclosures.

13.4 Health Information Disclosure Norms for the Age of AI

The cases considered in Section 13.3 show a spectrum of the possible situations in which the information holder (in those cases a health professional) may be called upon to exercise judgement on whether or not to disclose health information to the subject. Especially in cases where the patient did not solicit disclosure, such decisions may be finely balanced even after the event, it may not be very clear whether the disclosure was really justified. As discussed, in the medical ethical context, such cases implicate the opposing values of patient autonomy (wherein information is regarded positively as empowering) and non-maleficence (where it is seen as a source of potential harm due to its propensity to distress and confuse the patient). But sometimes there may be no conflict: as suggested earlier, if the effect of the information is to turn the recipient into a mental wreck (or if the nature of the information is not such as to allow, at least potentially, a reasonable choice of action), then autonomy is not served by disclosing it, nor sacrificed by its non-disclosure.

So what guiding principles might be suggested now for disclosure of the far greater amounts of information generated by health algorithms in the age of AI? As noted, such information will increasingly have been generated outside the traditional health care context, and the holders will not be trained health professionals used to dealing with such information, but an algorithm researcher or user (such as an insurance company), or even just an ordinary person who 'reads' the information off a photograph on a social media site.[43] Correspondingly, the putative recipient usually will

[43] Thus, a white-eye-flash in a photo may be a sign of retinoblastoma, a form of childhood eye-cancer: see *ITV News*, 'Facebook Picture Helps Save Life of Little Gracie', 19 May 2014, www.itv.com/news/anglia/2014-05-19/facebook-picture-helps-save-the-life-of-little-gracie. As noted, in Section 13.1, instances where the information is readable directly from the data in this way are exceptional.

lack the degree of forewarning they would have had in the health care context, where they typically would interact with a health care professional because they already felt unwell in some way.

13.4.1 *Unsolicited Disclosures of Diagnostic Information*

First, given the potential benefit of some kinds of information, it is hard to maintain that it should never be disclosed in an unsolicited way. This is true, in particular, where the information is clear and actionable, providing the subject with a reasonably straightforward path to avoid serious harm. Admittedly, we are here concerned with information holders who, as non-trained professionals, are unlikely to know, even approximately, what the chances, medically, of successfully treating the subject's condition are; but they are entitled to proceed on the commonsense assumption that, the earlier the subject receives treatment, the better these will stand.

Even so, the modalities of communication remain important. Here, the lay information holders will lack either the experience or resources for achieving a tactful and informed disclosure of potentially distressing information. Should they, in those circumstances, take upon themselves the task themselves of doing so? The answer to that appears to be a clear no: they should instead simply advise the subject to see a doctor. It is in any case only the latter who will be able to pronounce a conclusive diagnosis and initiate treatment.

The position here can be likened to a rescue situation, where it is generally accepted that a layperson should not intervene if there are professional rescuers to hand. Indeed, were they to do so, the former may potentially be liable in negligence for worsening the victim's situation relative to what it would have been had the rescue been left to the professionals.[44] This is not an exact analogy: the lay information discloser who officiously (possibly even maliciously)[45] provides direct diagnostic information does not worsen the subject's physical situation. Instead, the harm is of an emotional kind – shock, distress, and anxiety caused by the news, including the unexpected nature of its receipt. Even so, if this would have been less

[44] Relevant cases are rare, but see *Zelenko* v. *Gimbel Bros*, 287 NYS 134 (1935) (New York Sup Ct).

[45] For example, someone could use a diagnostic app on their mobile to study social media photos of people they dislike, to be able to trumpet to them that they have skin cancer; here, there would possibly be liability following the UK Supreme Court decision in *Rhodes* v. *OPO* (2015) UKSC 32. Issues of health app use are looked at further in Section 13.4.3.

had the information been provided by a doctor, the unnecessary added distress may – morally at least –[46] be imputed to the lay discloser.

A converse issue, though, is whether there might sometimes be a legal duty on the information holder (outside the health care context) to convey pressing diagnostic information to the relevant individual (by, as suggested, advising the latter to see a doctor). Here, it is suggested that – at least under the common law – the answer would be no: such a duty would go against the traditional principle that, outside situations of special reliance, there is no duty to rescue a person from a danger not of one's own making.[47] In this regard, there would be no duty even to notify the rescue services of the emergency.[48]

13.4.2 *Unsolicited Disclosures of Predictive Information*

As discussed in Section 13.2, the use of intelligent algorithms increasingly allows the generation of predictive information, couched in statistical or probabilistic terms. In these cases, it is submitted that ethically there will, in most cases, be no good reason for making an unsolicited disclosure, and insofar as it was thought justified, the greatest care would need to be taken over how the information is communicated and presented.

As a thought experiment, consider the following scenario: suppose an algorithm was able to show that a subgroup of persons (with attributes x, y, z, etc), who are presently in their 30s, have a 90–95% likelihood of developing a (presently incurable) form of lung cancer in 25–30 years' time. An initial question is whether there is any point in giving those persons this information. This would appear to depend in the first place on the element of actionability: is there some step that the knowledge allows the recipient to take (by altering their behaviour) to pre-empt or at least reduce the risk? Let us suppose the answer is no (based on the current state

[46] Legally, on traditional tort principles, the causation difficulty noted in *AB* v. *Tameside & Glossop HA* ((1997) PNLR 140) would arise – that is, the practical impossibility of separating out this added distress from that which the subject was bound in any case to experience on learning the diagnosis later from the doctor. For discussion of other scenarios, however, where this problem does not arise, see Section 13.4.2 below.

[47] See for example *Gorringe v. Calderdale MBC* (2004) UKHL 15. Here the law leaves the decision to the moral conscience of the potential rescuer.

[48] Or, in the present context, to advise the at-risk subject to see a doctor; the contrary rule would arguably be impossible to enforce in any event, given the need to prove the non-expert information holder appreciated the imminent risk to the subject's health posed by not informing them.

of knowledge, this is not an unlikely assumption, given the way that – as we saw in Section 13.2 – algorithms arrive at their predictions on the basis of pattern correlation, rather than detailed causal analysis). In this case, it appears the only effect of the information would be to cause distress.

It might perhaps be argued that having the knowledge that one is unlikely to survive into old age could be useful to a person in terms of life-planning, but this appears speculative; everyone must live with the possibility of their premature death, and to have detailed knowledge of its manner and timing appears more likely to induce a morbid state, paralysing both action and pleasure. But another key aspect of the scenario (weighing against disclosure) is that the most terrifying feature of the prediction – the incurable nature of the disease – is something that may in any case change, with advances in medical science, prior to the time when the subgroup members are predicted to develop the disease.

In the absence of any plausible reason for disclosure, it is certainly possible that there could be legal liability, at least where a recipient developed a proven psychiatric condition as a result of having the information. In particular, the causation problem discussed in the *AB* v. *Tameside and Glossop HA* case[49] does not arise: the person would simply have lived on in a normal (unaware) mental state for 25–30 years prior to the condition's onset.

What about cases where the predictive information could be acted on by the subject? Suppose, in the lung cancer scenario, an attribute of all the persons in the subgroup is that they are smokers, and the algorithm suggests that giving up smoking straightaway reduces the cancer risk to 50%. Here, it might be felt that unsolicited disclosure of these facts is justified – it allows the subjects to do something themselves to substantially improve their chances of not developing the disease. At this point, though, the way the information is presented becomes critical: to be told, 'Whatever you do, you have a 1 in 2 chance of dying prematurely from a (presently incurable) disease' is still highly distressing knowledge: many recipients may prefer simply to carry on smoking. But more constructively (and with no loss of veracity), the information could be given as, 'You have been identified as being at high risk of developing lung cancer later in life, but you can substantially reduce this by giving up smoking'.

This suggests that in cases where predictive health information is regarded as sufficiently compelling and actionable to warrant

[49] See the discussion at note 40.

disclosure,[50] it is something that should, in any event, be managed by trained professionals.

13.4.3 *Solicited Disclosures: The Case of Health and Apps*

As noted in Section 13.2, an important new source of health information generation is the data analyses performed by lifestyle or health apps, or health platforms/websites.[51] Usually, it is here the subjects themselves who instigate the process by inputting data into the relevant app. Accordingly, we are back in the realm of solicited information, where – as discussed in Section 13.3 – subject autonomy has traditionally been regarded as providing a sufficient justification for the informational disclosure.

Even so, an interesting issue arises with the increasing number of apps whose use is encouraged by insurance companies:[52] to what extent should the subject's use of the app (based on an incentive, such as lower-priced insurance) be regarded as voluntary? Similarly, doubts may arise over whether a given subject's request for the information was adequately informed: there might, for example, be a claim against an app which returned distressing information, where the subject argues they were insufficiently warned of the possibility of receiving such information.[53]

By contrast, in cases where the subject's consent is not in doubt, it appears that the app or platform developer's private law liability for distressing, accurate information, would often be foreclosed by the 'volenti' principle.[54] At the same time, it is hard to be categorical in this nascent area of the law. Thus, an interesting residual question of potential negligence liability concerns apps that (notwithstanding user consent to the receipt of the content) present the information in an unnecessarily distressing way and/or fail to manage its delivery in a safe way.

50 It should be reiterated that this chapter proceeds on the assumption (not necessarily satisfied in practice) that the probabilistic predictions provided by the algorithm are reliable and accurate to a high degree.

51 Such as the well-known '23andme' platform that allows people to obtain online genetic testing.

52 See Urs-Vito Albrecht (ed), *Chances and Risks of Mobile Health Apps* (*Charisma*) (Hannover Medical School 2016) 27–28.

53 The issues here also raise matters of the validity of the subject's consent under data protection law.

54 That is, that the subject agreed to assume the risk of suffering the relevant (distress) harm; there remains the possibility of other regulatory mechanisms – For example, requirements imposed under data protection law – to inhibit apps that provide information of no clear benefit, but with a propensity to cause distress.

In this regard, it appears an app or platform's degree of 'tact' in the way it presents information has as yet escaped any requirement for advance testing prior to marketing.[55] Nonetheless, it is clear in ethical terms that tools that purport to offer personalised diagnostic or predictive advice to users should be designed to minimise potential harms; in some cases (e.g., apps that reveal the likely or inevitable progression of a serious condition), direct physician involvement in the app use case should arguably be designed in.[56] Failing this, one could again imagine the potential for liability in negligence, or indeed under applicable consumer protection law.

Given the (partial) uncertainty of the existing law that has been identified in this section, there is finally a question of whether the legislature should seek to set out a clearer framework of obligations upon the new categories of health information holders in a specific legal instrument. This question is considered briefly in the concluding section.

13.5 Conclusion: Regulating Disclosures beyond the Health Care Context?

As this chapter has discussed, the algorithmic generation of health information beyond the traditional health care context raises interesting ethical and legal challenges with respect to deciding whether (and if so under what circumstances) it should be disclosed to the informational subject. In many situations, the information could be highly distressing and – especially when probabilistic in nature – difficult to act upon. However, sometimes its provision could also be life-saving.

The analysis of existing common law legal authorities suggests that, in cases where the rules are uncertain, the law would be flexible enough, given time, to find plausible solutions. At the same time, given the speed of technological advances – in which inexperienced non-professionals find themselves holding extremely telling diagnostic and/or predictive health information on complete strangers – there may be a case for legislating at

[55] That is, as part of the certification process that apps – at least those clearly aimed at health uses – should undergo pursuant to medical device regulation. So far, such regulations (such as the EU rules under the Medical Devices Regulation (EU) 2017/745) are primarily concerned with matters of reliability and accuracy of the information.

[56] See A Dahi and others, 'Using Patient Avatars to Promote Health Data Sharing Applications: Perspectives and Regulatory Challenges' (2016) 23 *European Journal of Health Law* 175.

least a simple framework of disclosure duties. This could include a bright-line rule that disclosure of certain kinds of health information should invariably be decided upon and managed by trained health professionals.

Particularly in the light of developments in predictive health apps and platforms (sometimes of a morbid character), this would arguably provide a useful steer and help prevent the overall online climate from descending too far towards 'cyberchondria'.

Bibliography

Albrecht U-V (ed), *Chances and Risks of Mobile Health Apps (Charisma)* (Hannover Medical School 2016).

Andorno R, 'The Right Not to Know – An Autonomy-Based Approach' (2004) 30(5) *Journal of Medical Ethics* 435–39.

Beauchamp T and Childress J, *Principles of Biomedical Ethics,* 5th ed. (Oxford University Press 2001).

Cate FH and others, *Data Protection Principles for the 21st Century* (Maurer Faculty Report 2013).

Chen JH 'Machine Learning and Prediction in Medicine – Beyond the Peak of Inflated Expectations' (2017) 376(26) *New England Journal of Medicine* 2507–25.

Cole C and others, '"Ethical Responsibility" or "A Whole Can of Worms": Differences in Opinion on Incidental Finding Review and Disclosure in Neuroimaging Research from Focus Group Discussions with Participants, Parents, IRB Members, Investigators, Physicians and Community Members' (2015) 41(10) *Journal of Medical Ethics* 841–47.

Dahi A and others, 'Using Patient Avatars to Promote Health Data Sharing Applications: Perspectives and Regulatory Challenges' (2016) 23(2) *European Journal of Health Law* 175–94.

Duncan RE, 'Predictive Genetic Testing in Young People: When Is It Appropriate?' (2004) 40(11) *Journal of Paediatrics and Child Health* 593–95.

Dworkin G, *The Theory and Practice of Autonomy* (Cambridge University Press 1988).

Epstein RM and others, 'Withholding Information from Patients – When Less Is More' (2010) 362(5) *The New England Journal of Medicine* 380–81.

EU Task Force on eHealth, 'Redesigning Health in Europe for 2020' (2012), https://joinup.ec.europa.eu/sites/default/files/document/2014-12/eHealth%20Task%20Force%20Report%20-%20Redesigning%20health%20in%20Europe%20for%202020%20-%20Part%20I_0.pdf

European Commission, 'Green Paper on Mobile Health ("mHealth")' COM(2014) 219 final, 2014, https://eur-lex.europa.eu/legal-content/EN/LSU/?uri=celex:52014DC0219

Fry H, *Hello World* (Norton 2018).

Gammon BL and others, 'Decisional Regret in Women Receiving High Risk or Inconclusive Prenatal Cell-Free DNA Screening Results' (2020) 33(8) *Journal of Maternal-Fetal and Neonatal Medicine* 1412–18.

Gilbar R, 'Communicating Genetic Information in the Family: The Familial Relationship as the Forgotten Factor' (2007) 33(7) *Journal of Medical Ethics* 390–93.

Godard B and others, 'Guidelines for Disclosing Genetic Information to Family Members: From Development to Use' (2006) 5(2) *Familial Cancer* 103–16.

Laurie G, 'In Defence of Ignorance: Genetic Information and the Right not to Know' (1999) 6(2) *European Journal of Health Law* 119–32.

Laurie G, 'Recognizing the Right Not to Know: Conceptual, Professional, and Legal Implications' (2014) 42(1) *The Journal of Law, Medicine and Ethics* 53–63.

Mackie JL, *The Cement of the Universe: A Study of Causation* (Clarendon Press 1980).

Mayer-Schönberger V and Cukier K, *Big Data* (John Murray 2013).

Mill JS, *A System of Logic* (John W Parker 1843).

Provost F and Fawcett T, *Data Science for Business* (O'Reilly Media 2013).

Stauch M, 'Causation, Risk, and Loss of Chance in Medical Negligence' (1997) 17(2) *Oxford Journal of Legal Studies* 205–26.

Teff H, *Causing Psychiatric and Emotional Harm* (Hart 2009).

Thorogood A and others, 'An Implementation Framework for the Feedback of Individual Research Results and Incidental Findings in Research' (2014) 15(1) *BMC Medical Ethics* 1–13.

Wright RW, 'Causation in Tort Law' (1985) 73(6) *California Law Review* 1735–1828.

14

Data Protection Implications of Forensic Genealogy

A Close Look at the Use of Forensic Genealogy in Solving a Double Murder in Sweden

DENA DERVANOVIĆ

14.1 Introduction

The industry of direct-to-consumer (DTC) genetic tests became increasingly more available in 2017, following the US Food and Drug Administration's approval of tests, as provided by 23andMe, that would show consumers what diseases they are at risk for.[1] The popularity of these tests is only growing, with more than 12 million people having done them as of 2018.[2]

This chapter aims to start a discussion on data protection issues arising in the context of DTC genetic tests and their growing use for law enforcement purposes. This chapter focuses on DTC genetic tests that involve no medical supervision – that is, such tests that are largely outside the scope of existing regulation (also called 'recreational testing')[3] and have to comply with the General Data Protection Regulation (GDPR) when offering services in the EU.[4] The upcoming EU Regulation on In Vitro Diagnostic Medical Devices[5] (IVDR), due to enter into effect in 2022, does encompass DTC genetic testing, albeit only to the extent that they provide

1 M Bates, 'Direct-To-Consumer Genetic Testing: Is the Public Ready for Simple, At-Home DNA Tests to Detect Disease Risk?' (2018) 9(6) *IEEE Pulse* 11.

2 Ibid., 13.

3 For a discourse on the concept of 'recreational', see H Feltzmann, '"Just a Bit of Fun": How Recreational is Direct-to-Customer Genetic Testing?', (2015) 21(1) *The New Bioethics* 22, https://doi.org/10.1179/2050287715Z.00000000062.

4 EU Regulation 2016/679 of the European Parliament and of the Council of 27 April 2016 on the Protection of Natural Persons with Regard to the Processing of Personal Data and on the Free Movement of Such Data, https://eur-lex.europa.eu/eli/reg/2016/679/oj.

5 Regulation (EU) 2017/746 of the European Parliament and of the Council of 5 April 2017 on In Vitro Diagnostic Medical Devices and Repealing Directive 98/79/EC and Commission Decision 2010/227/EU.

medical or health information and diagnosis, meaning that aspects of DTC genetic tests that provide information on aspects such as ancestry are not covered.[6] This chapter uses the term 'DTC genetic test provider' as an umbrella term for companies offering genetic sequencing services, including health and ancestry information through the probing of single nucleotide polymorphisms (SNP) contained in a genome through 'dense genotyping arrays',[7] as well as third-party interpretation service providers where a person can upload raw data and have it interpreted. The reasoning behind including third-party interpretation service providers lies in the fact that these providers also process vast amounts of personal data and their databases are increasingly being used by law enforcement authorities for solving crimes.

This chapter will not deal with aspects of DTC genetic testing from the perspective of public health, right to information, and so forth. The focus of the chapter is instead on the tests' impact on EU personal data protection from the aspect of their use for law enforcement purposes. The chapter discusses the possibilities granted to law enforcement to access the DTC genetic test providers' databases for the purposes of investigating crime. Are data subjects aware of this? More importantly, are the necessary legal prerequisites in place for this?

The DTC genetic test industry recently became an interesting target for law enforcement efforts. Most famously, and as a pioneer case, the mystery of the so-called Golden State Killer was solved by using forensic genealogy after law enforcement authorities obtained access to a DTC genetic provider's database.[8] The Golden State Killer was a serial rapist and murderer who committed a series of sexual crimes and homicides starting in 1976 and was only captured in 2018, thanks to forensic genealogy.[9] In Sweden, a double murder that shook the nation in 2004 remained unsolved for 16 years, despite it being the second-largest criminal investigation in Sweden

[6] SA Mahmoud-Davis, 'Direct-to-Consumer Genetic Testing: Empowering EU Consumers and Giving Meaning to the Informed Consent Process Within the IVDR and GDPR Frameworks' (2020) 19(1) *Washington University Global Studies Law Review* 14. See also L Kalokairinou and others, 'Legislation of Direct-to-Consumer Genetic Testing in Europe: A Fragmented Regulatory Landscape' (2018) 9(117) *Journal of Community Genetics* 127, https://doi.org/10.1007/s12687-017-0344-2.

[7] E Yaniv and others, 'Inference of Genomic Data Using Long-Range Familial Searches' (2018) 362(6415) *Science* 690–94 3, DOI: 10.1126/science.aau4832.

[8] The term 'forensic genealogy' is interchangeable with 'investigative genealogy'.

[9] S Zhang, 'How a Genealogy Website Led to the Alleged Golden State Killer' *The Atlantic*, 27 April 2018, www.theatlantic.com/science/archive/2018/04/golden-state-killer-east-area-rapist-dna-genealogy/559070/, accessed 12 June 2021.

(hereafter the 'Linköping case'). In an effort to resolve the Linköping case, which saw the tragic deaths of an 8-year-old boy and a 56-year-old woman, the *Polismyndigheten* (Swedish Police Authority, hereafter the 'Police') carried out swabs on about 6,500 persons and interrogated more than 9,000 persons without success.[10] Inspired by the Golden State Killer investigation, the Police launched a pilot project that was based on forensic genealogy.

Section 14.2 of this chapter focuses on the processing that occurs in a DTC genetic test provider's database and the processing by law enforcement. This is done in order to lay the foundation for the discussion that follows, specifically with respect to the legal landscape for allowing law enforcement to peruse these databases. This is done in Section 14.3, which goes into the details of the Linköping case outlining the circumstances and prerequisites in which such access may or may not occur.[11] The aim of Section 14.3 is to delineate and examine the premises on which law enforcement authorities can obtain access to personal data of the data subjects using the services of DTC genetic test providers and perform familial searches, when these measures can be resorted to, and what safeguards should be in place to ensure that the rule of law is upheld and that law enforcement authorities do not overreach when investigating crimes, as well as how personal data obtained in this manner should be treated once the relevant investigation ceases. For the purpose of a more specific delineation of the conditions and premises for such access, this section will reference the legal framework applicable in Sweden: the GDPR, the EU Law Enforcement Directive 2016/680 (Law Enforcement Directive),[12] the case law of the Court of Justice of the European Union (CJEU) and the European Court of Human Rights (ECtHR), as well as the Swedish legal framework regulating law enforcement authorities' processing of special categories of personal data, such as the Criminal Data Act (*Brottsdatalag*

[10] Nationellt Forensiskt Centrum, 'Pilot: Dna-spår och släktforskning, användning av släktforskningsdatabaser i brottsutredande syfte', reference number: A544.825/2020, 8.

[11] B Eriksson and P Snaprud, 'Dna-tekniken som löser dubbelmordet i Linköping' *SVT Nyheter*, 9 June 2020, www.svt.se/nyheter/vetenskap/dna-tekniken-som-kan-losa-dubbelmordet-i-linkoping, accessed 21 June 2020. Also, G Kolata and H Murphy, 'The Golden State Killer Is Tracked through a Thicket of DNA, and Experts Shudder' *The New York Times*, 27 April 2018, www.nytimes.com/2018/04/27/health/dna-privacy-golden-state-killer-genealogy.html, accessed 21 June 2020.

[12] Directive (EU) 2016/680 of the European Parliament and of the Council of 27 April 2016 on the Protection of Natural Persons with Regard to the Processing of Personal Data by Competent Authorities for the Purposes of the Prevention, Investigation, Detection or Prosecution of Criminal Offences or the Execution of Criminal Penalties, and on the Free Movement of Such Data, and Repealing Council Framework Decision 2008/977/JHA.

2018:1177) and the Act on processing of personal data within the scope of the Criminal Data Act (*Lag 2018:1693 om polisens behandling av personuppgifter inom brottsdatalagens område*, or Police Criminal Data Act). Lastly, Section 14.4 offers a conclusion.

14.2 The Personal Data Processed in the Context of DTC Genetic Testing and Access to Such Data by Law Enforcement

14.2.1 DTC Genetic Test Providers

In order to clarify the premises of discussing personal data processing by DTC genetic test providers, a brief discussion on the nature of the personal data processed in this context is necessary. In this discussion, it is important to understand what constitutes personal data and genetic data, what renders personal data anonymous and thus no longer personal data, and how these fit in the context of DTC genetic testing.

Personal data that is afforded a higher level of protection is exhaustively listed in Article 9(1) GDPR, which enumerates inter alia data concerning health, racial, or ethnic origin as well as biometric and genetic data as special categories of personal data. Genetic data is defined in Article 4(13) of the GDPR as personal data 'relating to the inherited or acquired genetic characteristics of a natural person which give unique information about the physiology or the health of that natural person and which result, in particular, from an analysis of a biological sample from the natural person in question'. Hence, it is not the mere act of spitting in a tube that automatically generates genetic data, nor personal data per se. Saliva, blood, or other human tissue are treated as sources from which personal data is derived.[13]

In order to understand the nature of the personal data processing at hand, let us briefly discuss the different processing operations that are relevant to this chapter. DTC genetic test providers go beyond processing genetic data alone. DTC genetic test providers may also process self-reported health data, where data subjects are encouraged to answer health-related questions, fill in forms and provide more information about their health conditions, as well as personal data that do not fall under special categories, such as information on familial bonds and relatives.

In a scenario where millions of people hand over not only their genetic data, but essentially the genetic data of their entire families too, it is important

[13] Article 29 Working Party, 'Opinion 4/2007 on the Concept of Personal Data, adopted on 20th June' (WP 136), 9.

to understand how this personal data is used, especially if it is shared with law enforcement. At the time of writing, the privacy notices and terms and conditions of the most prominent DTC genetic test providers have given information on potential disclosures of personal data to law enforcement authorities. The information varies among providers, but the majority state that they may disclose personal data to law enforcement authorities. There are nuances in the approach taken in this regard – providers such as Ancestry, 23andMe, MyHeritage and FamilyTreeDNA state that such disclosure will not occur on a voluntary basis, but it may occur when compelled.

The wordings differ somewhat, with some providers like 23andMe naming warrants and subpoenas as the conditions for disclosures, while others are more vague: Ancestry, for example, mentions 'due legal process' instead, and My Heritage states that they prohibit law enforcement access, only to specify later on in the document that such prohibition is conditional on the existence of a warrant or subpoena.[14] Stating that due legal process is necessary does not say much in the way of how the DTC genetic test provider interprets the notion of due legal process. It is also worth noting that these privacy notices and statements have improved over the years, but they are nonetheless lengthy documents that most data subjects do not read, as was indicated in 2015 when a Special Eurobarometer demonstrated that under a fifth of the barometer respondents fully read privacy notices, whereas 67% respondents stated that the reason for not reading privacy notices is because they find them too lengthy.[15]

Additionally, let us not forget that DTC genetic test provider FamilyTreeDNA had a collaboration with the Federal Bureau of Investigation to solve violent crimes, but did not inform its customers, sparking a backlash and raising concerns over transparency and privacy.[16] Providers such as GEDmatch.com, for example, nowadays openly state that law enforcement access will be granted.[17]

[14] See, for example, 23andMe, 'Privacy Highlights', www.23andme.com/en-eu/about/privacy/ accessed; Ancestry, 'Your Privacy', www.ancestry.com/cs/legal/privacystatement; FamilyTreeDNA, 'FamilyTreeDNA Privacy Statement', www.familytreedna.com/legal/privacy-statement; MyHeritage, 'MyHeritage sekretesspolicy', www.myheritage.com/privacy-policy?lang=SV, all accessed 19 July 2020.

[15] European Commission, 'Data Protection' Special Eurobarometer 431, June 2015, https://doi.org/10.2838/552336, 84–87.

[16] AM Dockser, 'Customers Handed Over Their DNA. The Company Let the FBI Take a Look', *Wall Street Journal*, 22 August 2019, www.wsj.com/articles/customers-handed-over-their-dna-the-company-let-the-fbi-take-a-look-11566491162, accessed 25 July 2020.

[17] C Guest, 'DNA and Law Enforcement: How the Use of Open-Source DNA Databases Violates Privacy Rights' (2019) 68(3) *American University Law Review* 13.

14.2.2 Processing by Law Enforcement Authorities

The processing of genetic data as done by law enforcement authorities for the purposes of criminal investigation within their own DNA databases differs from DTC genetic test providers' practices. While DTC genetic test providers use SNPs to derive a multitude of categories of personal data,[18] including appearance, ancestry and health information, law enforcement authorities normally use short tandem repeats (STRs) that create a numerical combination that constitutes a DNA profile. Processing via STRs generates a lot less information on the data subject than SNPs.[19]

With respect to law enforcement authorities using DTC genetic test providers' databases, one can make a reasonable assumption that there are two ways in which such processing may occur. The first would entail law enforcement agencies obtaining access privileges to the DTC genetic test provider's database and thereby also to genetic data and data pertaining to familial bonds of the users of the specific DTC genetic test provider. With such access, the law enforcement authority obtains an insight into a multitude of categories of personal data that it arguably does not need for the purpose of solving crimes. In this scenario, the law enforcement agency processes genetic data pertaining to (i) the suspect, (ii) any matches, (iii) familial bonds and (iv) possibly other data as well. In the second scenario, the law enforcement authority requests the DTC genetic test provider to feed the genetic data of the suspect into their database to produce a list of relevant matches that is provided to the law enforcement authority without actually giving access to the database. In this scenario, the law enforcement authority processes (i) the genetic data pertaining to the suspect and (ii) the personal data on familial bonds in relation to the relevant matches obtained (i.e., not genetic data).

14.3 Forensic Genealogy

14.3.1 Access to DTC Genetic Test Providers' Databases

As mentioned above, once DTC genetic testing services reached considerable popularity, law enforcement authorities followed suit and started requesting access to these services in order to resolve crimes. Examples of this can be found in the capture of the infamous Golden State Killer, who

[18] Yaniv and others, 'Inference of Genomic Data'.

[19] Nationellt Forensiskt Centrum, 'DNA och biologi, faktablad – DNA-undersökning', https://nfc.polisen.se/kriminalteknik/dna-och-biologi/, accessed 25 July 2020.

was suspected of having committed more than fifty rapes and twelve murders between 1976 and 1986, as well as in the resolution of the Linköping case.[20] Familial searching is arguably the main purpose of the law enforcement authorities' requests sent to DTC genetic test providers. It is based on comparing the DNA of the suspect with the profiles of DTC genetic test providers' end users in order to find matches and relatives of the suspect, presented as a ranking on the basis of familial proximity.[21] The purpose of this operation is to process more personal data than the personal data relating to the suspect, and as such, the operation encompasses the suspect's relatives as well.

Depending on the method used, the requesting law enforcement authority can either request that the DTC genetic test provider feed the suspect's DNA profile into its database and thereafter extract the relevant results containing relevant personal data of the matches, or it can request access to the database and perform the processing itself, thereby obtaining a larger amount of various types of personal data. One particular question arises in this context: by obtaining access to DTC genetic test providers' databases, are law enforcement authorities essentially circumventing the legal restraints that apply to their own databases? By obtaining uninhibited access to DTC genetic test providers' databases, the reach of law enforcement authorities suddenly becomes extensive and arguably goes beyond what their own databases have the capacity for, both technically and legally.

In order to understand the legal premises allowing for familial searching to occur, one must take into account the provisions set out in the Law Enforcement Directive, specifically the conditions for processing special categories of personal data contained in Article 10.

Article 10 of the Law Enforcement Directive stipulates criteria for processing of personal data, specifically with respect to special categories of personal data – that is, a category historically subject to higher protection in data protection legislation in general. Hence, Article 10 imposes a criterion that this processing may only occur where strictly necessary. This criterion is based on the case law of the CJEU, inter alia Digital Rights Ireland and Schrems, where the CJEU determined that derogations from the fundamental rights and freedoms as per the Charter of Fundamental Rights of the European Union (CFREU) may only occur where strictly

[20] Ibid.

[21] See also ECtHR, S. and *Marper* v. *The United Kingdom*, Applications nos. 30562/04 and 30566/04, para. 39.

necessary.[22] The test of strict necessity will have to take into account the balance between the public interests, and the interests, rights and freedoms of the data subject.

Furthermore, Article 10 of the Law Enforcement Directive continues to state that such processing must be subject to appropriate safeguards. According to the Article 29 Working Party (WP29), the term must entail a particular assessment of the necessity of processing of special categories of personal data, as well as foresee precise and solid justifications for the processing of such data.[23]

Appropriate safeguards in the context of access to DTC genetic test providers could be various technical and organizational measures, as an obligation generally imposed on controllers and processors of personal data. A safeguard in line with this could be, for example, conducting data protection impact assessments, since the technology used to find perpetrators via DTC genetic test providers' databases can be considered new and intrusive. Moreover, the threshold for law enforcement authorities to obtain access to these databases should be high. EU Member State law enforcement authorities shall perform relevant searches in their own national databases and searches pursuant to the Prüm Convention prior to resorting to other methods.

Furthermore, investigation of very serious crimes, including deadly violence and sexual crimes, may be justifiable reasons for law enforcement to obtain such access for the purpose of capturing the perpetrator. However, solving crimes such as credit card fraud are unlikely to be found to bear enough significance to would warrant such an intrusion of privacy and comprehensive personal data processing. Alas, it is not unheard of – in the United States, for example, Ancestry was approached with access requests for the purpose of solving credit card fraud and identity theft crimes.[24] Could the capture of the Golden State Killer have opened the flood gates of legal insecurity in this sense?

22 Digital Rights Ireland and Others, C-293/12 and C-594/12, para. 52; *Maximillian Schrems* v. *Data Protection Commissioner*, C-362/14, para. 92 et seq. See also Institut professionnel des agents immobiliers (IPI) C-473/12, para. 39 et seq.

23 Article 29 Working Party, 'Opinion on Some Key Issues of the Law Enforcement Directive' (EU 2016/680), WP 258, 8. Hereafter cited as WP 258.

24 Ancestry, 'Ancestry Transparency Report' version 10, July 2020, www.ancestry.com/cs/transparency, accessed 13 July 2020. See also, P Marinova, 'Ancestry CEO on Genetic Data Privacy: Consumers Need to Think About Who They Do Business With', *Fortune*, 16 July 2019, https://fortune.com/2019/07/15/dna-testing-privacy-ancestry/, accessed 13 July 2020.

Limitations on the possibility of resorting to access, as described above, could potentially constitute appropriate safeguards. It is of relevance to mention that the ECtHR has assessed the concept of familial searching in *S. and Marper* v. *The United Kingdom* in 2008, where it determined that familial searching is to be regarded as 'highly sensitive' and that it constitutes an interference with the right to private and family life, home and correspondence as enshrined in Article 8 of the European Convention on Human Rights (ECHR). In this particular case, the ECtHR deemed that the retention of genetic data relating to persons who have not been convicted of a crime failed to strike a balance between the competing public and private interests, and thereby amounted to a violation of Article 8 of the ECHR.[25]

S. and Marper v. *The United Kingdom* reminds us of the importance of limited retention periods – retaining personal data obtained through familial searching for unnecessarily long periods of time could be considered an unjustified interference. Thus, limited retention periods are to be regarded as yet another appropriate safeguard.

Data obtained through familial searching via DTC genetic test providers can result in a number of categories of personal data that the law enforcement authorities do not need for their purposes of solving crime. The risk with law enforcement authorities routinely using DTC genetic test providers' databases to perform this processing is that the processing becomes much more comprehensive than it is required, or indeed allowed by law.

An example of this is law enforcement authorities' use of GEDmatch to find the Golden State Killer. This was done without the knowledge of GEDmatch and through a violation of the terms of use of GEDmatch, where the law enforcement authority certified that the 'DNA was their own or belonged to someone for whom they were legal guardian' or that they had permission to upload the DNA.[26] After this, GEDmatch updated its terms to include that law enforcement may use the site for the purposes of investigating and solving violent crimes.[27] The issue, of course, is how a provider such as GEDmatch enforces this against law enforcement authorities and their use of GEDmatch for crimes that do not fit the definition of violent crimes.[28] Likewise, in the event of EU-based law

[25] *S. and Marper* v. *The United Kingdom*, ECtHR, para. 125.

[26] Guest, 'DNA and Law Enforcement', 13.

[27] Ibid., 6. see also S Zhang, 'How a Tiny Website Became the Police's Go-To Genealogy Database', *The Atlantic*, 1 June 2018, www.theatlantic.com/science/archive/2018/06/gedmatch-police-genealogy-database/561695/, accessed 25 July 2020.

[28] Guest, 'DNA and Law Enforcement', 13.

enforcement authorities using a non-EU DTC genetic test provider's database, the issue is how the EU-based authorities can enforce rules on the provider to ensure that appropriate safeguards are in place other than relying on their goodwill.

Furthermore, apart from the criteria of strict necessity and appropriate safeguards, Article 10 of the Law Enforcement Directive includes points (a), (b) and (c) that stipulate that the processing may only occur where authorized by EU or Member State law; where it serves the vital interests of the data subject or another natural person; or where the personal data was manifestly made public by the data subject, respectively.

According to the WP29, Article 10 is to be read in connection with Article 8 of the Law Enforcement Directive, signifying that processing of special categories of personal data pursuant to Article 10 must be based on a specific national legal basis, unless Union law allows for such basis.[29] This view is based on the interpretation of Recital 33 of the Law Enforcement Directive that states that references to Member State Law do not necessarily need to fulfil the criteria of a law passed by the legislative body in the Member State, but that the legal basis must follow the case law of the ECtHR and, to that end, that it should be clear, precise and foreseeable to those encompassed by it. Hence, WP29 seems to interpret that Article 10(a) is a prerequisite for the application of Article 10. Moreover, WP29 recommends that the interpretation of Article 10(b) and (c) is one of the illustrative examples which could be specifically addressed in national law, rather than alternatives on a list.

This may seem slightly odd, specifically when looking at how Article 10 is built: the first paragraph describes special categories of personal data and states the requirements of processing where strictly necessary and where secured by appropriate safeguards, and goes on to stipulate that this is only allowed where points (a), (b) *or* (c) are applicable. Owing to the word 'or' leading to point (c), an interpretation of the architecture of the provision would lead us to the conclusion that the list is alternative, and that any of the points (a), (b) or (c) can satisfy the application of Article 10, as long as the processing is strictly necessary and where appropriate safeguards have been undertaken. This interpretation is further supported by Recital 37 of the Law Enforcement Directive that states that where the processing of special categories of personal data is not already authorized by law, such processing may occur where it is necessary to protect the vital interests

[29] WP 258, 7.

of the data subject or of another person, or where the processing relates to data which are manifestly made public by the data subject. Hence, the WP29 interpretation may be considered a stretch. This chapter puts special focus on point (c), as analyzed in the following section.

14.3.2 *Manifestly Made Public by the Data Subject*

This section focuses on Article 10(c) of the Law Enforcement Directive, as this is one of the arguments the Police relied on in the Linköping case. This provision, stipulated as a derogation from the general prohibition on processing special categories of personal data in both Article 9(2)(e) of the GDPR and Article 10(c) of the Law Enforcement Directive, is difficult to assess. The main question pertaining to this exception is whether the data subject's use of DTC genetic test services can be considered a manifest publication of special categories of personal data that can thereby justifiably succumb to processing of personal data by law enforcement authorities for the purposes of solving crime.

There is little guidance on the matter of what constitutes personal data that has been manifestly made public by the data subject themself. WP29 offers some guidance in the interpretation of this derogation in the light of the Law Enforcement Directive, stating that one must discern between clear situations where the data subject manifestly makes public special categories of personal data, such as in the press, books, or similar publications, and situations where the possibility of the personal data being accessed by a wide audience, including public authorities, is described in terms and conditions of a service that the data subject wants to use.[30] WP29 also clarifies that this should mean that the data subject has voluntarily disclosed personal data to the public, including public authorities.[31]

In order to shed more light on the concept of manifestly making special categories of personal data public, one can look to the GDPR and the guidance provided in connection to it, seeing as Article 9(2)(e) of the GDPR provides for the same derogation from the prohibition of processing of special categories of personal data. The guidance is, however, scarce here as well. The provision being a derogation from a prohibition speaks to the fact that it should be construed narrowly.[32]

[30] Ibid., 10.

[31] Ibid.

[32] European Union Agency for Fundamental Rights and Council of Europe, Handbook on European data Protection Law (2018) 162.

The UK Information Commission Officer (ICO) regards this derogation to be two-fold. Firstly, this must be an active, 'unmistakably' deliberate act by the data subject that presupposes that the data subject has been given enough information to understand what their actions mean. The ICO continues to differentiate between blogging about one's own health conditions – an activity that falls within scope for the derogation – and posting about the same on social media for friends and family with the post audience being set to 'public' as a default – an activity which the ICO deems would be difficult to argue amounted to a manifest publication.[33]

The ICO clarifies that the personal data must also be realistically accessible to members of the general public and that this assessment should not be theoretical, but should be based on the practical circumstances of access. The ICO moves on to clarify that access provided to a limited audience would not amount to the criteria of being made public.[34] In contrast to this, and on the basis of a different legislative instrument that contained the same derogation (Regulation 45/2001, later repealed and replaced by Regulation 2018/1725),[35] the CJEU's then Court of First Instance deemed in *Esch-Leonhardt and Others* v. *ECB* that sending an e-mail within an organization amounted to such manifest publication of special categories of personal data within the organization, taking a tiered approach to what the term 'public' entails.[36] In the view of Dove and Chen, the term 'public' should not be delimited in this manner.[37] I, too, share this view.

In the context of DTC genetic test providers, there is doubt as to whether the data subject can be considered to have manifestly made their special categories of personal data public. The reasons for this lie in the

[33] Information Commissioner's Office, 'Special Categories of Personal Data, What Are the Conditions for Processing?', https://ico.org.uk/for-organisations/guide-to-data-protection/guide-to-the-general-data-protection-regulation-gdpr/special-category-data/what-are-the-conditions-for-processing/#conditions5, accessed 25 June 2021.

[34] Ibid.

[35] Regulation (EC) No 45/2001 of the European Parliament and of the Council of 18 December 2000 on the Protection of Individuals with Regard to the Processing of Personal Data by the Community Institutions and Bodies and on the Free Movement of Such Data; Regulation (EU) 2018/1725 of the European Parliament and of the Council of 23 October 2018 on the Protection of Natural Persons with Regard to the Processing of Personal Data by the Union Institutions, Bodies, Offices and Agencies and on the Free Movement of Such Data, and Repealing Regulation (EC) No 45/2001; and Decision No 1247/2002/EC.

[36] Case T-320/02, quoted in ES Dove and J Chen, 'What Does It Mean for a Data Subject to Make Their Personal Data "Manifestly Public"? An Analysis of GDPR Article 9(2)(e)', (2021) 13 *International Data Privacy Law* ipab005, https://doi.org/10.1093/idpl/ipab005.

[37] Dove and Chen, 'What Does It Mean for a Data Subject to Make Their Personal Data "Manifestly Public"?', 16.

fact that most data subjects will not have read the terms and conditions and privacy notices delineating this.[38] To add insult to injury, when different DTC genetic test providers state in their notice summaries that such disclosure will not happen only to clarify in fine print that it may occur under certain conditions, this further diminishes the possibility of interpreting the data subject's use of the service as having manifestly made the special categories of personal data public and undermines the possibility of law enforcement authorities being allowed to process such personal data on this basis. Moreover, seeing as DTC genetic test services usually require the payment of a fee or the creation of an account, it undermines the argument that these are publicly available databases where data subjects manifestly make their sensitive personal data public. The reason for discussing this derogation lies in the possibility of law enforcement relying on it as a fallback option in the event that there is a lack of clarity in the legal framework in which these authorities operate.

Lastly, with respect to Sweden, it should be noted that Article 10(c) of the Law Enforcement Directive allowing for this derogation has not been implemented in Swedish law. More specifically, neither the Criminal Data Act nor the Police Criminal Data Act implement this derogation. The Swedish preparatory works do not discuss this either, giving no rationale for why the legislature decided to exclude this from the implementation of the Law Enforcement Directive.

14.3.3 The Linköping Case

The result of the Police's efforts was a single arrest and a confession to the double murder by the person arrested with the help of forensic genealogy. The case ended in a trial with a conviction that has not been appealed. The person convicted had left his DNA at the crime scene, but despite swabbing more than 6,500 persons and interrogating more than 9,000 persons, the Police had not come any closer to solving the case. The Police carried out a familial search in its own registers, with no success.[39] Hence, the Police assessed that its usual investigative methods were unsuccessful, even so many years after the crime was committed, and that the circumstances of the crime and the investigation made it possible to go outside the usual framework of investigations and use DTC genetic test providers'

[38] Ibid.

[39] Nationellt Forensiskt Centrum, 'Pilot: Dna-spår och släktforskning', 8.

databases to try to identify the perpetrator.[40] This decision was followed by an argument that the public interest in the resolution of the case is compelling and therefore outweighs the data subjects' rights and freedoms. This being one of Sweden's largest criminal investigations, second only to the investigation of the murder of the Swedish Prime Minister Olof Palme, it is not difficult to see the pressure to solve the case.[41] How did the Police find him then? The person convicted had not shared his genetic data with a DTC genetic test provider. Instead, the Police had to trace back his ancestry by going as far as the late 1700s and thereafter reconstructing his family tree to identify him and his brother.[42] The Police couldn't discern which of them could be the perpetrator, so it had to obtain DNA swabs from both of them.[43]

In its pilot project report, the Police clarified the criteria used to resort to this investigation method. The Police stated the following criteria for the choice of the matter that was to be investigated: (i) that it was a matter of very severe crimes that included deadly violence or severe sexual crimes, (ii) that DTC genetic test providers' databases were deemed to be a prerequisite for the furtherance of the investigation, (iii) that the investigation had exhausted comprehensive investigation methods without success, and that it had undertaken relevant testing of DNA samples and analyses without progress, including searches in the Police's own databases and familial searches, swabs, and searches in international databases such as the Prüm register, (iv) that any DNA analysis not carried out by the Police's national forensic centre is carried out by a laboratory that follows the criteria placed upon it by the Police's national forensic centre, and (v) that there are prerequisites for a successful search.[44]

In terms of the choice of a DTC genetic test provider, the Police had three criteria: (i) that the users of the DTC genetic test provider's database (data subjects) have consented to the use of the database for investigative purposes by law enforcement and that the data subjects have accepted clear conditions under which they make their personal data public, (ii) that there are limitations on the use of the DNA data fed into it by law enforcement and that such data may not be used for other purposes in

[40] Ibid.

[41] A Brantemo, 'Linköpings trauma: Dubbelmördaren höll sig undan i 16 år', *SVT nyheter*, 1 October 2020, www.svt.se/nyheter/lokalt/ost/linkopings-trauma-daniel-nyqvist-gackade-polisen-i-16-ar, accessed 26 June 2021.

[42] Ibid.

[43] Nationellt Forensiskt Centrum, 'Pilot: Dna-spår och släktforskning', 27.

[44] Ibid., 6.

the DTC genetic test provider's database, and (iii) that the data uploaded to the database, as well as any results of matching and other data created in the process, can be erased once the comparative search is concluded.[45]

Based on these points, the Police delimited its use of DTC genetic test providers to those providers that specifically stated that they allowed the use of the databases for law enforcement purposes, such as GEDmatch and FamilyTreeDNA. This signifies that the Police was primarily relying on the exemption prescribed by Article 10(c) of the Law Enforcement Directive – that is, that the personal data has been manifestly made public – despite the fact that this provision of the Law Enforcement Directive does not seem to have been implemented in Swedish law. In its legal memorandum, the Police does, however, admit that the legal circumstances surrounding this are unclear and that a request for an amendment of the law should be considered.[46]

The legal framework for processing personal data is set out in the Criminal Data Act, the Swedish implementation of the Law Enforcement Directive. The Police Criminal Data Act is applicable beyond the Criminal Data Act and encompasses inter alia the Police and regulates the Police's processing of personal data for the purposes of detecting, preventing and solving crimes. Based on the legal memorandum provided by the Police in the scope of the prior consultation, the Police deemed that the access to and search in the DTC genetic test provider was uncharted territory, but that this processing should be allowed given that it is the National Forensic Center (the department that was in charge of the investigation) that would be the entity processing the personal data – that is, an entity specifically allowed to process genetic data pursuant to the Police Criminal Data Act, as long as it is done for forensic purposes.[47]

Chapter 2, Section 12 of the Criminal Data Act states that the processing of biometric and genetic data may only occur when this is prescribed by law and when it is absolutely necessary for the purpose of processing, whereas Chapter 2, Section 14 stipulates that searches with a purpose of producing a list of persons based on special categories of personal data, such as familial searching, is prohibited.

However, the prohibition of searches under the Criminal Data Act is subject to a derogation as per Chapter 6, Section 5 of the Police Criminal

[45] Ibid., 7.

[46] Polismyndigheten, 'Rättsutredning: Dna-spår och släktforskning' 2020 reference number: A637.388/2018 17.

[47] Ibid., 12.

Data Act that stipulates that searches may be performed in DNA registers, fingerprint registers or suspect description registers for the purposes of obtaining a list of persons based on health data, biometric data or genetic data. Hence, the Police may perform searches in the registers mentioned, as long as such searches are carried out in the registers held by the Police.[48] The preparatory works leave little room for an interpretation that familial searches on the basis of special categories of personal data may be carried out in databases operated and maintained by private companies are implicitly allowed under the derogation.[49]

14.3.4 Prior Consultation with the Swedish Authority for Privacy Protection

The aftermath of the resolution of the Linköping case resulted in a request for prior consultation with the Swedish Authority for Privacy Protection (*Integritetsskyddsmyndigheten*, hereafter SAPP). The request was sent to SAPP on 11 February 2021, eight months following the resolution of the Linköping case and the capture of the subject.[50]

Whether intentional or not, the timing of the prior consultation was poorly chosen, since the processing of personal data that constituted high risk for data subjects had already taken place in the course of the Linköping case and the relevant paragraph of the Criminal Data Act (Chapter 3, Section 7 second paragraph) does not specify an exemption for pilot projects of processing, and explicitly states that such consultation should take place prior to the processing and that this should be done with time to spare before the envisaged processing is to take place. This was also noted by the SAPP, which stated that it expects the Police to rectify this in the future.[51]

The SAPP concurred with the Police's assessment that the processing of personal data in this context is two-fold: genetic data is processed within the scope of the investigation, as is non-genetic data in the context of receiving information on family members and the familial bond to the suspect whose DNA is processed.

[48] Swedish Government Bill 2017/18:269, Criminal Data Act – complementary legislation (Sw. *Brottsdatalagen – kompletterande lagstiftning*) 173.

[49] Ibid.

[50] Polismyndigheten, 'Begäran om förhandssamråd – Dna-spår och släktforskning för brottsutredande ändamål', reference number: A071.932/2021.

[51] Integritetsskyddsmyndigheten, 'Förhandssamråd enligt brottsdatalagen; användning av dna-baserade släktforskningsdatabaser', reference number: DI-2021–1521 2.

With respect to the lawfulness of this processing, the SAPP clarified that it does not share the Police's view that the personal data was manifestly made public by the data subjects and concludes that this exemption is not applicable to the processing carried out in the pilot project as well as that the SAPP does not recommend the Police continue with this type of processing of personal data until an amendment of the applicable laws is in place. Interestingly, the SAPP completely accepted WP29's interpretation of Article 10(a) and stated that any such processing must have a basis in EU or Member State law and that Article 10(b) and (c) are to serve as illustratory examples.

The SAPP also noted, albeit merely in passing, that there are additional difficulties with this type of processing of special categories of personal data. Namely, the SAPP noted that issues surrounding the ability to enforce rules regarding appropriate security measures or protection against the unauthorized use of personal data in a private company established in a third country are questions that the SAPP deems to constitute obstacles to the lawfulness of this method. Moreover, the SAPP noted that any large-scale processing of personal data in this manner would involve large-scale transfers of personal data to third countries, which cannot be done on the same legal basis as the transfer carried out in the Linköping case, that is, Chapter 8, Section 8 and Chapter 8, Section 5 first paragraph, point 2 of the Criminal Data Act that regulate non-repetitive transfers in specific cases.

14.4 Conclusion

This chapter attempts to highlight that there is uncertainty in how law enforcement authorities may or may not resort to DTC genetic test providers to solve crimes. It is clearly difficult to argue that there is no clear and compelling public interest in solving crimes, especially if this method is resorted to for the resolution of serious crimes that include deadly or sexual violence. However, in all instances where new technologies are used, such as deploying DTC genetic databases, a balance must be struck between the rights and freedoms of the two types of data subjects – data subjects who have done DTC genetic tests for a personal purpose, and data subjects who have not done DTC genetic tests but who may be identified through their relatives who have done them –[52] and the interests of

[52] D Kennett, 'Using Genetic Genealogy Databases in Missing Persons Cases and To Develop Suspect Leads in Violent Crimes', (2019) 301 *Forensic Science International* 114, https://doi.org/10.1016/j.forsciint.2019.05.016.

the public in tackling and solving crime in an efficient manner. In this balancing exercise, law enforcement agencies must carefully consider the means deployed for the purpose of solving crime and whether the desired goal can be achieved in some other, less intrusive manner. The legal premises for this type of processing must be clear before this method of solving crime can be deployed on a large scale. As was noted in the Swedish example, the legislative prerequisites for this could be made clearer so as to define the lawfulness of such interventions.

The discussion started in this chapter could be continued from a myriad of perspectives: are data subjects blatantly unaware of the implications of DTC genetic tests? If so, whose responsibility is it to ensure that this awareness is raised to an adequate level so that data subjects can be considered truly and appropriately aware and able to make decisions regarding their genetic data – data that, if breached, cannot be changed as simply as a password – and how do we reach this level of awareness and personal data protection without entering the sphere of legal paternalism? Has the advent of DTC genetic testing opened the door for law enforcement to disregard their own DNA databases and the limitations attached to them? In this day and age, when genetic information is becoming more accessible, it is crucial to understand how this can be done in a manner that is in conformity with data protection laws and fundamental rights.

To say that the method of accessing DTC genetic test providers' databases for the purposes of law enforcement is uncharted territory would be an understatement. Inspired by the capture of the Golden State Killer in the US, Sweden has become the first European country to resort to this method of investigating crime.[53] The aftermath of the prior consultation with the SAPP was that the Police issued a request for an amendment of the law and, in what could be perceived as an expedited procedure, the Swedish government announced that it would initiate an inquiry into the possibilities of an amendment that may allow this type of processing of personal data to occur for law enforcement purposes, as per Swedish legislative procedures.[54]

The Linköping case was a trauma for the Swedish nation, a shock that lasted for 16 years and the resolution of the case has indubitably brought some form of closure to the victims' families but also restored the nation's faith in the Police. In today's Sweden, which continues to try to grapple

[53] Nationellt Forensiskt Centrum, 'Pilot: Dna-spår och släktforskning', 25.

[54] TT, 'Regeringen ska utreda släktforskningsmetoden' *Dagens Nyheter*, 12 May 2021, www.dn.se/sverige/regeringen-ska-utreda-slaktforskningsmetoden/?, accessed 26 June 2021.

with rising criminal activity, this case was an important pat on the back for the authorities and an important addition to the political agenda of fighting crime. Perhaps this is the reason behind such quick statements from the Swedish government in terms of announcing an official inquiry into the possibilities of an amendment.

What could the possible amendment mean for Sweden? According to the Police, some 100,000 Swedes have used a DTC genetic test provider service, thereby creating good scope for the continued use of this method, if one would look at the possibilities of succeeding with the method.[55] After all, the aforementioned 100,000 data subjects did not only share their own genetic data, but the genetic information pertaining to their entire families, dead or alive, living in Sweden or elsewhere, thus significantly expanding the perimeters of any potential future investigation.

What could this amendment end up looking like? To begin with, one can assume that Article 10(c) of the Law Enforcement Directive might be a crucial amendment to implement in Swedish law to ensure that this derogation is readily available to law enforcement. Will this be enough? As mentioned above, the threshold for treating special categories of personal data as manifestly made public by the data subject requires a level of knowledge of the data subject that can hardly be argued to exist when the relevant information is buried in pages of legal text in terms and conditions and privacy notices of DTC genetic test providers. Moreover, why would using an online service that a data subject pays for be considered public? DTC genetic test providers' databases are not open to the general public for browsing; one must create an account and pay for the service in order to gain access. Even then, the access is limited to viewing one's own personal data or, at best, the personal data of one's DNA relatives.

To consider this a manifest publication of personal data would be to disregard the general protections afforded to special categories of personal data. For the purposes of analogy, Article 9(1) GDPR stipulates a prohibition of processing of special categories of personal data, whereas Article 9(2)(e) GDPR (special categories of personal data manifestly made public by the data subject) is a derogation from this prohibition. To set a low threshold for meeting the criteria for this derogation would render Article 9(1) GDPR largely insignificant, seeing as personal data, sensitive or not, is constantly processed in a manner that can be equated with buying a service online and having access to such personal data behind a

[55] Nationellt Forensiskt Centrum, 'Pilot: Dna-spår och släktforskning', 31.

password-protected user account. In such a case, all of our personal data could very well be considered made public by ourselves – which leads to the question of whether the legislature truly intended this when drafting the derogation of manifestly making personal data public.

The result of the Swedish inquiry is much anticipated, as it may provide answers to the questions regarding the circumstances in which resorting to DTC genetic test providers is permissible and perhaps provide much-needed clarity on the delimitations of such processing.

Bibliography

23andMe, 'Privacy Highlights', www.23andme.com/en-eu/about/privacy/, accessed 19 July 2020.

Ancestry, 'Ancestry Transparency Report' version 10, July 2020, www.ancestry.com/cs/transparency, accessed 13 July.

Ancestry, 'Your Privacy', www.ancestry.com/cs/legal/privacystatement, accessed 19 July 2020.

Article 29 Working Party, 'Opinion 4/2007 on the Concept of Personal Data Adopted on 20th June' (WP 136), https://ec.europa.eu/justice/article-29/documentation/opinion-recommendation/files/2007/wp136_en.pdf

Article 29 Working Party, 'Opinion on Some Key Issues of the Law Enforcement Directive' (EU 2016/680), Adopted on 29 November 2017 (WP 258), https://ec.europa.eu/newsroom/article29/items/610178

Bates M, 'Direct-To-Consumer Genetic Testing: Is the Public Ready for Simple, At-Home DNA Tests to Detect Disease Risk?' (2018) 9(6) *IEEE Pulse Pulse, IEEE* 11–14.

Brantemo A, 'Linköpings Trauma: Dubbelmördaren höll sig undan i 16 år' *SVT nyheter*, 1 October 2020, www.svt.se/nyheter/lokalt/ost/linkopings-trauma-daniel-nyqvist-gackade-polisen-i-16-ar, accessed 26 June 2021.

Dockser AM, 'Customers Handed Over Their DNA. The Company Let the FBI Take a Look' *Wall Street Journal*, 22 August 2019, www.wsj.com/articles/customers-handed-over-their-dna-the-company-let-the-fbi-take-a-look-11566491162, accessed 25 July 2020.

Dove ES and Chen J, 'What Does It Mean for a Data Subject to Make Their Personal Data "Manifestly Public?" An Analysis of GDPR Article 9(2)(e)' (2021) 11(2) *International Data Privacy Law* ipab005, https://doi.org/10.1093/idpl/ipab005.

Eriksson B and Snaprud P, 'Dna-tekniken som löser dubbelmordet i Linköping' *SVT Nyheter*, 9 June 2020, www.svt.se/nyheter/vetenskap/dna-tekniken-som-kan-losa-dubbelmordet-i-linkoping, accessed 21 June 2020.

Esch-Leonhardt and Others v. ECB, T-320/02.

European Commission, 'Data Protection', Special Eurobarometer 431, June 2015, https://doi.org/10.2838/552336.

European Union Agency for Fundamental Rights and Council of Europe, *Handbook on European Data Protection Law* (2018), the European Union Agency for Fundamental Rights and Council of Europe, Publications Office of the European Union.

FamilyTreeDNA, 'FamilyTreeDNA Privacy Statement', www.familytreedna.com/legal/privacy-statement, accessed 19 July 2020.

Feltzmann H, '"Just a Bit of Fun": How Recreational is Direct-to-Customer Genetic Testing?' (2015) 21(1) *The New Bioethics* 20–32, https://doi.org/10.1179/2050287715Z.00000000062.

Guest C, 'DNA and Law Enforcement: How the Use of Open-Source DNA Databases Violates Privacy Rights' (2019) 68(3) *American University Law Review* 1015–52.

Information Commissioner's Office, 'Special Categories of Personal Data, What Are the Conditions for Processing?', https://ico.org.uk/for-organisations/guide-to-data-protection/guide-to-the-general-data-protection-regulation-gdpr/special-category-data/what-are-the-conditions-for-processing/#conditions5, accessed 25 June 2021.

Integritetsskyddsmyndigheten, 'Förhandssamråd enligt brottsdatalagen; användning av dna-baserade släktforskningsdatabaser', reference number: DI-2021-1521.

Kalokairinou L and others, 'Legislation of Direct-to-Consumer Genetic Testing in Europe: A Fragmented Regulatory Landscape' (2018) 9(2) *Journal of Community Genetics* 117–32, https://doi.org/10.1007/s12687-017-0344-2.

Kennett D, 'Using Genetic Genealogy Databases in Missing Persons Cases and to Develop Suspect Leads in Violent Crimes' (2019) 301 *Forensic Science International* 107–17, https://doi.org/10.1016/j.forsciint.2019.05.016.

Kolata G and Murphy H, 'The Golden State Killer is Tracked Through a Thicket of DNA, and Experts Shudder' *The New York Times*, 27 April 2018, www.nytimes.com/2018/04/27/health/dna-privacy-golden-state-killer-genealogy.html, accessed 21 June 2020.

Mahmoud-Davis SA, 'Direct-to-Consumer Genetic Testing: Empowering EU Consumers and Giving Meaning to the Informed Consent Process within the IVDR and GDPR Frameworks' (2020) 19(1) *Washington University Global Studies Law Review* 1–52.

Marinova P, 'Ancestry CEO on Genetic Data Privacy: Consumers Need to Think About Who They Do Business With' *Fortune*, 16 July 2019, https://fortune.com/2019/07/15/dna-testing-privacy-ancestry/, accessed 13 July 2020.

Maximillian Schrems v. Data Protection Commissioner C–362/14.

MyHeritage, 'MyHeritage sekretesspolicy', www.myheritage.com/privacy-policy?lang=SV, accessed 19 July 2020.

Nationellt Forensiskt Centrum, 'DNA och biologi, faktablad – DNA-undersökning', https://nfc.polisen.se/kriminalteknik/dna-och-biologi/, accessed 25 July 2020.

Nationellt Forensiskt Centrum, 'Pilot: Dna-spår och släktforskning, användning av släktforskningsdatabaser I brottsutredande syfte', reference number: A544.825/2020,https://polisen.se/aktuellt/nyheter/2020/november/dna-baserad-slaktforskning-kan-bli-nationellt-anvand-metod/

Polismyndigheten, 'Begäran om förhandssamråd – Dna-spår och släktforskning för brottsutredande ändamål', reference number: A071.932/2021.

Polismyndigheten, 'Rättsutredning: Dna-spår och släktforskning', reference number: A637.388/2018.

Swedish Government Bill, 2017/18:269, Criminal Data Act – complementary legislation (Sw. *Brottsdatalagen – kompletterande lagstiftning*), www.regeringen.se/49dff7/contentassets/560221d124cb46bda169c3e8f0eef2c5/prop-201718-269.pdf

TT, 'Regeringen ska utreda släktforskningsmetoden' *Dagens Nyheter*, 12 May 2021, www.dn.se31verigee/regeringen-ska-utreda-slaktforskningsmetoden/, accessed 26 June 2021.

Yaniv E and others, 'Identity Inference of Genomic Data Using Long-Range Familial Searches' (2018) 362(6415) *Science* 690–94, https://doi.org/10.1126/science.aau4832

Zhang S, 'How a Genealogy Website Led to the Alleged Golden State Killer' *The Atlantic*, 27 April 2018, www.theatlantic.com/science/archive/2018/04/golden-state-killer-east-area-rapist-dna-genealogy/559070/, accessed 12 June 2021.

Zhang S, 'How a Tiny Website Became the Police's Go-To Genealogy Database' *The Atlantic*, 1 June 2018, www.theatlantic.com/science/archive/2018/06/gedmatch-police-genealogy-database/561695/, accessed 25 July 2020.

15

Health Research, eHealth, and Learning Healthcare Systems

Key Approaches, Shortcomings, and Design Issues in Data Governance

SHAWN H. E. HARMON

15.1 Introduction

Dramatic demographic, biological, climate, and technological shifts are putting immense pressure on healthcare systems around the world, with many exhibiting a growing imbalance between the amount spent on care and the value patients receive.[1] Innovations aimed at improving technical knowledge and system efficiencies are necessary. One innovation has been to make personal information (PI) and personal health information (PHI) work more frequently and more effectively to achieve better health outcomes, and governments are investing significant funds to generate data that can be linked across networks and practices.[2] Healthcare has thus entered the realm of 'Big Data',[3] and the growing community of those interested in 'population data science'[4] is seeking to increase the number and broaden the range of datasets available for health research and practice, including data derived from wearable and implanted devices and the 'Internet of Things', and to make that data available to clinicians and others, including those training AIs designed

[1] B Barua and others, *Comparing Performance of Universal Health Care Countries, 2017* (Fraser Institute, 2017).

[2] NHS Digital, *Data Insights and Statistics: Information and Technology for Better Health and Care* (2018).

[3] This term refers to data characterised by volume (large amounts), variety (different types), and velocity (rapid distribution and analysis): N Price II and I Cohen, 'Privacy in the Age of Medical Big Data' (2019) 25 *Nature Medicine* 37.

[4] E Ford and others, 'Our Data, Our Society, Our Health: A Vision for Inclusive and Transparent Health Data Science in the UK and Beyond' (2019) 3 *Learning Health Systems* e10191.

to serve healthcare systems.[5] In this new environment, the boundary between clinical care and research is eroded,[6] with data continuously collected and continuously analysed so that processes can be amended to achieve improved patient outcomes, with the ambition to develop 'learning healthcare systems'.

However, there are risks associated with the increased collection, use, linkage, and dissemination of health data, which is generally considered to be exceptional and potentially damaging to data originator interests because it tends to reveal intimate details about lifestyle and personal choices (i.e., it goes to one's 'biographical core'). For example, information about prescription use and about mental health, around which there remains stigma, is biographically core.[7] And these risks have broad implications for both healthcare delivery and society. The risks include:

1. health data could increasingly be viewed as a commodity rather than a by-product of, and tool for, good healthcare service delivery;[8]
2. for-profit collecting/aggregating/mining companies could become disproportionately powerful, compounding the anxiety that people already feel about who is collecting and accessing that data, and what that data are being used for;[9]
3. insufficient attention could be paid to data deletion – indeed, it is easier to retain data than to erase it – with the result that digital records are retained in perpetuity and people lose the ability to be 'forgotten';[10]

[5] W Price II, 'Black-Box Medicine' (2016) 28 *Harvard Journal of Law & Technology* 419. AIs have been trained to analyse radiographic and other images, and to provide prognoses in a variety of contexts.

[6] N Kass, 'The Research-Treatment Distinction: A Problematic Approach for Determining Which Activities Should Have Ethical Oversight' (2013) 43 *Hastings Center Reports* S4.

[7] *R v Snowdon*, 2016 NSSC 278.

[8] Health information has gained value for purposes beyond patient care: Commission on the Future of Health Care in Canada, *Building on Values: The Future of Health Care in Canada* (2002).

[9] V Mayer-Schonberger, *Delete: The Virtue of Forgetting in the Digital Age* (Princeton University Press 2009); N Terry, 'Protecting Patient Privacy in the Age of Big Data' (2012) 81 *UMKC Law Review* 385.

[10] C Bennett and others, 'Forgetting, Non-Forgetting and Quasi Forgetting in Social Networking: Canadian Policy and Corporate Practice' in Gutwirth S and others (eds), *Reloading Data Protection: Multidisciplinary Insights and Contemporary Challenges* (Springer 2014) 41. Patients are initiating civil actions for intrusion on seclusion with respect to uses of electronic medical records: *Oliveira v Aviva Canada Inc.*, 2018 ONCA 321.

4. important policy decisions could be based solely on data-mining insights generated by interested parties, insights that are often generated by processes of inference rather than direct observation;[11]
5. our 'medical selves' come to exist outside the traditional health setting and its usual protections of 'informed consent' and 'anonymisation'; and
6. those traditional protections no longer align with evolving practices such that their protective potential is weakened even when they remain operative.[12]

Given these risks and the technological advancements being realised, the nature and content of information protection and access regimes are increasingly important, as are the secondary governance instruments and structures that are assembled around health data.

This chapter examines the Canadian health data ecosystem. Bearing in mind the ambitions for learning health systems and AIs in healthcare, it critiques this ecosystem, highlighting several shortcomings. Specifically, it questions the propertisation/marketisation trend, demonstrates the insufficiency of the existing foundational pillars and mechanisms of action, and highlights the need to improve the ethics element of the ecosystem. It then offers two key considerations for ecosystem design – social licence to operate and value foundation – both of which are important to foreground when developing health data governance frameworks.

15.2 A (Typical) Health Data Regulatory Ecosystem

While every jurisdiction has its nuances, data regulation around the world is increasingly aligned, a by-product of the need to protect a widely shared conception of privacy while also allowing for the collection, use, and sharing of data by public and private bodies across borders. This section examines the data ecosystem in Canada, which has both federal and provincial elements.

[11] J Skopek, 'Big Data's Epistemology and Its Implications for Precision Medicine and Privacy' in Cohen I and others (eds.), *Big Data, Health Law and Bioethics* (Cambridge University Press, 2018).

[12] For example, consent is perishable (i.e., it is obtained for specific actions and limited periods, and needs to be refreshed over time to remain valid), de-identification is impossible in some contexts, and medical confidentiality is a significant barrier to 'precision medicine': D Townend, 'Conclusion: Harmonisation in Genomic and Health Data Sharing for Research: An Impossible Dream?' (2018) 137 *Human Genetics* 657.

15.2.1 Federal Elements

The *Privacy Act*,[13] as well as the *Access to Information Act*,[14] applies to all PI that is collected, used, retained, or disclosed by the federal public sector, and it has provincial/territorial counterparts across the country. Under the *Privacy Act*, PI is defined broadly as information about an identifiable individual that is recorded in any form, including information relating to one's:[15]

- race, national/ethnic origin, colour, religion, age, marital status, fingerprint, and blood type;
- educational, medical, criminal, employment, or financial history;
- address and assigned identifying numbers, symbols, or particulars;
- personal opinions or views, except in certain circumstances;
- correspondence to a government institution that is implicitly or explicitly of a private or confidential nature, and replies to such correspondence;
- views or opinions about another individual, or about certain specified events; and
- name where it appears with other PI relating to the individual, or where the disclosure of the name itself would reveal information about the individual.

In *Mountain Province Diamonds Inc. v De Beers Canada Inc.*,[16] it was held that privacy rights, and an individual's ability to control the use of PI, are *quasi-constitutional rights* that help preserve a free and democratic society. Thus, the baseline is that no PI is to be collected by government institutions unless it relates directly to the institution's programmes or activities.[17] Where PI *is* collected, the institution must, wherever possible, collect it directly from the individual to whom it relates, indicating the purpose for the collection, except where the individual authorises otherwise, or where PI may be disclosed to the institution under Section 8(2),[18] which states that an institution may disclose information for specified reasons. Every citizen or permanent

[13] RSC 1985, c. P-21.

[14] Ibid., c. A-1.

[15] *Privacy Act*, RSC 1985, c. P-21, s 3, at https://laws-lois.justice.gc.ca/eng/acts/P-21/index.html.

[16] (2014) 25 BLR (5th) 141 (OSC), citing *Alberta (IPC) v United Food and Commercial Workers, Local 401* (2013) 3 SCR 733.

[17] *Privacy Act*, s 4.

[18] Ibid., ss 5(1) and (2).

resident shall be given, on request, any PI about him or her under the control of a government institution, so long as it is reasonably retrievable.[19]

Another important statute is the *Personal Information Protection and Electronic Documents Act* (PIPEDA).[20] PIPEDA governs the collection, use, or disclosure of PI in the course of (private sector) commercial activities, or federal works, including healthcare, and it can extend to foreign organisations if there are sufficient connections to Canada.[21] PIPEDA must be interpreted based on its own language, not with reference to the *Privacy Act*,[22] so a siloed approach has been adopted. Nonetheless, in *Royal Bank of Canada v Welton*,[23] it was held that PIPEDA is, in essence, a 'privacy statute' in keeping with the *Privacy Act*, so significant weight must be given to the public and individual value of privacy.

PIPEDA applies throughout Canada, unless it has been displaced by provincial legislation that the Governor-in-Council has declared to be substantially similar. To date, Québec, Alberta, and British Columbia have adopted substantially similar general legislation, and Newfoundland & Labrador, Nova Scotia, New Brunswick, and Ontario have adopted substantially similar legislation with respect to PHI. Nonetheless, PIPEDA continues to apply to all interprovincial and international transactions by all organisations subject to the act, as well as to federally regulated organisations such as banks, telecommunications, and transportation companies.

PIPEDA has the dual role of promoting commercial enterprises (and e-commerce) while also supporting consumers and protecting privacy interests. This dual role was acknowledged in *Englander v TELUS*

[19] Ibid., s 12(1).

[20] *Personal Information Protection and Electronic Documents Act*, SC 2000, c. 5, https://laws-lois.justice.gc.ca/ENG/ACTS/P-8.6/index.html.

[21] In the webspace context, connecting factors include: (1) the location of the target audience of the website, (2) the source of the content on the website, (3) the location of the website operator, and (4) the location of the host server. *Desjean v Intermix Media Inc.*, (2007) 4 FCR 151 (TD), aff'd (2007) FCJ No. 1523 (CA). See also, *Douez v Facebook Inc.*, (2017) 1 SCR 751, on the validity of the forum selection clause used by Facebook in its terms of use; and *Google Inc. v. Equustek Solutions Inc.*, (2017) 1 SCR 824, on the validity of a BC court-ordered injunction against Google to globally deindex websites of a certain distributor who was continuing to act unlawfully.

[22] *Canada (PCC) v Blood Tribe Department of Health*, (2008) 2 SCR 574.

[23] (2009), 93 OR (3d) 403 (CA).

Communications Inc.,[24] wherein Décary JA described PIPEDA as a compromise both in terms of substance and form, and indicated that the competing interests at stake must be balanced. This is apparent from the ten interrelated Fáir Information Principles that are contained in Schedule 1: accountability; identifying purposes; consent; limiting collection; limiting use, disclosure and retention; accuracy; safeguards; openness; individual access; and challenging compliance.

In PIPEDA, as in the *Privacy Act*, PI is defined as any factual or subjective information, recorded or not, about an identifiable individual, including information in any form.[25] Courts have interpreted PI broadly to include any information that has a 'serious possibility' of identifying an individual through the use of the information alone or in combination with other available information.[26] In *Gordon v Canada (Minister of Health)*,[27] a case arising from a journalist's request for data from Health Canada's adverse drug reaction reporting system (CADRIS), the Federal Court found that information as to a person's provincial place of residence is PI.

Commercial activities are defined as any transaction, act, or conduct, or any regular course of conduct that is of a commercial character, including the selling, bartering, or leasing of donor, membership, or other fundraising lists.[28] Organisations may collect, use, or disclose PI only for purposes that a reasonable person would consider appropriate in the circumstances, and they must obtain consent when they collect, use, or disclose PI, unless they are otherwise authorised to do so by law.[29] With respect to what a reasonable person would consider appropriate, expectations must be assessed objectively but within the context of the relationship between the subject individual(s) and organisation(s),[30] and

[24] [2005] 2 FCR 572 (CA).

[25] PIPEDA, s 2(1).

[26] *MG Canada Inc. v John Doe* (2004) 3 FC 241 (TD).

[27] (2004) 324 FTR 94 (TD).

[28] PIPEDA, s 2(1).

[29] Ibid., ss 4, 5(3) and 7. For a discussion of when PI can be disclosed without the consent of the data subject, see *R v Spencer* (2011), 377 Sask R 280 (CA), which involves the disclosure of a client's name and address to the police by an Internet carrier in a case of suspected child pornography. The court held that, while the police inquiry was intrusive and could reveal intimate details of lifestyle and personal choices, in the light of the nature of the investigation, the inquiry was not unduly intrusive and the defendant could have no reasonable expectation of privacy in relation to the disclosed information.

[30] *Wansink v TELUS Communications Inc.*, (2007) 4 FCR 368 (CA).

not as necessarily determined by industry practice.[31] Thus, it is the parties' expectations and the circumstances around their interaction that drive the balancing process.[32]

An individual may complain to the organisation in question or to the Privacy Commissioner of Canada (PCC) about any alleged breaches of the law.[33] The PCC may also initiate a complaint and may audit the data management practices of an organisation.[34] Breaches of information safeguards must be reported to the PCC.[35] It is an offence to destroy PI that an individual has requested, to retaliate against an employee who has complained to the PCC, or who refuses to contravene sections 5–10 of the Act or to obstruct a complaint investigation or audit by the PCC.[36]

15.2.2 Provincial Elements

These national laws work in combination with provincial laws, which vary from province to province. The primary statute relevant to PHI in Nova Scotia is the *Personal Health Information Act* (PHIA),[37] which is recognised as substantially similar to PIPEDA in the health data context, and so displaces it in certain situations. PHIA applies to the collection, use, and disclosure of health card numbers and PHI.[38] It does *not* apply to statistical, aggregate or de-identified health information, or to PHI about an individual after 120 years after a record containing the information was created or 50 years after the death of the individual, whichever is earlier.[39] It defines PHI broadly to include identifying information about an individual, whether living or deceased, and in both recorded and unrecorded forms, if the information relates to:[40]

31 *Nammo v TransUnion of Canada Inc.*, (2012) 3 FCR 600 (TD).

32 In *Eastmond v Canadian Pacific Railway* (2004), 254 FTR 169 (TD), an employer erected surveillance cameras which captured images of employees at work and other people. The court found this to constitute collection of PI. In determining that it was reasonable, the court offered the following questions: is privacy invasion necessary to meet a specific need? Is the invasion likely to be effective in meeting that need? Is the loss of privacy proportional to the benefit gained? Is there a less invasive way of achieving the same end? The court also observed that the appropriate purposes for collection may be different than the appropriate purposes for use.

33 PIPEDA s 11(1).

34 Ibid., ss 11(2), 12 and 18.

35 Ibid., s 10.1.

36 Ibid., ss 27 and 28.

37 SNS 2010, c. 41.

38 PHIA s 5(1).

39 Ibid., s 5(2).

40 Ibid., s 3(r).

(i) the physical or mental health of the individual, including information that consists of the health history of the individual's family;[41]
(ii) the application, assessment, eligibility, and provision of healthcare to the individual, including the identification of one as a provider of healthcare to the individual;
(iii) payments or eligibility for healthcare in respect of the individual;
(iv) the donation by the individual of any body part or bodily substance of the individual, or is derived from the testing or examination of same;
(v) the individual's registration information, including health card number; or
(vi) an individual's substitute decision-maker identity.

PHIA also states that identifying information that does not fall within one or more of the above categories but is nevertheless 'contained in a record that contains [PHI]' will be treated as PHI under the Act.[42]

The central concept around which PHIA is structured is 'privacy', tempered by a recognition of the need to use PHI to provide, support, and manage healthcare.[43] The foundational proposition is that PHI will not be collected, used, or disclosed. Assuming the information does not fall within one of the exceptions under Section 5(2), PHIA directs that a 'custodian'[44] *shall not* collect, use, or disclose PHI about an individual unless:

[41] In *Nova Scotia (PPS) v Fitzgerald Estate*, 2015 NSCA 38, it was acknowledged that information in a publicly held record may engage the privacy rights of several individuals, in which case the decision-maker must balance the competing interests. *Re Department of Community Services*, FI-10-95, 19 November 2015 (NSPC) and *Re Department of Community Services*, FI-11-71, 19 November 2015 (NSPC) were both cases in which an individual sought information about their entrance into foster care. Commissioner Tully held that disclosing the PI of the implicated third parties, including family health history, would serve an important purpose, and that that disclosure was also favoured by the fact that there was no other source from which the applicants could obtain some of the PI.

[42] PHIA, s 4(1). In *Re Office of the Premier*, IR16-01, 11 February 2016 (NSPC), a recording was released that contained revelations about the health status of a public individual. In holding it to be PHI, Commissioner Tully noted that (1) privacy protections safeguard democratic societies by furthering autonomy, self-fulfilment and freedom, (2) public bodies must be vigilant to ensure that their privacy controls are current and effective, and (3) much of the government training around privacy is inadequate.

[43] PHIA, s 2.

[44] Ibid., s 3(f) defines 'custodian' as an individual or organisation who has custody or control of PHI as a result of, or in connection with, performing the duties or exercising the powers of the person or organization, including a number of specified entities (e.g., a regulated health professional, a person who operates a group practice of such professionals, the minister, a district health authority, Canadian Blood Services, and other individuals or organisations prescribed by regulation).

the custodian has the individual's consent, *and* the collection, use, or disclosure is reasonably necessary for a lawful purpose; or the collection, use, or disclosure is permitted or required by PHIA.[45] Consent is required at the point of collection. Where it is required, consent can be express, either written or oral,[46] or implied.[47] In either case, it must be 'knowledgeable',[48] voluntary, applicable to the specific information at issue, and given by the data subject or their substitute decision-maker.[49] Where the information is collected for a purpose unrelated to health, such as fundraising or marketing, explicit consent is required.[50] Multiple provisions further embed and advance the privacy disposition of the act:

- An individual can limit or revoke their consent to the collection, use, or disclosure of PHI at any time, at which point the custodian must inform the individual of the consequences of this course and take reasonable steps to comply.[51]
- A custodian cannot collect, use, or disclose PHI if other information will suffice.[52]
- A custodian must limit the collection, use, or disclosure of PHI to only that which is necessary to achieve the (lawful) purpose.[53]

PHIA goes on to state that a custodian may use PHI (1) for the purpose for which it was collected or created and all functions reasonably necessary for carrying out that purpose, (2) for a purpose which PHIA permits, and (3) for educating healthcare professionals.[54] It also enumerates circumstances in which consent is *not required*, including:[55]

- planning or delivering programmes or services, and detecting and preventing fraudulent receipt of services or benefits;
- ensuring standards of care within a quality review programme within the custodian's organisation;

45 PHIA s 11.
46 Ibid., s 16.
47 Ibid., s 12.
48 This means that the individual knows, or it is reasonable in the circumstances to believe that s/he knows, the purpose for the collection, use, or disclosure, and that s/he can give or withhold consent: PHIA ss 14 and 15.
49 PHIA ss 13 and 21–23.
50 Ibid., ss 32(a) and (b).
51 Ibid.
52 Ibid.
53 Ibid., s 25.
54 PHIA s 33.
55 Ibid., ss 35 and 38.

- creating or maintaining an electronic health record, if the custodian is the minister and the information was collected from another custodian for that purpose;
- risk management or patient safety within the custodian's organisation; or
- research conducted by the custodian, in accordance with sections 52–60.

These permitted (or lawful) uses represent derogations from the primary proposition (no collection, use, or disclosure without consent), inserting flexibilities that permit PHI sharing.[56]

With respect to research, a custodian may use and/or disclose PHI for research purposes provided (1) the research has been approved by a Research Ethics Board (REB), (2) the researcher(s) involved (whether the custodian or others) have submitted a research plan, and (3) the researcher(s) and custodian have in place a sharing agreement.[57] The custodian must be satisfied that: the research cannot be conducted without the PHI; the amount of PHI to be used is limited to the amount that is actually needed; the PHI has been de-identified as much as possible; the PHI will be used in a manner that ensures confidentiality; and it is impracticable to obtain consent.[58] The REB must determine that the consent of the individuals whose PHI is implicated is not required.[59] The wording of the research-related provisions thus set a high bar for conducting research with PHI in the absence of prior consent.

Curiously, PHIA contains no penalties for failures to comply on the part of custodians or others. It states that privacy breaches (i.e., circumstances in which PHI has been stolen, lost, or subject to unauthorised access, use, disclosure, copying, or modification) must be reported to the subject individual,[60] unless the custodian considers that there is no potential for harm or embarrassment to the individual, in which case the custodian must inform the Nova Scotia Privacy Commissioner (NSPC).[61]

[56] In *Finney v Joshi*, 2016 NSSC 227, the Court held that a physician's request for disclosure of hospital records so he could identify his whereabouts during rounds would not need PHI about patients, and was not therefore a request for PHI. The records could be de-identified and supplied to the physician with reasonable effort.

[57] PHIA, ss 55 and 56. For more on the Research Plan and Research Agreement, see PHIA, ss 59 and 60.

[58] Ibid., s 57. Reiterated in PHIA, s 54.

[59] Ibid.

[60] Ibid., s 69.

[61] Ibid., s 70.

The result is that minor breaches are relayed to the NSPC and not to the individual, and major breaches are relayed to the individual, but not necessarily to the NSPC. In Nova Scotia, there have been serious breaches relating to PHI,[62] including intentional breaches resulting from ineffective breach management protocols and technical auditing capacities,[63] but inadequate training and enforcement has been identified as a problem across Canada.[64]

A further feature of the Nova Scotia ecosystem is the *Personal Information International Disclosure Protection Act* (PIIDPA).[65] It applies to all records in the custody or under the control of any public body.[66] All public bodies must ensure that PI in its custody or control, or that of a service provider or associate of a service provider, is stored and accessed only in Canada, unless consent has been obtained for storage and access to be outside Canada, or such is otherwise permitted by the Act (i.e., such as when the head of a public body considers the storage or access to meet the requirements of the body's operation).[67] PI can be disclosed for research purposes.[68] When storage, access, or disclosure of PI is outside Canada, only that information which is necessary to fulfil the public body's obligation shall be used, and the service provider must have in place reasonable security arrangements to protect the data.[69] Those found in breach of the Act are liable on summary conviction to a fine of up to $2,000 and imprisonment of fewer than six months.[70]

62 Y Colbert, 'More Than 2,500 Privacy Breaches at NS Health Authority in Recent Years, Report Says', *CBC News*, 22 May 2019, www.cbc.ca/news/canada/nova-scotia/privacy-breaches-nsha-privacy-comissioner-1.5138360?cmp=rss, accessed 28 July 2021.

63 *Re Nova Scotia Department of Health and Wellness*, IR18-01, 1 August 2018 (NSPC); *Re Sobeys National Drug Pharmacy Group*, IR18-02, 1 August 2018 (NSPC).

64 PCC, 'Appearance Before the Standing Committee on Access to Information, Privacy and Ethics (ETHI) Before the International Grand Committee on Big Data, Privacy and Democracy', 28 May 2019, www.priv.gc.ca/en/opc-actions-and-decisions/advice-to-parliament/2019/parl_20190528/, accessed 28 July 2021; PCC, 'Guidance on Inappropriate Data Practices: Interpretation and Application of s 5(3) PIPEDA' 2018, www.priv.gc.ca/en/privacy-topics/collecting-personal-information/consent/gd_53_201805/, accessed 28 July 2021.

65 SNS 2006 c. 3.

66 PIIDPA, ss 3 and 4.

67 Ibid., ss 5(1–3). In *R v Clarke* (2015), 363 NSR (2d) 337 (SC), it was held that public bodies like the Securities Commission and the RCMP could share information internationally in pursuit of investigations.

68 Ibid., s 10.

69 Ibid., s 5(4).

70 Ibid., ss 12 and 13.

15.3 Shortcomings in the Ecosystem

It should be clear from the above that Nova Scotia's ecosystem, a typical Canadian exemplar, has uncertainties and tensions. This section explores some areas of concern that are of broader (international) interest.

15.3.1 Slippage towards Commodification

Traditionally, ownership was not recognised in facts or information; they were viewed as unencumbered phenomena in the public domain that could be used by anyone (i.e., they represented the 'knowledge commons'). However, key actors in the *knowledge economy* have pushed for information enclosure and/or monetisation. A central idea that now informs the data ecosystem is that of 'ownership', which encourages propertisation of data. It has been held, for example, that healthcare professionals – who hold PHI in trust and for the benefit of patients – 'own' the record, and can pledge it as an asset or post it as a security in pursuit of their own interest, so long as doing so does not conflict with the duty to act in the patient's best interests.[71] The control furnished by consent and its withdrawal also encourages the idea of 'ownership' by patients, which gives rise to the idea of property in the data. This sense of ownership is bolstered by the individual right to exclude or withdraw data from further use at any time, or narrow consent to use after the original consent has been given, thus compromising the stability of existing data resources.[72] This property/ownership model is further supported by the rights of portability, erasure, and correction.[73]

While ownership does *not* necessitate a right to sell, some argue that patients should be given both ownership and monetisation rights over their PI.[74] Advocates have long drawn on debates around human tissue, body parts, and Indigenous resources to argue for individual

[71] *McInerney v MacDonald*, (1992) 2 SCR 138; *Maximum Financial Services Inc. v 1144517 Alberta Ltd.*, 2015 ABQB 646; *Re Axelrod* (1994), 20 OR (3d) 133 (CA).

[72] J Contreras and F Nordfalk, 'Liability (and) Rules for Health Information' (2019) 29 *Health Matrix* 1.

[73] J Rumbold and B Pierscionek, 'Why Patients Shouldn't "Own" Their Medical Records' (2016) 34 *Nature Biotechnology* 586. It can also be detected in US statutes from Alaska, Colorado, Florida, Georgia, and Louisiana which give individuals 'ownership' over their genetic information.

[74] M Hall, 'Property, Privacy and the Pursuit of Interconnected Electronic Health Records' (2010) 95 *Iowa Law Review* 631.

property rights in PI and PHI.[75] These arguments have relied on claims that individuals:

- must have their autonomy, privacy, and dignity protected (in this particular way);[76]
- should be able to share in the financial rewards that are being enjoyed by some (such as big pharma);[77]
- could thereby re-balance the power being accumulated by large data-holding corporations.[78]

However, a property approach based on consent will have limited potential to positively influence these matters. A property approach that additionally monetises PI for individuals, injecting a sense of negotiated participation and individual gain, will significantly undermine the possibilities for maximal use of data within healthcare systems and by researchers. As such, it has been challenged morally,[79] doctrinally,[80] and practically (e.g., increased upfront costs and instability of data resources).[81] Further, commodification may be contrary to professional ethical values and standards and may undermine the patient–caregiver relationship.

75 J Cohen, 'Examined Lives: Informational Privacy and the Subject as Object' (2000) 52 *Stanford Law Review* 1373; P Schwartz, 'Property, Privacy, and Personal Data' (2004) 117 *Harvard Law Review* 2056; R Thaler, 'Show Us the Data (It's Ours, After All)', *New York Times*, 23 April 2011; M Rothstein, 'Ethical Issues in Big Data Health Research' (2015) 43 *Journal of Law, Medicine & Ethics* 425.

76 J Roberts, 'Progressive Genetic Ownership' (2018) 93 *Notre Dame Law Review* 1105. *Beleno v Lakey* (2009) 306 F.Supp.3d 930 (Tex. Dist. Ct.), resulted in a settlement under which the state destroyed its repository of 5.3 million infant blood samples.

77 M Hall and K Schulman, 'Ownership of Medical Information' (2009) 301 *JAMA* 1282.

78 N Purtova, 'Do Property Rights in Personal Data Make Sense After the Big Data Turn?' (2017) 10 *Journal of Law & Economic Regulation* 208.

79 Dignitarian claims that certain things should never be alienable or subject to market transactions have long persisted: M Radin, 'Market-Inalienability' (1987) 100 *Harvard Law Review* 1849; R Brownsword, 'The Cult of Consent: Fixation and Fallacy' (2004) 15 *King's Law Journal* 223. It has been argued that corporate ownership in particular is morally and socially inimical: M Rodwin, 'The Case for Public Ownership of Patient Data' (2009) 302 *JAMA* 86.

80 I Cohen, 'Is There a Duty to Share Healthcare Data?' in Cohen I and others (eds), *Big Data, Health Law and Bioethics* (Cambridge University Press 2018) 209. It has been argued that many protections sought to be achieved through property law already exist in regulatory frameworks applicable to medical records and research, and no greater level of patient confidentiality will be enjoyed if patients 'own' their samples and data: B Evans, 'Barbarians at the Gate: Consumer-Driven Health Data Commons and the Transformation of Citizen Science' (2016) 42 *American Journal of Law & Medicine* 651.

81 J Contreras, 'Genetic Property' (2016) 105 *Georgetown Law Journal* 1.

While the rights of data subjects to access data about them are important and valuable (for matters ranging from accuracy to self-care to personal identity), there is little value in extending avenues of gain to the many data subjects that will contribute to existing and emerging datasets, and whose mass contribution is necessary to make the datasets useful. Indeed, serious consideration might be given to restricting the 'ownership' rights to PHI and health datasets to *public institutions* that have the 'common good' as their primary objective.[82] But most regulatory frameworks have very little to say about the commercial use of data, with the result that it is not entirely clear who 'owns' the accumulating health data, although note that commercial use is one of the premises of PIPEDA. In the US context, the following has been reported:

> [It] is not clear where those who sell data analytics services obtain the data, or how they might use them. Well-known electronic health records vendors have sold de-identified copies of their patient databases to pharmaceutical companies, medical device makers, and health services researchers. Vendor contracts are unusual in that some vendors lay claim to patient record data, whereas businesses and financial institutions typically do not give up their data to their software vendors. Regardless of whether the data themselves or the means of access to them are owned by...vendors, some academic medical centers pay to get data from their own patients' records. Vendors often consider their contracts intellectual property and do not reveal these and other contract provisions, a practice the American Medical Informatics Association considers unethical.[83]

Ultimately, the matter of ownership is worth direct and explicit legislative clarification, with specific attention to the needs of the public (and public goods). Currently, proprietary claims are advanced in relation to records, aggregated data, and databases themselves, with a range of actors having interests, and it is not clear how these claims and interests should be balanced.

15.3.2 Insufficient Foundational Pillars

Like many others, the ecosystem conceptualises PI and PHI collection and use as a *competition* between the individual right to privacy and the social utility of information disclosure, both of which are erected as pillars of the

[82] There are many cases exposing unethical business practices in accessing and controlling consumer PI: *Re Ticketmaster Canada Ltd.*, Investigation Report 2008-388, 12 February 2008 (PCC); *Re Facebook Inc.*, Investigation Report 2009-008, 16 July 2009 (PCC).

[83] B Kaplan, 'How Should Health Data Be Used?' (2016) 25 *Cambridge Quarterly of Healthcare Ethics* 312, 322–23.

regime. As such, it emphasises the need to *balance* conflicting interests, individual on the one hand and social on the other. This conceptualisation of data use as competition is exemplified by *Fontaine v Canada (AG)*,[84] wherein the court understood individual privacy as *competing* with the public good of having information available in perpetuity. It also acknowledged the *social value* of avoiding group harms by permitting individuals and groups to distance themselves from their past and to forge new identities through information enclosure.

However, there are other fundamental interests at play which should serve as foundational pillars, but do not. The most obvious one is 'equity' (i.e., the multifaceted interest in legal, social and healthcare equality, and a reduction of distributive inequity). Equity ought to be a core concern, particularly in relation to historically marginalised groups, many of whom have had consistently negative experiences within the healthcare system.[85] The general and health-related inequity suffered by Indigenous communities in Canada and elsewhere, for example, is well documented.[86] Dismay has been expressed at the delivery of Indigenous data to commercial entities who then sell that processed data back to the healthcare system.[87] While there is value in more data and more useful data being generated about Indigenous peoples, these data must be generated *with* Indigenous communities and *for* Indigenous communities:

> In the past, Aboriginal people have not been consulted about what information should be collected, who should gather that information, who should maintain it, and who should have access to it. The information gathered may or may not have been relevant to the questions, priorities and concerns of Aboriginal peoples. Because data gathering has frequently been imposed by outside authorities, it has met with resistance in many quarters.[88]

It has thus been argued that data must be generated using Indigenous 'frames of view', relying on greater engagement with Indigenous people

[84] (2014) 122 OR (3d) 1 (SCJ), var'd (2016) 130 OR (3d) 1 (CA) aff'd (2017) 2 SCR 205.

[85] E Callahan and others, 'Eliminating LGBTIQQ Health Disparities: The Associated Roles of Electronic Health Records and Institutional Culture' (2014) 44 *Hastings Center Report* S48.

[86] J Reading and E Nowgesic, 'Improving the Health of Future Generations: The Canadian Institutes of Health Research Institute of Aboriginal Peoples' Health' (2002) 92 *American Journal of Public Health* 1396; M King, 'An Overall Approach to Health Care for Indigenous Peoples' (2009) 56 *Pediatric Clinics* 1239.

[87] C Paul and others, 'Being Sorry Is Not Enough: The Sorry State of the Evidence Base for Improving the Health of Indigenous Populations' (2010) 38 *American Journal of Preventive Medicine* 566.

[88] Royal Commission on Aboriginal Peoples, *Report of the Royal Commission on Aboriginal Peoples: Gathering Strength* (1997) ch. 5, p. 4.

in data conceptualisation, design, collection, analysis and reporting, and offering greater levels of control by Indigenous groups over data relevant to their communities.[89] The need for greater Indigenous involvement in PHI generation, curation, and application is supported by the 2007 UN Declaration on the Rights of Indigenous Peoples,[90] which serves to emphasise that the locus of authority over data relating to Indigenous peoples, their lands, and ways of life must rest with Indigenous peoples.

Obviously, the need to ensure that data custodians and users are not benefitting from access to, and control over, PI at the cost of those who supply and are the subjects of the data implicates the data ecosystem profoundly. Both equity and the associated notion of data sovereignty demands a more nuanced and non-dichotomous approach to PHI collection, use, and disclosure. Moving from the two-pillar foundation that prevails to a tripartite foundation that includes equity makes sense when one recognises that privacy, data access/use, and equity (with its elements of social and cultural reparation) *are all public goods*. Such might mean explicit recognition in the framework of the role of further and community-based decisional bodies.

15.3.3 Misaligned Mechanisms of Action

Setting aside the absence of the desired third pillar, the ecosystem does a relatively poor job of actually advancing its existing pillars; it hardly treats privacy like the socially and constitutionally significant right that it is,[91] and it hampers maximal data use, which undermines the utility imperative.

In support of privacy protection, the framework adopts very broad definitions of PI and PHI. It then negates this breadth by removing all data that has been 'de-identified' from any statutory protection. Indeed, anonymisation has become the primary means of avoiding statutory standards. The difficulty is that true anonymisation is often difficult, and

[89] First Nations Information Governance Centre, *Ownership, Control, Access and Possession (OCAP™): The Path to First Nations Information Governance* (2014); T Kukutai and J Taylor (eds.), *Indigenous Data Sovereignty: Toward an Agenda* (ANU Press, 2016).

[90] UN General Assembly Resolution 61/295, United Nations Declaration on the Rights of Indigenous Peoples (13 September 2007).

[91] Although individuals seem willing to abandon their privacy in certain contexts (e.g., social media), and the rise of 'surveillance capitalism' has undermined many privacy protections, personal and informational privacy have been characterised as quasi-constitutional rights necessary for the realisation of autonomy, dignity, integrity and a democratic society: *R v Dyment*, (1988) 2 SCR 417.

anonymisation can diminish the value of the data.[92] One could argue, therefore, that the protections enumerated, or at least some of them, should operate even in the context of de-identified data.

The framework also relies on notice and consent as a means of empowering data subjects.[93] Collection, use, and disclosure generally requires the consent of the data subject and is limited to the minimum amount of data necessary to achieve the purpose(s) identified in the notice used to secure that consent (i.e., data may not be used for other unrelated purposes without new consent). However, this approach does little to protect individuals or to support the valuable uses of data that are unknown at the time of collection.[94] The following has been observed:

> The narrower the scope of notice and consent, the greater the restrictions imposed on future, often unknown uses of data. This can interfere with future benefits and hinder valuable new discoveries. On the other hand, because privacy notices…constrain future data uses, notices have become increasingly broad and permissive. The result has been the increasing erosion of information privacy. In both cases, the reliance on notice and choice has had the effect of shifting much of the responsibility for data protection away from data collectors and data users and onto data subjects.[95]

Notice and consent systems may provide protection in certain contexts but are increasingly ineffective as the primary mechanism for ensuring information privacy. Ultimately, the ecosystem furnishes data subjects with the very limited power to say 'yes' or 'no' to data disclosure, while data users are subject to relatively weak regimes, the oversight of which is negligible.

Obviously, data use is facilitated by limiting the legislative protections to *identifying* PI and PHI, but some of the other conditions in the framework have the effect of seriously hampering maximal data use. For example, the minimisation imperative, which withholds potentially important

92 J Henriksen-Bulmer and S Jeary, 'Re-Identification Attacks – A Systematic Literature Review' (2016) 36 *International Journal of Information Management* 1184.

93 This approach derives from the OECD, *Guidelines on the Protection of Privacy and Transborder Flows of Personal Data* (2013), www.oecd.org/sti/ieconomy/privacy.htm, accessed 28 July 2021.

94 New uses enabled by Big Data include (1) examining health records and lab results for medical research, (2) analysing billions of internet search records to map flu outbreaks and identify dangerous drug interactions, (3) searching financial records to detect and prevent money laundering, and (4) tracking vehicles and pedestrians to aid in infrastructure planning.

95 F Cate and others, 'Data Protection Principles for the 21st Century: Revising the 1980 OECD Guidelines' 2014, www.oii.ox.ac.uk/archive/downloads/publications/Data_Protection_Principles_for_the_21st_Century.pdf, accessed 28 July 2021.

data from use, might be criticised as being overly restrictive. The 'types of use' approach – by which processes and limitations for access obtain based on whether the data are intended for systems assessment purposes or research purposes – can be described as confusing and counterproductive insofar as it creates regulatory categories that do not effectively reflect how data are collected, or how it can be used to help inform decisions.

The difficulties generated by these imperatives are compounded by the fact that there is very little guidance as to how they should be interpreted. Presently, data custodians interpret legislative standards according to their own institutional culture and practices. This has led to several sub-optimal phenomena. First, the rules receive considerably different treatments depending on the actor; some data custodians are very risk averse, which limits the possibilities for effective data use. Second, an approach has evolved whereby access to, and use of, data for research is limited by the need for a hypothesis-based protocol, but this is not reflective of how value is typically generated from Big Data. In the end, the framework is both over- and under-inclusive.

15.3.4 Underdeveloped Ethics Element

Given the importance of research in this setting, ethics is an important feature of the landscape. Unless research is ethical (i.e., exhibits necessity, coherence, and excellence), it will have questionable veracity and little value, and will not be worthy of the public's trust.[96] Ethics frameworks are intended to ensure that all research undertaken is both warranted and properly designed, and is pursued such that rights are protected and outcomes are reliable. However, ethics review of research remains a distributed task in Nova Scotia, with no legislative foundation. The ethics environment is therefore fragmented and uneven, with standards interpreted and enforced through local institutions such as university-based REBs, the Nova Scotia Health Authority REB, and the IWK Health Centre REB.

In addition to being fragmented, the existing ethics architecture has little systematised communication between major REBs, and no systematised shared learning platforms for members of the REBs.[97] This means that learning is not shared, common practices and forms are not efficiently

[96] Council of Canadian Academies, *Honesty, Accountability and Trust: Fostering Research Integrity in Canada* (2010), 38.

[97] The Canadian Association of Research Ethics Boards hosts annual conferences, but funds are not readily available to REB members to attend these conferences.

developed, and ethics reviews (and experiences) are unlikely to be consistent throughout the region, or even within large and diffuse institutions with multiple REBs. Aside from the online 'TCPS2 Core Tutorial',[98] there is no mandatory, in-depth, and systematised individual training or certification for REB members, and no recertification after the passage of time.[99] This, combined with the absence of experiential sharing events, means that REBs (and reviewers) will most likely approach new research methods and problems in an ad hoc rather than a systematic and informed manner.[100]

Given the importance of effective and consistent ethics review and monitoring to good science, there have been calls for empirical research into the workings of REBs,[101] with some arguing for legislation.[102] In the context of data-intensive health research specifically, the following have been identified as impediments to good research design and administration: (1) variability, inconsistency, and duplication; (2) lack of communication between REBs; (3) insufficient expertise of REB members; and (4) local sensitivity and jurisdictional politics.[103] Recommendations that have been advanced are regulatory-based leadership for REBs and the development of mutual recognition agreements between REBs.

Of course, these reforms will have little impact if researchers are not using the system; much AI research, for example, is conducted in the absence of civil society or ethical review, or any true social-systems analysis.[104] In the United Kingdom, there have been calls for the NHS AI Lab to create an Ethics Advisory Board, which might monitor,

98 Panel on Research Ethics, 'TCPS2 Tutorial Course on Research Ethics (CORE)', www.pre.ethics.gc.ca/eng/education/tutorial-didacticiel/, accessed 28 July 2021.

99 Some REB members have access to the CITI Program 'Research Ethics and Compliance Training', https://about.citiprogram.org/en/homepage/, accessed 28 July 2021.

100 For more on training, see R Egan and others, 'Research Ethics Board (REB) Members' Preparation for, and Perceived Knowledge of Research Ethics' (2016) 14 *Journal of Academic Ethics* 191.

101 S Page and J Nyeboer, 'Improving the Process of Research Ethics Review' (2017) 2 *Research Integrity and Peer Review* 14.

102 J Kotecha and others, 'Ethics and Privacy Issues of a Practice-based Surveillance System: Need for a National-level Institutional Research Ethics Board and Consent Standards' (2011) 57 *Canadian Family Physician* 1165; M Herder, 'When Everyone Is an Orphan: Against Adopting a U.S.-Styled Orphan Drug Policy in Canada' (2013) 20 *Responsibility in Research* 227.

103 E Dove and C Garattini, 'Expert Perspectives on Ethics Review of International Data-Intensive Research: Working Towards Mutual Recognition' (2018) 14 *Research Ethics* 1.

104 K Crawford and R Calo, 'There Is a Blind Spot in AI Research' (2016) 538 *Nature News* 311; B Stahl and D Wright, 'Ethics and Privacy in AI and Big Data: Implementing Responsible Research and Innovation' (2018) 16 *IEEE Security & Privacy* 26.

analyse, and address the normative and ethical issues that arise at the individual, interpersonal, group, institutional, and societal levels in AI for healthcare.[105]

15.4 Data Ecosystem Design Considerations

Bearing in mind the above critique, this final section suggests matters of importance for the design of the data ecosystem (legal regulation and the operation of repositories), namely support for social licence and the exploration of social values.

15.4.1 Social Licence to Operate

The term 'social licence to operate' (SLO) has two primary applications. It relates to the relationship between a profession and society, comprising the licence of certain occupational groups to carry out particular activities, and the mandate of its members to define proper conduct.[106] It also relates to the expectations of society regarding the conduct and activities of corporations that go beyond the requirements of formal regulation.[107] Wider usage of SLO has prompted a merged understanding which relates to the need in social undertakings of acceptance, engagement, and mutual benefit as between implicated actors.[108] It is understood as an articulation of the social contract that characterises a field.

In the health sciences, concerns over the social contract revolve around stakeholder empowerment, democratic decision-making, decision-maker competence, and conflicts of interest.[109] With respect to health

[105] J Morley and L Floridi, 'NHS AI Lab: Why We Need to Be Ethically Mindful About AI for Healthcare' (2019) SSRN 3445421, http://dx.doi.org/10.2139/ssrn.3445421. See also EU High-Level Expert Group on Artificial Intelligence, *Ethics Guidelines for Trustworthy AI* (2019), https://ec.europa.eu/digital-single-market/en/news/ethics-guidelines-trustworthy-ai, accessed 28 July 2021.

[106] M Dixon-Woods and R Ashcroft, 'Regulation and the Social Licence for Medical Research' (2008) 11 *Medicine, Health Care and Philosophy* 381.

[107] K Moffat and others, 'The Social License to Operate: A Critical Review' (2016) 89 *Forestry* 477.

[108] S Ramon and A Mohr, 'A Social License for Science: Capturing the Public of Co-Constructing Research?' (2014) 28 *Social Epistemology* 258.

[109] Academy of Medical Sciences, *Exploring a New Social Contract for Medical Innovation* (2015); C Gough and others, 'Understanding Key Elements in Establishing a Social License for CCS: An Empirical Approach' (2018) 68 *International Journal of Greenhouse Gas Control* 16.

data, SLO is required for both researchers and custodians.[110] Building that SLO demands multiple strategies sensitive to time, context, culture, social concerns, and technical, economic and social risks. Core elements of SLO-building/testing strategies are:

- identifying and involving the full range of communities of interest, ensuring that all actors have a role that permits meaningful contributions;
- crafting processes that allow for open and frank discussion, respectful contestation, negotiation of terms and objectives, meaningful discourse around risk/benefit balance, and that build trust through positive actions with discernable outcomes;
- developing a dynamic framework for ongoing engagement that is respectful of capacities and ways of working, and that can strengthen relationships and encourage foresight.

A key mechanism for defining the social contract under which actors will pursue an undertaking for building and measuring SLO, and for encouraging *justified* trust in the PHI setting is early, meaningful, and ongoing stakeholder engagement and participation in governance. This engagement becomes even more important when commercial actors are accessing PHI.[111] Publics can and do hold considerably nuanced views on health data sharing (i.e., they are not 'for' or 'against' it, but are concerned about context and objectives),[112] and are often concerned about ignorance as to what is being done with their data, undue profit by aggregators and users, and the potential for data to be used 'against' them in other contexts (e.g., employment, insurance). Unfortunately, policymaking is replete with examples of flawed or insufficient engagement with affected communities.[113]

[110] J Allen and others, 'The Role of Data Custodians in Establishing and Maintaining Social License for Health Research' (2019) *Bioethics Online*.

[111] A US survey found that 67% of participants agreed that clear notification of potential commercialisation is warranted, only 23% were comfortable with such use, and 62% believed that profits should be used to support future research: K Spector-Bagdady and others, 'Encouraging Participation and Transparency in Biobank Research' (2018) 37 *Health Affairs* 1313.

[112] M Aitken and others, 'Who Benefits and How? Public Expectations of Public Benefits From Data-Intensive Health Research' (2018) 5 *Big Data & Society* 1; N Howe and others, 'Systematic Review of Participants' Attitudes Towards Data Sharing: A Thematic Synthesis' (2018) 23 *Journal of Health Service Research Policy* 123.

[113] P Carter and others, 'The Social License for Research: Why *Care.Data* Ran into Trouble' (2015) 41 *Journal of Medical Ethics* 404.

With respect to ongoing engagement around repository operation and AI, and learning health system research itself, special challenges include: scale and nature of the research, which can be difficult appreciate; changing capacities of collection, use, and disclosure, which shift with technologies; separation of data researcher from subject(s); and scope of the populations implicated, which are often varied.[114] Engagement can take many forms depending on organisational context, governance structures, and patient populations, but they must be broadly inclusive of all stakeholders, with particular attention to traditionally marginalised groups. It is important that data use aligns with culturally appropriate objectives, and avoids the appropriation of knowledge.

Ultimately, it is important to explore social desires and tolerances, and to build support for data sharing by generating good evidence about how it will actually deliver the promised benefits. Governments can lead by example by moving more of their data holdings into the open data commons, and by requiring that clinical trial data be transparent.[115] SLO will be enhanced if it is not only individuals/patients who are expected to contribute data, but also users, including commercial users.

15.4.2 Social Values Explored

Science is not value-free, and health research ought to be solidly grounded on essential human values.[116] Similarly, laws should have some moral basis, particularly where there exists some potential for harm. Values are therefore important to the realisation of both good science and good governance, particularly where human health and well-being is implicated. However, values are often more assumed than explicit, and are often opaque or hidden, and therefore invisible, or they are stated and then under-operationalised, and therefore remain rhetorical.

Notions of justice and transparency make it imperative that both regulatory frameworks and repository governance structures clearly identify and define core values, and that the platform designed for processing and curating data embed and operationalise those values. A

[114] M Aitken and others, 'Consensus Statement on Public Involvement and Engagement with Data Intensive Health Research' (2019) 4 *International Journal of Population Data Science* 6.

[115] A Heitmueller and others, 'Developing Public Policy to Advance the Use of Big Data in Health Care' (2014) 33 *Health Affairs* 1523.

[116] F Mayor, 'Preface' in *Proceedings of the First Session of the IBC* (UNESCO 1994).

value-based and/or value-explicit regulatory approach for health has long been espoused,[117] and this is now being echoed in the information technologies context:

> government should develop a statement of values for our digital society. This will inform how laws are developed, interpreted, and applied, and will make explicit the principles that should guide the adoption of new technologies.[118]

These values serve as signals to all about what will inform actions and decisions (i.e., they are both descriptive and normative). While they should be informed by rights and ethics instruments, they should be discussed, developed, defined, and unpacked through the engagement exercises noted above.

To date, risk-based and autonomy-based approaches have heavily influenced structures and practices. Though autonomy is a central feature of regulatory and governance frameworks, true autonomy is not often achieved through existing practices.[119] Thus, in addition to reconceptualising autonomy so it is more relational, a broader value base might uncover a wider range of acceptable practices and outcomes. Some of these values will be general (i.e., applicable to the data ecosystem broadly), and some more procedural (i.e., applicable to the specific undertaking and its key actors). Attention should be paid to *all the values* within our moral and rights canon.[120]

Core general values include dignity, well-being, solidarity, knowledge, and equity. Narrower values aimed at the governance and research undertaking more specifically, include transparency, accountability, democracy, proportionality, reflexivity, honesty, confidentiality, and reciprocity. Each of these values can be associated with specific duties and rights and processes of action. Moreover, they produce a balance that might allow for more than existing uses, and more than prevailing 'altruism in, profit out'

[117] S Harmon, 'Solidarity: A (New) Ethic for Global Health Policy' (2006) 14 *Health Care Analysis* 215; S Harmon, 'Semantic, Pedantic or Paradigm Shift? Recruitment, Retention and Property in Modern Population Biobanking' (2008) 16 *European Journal of Health Law* 27; S Harmon and A McMahon, 'Banking (on) the Brain: From Consent to Authorisation and the Transformative Potential of Solidarity' (2014) 22 *Medical Law Review* 572.

[118] T Scassa, 'As Our Economy Becomes More Data Driven, Canadians Need a National Data Strategy that Encourages Innovation and Provides Security and Privacy' *Policy Options*, 15 January 2019.

[119] Autonomy is exercised in a social context that often has elements of oppression: C McLeod and S Sherwin, 'Relational Autonomy, Self-Trust, and Health Care for Patients Who Are Oppressed' (2000) 345 *Philosophy Publications* 259.

[120] B Knoppers and others, 'A Human Rights Approach to an International Code of Conduct for Genomic and Clinical Data Sharing' (2014) 133 *Human Genetics* 895.

paradigms. They should help inform an ecosystem and resource practices that accept that, without significantly greater social solidarity and attention to stakeholder obligations to others, the equitable and effective translation of scientific advances will not be realised.[121]

15.5 Conclusion

Healthcare systems are coming under immense pressure to deliver better services to more people at sustainable costs. One means of pursuing this objective is to make PI, PHI, and administrative health information (AHI) work harder. Efforts at realising this include marshalling under-utilised datasets for impactful research, designing learning healthcare systems with sensitive data feedback loops, and training AIs to undertake certain healthcare services. Some of the risks posed by this turn in data use are well rehearsed, and some are hardly contemplated. The above analysis suggests that the (health) data ecosystem in Nova Scotia, Canada, like many other data ecosystems, is not up to the task of ensuring that this data is used effectively for the common good while also meeting the expectations that people have for their personal well-being, autonomy, and privacy. In particular, the ecosystem exposes a trend towards propertisation and monetisation of data to the exclusion of key participants, a dual foundation when a tripartite foundation is more appropriate, poorly aligned mechanisms for advancing its foundational principles, and inadequate attention to the formation of a robust and resilient ethics component. When considering the warranted ecosystem redesign, actors should pay careful attention to ensuring and revisiting the existence of an unambiguous SLO, and should take efforts to explore and expand the value foundation of the regime, which might open up whole new use and governance options.

Bibliography

Academy of Medical Sciences, *Exploring a New Social Contract for Medical Innovation* (Academy of Medical Sciences 2015).

Aitken M, Porteous C and others, 'Who Benefits and How? Public Expectations of Public Benefits from Data-Intensive Health Research' (2018) 5 *Big Data & Society* 1–12.

[121] Harmon, 'Solidarity'; Harmon, 'Semantic, Pedantic or Paradigm Shift'; Harmon and McMahon, 'Banking (on) the Brain'; D Townend, 'Privacy, Politeness and the Boundary Between Theory and Practice in Ethical Rationalism' in Capps P and Pattinson S (eds), *Ethical Rationalism and the Law* (Hart Publishing, 2017) 171.

Aitken M, Porteous C and Tully M and others, 'Consensus Statement on Public Involvement and Engagement with Data Intensive Health Research' (2019) 4 *International Journal of Population Data Science* 6.

Allen J, Adams C and Flack F, 'The Role of Data Custodians in Establishing and Maintaining Social License for Health Research' (2019) *Bioethics Online*.

Barua B, Hasan H and Timmermans I, *Comparing Performance of Universal Health Care Countries, 2017* (Fraser Institute 2017).

Bennett C, Parsons C and Molnar A, 'Forgetting, Non-Forgetting and Quasi Forgetting in Social Networking: Canadian Policy and Corporate Practice' in Gutwirth S, Leenes R and De Hert P (eds), *Reloading Data Protection: Multidisciplinary Insights and Contemporary Challenges* (Springer 2014) 41.

Brownsword R, 'The Cult of Consent: Fixation and Fallacy' (2004) 15 *King's Law Journal* 223.

Callahan E, Hazarian S and others, 'Eliminating LGBTIQQ Health Disparities: The Associated Roles of Electronic Health Records and Institutional Culture' (2014) 44 *Hastings Center Report* S48.

Carter P, Laurie G and Dixon-Woods M, 'The Social License for Research: Why *Care.Data* Ran into Trouble' (2015) 41 *Journal of Medical Ethics* 404.

Cate F, Cullen P and Mayer-Schönberger V, 'Data Protection Principles for the 21st Century: Revising the 1980 OECD Guidelines' 2014, www.oii.ox.ac.uk/archive/downloads/publications/Data_Protection_Principles_for_the_21st_Century.pdf, accessed 28 July 2021.

Cohen I, 'Is There a Duty to Share Healthcare Data?' in Cohen I, Fernandez Lynch H and others (eds), *Big Data, Health Law and Bioethics* (Cambridge University Press 2018) 209–22.

Cohen J, 'Examined Lives: Informational Privacy and the Subject as Object' (2000) 52 *Stanford Law Review* 1373.

Colbert Y, 'More Than 2,500 Privacy Breaches at NS Health Authority in Recent Years, Report Says' *CBC News*, 22 May 2019, www.cbc.ca/news/canada/nova-scotia/privacy-breaches-nsha-privacy-comissioner-1.5138360?cmp=rss, accessed 28 July 2021.

Commission on the Future of Health Care in Canada, *Building on Values: The Future of Health Care in Canada* (Queen's Printer 2002).

Contreras J, 'Genetic Property' (2016) 105 *The Georgetown Law Journal* 1.

Contreras J and Nordfalk F, 'Liability (and) Rules for Health Information' (2019) 29 *Health Matrix* 1.

Council of Canadian Academies, *Honesty, Accountability and Trust: Fostering Research Integrity in Canada* (Council of Canadian Academies 2010).

Crawford K and Calo R, 'There Is a Blind Spot in AI Research' (2016) 538 *Nature News* 311.

Dixon-Woods M and Ashcroft R, 'Regulation and the Social Licence for Medical Research' (2008) 11 *Medicine, Health Care and Philosophy* 381.

Dove E and Garattini C, 'Expert Perspectives on Ethics Review of International Data-Intensive Research: Working Towards Mutual Recognition' (2018) 14 *Research Ethics* 1.

Egan R, Stockley D and others, 'Research Ethics Board (REB) Members' Preparation for, and Perceived Knowledge of Research Ethics' (2016) 14 *Journal of Academic Ethics* 191.

EU High-Level Expert Group on Artificial Intelligence, *Ethics Guidelines for Trustworthy AI* (2019), https://ec.europa.eu/digital-single-market/en/news/ethics-guidelines-trustworthy-ai, accessed 28 July 2021.

Evans B, 'Barbarians at the Gate: Consumer-Driven Health Data Commons and the Transformation of Citizen Science' (2016) 42 *American Journal of Law & Medicine* 651.

First Nations Information Governance Centre, *Ownership, Control, Access and Possession (OCAP™): The Path to First Nations Information Governance* (2014).

Ford E, Boyd A and others, 'Our Data, Our Society, Our Health: A Vision for Inclusive and Transparent Health Data Science in the UK and Beyond' (2019) 3 *Learn Health Systems* 10191.

Gough C, Cunningham R and Mander S, 'Understanding Key Elements in Establishing a Social License for CCS: An Empirical Approach' (2018) 68 *The International Journal of Greenhouse Gas Control* 16.

Hall M, 'Property, Privacy and the Pursuit of Interconnected Electronic Health Records' (2010) 95 *Iowa Law Review* 631.

Hall M, and Schulman K, 'Ownership of Medical Information' (2009) 301 *JAMA* 1282.

Harmon S, 'Semantic, Pedantic or Paradigm Shift? Recruitment, Retention and Property in Modern Population Biobanking' (2008) 16 *European Journal of Health Law* 27.

Harmon S, 'Solidarity: A (New) Ethic for Global Health Policy' (2006) 14 *Health Care Analysis* 215.

Harmon S and McMahon A, 'Banking (on) the Brain: From Consent to Authorisation and the Transformative Potential of Solidarity' (2014) 22 *Medical Law Review* 572.

Heitmueller A, Henderson S and others, 'Developing Public Policy to Advance the Use of Big Data in Health Care' (2014) 33 *Health Affairs* 1523.

Henriksen-Bulmer J and Jeary S, 'Re-Identification Attacks – A Systematic Literature Review' (2016) 36 *The International Journal of Information Management* 1184.

Herder M, 'When Everyone Is an Orphan: Against Adopting a U.S.-Styled Orphan Drug Policy in Canada' (2013) 20 *Responsibility in Research* 227.

Howe N, Giles E and others, 'Systematic Review of Participants' Attitudes Towards Data Sharing: A Thematic Synthesis' (2018) 23 *Journal of Health Services Research and Policy* 123.

Kaplan B, 'How Should Health Data Be Used?' (2016) 25 *Cambridge Quarterly of Healthcare Ethics* 312.

Kass N, 'The Research-Treatment Distinction: A Problematic Approach for Determining Which Activities Should Have Ethical Oversight' (2013) 43 *Hastings Center Reports* S4.

King M, 'An Overall Approach to Health Care for Indigenous Peoples' (2009) 56 *Pediatric Clinics* 1239.

Knoppers B, Dove E and others, 'A Human Rights Approach to an International Code of Conduct for Genomic and Clinical Data Sharing' (2014) 133 *Human Genetics* 895.

Kotecha J, Manca D, and others, 'Ethics and Privacy Issues of a Practice-based Surveillance System: Need for a National-level Institutional Research Ethics Board and Consent Standards' (2011) 57 *Canadian Family Physician* 1165.

Kukutai T and Taylor J (eds), *Indigenous Data Sovereignty: Toward an Agenda* (ANU Press 2016).

McLeod C and Sherwin S, 'Relational Autonomy, Self-Trust, and Health Care for Patients Who Are Oppressed' (2000) 345 *Philosophy Publications* 259.

Mayer-Schonberger V, *Delete: The Virtue of Forgetting in the Digital Age* (Princeton University Press 2009).

Mayor F, 'Preface' in *Proceedings of the First Session of the IBC* (UNESCO 1994).

Moffat K, Lacey J and others, 'The Social License to Operate: A Critical Review' (2016) 89 *Forestry* 477.

Morley J and Floridi L, 'NHS AI Lab: Why We Need to Be Ethically Mindful About AI for Healthcare' (2019) SSRN 3445421, http://dx.doi.org/10.2139/ssrn.3445421.

NHS Digital, *Data Insights and Statistics: Information and Technology for Better Health and Care* (2018).

OECD, *Guidelines on the Protection of Privacy and Transborder Flows of Personal Data* (2013), www.oecd.org/sti/ieconomy/privacy.htm, accessed 28 July 2021

Page S and Nyeboer J, 'Improving the Process of Research Ethics Review' (2017) 2 *Research Integrity and Peer Review* 14.

Panel on Research Ethics, 'TCPS2 Tutorial Course on Research Ethics (CORE)', www.pre.ethics.gc.ca/eng/education/tutorial-didacticiel/, accessed 28 July 2021.

Paul C, Sanson-Fisher R and others, 'Being Sorry Is Not Enough: The Sorry State of the Evidence Base for Improving the Health of Indigenous Populations' (2010) 38 *American Journal of Preventive Medicine* 566.

PCC, 'Appearance Before the Standing Committee on Access to Information, Privacy and Ethics (ETHI) Before the International Grand Committee on Big Data, Privacy and Democracy', 28 May 2019, www.priv.gc.ca/en/opc-actions-and-decisions/advice-to-parliament/2019/parl_20190528/, accessed 28 July 2021.

PCC, 'Guidance on Inappropriate Data Practices: Interpretation and Application of s 5(3) PIPEDA' 2018, www.priv.gc.ca/en/privacy-topics/collecting-personal-information/consent/gd_53_201805/, accessed 28 July 2021.

Price W, 'Black-Box Medicine' (2016) 28 *The Harvard Journal of Law & Technology* 419.

Price W and Cohen I, 'Privacy in the Age of Medical Big Data' (2019) 25 *Nature Medicine* 37.

Purtova N, 'Do Property Rights in Personal Data Make Sense After the Big Data Turn?' (2017) 10 *Journal of Law & Economic Regulation* 208.

Radin M, 'Market-Inalienability' (1987) 100 *Harvard Law Review* 1849.
Ramon S and Mohr A, 'A Social License for Science: Capturing the Public of Co-Constructing Research?' (2014) 28 *Social Epistemology* 258.
Reading J and Nowgesic E, 'Improving the Health of Future Generations: The Canadian Institutes of Health Research Institute of Aboriginal Peoples' Health' (2002) 92 *American Journal of Public Health* 1396
Roberts J, 'Progressive Genetic Ownership' (2018) 93 *Notre Dame Law Review* 1105.
Rodwin M, 'The Case for Public Ownership of Patient Data' (2009) 302 *JAMA* 86.
Rothstein M, 'Ethical Issues in Big Data Health Research' (2015) 43 *Journal of Law, Medicine & Ethics* 425.
Royal Commission on Aboriginal Peoples, *Report of the Royal Commission on Aboriginal Peoples: Gathering Strength* (1997).
Rumbold J and Pierscionek B, 'Why Patients Shouldn't "Own" Their Medical Records' (2016) 34 *Nature Biotechnology* 586.
Scassa T, 'As Our Economy Becomes More Data Driven, Canadians Need a National Data Strategy that Encourages Innovation and Provides Security and Privacy', *Policy Options*, 15 January 2019.
Schwartz P, 'Property, Privacy, and Personal Data' (2004) 117 *Harvard Law Review* 2056.
Skopek J, 'Big Data's Epistemology and Its Implications for Precision Medicine and Privacy' in Cohen I, Fernandez Lynch H and others (eds), *Big Data, Health Law and Bioethics* (Cambridge University Press 2018).
Spector-Bagdady K, DeVries R and others, 'Encouraging Participation and Transparency in Biobank Research' (2018) 37 *Health Affairs* 1313.
Stahl B and Wright D, 'Ethics and Privacy in AI and Big Data: Implementing Responsible Research and Innovation' (2018) 16 *IEEE Security and Privacy* 26.
Terry N, 'Protecting Patient Privacy in the Age of Big Data' (2012) 81 *UMKC Law Review* 385.
Thaler R, 'Show Us the Data (It's Ours, After All)' *New York Times*, 23 April 2011, www.nytimes.com/2011/04/24/business/24view.html?_r=1&partner=rss&emc=rss
Townend D, 'Conclusion: Harmonisation in Genomic and Health Data Sharing for Research: An Impossible Dream?' (2018) 137 *Human Genetics* 657.
Townend D, 'Privacy, Politeness and the Boundary Between Theory and Practice in Ethical Rationalism' in Capps P and Pattinson S (eds), *Ethical Rationalism and the Law* (Hart Publishing 2017) 171–90.

INDEX

Books in the Series

Marcus Radetzki, Marian Radetzki and Niklas Juth
Genes and Insurance: Ethical, Legal and Economic Issues

Ruth Macklin
Double Standards in Medical Research in Developing Countries

Donna Dickenson
Property in the Body: Feminist Perspectives

Matti Häyry, Ruth Chadwick, Vilhjálmur Árnason and Gardar Árnason
The Ethics and Governance of Human Genetic Databases: European Perspectives

J. K. Mason
The Troubled Pregnancy: Legal Wrongs and Rights in Reproduction

Daniel Sperling
Posthumous Interests: Legal and Ethical Perspectives

Keith Syrett
Law, Legitimacy and the Rationing of Health Care: A Contextual and Comparative Perspective

Alasdair Maclean
Autonomy, Informed Consent and Medical Law: A Relational Change

Heather Widdows and Caroline Mullen
The Governance of Genetic Information: Who Decides?

David Price
Human Tissue in Transplantation and Research: A Model Legal and Ethical Donation Framework

Matti Häyry
Rationality and the Genetic Challenge: Making People Better?

Mary Donnelly
Healthcare Decision-Making and the Law: Autonomy, Capacity and the Limits of Liberalism

Anne-Maree Farrell, David Price and Muireann Quigley
Organ Shortage: Ethics, Law and Pragmatism

Sara Fovargue
Xenotransplantation and Risk: Regulating a Developing Biotechnology

John Coggon
What Makes Health Public?: A Critical Evaluation of Moral, Legal, and Political Claims in Public Health

Mark Taylor
Genetic Data and the Law: A Critical Perspective on Privacy Protection

Anne-Maree Farrell
The Politics of Blood: Ethics, Innovation and the Regulation of Risk

Stephen W. Smith
End-of-Life Decisions in Medical Care: Principles and Policies for Regulating the Dying Process

Michael Parker
Ethical Problems and Genetics Practice

William W. Lowrance
Privacy, Confidentiality, and Health Research

Kerry Lynn Macintosh
Human Cloning: Four Fallacies and Their Legal Consequence

Heather Widdows
The Connected Self: The Ethics and Governance of the Genetic Individual

Amel Alghrani, Rebecca Bennett and Suzanne Ost
Bioethics, Medicine and the Criminal Law Volume I: The Criminal Law and Bioethical Conflict: Walking the Tightrope

Danielle Griffiths and Andrew Sanders
Bioethics, Medicine and the Criminal Law Volume II: Medicine, Crime and Society

Margaret Brazier and Suzanne Ost
Bioethics, Medicine and the Criminal Law Volume III: Medicine and Bioethics in the Theatre of the Criminal Process

Sigrid Sterckx, Kasper Raus and Freddy Mortier
Continuous Sedation at the End of Life: Ethical, Clinical and Legal Perspectives

A. M. Viens, John Coggon and Anthony S. Kessel
Criminal Law, Philosophy and Public Health Practice

Ruth Chadwick, Mairi Levitt and Darren Shickle
The Right to Know and the Right Not to Know: Genetic Privacy and Responsibility

Eleanor D. Kinney
The Affordable Care Act and Medicare in Comparative Context

Katri Lõhmus
Caring Autonomy: European Human Rights Law and the Challenge of Individualism

Catherine Stanton and Hannah Quirk
Criminalising Contagion: Legal and Ethical Challenges of Disease Transmission and the Criminal Law

Sharona Hoffman
Electronic Health Records and Medical Big Data: Law and Policy

Barbara Prainsack and Alena Buyx
Solidarity in Biomedicine and Beyond

Camillia Kong
Mental Capacity in Relationship: Decision-Making, Dialogue, and Autonomy

Oliver Quick
Regulating Patient Safety: The End of Professional Dominance?

Thana Cristina de Campos
The Global Health Crisis: Ethical Responsibilities

Jonathan Ives, Michael Dunn and Alan Cribb
Empirical Bioethics: Theoretical and Practical Perspectives

Alan Merry and Warren Brookbanks
Merry and McCall Smith's Errors, Medicine and the Law (second edition)

Donna Dickenson
Property in the Body: Feminist Perspectives (second edition)

Rosie Harding
Duties to Care: Dementia, Relationality and Law

Ruud ter Meulen
Solidarity and Justice in Health and Social Care

David Albert Jones, Chris Gastmans and Calum MacKellar
Euthanasia and Assisted Suicide: Lessons from Belgium

Muireann Quigley
Self-Ownership, Property Rights, and the Human Body: A Legal Perspective

Françoise Baylis and Alice Dreger
Bioethics in Action

John Keown
Euthanasia, Ethics and Public Policy: An Argument against Legislation (second edition)

Amel Alghrani
Regulating Assisted Reproductive Technologies: New Horizons

Britta van Beers, Sigrid Sterckx and Donna Dickenson
Personalised Medicine, Individual Choice and the Common Good

David G. Kirchhoffer and Bernadette J. Richards
Beyond Autonomy: Limits and Alternatives to Informed Consent in Research Ethics and Law

Markus Wolfensberger and Anthony Wrigley
Trust in Medicine: Its Nature, Justification, Significance, and Decline

Catriona A. W. McMillan
The Human Embryo in vitro: Breaking the Legal Stalemate

Benjamin Peter White and Lindy Willmott (editors)
International Perspectives on End-of-Life Law Reform: Politics, Persuasion and Persistence

Carolyn Adams, Judy Allen and Felicity Flack
Sharing Linked Data for Health Research: Toward Better Decision Making

Emily Postan
Embodied Narratives: Protecting Identity Interests through Ethical Governance of Bioinformation

Jaime Lindsey
Reimagining the Court of Protection: Access to Justice in Mental Capacity Law

Marcelo Corrales Compagnucci, Michael Lowery Wilson, Mark Fenwick, Nikolaus Forgó and Till Bärnighausen
AI in eHealth: Human Autonomy, Data Governance and Privacy in Healthcare

www.ingramcontent.com/pod-product-compliance
Lightning Source LLC
LaVergne TN
LVHW011656200926
848484LV00004B/964
* 9 7 8 1 1 0 8 8 3 0 9 6 6 *

Acknowledgments

AF707351

This curriculum was developed through funds from a USDA-NIFA Grant (Award # 2012-68003-19621) titled "Development of Novel Salmonella Control Practices and Integrated Education Program to Reduce Salmonellosis." Research **Principal Investigators** include Dr. Hosni Hassan, Dr. Matthew Koci at North Carolina State University, and Dr. Andrea Azcarate-Peril at the University of North Carolina at Chapel Hill. Extension and education components for this grant were provided by North Carolina 4-H and the North Carolina Kenan Fellows Program, both at North Carolina State University.

Also instrumental in the creation of this curriculum:

Kenan Fellow Authors
Kristen Bedell
Shannon Page
Cortney Gordon

4-H Curriculum Specialist
Amy Chilcote

4-H Evaluation Specialist
Autumn Guin

4-H Microbiology Program Coordinator
Anne Greenaway

4-H Graphic Design/Illustration
Tabitha Barnes

4-H Illustrator
Uyen Nguyen- NCSU Chemistry Undergraduate

4-H curriculum is vetted through both formal and non formal educational environments. This curriculum has been piloted through the NC 4-H Curriculum Guidelines and evaluated through the following youth directed systems: summer camp, school enrichment, and 4-H community clubs. The following counties assisted in piloting this curriculum: Bladen, Cabarrus, Catawba, Cherokee, Currituck, Guilford, Iredell, Johnston, Jones, Lincoln, Pasquatank, Rowan, Sampson, Warren, and Wayne County Cooperative Extensions.

Your purchase helps ensure that this curriculujm will stay current with state and national educational standards as well as provide additional curricula materials locally to North Carolina 4-H agents, youth, and volunteers.

Introduction to "I am an Ecosystem"

"We are not alone."

Historically, this phrase has conjured up images of aliens waiting in space to descend on our unsuspecting planet. However, advances in technology over the years have meant that "we are not alone" applies to our own bodies, our own sense of self in the universe.

It turns out that we are colonial creatures. For every one of our cells that is "us," we also host ten times as many bacterial cells. Our digestive system alone is estimated to contain between 500 and 1,000 different bacterial species. Furthermore, we are learning that these bacteria and other microbes that inhabit our bodies, known collectively as our "microbiome," are essential for our survival. Our microbiome helps to train our immune system to recognize invaders. It also helps us to better process food and nutrients. Some studies even suggest that our microbiome may affect our moods! Without our trillions of hitchhikers, we would be lost.

However, despite our close relationship with our microbiome, not all bacteria are helpful to us. Many bacteria, which are fine outside of our bodies, become disease-causing pathogens once they get inside. Our bodies have many natural defenses against these invaders, including our skin, our mucous membranes, and our immune system. However, some do find their way in. For example, every year, thousands of people become sickened by a bacteria known as Salmonella. Salmonella bacteria cause a disease known as salmonellosis which results in fever, abdominal cramping, and diarrhea. In some cases, salmonellosis can be fatal.

Salmonella bacteria are found normally in the ground, in water, and in poultry and eggs. Proper food safety procedures, including thoroughly washing vegetables, storing food correctly, and cooking all foods to proper temperatures, can help prevent salmonellosis.

In this unit, youth will confront some of the myths and facts surrounding microbes in general and Salmonella in particular. Youth will examine where microbes grow in the environment and under what conditions. They will investigate the roles that microbes play in a healthy ecosystem as well as the roles that microbes play in our own bodies.

Youth will also examine the negative effects of microbes as they investigate a disease outbreak.

Finally, youth will apply their knowledge by designing technologies to help keep people safe from dangerous, food-borne microbes in our world.

Table of Contents

ADDITIONAL MATERIALS

There are additional materials for each lesson available on our NC 4-H curriculum website (nc4hcurriculum.org).

Content for lessons 1-6:

- Lesson variations for remote learning
- Videos
- PowerPoint presentations
- Interactive content
- PDFs separated by activity for easy printing
- Fillable PDFs for online submission of worksheets
- New content added regularly

Visit *NC4HCurriculum.org* under the Virtual Resources menu section.

Bonus access to all "Grab and Go" content on the menu under Grab and Go. Those are not lessons from this microbiology curriculum.

Access Code for "*I Am An Ecosystem*" and all "*Grab and Go*" content:

60007734c48ed

Elementary Microbiology Unit
Scope and Sequence Variations

Teaching Lessons over 5 days for 1 ½-2 hours a day:

DAY	LESSONS
1	Lesson 1: Microbes All Around and Inside Us (Have cantaloupes prepared) Lesson 2: The Role of Microbes in an Ecosystem (begin)
2	Lesson 1: Observe cantaloupes Lesson 2: Completion of activities Lesson 3: The Ecosystems Inside Us
3	Lesson 1: Observe cantaloupes Lesson 3: Complete any activities needed Lesson 4: The Body's Natural Defenses--All Parts (Make sure materials have been collected to complete activity)
4	Lesson 1: Observe cantaloupes Lesson 5: CSI Bacteria- All parts
5	Lesson 1: Observe cantaloupes and finish activities Lesson 6: Engineering a Solution – All parts Wrap-up and conclusions

Teaching Lessons over 3 days: 2-3 hours a day:

DAY	LESSONS
1	Lesson 1: Microbes All Around and Inside Us (Have cantaloupes already prepared—Have some showing the decomposition over certain days for participants to observe) Lesson 3: The Ecosystems Inside Us
2	Lesson 1: Observe cantaloupes Lesson 4: The Body's Natural Defenses Lesson 2: The Role of Microbes in an Ecosystem
3	Lesson 1: Observe cantaloupes and finish activities Lesson 5: CSI Bacteria Lesson 6: Engineering a Solution (Make sure to collect materials to complete activity)

Teaching all lessons in 1 day: 6-7 hours:

DAY	LESSONS
1	**If curriculum is only taught in one day, these are the top 4 suggested lessons to cover: Lesson 3: The Microbes Inside Us Lesson 4: The Body's Natural Defenses Lesson 6: Engineering a Solution (Make sure to have all materials ready for lesson) Lesson 5: CSI Bacteria

Experiential Learning: A Holistic Approach to Learning

Experiential Learning is youth centered. It is an active learning process, which first involves youth in an activity, asks them to reflect on the activity to determine what was useful or important to remember, and then tasks youth with understanding how the information they learned applies to their lives now and in the future. This learning process is holistic and allows youth to consume, apply, and build upon life experiences.

Pfeiffer and Jones' experiential learning model is commonly used in 4-H. However, other pioneers such as Kolb provide a wealth of research that emphasizes the importance of the adult facilitator. According to Kolb, the experiential learning model allows the learner actively participate in what is learned. The facilitator's role is to connect with the youth to spark their interest and intrinsic motivation so that the youth can gain, revise, or enhance their life skills. The facilitator plays multiple rolls during this process: balancing the attention of the learner, engaging with the subject matter, and creating a safe and holistic learning environment.

Tips to think about when creating a welcoming environment for learning:

- Patience is a virtue. When waiting for youth to respond fully, having patience and allowing time for them to think is important.
- You are not the judge. Accept all responses.
- Experiential questions are open-ended to allow for expression. Make sure that you acknowledge youth who respond to you. Not acknowledging all youth can stop the flow of answers and make youth less likely to respond in the future.
- You are not the young person. Don't answer the question.
- Encourage deep conversation. If a young person gives a short response, provide follow up questions to allow for deeper conversation. Examples could be: "Would you provide an example of what you mean? Can you tell me more about your thoughts?"
- Avoid yes or no questions. These are not open-ended and stop the flow of conversation.
- Don't lead the youth to answers you want to hear.
- Allow the youth to share their responses in pairs rather than with the entire group.

1. Experience: Let's Do It!!!
Key Reminders to Leader:
- "Sit on Your Hands"
- Observe
- Facilitate to the "bigger picture"

Key Objectives for Discovery:
- To Explore
- To Examine
- To Construct
- To Arrange

2. Share
Key Concept: Respond
Key Question: "What Happened?"

3. Reflect
Key Concept: Analyze Patterns
Key Question: "What's Important?"

Leader Role
- Allow adequate processing time for sharing.
- Use open-ended questions to stimulate thinking and feeling.
- Encourage "pair share" and large group share.

4. Generalize
Key Concept: Inference
Key Question: "So What?"

5. Apply
Key Concept: Application
Key Question: "Now What?"

Leader Role
- Facilitate youth finding ways to use what they have learned in new situations.
- Guide youth in making connections between the inner meaning of the activity and the broader world.

Share Questions (What Happened?)
What did you like about this activity?
What part of the activity was the hardest to do?
How did you decide what to choose?
What was the most fun about doing the activity?
How did your group work together?
How did you feel about successfully being able to____?
What are some decisions you had to make to carry out this activity?

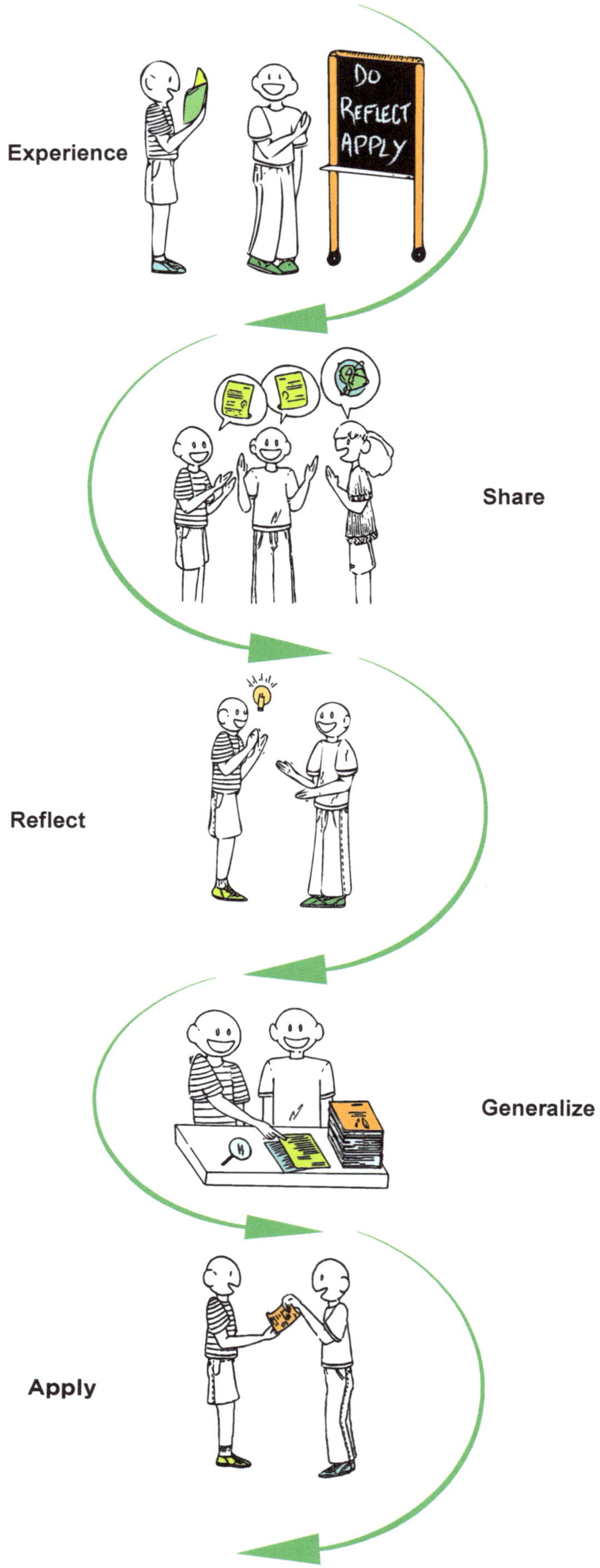

What steps did you go through before you made your decision?
Why do you think everyone in your group didn't agree about everything?
What was it like to have to make quick decisions?
How did you keep track of everyone's ideas?
Do you think you get more ideas working alone or in a group? Why?
What kind of feelings did you have when group members argued?
What did you observe about the way the groups disagreed (or agreed)?
How did you use your various senses to ___?
What new words did you learn?
Why do you think people have different ideas about what is correct?

Reflect Questions (What's Important?)
What did you learn about yourself by doing this activity?
Why is it important to know___?
How did your group decide ___?
What did you learn as a group that you might not have learned alone?
What were some common themes or thoughts you heard?
How were each person's viewpoints the same? How were they different?
What problems came up over and over?
What would you do if_____ were to happen?
What was easy or difficult about working with a group to____?
What did you do if everyone in the group didn't agree on___?
How did this differ from the way you are usually taught in school?
Give an example of a challenge you had and what you did to solve it.
What works best to get people involved and excited about doing this type of activity?
Why is learning with others sometimes more fun than learning alone?
What suggestions would you have for someone who wanted to____?

Generalize Questions (So What?)
What other situations like this have you experienced?
Why is it important that each person has his/her own view?
When have you had to___ before?
Where can you find resources to help you make some of your decisions about__?
When else have you had fun and learned new things at the same time?
Why is it important to have plenty of information before making decisions?
When do you make decisions that require everyone in the group to agree?
What do you do when you don't agree with the group?
What did you learn about your own skill in making decisions?
What did you learn about your own skill in communicating with others?
Describe five ways in which new ideas can be communicated to you.
In what ways do people help each other learn new things?
What are some ways you like to learn?
What did you learn?

Apply (What was Learned?)
How would you teach someone about this activity or concept?
What did you learn today that you will be able to use in school....at home?
What did you learn by participating in this process that will help you in the future?
Describe a time when you might need the skills/knowledge you learned today.
What are some other situations when you will need to use the skills you learned today?
What would you do differently if you conducted this activity again?

Lesson 1 Microbes All Around and Inside Us

Introduction

Look around you. What types of organisms, or living things, can you see? For example, you might see different grasses, trees, or flowers. You might see ants, spiders, birds, or other humans. The biodiversity, or variety of living species, of our planet, is amazing. Even now, new species are discovered every day.

However, what you see with your eyes only tells a tiny piece of the biodiversity story. The world we live in is mostly microscopic. Microorganisms, tiny living things too small to see with our eyes alone, vastly outnumber the organisms we can easily see. An entire world of bacteria, fungi, viruses, protists, and other microscopic organisms exists under (and even inside of) our very noses. Sometimes, the term "micro biodiversity" is used to describe the enormous variety of microorganisms that exist on our planet.

Microorganisms (also called "microbes") can be extremely tiny. For example, a single E. coli bacterium is approximately one micrometer across. A micrometer is one-millionth of a meter, or one-thousandth of a millimeter, and is written as 0.000001 m. Compare this to a single grain of sugar, which is about one-half of a millimeter across, or 0.0005 m. In other words, 500 E. coli bacteria could easily fit on a grain of sugar. Ten thousand E. coli bacteria could fit on the period at the end of this sentence. In your body alone, 100 trillion different microbes make their home. In an average, healthy adult, these bacteria, fungi, viruses, and protists can weigh as much as five pounds!

bacteriophage: any of a group of viruses that infect specific bacteria, usually causing their disintegration or dissolution.

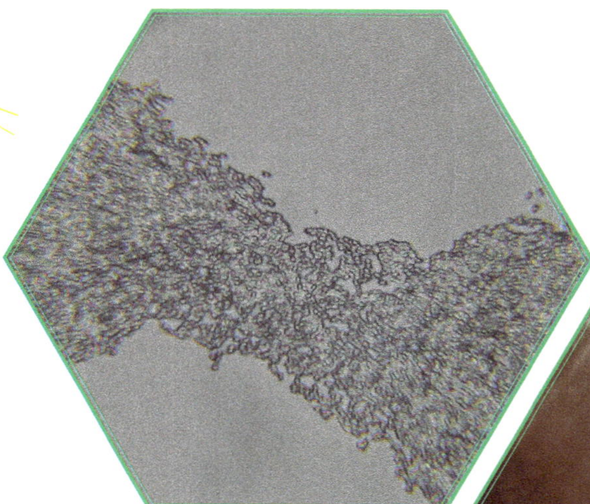

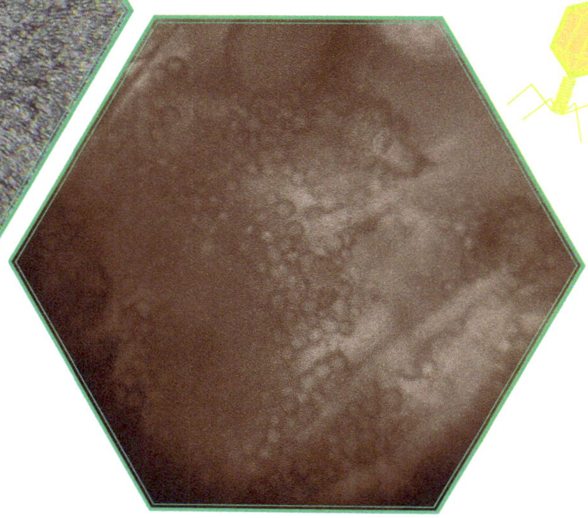

Lesson 1 Microbes All Around and Inside Us

Key Teaching Points

1. Microbes (organisms too small to see unaided) make up most of the biomass (living matter) on our planet.
2. Scientists use evidence and reasoning to talk about their claims.

Learner Outcomes

- Develop an understanding of bacteria, microbes, biodiversity, and microbiodiversity.

Make predictions about the growth of microbes on pieces of cantaloupe that have been swiped across different surfaces.

- Predict which surfaces and environments will promote the most and least microbial growth.
- Make observations and draw conclusions while observing the microbial growth throughout the experiment.

Skill Level: Elementary, Beginning

Success Indicators

- Youth will state claims using reasoning from prior knowledge and discussions.
- Youth will make predictions using schema and information shared before the experiment.

Life Skills

Critical Thinking, Keeping Records, Communication, Team Work, Healthy Life-style Choices

Time Needed

90 minutes or two 45 minute sessions

Space

Classroom or kitchen

Suggested Group Size

Groups of 4-5 youth

No tasting the cantaloupe

Materials List

- 5 pound bag of sugar (this will be used again in Lesson 3)
- A small cup of loose sugar or individual sugar packets
- Sticky Notes
- 1 KWL (poster size)- A graphic organizer used to find out what youth Know, Want to know or questions, and what they Learn
- Microbe Comic (1 per youth)
- Claim-Evidence-Reasoning poster (1 for the class)
- Claim-Evidence-Reasoning chart (1 per youth)
- Cantaloupe Lab packet (1 per group)

For experiment

Facilitator materials

- Clean knife
- Clean cutting surface
- Clean spoon to scoop seeds from cantaloupe
- Clean bowl or container to hold sliced cantaloupe (1 per group)

Youth materials

- Cantaloupe slices (14 slices per group)
- Plastic bags that can be sealed (14 per group)
- Box or other container that blocks light to collect prepared bags of room temperature cantaloupe (1 per group)
- Container to collect prepared bags of refrigerated cantaloupe (1 per group)
- Hand sanitizer
- Soap and water (to wash hands)
- Permanent marker (1 per group to write the surface name on each bag, or stickers)
- Bag Stickers (1 set per group)
  ** Alternative: provide labels printed on regular paper, scissors, and tape to label the bags.

Lesson 1 Microbes All Around and Inside Us

Background information

Microbes make up most of the life on our planet, but we are only just beginning to understand them. Microbiology is the branch of science that studies microbes, particularly bacteria. For decades, the major focus was on how to eliminate microbes, hoping that doing so would eliminate diseases. Now, microbiologists are discovering that our relationships with microbes are far more complex and complicated than we ever imagined. In fact, our bodies are teeming with microbes, and while some cause us harm, most are essential to our very survival.

Before the Activity

1. Have a 5-pound bag of sugar out.
2. Have a small cup of loose sugar or individual sugar packets out.
3. Print copies of the Claim-Evidence-Reasoning chart for each youth.
4. Print copies of the Claim-Evidence-Reasoning Self-Assessment for each youth.
5. Print copies of the Cantaloupe Experiment lab packet for each group.
6. Print labels for bags of cantaloupe, either on regular paper or on sticker paper.
7. Have sticky notes available for all youth.
8. Label corners of the room with "I agree with Shannon," "I agree with Brad," "I agree with Courtney," and "I agree with Whitney." [Note: Names may be changed to reflect the community in which you teach.]
9. Divide the youth into pairs and groups of 4-5. For easy labeling of materials during the cantaloupe experiment, you may assign each group a name or a number; alternatively, each group can be allowed to choose a name.
10. Have 2 copies of the Microbe Comic for each group of youth to use during the lesson.
11. Make sure that each group has 14 slices of cantaloupe, 14 plastic bags, stickers or labels for the bags, access to hand sanitizer, and access to a sink with soap and water.

To prepare the cantaloupe

1. Wash cantaloupe outer surface with water.
2. Clean and sterilize the working area as much as possible to avoid contaminating the cantaloupe.
3. Cut the cantaloupe in half and remove the seeds. Discard the seeds.
4. Cut the outer rind off the cantaloupe. Dispose of the rind.
5. Cut the cantaloupe into slices. The slices do not have to be exactly the same size or shape, as long as approximately the same amount of surface area is available for most of the slices.
6. Place 14 slices of cantaloupe into a bowl or other clean container for each group.
7. One small to medium cantaloupe can provide enough slices for 2-3 groups.
8. If preparing in advance, cover the bowls or containers with plastic wrap to avoid contamination as much as possible. Do not touch the cantaloupe with the plastic wrap.

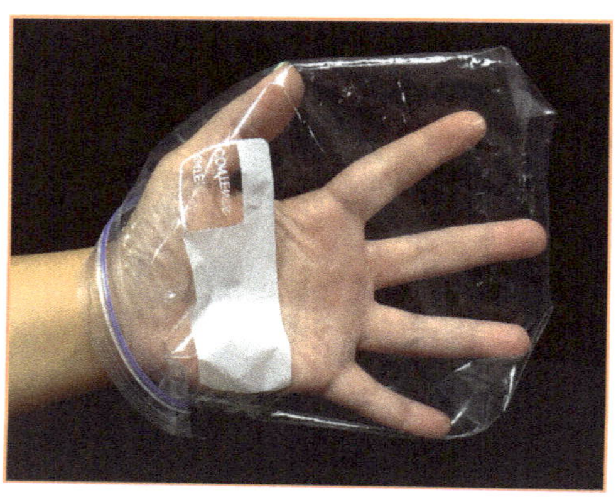

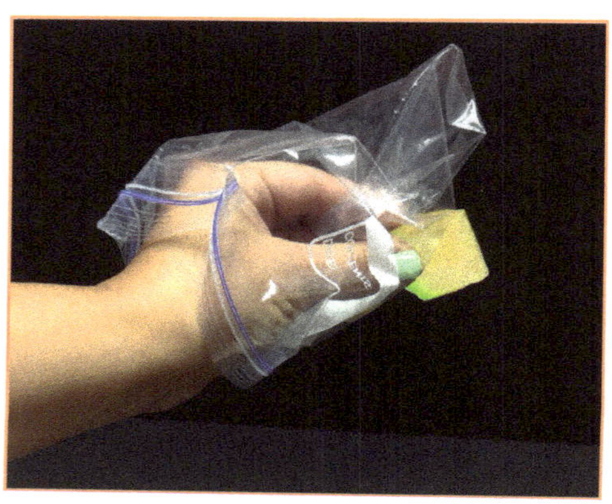

Lesson 1 Microbes All Around and Inside Us

PART ONE

Opening Questions

- Have you ever heard of bacteria, fungi, or viruses?
- If so what do you know about them and where have you heard of them before?

Follow-up Questions

- Do you know if all bacteria, fungi, or viruses are good or bad?
- Do you know where bacteria, fungi, and viruses live?
- What do microbes do for humans? Are they helpful or harmful?

Let's Do It!

1. Activate the youth's background knowledge by asking the Opening Questions.

2. Give youth sticky notes and a few minutes to record anything that they personally think to be true. Youth should only record one idea on each sticky note. If they have three things to say, they should end up with three sticky notes.

3. Have youth share their work ideas with their group members. Any new ideas that arise during their conversations should also be recorded with one idea per sticky note.

4. Show the youth the class KWL poster. Tell youth that the letters "KWL" stand for "What I Know," "What I Want to Know," and "What I Have Learned." Explain that they will be using this tool to help them record their questions and their learning, and that they will start by placing their sticky notes in the first column.

5. Allow youth to bring their sticky notes to the poster and place them on the Know section.

6. Summarize the group knowledge. If there are conflicting ideas, move those sticky notes to the "W" column. Remind youth that what they know at the start of the lesson may change as they work, and that is simply a sign of learning.

7. Point out the "W" column. Explain to youth that, as they have questions, they are welcome to write their questions down during the course of their work and add those sticky notes to the W section.

8. Inform the youth that bacteria, fungi, and viruses are actually types of organisms known as microbes. Write the following terms on the board: "microbes," "biodiversity," "organisms," "microorganisms," and "micro biodiversity." Ask youth what they know about these words. Break down each of the words to find out if the youth know what the parts of the words mean:
   a. bio- means "life"
   b. micro- means "small"
   c. diversity means "variety"
   d. organism means "living thing"

9. Give the youth time to collaboratively discuss these words to develop an understanding. Possible questions to support this discussion:

    a. What is an organism? If an organism is a living thing, then what is a microorganism or a microbe? What does micro- mean?
    b. What does the word biodiversity mean? Do you know what the root bio- means? What is diversity? Do you have any connections to either word or have you heard of biodiversity before?

10. Now that you have an understanding of what a microorganism is, what do you think micro biodiversity is?

11. Ask youth to estimate the number of microbes in their bodies. Have youth write down their estimates and line up in order based on the number they chose. Reveal that there are over one trillion bacterial cells in our bodies and that bacterial cells outnumber human cells by a 10:1 ratio. In other words, for every human cell, there are ten bacterial cells.

12. Give the 5-pound bag of sugar to the youth and let them pass it around. Explain that approximately 5 pounds of microbes inhabit our bodies.
[Note: This bag of sugar will be used again in Lesson 3.]

13. Pour a small amount of sugar in a cup or pass out individual sugar packets. Have youth each try to pick up a single granule of sugar. Ask youth to estimate the size of the granule. Again, youth can rearrange themselves based on their estimates.

14. Inform youth that a single grain of sugar is approximately 0.5 mm, whereas a single E. coli bacterium is 0.001 mm (one micrometer, or one-millionth of a meter). Explain that microbes are so small that they cannot be seen without a microscope. If we see bacteria with our eyes alone, then we are actually looking at colonies of bacteria.

15. Introduce the Microbes Comic to the youth and let them know that they will be working in groups to learn more about microbes and how they interact with our bodies. Ask youth to work with 1-2 partners to read the booklet. They should use sticky notes to record at least five facts that they learn and at least three questions they have. After youth navigate through this resource, have them place their sticky notes on the KWL poster. Summarize the information on the KWL chart for the group.

[for 45 minute classes, this is a good breaking point]

PART TWO

1. If a second class period has begun, review the KWL chart from the previous lesson.

2. Ask the Share question.

   - Before learning about microbes, what did you think a microbe was?
   - Where did you think they lived?

3. Ask the first Reflect question.

   - How did your thinking change as you read about microbes?

4. Introduce the Claim-Evidence-Reasoning poster to the youth. Inform youth that they will be using the Claim-Evidence-Reasoning framework in order to craft a scientific argument.

5. As a class, you will be modeling how to use the Claim-Evidence-Reasoning format. Share with youth the following Microbe Probe question. You may change the names to names that are representative of the community in which you teach:

   Four friends were talking about microbes and where they would grow best.

   Shannon said, "I think that microbes would grow best on counters."

   Brad said, "I think that microbes would grow best in the refrigerator."

   Courtney said, "I think that microbes would grow best on our hands."

   Whitney said, "I think that microbes would grow best somewhere else."

   With which friend do you most agree? Why?

6. Use a Four-Corners activity for youth to share their ideas. Designate one corner as "I agree with Shannon," one corner as "I agree with Brad," one corner as, "I agree with Courtney," and one corner as "I agree with Whitney." Youth move to the corner that most closely matches their ideas. Allow one or two youth to defend their position.

7. Randomly choose one of the corners to use as the model claim. Model how to complete the "Claim" section by writing, "Bacteria will grow best on [the surface] because [use a reason from one or two of the youth in that corner]." Explain that a claim is a complete sentence that stands alone and includes at least one supporting reason. "I agree with Courtney" is not an example of a claim.

8. Pass out the Claim-Evidence-Reasoning charts to each youth. Provide a few minutes for youth to record their individual claims.

9. Tell youth that they will be testing their claims by collecting microbes from a variety of locations. They will use cantaloupe slices in order to determine which environments have the most microbes and to determine what makes bacteria grow faster in certain environments. Pass out the Cantaloupe Experiment sheet. Read the Procedure with youth to ensure that they know the expectations.

10. **Review lab observation and safety procedures, especially procedures for tasting food in the lab. After the lab has been completed, youth will not directly touch or smell the cantaloupe again. The bags will remain sealed. Youth will observe the experiment by visual inspection.**

    - **Seeing: youth will use their sense of sight to make visual observations of the cantaloupe experiment once it has been set up.**
    - **Tasting: youth are to eat in the lab only when directly instructed to do so by the teacher. Otherwise, there should not be anything to eat or drink in the lab setting.**
    - **Touching: youth will not directly touch the cantaloupe again after the experiment has been set up.**
    - **Smelling: youth will not observe the cantaloupe by smelling again after the experiment has been set up.**
    - **Hearing: this sense is not applicable to this experiment.**

11. Youth will use their cantaloupe slices to gather microbes from each of the following locations- single human contact, multiple human contact, two different surface areas, hands that have been cleaned with hand sanitizer, hands that have been washed with soap and water, and one pair of slices that has not been used to swipe a surface (controls for room temperature and refrigerator). They will need to swipe each surface with two pieces of cantaloupe because one will be placed in a refrigerated environment and the other will remain in a room temperature environment.

12. Tell youth to take two pieces of cantaloupe, place them in sealed bags, and label the bags. One bag should be labeled “Control: Room Temperature,” while the other bag should be labeled “Control: Refrigerator.” Model how to use the bags as gloves to pick up the cantaloupe.

13. Instruct each group to select one member to be the “Single Human Contact” member of their group.

14. Have the Single Human Contact group member swipe two cantaloupe pieces across his/her hands and put into sealed bags. One bag should be labeled "Single Human Contact: Room Temperature" and the other should be labeled "Single Human Contact: Refrigerator."

15. Have youth pass two pieces of cantaloupe around in their group so that every person touches each piece. Put these pieces in sealed bags labeled "Multiple Human Contact: Room Temperature" and "Multiple Human Contact: Refrigerator."

16. Tell youth to wash their hands.

17. Have the Single Human Contact group member for each group swipe their freshly-washed hands with the cantaloupe. Place the pieces in sealed, labeled bags.

18. The Single Human Contact group members now wash their hands again.

19. Have the Single Human Contact group member for each group clean their hands with hand sanitizer. Swipe their hands with the cantaloupe and place the pieces in sealed, labeled bags.

20. The Single Human Contact group members now wash their hands again.

21. Have youth choose two different surfaces in the room that they would like to swipe with cantaloupe. Have them swipe the first surface with two pieces of cantaloupe and put them in sealed, labeled bags. Repeat for the second surface. Youth should use the bag-as-glove method demonstrated earlier in the lab.

22. Tell youth that they will revisit the cantaloupe throughout the course of the unit to observe what might start growing.

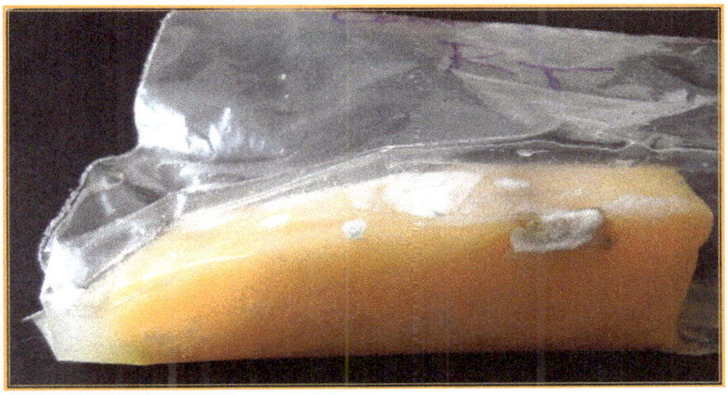

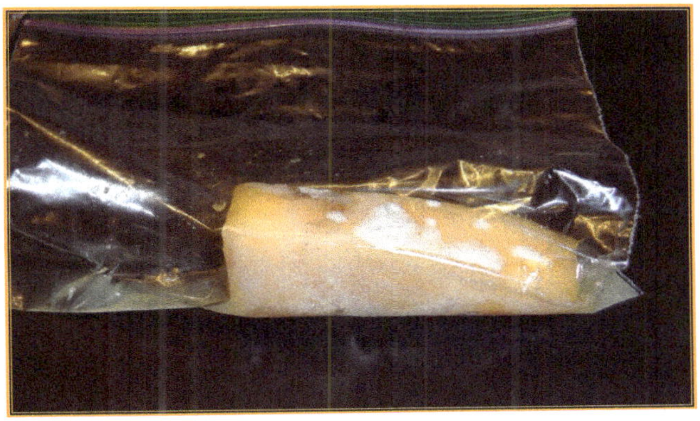

23. Ask the second Reflect question.
    - Did your thinking about where bacteria might grow best change throughout the experiment preparation?

24. Ask the Generalize questions.
    - After setting up the cantaloupe experiment, which cantaloupe slices do you think will show the greatest and least microbial growth?
    - Why do you think this? Do you think that each of the cantaloupe slices will look the same throughout the experiment? Why and in what ways?

25. Ask the Apply questions.
    - Using the predictions that you made today about the growth of microbes in different environments, where do you think microbes tend to grow best inside of our bodies? What do microbes do to our bodies?
    - Are they harmful or helpful?

Term and Concept Discovery

Bacteria: a type of single-celled organism. Bacteria are classified as prokaryotic organisms, as they do not have membrane-enclosed nuclei or other similar structures (organelles). Bacteria are the most abundant life forms on our planet. Singular: bacterium

Biomass: the total mass of all the organisms in an ecosystem

E. coli: Escherichia coli is the most well-studied bacteria. It is a very common bacteria and one of the major microbes in the gut of healthy humans. However, some strains are pathogenic and can cause severe cramps, bloody diarrhea, and vomiting.

Fungi: Fungi are eukaryotic, since their cells do contain a nucleus. Mushrooms are fungi, as are microorganisms such as yeasts and molds. Singular: fungus

Microbe: any one of a number of organisms too small to be seen without a microscope. Bacteria, viruses, and many fungi are all considered microbes.

Microbiodiversity: the variety of microbes that inhabit an ecosystem.

Microbiome: the term given to the microbes that live within/on a particular organism

Virus: a microbe that replicates itself by taking over cells in a host organism. At this time, there is debate among scientists as to whether viruses are actually considered to be living organisms. Unlike pathogenic bacteria, viruses cannot be killed using antibiotic medicines.

Talk It Over

Share 1	**Reflect 2**
Before learning about microbes, what did you think a microbe was? Where did you think they lived?	How did your thinking change as you read about microbes? Did your thinking about where bacteria might grow best change throughout the experiment preparation?
Generalize 3	**Apply 4**
After setting up the cantaloupe experiment, which cantaloupe slice do you think will show the greatest and least microbial growth? Why do you think this? Do you think that each of the cantaloupe slices will look the same throughout the experiment? Why and in what ways?	Using the predictions that you made today about the growth of microbes in different environments, where do you think microbes tend to grow best inside of our bodies? What do microbes do to our bodies? Are they harmful or helpful?

Variations

- Demonstrate how to write the number "one trillion" in US standard form (1,000,000,000,000) and scientific form (1.0×10^{12}). Have youth represent the size of a E. coli bacterium using a decimal, a fraction, and scientific notation (0.000001; 1/1,000,000; 1.0×10^{-6}).

- You can provide the youth with different kinds of fruits or vegetables so that they can observe the differences of microbial growth on a variety of produce. Potatoes and sugar pumpkins are possible alternatives if cantaloupe is not available.

- You may choose to use electronic versions of the Claim-Evidence-Reasoning chart and Cantaloupe Experiment lab packet. Youth can digitally photograph any changes in their cantaloupe over the course of the experiment and share their findings through Edmodo or other locally-approved platforms.

Take It Home!

With an adult, take a walk in your neighborhood.

Draw pictures in your notebook or take photographs to document the biodiversity in your neighborhood.

How many different types of organisms can you find?

Education Standard(s)

5.L.2.3- Infer the effects that may result from the interconnected relationship of plants and animals to their ecosystem.
Youth know that all of the organisms in an ecosystem have interconnected relationships. Youth know that because of this, factors that impact one population within an ecosystem may impact other populations within that ecosystems.
5-LS2-1 Develop a model to describe the movement of matter among plants, animals, decomposers, and the environment.
Variation: 5.NBT.1 -Recognize that in a multi-digit number, a digit in one place represents 10 times as much as it represents in the place to its right and 1/10 of what it represents in the place to its left.
Variation: 5.NBT.2 - Explain patterns in the number of zeros of the product when multiplying a number by powers of 10, and explain patterns in the placement of the decimal point when a decimal is multiplied or divided by a power of 10. Use whole-number exponents to denote powers of 10.

Tags

Microbes, Microorganisms, bacteria, fungi, viruses, biodiversity, microbiome, microbiodiversity

Lesson 1 Print Materials

Facilitator
KWL poster
(one large scale poster per class)
Claim-Evidence-Reasoning poster (one large scale poster per class)

See page 5 for information on digital assets and extra enrichment.

Group Handouts
Cantaloupe Lab packet
Bag stickers or labels

Youth Handouts
Microbe Comic
Claim-Evidence-Reasoning chart
Claim-Evidence-Reasoning Self-Assessment

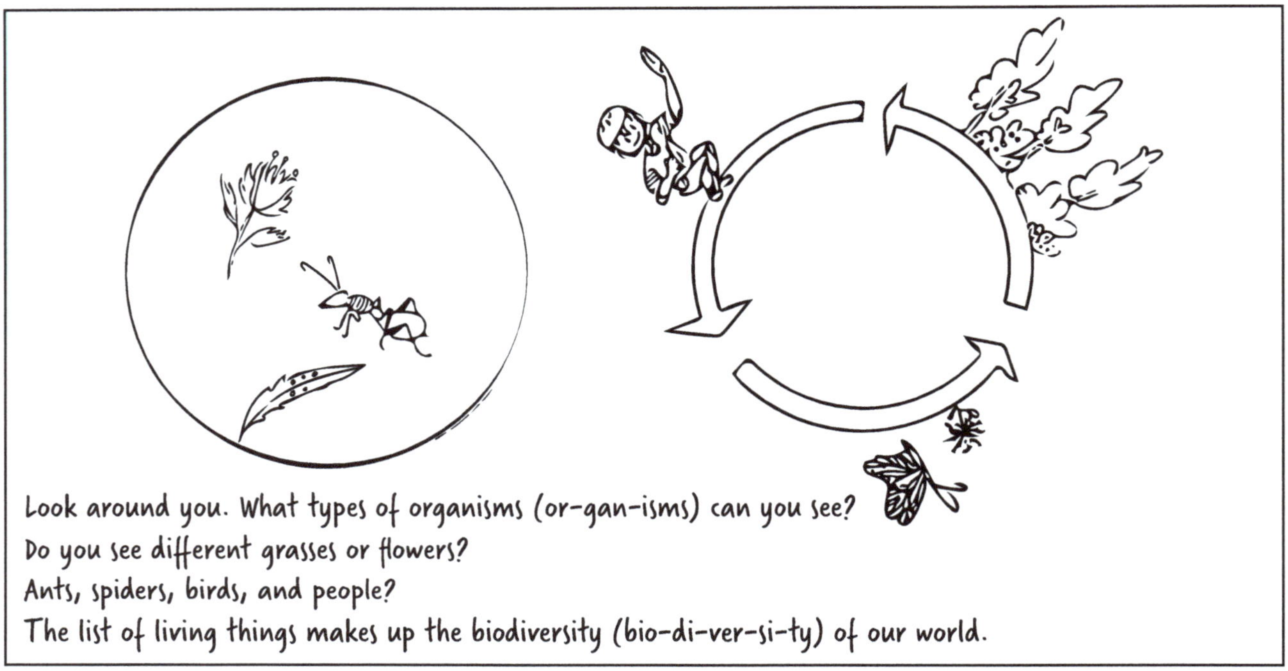

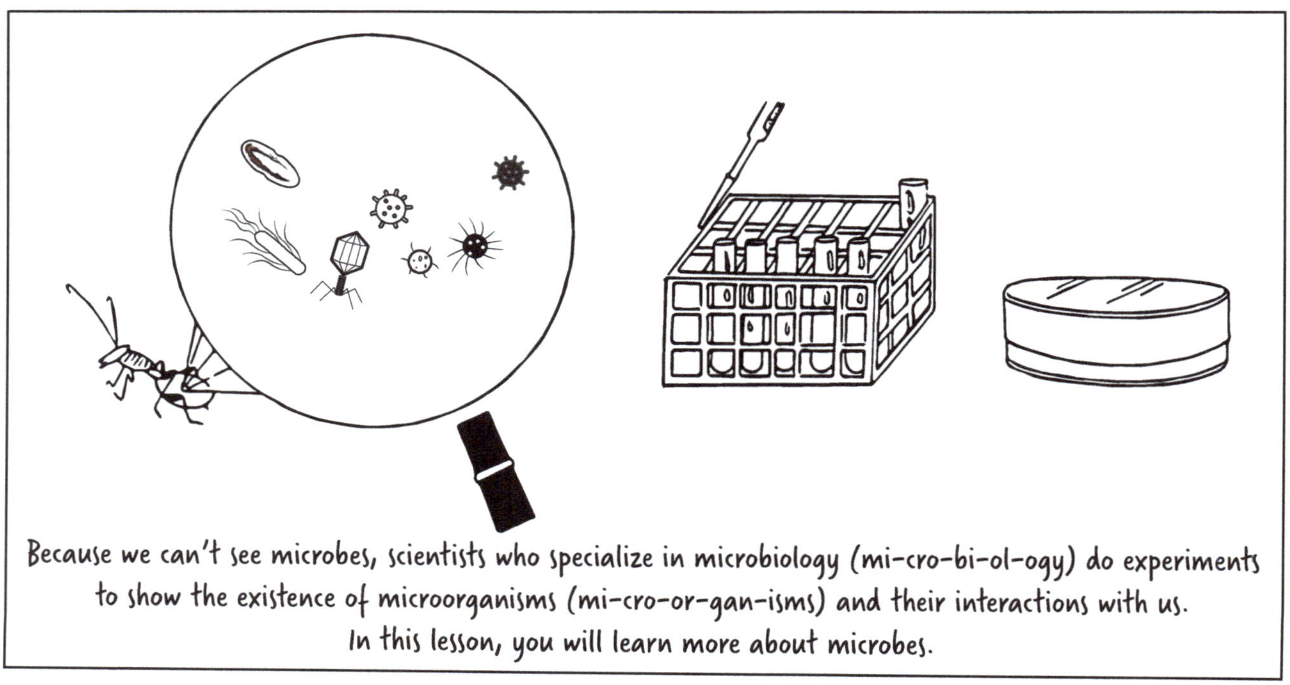

What I Know	What I Want to Know	What I Have Learned

KWL poster

Your name: ______________________ Date: ______________

Claim - Evidence - Reasoning Chart

Investigative Question

On what surface will microbes grow best?

Claim

Microbes will grow best on ______________ because

Cantaloupe Lab

Materials

Your group will need:

- ☐ 14 slices of cantaloupe
- ☐ 14 plastic sealable bags
- ☐ A permanent marker
- ☐ Bag Stickers, or Bag Labels that you can cut and tape to the sealable bags
- ☐ Hand sanitizer
- ☐ Access to a sink with soap and water

Procedure

1. With your group, decide on two different surfaces that you want to test. Write those surfaces on the blanks in the chart below.

	Room Temperature	Refrigerator
Control		
Single Human Contact		
Multiple Human Contact		
Soap and Water (single contact)		
Hand Sanitizer (single contact)		
Surface 1: ______________ ______________		
Surface 2: ______________ ______________		

2. Use the Bag Stickers and permanent marker to label each of the bags with your group name or number and the surface. For example, you will have a bag labeled "Control: Room Temperature" and another bag labeled "Control: Refrigerator." Check off the bags in the chart above as you label them.

3. Begin with the "Control" slices. Carefully scoop a cantaloupe slice into each of the "Control" bags. Use the bag like a glove to help you pick up the slice. Do not let the cantaloupe touch anything other than the inside of the bag, including your skin.

4. Next, choose a group member to be the "Single Human Contact." That group member should pick up two pieces of cantaloupe and rub the cantaloupe over their hands. The group member should then carefully place the cantaloupe inside the bags with the Single Human Contact labels.

5. For the Multiple Human Contact bags, every group member should touch the cantaloupe. Choose two pieces for your group to use. Pass the pieces around so that every person in your group has touched each piece. Then, carefully place the pieces inside the "Multiple Human Contact" bags.

6. Every group member should now go wash their hands thoroughly with soap and water.

7. The "Single Human Contact" group member should pick up two pieces of cantaloupe and rub the cantaloupe over their hands. The group member should then carefully place the cantaloupe inside the bags labeled "Soap and Water."

8. The "Single Human Contact" group member should wash their hands with soap and water before the next step.

9. The "Single Human Contact" group member should then clean their hands with hand sanitizer. They should pick up two pieces of cantaloupe and rub the cantaloupe over their hands. The group member should then carefully place the cantaloupe inside the bags labeled "Hand Sanitizer."

10. The "Single Human Contact" group member should wash their hands again.

11. Bring the cantaloupe to the surfaces that your group identified. Using the bags as gloves, swipe the surfaces. Be careful not to let the cantaloupe touch anything other than the surfaces or the inside of the bags. Place the slices into the correct bags.

12. Seal all of your bags. You will not open them back up.

13. Clean up all of your work surfaces, including anywhere that your group swiped with cantaloupe.

14. Sort the bags into "Refrigerator" and "Room Temperature." Place the bags where your teacher directs you to put them.

Discuss the following questions with your group.

Which **temperature** do you think will promote the <u>most</u> microbial (mi-cro-bi-al) growth?

Room Temperature ☐ Refrigerator ☐

Support your claim:

Which **surface** do you think will promote the <u>most</u> microbial (mi-cro-bi-al) growth?

Control ☐ Soap and Water ☐ Hand Sanitizer ☐
Single human contact ☐ Multiple human contact ☐
Surface contact 1____________________ ☐ Surface contact 2____________________ ☐

Support your claim:

Which **surface** do you think will promote the <u>least</u> microbial (mi-cro-bi-al) growth?

Control ☐ Soap and Water ☐ Hand Sanitizer ☐
Single human contact ☐ Multiple human contact ☐
Surface contact 1____________________ ☐ Surface contact 2____________________ ☐

Support your claim:

Record your observations

Each day, you will examine your cantaloupe. Record your observations here using words and/or pictures. You may add more pages as needed. Be sure to wear safety equipment when handling the bags. Wash your hands thoroughly afterwards.
Date: Changes you observe:
Date: Changes you observe:
Date: Changes you observe:

Date:
Changes you observe:

Date:
Changes you observe:

Date:
Changes you observe:

Date:
Changes you observe:

Analyze your results

Which temperature promoted the most microbial (mi-cro-bi-al) growth? Which promoted the least growth? Why might this have happened? Why might it be important?
Which surface promoted the most microbial (mi-cro-bi-al) growth? Which promoted the least growth? Why might this have happened? Why might it be important?
Describe one observation or finding that was the most surprising or interesting. Why did you think it was surprising or interesting?

Cantaloupe Lab packet 6/6

Bag Stickers

Control Room Temperature Group	Control Refrigerator Group
Single Human Contact Room Temperature Group	Single Human Contact Refrigerator Group
Multiple Human Contact Room Temperature Group	Multiple Human Contact Refrigerator Group
Soap and Water Room Temperature Group	Soap and Water Refrigerator Group
Hand Sanitizer Room Temperature Group	Hand Sanitizer Refrigerator Group
Surface 1: Room Temperature Group	Surface 1: Refrigerator Group
Surface 2: Room Temperature Group	Surface 2: Refrigerator Group

Bag stickers or labels

Microbe Comic

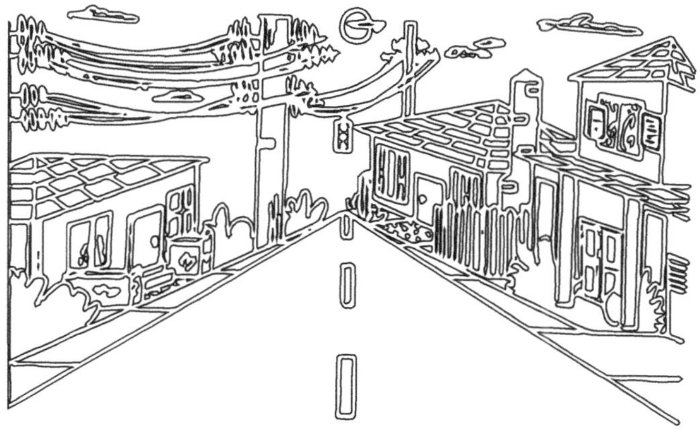

Microbes are all around us.

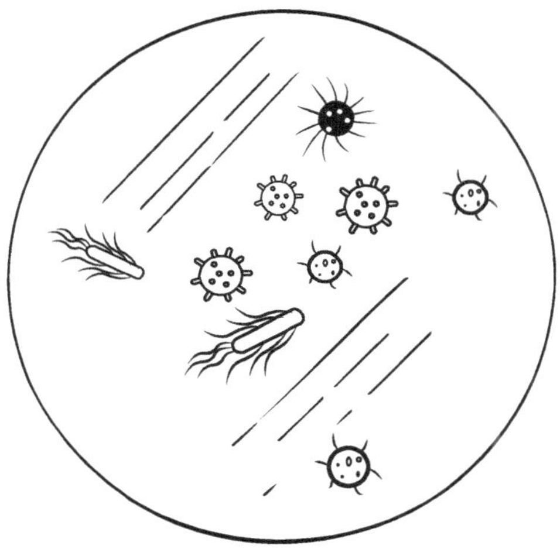

They vary in type and make up most of the biomass (bio-mass) on Earth.
They create what we call micro biodiversity (mic-ro-bio-di-ver-si-ty).

Microbes live in and on trees. . .

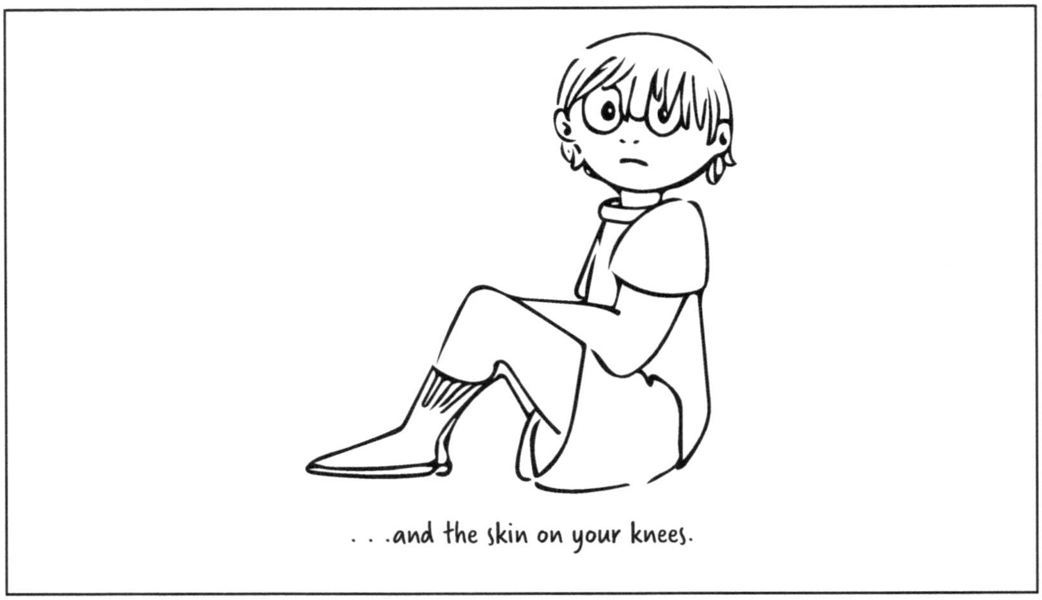
. . .and the skin on your knees.

18047
Microbes even live on these keys... although really,
someone should turn them in to the lost and found.

The main point is, there are many of them, about 5 nonillion
(no-nil-lion) on earth. They inhabit most things around us.
(5,000,000,000,000,000,000,000,000,000,000)

There is more than one type of microbe, just like there are different ice cream flavors.

But, be careful! Not all microbes are as good as ice cream.

There are good guys like Laci Pacey and Mr. Blue, also known as Cyano.

These microbes help plants grow by enriching the soil.
KAPOW!
They protect the body by fighting off the bad guys.
And at the end of the day, they return to the secret lair, the Gut.

Beat it kid!
Just as there are heros like Laci and Mr. Blue, there are also villains that can make you sick, like old Strep over here.

The bad guys can cause diseases and spread them to others.

Yes! Eat us!
They cause infections and food poisoning if you eat spoiled food.

But that's enough lip from me!
Why don't I let each microbe
introduce themselves?
Hi, I'm "Lactobacillus"(lac-to-ba-cil-lus), but I go by Laci for short.
I am responsible for creating a lot of food that you guys probably eat.
Things like yogurt, cheese, pickles, and salami are all made with my kind of microbes.

BAM!
But part of my job is to keep the bad bacteria (bac-te-ria) from getting into our food. These guys can give you tummy pain, sickness, and diarrhea from spoiled food.
It can be hard work sometimes, but I like seeing people happy and healthy.
Hey guys, it's Mr. Blue here. I also go by "Cyanobacteria" (cy-an-o-bac-te-ri-a), but in my country Cyano means blue, so I just go by Mr. Blue.
C

BLUE!
SMASH!
I'm responsible for breaking down and recycling dead animals and plants to make more food for plants and trees to grow.
I also make oxygen that we all breathe.
Sooorrrrry
I do get a bit carried away sometimes and make too much oxygen. This can cause water to be poisonous and not safe to drink.

I'm Strep, also known as "Streptococcus pyogenes" (st-rep-to-coc-cus py-o-gen-es). I can give you tonsillitis (ton-sil-li-tis) by growing in your tonsils, causing them to be swollen and red.
Can I go now?
I will also give you a high temperature, sickness, and headaches. Blah, blah, blah.
Cheer up Strep! You can go now because we are out of time for today.

We will return another day to continue exploring the world of microbiology.

See you next time...

Your name: ______________________ Date: ______________

Claim - Evidence - Reasoning Chart

Investigative Question

On what surface will microbes grow best?

Claim

Microbes will grow best on ______________________ because

Evidence

List key ideas that you learn. Your ideas may come from scientific experiments or personal experiences. You may use your own work or work from other experts.

Evidence From Personal Experiences

Evidence From Books, Videos, Websites, or other Research Sources

EVIDENCE FROM SCIENTIFIC MODELS, EXPERIMENTS, OR INVESTIGATIONS
REASONING
Decide if your claim is supported or not supported by your evidence. Explain what you think the evidence means and how it helps to answer our investigative question.

Claim-Evidence-Reasoning Self-Assessment

Name: ________________________________ Date: ________________

Check off each statement when you feel that you have completely met the criteria. If you can't check off something, go back and revise your work until you can.

Claim:

- ☐ I have stated my claim using complete sentences.
- ☐ My claim focuses on important scientific ideas.
- ☐ A reader would not need to see the question my teacher gave me in order to understand my claim because I have provided details in my work.
- ☐ I have included at least one reason that I feel supports my claim.

Evidence:

- ☐ I have carefully recorded all of my evidence.
- ☐ I have tried to locate multiple pieces of evidence.

Reasoning:

- ☐ I have looked for patterns in my evidence.
- ☐ I have I have decided which pieces of evidence are the best pieces for me to use in my argument.
- ☐ I have explained why those pieces of evidence are the strongest pieces.
- ☐ I have compared my strongest evidence to my claim.
- ☐ I have explained why my strongest evidence supports or does not support my claim.
- ☐ I have revised my original claim to include the information from my strongest evidence, if possible.

Lesson 2 The Role of Microbes in an Ecosystem

Introduction

An **ecosystem** is made up of all of the living and nonliving things in one place. Scientists study ecosystems to better understand how organisms relate to - and depend on - other organisms and nonliving things in order to survive.

One way to study ecosystems is to look at the different ways organisms get food. Organisms (such as plants) that are able to make their own food are called **producers**. The organisms use sunlight, water, and carbon dioxide to make food and oxygen. **Consumers** are organisms that need to eat in order to survive. Some consumers eat plants, while other consumers eat animals, and still others eat both plants and animals. Finally, some organisms, known as **decomposers**, break down waste products and dead organisms. Decomposers release nutrients back into the ecosystem.

producer

decomposer

consumer

Lesson 2 The Role of Microbes in an Ecosystem

Key Teaching Points

1. Organisms (including humans) in ecosystems are interdependent.
2. Microbes act as decomposers. They recycle matter throughout ecosystems.

Learner Outcomes

- Classify organisms as consumers, producers, or decomposers.
- Infer changes in one ecosystem based on changes in another.

Skill Level: Elementary, Beginning

Success Indicators

- Youth will classify organisms correctly.
- Youth will use evidence to support a claim.
- Youth will explain the role of bacteria in an ecosystem.

Life Skills

Critical Thinking, Keeping Records

Time Needed

90 minutes or two 45 minute sessions

Space

Classroom or similar sized area with access to an outdoor space or a gymnasium

Suggested Group Size

Groups of 4-5 youth

Materials List

- Examples of antibacterial products, such as hand soap and counter wipes
- 2 sticky notes per child or access to an online collaborative notation system, such as Padlet or Lino
- Technology to display producer/consumer/decomposer presentation
- Classroom whiteboard or chalkboard OR a piece of poster board
- 100 fake flowers or leaves for the Ecosystem Game
- 2 bins for the Ecosystem Game
- Claim-Evidence-Reasoning chart (1 per youth)
- Claim-Evidence-Reasoning Self-Assessment (1 per youth)
- Introduction (1 per youth)
- Ecosystem diagram (1 per group)
- Frayer models (optional)

Cantaloupe Experiment (ongoing)

- 1 pair of safety glasses for each youth
- 1 pair of safety gloves for each youth
- Alcohol solution (to be used by facilitator to clean goggles after the lesson)
- Bags of cantaloupe from Lesson 1
- Youth recording forms from Lesson 1

Remind youth about handling cantaloupe safely.

Show the presentation about putting on and taking off gloves appropriately (available on nc4hcurriculum.org, see page 5 for information.)

Lesson 2 The Role of Microbes in an Ecosystem

Background information

Microbes are essential to healthy, functioning ecosystems. Bacteria and fungi act as decomposers. This means that they survive by breaking down waste products and decaying dead organisms. In doing so, they release organic compounds and nutrients back into the ecosystem for use by other, living organisms.

In the past several decades, there has been a rapid increase in the number of products containing triclosan, a common antibacterial agent. Youth are likely familiar with the heavily-marketed idea that "germs are bad" and may be resistant to the idea that bacteria and other microbes actually are necessary components of healthy ecosystems. As you teach the lesson, encourage youth to reflect on the data that they gather and to revise their thinking in order to account for new data. Youth may also fail to see how they personally are organisms involved in ecosystems, and are thus dependent upon the same bacteria that many advertisements seek to destroy.

Before the Activity

1. Prepare technology to display the producer/consumer/decomposer presentation.(See page 5 for presentation access online).
2. Thoroughly read through the directions for the Ecosystem Game.
3. Print copies of the Claim-Evidence-Reasoning chart for each youth.
4. Print copies of the Claim-Evidence-Reasoning Self-Assessment for each youth.
5. Print copies of the Ecosystem diagram for each small group.
6. Print copies of the Frayer models for each youth (optional).
7. Print copies of the Introduction for each youth.
8. Scatter approximately 100 fake flowers or leaves on a playing field large enough for youth to run.
9. Provide two bins that "microbes" can use to return "nutrients" to the soil.
10. Ensure that safety materials are clean and in proper working order.
11. Prepare to distribute safety glasses and safety gloves to each youth.

Lesson 2 The Role of Microbes in an Ecosystem

PART ONE

Opening Question

- Would the world be better off if we could get rid of all of the microbes?
- Justify (provide reasons for) your ideas.

Let's Do It!

1. Ask youth to share the big ideas from their work in Lesson 1 as a quick review. Pass out the various antibacterial products. Ask youth what they know about these products and why these products might exist. Give youth a minute to talk with their learning partners and then share their ideas.

2. Pass out sticky notes, 1 per child. Ask the opening question.

   - Would the world be better off if we could get rid of all of the microbes? Justify (provide reasons for) your ideas.

   On their sticky notes, they will write down "Agree," "Disagree," or "Unsure" as well as at least one reason for their choice. Write "Agree," "Disagree," and "Unsure" on the board (or the wall or even a piece of poster board if needed). When youth are finished writing, they will add their sticky notes to the correct category in order to make a bar graph.

3. With the youth, look at trends with the initial ideas. Ask youth to share some of their reasoning. Leave the graph on the board so youth will be able to refer to it throughout the lesson.

4. Distribute the Claim-Evidence-Reasoning chart. With youth, locate the different boxes on the organizer. Explain to youth that scientists make claims by stating what they believe might be true. Scientists then gather evidence as they test their claims. Finally, scientists explain how their reasoning supports their claims OR supports new claims.

5. Tell youth that they will be making a claim and then testing that claim. Ask youth to write a sentence that states whether they think the world would be better off without microbes and provides at least one reason to support it. Remind them that their ideas might change as they learn more.

6. Explain to youth that they will be collecting data from two different sources during this lesson. First, they will play a game that simulates, or acts as a model of real-world relationships. Second, they will use their senses to observe the cantaloupe experiment they began in Lesson 1.

7. Take youth to the playing surface. Play the Ecosystem Game using the first variation in the directions.

8. After the game has collapsed once, give youth 2 minutes to turn and talk to a partner about what happened. Provide an additional minute for youth to record their observations on the "Evidence from Scientific Experiments or Models" section of their Claim-Evidence-Reasoning chart.

9. Play the Ecosystem Game again, using the second variation where youth act as microbes. Play until the Ecosystem is stable. Then, give youth 1 minute to turn and talk to a neighbor about their observations and an additional minute for them to record their observations.

10. Clean up the playing field and then return to the classroom. Ask the Share question.

    - Before playing the Ecosystem Game, what did you think the role of microbes might have been?

11. Ask the Reflect question.

    - What happened in the first version of the Ecosystem Game?
    - What happened in the second version?
    - What caused the change to happen?

12. Explain to youth that scientists use language to describe what they observed. Introduce the vocabulary words **ecosystem, producer, consumer,** and **decomposer**.

13. Distribute the Introduction to each youth and the Ecosystem diagram to each group.

14. Have youth work in small groups to read the Introduction.

15. Present the The Role of Microbes in an Ecosystem presentation.

16. Have youth work in small groups to complete the Ecosystem diagram.

17. Optional: Youth may define the terms in their own words using the Frayer model cards.

[For 45 minute classes, this is a good breaking point.]

PART TWO

1. If a second class period has begun, review the Ecosystem diagram from the previous lesson.

2. Provide youth with safety glasses and safety gloves.
   Show presentation to demonstrate proper use, removal, and disposal of gloves.

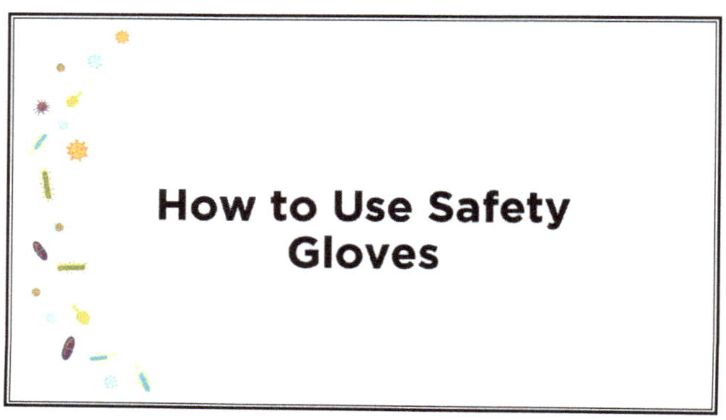

3. Instruct youth to observe their cantaloupe slices from the previous lesson in order to gather more evidence of microbes in the ecosystem. **Remind youth that they are not to open the bags, nor are they to taste anything.**

4. Youth should be able to see evidence of decomposition. They will add their observations to their Claim-Evidence-Reasoning chart from Lesson One and the group Cantaloupe Lab packet.

5. When youth have finished observing their cantaloupe experiment and cleaned their workspace thoroughly, they will wash their hands with soap and water.

6. Direct youth to work with their groups in order to brainstorm additional times that they have observed the effects of microbes in the ecosystem (e.g., rotting leaves, decaying food, etc.). They will add this information to their Claim-Evidence-Reasoning chart under "Evidence from Personal Experiences."

7. Finally, guide youth to decide if their evidence supports their initial claims about microbes. If youth feel that their initial claim is supported by their evidence, they will write a paragraph that explains how their evidence supports their initial claim. If youth do not feel that their evidence supports their initial claim, they will write a paragraph that includes a revised claim and the evidence that supports their new claim.

8. Youth will complete the Claim-Evidence-Reasoning Self-Assessment.

9. Ask the Generalize question.

   - After playing the Ecosystem Game, how might you describe the role of microbes in a healthy ecosystem?
   - What would happen to our ecosystem if there were no microbes?

10. Pass out one new sticky note to each child. Re-read the Opening Question.

    - Would the world be better off if we could get rid of all of the microbes?
    - Justify (provide reasons for) your ideas.

    Provide the same three categories, "Agree," "Disagree," and "Unsure." Ask youth to answer the question on their sticky notes and to provide a reason. Again, create a bar graph that shows youth responses. Compare this graph to the graph from the beginning of the lesson. Ask youth if they changed their responses from the beginning of the lesson and to share what evidence made them change their ideas.

11. Close the lesson by asking the Apply question.

    - Imagine a scientist has created a product called "Microbe-B-Gone" that is guaranteed to kill 100% of all microbes, including bacteria, in the area in which the product is used. Your local school board is planning to use Microbe-B-Gone as their main cleaning supplier. Is this a good idea? Why or why not? What would you tell the school board about this decision?

12. After the lesson has ended, be sure to clean all safety glasses thoroughly with the alcohol solution. Allow the glasses to dry before returning them to the kit.

Lesson 2 The Role of Microbes in an Ecosystem

Term and Concept Discovery

Abiotic factor: a non-living factor that affects the way organisms live in an ecosystem. Light, climate, water quality, and soil type are all examples of abiotic factors.

Antibiotic: chemicals that are known to kill or weaken bacteria. Antibiotics are used in medicines designed to treat bacterial infections. In the past few decades, there has been a rapid increase in the number of antibiotics used in non-medical products, including soap, hand sanitizer, and cleaning products. Antibiotics are also widely used in animal feed to prevent disease among livestock. The use of antibiotics is controversial, as bacteria can develop resistance to the chemicals, making them ineffective.

Biotic factor: the living factors in an ecosystem. For example, a forest ecosystem may include competing populations of deer, squirrels, owls, snakes, worms, and oak trees among its many biotic factors.

Consumer: an organism that gets energy by eating other organisms. For example, a grasshopper eats grass. Lions eat zebras. Bears eat berries and fish. Fish eat grasshoppers. These are all consumers because they eat other organisms to survive.

Decomposer: an organism that gets energy by chemically breaking down the remains of other organisms. The decomposition process also returns stored nutrients from the dead organisms back to the ecosystem. Fungi and bacteria are common decomposers.

Ecosystem: the movement of energy and recycling of matter in a particular location. Ecosystems are defined by the relationships among biotic and abiotic factors. Commonly studied ecosystems include tundra, desert, forest, grassland, and estuarine ecosystems.

Producer: an organism that is able to make its own food using energy from the environment. Plants are producers, as are some photosynthetic and chemosynthetic bacteria.

Talk It Over

Share 1

Before playing the Ecosystem Game, what did you think the role of microbes might have been?

Reflect 2

What happened in the first version of the Ecosystem Game?

What happened in the second version? What caused the change to happen?

Generalize 3

After playing the Ecosystem Game, how might you describe the role of microbes in a healthy ecosystem?

What would happen to our ecosystem if there were no microbes?

Apply 4

Imagine a scientist has created a product called "Microbe-B-Gone" that is guaranteed to kill 100% of all microbes,including bacteria, in the area in which the product is used. Your local school board is planning to use Microbe-B-Gone as their main cleaning supplier.

Is this a good idea? Why or why not?

What would you tell the school board about this decision?

Variations

- If an interactive whiteboard is available, you may choose to do the diagram as a whole-class activity.
- If Internet access is available, you may choose to use a website such as http://en.linoit.com, http://www.padlet.com, or another collaborative notation tool to use in place of sticky notes.
- Frayer Model templates have been provided for key vocabulary in this section. You may choose to use the Frayer Models to support vocabulary development among youth.
- You may choose to assign the "Apply" question as homework. Youth may choose to perform a skit, write a letter, or film a public service announcement video in response to the "Apply" question.

Take It Home!

Go for a walk with a family member. Take pictures or record in your notebook examples of producers, consumers, and decomposers that you find on your walk.

Include the evidence that helped you to classify the organism as a producer, consumer, or a decomposer.

You may choose to include pictures if you wish.

Education Standard(s)

North Carolina Essential Standards in Science:
5.L.2.2 Classify the organisms within an ecosystem according to the function they serve: producers, consumers, or decomposers (biotic factors)
5.L.2.3 Infer the effects that may result from the interconnected relationship of plants and animals to their ecosystem.
Common Core State Standards
CCSS.ELA-Literacy.W.5.1 Write opinion pieces on topics or texts, supporting a point of view with reasons and information.
Next Generation Science Standards
5-LS2-1. Develop a model to describe the movement of matter among plants, animals, decomposers, and the environment

Tags

Ecology, ecosystems, producer, consumer, decomposer, game, scientific thinking

Lesson 2 Print Materials

Facilitator Print Materials
Instructions for Ecosystem Game
Ecosystem diagram answers

Group Handouts
Ecosystem diagram

Youth Handouts
Introduction
Claim-Evidence-Reasoning chart
Claim-Evidence-Reasoning Self-Assessment
Frayer models (optional)

See page 5 for information on digital digital assets and extra enrichment.

We each have a purpose and connections to other organisms (or-gan-isms) on this planet.

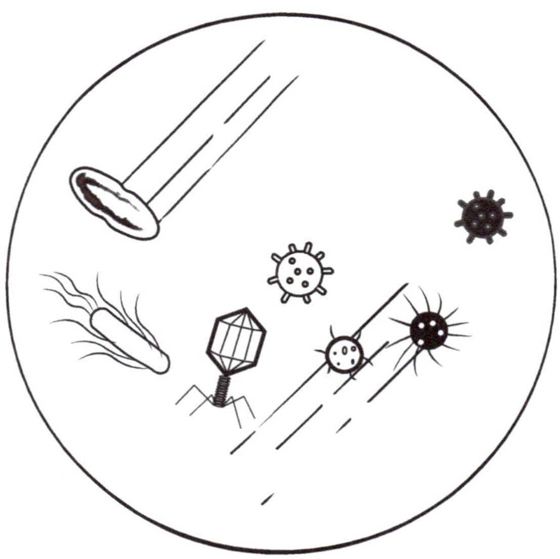

In this lesson, we will explore how we depend on microbes to survive and the different roles they play.

The Ecosystem Game

The Ecosystem Game is a way to model population growth and the recycling of matter and nutrients in an ecosystem. Many different variations of this game exist. The directions below are for one possible variation designed to help introduce the importance of bacteria and other microbes in an ecosystem.

Materials:

- 100 fake flowers
- A large open space, such as a playground or soccer field.

Directions:

1. Scatter the flowers on the playing field.
2. Ask youth how the flowers get nutrients. If needed, remind youth that flowers (plants) produce their own food through photosynthesis using energy from the sun, carbon from the air, and water, but that they use nutrients from the soil as well in order to grow.
3. Explain to the youth that they are going to pretend to be animals. Ask them how they might get their nutrients. [*possible answer: by eating plants*]
4. Explain to the youth that they will need to collect 5 flowers when the game starts in order to "survive". If they collect fewer than 5 flowers, they will "die" and have to sit out.
5. When the youth are ready, begin the game. Give youth 30 seconds to 1 minute (depending on number of youth and the size of your space) to pick up as many flowers as possible. Once time is up, bring the youth back together.
6. Collect all of the flowers that the youth have picked up and set them aside into one of the bins. Ask youth who collected fewer than 5 flowers to remain at the side of the playing field.
7. Ask youth who collected at least 5 flowers to return to the field in order to begin the second round. Repeat steps 5-7 until no more flowers remain on the field. This usually takes about 3 rounds.
8. Once youth notice that there are no more flowers and that everyone has died, explain that the ecosystem has collapsed. Ask youth to generate reasons why the ecosystem might have collapsed. [*possible answer: there were no more flowers for the animals to eat*]
9. Explain to youth that the model was missing something. Designate two youth to be "microbes." Explain that they will be responsible for collecting flowers from the youth in between rounds and returning them to the playing field.
10. Hand a bin to each of the "microbes." Ask the microbes to put all of the flowers back out to the field.
11. Run the game again with all of the youth who are not designated as "microbes."
12. When time for the round is up, have youth put their collected flowers into the microbes' bins.
13. Repeat Steps 10-12 for 3 more rounds. Ask youth to compare the model without bacteria to the model with bacteria. [*possible answers: the first was unbalanced, the second was balanced; the system with bacteria was healthy; the second system had the bacteria to help return nutrients to the soil, but the first did not; etc.*]

Ecosystem Diagram

Work with your partner to label the diagram. Be ready to explain your work.

Words to use: **producer** **consumer** **decomposer**

producer

decomposer

consumer

Ecosystem Diagram answers

Ecosystem Diagram

Work with your partner to label the diagram. Be ready to explain your work.

Words to use: **producer (pro-du-cer)** **consumer (con-su-mer)** **decomposer (de-com-po-ser)**

Introduction to Ecosystems

An **ecosystem (e-co-sys-tem)** is made up of all of the living and nonliving things in one place. Scientists study ecosystems to better understand how organisms (or-gan-isms) relate to - and depend on - other organisms and nonliving things in order to survive.

One way to study ecosystems (e-co-sys-tems) is to look at the different ways organisms (or-gan-isms) might get food. Organisms (such as plants) that are able to make their own food are called **producers (pro-du-cers)**. The organisms use sunlight, water, and carbon dioxide to make food and oxygen. **Consumers (con-su-mers)** are organisms that need to eat in order to survive. Some consumers eat plants, while others eat animals, and still others eat both plants and animals. Finally, some organisms, known as **decomposers (de-com-po-sers)**, break down waste products and dead organisms. Decomposers release nutrients back into the ecosystem.

Your name: ______________________ Date: ______________

Claim - Evidence - Reasoning Chart

Investigative Question Should microbes be removed from the ecosystem?
Claim
Microbes should / should not be removed from the ecosystem (e-co-sys-tem) because
Evidence
List key ideas that you learn. Your ideas may come from scientific experiments or personal experiences. You may use your own work or work from other experts.
Evidence From Personal Experiences
Evidence From Books, Videos, Websites, or other Research Sources

Evidence From Scientific Models, Experiments, or Investigations

Reasoning
Decide if your claim is supported or not supported by your evidence. Explain what you think the evidence means and how it helps to answer our investigative question.

Claim-Evidence-Reasoning Self-Assessment

Name: ________________________________ Date: ________________

Check off each statement when you feel that you have completely met the criteria.
If you can't check off something, go back and revise your work until you can.

Claim:

- ☐ I have stated my claim using complete sentences.
- ☐ My claim focuses on important scientific ideas.
- ☐ A reader would not need to see the question my teacher gave me in order to understand my claim because I have provided details in my work.
- ☐ I have included at least one reason that I feel supports my claim.

Evidence:

- ☐ I have carefully recorded all of my evidence.
- ☐ I have tried to locate multiple pieces of evidence.

Reasoning:

- ☐ I have looked for patterns in my evidence.
- ☐ I have I have decided which pieces of evidence are the best pieces for me to use in my argument.
- ☐ I have explained why those pieces of evidence are the strongest pieces.
- ☐ I have compared my strongest evidence to my claim.
- ☐ I have explained why my strongest evidence supports or does not support my claim.
- ☐ I have revised my original claim to include the information from my strongest evidence, if possible.

Definition in your own words	Characteristics (features that identify it)

Ecosystem
(e-co-sys-tem)

Examples	Non-examples

Definition in your own words

Characteristics (features that identify it)

Producer (pro-du-cer)

Examples

Non-examples

Definition in your own words	Characteristics (features that identify it)

Consumer
(con–su–mer)

Examples	Non-examples

Definition in your own words	Characteristics (features that identify it)
Examples	**Non-examples**

Decomposer
(de-com-po-ser)

Lesson 3 The Ecosystems Inside Us

Introduction

It is estimated that there are ten times as many bacterial cells as there are human cells living in and on your body. Scientists call these bacteria your **microbiome**. The word "microbiome" comes from the words "micro," which means "small," and "biome," which means "ecosystem." Your microbiome acts like a small ecosystem in and on your body because many different types of microbes compete against each other for the scarce resources they need to survive.

The microbes in your microbiome are examples of **matter**. Matter is all of the "stuff" in our universe. Anything that you can touch, taste, or smell is matter. Desks are matter. Dogs are matter. Decomposers are matter.

Scientists talk about the properties of matter in order to describe different types of matter. Think about gold. The way it reflects light is one of its properties. The way gold feels is another. Gold can melt or be a solid. It tends not to react with other chemicals. These are all properties of gold. When matter interacts with other types of matter, changes can occur. Sometimes, matter changes shape or size. The way the matter looks changes, but the actual "stuff" doesn't. Melted gold is still gold. Sugar dissolved in tea is still sugar, and will eventually fall to the bottom of the glass if you wait long enough. These types of changes are called **physical changes**.

Sometimes when matter interacts, the changes are more than physical changes. **Chemical changes** occur when new types of matter are made or released. Bubbles, odors, color changes, and heat are all indicators that chemical changes are taking place. For example, plants use photosynthesis to turn carbon dioxide and water into sugar and oxygen. Oxygen is released and the sugars are very different from the carbon dioxide. The plants have transformed one type of matter into another through chemical changes.

In our bodies, we change matter through **digestion**. Our digestive system is a special group of organs that help us decompose our food so we can get the energy and nutrients we need. Most of our microbiome can be found in our digestive system.

Lesson 3 The Ecosystems Inside Us

Key Teaching Points

1. Matter can undergo changes. Some changes are physical, meaning the type of matter doesn't change. Other changes are chemical, meaning that the type of matter is transformed into another type of matter.
2. Microbes cause chemical changes as they decompose matter.
3. When we digest food, with the help of microbes, we cause chemical changes.

Learner Outcomes

- Explain how organisms are able to obtain nutrients.
- Classify changes as chemical or physical changes.

Skill Level: Elementary, Beginning

Success Indicators

- Youth will make and record observations about properties of matter.
- Youth will classify changes.

Life Skills

Critical Thinking, Keeping Records

Time Needed

90 minutes or two 45 minute sessions

Space

Classroom or similar sized area with at least one tabletop available for the burning paper demonstration

Suggested Group Size

Groups of 4 youth

Materials List

- 5 lb. bag of sugar from Lesson 1
- 3 sticky notes per youth
- Whiteboard or 2 pieces of poster board to use as graph templates
- Piece of scrap paper
- Large, clear, glass mixing bowl or beaker
- Tabletop
- Match or lighter
- 1 pair safety goggles for instructor use
- Large pitcher of water (for safety purposes)
- 1 copy of the Introduction for each pair
- 1 set of Frayer models for each youth (optional)
- 1 set of sort cards for each group of 4 youth
- 1 small plastic bottle, like a 12-ounce soda bottle or small water bottle, for each group
- 1 small pitcher of warm water (approximately 100 to 105 degrees Fahrenheit) for each group
- 2 tablespoons of molasses for each group
- 1 packet of yeast for each group
- 1 balloon for each group
- 1 funnel for each group
- Clock with a minute hand or a timer
- 1 sheet of chart paper per group of 4 youth
- 1 marker per group of 4 youth
- Balloon Bottle Observation Log (1 per group)
- Anticipation Guides (1 per youth)
- Computer with projection capabilities and Internet access to watch the video

Cantaloupe Experiment (ongoing)

- 1 pair of safety glasses for each youth
- 1 pair of safety gloves for each youth
- Alcohol solution (to be used by facilitator to clean goggles after the lesson)
- Bags of cantaloupe from Lesson 1
- Youth recording forms from Lesson 1

Lesson 3 The Ecosystems Inside Us

Background information

Microbes are essential to healthy, functioning ecosystems. In Lesson 2, youth learned that bacteria and fungi act as decomposers. This means that they survive by breaking down waste products and decaying dead organisms. In doing so, they release organic compounds and nutrients back into the ecosystem for use by other, living organisms.

The process of decomposition involves matter undergoing changes. **Matter** is all of the "stuff" in our world, the things we can see and the things we can't. Water is a type of matter. Trees are another type of matter. Every atom, every star, every person: they are all matter.

When matter interacts, changes may result. Sometimes, the changes only affect the way matter looks or feels. For example, melting ice changes water from a solid to a liquid. Chopping a tree changes it from a large piece of wood into smaller pieces. However, in both examples, the type of matter stays the same. The water is still water. The wood is still wood. These types of changes are called **physical changes**.

Chemical changes change one type of matter into another completely different type of matter. For example, burning wood changes the wood into ash and gas. Adding baking soda to vinegar creates a reaction that results in a type of (inedible) salt, water, and carbon dioxide gas. These new types of matter have different chemical **properties** than the original types: they look and behave differently.

Digestion is the process that living organisms, including microbes, use to obtain nutrients through decomposition. Humans have a specialized system of organs, known as the digestive system, to help them obtain energy from food. Most of the human **microbiome**, the billions of microbes living on and in the human body, is located within the digestive tract (the gut).

Scientists are just beginning to understand the relationships we have with the billions of bacteria that live in and on our bodies. Thanks to advances in scientific techniques such as DNA sequencing, scientists are better able to understand which bacteria are present in individuals and in which proportions they are found. Scientists are also starting to understand how the bacteria are interacting with each other and with us.

Some scientists feel that the bacteria in our microbiome benefit from their relationships with us, but that we see no effect. If this is indeed the case, then our relationship with our microbiome would best be classified as an example of **commensalism** (A symbiotic relationship in which one organism derives benefit and the other is unharmed). On the other hand, other scientists feel that our relationship with our microbiome is an example of **mutualism** (A symbiotic relationship in which both species benefit). They argue that both humans and bacteria benefit from the microbiome relationship. These scientists suggest that the bacteria help train our immune systems to be ready for invaders. They also suggest that the bacteria are helping our digestive tracts to break down food and that we would be unable to digest many types of foods without our microbiome.

In the past several decades, there has been a rapid increase in the number of products containing triclosan, a common antibacterial agent. Youth are likely familiar with the heavily-marketed idea that "germs are bad" and may be resistant to the idea that bacteria and other microbes actually are necessary components of healthy ecosystems. As you teach the lesson, encourage youth to reflect on the data that they gather and to revise their thinking in order to account for new data.

Lesson 3 The Ecosystems Inside Us

Before the Activity

1. Set out the bag of sugar.
2. Prepare the demonstration materials:
   - One piece of scrap paper
   - One large, clear, glass mixing bowl or beaker
   - Match or lighter
   - One pair of safety glasses
   - Large pitcher of water
3. Print copies of the handouts:
   - Balloon Bottle Observation Log (one per group)
   - Anticipation Guide (one per youth)
   - Introduction (one per pair)
   - Frayer models (one per youth, optional)
4. Print copies of Sort Cards for each group and cut them apart.
5. Prepare the lab materials for each group:
   - 2 tablespoons of molasses in a small cup
   - One plastic water or soda bottle with a lid.
   - One small cup of warm water (100-105 degrees F)
   - One packet of yeast
   - One balloon
   - One funnel
   - One sheet of chart paper
   - One marker
6. Prepare a clock with a minute hand or a timer
7. Ensure that safety materials are clean and in proper working order.
8. Prepare to distribute safety glasses and safety gloves to each youth.

This learning experience has the potential to be quite messy. Please plan for containment & cleanup according to the needs of your group.

Note: The Introduction for youth provided in this lesson is identical to the Introduction for Grab and Go 2: Microbial Munchies. Please plan appropriately if these youth will complete both lessons.

Lesson 3 The Ecosystems Inside Us

PART ONE

Opening Question

- What happens when microbes inside our bodies act as decomposers?

Let's Do It!

1. Distribute the Introduction and read with youth. Display the bag of sugar from Lesson 1. Remind youth that it represented the total weight of the **microbiome**, the microbes that live in and on each of our bodies.

2. Show youth the Ecosystem Diagram correctly labeled with the key vocabulary (producer, consumer, decomposer, and ecosystem) from Lesson 2. Ask youth the Opening Question.

    - What happens when microbes inside our bodies act as decomposers?

3. Emphasize to youth that when objects or organisms interact, they might change. Sometimes the changes involve the way things look or feel, but the type of matter stays the same. Crumble up a piece of paper as a demonstration. (The matter looks different and feels different, but it is still a piece of paper). These changes are called **physical changes.**

4. Put on the safety goggles. Distribute safety glasses to youth to put on.

5. Use the match to light the paper on fire. Drop the paper into the glass bowl on the table and let it burn to ash. **Make sure to have the pitcher of water next to the bowl in case it is needed.** Tell youth that other interactions can cause matter to change into new types of matter. These changes are called **chemical changes**.

6. Pass out the Sort Cards, 1 set for each group of four youth. Give youth five minutes to sort the cards. You may need to read the cards aloud for youth who are still developing academic English language. Review the sorts using the Answer Key.

7. Point out to youth that the examples in the cards all involved interactions large enough to easily see with the unaided eye. Microbes, on the other hand, present different challenges for scientists because of their small size. Solicit ideas about how scientists might study the interactions among microbes.

8. Tell youth that one-way scientists understand microbial activity is by observing changes in the **properties** of matter. Explain that properties can be chemical, like rust, or physical, like the color of a rock. Tell youth that they will practice by observing the properties in their ongoing cantaloupe experiment.

9. Pass out safety gloves, 1 pair per youth. Demonstrate proper use, removal, and disposal of safety gloves again if necessary.

10. Give youth five minutes to observe their cantaloupe and record their observations. **Make sure youth understand that they are not to open the bags, nor are they to taste anything.**

11. Youth should be able to see evidence of decomposition. They will add their observations to their Claim-Evidence-Reasoning chart from Lesson One and the group Cantaloupe Lab Packet.

12. When youth have finished observing their cantaloupe experiment and cleaned their workspace thoroughly, they will wash their hands with soap and water.

13. While youth are working, write the following words on the board: Appearance, Odor, Texture, Sound, and Other.

14. Ask the Share question.

    • When you examined the cantaloupe today, what properties did you observe?

    Ask youth to share out the properties they observed and to classify them according to the criteria listed on the board. Listen to ensure that youth are correctly classifying.

15. Pass out sticky notes, 1 to each youth. Ask the Reflect question.

    • Based on your observations so far, do you believe that your cantaloupe is undergoing a chemical change, a physical change, or some other type of change?

    Ask youth to write "Chemical Change," "Physical Change," or "Other" and at least one reason on the sticky note to justify the answer.

16. Write "Chemical Change," "Physical Change," and "Other" on the board (or another display surface). When youth are finished writing, they will add their sticky notes to the correct category in order to make a bar graph.

17. As a group, analyze trends on the graph. Ask youth to share their reasoning.

[For 45 minute classes, this is a good breaking point.]

PART TWO

1. If a second class period has begun, review chemical and physical changes from the previous lesson.

2. Pass out the Balloon Bottle Observation Log and Procedure. You may also choose to provide the word bank version of the Observation Log to youth who are still developing academic English vocabulary. With youth, read through the Balloon Bottle Observation Log and Procedure to ensure that youth understand the directions.

3. **Review lab observation and safety procedures, especially procedures for tasting food in the lab.**
    - **Seeing: youth will use their sense of sight to make visual observations of the balloon.**
    - **Tasting: youth are to eat in the lab only when directly instructed to do so by the teacher. Otherwise, there should not be anything to eat or drink in the lab setting.**
    - **Touching: youth will not touch the molasses or yeast.**
    - **Smelling: youth will not observe the experiment by smelling the experiment directly.**
    - **Hearing: youth may be able to hear the yeast, warm water, and molasses interacting if they carefully place the balloon bottle near their ear**

4. Ask youth if they have ever seen any of the materials before. Make sure that youth know that yeast is an organism and that molasses is a sugar.

a. Carefully fill a small plastic bottle, like a water or soda bottle, with warm water until it is approximately 2/3 full. If you are using a soda bottle, the top of where the label would have been is a good marker.

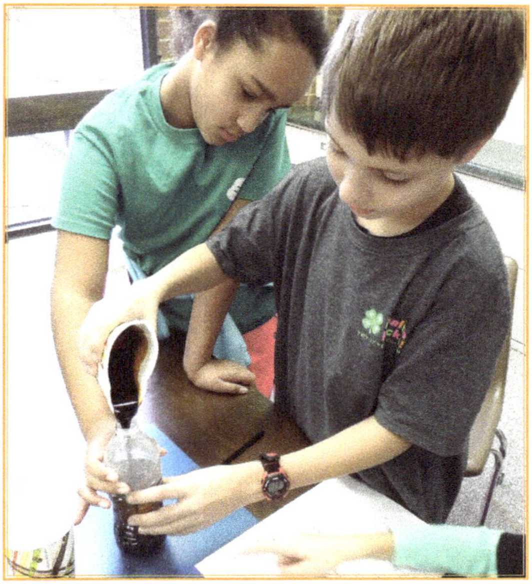

b. Add the molasses.

c. Add the yeast.

d. Screw the cap back on the bottle.

e. Gently swirl the bottle for two minutes.

f. Remove the cap.

g. Place the balloon over the opening at the top of the bottle.

h. Wait 5 minutes while youth observe the bottle.
Depending on the age of the yeast and the temperature of the water, it can take up to 20 minutes for the process to start. If 5 minutes pass and nothing appears to have changed, skip ahead and complete steps 8-11. You may return to steps 6-7 once the reaction occurs.

Balloon at 10 minutes.

Balloon at 5 minutes.

The bottle will make some noise.

5. You may want to demonstrate "gentle swirling" as opposed to shaking.
6. Have youth compare their Observation Logs. Ask the Share question.

    - What changes did you observe in your Balloon Bottle system?

    Direct youth to create a poster on chart paper that summarizes the changes that occurred.

7. Ask the Reflect question.

    - What might have caused the balloon to inflate? (Solicit ideas)

    Explain that the yeast digested (ate) the sugars in the molasses. The digestion process produced a gas called carbon dioxide that inflated the balloon. Ask youth to work with their learning partners in order to classify the changes to the molasses as physical or chemical changes. If your youth have whiteboards available, they could record their ideas on the whiteboards and flip them up. If not, listen to see if youth are correctly using the definitions of the terms in their justifications. (When the yeast digested or decomposed, the sugars (molasses) underwent a chemical change. The carbon dioxide gas is one indicator that a chemical change took place.)

8. Review the Opening Question.

    - What happens when microbes inside our bodies act as decomposers?

    Tell youth the human microbiome contains gut microbes that help digest food. Explain that youth will watch a brief video about the digestion process in humans in order to understand help answer this question.

9. Give youth time to complete side 1 of the Video Anticipation Guide. Watch the video. (Video is available online at http://youtu.be/PO9WRIlxvww or on nc4hcurriculum.org). You may want to let youth watch twice, depending on time.

10. After the video, youth should complete side 2 of the Anticipation Guide.

11. Ask youth to share their work from side 2 of the Anticipation Guide.

12. Ask youth to use evidence from the visualization to talk about the role that microbes play in digestion. Make sure youth understand that gut microbes help to break down food that we can't break down on our own. Some of the calories we get from food are actually due to the activity of our gut microbes.

13. Ask the Generalize question.

    - Are digestion and decomposition examples of chemical change, physical change, or some other type of change?

    Pass out 1 sticky note per youth. Ask youth to write "Chemical Change," "Physical Change," or "Other" on their sticky note and to place their sticky note on a new graph. Ask youth to share their reasoning and to summarize their understanding.

14. Hand youth the final sticky note. As a ticket out the door, ask the Apply questions. Have them write their response on the sticky note and hand it to you as they leave.

- What evidence do you have that chemical changes are taking place inside your digestive system? How would you explain this process to a friend?

15. After the lesson, use the alcohol solution to thoroughly clean the safety glasses. Allow glasses to dry before returning them to the kit.

Term and Concept Discovery

Chemical Change: a change in the chemical structure and atomic bonding of matter. Chemical changes are often accompanied by a gas being released, a temperature change, a change in color, or a change in odor. Burning paper causes a chemical change, changing paper into ash.

Commensalism: a relationship between species in which one organism benefits while the other is neither harmed nor benefitted. For example, some tropical plants known as epiphytes grow on host trees. The epiphytes get nutrients from the atmosphere and are better able reach sunlight and water. They do not appear to affect the host trees in any way, either positively or negatively.

Decomposition: the process by which dead organisms are broken down chemically into component nutrients. For example, as dead trees decompose, they are broken into carbon and nitrogen, among other elements.

Digestion: the process through which organisms chemically break down food into component nutrients that can be used by their cells.

Digestive System: the system of organs in the human body that helps humans to extract nutrients and energy from food. The tongue, esophagus, stomach, and intestines are some components of the human digestive system.

Mass: the amount of matter something has

Matter: all of the "stuff" in the universe. Anything made of atoms or subatomic particles is matter. Matter has mass and thus can be measured.

Microbiome: the term given to the microbes that live within/on a particular organism.

Mutualism: a relationship between species in which both organisms benefit. Cleaning stations on coral reefs are examples of mutualism; the cleaner fish benefits by getting food, while the other fish benefit by having their parasites cleaned away.

Physical Change: a physical change occurs when matter changes shape or state, but the chemical bonds between atoms are not affected. For example, tearing paper into bits and melting ice are examples of physical changes.

Talk It Over

Share 1	Reflect 2
When you examined the cantaloupe today, what properties did you observe? What changes did you observe in your balloon bottle system?	Based on your observations so far, do you believe that your cantaloupe is undergoing a chemical change, a physical change, or some other type of change? Write at least one reason on your sticky note to justify your answer. What might have caused the balloon to inflate?
Generalize 3	**Apply 4**
Are digestion and decomposition examples of chemical change, physical change, or some other type of change?	What evidence do you have that chemical changes are taking place inside your digestive system? How would you explain this process to a friend?

Variations

- You may choose to use the provided Frayer models with youth who are still developing academic English language. These models can be completed as a pre-teaching activity in class with support or as a homework assignment.

Learn More

Bellybutton Biodiversity:
http://robdunnlab.com/projects/belly-button-biodiversity/

Take It Home!

Yogurt is another food many of us eat that is a product of microbial work. Yogurt begins with milk and goes through changes to end up as something different. With the help of an adult, compare milk to yogurt.

What observations can you make?

What is the same about milk and yogurt?

What is different?

Education Standard(s)

North Carolina Essential Standards in Science:

5.L.1 Understand how structures and systems of organisms (to include the human body) perform functions necessary for life.

5.P.2 Understand the interactions of matter and energy and the changes that occur.

Next Generation Science Standards:

5-LS2-1. Develop a model to describe the movement of matter among plants, animals, decomposers, and the environment.

5-PS1-1: Develop a model to describe that matter is made of particles too small to be seen.

Tags

Ecology, microbiome, scientific thinking

Lesson 3 Print Materials

Facilitator Print Materials

Balloon Bottle Observation Log and Procedure (alternative front page) -
Word Bank version for youth
Sort Cards answer key

See page 5 for information on digital assets and extra enrichment.

Group Handouts

Introduction (one per pair)
Sort Cards (one per group of four youth)
Balloon Bottle Observation Log and Procedure (one per group)

Youth Handouts

Video Anticipation Guide
Frayer models (optional)

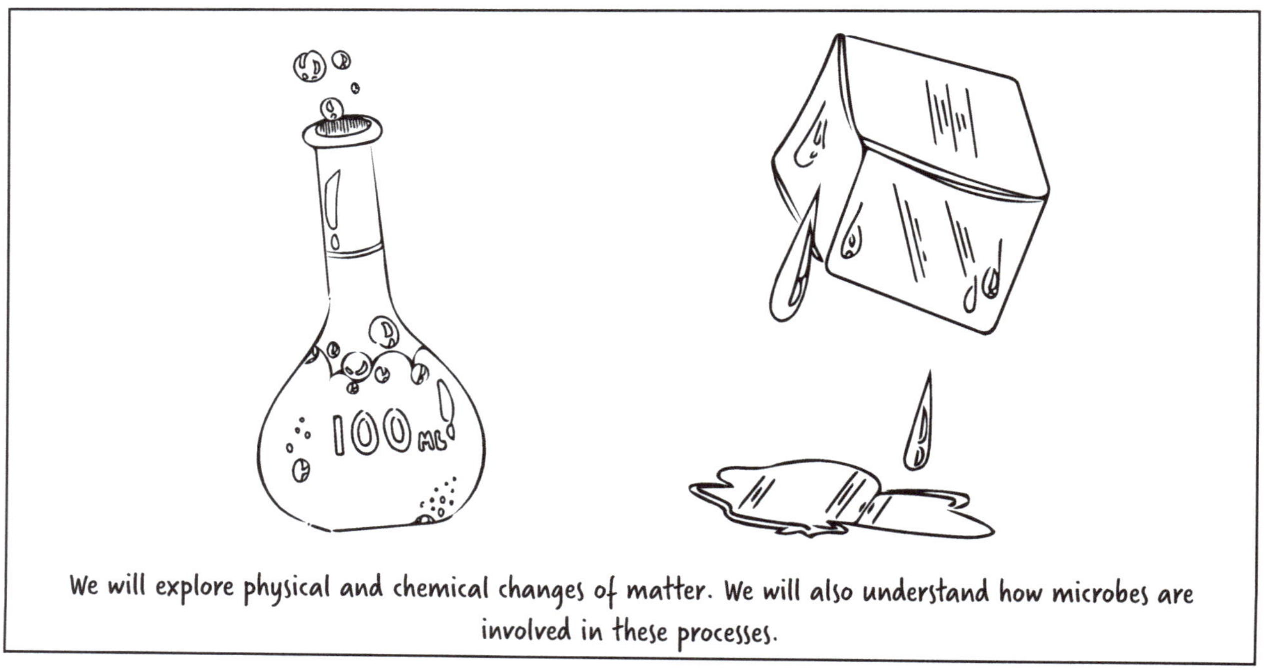

Balloon Bottle Observation Log and Procedure - Word Bank version

1. With your partner, circle the words that describe the properties of each item listed below.

Item	Observations			
Yeast	small Other words:	grainy	large	soft
Water	brown Other words:	clear	liquid	solid
Molasses	brown Other words:	clear	liquid	solid
Balloon	stiff Other words:	stretchy	liquid	solid

2. Using the funnel, carefully fill the small plastic bottle with warm water until it is approximately 2/3 full. If you are using soda bottles, the top of where the label would have been is a good marker.
3. Add the molasses.
4. Add the yeast.
5. Screw the cap back on the bottle.
6. Gently swirl the bottle for two minutes.
7. Remove the cap.
8. Carefully stretch the balloon over the opening at the top of the bottle.
9. Set the bottle on the table.

In the box below, draw your balloon bottle system as it looks right now.
Label the parts.

Time:

Ingredients are baked into a cake. **(Chemical change. Indicators include smell, color, and bubbles)**	You make a "volcano" by adding baking soda to vinegar. **(Chemical change: bubbles)**
An old nail rusts. **(Chemical change: color, smell)**	Ice melts. **(Physical change: change of state)**
You chop firewood. **(Physical change: change of size)**	Melted chocolate hardens in a candy mold. **(Physical change: change of state)**
Fireworks explode. **(Chemical change: odor, color, gas)**	You tie-dye a white shirt. **(Chemical change to the dye: change of color)**
Boiling water evaporates. **(Physical change: change of state)**	You dissolve salt in water. **(Physical change: solution)**

Introduction

It is estimated that there are ten times as many bacterial (bac-te-ri-al) cells as there are human cells living in and on your body. Scientists call these bacteria your **microbiome (mi-cro-bi-ome)**. The word "microbiome" comes from the words "micro," which means "small," and "biome," which means "ecosystem" (e-co-sys-tem). Your microbiome acts like a small ecosystem in and on your body because many different types of microbes compete against each other for the scarce resources they need to survive.

The microbes in your microbiome (mi-cro-bi-ome) are examples of **matter**. Matter is all of the "stuff" in our universe. Anything that you can touch, taste, or smell is matter. Desks are matter. Dogs are matter. Decomposers (de-com-po-sers) are matter.

Scientists talk about the properties of matter in order to describe different types of matter. Think about gold. The way it reflects light is one of its properties. The way gold feels is another. Gold can melt or be a solid. It tends not to react with other chemicals. These are all properties of gold. When matter interacts with other types of matter, changes can occur. Sometimes, matter changes shape or size. The way the matter looks changes, but the actual "stuff" doesn't. Melted gold is still gold. Sugar dissolved in tea is still sugar, and will eventually fall to the bottom of the glass if you wait long enough. These types of changes are called **physical changes**.

Sometimes when matter interacts, the changes are more than physical changes. **Chemical changes** occur when new types of matter are made or released. Bubbles, odors, color changes, and heat are all indicators that chemical changes are taking place. For example, plants use photosynthesis (pho-to-syn-the-sis) to turn carbon dioxide and water into sugar and oxygen. Oxygen is released and the sugars are very different from the carbon dioxide. The plants transform one type of matter into another through chemical changes.

In our bodies, we change matter through **digestion (di-ges-tion)**. Our digestive (di-ges-tive) system is a special group of organs that help us decompose (de-com-pose) our food so we can get the energy and nutrients (nu-tri-ents) we need. Most of our microbiome (mi-cro-bi-ome) can be found in our digestive system.

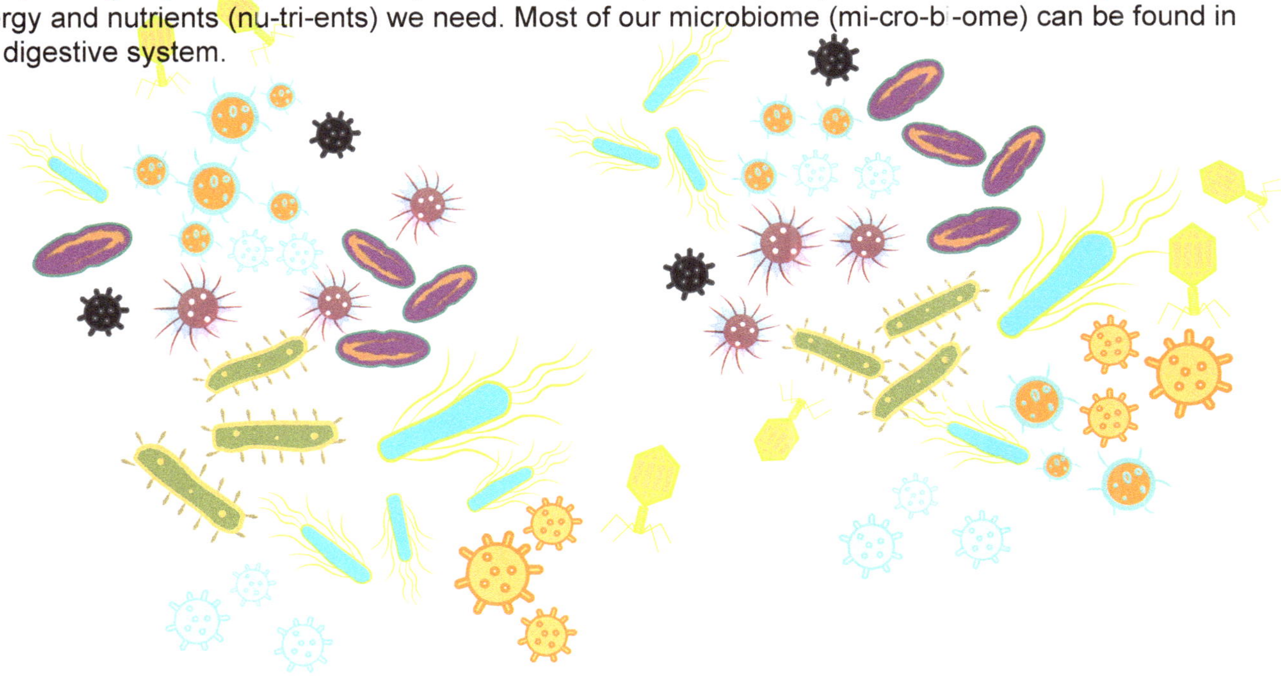

Ingredients are baked into a cake.	You make a “volcano” by adding baking soda to vinegar.
An old nail rusts.	Ice melts.
You chop firewood.	Melted chocolate hardens in a candy mold.
Fireworks explode.	You tie-dye a white shirt.
Boiling water evaporates.	You dissolve salt in water.

Balloon Bottle Observation Log and Procedure

1. With your partner, describe the properties of each item listed below.

Item	Observations
Yeast	
Water	
Molasses	
Balloon	

2. Using the funnel, carefully fill the small plastic bottle with warm water until it is approximately 2/3 full. If you are using a soda bottle, the top of where the label would have been is a good marker.
3. Add the molasses.
4. Add the yeast.
5. Screw the cap back on the bottle.
6. Gently swirl the bottle for two minutes.
7. Remove the cap.
8. Carefully stretch the balloon over the opening at the top of the bottle.
9. Set the bottle on the table.

In the box below, draw your balloon bottle system as it looks right now.
Label the parts.

Time:

10. Wait five minutes. Draw your balloon bottle system again. Label the parts.

Time:

11. Wait five minutes. Draw your balloon bottle system again. Label the parts.

Time:

12. Wait five minutes. Draw your balloon bottle system again. Label the parts.

Time:

In what ways has your system changed since your first observation?

What might be causing those changes?

Your name: ______________________ Date: ______________

Video Anticipation Guide, Side 1

Before watching the video, mark the boxes below that best describe you.

	I know a lot about this.	I know something about this.	I know just a little bit about this.	This is completely new to me.
I know the steps in the digestive (di-ges-tive) system.				
I understand the role of saliva in digestion.				
I know what an enzyme is.				
I can locate places where microbes live in the digestive tract.				
I can explain how microbes aid in digestion.				

Use the space below to take notes on the video. Add extra pages if needed.

Video Anticipation Guide, Side 2

Now that you've watched the video and taken notes, mark the boxes below that best describe you. Demonstrate your knowledge by finishing the sentences in **bold**.

	I know a lot about this.	I know something about this.	I know just a little bit about this.	This is completely new to me.
I know the steps in the digestive system. **They are...**				
I understand the role of saliva in digestion. **It...**				
I know what an enzyme is. **It is...**				
I can locate places where microbes live in the digestive tract. **(Draw a map.)**				
I can explain how microbes aid in digestion. **They...**				

Definition in your own words

Characteristics
(features that identify it)

Chemical Change

Examples

Non-examples

Definition in your own words	Characteristics (features that identify it)

Digestion
(di-ges-tion)

Examples	Non-examples

Definition in your own words

Characteristics (features that identify it)

Matter

Examples

Non-examples

Definition in your own words	Characteristics (features that identify it)

Microbiome (mi-cro-bi-ome)

Examples	Non-examples

Definition in your own words

Characteristics (features that identify it)

Physical Change

Examples

Non-examples

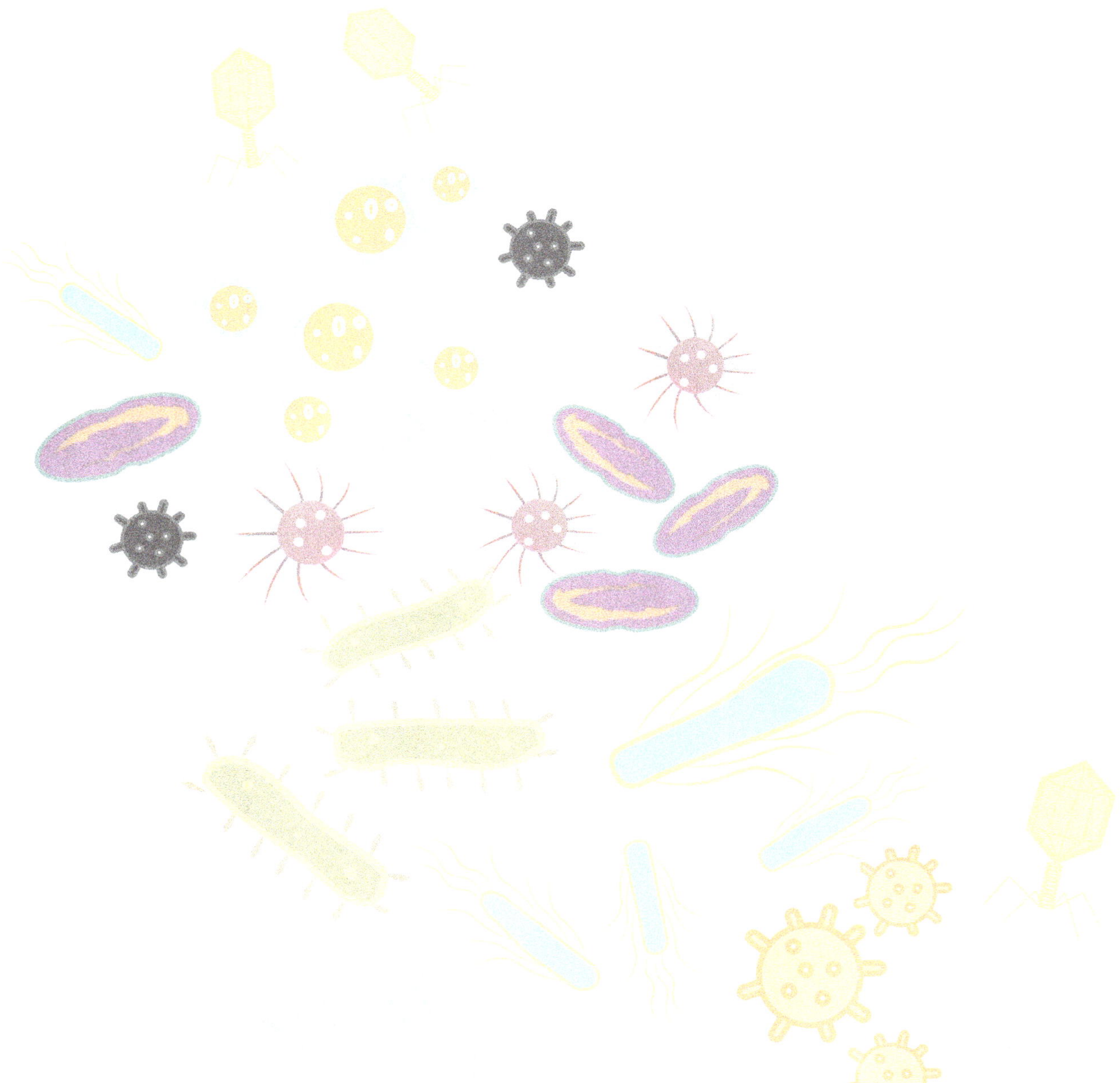

Lesson 4 — The Body's Natural Defenses

Introduction

Our bodies constantly battle against invaders. These microscopic invaders can enter our bodies in a variety of ways. Luckily, our body has many ways to defend itself against these unwanted guests. The body has several lines of defense to protect us from everything unseen (such as microorganisms) and attackers that are seen (such as insects and injury). The **first line of defense** that our body depends upon involves 3 major areas: **skin, mucous membranes, and airway filters**. Our skin is made up of three layers (epidermis, dermis, and hypodermis) and is the largest of all the body's organs. **Skin** protects our bodies and helps regulate temperature. **Mucous membranes** are similar to skin; just like skin protects the outer parts of the body, mucous membranes line the inside of our nose, mouth, lungs, and many other parts of the body. Mucous membranes make mucus, which keeps our airways and other body parts moist. The **airway filters** that lead to the lungs are one of many things in the body coated with mucus. This mucus traps invaders, such as air pollutants and microorganisms, which tiny hairs, called **cilia**, can then help to move out of our bodies. This ultimately rids the body of invaders in order to provide one of the first lines of defense for our immunity.

Lesson 4 – The Body's Natural Defenses

Key Teaching Points

1. Our body has a variety of defense structures that can prevent pathogens from causing harm.
2. Scientists use models to build explanations and make predictions.

Learner Outcomes

- Determine how the body provides natural defenses against bacteria.
- Determine ways in which humans can avoid contracting harmful bacteria.

Skill Level: Elementary, Beginning

Success Indicators

- Youth will articulate how the body uses natural defenses to protect against bacteria and other invaders.
- Youth will describe how skin, mucous membranes, and airway filters are natural barriers in the body, based on hands-on creation of these three defense systems.

Life Skills

Healthy Lifestyle Choices, Disease Prevention

Time Needed

90 minutes or two 45 minute sessions
(This time does not include the 3 hour period needed to collect pollutants on the petroleum jelly index cards. This step can be completed prior to youth arriving and youth can simply observe what was collected on the cards.)

Space

Classroom or similar sized area with access to water and an outdoor space

Suggested Group Size

Groups of 2-3 youth (Partners or a group of 3 youth are ideal for conversation in this lab; however, if your whole group consists of a small number of youth, each child can complete the lab individually and a whole group discussion can be facilitated in place of group work.)

Materials List

(Note that some materials are used in more than one lab and may only need to be purchased once.)

- Copy of Introduction for each youth or group (optional, only if desired)
- Whiteboard or other surface for recording youths' ideas
- Computer connected to a projector
- Goggles (1 per youth)
- Alcohol solution
  (to be used by the facilitator to clean the goggles after the lesson)
- Lab Observation sheets 1 per youth
- Old newspapers, plastic tablecloths, or something else that can be used to protect work surfaces

Lab Station #1 (Skin)

- 2 wax paper squares per group (approximately 8 inches)
- Blue food dye (1 bottle)
- Water for spray bottle
- 1 spray bottle (empty and clean)
- 2 pieces of white construction paper per group
- 1 ruler
- 1 sharp pencil, pair of scissors, or other acceptable items for poking holes in the wax paper
- Station Directions (1 per group)

Lab Station #2 (Mucous Membrane)

- "Goo" to simulate mucus (see recipe in the Before the Activity section). Ingredients:
  * Clear glue (white will work if necessary)
  * Warm water
  * Borax
- 1 wax paper square (approximately 8 inches)
- 1 ruler
- 1 sharp pencil, pair of scissors, or other acceptable items for poking holes in the wax paper
- Blue food dye (1 bottle)
- Water for spray bottle
- 1 spray bottle (empty and clean)
- 1 piece of white construction paper per group
- 1 craft stick per youth
- Station Directions (1 per group)

Materials List (continued)

Lab Station #3 (Airway Passages)

- 2 large (e.g. 4x6) index cards per group
- Petroleum jelly
- 1 craft stick
- 1 cheesecloth square cut to fit the index cards per group
- Fine sand or glitter
- Station Directions (1 per group)

Cantaloupe Experiment (ongoing)

- 1 pair of safety glasses for each youth
- 1 pair of safety gloves for each youth
- Alcohol solution (to be used by facilitator to clean goggles after the lesson)
- Bags of cantaloupe from Lesson 1
- Youth recording forms from Lesson 1

Background Information

Youth may notice that "mucous membrane" is spelled differently than "mucus". **Mucus** is the correct spelling of the noun (indicating the substance), while **mucous** is the correct spelling of the adjective telling us what kind of membrane.

> **Youth will be active during this learning experience and may need more direction than normal. Consider recruiting volunteers to help groups as they participate in different stations.**

Before the Activity

1. Print the Introduction for each youth or group (if desired).
2. Print directions for each station.
3. Print copies of Lab Observation sheets, 1 per youth.
4. Cover workspaces to protect them.
5. Have materials ready for youth in three separate stations, one for each of the first lines of defense.
6. Station #1 Skin
   - 2 wax paper squares (approximately 8 inches)
   - 1 spray bottle with water and blue food dye
   - 2 pieces of white construction paper per group
   - 1 ruler
   - 1 sharp pencil, pair of scissors, or other acceptable items for poking holes in the wax paper
   - Station Directions (1 per group)
7. Station #2 Mucous Membrane
   - "Goo" to simulate mucus
   - 1 wax paper square per group (approximately 8 inches)
   - 1 spray bottle with water and blue food dye
   - 1 ruler
   - 1 sharp pencil, pair of scissors, or other acceptable items for poking holes in the wax paper
   - 1 piece of white construction paper per group
   - 1 craft stick per group
   - Station Directions (1 per group)
8. Station #3 Airway Filters
   - 2 large index cards per group
   - petroleum jelly
   - craft sticks
   - cheesecloth cut to size of index cards
   - fine sand or glitter
   - Station Directions (1 per group)
9. Ensure that safety materials are clean and in proper working order.
10. Prepare to distribute safety glasses and safety gloves to each youth.

11. Recipe for creating the "goo" for the second station:
    - Mix 4 oz. of clear or white glue with 1 cup of warm water
    - Mix 2 tsp of Borax with ⅓ cup of warm water
    - Add small amounts of the Borax and water to the glue and water mixture until the proper consistency is reached

Note: The above recipe creates enough "goo" for two groups. Multiply the recipe as necessary to accommodate your number of groups. If you plan to give youth small baggies of the "goo" to use in the classroom or to take home, prepare enough for each youth and portion into plastic bags before the lesson.

Pre-Lesson Option:

As time permits, you may allow the youth to make the "goo" in a session prior to the main lesson. Be mindful of the distraction that the hands-on craft may present to some youth and plan accordingly so that the actual lesson content is not overshadowed by the craft.

PART ONE

Opening Question

- Why do we have snot?

Let's Do It!

1. Ask youth the Opening Question. Collect youths' responses on the whiteboard.

2. Read the Introduction to youth. If you have a computer and projector, it can be projected on the whiteboard, or you may print it for each youth or group if desired. Guide youth to understand that our bodies have many ways to react and defend against bacteria and other microorganisms; however, focus on natural barriers: skin, mucous membranes, and airway filters. Continue the discussion and have youth brainstorm ways in which these natural defenses can be most useful and ways in which they might be defective and allow bacteria to enter the body.

3. Explain to youth that scientists use models to help them understand the natural world. Ask youth to share examples of models they have used. Collect youths' responses on the whiteboard.

4. Tell youth that they will be building three models to understand how the body can protect them from invaders. Divide youth into pairs, and then assign the pairs to teams. Tell youth that they will have approximately 5 minutes at each station to build and observe their models and 3 minutes to write notes for each station.

5. Distribute safety glasses to all youth.

6. **Review lab safety procedures. Remind youth that they will not be eating any of the lab materials today, nor should they try to detect odors. Ensure that all youth have properly fitting goggles.**

7. Move youth to their lab stations. Instruct youth to read the directions aloud prior to beginning the station.

8. **Lab Station #1: Skin**
In order to replicate the natural defense our skin provides, each group will receive two squares of wax paper. Youth will place one square of the wax paper on a flat surface on top of a layer of white construction paper. A colored solution of blue food dye and water will be sprayed on top of the wax paper. Youth will observe for 1 minute before lifting the wax paper to determine whether the solution (bacteria) passed through a wound in the skin or if the skin provided a barrier for protection. Youth will then discuss how the wax paper acts like their skin and use the tools available at the station to simulate "wounds" in the second piece of wax paper that may allow the water to pass through. "Wounds" should not be more than one inch in any direction. Finally, youth will place the second piece of wax paper on the second piece of white construction paper and spray blue food dye and water onto the "wounded" skin.

9. **Lab #2: Mucous membrane**
The mucous membrane will be simulated by using one handful of "goo." One square of wax paper will act as the membrane. Youth will use the tools available at the station to simulate openings in the membrane (intestines, sinuses, etc.) that may allow the water to pass through. Openings should not be more than one inch in any direction. Youth will use the craft stick and their hands to coat the wax paper with the "goo" to mimic the secretions that fight microbes that line our intestines and airways. Youth will then spray a colored solution of blue food dye and water onto the "goo" to determine the differences in how skin and mucous membranes protect the body.

    Note: Consider providing each youth with a small baggie of the "goo." Youth can use the goo to collect dust and small particles from around the classroom or school to model how mucus traps them. Alternatively, youth may take the goo home and collect small particles from their home environment and then bring it back the next day to share with the class.

10. **Lab #3: Airway Defense System**
In order to simulate the body's airway defense system, youth will coat large index cards with petroleum jelly. One card will simply be coated with petroleum jelly and the other card will be coated with petroleum jelly and then covered with cheesecloth. The cheesecloth stands in place of cilia - the tiny "hairs" that line the human nasal passage and the walls of your airways. Explain to youth that these "hairs" are actually controlled by muscles that help transport mucus and ultimately trap unwanted particles (chemicals, dust, soot, fungi, mold, bacteria, viruses, and many other pollutants), keeping them from making us sick. Youth will sprinkle the fine sand or glitter on both index cards. Allow the cards to sit for about a minute. After a minute, youth will peel the cheesecloth carefully from one index card. Youth will observe their specimens to determine what difference the cloth made in protecting the card from possible pollutants.

Lesson 4 The Body's Natural Defenses

PART TWO

1. If a second class period has begun, review the labs completed during the previous lesson.

2. Share The Body's Natural Defenses presentation. Ask youth to connect the models they built to the information on the presentation. Give youth 3 minutes to talk in their groups. Then, ask the Share question.

   - What new learning did you gain about the body's first line of natural defense?

   Collect youths' responses on the board.

3. Ask the Reflection questions.

   - How did the models we created mimic how the body defends against invaders?
   - What might be some of the limitations of our models?

   Collect youths' responses on the board.

4. Ask the Generalize question.

   - Two youth decided that their bodies only produced snot after they became ill. Using evidence from the models you explored today, what would you tell the youth about first-line defenses?

   Collect youths' responses on the board.

5. Ask the Apply question.

   - What information would you share with others to help them protect their bodies from microscopic invaders?

   Collect youths' responses on the board.

6. Pass out safety glasses and safety gloves, 1 pair per youth. Demonstrate proper use, removal, and disposal of safety gloves again if necessary.

7. Direct youth to observe their ongoing cantaloupe experiments and to add their observations to their records. Make sure youth understand that they are not to open the bags nor are they to taste anything. Remind youth that they will be sharing their ideas during the next learning opportunity about the best conditions for microbes.

8. Youth should be able to see evidence of decomposition. They will add their observations to their Claim-Evidence-Reasoning chart from Lesson One and the group Cantaloupe Lab Packet.

9. When youth have finished observing their cantaloupe experiment and cleaned their workspace thoroughly, they will wash their hands with soap and water.

Lesson 4 The Body's Natural Defenses

Talk It Over

Share 1	Reflect 2
What new learning did you gain about the body's first line of natural defense?	How did the models we created mimic how the body defends against invaders? What might be some of the limitations of our models?
Generalize 3	**Apply 4**
Two youth decided that their bodies only produced snot after they became ill. Using evidence from the models you explored today, what would you tell the youth about first-line defenses?	In what ways would you share with others to help protect their bodies from microscopic invaders?

Variations

- In order to extend the knowledge youth have gained about the invaders and defenders of our body's first lines of defense, allow youth to create a series of wanted posters.

Ask youth, "Imagine that the Malicious Microbe manages to break through one of your superpowers. How might Malicious Microbe enter your body? In what ways can you defend against this invader? Are there any superpowers your body uses that are 100% effective all the time? Explain your thinking."

Explain that youth will create posters searching for enemies (invaders against the body) as well as posters in search of first line defenders. One poster might include the "Malicious Microbe" who is able to make himself so small that he is able to elude defenders by sneaking into tiny areas undetected, leap tall cilia in a single bound, and fly through airway passages faster than the speed of a sneeze. Similarly, youth may choose to create a wanted poster for those that are defenders within the human body. For example, they could create a poster in search of Super Cilia who can transport pollutants through rivers of mucus, hurl bacteria toward the digestive tract, and form a barrier of armor inside the nasal passages. Rewards should be fitting for the posters, including a lifetime supply of antibiotics or tissues. If appropriate, youth may even want to research more advanced immune system responses, including "helper-T" cells, for their posters.

Lesson 4 The Body's Natural Defenses

Term and Concept Discovery

Airway passage filters: a first-line defense system in the human body. The shape of the airway passages in the human body can help trap pathogens. For example, pathogens can get trapped in the curve of the nasal cavity and thus prevented from infecting the body.

Cilia: minute hairlike organelles, identical in structure to flagella, that line the surfaces of certain cells and beat in rhythmic waves, providing locomotion to ciliate protozoans and moving liquids along internal epithelial tissue in animals.

First line of defense: the passive defense systems of the body that do not require active immune response. These are defense systems that are preventative in nature and include skin, mucous, and airway passage filters.

Immune System: the system of first-line defenses and active responses that prevent pathogens from causing harm to an organism

Immune System Response: the active phase of the immune system. When an invading pathogen breaches the first-line defenses, the immune system sends cells to seek out the pathogen and destroy it.

Mucous membranes: a first-line defense. Mucous membranes are the sticky membranes that line the inside of the nose, the airway, and the throat, as well as other openings in the human body. Pathogens are trapped by the sticky mucous and prevented from doing harm.

Pathogen: a disease-causing agent, such as a microbe, that harms the host organism

Skin: the outer covering of the human body. This organ is an important first-line defense system.

Take It Home!

Talk with a family member about your body's first-line defenses. Share your ideas for protecting your body against invaders.

Find out how you can protect your skin from damage so that it can protect you.

Education Standard(s)

North Carolina Essential Standards in Science:

3.L.1.2 Explain why skin is necessary for protection and for the body to remain healthy.

5.L.1 Understand how structures and systems of organisms (to include the human body) perform functions necessary for life.

Tags

Body's First Line of Defense, Natural Defenses, Bacteria, Skin, Mucous Membrane, Airway Filters

Lesson 4 Print Materials

Facilitator Print Materials
None

Group Handouts
Lab Direction Sheets (1 per station)

Youth Handouts
Introduction (optional to print) Lab Observation sheets

See page 5 for information on digital assets and extra enrichment.

Our body is one giant machine with different parts that work together to keep it growing and healthy. Some of these parts make up a variety of defense structures that keep pathogens (path-o-gens) from doing harm.

In this lesson, we are going to discover how the body fights against bacteria (bac-te-ria), and what we can do to avoid these bad microbes.

Directions for Lab Station #1: Skin

Your group will make a model of skin in order to understand how it helps protect our body.

You will need:

- ✓ 2 squares of wax paper
- ✓ A sharp pencil and/or scissors
- ✓ 2 pieces of white construction paper
- ✓ 1 ruler
- ✓ A spray bottle of liquid (share with your table)

You will do:

Step 1: With your partner(s), make a prediction about how skin might protect our body.

Step 2: Carefully lay ONE piece of wax paper on top of ONE piece of white paper. Move the other wax paper and white paper out of the way.

Step 3: Gently spray the wax paper using the spray bottle (2-3 gentle pumps per team member).

Step 4: Observe the model for 1 minute.

Step 5: Make a prediction about what the paper will look like when you remove the wax paper. Record your prediction on your lab recording sheet.

Step 6: Remove the wax paper and carefully throw it in the trash bag.

Step 7: Record what you observe.

Step 8: Discuss how the wax paper acts like skin and use the tools available at the station to simulate wounds in the second piece of wax paper that may allow the water to pass through. "Wounds" should not be more than one inch in any direction.

Step 9: Repeat Steps 2-7 with the second piece of wax paper.

Step 10: Clean up your station.

Step 11: Record your ideas on your Lab Observation sheets.

Directions for Lab Station #2: Mucous Membrane

Your group will make a model of mucous membrane in order to understand how it helps protect our body.

You will need:

- ✓ "Goo" to simulate mucus
- ✓ 1 wax paper square (approximately 8 inches)
- ✓ 1 spray bottle with water and blue food dye
- ✓ 1 ruler
- ✓ 1 sharp pencil, pair of scissors, or other acceptable items for poking holes in the wax paper
- ✓ 1 piece of white construction paper
- ✓ 1 craft stick

You will do:

Step 1: With your partner(s), make a prediction about how mucous membrane might protect our body.

Step 2: Use the tools available at the station to simulate openings in the membrane (intestines, sinuses, etc.) that may allow the water to pass through. Openings should not be more than one inch in any direction.

Step 3: Carefully lay the piece of wax paper on top of the piece of white paper.

Step 4: Using the craft stick and your hands, smear "mucus" on top of the damaged wax paper.

Step 5: Gently spray the wax paper using the spray bottle (2-3 gentle pumps per team member).

Step 6: Observe the model for 1 minute.

Step 7: Make a prediction about what the paper will look like when you remove the wax paper. Record your prediction on your lab recording sheet.

Step 8: Remove the wax paper and carefully throw it in the trash bag.

Step 8: Record what you observe.

Step 9: Clean up your station.

Step 10: Record your ideas on your Lab Observation sheets.

Directions for Lab Station #3: Airway Filters

Your group will make a model of airway filters in order to understand how they help protect our body.

You will need:

- ✓ A craft stick
- ✓ 2 index cards
- ✓ 1 piece of cheesecloth
- ✓ Petroleum jelly (share with your table)
- ✓ Fine sand or glitter

You will do:

Step 1: With your partner(s), make a prediction about how airway filters might protect our body.

Step 2: Using the craft stick, smear petroleum jelly on one side of each index card.

Step 3: Carefully lay the piece of cheesecloth on top of one of the index cards.

Step 4: Sprinkle the fine sand or glitter on top of both index cards.

Step 5: Make a prediction about what the paper will look like when you remove the cheesecloth. Record your prediction on your lab recording sheet.

Step 6: Peel the cheesecloth off the index card and carefully throw it in the trash bag.

Step 7: Record what you observe.

Step 8: Clean up your station.

Step 9: Record your ideas on your lab recording sheet.

Introduction

Our bodies are constantly in battle against invaders. These microscopic (mi-cro-scop-ic) invaders can enter our bodies in a variety of ways. Luckily, our body has many ways to defend itself against these unwanted guests. The body has several lines of defense to protect us from everything unseen (such as microorganisms (mi-cro-or-gan-isms)) and attackers that are seen (such as insects and injury).

The **first line of defense** that our body depends upon involves 3 major areas: **skin, mucous membranes,** and **airway filters**. Our skin is made up of three layers (epidermis (epi-der-mis), dermis (der-mis), and hypodermis (hy-po-der-mis)) and is the largest of all the body's organs. **Skin** protects our bodies and helps regulate temperature.

Mucous membrane is similar to skin, in that just like skin protects the outer parts of the body, mucous membranes line the inside of the body. **Mucous membranes** line the inside of our nose, mouth, lungs, and many other parts of the body. Mucous membranes make mucus, which keeps our airways and other body parts moist.

The **airway filters** that lead to the lungs are one of many things in the body coated with mucus. This mucus traps invaders, such as air pollutants (pol-lut-ants) and microorganisms (mi-cro-or-gan-isms), which tiny hairs, called **cilia (cil-i-a)**, can then help to move out of our bodies. This ultimately rids the body of invaders in order to provide one of the first lines of defense for our immunity.

Your name: ______________________

Partner(s): ______________________

Lab Observations

I. Why do we have snot? Write your initial ideas here.

II. **Lab Station #1: Skin**

1. How does our skin protect us? Write your prediction here.

2. Draw your prediction for what your model will look like when you remove the wax paper.

Without holes	With holes

3. Draw your observations after you remove the wax paper.

Without holes	With holes

4. Based on your model, how can skin protect us?

5. How might you improve your model? What are some of the limitations?

III. **Lab Station #2: Mucous Membrane**

1. How does mucus protect us? Write your prediction here.

2. Draw a picture of your model before you remove the wax paper.

3. Draw a prediction for what your model will look like when you remove the wax paper.

4. Draw your observations after you remove the wax paper.

5. Based on your model, how can mucous membrane protect us?

6. How might you improve your model? What are some of the limitations?

IV. **Lab Station #3: Airway Filters**

1. How do our airway filters protect us? Write your prediction here.

2. Draw a picture of your model before you remove the cheesecloth.

Card that has cheesecloth	Card with petroleum jelly only

3. Draw your prediction for what your model will look like when you remove the cheesecloth.

Card that has cheesecloth	Card with petroleum jelly only

4. Draw your observations after you remove the cheesecloth.

Card that has cheesecloth	Card with petroleum jelly only

5. Based on your model, how can airway filters protect us?

6. How might you improve your model? What are some of the limitations?

V. Use this space to jot down new ideas you have while viewing the Background PowerPoint.

VI. Connect your new ideas to each of the models you explored.

Skin	Mucous Membranes	Airway Filters

VII. How can models help scientists to learn?

VIII. Two people decided that their bodies only produced snot after they became ill. Using evidence from the models you explored today, what would you tell them about first-line defenses?

Lesson 5 CSI Bacteria

Introduction

Different microbes, such as bacteria, fungi, and viruses, can cause people to become sick. There are many different types of bacteria that humans come in contact with that can either make them sick or help to balance the ecosystem within their bodies. Microbes that cause humans to get sick are known as **pathogens**. When our body is infected with a pathogen, our immune system responds by trying to get rid of it. Sometimes the way that our immune system responds is by vomiting or diarrhea. Our body responds in different ways depending on the pathogen that has entered our body. Sometimes when our immune system cannot defend itself, we must go to a doctor to get medicine in order to help fight off the bacteria, fungus, or virus.

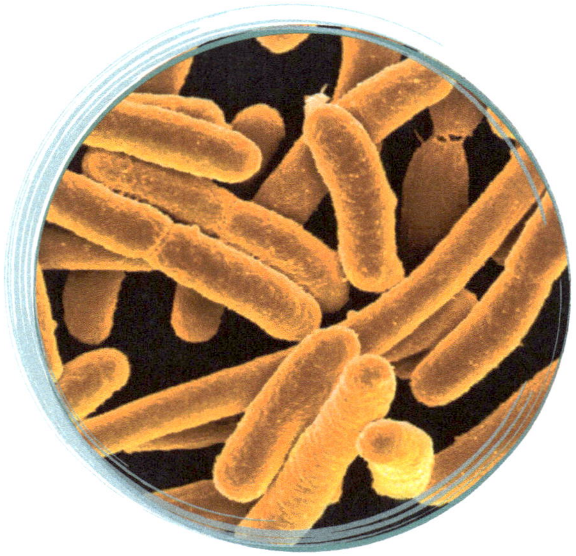

Colorized scanning electron micrograph of Escherichia color (E. coli), grown in culture and adhered to a cover slip. Credit: NIAID

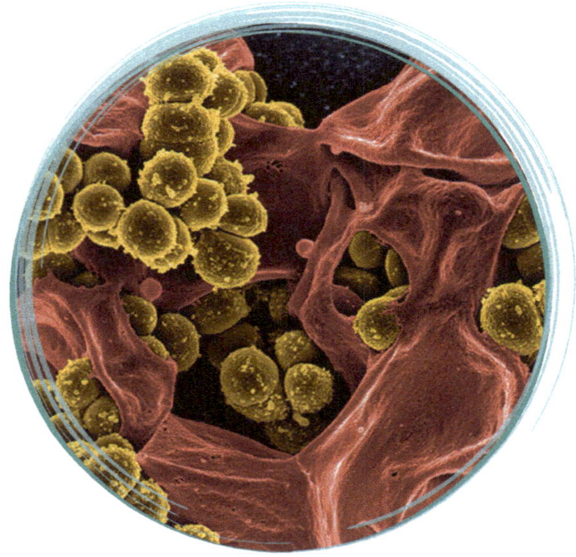

Scanning electron micrograph of methicillin-resistant Staphylococcus aureus and a dead neutrophil. Credit: NIAID

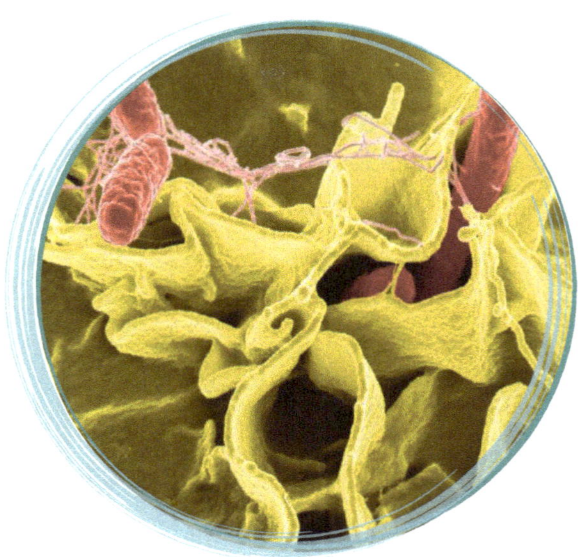

Salmonella bacteria, a common cause of foodborne disease, invade an immune cell. Credit: NIAID

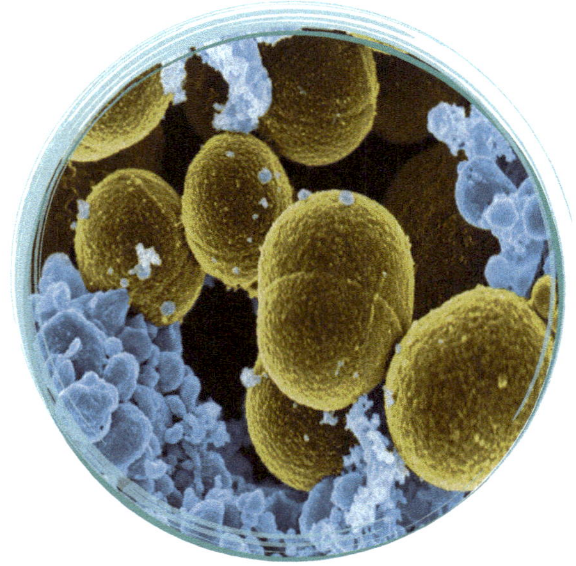

Scanning electron micrograph of S. aureus bacteria escaping destruction by human white blood cells. Credit: NIAID

Lesson 5 CSI Bacteria

Key Teaching Points

1. Epidemiologists are scientists who study the spread of diseases, including diseases caused by microbes.
2. Good research techniques help researchers find useful evidence.

Learner Outcomes

- Analyze texts to make a claim about what has made Sam E. sick.
- Gather evidence to support their claim.
- Develop an understanding of bacteria and how it interacts with humans.

Skill Level: Elementary, Beginning

Success Indicators

- Youth will use a graphic organizer to record information that they find while learning about specific microbes that cause people to become ill.
- Youth will record information while reading multiple resources to support their claim.

Life Skills

Critical Thinking, Problem Solving, Teamwork, Communication

Time Needed

One 90 minute session or
two 45 minute sessions

Space

Classroom or a large meeting room

Suggested Group Size

Groups of 5 youth

Materials List

- Case File (manila folder)- one per group
    - 1 copy of Sam E.'s medical information
    - 1 CSI Microbes Claim-Evidence-Reasoning chart per group
    - 1 copy of Information Critical Review per group
    - 1 of four Investigation handouts (a different one per Case File)
- Minimum of 1 piece of technology per group with which to conduct research OR several articles previously selected by the facilitator dealing with the subjects of Strep, Salmonella, MRSA, and E. Coli

Cantaloupe Experiment (ongoing)

- 1 pair of safety glasses for each youth
- 1 pair of safety gloves for each youth
- Alcohol solution (to be used by facilitator to clean goggles after the lesson)
- Bags of cantaloupe from Lesson 1
- Youth recording forms from Lesson 1

The ongoing Cantaloupe Lab ends with this lesson. Remind youth that they may NOT open the bags, even though the experiment has ended. Dispose of the cantaloupe carefully.

Lesson 5 CSI Bacteria

Background Information

There are many different kinds of bacteria; some of them are helpful and some are harmful. Different bacteria may have different effects on humans and on other animals. For example, Salmonella can be harmful to humans, but it is not harmful to chickens. When humans are contaminated with Salmonella and it moves into their intestines, they tend to vomit or have diarrhea. Humans can get Salmonella from different sources such as water, fruits and vegetables, eggs, and meat. Harmful bacteria, viruses, or fungi that infect people are called **pathogens**. Pathogens are considered to be any microbe that causes disease or harm to the host, which can be a person or any other living organism.

Before the Activity

1. Have Case Files prepared with 1 copy of Sam E.'s medical file, 1 Information Critical Review, 1 Investigation handout (a different one in each Case File), and 1 copy of the Claim-Evidence-Reasoning chart.
2. As a hook for the youth, the facilitator may choose to set up a medical crime scene which could include crime scene tape, a masking tape outline, magnifying glass, and other items that might be found at a crime scene or doctor's office.
3. Ensure that safety materials are clean and in proper working order.
4. Prepare to distribute safety glasses and safety gloves to each youth.

PART ONE

Opening Questions

Questions to assess prior knowledge from previous lessons:

- What are some examples of microorganisms that thrive in human bodies?
- What can bacteria, fungi, and viruses do to our bodies?

Questions to introduce this lesson:

- Have you ever heard of people getting sick because of a bacteria or a pathogen?
- Do you know the names any microbes that sometimes make people or other living organisms sick?
- What happens if someone gets sick because of bacteria?

Let's Do It!

1. Begin by activating interest and giving youth the following scenario:

   Have you ever imagined what it would be like to work as an investigator on a crime scene? To dig through evidence in order to find one clue or one fingerprint that would break open the case? Maybe instead you have thought about what it might be like to be a doctor, searching for symptoms and analyzing lab tests and patient files in order to discover the hidden reason behind a mysterious illness. The process used by investigators and doctors is somewhat similar-they are both searching for something just below the surface that can't be seen without some research. In our lesson today you will need to combine the skills used by a trained Crime Scene Investigator with those used by a doctor diagnosing a patient.

2. Explain to youth that they will be working as an investigative team to solve a case involving a person, Sam E., who was contaminated with a microbe in the past 72 hours.

3. Ask youth the questions to assess prior knowledge from previous lessons and allow them time to discuss their thinking in small groups. Allow time for youth to share their knowledge with the whole group.

   - What are some examples of microorganisms that thrive in human bodies?
   - What can bacteria, fungi, and viruses do to our bodies?

4. Explain to youth that a pathogen is a microbe that causes diseases in humans. Provide youth with a few examples (chickenpox, salmonella, strep, E. Coli, etc.) so that youth can start to make connections.

5. Ask the questions to introduce this lesson.

   - Have you ever heard of people getting sick because of a bacteria or a pathogen?
   - Do you know the names any microbes that sometimes make people or other living organisms sick?
   - What happens if someone gets sick because of bacteria?

6. Introduce the CSI case to the youth by directing them to the information about Sam E.'s symptoms and interactions in his medical file. Tell them they will need to reference Sam E.'s symptoms and interactions throughout the lesson in order to help determine which pathogen might be responsible for making Sam sick. Explain to youth that just as in real CSI work, there are some pieces of information missing from the case file. Doctors have a few ideas about what might be making Sam sick; however, they need more specific information in order to make a conclusive diagnosis. Tell the youth that they will add to a case file by researching about one specific pathogen in order to determine if it could be the cause of the illness. Remind youth that the world in which we live often provides an overload of information. In fact there is so much information on nearly every topic and subject that we could never possibly learn everything there is to know about any subject. As researchers looking for information, we must be critical in our evaluations in order to determine the credibility and usefulness of a source. In a way we must be reading detectives in our hunt for quality sources. Today their detective work will take them through the past 72 hours in the life of the man whom we will refer to as Sam E. Before simply choosing a resource or article, youth must evaluate its credibility by answering the questions on the Information Critical Review. Each group will be assigned a different research topic: Strep, Salmonella, MRSA, or E. Coli. Inform them that his disease has been narrowed down to these four different microbes.

7. Before the youth start investigating the cause of Sam E. becoming ill, tell them to make a prediction with their team of investigators about which microbe they believe was the cause. Ask the Share question.

   - When you first heard the symptoms and activities of the contaminated person, what did you think was the cause?

   Give them a couple of minutes to discuss and then ask the youth to vote on which microbe they believe made Sam E. ill simply based upon what they have read in his medical file so far.

8. While the youth read the information that they find online or in articles based on the topic in their case files, have them fill out the Claim-Evidence-Reasoning chart as well as their Information Critical Review. Once the youth have determined that a source is valid and useful, they should read through the documents and start collecting clues that match the symptoms and interactions of Sam E. over the past 72 hours. Inform the youth that they will state their claim on the handout and provide evidence and reasoning to support their conclusion.

PART TWO

1. If a second class period has begun, review the case file for Sam E. and have youth review their Claim-Evidence-Reasoning form from the previous lesson in small groups.

2. After the youth have conducted research and stated their claim, reasoning, and evidence, they will report their case to the whole group.
   Ask the Reflect question.

   - How and why did your thinking change after you began to research the bacteria that you were assigned?

3. The whole group will then determine (together as a group) based on the research they collected that the person was contaminated with the bacteria Salmonella.
   Ask the Generalize questions.

   - What made you realize that Salmonella was the bacteria that made the person sick?
   - Now that you know how a person can be contaminated with Salmonella, how can a person protect him/herself from getting it?

4. Pass out safety gloves. **Make sure youth understand that they are not to open the bags, nor are they to taste anything.** Have youth check on their cantaloupe experiment. Youth will be able to see evidence of decomposition of the cantaloupe and evidence of microbes growing on the slices. They should add their observations to their Claim-Evidence-Reasoning chart from Lesson One and the group Lab Packet, as well as complete the Claim-Evidence-Reasoning Self-Assessment provided in Lesson 1. (This is the end of the cantaloupe experiment.)

5. When youth have finished observing their cantaloupe experiment and cleaned their workspace thoroughly, they will wash their hands with soap and water.

6. Provide youth with a few minutes to collect their thoughts, and then allow them to share their ideas about the best conditions for microbes. Prompt youth to provide evidence to support their claims.

7. Ask youth to hypothesize how the cantaloupe experiment might connect to Sam E.'s unfortunate condition.

8. After the lesson has ended, be sure to clean all safety glasses thoroughly with the alcohol solution. Allow the glasses to dry before returning them to the kit.

Lesson 5 CSI Bacteria

Term and Concept Discovery

Antibiotic: chemicals that are known to kill or weaken bacteria. Antibiotics are used in medicines designed to treat bacterial infections. In the past few decades, there has been a rapid increase in the number of antibiotics used in non-medical products, including soap, hand sanitizer, and cleaning products. Antibiotics are also widely used in animal feed to prevent disease among livestock. The use of antibiotics is controversial, as bacteria can develop resistance to the chemicals, making them ineffective.

Bacteria: a type of single-celled organism. Bacteria are classified as prokaryotic organisms, as they do not have membrane-enclosed nuclei or other similar structures (organelles). Bacteria are the most abundant life forms on our planet. Singular: bacterium

E. Coli: Escherichia coli is the most well-studied bacteria. It is a very common bacteria and one of the major microbes in the gut of healthy humans. However, some strains are pathogenic and can cause severe cramps, bloody diarrhea, and vomiting.

Epidemiologist: a scientist who studies epidemiology

Fungi: Fungi are eukaryotic, since their cells do contain a nucleus. Mushrooms are fungi, as are microorganisms such as yeasts and molds. Singular: fungus

Immune System: the system of first-line defenses and active responses that prevent pathogens from causing harm to an organism

Microbe: any one of a number of organisms too small to be seen without a microscope. Bacteria, viruses, and many fungi are all considered microbes.

MRSA: methicillin-resistant Staphylococcus aureus, a bacterium that is highly resistant to methicillin, penicillin, and certain other antibiotics, and may cause infections of the skin, blood, lungs, etc.

Pathogen: a disease-causing agent, such as a microbe, that harms the host organism

Salmonella: a bacterium widely found in the environment that is also pathogenic to humans. Salmonella can be transmitted through contact with reptiles, particularly turtles. It can also be transmitted through undercooked food, particularly poultry products, and through unwashed vegetables. In humans, the Salmonella bacterium commonly causes a disease known as salmonellosis. Some strains of Salmonella are also responsible for typhoid fever.

Salmonellosis: a disease caused in humans by the Salmonella bacteria. Symptoms of salmonellosis include diarrhea, fever, and severe abdominal cramps, usually lasting for several days. Salmonellosis is a very common form of food poisoning and can be very dangerous for children, the elderly, and persons with compromised immune systems.

Streptococcus pharyngitis: the bacteria responsible for strep throat.

Virus: a microbe that replicates itself by taking over cells in a host organism. At this time, there is debate among scientists as to whether viruses are actually considered to be living organisms. Unlike pathogenic bacteria, viruses cannot be killed using antibiotic medicines.

Talk It Over

Share 1	**Reflect 2**
When you first heard the symptoms and activities of the contaminated person, what did you think was the cause?	How and why did your thinking change after you began to research the bacteria that you were assigned?
Generalize 3	**Apply 4**
What made you realize that Salmonella was the bacteria that made the person sick? Now that you know how a person can be contaminated with Salmonella, how can a person protect him/herself from getting it?	Check out the news across the United States and around the world to find out more about cases of Salmonella and other microbes. Find a news story about someone getting sick from bacteria such as Salmonella. How did that person get sick and how did they know that it was caused from that bacterium?

Lesson 5 CSI Bacteria

Learn More

Challenge the youth to do research to find out more about people getting sick from different bacterias, fungi, and viruses. They can search through news articles and other resources on the internet.

Take It Home!

Many diseases are spread through contact, so hand washing is a key step in preventing diseases from spreading. Create posters for your home that show good hand washing techniques and post them to remind everyone about the importance of proper hand washing.

Education Standard(s)

CCSS.ELA-Literacy.RI 5.3 Explain the relationships or interactions between two or more individuals, events, ideas, or concepts in a historical, scientific, or technical text based on specific information in the text.

CCSS.ELA-Literacy.W.5.1 Write opinion pieces on topics or texts, supporting a point of view with reasons and information.

CCSS.ELA-Literacy.RI 5.7 Draw on information from multiple print or digital sources, demonstrating the ability to locate an answer to a question quickly or to solve a problem efficiently.

Tags

Bacteria, Viruses, Fungi, E. Coli, Salmonella, Strep

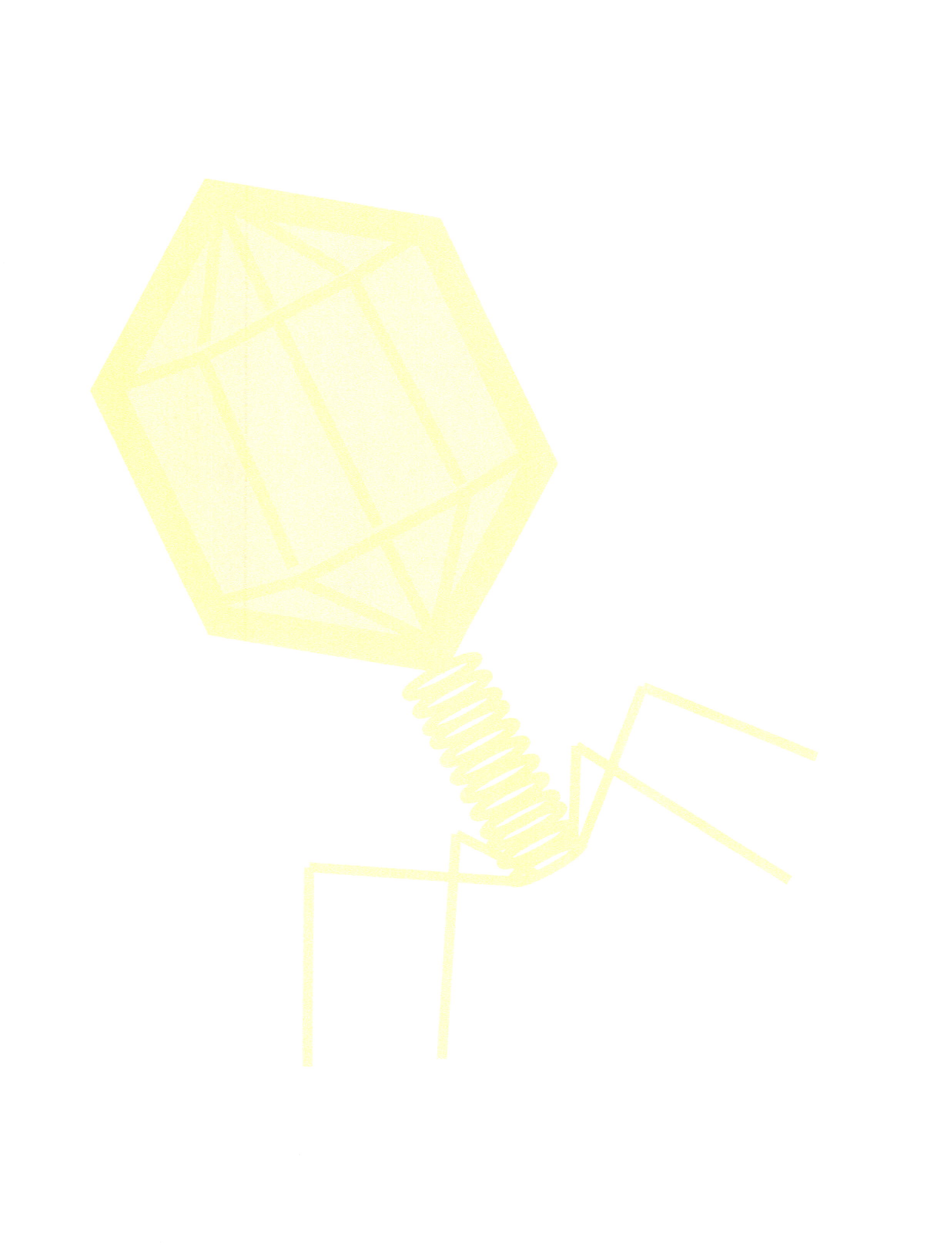

Lesson 5 Print Materials

Facilitator Print Materials None

Youth Handouts
None

See page 5 for information on digital assets and extra enrichment.

Group Handouts
Include in the Case File inside a manila envelope 1 copy of each (1 Case File per group):

Information Critical Review
Investigation handouts (one per envelope, a different investigation in each Case File)
Claim-Evidence-Reasoning chart
Sam E.'s medical file

Information Critical Review

As you search for sources on your pathogenic (path-o-gen-ic) bacteria (bac-te-ria), use the questions below to help determine the usefulness of the article or website. Credible sources should allow you to answer most, if not all, of these questions easily. If you find that it is difficult to answer the questions below, then choose another article or site to review and consider as your resource.

Who is the author of the article/site you wish to use? ______________________

Is there a way to contact the author listed on the article/site? If so, how? ______________

____

____

When was the article written? ______________________________

Would you consider the information current based on its topic? ________________

Were you able to form an opinion based on the information provided in the article? __________

Did you gain new information when reading the information provided by the article? __________

What is one new piece of information you gained as read through the article/site? __________

____

____

Did the author provide a bibliography or reference list of sources as to where they gained their information? ______________________________

If you were able to answer the above questions easily, then the resource you have selected can be used for your Claim-Evidence-Reasoning chart to determine what is making Sam E. sick.

E. coli Investigation

Breaking News

The Super-Peanutman Peanut Butter company has been forced to recall millions of jars of peanut butter after tests confirmed the presence of *E. coli.* Already, 43 people in four states have been sickened with *E. coli*, which causes diarrhea and stomach cramping in patients. Although most patients will recover within a few days, children, the elderly, and patients with compromised immune systems are at risk for serious, even fatal, complications.

E. coli is caused by the bacteria, *Escherichia coli*, which is normally found in human and animal digestive systems. It can be transmitted through unsafe food handling practices or through contaminated water. Jaylyn Brown, spokesman for Super-Peanutman, stated today that the company has traced the outbreak to a farm where contaminated water was used to irrigate the growing peanut plants. Mr. Brown continued, “Here at Super-Peanutman, we are saddened by what has happened. We send our deepest apologies to the victims of this outbreak, and we sincerely hope that they recover quickly. In the meantime, we have doubled our efforts to educate our producers about safe food and farm practices.”

If you have jars of Super-Peanutman Peanut Butter, do not eat them. Instead, take them to the nearest store where you will receive a full refund and a replacement product. If you have questions, you can visit the company’s website for more information.

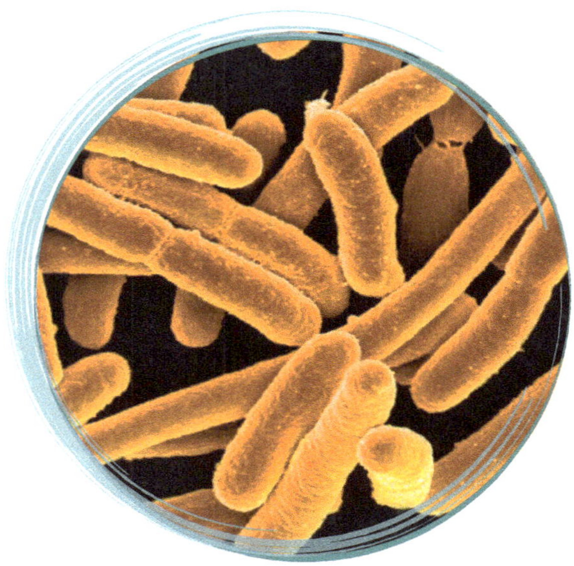

Colorized scanning electron micrograph of Escherichia color (E. coli), grown in culture and adhered to a cover slip. Credit: NIAID

Strep Investigation

Dear Parents and Guardians,

The Beech Tree County Health Department has reported that cases of strep throat are on the rise in the school system. Strep throat is caused by the Streptococcus bacteria, group A, a bacteria that normally lives on the skin and throat. Symptoms include a low-grade fever (usually around 101 degrees), headache, and an extremely sore throat. White patches are often visible in the back of the throat, and a rash may be present. Strep can also cause vomiting in some cases.

Signs of a more serious infection include high fever, swelling, and open sores. These symptoms indicate possible complications, including scarlet fever, impetigo (a skin disease), or even necrotizing fasciitis (the so-called "flesh-eating disease"). See a doctor immediately if you experience any of these symptoms.

If you feel like you might be ill, see your doctor. Strep throat infections can be confirmed with a simple test and are usually easy to treat with antibiotics. However, the best treatment is prevention. Strep throat is spread through contact with the bacteria. To protect yourself and others, practice proper hand-washing techniques, cover your coughs and sneezes, and avoid sharing food or drinks. If your child is sick, please remember to keep him or her home from school to avoid spreading the illness to others.

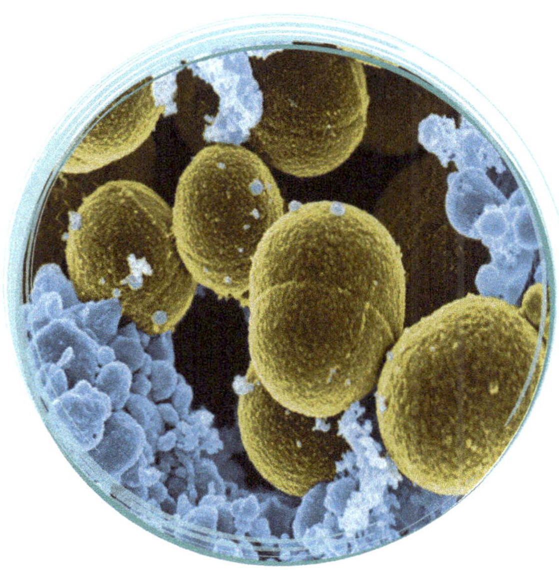

Scanning electron micrograph of S. aureus bacteria escaping destruction by human white blood cells. Credit: NIAID

Salmonella Investigation

Today's Top Story: Salmonella Outbreak Traced to Local Restaurant

Health Department officials shut down the popular Chicken Feathers restaurant on Oak Road today after several people were diagnosed with salmonellosis. One elderly man remains hospitalized in critical condition.

Salmonellosis is a disease caused by the salmonella bacterium. Symptoms include severe stomach cramps, fever, vomiting, and diarrhea, and they usually last for up to one week. In rare cases, salmonella bacteria can even enter the bloodstream and cause potentially fatal infections.

Salmonellosis is typically spread through unsafe food practices, as the bacteria are found in uncooked meat, eggs, poultry, fruits, and vegetables.

In addition to food, salmonella bacteria are also found in dirt and water contaminated with animal feces. Salmonella can even be found on animals, especially on reptiles including snakes and turtles. Proper hand-washing is critical to preventing the spread of salmonellosis.

The Oak Road location of Chicken Feathers will remain closed until the Health Department investigation is complete. Other locations are still operating at this time. If you have eaten at the Oak Road Chicken Feathers at any point in the past two weeks, please contact the Health Department as soon as possible.

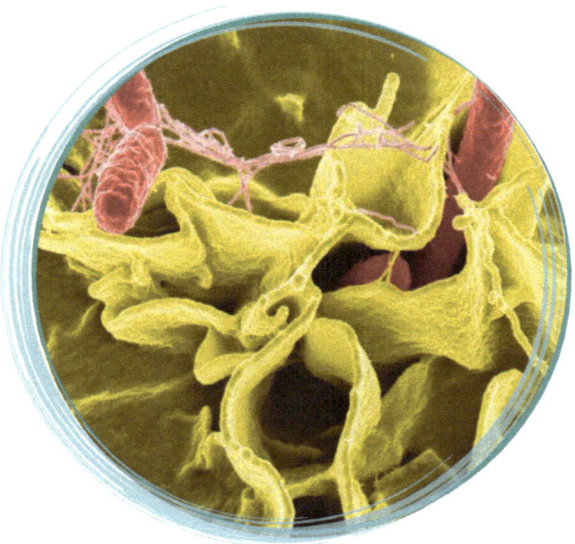

Salmonella bacteria, a common cause of foodborne disease, invade an immune cell. Credit: NIAID

MRSA Investigation

Hospital Staff Bulletin

Attention, all doctors and nurses:

We have seen an increase in the number of cases of MRSA (methicillin-resistant *Staphylococcus aureus*) infections here at the hospital. As you know, MRSA infections do not respond easily to most antibiotics. Therefore, these infections pose serious dangers to our patients. We need to take action now to prevent the spread of the bacteria.

If you have a patient who develops a large, swollen area on his or her skin, similar to a boil or giant pimple, please notify the area manager at once. Staph (pronounced "staff") infections also can present as impetigo, a condition that results in crusty sores appearing on the skin. Occasionally, staph infections can affect the trachea, the lungs, or even the heart.

In order to protect our patients and ourselves, practice good hygiene. Thoroughly wash your hands and change your gloves before every patient. Keep all surfaces clean and sterilized and follow hospital guidelines at all times. If you see unsafe conditions, report them at once to your area manager.

Remember, it takes all of us to keep our patients safe!

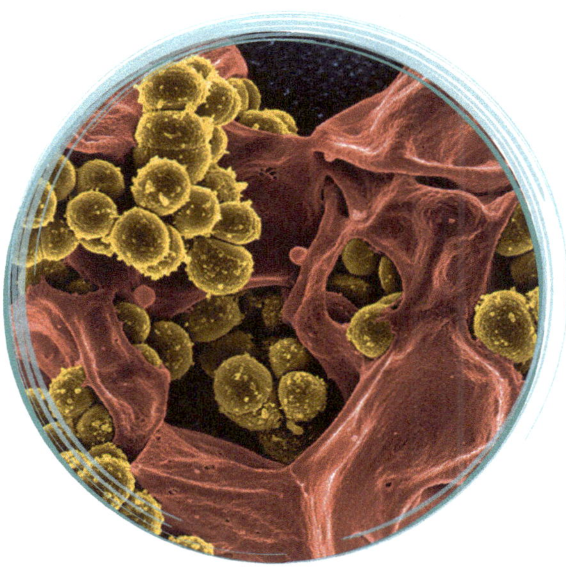

Scanning electron micrograph of methicillin-resistant Staphylococcus aureus and a dead neutrophil. Credit: NIAID

Your name: ______________________ Date: ______________

Claim - Evidence - Reasoning Chart

Investigative Question

Why do you think Sam E. is sick? Which bacteria do you think made him sick?

Claim

Sam E. was sickened by the bacteria ______________ because

Evidence

List key ideas that you learn. Your ideas may come from scientific experiments or personal experiences. You may use your own work or work from other experts.

Evidence From Personal Experiences

Evidence From Books, Videos, Websites, or other Research Sources

Evidence From Scientific Models, Experiments, or Investigations

Reasoning
Now that you have researched a specific bacteria, do you think that bacteria was the main cause for Sam E.'s immune system responding the way it did? Why or why not? If this bacteria wasn't the reason, do you know what was most likely the cause of this illness?

Explanation
Now that all of the investigators have researched different types of bacteria, it is time to find out which bacteria is the cause of Sam E. getting sick. Which bacteria was the cause of Sam E.'s immune system responding the way it did? Why and how did this bacteria infect Sam E.'s immune system? What could have been done to prevent this from happening?

Urgent Care Admission Form

PATIENT INFORMATION

Patient Name Collie (last) Samuel (first) E. (middle) ID# 1342657

Date of Birth 9/28/1990 Gender male Race human

Occupation Animal care at Raulston Aquarium

Anyone else currently living in your home? one cat (Rascal), two dogs (Rex and Toby), and one turtle (Twinkle)

Any known allergies? Circle One: NO (YES) (If you selected yes, then please list below)
bee stings

PRIMARY COMPLAINT AND REASON FOR TODAY'S VISIT

What is your reason for scheduling an urgent care appointment today?
severe stomach upset and fever

What symptoms have you experienced over the past 72 hours? Be specific.
vomiting and diarrhea and also fever

If your symptoms are related to gastric distress, list items you have eaten in the past 4-7 days.
I ate eggs and toast for breakfast each day, turkey sandwich for lunch with yogurt each day, and spaghetti and meatballs for dinner.

PLEASE CIRCLE ANY SYMPTOMS BELOW THAT YOU ARE CURRENTLY EXPERIENCING:

Cough	(Vomiting)	Nose Bleeds
Insomnia	Hives/Swelling	Sore Throat
(Chills)	Muscle Aches	(Headache)
(Nausea)	Confusion	Joint Pain
Congestion	Fainting	Sweating
(Diarrhea)	Sprain	(Fever)

Sam E.'s Medical file

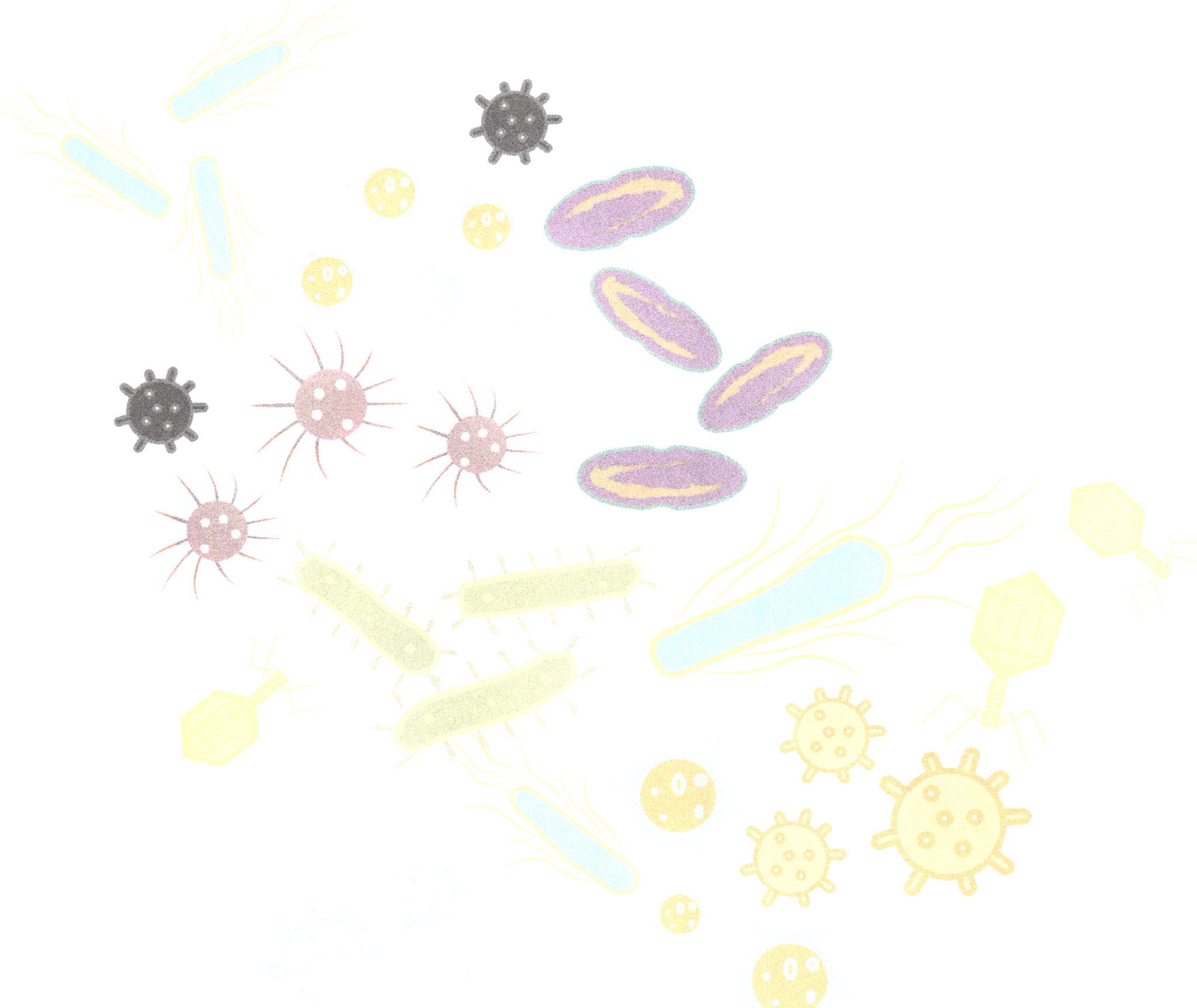

Lesson 6 Engineering a Solution: Defense in Food Safety

Introduction

When we hear the term Food Safety, we generally think about product recalls and raw meat; however, the food safety battle begins with a much more basic attack. What happens to our food supply when we are without power? On average, frozen food can be safely eaten for up to 48 hours. But imagine if you suddenly lost power and it was unable to be repaired for 5 days or even 10? What would we do if our water supply suddenly vanished?

Although we depend on the body's natural lines of defense, there are many ways we can provide aid and support to prevent the invasion of unwanted microorganisms. One of the most basic ways to protect our personal microbiome is simply to wash our hands regularly and with vigilance after exposure to unclean situations. By cooking meat to proper temperatures and by not cross-contaminating foods in our own kitchens, we can offer support to our first line defense systems. But what would happen if some of our most basic conveniences were taken from us?

Lesson 6 – Engineering a Solution: Defense in Food Safety

Key Teaching Points

1. Food safety can be impacted by events such as natural disasters.
2. Clean water is one of the most important food safety concerns for a community as a whole.

Learner Outcomes

- Analyze the information learned throughout this unit in order to solve a possible problem in food safety.
- Create and test a prototype to solve a problem in food safety that arises after a natural disaster.

Skill Level: Elementary, Beginning

Success Indicators

- Youth will be able to identify the most critical problem facing their community after a natural disaster.
- Youth will work in teams as valuable contributors in both design and collaboration.

Life Skills

Communication, Critical Thinking, Healthy Lifestyle Choices, Problem Solving, Teamwork

Time Needed

120 minutes or two 60 minute lessons

Space

Classroom or comparable space where teams can spread out and work during the build with access to running water.
It is recommended to test the water filtration systems outside if possible as some may leak or splash.

Suggested Group Size

Groups of 5 youth

Materials List

- Large trash bags to be given out a week ahead of this lesson (1 per youth)
- Global Sanitation letter to be distributed with trash bag (1 per youth)
- 1 craft drill to be used only by facilitator
- 1 pair of large scissors to be used only by facilitator
- Pencils, rulers, and other drawing tools for youth to use when creating designs
- Graph paper (1-2 pieces per youth)
- Engineering a Solution Youth Response Form (1 per youth)
- Sand (to add to water to be filtered)
- Marbles (to add to water to be filtered)
- Access to water or 1 gallon of water per group to use while testing the filtration process
- Masking Tape
- Note: Each group should build into their design a water collection reservoir. One bucket or gallon-sized container (e.g. a clean, empty milk container) may be provided for each group if desired.

Materials for experiment provided by youth

- Youth will collect all of their personal recyclable trash for a 48 period prior to the lesson. All trash collected will be used to build a water filtration system during the build. The facilitator will give each youth a trash bag and a letter from Global Sanitation in the lesson prior to Engineering a Solution.

Make sure to emphasize that no one should drink the water that has been "cleaned."

Lesson 6 - Engineering a Solution: Defense in Food Safety

Background Information

Youth will have the opportunity to role-play in a natural disaster situation by participating in a town meeting in order to determine the greatest need facing their community. Although many problems could be present, lead youth to determine that the need for clean drinking water is most crucial at the moment. Facilitate a discussion that will challenge youth to think beyond the modern conveniences they currently enjoy by allowing only recyclables they have collected, masking tape, and facilitator use scissors/craft drill to complete their build. Do not give youth any information on why they are collecting recyclable materials other than what the Global Sanitation Letter explains to them. The builds are more authentic if youth do not know how they will be using the materials.

Before the Activity

1. Give youth a Global Sanitation letter and a trash bag to collect their personal recyclables for a 48 hour period prior to the lesson.
2. Make copies of the Engineering a Solution Youth Response Form (1 per youth).

Lesson 6 – Engineering a Solution: Defense in Food Safety

PART ONE

Opening Questions

- What does it mean to take food safety precautions?
- What are some ways your family practices food safety?
- What are some advances in food safety technology?
- What would happen if some of those technological advances were taken away?

Let's Do It!

1. Ask the Opening Questions and facilitate discussion among the youth.

2. Assemble youth on the floor of the classroom or learning space with their bag of recyclables. Ask youth to imagine a scenario where 72 hours ago their community suffered a devastating natural disaster. Since that time, there has been no electricity or running water available. People in the community are in need of food, water, and shelter. Time is critical after a disaster. During this Town Meeting, ask the youth to think about the biggest problem currently facing the community. Remind youth that the safety of food and water supplies is critical. Challenge youth to think about what they already know about food safety. What are some current technologies and innovations that have been put in place to improve the safety of our food? Point out to youth items as simple as a sneeze guard in cafeterias and water filters are considered products in food safety. During the discussion ask youth what issues in food safety arise during times of natural disaster (aftermath of a hurricane or tornado, or during a blizzard) and how they might address such issues. Show youth a roll of masking tape, one pair of adult scissors, and one craft drill. Explain to youth that these materials were the only salvageable tools found in the community aside from the recyclables they have collected over the past 48 hours.

3. Hand out the Engineering a Solution Youth Response Form and graph paper to each youth. Allow youth time to fill in the first box, listing three problems facing their community after the natural disaster. Explain to youth that they will be designing a new piece of food safety equipment to address the community's greatest need. Facilitate a discussion and challenge youth by suggesting that the next closest town is more than 20 miles away, that temperatures are reaching more than 100 degrees during the heat of the day, and that there are many available ponds and puddles due to the amount of rain that has fallen over the past 3 days.

4. Once youth have been given time to brainstorm food safety problems, ask them to take 2-3 minutes as a group to isolate the greatest need of the community. Lead the discussion in such a way as to guide youth into choosing water filtration if this is something that they don't naturally choose. Allow time for youth to complete the second box by explaining what they believe the biggest problem facing the community might be as well as what resources are needed to solve the problem.

5. Youth should work together to isolate one problem with which to move forward at this point by recording it in the third box.

6. Ask the Share question.

   - When we first began discussing food safety during a natural disaster, what did you anticipate would be the greatest need of the community?

7. In the next phase, youth will begin to make a plan for their group design. Following the directions in the Design section of their graphic organizer, youth should use graph paper to draw out a design of how their product should look, what materials might be needed to develop a prototype, and how it would work to end the water problem facing the community. Before youth begin to design their water filtration system, allow the group to ask questions. Participants are allowed to trade or barter materials within their recycling bags and may choose to work together as teams to find a solution. Do not offer these options, however, unless a participant asks these questions. You may choose to limit questions if they are not productive to the outcome of the project. Remind youth that they are limited to only 15 minutes to design their water filtration system.

PART TWO

1. If a second class period has begun, review the scenario and model design from the previous lesson. Youth may be given time to modify their design if they have thought of improvements and time allows.

2. Once youth have worked through the first 4 sections on their graphic organizer, they should begin to build a model of their idea. Youth will use the drawing they created during the previous step as a blueprint to create their solution. Remind youth to incorporate their recyclable materials throughout the build. Additionally, each group will be allowed 6 inches of masking tape per person as 1 roll of masking tape has been found in the rubble of the community. This means if 4 youth work together then they may have 24 inches of tape. **As the Head of Facilities, you (the facilitator) alone are allowed to use scissors or the craft drill.** This will ensure safety for youth while still allowing for water to pass through plastic bottles or metal cans. Remind youth that they are limited to only **15 minutes** to build their water filtration system.

3. When groups have been given time to create their design, youth will move their builds outdoors or to an area where they can test their product without worrying about water spilling. Each youth/team will test their filtration system to ensure the following:

   - Water will pass through the filter
   - The filter will sift marbles from entering the final water source
   - The filter will sift sand from entering the final water source

   NOTE: Make sure to emphasize that no one should drink the water that has been "cleaned."

4. As audience members, youth will watch the ideas/builds as they are presented and tested and offer constructive feedback to improve the design or function of other water filtration systems. Based on observations during their own tests and the tests of other water filtration systems, youth will then make adjustments in order to create a more effective water filtration system. Allow 10 minutes for youth to make changes and improvements to their designs based on what they learned during the testing process.

5. Ask the Reflect questions.

   - What made solving the problem of not having clean water so difficult?
   - If you were able to complete this project again, what changes would you make to the way you designed or built your water filtration system?
   - How would these changes positively impact the final system?

6. Ask youth independently/as a team to fill in the adjustments section on their graphic organizer by rating their initial design and build. Youth will consider 1 or 2 of the ideas that were shared by classmates and make improvements to their initial design.

7. Youth will fill out the last section on their Youth Response Form after they have made final adjustments. Allow youth the opportunity to test their product once again in order to determine whether or not their changes yielded greater productivity or cleaner water.

   NOTE: Again, make sure to emphasize that no one should drink the water that has been "cleaned."

8. Ask the Generalize questions.

   - Of the designs shared today, which one(s) do you believe could make the biggest impact in a community after a natural disaster? Why?
   - What other materials would have been useful in building and testing your design?

9. Ask the Apply questions.

   - Using what you have learned today and throughout this unit, what are ways that you can help to ensure you and your family practice proper food safety at home?
   - What is one thing you will try to change in your household to make food preparation safer?

References

http://www.foodsafety.gov/

Lesson 6 - Engineering a Solution: Defense in Food Safety

Term and Concept Discovery

Bacteria: a type of single-celled organism. Bacteria are classified as prokaryotic organisms, as they do not have membrane-enclosed nuclei or other similar structures (organelles). Bacteria are the most abundant life forms on our planet. Singular: bacterium

Design: Problem-solving choices made consciously by an individual or a group in order to most effectively reach a goal within agreed-upon constraints.

Engineering: a branch of applied science and math with a focus on real-world problem-solving.

Foodborne Illness: a disease caused by a microbe that was transmitted to its host through the food supply. "Food poisoning" refers to a variety of foodborne illnesses, including salmonellosis and E. coli infections.

Food Safety: a series of practices designed to minimize risks posed by microbes in the food supply. Food safety practices include proper handwashing, cooking food thoroughly, keeping perishable items chilled, cleaning food preparation surfaces and tools, and keeping different types of food separated to avoid cross-contamination.

Talk It Over

Share 1	**Reflect** 2
When we first began discussing food safety during a natural disaster, what did you anticipate would be the greatest need of the community?	What made solving the problem with not having clean water so difficult? If you were able to complete this project again, what changes would you make to the way you designed or built your water filtration system? How would these changes positively impact the final system?
Generalize 3	**Apply** 4
Of the designs shared today, which one(s) do you believe could make the biggest impact in a community after a natural disaster? Why? What other materials would have been useful in building and testing your design?	Using what you have learned today and throughout this unit, what are ways that you can help to ensure you and your family practice proper food safety at home? What is one thing you will try to change in your household to make food preparation safer?

Lesson 6 - Engineering a Solution: Defense in Food Safety

Variations

As an extension, ask youth to consider what it would take to sell the new food safety product they engineered.

Using what they have learned about food safety and the needs that various populations have around the world, create a campaign to sell the water filtration product the youth created. Youth may choose to design a pamphlet, a commercial, or an infographic to share their new product with the world. As they create their campaign, consider the audience. Will this product be best used in times of disaster? Then perhaps the product should be marketed to organizations such as the Red Cross or FEMA. Will this product revolutionize a restaurant kitchen? Then it could be marketed toward chefs and restaurant managers. Once youth have determined their audience, it is then their job to choose a quick way for the audience to hear their message. Youth will sell them on the idea by giving them all the benefits this product will provide. Campaigns should be creative and convincing! When the advertisement is complete, youth will make a 60 second presentation to their fellow entrepreneurs highlighting the benefits of this fabulous new food safety design.

Education Standard(s)

5.L.1 Understand how structures and systems of organisms (to include the human body) perform functions necessary for life.

ELA-Literacy.SL.5.1 Engage effectively in a range of collaborative discussions (one-on-one, in groups, and teacher-led) with diverse partners on grade 5 topics and texts, building on others' ideas and expressing their own clearly.

ELA-Literacy.SL.5.1b Follow agreed-upon rules for discussions and carry out assigned roles.

ELA-Literacy.SL.5.1d Review the key ideas expressed and draw conclusions in light of information and knowledge gained from the discussions.

3-5-ETS1-1.Define a simple design problem reflecting a need or a want that includes specified criteria for success and constraints on materials, time, or cost.

3-5-ETS1-2.Generate and compare multiple possible solutions to a problem based on how well each is likely to meet the criteria and constraints of the problem.

Tags

Food Safety, Foodborne Illness, Bacteria, Engineering, Engineering Design Process

Lesson 6 Print Materials

Facilitator Print Materials
None

Group Handouts
None

Youth Handouts
Global Sanitation Letter
Engineering a Solution Youth Response Form

See page 5 for information on digital assets and extra enrichment.

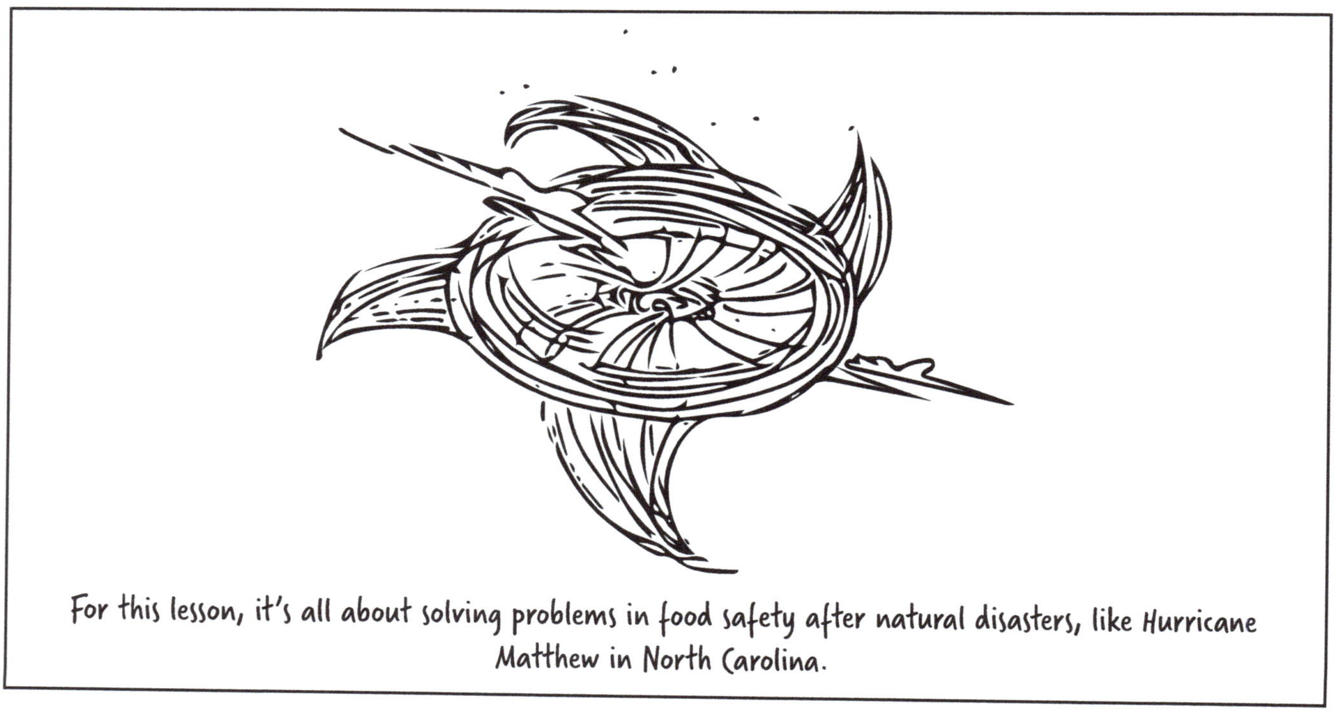

Congratulations!

You have been selected to participate in an engineering challenge. In order to participate, you will need to collect your own recyclable items over a 48 hour time period.

You have been given a clean garbage bag. This bag should travel with you wherever you go over the next 2 days. It will be used to collect any **CLEAN** recyclable waste materials **YOU** produce. For example: If **YOU** drink the last glass of orange juice at your house, rinse out the juice container and place it in your bag. If **YOU** use the last paper towel on the roll, place the empty cardboard tube in your bag. It is very important that everything you place inside your garbage bag is clean-this means you must rinse/wash the items prior to placing them inside the bag. You should include lids and all other parts of containers in the bag as well.

Some items are **OFF LIMITS** and should not be placed in the bag. Examples include: used tissues, bathroom waste, glass, and any food waste or scraps. Remember to only include recyclable materials other than glass in your bag.

In order to participate, you must bring your bag of recyclable materials with you on (date) ________.
Not having these items with you will make your challenge very difficult!

Good luck and happy recycling!!

Global Sanitation

Global Sanitation letter

Your community has just been devastated by a natural disaster, what are some of the problems you might be facing? 1. 2. 3. (1)	What do you believe is the greatest problem facing your community? Why? What resources will you need to solve this problem? (2)	Which problem has your community decided to tackle? Why? (3)
How did the changes you made after the first test alter the performance of your design either positively or negatively? How you would approach this project differently if you could do it again? (8)	**Engineering a Solution Youth Response Form**	Using graph paper, begin to design a solution to the problem your community has decided to tackle. Label each part of the design according to which piece of recyclable material you will use. (4)
What were the results of the first test? How would you rate your water filtration system? 1-Your system did not allow water to pass through for collection 2-Your system allowed water to pass but did not filter the particles 3-Your system filtered the larger particles but not the smaller particles 4-You system filtered all particles but the water has a cloudy appearance 5-The filtered water has a clear appearance (7)	Questions you should ask as you conduct your first test: 1. Will water pass through the filter? 2. Will the filter sift marbles to prevent them from entering the final water source? 3. Will the filter sift sand to prevent it from entering the final water source? (6)	As you build, list each material you used below, as well as how much tape you needed and if you required the Facilities Manager to drill holes or cut anything. Materials List: Tape in inches used= ______ Did you use the Facilities Manager? (5)

Engineering a Solution youth response form

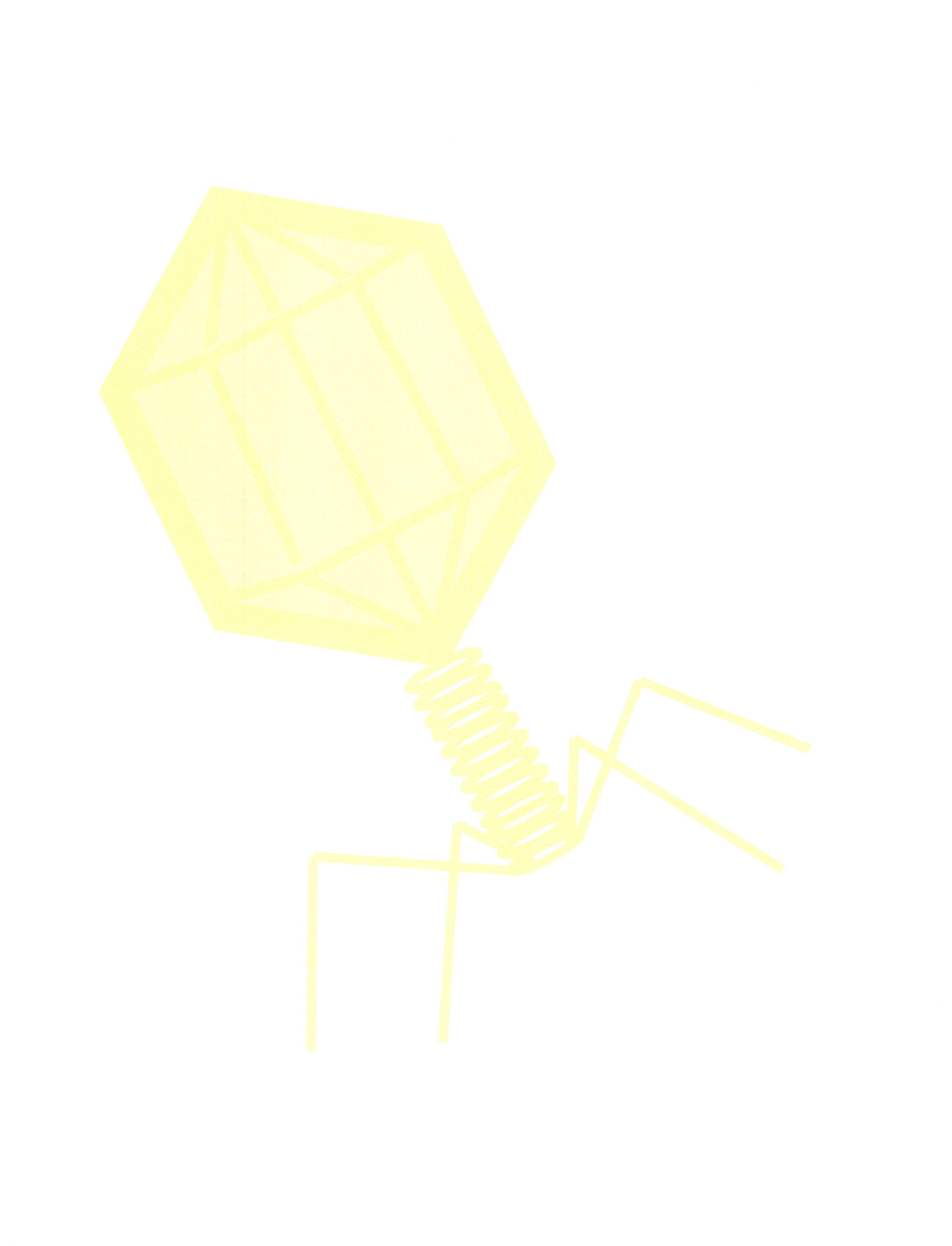

Appendix A

Grab and Go Lessons

Grab and Go #1 Germs All Around

Introduction

Microorganisms are living things that are all around us, but they are so small that you need a microscope to see them. While most microorganisms on our planet are harmless, or even beneficial, to humans, some microorganisms are dangerous. These microorganisms are known as pathogens or more commonly as "germs." Bacteria, fungi, viruses, and protozoans (single-celled organisms that move and consume other organisms) are all different types of pathogens that can make humans ill.

Some of the ways in which pathogens can enter the body include breaks in the skin, airway passages, and the mouth. Pathogens spread through the air when we sneeze and through contact with infected surfaces. Epidemiology is a branch of science that studies how diseases spread.

Key Teaching Points

1. Germs are microorganisms that are pathogenic, or harmful, to humans.
2. Germs can spread in a variety of ways.

Learner Outcomes

- Youth will develop an understanding of microbes and how they spread from one place to another.
- Youth will develop an understanding of microbes that are considered germs.

Skill Level: Elementary, Beginning

Success Indicators

- States claims using reasoning from prior knowledge and discussions
- Makes predictions using schema and information shared during the activity
- Creates a multimedia presentation informing others about how germs spread and how they affect humans (optional)

Life Skills

Critical Thinking, Communication, Teamwork, Healthy Lifestyle Choices

Time Needed

90 minutes or two 45 minute sessions

Space

Classroom or kitchen

Suggested Group Size

Groups of 4 youth

Materials List

- Germs All Around KWL chart – 1 per group
- Introduction: Germs All Around – 1 per group
- Petroleum jelly and paper towel (put a small amount of jelly on one paper towel for each youth before activity starts)
- Glitter, 4 different colors
- Spray bottle with water
- Baby powder in bottle
- Soap and water (to wash hands)
- Germs Multimedia Presentation Planning sheet -1 copy per group (optional)
- Computer with Internet access

Be aware of any youth in your class who may be sensitive to the feeling of petroleum jelly or glitter on their hands. Consider creating "observer" positions for youth who will not or cannot participate in the hands-on activity to model the spread of germs.

Grab and Go #1 – Germs All Around

Before the Activity

1. Read the article on KidsHealth (http://kidshealth.org/kid/talk/qa/germs.html)

2. Have the following materials ready:

   - Spray bottle filled with water
     (to show how germs spread when someone coughs or sneezes).

   - A bottle of baby powder
     (to show how germs can stay in the air for an extended period of time).

   - Paper towels with a small amount of petroleum jelly
     (for youth to rub on their hands).

3. Bottles of glitter - 4 different colors (to sprinkle on youth hands).

4. Make copies of the Introduction, the KWL chart, and Germs Multimedia Presentation Planning sheet (optional) for each group.

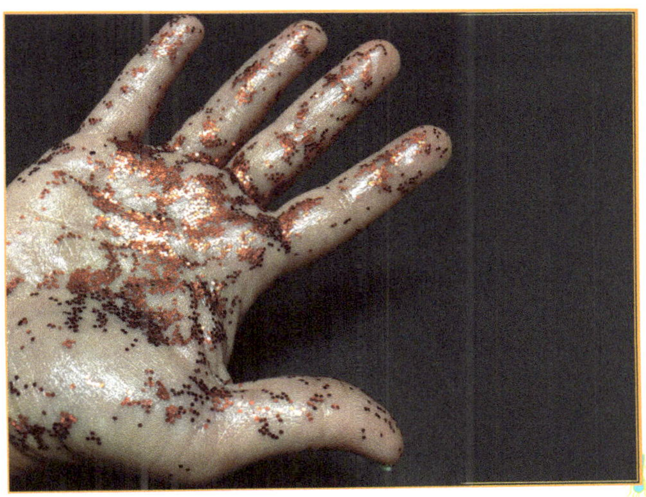

Grab and Go #1 – Germs All Around

Opening Questions

- What is a germ?
- How do germs spread from one place or person to another?

Potential follow-up questions

- Do you know if all microbes, such as bacteria, fungi, or viruses, are good or bad for humans?
- What do you know about microbes that are considered harmful to humans?
- Where do microbes such as bacteria, fungi, and viruses live?
- How do protect yourself from germs?

Let's Do It!

1. Activate youth's background knowledge by asking the Opening Questions.

   - What is a germ?
   - How do germs spread from one place or person to another?

2. Give each group a KWL chart. Tell youth that the letters "KWL" stand for "What I Know," "What I Want to Know," and "What I Have Learned." Explain that they will be using this tool to help them record their questions and their learning. Give groups a few minutes to record anything that they think to be true.

3. Have youth share their work ideas with their group members.

4. Point out the "W" column. Explain to youth that, as they have questions, they are welcome to write their questions down during the course of their work.

5. Pass out the Introduction. Read the Introduction out loud as youth follow along. Provide groups with a few minutes to write down questions on their KWL charts.

6. Have one representative from each group share their questions.

7. Using a computer with Internet access, take youth to the KidsHealth website. If possible, project the website onto a wall so all youth can see the information. Read aloud the sections on the website labeled "What Types of Germs are There?" (pg.1) and "What do Germs Do?" (pg. 2).

8. Provide a few minutes for groups to record their ideas. Questions should be placed on the "W" column. New information should be placed in the "L" column.

9. Explain that you will be modeling some of the ways that germs spread and move through the air. Remind youth that germs are microscopic and that we normally cannot see them. Explain that scientific models help us understand things that we may not be able to directly see.

10. Ask youth to think about how germs spread when someone coughs or sneezes and to predict where germs might end up afterwards. Tell youth that the spray bottle of water will represent the spread of germs following a cough or sneeze.

11. Spray the bottle several times around the room so that youth can feel water dropping from the air. Point out how water is moving in the air and down to different surfaces.

12. Explain that even though germs seem very tiny to us, they still come in different sizes. Some germs move slowly through the air, while others move more quickly. Show youth the bottle of baby powder. Explain that the baby powder will represent slow-moving germs.

13. Squeeze the baby powder bottle several times so that youth can see the powder floating in the air.

14. Give youth 2 minutes in their groups to compare and contrast what they observed about the different models. Ask youth to reflect on the different types of movements and how they might affect people.

15. Provide youth with a few minutes to reflect on their learning and add new information in the "L" column.

16. Ask youth to describe other ways in which germs can spread. Tell youth that they will take part in an activity that will allow them to see how germs travel around us.

17. Give each youth a paper towel smeared with a pea sized amount of petroleum jelly. Tell them to spread the petroleum jelly on their hands.

18. Go around the room and sprinkle glitter on the hands of each youth. Use different colors of glitter for each group, up to four different colors (there may be some overlap among groups).

19. Instruct the youth to touch objects and surfaces in the areas immediately around them. Provide about 1-2 minutes for them to complete this task, and then ask them what they notice.

20. Explain to youth that the glitter represents germs.

21. Using the "Stay-Stray" technique, provide youth with a few minutes to share the information that they have recorded on their KWL charts. In this technique, one member of each group is designated as the "Stayer" while the other group members are the "Strayers." The Stayer remains at the group's designated work area and has possession of the group's KWL chart. The Stayer's responsibility is to share the group's work with members from other groups. They "Strayers" are responsible for visiting the other groups in the class and learning about their work. Strayers need to initial the KWL chart of each group they visit.

22. Bring youth back together in their original groups. Provide a few minutes for Strayers to share what they have learned and for groups to update their own KWL charts.

23. Ask youth to stand up and try to trace the path of their germs around the room. Ask them to carefully look at surfaces, including hands, to determine the number of colors of glitter. Have them observe the colors of glitter on the Strayers and explain why there might be multiple colors present.

24. Ask youth to brainstorm ways they might protect themselves and others from germs. Share out ideas.

25. Return to the KidsHealth website (http://kidshealth.org/kid/talk/qa/germs.html#) and read aloud the section, "How Can You Protect Yourself From Germs?" (pg. 2).

26. Instruct youth to wash their hands with soap and water in order to remove the petroleum jelly and the glitter. Provide damp paper towels so that youth may clean their work stations.

27. Allow youth to share the ideas that they have written in the "L" column on their KWL charts.

28. Ask the Share question.

    - What was the most interesting idea that you learned today during the lesson?

29. Ask the Reflect questions.

    - How did your thinking change as you learned about germs today?
    - Is there something that you will do differently now that you know more about germs?

30. Ask the Generalize questions.

    - After participating in the spray bottle, baby powder, and glitter germ activity, what did you learn about the spread of germs?
    - How did the water, powder, and glitter act like germs?

31. Ask the Apply question.

    - Using the information that you learned today, what could you do to spread knowledge to other people so that they are more aware of germs?

32. Optional: Invite youth to work in groups to create a multimedia presentation, skit, song, or poster that will inform the public about germs, the spread of germs, and precautions that people can take to protect themselves.

33. Pass out the Germs Multimedia Presentation Planning sheet. Provide time for youth to complete the planning sheet. Once they are ready, they may begin their projects. If time permits, allow groups to share their work.

Variations

Depending on time, computer access, and/or materials availability, you may wish to end the lesson at Step 27 or you may choose to skip the steps that use the KidsHealth website.

References

KidsHealth from Nemours - http://kidshealth.org/kid/talk/qa/germs.html#

Grab and Go #1 — Germs All Around

Term and Concept Discovery

Bacteria: a type of single-celled organism. Bacteria are classified as prokaryotic organisms, as they do not have membrane-enclosed nuclei or other similar structures (organelles). Bacteria are the most abundant life forms on our planet. Singular: bacterium

Epidemiology: the study of the spread of disease

Fungi: Fungi are eukaryotic, since their cells do contain a nucleus. Mushrooms are fungi, as are microorganisms such as yeasts and molds. Singular: fungus

Germ: a microorganism, especially when disease-producing; microbe.

Host: the organism that provides food, shelter, or other benefits for another organism. For example, chickens can host the Salmonella bacterium.

Microbe: any one of a number of organisms too small to be seen without a microscope. Bacteria, viruses, and many fungi are all considered microbes.

Pathogen: a disease-causing agent, such as a microbe, that harms the host organism

Protozoa: single-celled eukaryotic organisms that behave in ways more similar to animals than to plants, particularly with regards to mobility and heterotrophy (they do not make their own food). Some protozoa, such as certain amoebas, are human pathogens. Singular: protozoan

Virus: a microbe that replicates itself by taking over cells in a host organism. At this time, there is debate among scientists as to whether viruses are actually considered to be living organisms. Unlike pathogenic bacteria, viruses cannot be killed using antibiotic medicines.

Talk It Over

Share 1	**Reflect** 2
What was the most interesting idea that you learned today during the lesson?	How did your thinking change as you learned about germs today? Is there something that you will do differently now that you know more about germs?
Generalize 3	**Apply** 4
After participating in the spray bottle, baby powder, and glitter germ activity, what did you learn about the spread of germs? How did the water, powder, and glitter act like germs?	Using the information that you learned today, what could you do to spread knowledge to other people so that they are more aware of germs?

Education Standard(s)

North Carolina Essential Standards:
5.L.2.3. Infer the effects that may result from the interconnected relationship of plants and animals to their ecosystem.

Next Generation Science Standards:
5-LS2-1. Develop a model to describe the movement of matter among plants, animals, decomposers, and the environment.

Tags

Microbes, germs, bacteria, fungi, viruses

Grab and Go #1 Print Materials

Facilitator Print Materials
None

Group Handouts
Introduction
KWL Chart
Presentation Planning sheet (optional)

Youth Handouts
None

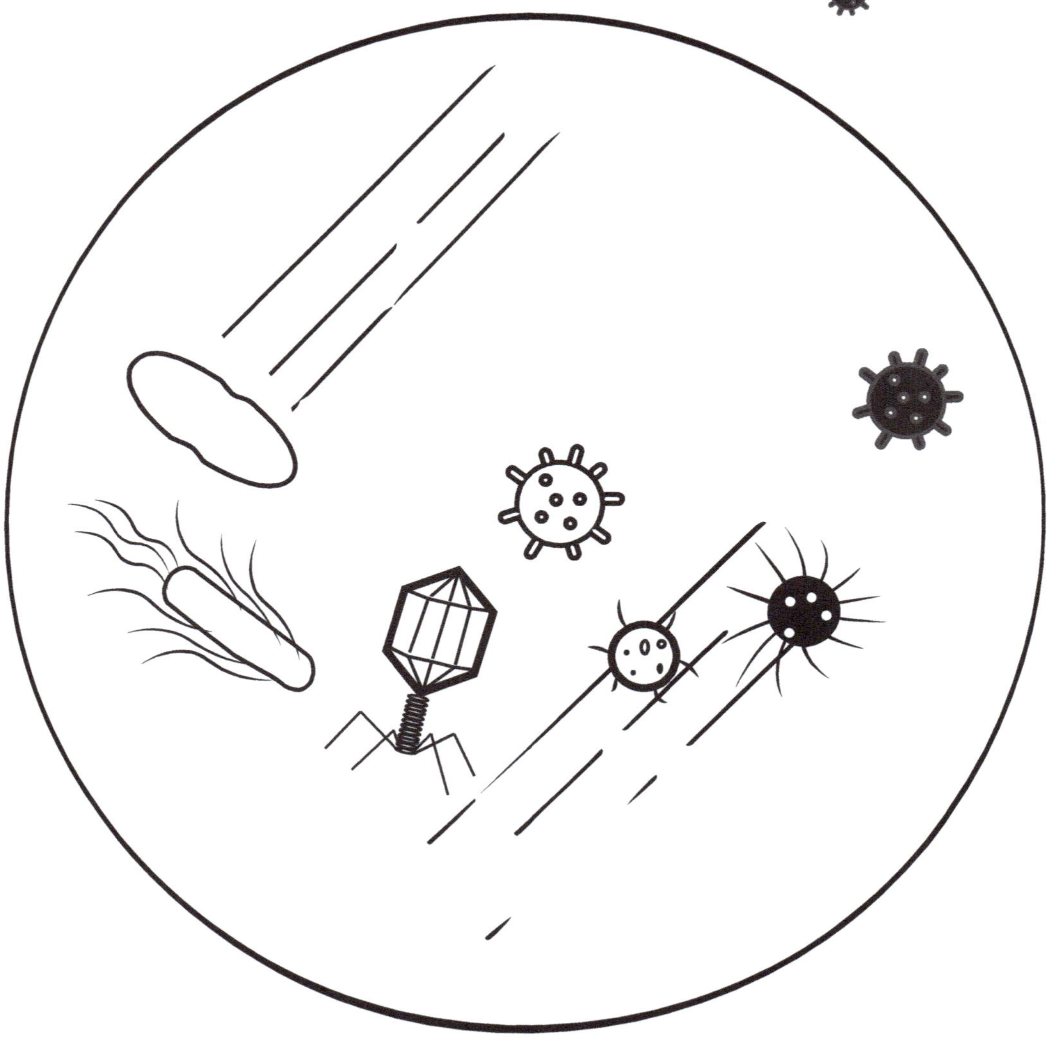

Introduction

Microorganisms (mi-cro-or-gan-isms) are living things that are all around us, but they are so small that you need a microscope to see them. While most microorganisms on our planet are harmless or even beneficial (ben-e-fi-cial) to humans, some microorganisms are dangerous. These microorganisms are known as **pathogens (path-o-gens)** or more commonly as "germs." Bacteria (bac-te-ria), fungi, viruses, and **protozoans (pro-to-zo-ans)** (single-celled organisms that move and consume other organisms) are all different types of pathogens that can make humans ill.

Some of the ways in which pathogens (path-o-gens) can enter the body include breaks in the skin, airway passages, and the mouth. Pathogens spread through the air when we sneeze and through contact with infected surfaces. **Epidemiology (ep-i-de-mi-o-lo-gy)** is a branch of science that studies how diseases spread.

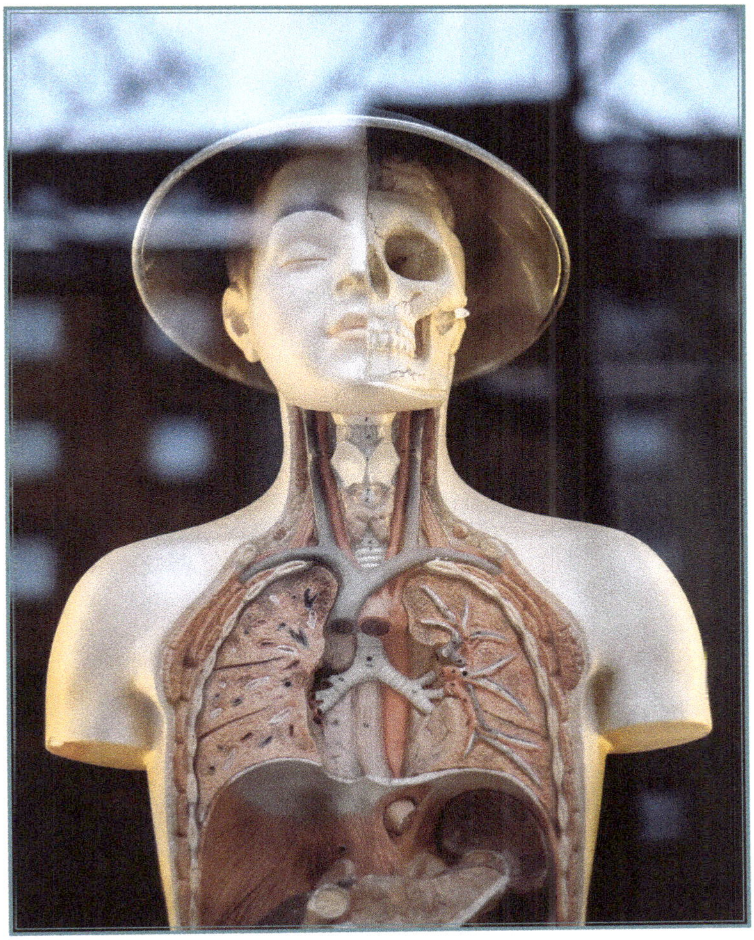

What I Know	What I Want to Know	What I Have Learned

KWL chart

What type of presentation will we create? examples: brochure, poster, video, slideshow, etc. (1)	Who will my audience be? Adults, children, teenagers, everyone, etc. (2)	What is the goal of your presentation? What do you want people to take away from it? (3)
What materials do you need to create your presentation? (8)	**Germs** **Multimedia Presentation Planning**	What information will we share about what germs are? (4)
What images will your include in your video? (7)	What information will we share about how we can protect people from germs and how we can keep them from spreading? (6)	What information will we share about how germs spread? (5)

Grab and Go #2 Microbial Munchies

Introduction

It is estimated that there are ten times as many bacterial cells as there are human cells living in and on your body. Scientists call these bacteria your microbiome. The word "microbiome" comes from the words "micro," which means "small," and "biome," which means "ecosystem." Your microbiome acts like a small ecosystem in and on your body because many different types of microbes compete against each other for the scarce resources they need to survive.

The microbes in your microbiome are examples of matter. Matter is all of the "stuff" in our universe. Anything that you can touch, taste, or smell is matter. Desks are matter. Dogs are matter. Decomposers are matter.

Scientists talk about the properties of matter in order to describe different types of matter. Think about gold. The way it reflects light is one of its properties. The way gold feels is another. Gold can melt or be a solid. It tends not to react with other chemicals. These are all properties of gold.

When matter interacts with other types of matter, changes can occur. Sometimes, matter changes shape or size. The way the matter looks changes, but the actual "stuff" doesn't. Melted gold is still gold. Sugar dissolved in tea is still sugar, and will eventually fall to the bottom of the glass if you wait long enough. These types of changes are called physical changes.

Sometimes when matter interacts, the changes are more than physical changes. Chemical changes occur when new types of matter are made or released. Bubbles, odors, color changes, and heat are all indicators that chemical changes are taking place. For example, plants use photosynthesis to turn carbon dioxide and water into sugar and oxygen. Oxygen is released and the sugars are very different from the carbon dioxide. The plants have transformed one type of matter into another through chemical changes.

Digestion is the process that living organisms, including microbes, use to obtain nutrients through decomposition. Humans have a specialized system of organs, known as the digestive system, to help them obtain energy from food. Most of the human microbiome, the billions of microbes living on and in the human body, is located within the digestive tract. These microbes help release energy and nutrients from the foods that humans eat.

Grab and Go #2 – Microbial Munchies

Key Teaching Points

1. Matter can undergo physical and chemical changes.
2. Decomposition and digestion are chemical changes.
3. Properties of matter, including odor, taste, texture, and pH, change when the matter undergoes decomposition.

Learner Outcomes

- Youth will describe changes in matter resulting from digestion and decomposition.

Skill Level: Grades 3-5

Success Indicators

- Youth make and record observations about properties of matter.
- Youth classify relationships among organisms.

Life Skills

Critical Thinking, Keeping Records

Time Needed

60 minutes

Space

Classroom or similarly-sized space

Suggested Group Size

Pairs that turn into groups of 4

Materials List

- Commercial unflavored or "plain" Greek-style yogurt
- Whole milk
- Small sample cups (2 per pair if tasting is not permitted, 4 per youth if tasting is permitted)
- Spoons (1 per youth if tasting is permitted)
- 8 oz cup of water (1 per youth if tasting is permitted)
- Litmus paper strips (2 per pair)
  Note: Cabbage juice indicator solution can be prepared and used in place of litmus paper strips. Please see Appendix A
- Observation Logs (1 per youth)
  Note: there are four versions of the Observation Logs: Tasting Permitted, Tasting Permitted with a Word Bank (to support youth who are still acquiring academic English), Tasting Not Permitted, and Tasting Not Permitted with a Word Bank. We recommend allowing youth to taste the samples, provided that allergies or food safety standards are not concerns. Please choose the version of the Observation Log that best fits the needs of your class.
- 1 sheet of chart paper per group of 4 youth
- 1 marker per group of 4 youth

Note:

The Introduction for youth provided in this lesson is identical to the Introduction for Lesson 3: The Ecosystems Inside Us. Please plan appropriately if these youth will complete both lessons.

Grab and Go #2 – Microbial Munchies

Before the Activity

1. Determine allergy status of the youth with whom you will be working.

2. Prepare enough milk and yogurt samples so that each pair has one milk sample and one yogurt sample. If youth are to taste the samples (recommended), prepare enough samples so that each individual youth has a milk sample and a yogurt sample in addition to the working samples prepared for each pair. Refrigerate the samples until you are ready to use them.

3. If youth will taste the samples, prepare an 8-ounce cup of water for each individual.

4. Prepare copies of the Introduction for each youth or pair or group (optional, only if desired).

5. Prepare copies of the Observation Log version (or versions) to meet your needs.

6. If you are planning to use cabbage juice indicator instead of pH strips, prepare the indicator following the steps on the sheet, "Instructions for Cabbage Juice Indicator." (Appendix A) This must be done at least a day in advance.

Grab and Go #2 — Microbial Munchies

Opening Question

- How might microbes get energy?

Let's Do It!

1. Introduce the term **matter**. Matter is the "stuff" that makes up our universe. Ask youth to share some ideas. Listen to make sure they are talking about actual matter rather than ideas, such as love, movements, or words that describe (adjectives). Point out to youth that they, too, are matter.

2. Explain to youth that when objects or organisms interact, they might change. Sometimes, the changes involve the way things look or feel, but the type of matter stays the same. These changes are called **physical changes**.

3. Tell youth that other interactions can cause matter to change into new types of matter. These changes are called **chemical changes**.

4. Read the Introduction with youth.

5. Tell youth that one way scientists understand microbial activity is by observing changes in **properties** of matter. Explain that properties can be chemical, like the rust, or physical, like the color of a rock. Explain to youth that they will use their senses, as well as chemical indicators, to observe and record properties for two samples: a milk sample and a yogurt sample.

6. Pass out the Observation Log version that you have chosen. With youth, walk through the Observation Log to ensure that youth understand the directions.

7. **Review lab safety procedures, especially procedures for tasting food in the lab.**

8. Transition youth from their small groups into their learning partners. Pass out milk and yogurt samples to each pair and pH strips or cabbage juice indicator solution. **Explain that youth will NOT taste from the samples in front of them. Ensure that youth understand that they will NOT taste from the samples in front of them.**

9. Demonstrate using the litmus paper strips or cabbage juice indicator solution.

10. Direct youth to observe the samples and complete the Observation Log with their partners.

11. Clean up the samples. If youth will taste the samples (recommended), pass out fresh samples of milk and yogurt, 1 sample of each per youth, as well as one cup of water per youth. Demonstrate drinking water between tasting samples to clear out the flavors and cleanse the palate. Guide youth to work together in order to complete the remaining boxes on the Observation Log.

12. Clean up the samples and water. Transition youth from learning partners back into small groups of four youth. Give each group a marker and a sheet of chart paper.

13. Ask the Share Questions.

    - What differences did you observe between the milk and the yogurt?
    - What properties were similar?

Have youth compare their completed Observation Logs with those belonging to the other members of their group. Direct youth to create a poster on chart paper that summarizes the differences between milk and yogurt. Provide 5-10 minutes for youth to complete their posters.

14. Allow youth 5-10 minutes to complete a "gallery walk." During the gallery walk, youth walk around the room and read the other groups' posters.

15. Return youth to their seats. Explain to youth that yogurt is made from milk. Solicit their ideas about what happened to cause the change from milk to yogurt. Ask the Reflect Question.

    - What caused the properties to change?

16. Ask the Generalize Question.

    - Based on your observations, does digestion seem to be a chemical or physical change? Explain.

17. Close with the Apply Question.

    - What are other examples of foods that rely on changes caused by microbes?
    - Which ones do you eat in your home?

Take it Home

Go on a microbe hunt at your home. What other kinds of foods can you find that are made using microbes? What properties do you observe for each of these foods?

Grab and Go #2 – Microbial Munchies

Term and Concept Discovery

Airway passage filters: a first-line defense system in the human body. The shape of the airway passages in the human body can help trap pathogens. For example, pathogens can get trapped in the curve of the nasal cavity and thus prevented from infecting the body.

Chemical Change: a change in the chemical structure and atomic bonding of matter. Chemical changes are often accompanied by a gas being released, a temperature change, a change in color, or a change in odor. Burning paper causes a chemical change, changing paper into ash.

Decomposition: the process by which dead organisms are broken down chemically into component nutrients. For example, as dead trees decompose, they are broken into carbon and nitrogen, among other elements.

Digestion: the process through which organisms chemically break down food into component nutrients that can be used by their cells.

Matter: all of the "stuff" in the universe. Anything made of atoms or subatomic particles is matter. Matter has mass and thus can be measured.

Microbiome: the term given to the microbes that live within/on a particular organism

Pathogen: a disease-causing agent, such as a microbe, that harms the host organism

Physical Change: a physical change occurs when matter changes shape or state, but the chemical bonds between atoms are not affected. For example, tearing paper into bits and melting ice are examples of physical changes.

Talk It Over

Share 1	**Reflect** 2
What differences did you observe between the milk and the yogurt? What properties were similar?	What caused the properties to change?
Generalize 3	**Apply** 4
Based on your observations, does digestion seem to be a chemical or physical change? Explain.	What are other examples of foods that rely on changes caused by microbes? Which ones do you eat in your home?

Education Standard(s)

North Carolina Essential Standards:
5.P.2 Understand the interactions of matter and energy and the changes that occur.
5.L.2.2 Classify the organisms within an ecosystem according to the function they serve: producers, consumers, or decomposers (biotic factors)

Next Generation Science Standards:
5-LS2-1. Develop a model to describe the movement of matter among plants, animals, decomposers, and the environment.
5-PS1-1. Develop a model to describe that matter is made of particles too small to be seen.

Tags
Ecology, microbiome, decomposer, properties, matter, scientific thinking

Grab and Go #2 ✹ Print Materials

Facilitator Print Materials
None

Group Handouts
Introduction (optional, 1 per youth or pair)

Note: there are four versions of the Observation Logs: Tasting Permitted with a Word Bank (to support youth who are still acquiring academic English), Tasting Permitted, Tasting Not Permitted with a Word Bank, and Tasting Not Permitted. We recommend allowing youth to taste the samples, provided that allergies or food safety standards are not concerns. Please choose the version of the Observation Log that best fits the needs of your class.

Observation Log (word bank, tasting)
Observation Log (no word bank, tasting)
Observation Log (word bank, non-tasting)
Observation Log (no word bank, non-tasting)

Youth Handouts
None

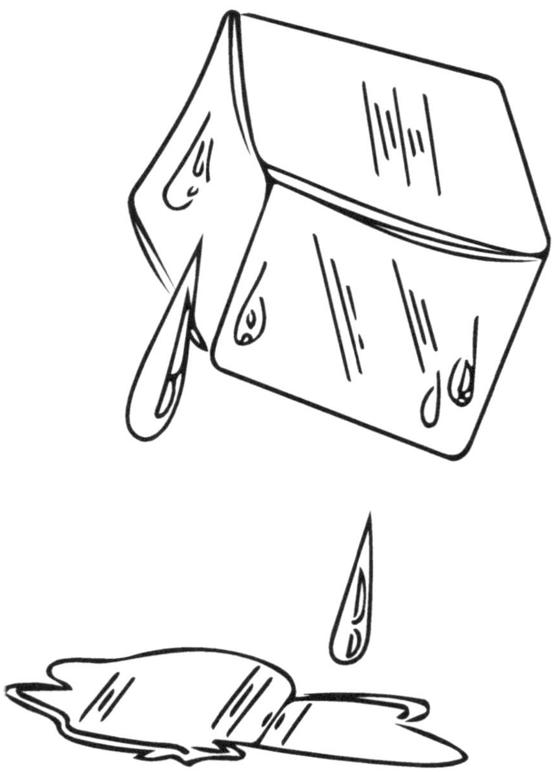

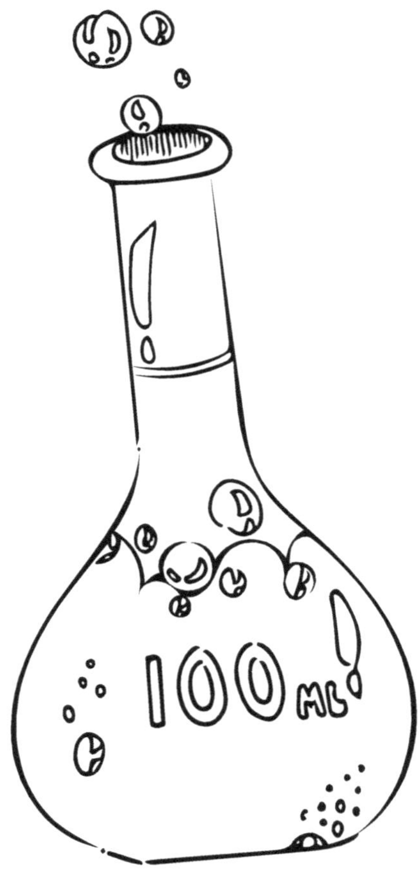

Introduction

It is estimated that there are ten times as many bacterial (bac-te-rial) cells as there are human cells living in and on your body. Scientists call these bacteria your **microbiome (mi-cro-bi-ome)**. The word "microbiome" comes from the words "micro," which means "small," and "biome," which means "ecosystem" (eco-sys-tem). Your microbiome acts like a small ecosystem in and on your body because many different types of microbes compete against each other for the scarce resources they need to survive.

The microbes in your microbiome (mi-cro-bi-ome) are examples of **matter**. Matter is all of the "stuff" in our universe. Anything that you can touch, taste, or smell is matter. Desks are matter. Dogs are matter. Decomposers are matter.

Scientists talk about the properties of matter in order to describe different types of matter. Think about gold. The way it reflects light is one of its properties. The way gold feels is another. Gold can melt or be a solid. It tends not to react with other chemicals. These are all properties of gold. When matter interacts with other types of matter, changes can occur. Sometimes, matter changes shape or size. The way the matter looks changes, but the actual "stuff" doesn't. Melted gold is still gold. Sugar dissolved in tea is still sugar, and will eventually fall to the bottom of the glass if you wait long enough. These types of changes are called **physical changes**.

Sometimes when matter interacts, the changes are more than physical changes. **Chemical changes** occur when new types of matter are made or released. Bubbles, odors, color changes, and heat are all indicators that chemical changes are taking place. For example, plants use photosynthesis (pho-to-syn-the-sis) to turn carbon dioxide and water into sugar and oxygen. Oxygen is released and the sugars are very different from the carbon dioxide. The plants have transformed one type of matter into another through chemical changes.

In our bodies, we change matter through **digestion (di-ges-tion)**. Our digestive (di-ges-tive) system is a special group of organs that help us decompose (de-com-pose) our food so we can get the energy and nutrients (nu-tri-ents) we need. Most of our microbiome (mi-cro-bi-ome) can be found in our digestive system.

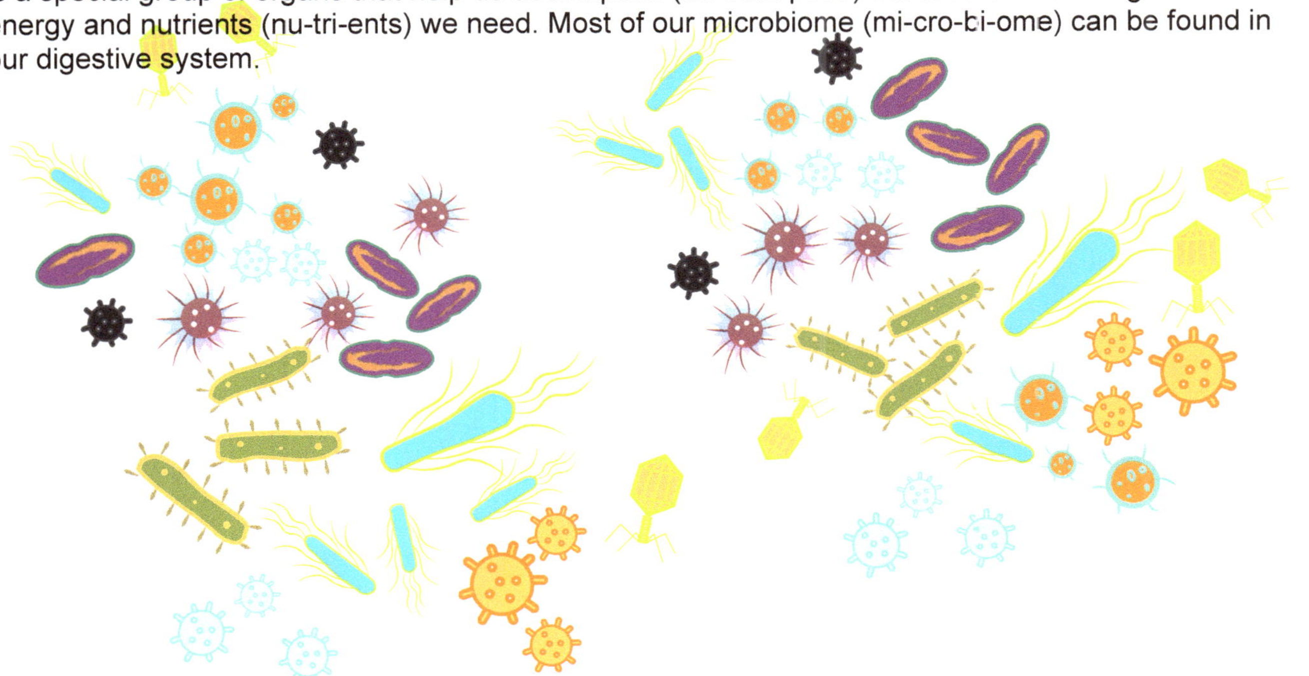

Observation Log: Comparing Milk and Yogurt Samples

Use this chart to record your observations. Circle words that match what you observe. You may add your own words as well. Do not taste anything until your teacher tells you to do so.

	Properties of Milk	Properties of Yogurt
Appearance	Liquid Semi-solid Solid Color	Liquid Semi-solid Solid Color
Odor	Sweet Mild Strong Tangy	Sweet Mild Strong Tangy
Texture	Silky Creamy Chunky Grainy Hard Oily	Silky Creamy Chunky Grainy Hard Oily
Sound	Sloshes Rattles No Sound	Sloshes Rattles No Sound
Taste (Wait for directions from your teacher!)	Sweet Mild Strong Tangy Sour	Sweet Mild Strong Tangy Sour
Other (e.g., pH)		

Which properties do the samples seem to share?

Observation Log (word bank, tasting)

Observation Log: Comparing Milk and Yogurt Samples

Use this chart to record your observations.
Do not taste anything until your teacher tells you to do so.

	Properties of Milk	Properties of Yogurt
Appearance		
Odor		
Texture		
Sound		
Taste (Wait for directions from your teacher!)		
Other (e.g., pH)		

Which properties do the samples seem to share?

Observation Log: Comparing Milk and Yogurt Samples

Use this chart to record your observations. Circle words that match what you observe. You may add your own words as well. Do not taste anything.

	Properties of Milk	Properties of Yogurt
Appearance	Liquid Semi-solid Solid Color	Liquid Semi-solid Solid Color
Odor	Sweet Mild Strong Tangy	Sweet Mild Strong Tangy
Texture	Silky Creamy Chunky Grainy Hard Oily	Silky Creamy Chunky Grainy Hard Oily
Sound	Sloshes Rattles No Sound	Sloshes Rattles No Sound
Other (e.g., pH)		

Which properties do the samples seem to share?

Observation Log: Comparing Milk and Yogurt Samples

Use this chart to record your observations. Do not taste anything.

	Properties of Milk	Properties of Yogurt
Appearance		
Odor		
Texture		
Sound		
Other (e.g., pH)		

Which properties do the samples seem to share?

Grab and Go #3 Microbes on the Menu

Introduction

As you gaze out across the school cafeteria you may see a variety of foods ranging from pepperoni pizza prepared in the cafeteria to sushi brought from home. Youth may purchase a salad from the lunch line or they may bring a turkey and cheese sandwich in their lunch box. Many youth and teachers choose to bring lunch from home every day. Perhaps they have food allergies or specific dietary restrictions or maybe they believe that eating lunch from home is healthier or even safer to eat. However, in the world of food safety there is a "Danger Zone" to avoid. When food that should be cold reaches a temperature greater than 40 degrees Fahrenheit and food that should be hot drops to temperatures below 140 degrees Fahrenheit, microbes thrive. There are a variety of foods that can be served at any temperature (within reason to remain appetizing) and continue to maintain freshness and be safely eaten. Whole fresh fruits or vegetables, breads and crackers, chips, hard cheeses, and peanut butter and jelly are some of the foods that do not require a constant temperature in order to maintain safety. However, many of the foods we eat and carry in our lunches need certain temperature conditions in order to be safely consumed. When cold foods become too warm and hot foods become too cold, they enter a world known as the food safety danger zone. Microbes require certain conditions in order to grow and lunch boxes can provide the ideal environment for microbe multiplication. In fact, many foods that are left unrefrigerated for periods longer than two hours can lead to microbe growth rates that double every 20-30 minutes. Imagine if your turkey sandwich had only one microbe present when you left your house at 7a.m. How many microbes would there be when you ate the sandwich at 12:00? Ten? A hundred? Actually there would be more than 32,000 by 12:00 if the first microbe doubled every 20 minutes! That's a lot of microbes on the lunch menu!

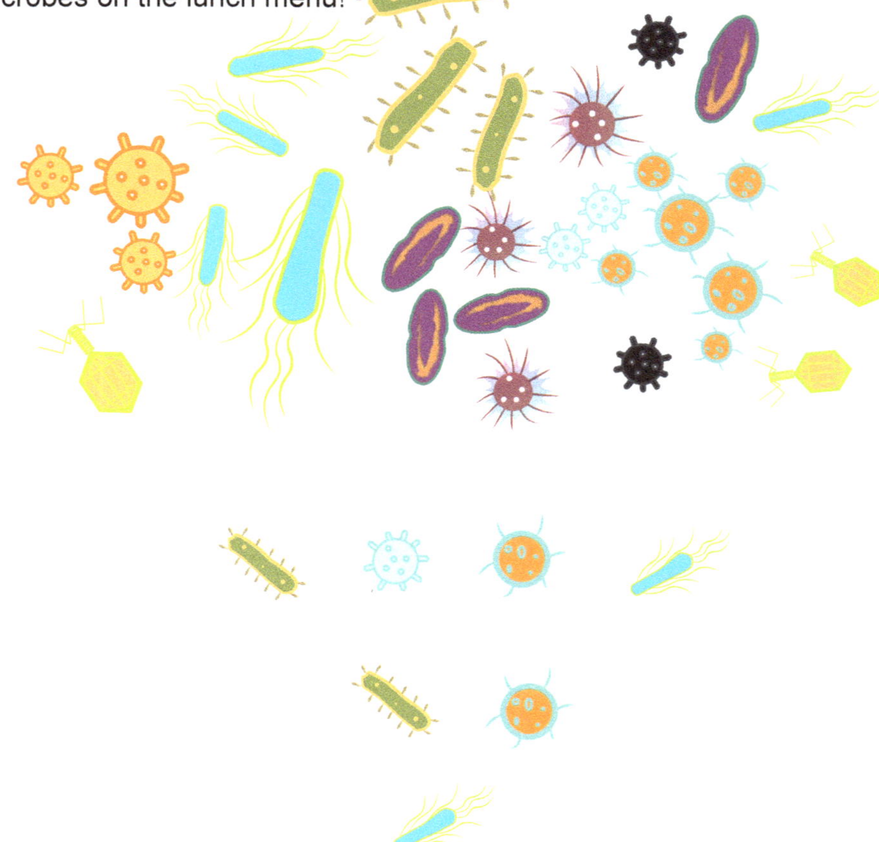

Grab and Go #3 – Microbes on the Menu

Key Teaching Points

1. Microbes grow and reproduce under certain conditions.
2. Keeping foods at temperatures to inhibit microbial growth is an important aspect of food safety.

Learner Outcomes

- Youth will develop an understanding of microbes and how they multiply at room temperature.
- Youth will develop an understanding of food safety when packing lunch for school.
- Youth will develop an understanding of which foods are safe to pack in lunches without refrigeration.

Skill Level: Elementary, Beginning

Success Indicators

- Makes predictions about microbes and food safety using prior knowledge and information shared in previous activities.
- Creates a graph demonstrating the multiplication rate of one microbe over the course of a given time.

Life Skills

Critical Thinking, Communication, Team Work, Healthy Life-style Choices

Time Needed

30-40 minutes

Space

Classroom or similar space with access to microwave and refrigerator prior to lesson.

Suggested Group Size

Groups of 5

Materials List

- Microbes on the Menu Recording Sheet (1 per youth)
- Variety of lunch boxes (4 different kinds)
- Variety of thermos-type containers (5 different kinds)
- 1 Brown paper lunch bag
- Food thermometer (one per each group of youth)
- Freezable cold packs (one per group)
- 5 cans of spaghetti, ravioli, or other meat filled canned pasta item (must be the same brand and same variety)
- 5 containers of yogurt (must be the same brand and same variety)
- 5 prepackaged lunch meal kits containing meat and cheese (must be the same brand and same variety)
- Access to a microwave prior to beginning the lesson
- Access to a refrigerator prior to beginning the lesson
- 1 piece of chart paper
- Graph paper (1 sheet per youth)
- Markers (1 pack of 8 different colors)
- Pencils (1 per youth)

Caution:

Please remind youth that the lunch foods in this learning experience are lab materials and not to be eaten.

Grab and Go #3 – Microbes on the Menu

Consider enlisting help from youth or parents to collect the thermos-type containers and different types of lunch boxes.

Before the Activity

1. Take the following steps four hours before the activity starts:

    a. Heat the cans of meat filled pasta to a temperature greater than 140 degrees and divide into 5 different thermos-type containers. Place one in each of the 4 lunch boxes and 1 into the paper lunch bag.
    b. Keep the 5 yogurt containers in the refrigerator until 4 hours prior to the lesson. Once removing them from the refrigerator, place one in each of the 4 lunch boxes and 1 into the paper lunch bag.
    c. Keep the 5 pre-packaged lunches refrigerated until 4 hours prior to the lesson. Once removing them from the refrigerator, place one in each of the 4 lunch boxes and 1 into the paper lunch bag.
    d. You may choose to include other foods that are stable and safe to eat at room temperature such as: whole fruit, crackers, or chips. Although these items do not allow for easy temperature gauging, they can certainly add to the conversation of food safety and items that are lunch box safe at any temperature.
    e. Keep lunch boxes and the paper lunch bag at room temperature for 4 hours prior to the start of the lesson.

2. Make copies of Microbes on the Menu recording sheet (1 per youth).

3. At the beginning of the day when you are conducting this lesson, place a sheet of chart paper where youth can easily view it throughout the day. Make available to youth 8 different colored markers. Begin at 8:00 (or during the start of your day when all youth can view the chart) by drawing one dot in the center of the chart. Tell youth that in twenty minutes you would like for a youth to come up to the board and double the number of circles on the chart using a green marker. After an additional 20 minutes have another youth with a different color to then come up and double the number of circles now on the chart. By going through this process 8 times, you will have 128 circles drawn on the board. You may choose to simply assign youth a time to walk up to the board, or you may choose to call attention to the board every 20 minutes throughout the day. You can continue to double the circles if time allows until the start of the Microbes on the Menu lesson. However, seeing the multiplication process of microbes from 1 to 128 will be very visual for youth and will help them understand that under the right conditions, microbes thrive. If continuing the microbe multiplication process through the first 8 cycles, your pattern will look like this: 1, 2, 4, 8, 16, 32, 64, 128.

Grab and Go #3 — Microbes on the Menu

Opening Questions

- Have you ever brought your lunch to school in a lunch box? A brown paper bag?
- What are some of the foods you might pack in your lunch?
- What do you find to be one difficulty when eating food that you bring from home?

Follow-Up Questions

- What do you know about microbes and how they are able to grow and multiply?

Let's Do It!

1. Activate youths' interest by asking the Opening Questions.

2. Tell youth that many youth/teachers choose to bring their lunch from home because they consider this to be a healthy eating option and that this is one way they can be sure they know what they are eating. Many people, however, don't consider that they may be eating not only what they packed in their lunch, but they may also be eating millions of other items that they don't remember packing at all.

3. Ask youth to think back about what they know about microbes. Ask the Follow-Up Question.

   What do you know about microbes and how they are able to grow and multiply?

4. Explain to youth that today they will be taking a look an environment that can foster microbe growth at a quick rate. Tell youth that in food safety, there is a danger zone where temperature is concerned. All food that is meant to be consumed cold should remain at or below 40 degrees Fahrenheit in order to be considered safe to eat. Likewise, foods that are heated and meant to be consumed hot should remain at or above 140 degrees Fahrenheit. Unfortunately, foods left out at room temperature for as little as two hours can become unsafe to eat due to the number of microbes that quickly multiply under the right conditions and in the temperatures between 40 and 140 degrees. Refer back to the chart paper from earlier in the day. Point out the first dot on the chart. Explain to youth that this dot represents one microbe under ideal growing conditions. For the purpose of this activity, it is one microbe on a food item inside a lunch box. Explain that in the right environment, microbes can double every 20-30 minutes, meaning that within several hours, food can go from safe to dangerous. At this point in the lesson lead youth to graph the results of the first 8 cycles represented on the chart. Lead youth to label the x and y-axis and to create a title for their graph. Discuss the intervals needed for each axis and the reason behind them.

   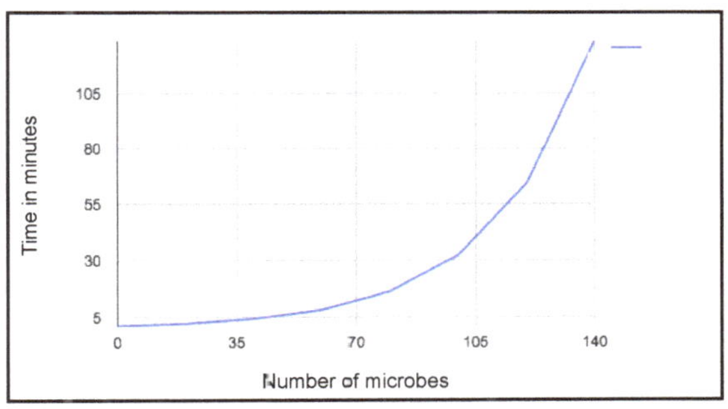

5. Show youth the 5 different lunch containers that have been sitting out at room temperature since arrival this morning. Explain to youth that each lunch contains the exact same foods and that they have been kept under the same conditions. Show them the contents of one of the lunch containers and explain that the yogurt and the meat and cheese in the prepackaged lunch kits are meant to be cold and that in order to limit microbial growth they should maintain a temperature at or below 40 degrees Fahrenheit. Additionally, the meat filled pasta should maintain at a temperature at or above 140 degrees Fahrenheit in order to limit microbial growth.

6. Explain to youth that they will be working in teams to evaluate the safety of the food inside a variety of lunch containers. With their team, youth will record the temperature of each item inside their given lunch container and determine whether or not the food in the lunch container should be considered safe to eat based on the potential microbial growth that may have occurred due to temperature.

7. Divide youth into teams and allow them the opportunity to unpack their lunch box and begin recording the appearance, smell, texture, and temperature of the contents on their recording sheets.

8. Once youth have completed their assessment of the lunch box contents, have them rate the overall safety of each food item inside. Remind youth that they must be able to defend the reasoning behind their decisions as to whether or not the food is safe to eat.

9. As a closing to the lesson, number the youth within each team 1-5. Then have youth to Jigsaw in order that one youth from each original team is now part of a new team. Allow several minutes for the new teams to discuss their conclusions. If needed, prompt them with the following discussion questions: Were the temperatures among the same foods consistent in every group? If not, why do you think they were different? Did everyone rate the same foods safe or unsafe to eat? If not, why do you think the results were inconsistent?

10. Ask the Share questions of the whole class.

    Which foods (if any) were consistently safe or unsafe to eat?
    Why do you think this was true?
    What factor(s) other than room temperature played a part in the different results we recorded?

11. Ask the Reflect questions.

    Which method(s) proved safest when packing certain foods?
    Why was this more effective that another way?
    What is one way you can change your lunch packing process in order to make the food you eat safer?

12. Ask the Generalize question.

    What generalizations could we possibly make about certain types of food such as proteins, dairy, grains, fruits, or vegetables?

13. Ask the Apply question.

    Using the information that you learned today, how can you inform those in your school setting and in your family about the need for safer food practices in order to reduce the risk of foodborne illness when packing food from home?

Grab and Go #3 – Microbes on the Menu

Talk It Over

Share 1

Which foods (if any) were consistently safe or unsafe to eat? Why do you think this was true?

What factor(s) other than room temperature played a part in the different results we recorded?

Reflect 2

Which method(s) proved safest when packing certain foods? Why was this more effective that another way?

What is one way you can change your lunch packing process in order to make the food you eat safer?

Generalize 3

What generalizations could we possibly make about certain types of food such as proteins, dairy, grains, fruits, or vegetables?

Apply 4

Using the information that you learned today, how can you inform those in your school setting and in your family about the need for safer food practices in order to reduce the risk of foodborne illness when packing food from home?

Term and Concept Discovery

Bacteria: a type of single-celled organism. Bacteria are classified as prokaryotic organisms, as they do not have membrane-enclosed nuclei or other similar structures (organelles). Bacteria are the most abundant life forms on our planet. Singular: bacterium

Foodborne Illness: a disease caused by a microbe that was transmitted to its host through the food supply. "Food poisoning" refers to a variety of foodborne illnesses, including salmonellosis and E. coli infections.

Food Safety: a series of practices designed to minimize risks posed by microbes in the food supply. Food safety practices include proper handwashing, cooking food thoroughly, keeping perishable items chilled, cleaning food preparation surfaces and tools, and keeping different types of food separated to avoid cross-contamination.

Microbe: any one of a number of organisms too small to be seen without a microscope. Bacteria, viruses, and many fungi are all considered microbes.

Education Standard(s)

CCSS.Math.Content.5.G.A.1 Use a pair of perpendicular number lines, called axes, to define a coordinate system, with the intersection of the lines (the origin) arranged to coincide with the 0 on each line and a given point in the plane located by using an ordered pair of numbers, called its coordinates. Understand that the first number indicates how far to travel from the origin in the direction of one axis, and the second number indicates how far to travel in the direction of the second axis, with the convention that the names of the two axes and the coordinates correspond (e.g., x-axis and x-coordinate, y-axis and y-coordinate

Tags

Microbes, germs, bacteria, food safety, lunch box, brown bag, microbial growth

Grab and Go #3 Print Materials

Youth Handouts
Microbes on the Menu Recording Sheet

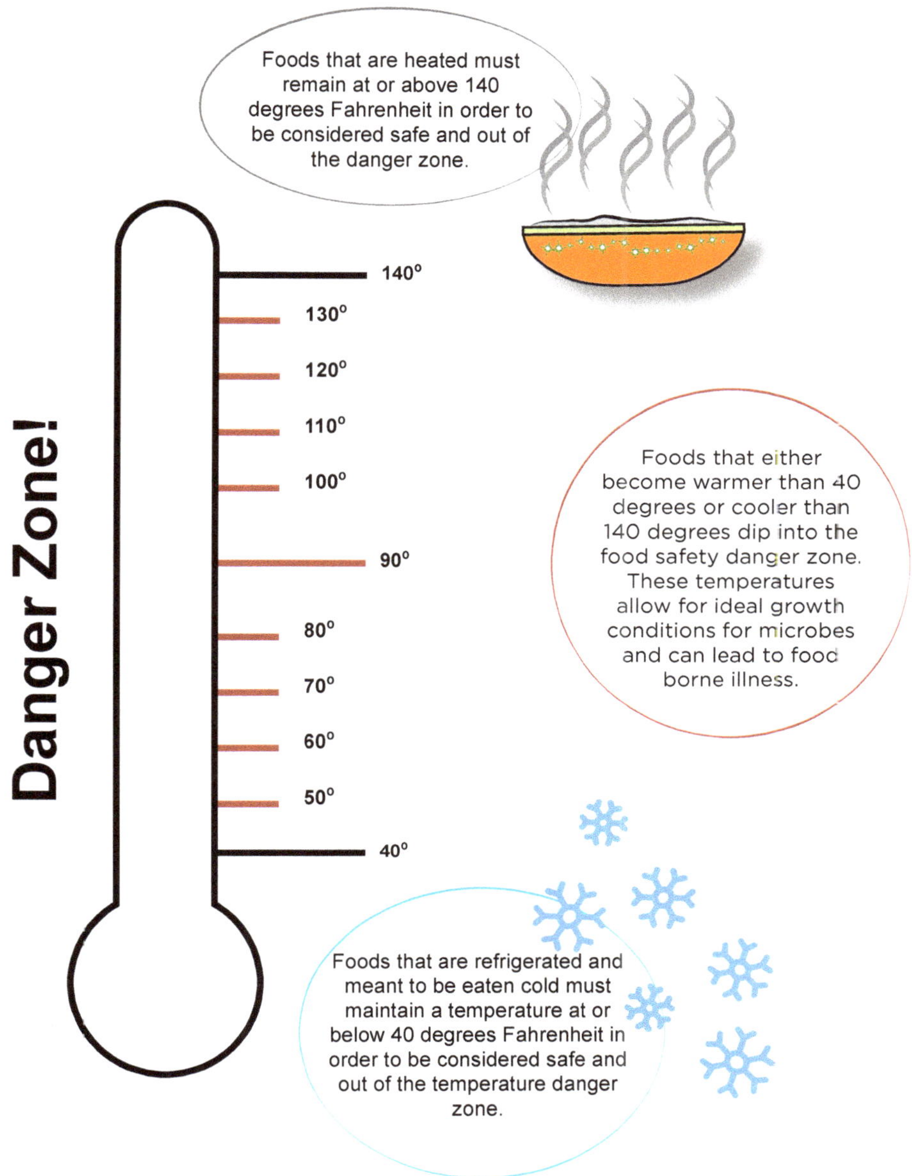

Food 1:	Food 2:	Food 3:
Appearance-	Appearance-	Appearance-
Temperature-	Temperature-	Temperature-
Smell-	Smell-	Smell-
Texture-	Texture-	Texture-
Overall Safety Rating-	Overall Safety Rating-	Overall Safety Rating-

Microbes on the Menu Recording Sheet

Appendix B

Support Materials

Permission Form
Complete Materials List
Alcohol Solution for Cleaning Goggles
Instructions for Red Cabbage Juice Indicator

Date: ____________

Dear families,

Your child, __________________, will be participating in a microbiology unit, "I am an Ecosystem." The unit, which consists of six lessons, is designed to help youth better understand microbes, food safety, and careers in microbiology.

A variety of labs and hands-on experiences are built into the unit so that youth may practice thinking and problem solving as a scientist. One lab, which runs over the course of five lessons, involves youth swiping surfaces in the everyday environment with a nutrient-rich medium and then growing microbes from those surfaces under different conditions. Safety precautions embedded in the lesson include the use of sealed bags, gloves, goggles, and hand-washing; however, there is always the slight potential for risk. While we do not expect any problems to arise, this letter is to inform you of the potential for risk so that you may make the best decisions for your family.

Please check the space below that best describes your choice and return the form to ______________.
If you have questions, please contact _________________ at _________________.

Sincerely,

Cut on the line below and return the lower part of the form.

....

My child's name:

___YES! Please allow my child to participate in all activities associated with the "I am an Ecosystem" unit.

___Maybe. I would like some more information. Please contact me at _______________.

___Yes and no. I would like my child to participate in the unit, but not the lab in which youth grow microbes.

___No, thank you. I would not like my child to participate in any part of this unit.

Optional: Please share the reasons why you checked the space you did:

Your name (printed): ________________________________ Date: ________________

Your signature: ________________________________

Materials List for Elementary Group

1 group=4 youth

Lesson 1		
Consumables	Non Consumables	Items to be printed
5 pound bag of sugar (used again in Lesson 3)	Clean knife	Claim Evidence Reasoning chart (1 per youth)
Sticky Notes	Cutting surface	Microbes Comic (1 per youth)
Cantaloupe	Spoon to scoop seeds from cantaloupe	1 KWL poster
Resealable plastic bags (14 per group)	Container to hold sliced cantaloupe (1 per group)	Claim-Evidence-Reasoning poster
Hand sanitizer	Box or other container that blocks light to collect prepared bags of room temperature cantaloupe (1 per group)	Cantaloupe Lab packet (1 per group)
Permanent markers to label bags (1 per group)	Container to collect prepared bags of refrigerated cantaloupe (1 per group)	Bag Stickers (1 set per group) ** Alternative: provide labels printed on regular paper, scissors, and tape to label the bags.
A small cup of loose sugar or individual sugar packets	Permanent marker (1 per group to write the surface name on each bag, or stickers)	
Plastic bags that can be sealed (14 per group)		
Soap and water (to wash hands)		

Lesson 2		
Consumables	Non Consumables	Items to be printed
1 or 2 Antibacterial products per group (examples: hand sanitizer, hand soap, counter wipes, etc.)	Fake flowers (approximately 100 for a class of 25)	Claim-Evidence-Reasoning chart (1 per youth)
Sticky Notes	2 bins for the Ecosystem Game	Claim-Evidence-Reasoning Self-Assessment (1 per youth)
Alcohol solution (to be used by facilitator to clean goggles after the lesson)	1 pair of safety glasses for each youth	Introduction (1 per youth)
1 pair of safety gloves for each youth		Ecosystem Diagram (1 per group)
		Frayer models (optional)

Lesson 3		
Consumables	Non Consumables	Items to be printed
5 lb. bag of sugar from Lesson 1	Large, clear, glass mixing bowl or beaker	Introduction (1 per pair)
Sticky Notes	Match or lighter	Balloon Bottle Observation Log (1 per group)
Large pitcher of water (for safety purposes)	Clock with a minute hand or a timer	Sort cards (1 set per group)
Small Plastic bottle (1 per pair) (small water bottle or soda bottle)	1 pair safety goggles for instructor use	Video Anticipation Guide (1 per youth)
Small pitcher of warm water (1 per group)	Marker (1 per group)	Frayer models (optional)
2 tbsp of molasses (1 per group)	1 pair of safety glasses for each youth	
Packet of yeast (1 per group)		
Balloon (1 per group)		
Plastic funnel (1 per group)		
Sheet of chart paper (1 per group)		

Lesson 4		
Consumables	Non Consumables	Items to be printed
Cheesecloth squares (1 per group cut to fit the index cards)	1 pair of safety glasses for each youth	Introduction (optional, one per youth or group if desired)
1 large bottle of white glue OR 1 small bottle per group	2 clear plastic spray bottles	Lab Observation sheets (1 per youth)
1 package of 11 x 17 white construction paper (approx. 50 sheets)	1 stopwatch or timer that counts seconds	Station Directions (1 of each per station)
1 pack of large index cards (divide among groups)		
1 roll of wax paper		
Wooden craft sticks (2 per group)		
1 bottle of blue food coloring		
Several plastic cups for holding glitter or fine sand		
borax (1 per group)		
1 jar of petroleum jelly		
Old newspapers, plastic tablecloths, or something else that can be used to protect work surfaces		

Lesson 5		
Consumables	Non Consumables	Items to be printed
Manilla folder (1 per group to hold printed materials)	1 pair of safety glasses for each youth	Sam E.'s medical information (one per group)
Alcohol solution (to be used by facilitator to clean goggles after the lesson)		CSI Microbes Claim-Evidence-Reasoning chart (1 per group)
1 pair of safety gloves for each youth		Information Critical Review (1 per youth)
		Investigation handouts (a different one per Case File)

Lesson 6		
Consumables	Non Consumables	Items to be printed
Large drawstring trash bag (1 per youth)	1 craft drill	Global Sanitation letter (1 per youth)
1 roll of masking tape	1 pair of large scissors	Engineering a Solution Youth Response Form (1 per youth)
1 clean gallon sized container	Pencils, rulers, and other drawing tools for youth to use when creating designs	
2 dozen marbles		
1 five pound bag of large grain sand (to be divided into 1 pound amount for each class)		
Graph paper (1-2 pieces per youth)		

Grab and Go 1		
Consumables	Non Consumables	Items to be printed
Petroleum jelly	Spray bottle (1 for the class)	Germs All Around KWL chart (1 per group)
Paper towels		Introduction: Germs All Around (1 per group)
Glitter (4 different colors)		Presentation Planning sheet (1 per group)
Baby powder in bottle		

Grab and Go 2		
Consumables	Non Consumables	Items to be printed
Commercial unflavored or "plain" Greek-style yogurt	Markers (1 per group)	Observation Logs (1 per youth)
Whole milk		
Small sample cups (2 per pair if tasting is not permitted, 4 per youth if tasting is permitted)		
Spoons (1 per youth if tasting is permitted)		
8 oz cup of water (1 per youth if tasting is permitted)		
Litmus paper strips (2 per pair) or cabbage juice indicator solution		
Chart paper (1 sheet per group)		
Note: there are four versions of the Observation Logs: Tasting Permitted, Tasting Permitted with a Word Bank (to support youth who are still acquiring academic English), Tasting Not Permitted, and Tasting Not Permitted with a Word Bank. We recommend allowing youth to taste the samples, provided that allergies or food safety standards are not concerns. Please choose the version of the Observation Log that best fits the needs of your class.		

Grab and Go 3		
Consider enlisting help from youth or parents to collect the thermos-type containers and different types of lunch boxes.		
Consumables	Non Consumables	Items to be printed
1 Brown paper lunch bag	Variety of lunch boxes (4 different kinds)	Microbes on the Menu Recording Sheet (1 per youth)
5 cans of spaghetti, ravioli, or other meat filled canned pasta item (must be the same brand and same variety)	Variety of thermos-type containers (5 different kinds)	
5 containers of yogurt (must be the same brand and same variety)	Food thermometer (one per group)	
5 prepackaged lunch meal kits containing meat and cheese (must be the same brand and same variety)	Freezable cold packs (one per group)	
Chart paper (1 piece for the class)	Markers (1 pack of 8 different colors)	
	Pencils (1 per youth)	

Alcohol Solution for Cleaning Goggles

Instructions

Materials:

- 1 spray bottle to hold at least 100mL of liquid
- 70% rubbing alcohol solution
- Measuring device (graduated cylinder)
- Water
- Paper towels

Procedure:

- Measure 40mL of rubbing alcohol and place it into the spray bottle.
- Measure 60mL of water and place it into the spray bottle.
- Tightly place the spray lid on the bottle.
- Carefully invert the bottle a couple of times to mix the solution.

Application:

- Place paper towels on a clean, dry surface. Place goggles on top of the paper towels.
- Generously spay goggles with cleaning solution.
- Allow goggles to air dry.

Instructions for Red Cabbage Juice Indicator

You will need

1. A large red cabbage
2. A large stock pot and lid
3. Water
4. A strainer
5. An empty plastic ice cube tray
6. A large plastic freezer bag

To Do:

1. Place the cabbage in the pot.
2. Fill the pot with water to cover the cabbage.
3. Place the pot on a stove burner.
4. Turn the burner on to medium high.
5. When the water comes to a rapid boil, turn the heat down to medium.
6. Place the lid on the pot.
7. Let simmer for 30 minutes.
8. Once the liquid is good and dark, strain the cabbage leaves out. These may be composted or otherwise disposed of.
9. Pour the liquid into the ice cube tray.
10. Freeze the ice cubes overnight or until solid.
11. Pop the cubes out. Place them in the freezer bag and store them in the freezer until needed.

To use the cabbage juice indicator:

1. Thaw out a cube.
2. Add a few drops of thawed indicator to the item you are testing. You can use an eyedropper, a straw, or even a small spoon to do this.
3. If the item is acidic, the indicator will remain pink.
   If the item is basic, the indicator will turn light blue.

Appendix C

Teaching Tips and Techniques

Appendix C: Teaching Tips and Techniques

In this section, you will find information about some of the terms and structures used in designing the actual lessons. For information about the scientific vocabulary, please see the glossary.

The decision has been made to use the term "learners" instead of "youth" in this section, as these techniques work with adults as well.

Term	Anticipation Guides (also sometimes called Anticipation Sets)
What it is	Anticipation Guides are questions or checklists that learners complete prior to viewing or reading informational text.
How it works	Learners use their background knowledge to complete the Anticipation Guide prior to learning the information. This helps them to know what concepts they will encounter. It also helps learners to actively seek out and pay attention to the important ideas and major underlying concepts. After viewing or reading the informational text, learners go back and complete the same questions again. They are able to then compare their old knowledge with the knowledge gained as a result of the text.
When to use it	Use Anticipation Guides before and after viewing videos or reading informational text. Anticipation Guides are especially helpful for language learners who might otherwise be overwhelmed by the amount of information in a text or video.

Term	Claim-Evidence-Reasoning
What it is	Claim-Evidence-Reasoning is a lesson format that is based on scientific writing, argumentation, and thinking.
How it works	Learners encounter a research question and are asked to take a stand on a possible answer. At this point, the claim functions partly like a prediction and partly like a hypothesis, to use the language of the traditional scientific method. Learners then set about gathering evidence, which may include evidence from their personal experiences, evidence from printed or digital materials, and/or evidence from hands-on investigations. Once evidence has been gathered, youth re-evaluate their initial claim. They have to decide which pieces of evidence are strongest and why. They also need to decide whether that evidence supports their initial claim, or if their initial claim needs to be revised.
When to use it	Use Claim-Evidence-Reasoning to support learners in developing scientific language and argument. Because the language mirrors the language in the Common Core State Standards, it can be used to support lessons in a variety of disciplines that require learners to identify and use evidence to support their thinking.

Term	Fishbowl Seminar
What it is	An alternative to a whole class discussion, the Fishbowl Seminar allows small group interaction and among youth while involving the entire class.
How it works	The class creates two circles, an inner circle and an outer circle. The inner circle should have 6-8 seats or fewer. The facilitator asks open-ended, higher-order thinking questions. Participants on the outer circle take notes on the participants speaking in the inner circle. They are not allowed to speak or answer any questions. Participants in the inner circle discuss openly about the higher-order thinking questions that the facilitator poses. Participants in the outer circle can tap the shoulder of a participant in the inside circle when they have a strong point to make. This is how the circles change and how everyone gets incorporated into the discussion. Circle sizes can be changed to meet the needs of the group, but make sure to have more people in the outer circle than the inner circle. It is recommended to have at least 3-4 participants in the inner circle.
When to use it	The Fishbowl Seminar can be used as a class discussion tool when participant evaluation is important or to better hear each individual participant's input in a large group discussion.

Term	Four Corners
What it is	Four Corners is a formative technique for sharing out answers to a selected-response (multiple choice) question.
How it works	Learners are given a question along with several potential answers. The answers are displayed around the room, often in the corners. Learners move to the corner that matches their preferred response. Learners are allowed to share their reasons for their choice. They are also allowed to change their minds and move to a new location. A variation of Four Corners has youth line up in front of their preferred choice. This creates a "human graph" which can be used to provide class data about misconceptions.
When to use it	Use Four Corners to determine what learners are thinking about key concepts and ideas in a quick, movement-based format.

Term	Formative Assessment Probes
What it is	A formative assessment probe is a question posed to gain an understanding of where learners are in their thinking. Frequently, assessment probes feature possible responses that mirror common thinking patterns among learners.
How it works	Formative Assessment Probes can be checklists, selected response questions, sorts, or other tasks that require youth to articulate and apply scientific concepts. They are not used for grades; rather, they provide the base for the direction of the instruction. Learners are encouraged to explain their thinking as they complete the tasks.
When to use it	Use Formative Assessment Probes throughout a unit cycle to track learners' understanding of key concepts. Probes are especially useful at the beginning of a lesson to uncover existing misconceptions and prepare learners for the activity. The same probe can then be used at the close of the lesson to determine if learners' thinking changed or grew as a result of their work.

Term	Frayer Model
What it is	Frayer models are graphic organizer tools for developing vocabulary. It looks like this: 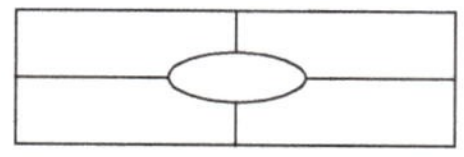 In the center of the rectangle is an oval. The new vocabulary word is written in the oval. Around the oval, the rectangular sections are labeled "Definition," "Characteristics," "Examples," and "Non-Examples." Occasionally, "Picture" or "Facts" is used in place of "Characteristics."
How it works	Learners write the new vocabulary word in the oval. Then, they complete the information in each of the rectangle sections. By having to go beyond the dictionary definition, learners develop a deeper connection to the vocabulary and a deeper understanding of the concepts.
When to use it	Frayer models can be used after new vocabulary has been introduced or as a pre-teaching tool. They are most effective once learners have had some experience with the vocabulary in context, as those experiences help learners to determine characteristics, examples, and non-examples. Frayer models can be done in class and/or as homework.

Term	Gallery Walk
What it is	A Gallery Walk is a technique for sharing ideas that have been organized in a poster, 3D model, or other highly-visual format. A variation of the Gallery Walk is the Graffiti Wall.
How it works	Learners, often in groups, create posters or 3D models in response to a question. These models are displayed, either on walls or on tables. All learners then proceed in an orderly fashion around the room, paying close attention to the work of other groups. The debrief phase of the lesson usually asks learners to summarize what they noticed during the Gallery Walk. Sometimes, learners use sticky notes to ask questions or leave feedback for the model's creator(s). In the Graffiti Wall variation, learners leave feedback or add new information directly on the original model.
When to use it	Use a Gallery Walk when learners are ready to share ideas about concepts and need a movement break.

Term	Jigsaw (sometimes called "Numbered Heads Together")
What it is	A Gallery Walk is a technique for sharing ideas and work among groups
How it works	Each group is assigned a particular component of a larger task. Group members complete the assigned component and are then reshuffled into new groups. These groups are comprised of members from each of the original groups. Together, they put the "jigsaw" together to complete the entire task.
When to use it	Use a Jigsaw to support learners as they work through large, complex tasks.

Term	"KWL"
What it is	"KWL" stands for "What I Know, What I Want to Know, and What I've Learned." KWLs are charts that learners use to track their understanding across a lesson. Variations include "TWD" (Think, Wonder, Learned) and "KWHL" (Know, Want to Know, How I Plan to Find Out, and Learned)
How it works	At the beginning of a lesson, learners complete the "K" section by listing out everything they believe to be true about a topic. Next, learners add their questions about the topic in the "W" section. The "W" section can also be used to list conflicting ideas that the class might have about a topic. Once the "W" section is complete, learners begin researching the topic through the lesson activities. Youth add their new or clarified knowledge to the "L" section at the end of the lesson. During the lesson debrief at the end, youth compare their ideas in "K" to their understandings in "L." They also check to see which questions were answered and which remain as topics for future investigation.
When to use it	KWL charts can be used to see what youth know (or think they know) when beginning a new topic of study. They are also useful when youth are going to use print or digital materials to research a topic.

Term	Stay-Stray
What it is	Stay-Stray is a technique used for sharing ideas among groups. It is similar to a Gallery Walk, but the focus is on conversation.
How it works	When it is time for groups to share their work, one group member is designated as the "speaker." The speaker stays at the group's assigned work space and is responsible for explaining the group's ideas. The other group members are designated as "strayers." Strayers are responsible for visiting the other groups and learning how they approached their work. After a few minutes, all group members return to their assigned work areas. Strayers share with their group members what they learned by visiting the other stations. The speaker shares any questions or new ideas that came up in conversation with strayers from other groups.
When to use it	Use Stay-Stray as a tool for promoting conversation among learners while sharing group work results. It is especially useful when learners have been sitting and need a movement break.

Term	Think Time
What it is	Think Time is just what it says: time given to learners to think. "Think-Pair-Share," "Think-Write-Pair-Share," "Turn and Talk," and "Wait Time" are all common variations of Think Time.
How it works	After asking a question, wait at least 5 seconds before collecting youth responses. This is "Wait Time." Think Time can be extended by having learners jot ideas down and/or share their responses with a partner ("Think-Pair-Share" or "Turn and Talk") prior to sharing with the whole group. Providing Think Time is important because it allows learners time to gather their thoughts and mentally practice their responses. It also allows learners to think more deeply about questions, opening up opportunities for richer discussion. Finally, it holds more learners accountable. All learners are more likely to think about the question when they know that "the answer" won't be shared immediately. Using partner talk increases the accountability even more, as all learners then need to participate in the lesson.
When to use it	Every time a question is posed.

Term	Ticket Out the Door (also known as "Exit Ticket")
What it is	Ticket Out the Door is a quick (2-3 minute) task that learners complete at the very end of the lesson.
How it works	At the very end of a lesson, learners complete a quick task, no more than 2-3 minutes in length. Common tasks include application questions that learners answer based on the lesson, sketching activities, or reflective activities. Sometimes, Tickets Out the Door ask learners to write down areas of confusion. Tickets Out the Door provide immediate, formative feedback for teachers to help plan for the next lesson. They allow teachers to see what learners have taken away from the lesson as well as what items are still confusing and need further clarification.
When to use it	Tickets Out the Door can be used when new material is introduced or learners encounter particularly difficult material in a unit. Use them any time more information is needed about learner progress.

Appendix D

Glossary of Scientific Terms

Appendix D: Glossary of Scientific Terms

In this section, you will find definitions for the scientific vocabulary terms that appear throughout the unit. If you have questions about terms that refer to teaching activities, please see the section entitled, "Teaching Tips and Techniques."

Abiotic factor: a non-living factor that affects the way organisms live in an ecosystem. Light, climate, water quality, and soil type are all examples of abiotic factors.

Airway passage filters: a first-line defense system in the human body. The shape of the airway passages in the human body can help trap pathogens. For example, pathogens can get trapped in the curve of the nasal cavity and thus prevented from infecting the body.

Antibiotic: chemicals that are known to kill or weaken bacteria. Antibiotics are used in medicines designed to treat bacterial infections. In the past few decades, there has been a rapid increase in the number of antibiotics used in non-medical products, including soap, hand sanitizer, and cleaning products. Antibiotics are also widely used in animal feed to prevent disease among livestock. The use of antibiotics is controversial, as bacteria can develop resistance to the chemicals, making them ineffective.

Bacteria: a type of single-celled organism. Bacteria are classified as prokaryotic organisms, as they do not have membrane-enclosed nuclei or other similar structures (organelles). Bacteria are the most abundant life forms on our planet.
Singular: bacterium
Biodiversity: the variety of species that inhabit an ecosystem

Biomass: the total mass of all the organisms in an ecosystem

Biotic factor: the living factors in an ecosystem. For example, a forest ecosystem may include competing populations of deer, squirrels, owls, snakes, worms, and oak trees among its many biotic factors.

Chemical Change: a change in the chemical structure and atomic bonding of matter. Chemical changes are often accompanied by a gas being released, a temperature change, a change in color, or a change in odor. Burning paper causes a chemical change, changing paper into ash.

Cilia: minute hairlike organelles, identical in structure to flagella, that line the surfaces of certain cells and beat in rhythmic waves, providing locomotion to ciliate protozoans and moving liquids along internal epithelial tissue in animals.

Commensalism: a relationship between species in which one organism benefits while the other is neither harmed nor benefitted. For example, some tropical plants known as epiphytes grow on host trees. The epiphytes get nutrients from the atmosphere and are better able reach sunlight and water. They do not appear to affect the host trees in any way, either positively or negatively.

Consumer: an organism that gets energy by eating other organisms. For example, a grasshopper eats grass. Lions eat zebras. Bears eat berries and fish. Fish eat grasshoppers. These are all consumers because they eat other organisms to survive.

Decomposer: an organism that gets energy by chemically breaking down the remains of other organisms. The decomposition process also returns stored nutrients from the dead organisms back to the ecosystem. Fungi and bacteria are common decomposers.

Decomposition: the process by which dead organisms are broken down chemically into component nutrients. For example, as dead trees decompose, they are broken into carbon and nitrogen, among other elements.

Design: Problem-solving choices made consciously by an individual or a group in order to most effectively reach a goal within agreed-upon constraints.

Digestion: the process through which organisms chemically break down food into component nutrients that can be used by their cells.

Digestive System: the system of organs in the human body that helps humans to extract nutrients and energy from food. The tongue, esophagus, stomach, and intestines are some components of the human digestive system.

E. coli: Escherichia coli is the most well-studied bacteria. It is a very common bacteria and one of the major microbes in the gut of healthy humans. However, some strains are pathogenic and can cause severe cramps, bloody diarrhea, and vomiting.

Ecosystem: the movement of energy and recycling of matter in a particular location. Ecosystems are defined by the relationships among biotic and abiotic factors. Commonly studied ecosystems include tundra, desert, forest, grassland, and estuarine ecosystems.

Engineering: a branch of applied science and math with a focus on real-world problem-solving

Epidemiologist: a scientist who studies epidemiology

Epidemiology: the study of the spread of disease

First-line defenses: the passive defense systems of the body that do not require active immune response. These are defense systems that are preventative in nature and include skin, mucus, and airway passage filters.

Foodborne Illness: a disease caused by a microbe that was transmitted to its host through the food supply. "Food poisoning" refers to a variety of foodborne illnesses, including salmonellosis and E. coli infections.

Food Safety: a series of practices designed to minimize risks posed by microbes in the food supply. Food safety practices include proper hand washing, cooking food thoroughly, keeping perishable items chilled, cleaning food preparation surfaces and tools, and keeping different types of food separated to avoid cross-contamination.

Fungi: Fungi are eukaryotic, since their cells do contain a nucleus. Mushrooms are fungi, as are microorganisms such as yeasts and molds. Singular: fungus

Germ: a microorganism, especially when disease-producing; microbe.

Host: the organism that provides food, shelter, or other benefits for another organism. For example, chickens can host the Salmonella bacterium.

Immune System: the system of first-line defenses and active responses that prevent pathogens from causing harm to an organism

Immune System Response: the active phase of the immune system. When an invading pathogen breaches the first-line defenses, the immune system sends cells to seek out the pathogen and destroy it.

Matter: all of the "stuff" in the universe. Anything made of atoms or subatomic particles is matter. Matter has mass and thus can be measured.

Mass: the amount of matter something has

Microbe: any one of a number of organisms too small to be seen without a microscope. Bacteria, viruses, and many fungi are all considered microbes.

Microbiodiversity: the variety of microbes that inhabit an ecosystem

Microbiome: the term given to the microbes that live within/on a particular organism
MRSA: methicillin-resistant Staphylococcus aureus, a bacterium that is highly resistant to methicillin, penicillin, and certain other antibiotics, and may cause infections of the skin, blood, lungs, etc.

Mucous Membranes: a first-line defense. Mucous membranes are the sticky membranes that line the inside of the nose, the airway, and the throat, as well as other openings in the human body. Pathogens are trapped by the sticky mucus and prevented from doing harm.

Mutualism: a relationship between species in which both organisms benefit. Cleaning stations on coral reefs are examples of mutualism; the cleaner fish benefits by getting food, while the other fish benefit by having their parasites cleaned away.

Pathogen: a disease-causing agent, such as a microbe, that harms the host organism

Protozoa: single-celled eukaryotic organisms that behave in ways more similar to animals than to plants, particularly with regards to mobility and heterotrophy (they do not make their own food). Some protozoa, such as certain amoebas, are human pathogens. Singular: protozoan

Physical Change: a physical change occurs when matter changes shape or state, but the chemical bonds between atoms are not affected. For example, tearing paper into bits and melting ice are examples of physical changes.

Producer: an organism that is able to make its own food using energy from the environment. Plants are producers, as are some photosynthetic and chemosynthetic bacteria.

Salmonella: a bacterium widely found in the environment that is also pathogenic to humans. Salmonella can be transmitted through contact with reptiles, particularly turtles. It can also be transmitted through undercooked food, particularly poultry products, and through unwashed vegetables. In humans, the Salmonella bacterium commonly causes a disease known as salmonellosis. Some strains of Salmonella are also responsible for typhoid fever.

Salmonellosis: a disease caused in humans by the Salmonella bacteria. Symptoms of salmonellosis include diarrhea, fever, and severe abdominal cramps, usually lasting for several days. Salmonellosis is a very common form of food poisoning and can be very dangerous for children, the elderly, and persons with compromised immune systems.

Skin: the outer covering of the human body. This organ is an important first-line defense system.

Streptococcus pharyngitis: the bacteria responsible for strep throat.

Virus: a microbe that replicates itself by taking over cells in a host organism. At this time, there is debate among scientists as to whether viruses are actually considered to be living organisms. Unlike pathogenic bacteria, viruses cannot be killed using antibiotic medicines.

References

Lesson 2

Arias, R. Mushroom in Forest [Online Image].
Retrieved December 9, 2016 from https://unsplash.com/@rariasg?photo=ihpiRgog1vs licensed under CC0

Dennis, D. (2007). Millipede [Online Image].
Retrieved December 9, 2016 from https://www.flickr.com/photos/davidden/ licensed under CC BY-SA 2.0

Balazs, B. Mushroom/Ladybug [Online Image].
Retrieved December 9, 2016 from https://unsplash.com/@brenkee?photo=fc_tWL1W3TI licensed under CC0

Cessati, G. Alligator, Italy [Online Image].
Retrieved December 9, 2016 from https://unsplash.com/gaetanocessati?photo=YOX8ZMTo7hk licensed under CC0

Gallarotti, F. Seedlings [Online Image].
Retrieved December 9, 2016 from https://unsplash.com/@gallarotti?photo=ruQHpukrN7c licensed under CC0

Hail, E. Meadows Farms Nurseries, Sunflowers [Online Image].
Retrieved December 9, 2016 from https://unsplash.com/@elijahhail?photo=29GUdIWrink licensed under CC0

Hobbs, A. Lily Pads [Online image].
Retrieved March 13, 2017 from https://flic.kr/p/9YTx86 licensed under CC BY-ND 2.0

Kinghorn, J. Walking the Dog [Online image].
Retrieved March 13, 2017 from https://flic.kr/p/nVVy8a licensed under CC BY-SA 2.0

Lastra, P. Dragonfly [Online Image].
Retrieved December 9, 2016 from https://unsplash.com/@peterlaster?photo=5oRzZU5uwSM licensed under CC0

Matthew. Picking Strawberries [Online image].
Retrieved March 13, 2017 from https://flic.kr/p/M6fVz licensed under CC BY-SA 2.0

Mayer, K. Caspian and the house [Online image].
Retrieved March 13, 2017 from https://flic.kr/p/bNfBZX licensed under CC BY 2.0

McCurdy, G. Red Maple Leaves [Online Image].
Retrieved December 9, 2016 from https://unsplash.com/@gmccurdy?photo=KOKxOB8550Q licensed under CC0

Morgan, B. Child on water with camera. [Online Image].
Retrieved December 9, 2016 from https://unsplash.com/@littleppl85?photo=lTbvhkaTfGU licensed under CC0

Pons, A. Puppy on Beach [Online Image].
Retrieved December 9, 2016 from https://unsplash.com/@a_pons?photo=oH9AuO20kbk licensed under CC0

Robinson, W. Palm Trees [Online Image].
Retrieved December 9, 2016 from https://unsplash.com/@wrrobinson?photo=Ud9lKknu9c0 licensed under CC0

Sauvin, T. Sea Turtle [Online Image].
Retrieved December 9, 2016 from https://unsplash.com/@tanguysauvin?photo=IBEXUZBmlXg licensed under CC0
Selena N. B. H. Mushrooms {Online image].
Retrieved March 13, 2017 from https://flic.kr/p/af7HgQ licensed under CC BY 2.0

Smith, M. Trees on a Beach [Online Image].
Retrieved December 9, 2016 from https://unsplash.com/@whale?photo=5YJSXfUONqA licensed under CC0

Stainless Images. Bull [Online Image].
Retrieved December 9, 2016 from https://unsplash.com/@ramone?photo=9uOasewOoXc licensed under CC0

Vigerova, M. Red/Orange Mushroom [Online Image].
Retrieved December 9, 2016 from https://unsplash.com/@mili_vigerova?photo=on6575qnuzg licensed under CC0

Romero, X. Orange Sunflowers [Online Image].
Retrieved December 9, 2016 from https://unsplash.com/@xromero?photo=FqpYln_x_Jl licensed under CC0

Trudeau, F. Lizard [Online image].
Retrieved March 13, 2017 from https://flic.kr/p/9LGZ8N licensed under CC BY-SA 2.0

Wylie, S. Forest Sunlight [Online image].
Retrieved March 13, 2017 from https://flic.kr/p/bkdtAF licensed under CC BY 2.0

Young, J. Pine Trees in the Sun. [Online Image].
Retrieved December 9, 2016 from https://unsplash.com/@duffuff?photo=MZVXrjKYgow licensed under CC0

Lesson 3

“commensalism”. The American Heritage® Science Dictionary. Houghton Mifflin Company. 27 Feb. 2017. <Dictionary.com http://www.dictionary.com/browse/commensalism>.

Doncaster, K. Erosion [Online image].
Retrieved March 13, 2017 from https://flic.kr/p/HHpMiF licensed under CC BY 2.0

Gube, J. Burnt Paper Texture 01 [Online image].
Retrieved March 13, 2017 from https://flic.kr/p/6DD7ng licensed under CC BY-SA 2.0

Mai, A. Tuesday nights are for red velvet cupcakes [Online image].
Retrieved March 13, 2017 from https://flic.kr/p/bCV75t licensed under CC BY-SA 2.0

m01229. Cutting wrapping paper with scissors [Online image].
Retrieved March 13, 2017 from https://flic.kr/p/imbPYH licensed under CC BY 2.0

“mutualism”. The American Heritage® Science Dictionary. Houghton Mifflin Company. 27 Feb. 2017. <Dictionary.com http://www.dictionary.com/browse/mutualism>.

west, I. melting [Online image].
Retrieved March 13, 2017 from https://flic.kr/p/5Sfz58 licensed under CC BY 2.0

Grigoras, I. Yogurt in Mason Jars [Online Image].
Retrieved January 3, 2018 from https://unsplash.com/photos/ZzZzXCsgl3w licensed under CC0

Lesson 4

"cilia". Dictionary.com Unabridged. Random House, Inc. 13 Dec. 2016. <Dictionary.com http://www.dictionary.com/browse/cilia>.

Gathany, J. Sneeze in progress. CDC/ Brian Judd [Online image].
Retrieved March 13, 2017 from https://phil.cdc.gov/phil/details.asp?pid=11162 Public Domain

Gold, D. Desert Floor. [Online Image].
Retrieved December 14, 2016 from https://unsplash.com/@dangold?photo=6sVGW87o8tM licensed under CC0

Howard, L. Scanning electron microscope image of lung trachea epithelium [Online image].
Retrieved March 13, 2017 from https://commons.wikimedia.org/wiki/File%3ABronchiolar_epithelium_4_-_SEM.jpg
Public Domain

Scottow, A. Skin [Online image].
Retrieved March 13, 2017 from https://flic.kr/p/dwkMY8 licensed under CC BY-SA 2.0

Lesson 5

Joel, J. 90111-050-E8E8B313 SEM of Streptococcus pyrogens bacteria [Online image].
Retrieved March 13, 2017 from https://flic.kr/p/fbwY35 licensed under CC BY-ND 2.0

Keenan, A. Children washing hands, Chiang Mai, Pa Daet, Thailand. [Online Image].
Retrieved December 19, 2016 from https://unsplash.com/@akeenster?photo=_h_weGa3eGo licensed under CC0

"mrsa". Dictionary.com Unabridged. Random House, Inc. 19 Dec. 2016. <Dictionary.com http://www.dictionary.com/browse/mrsa>.

NIAID. E. coli Bacteria [Online Image].
Retrieved December 14, 2016 from www.flickr.com licensed under CC BY 2.0

NIAID. E. coli Bacteria [Online image].
Retreived March 13, 2017 from https://flic.kr/p/rg1p9H licensed under CC BY 2.0

NIAID. Micrograph of Methicillin-Resistant Staphylococcus aureus (MRSA) [Online Image].
Retrieved December 14, 2016 from www.flickr.com licensed under CC BY 2.0

NIAID. Methicillin-Resistant Staphylococcus aureus (MRSA) Bacteria [Online image].
Retrieved March 13, 2017 from https://flic.kr/p/9y4sDM licensed under CC BY 2.0

NIAID. Salmonella Bacteria [Online image].
Retrieved March 13, 2017 from https://flic.kr/p/9y4sD6 licensed under CC BY 2.0

NIAID. Salmonella Bacteria [Online Image].
Retrieved December 14, 2016 from www.flickr.com licensed under CC BY 2.0

NIAID. Staphylococcus aureus Bacteria [Online Image].
Retrieved December 14, 2016 from www.flickr.com licensed under CC BY 2.0

Lesson 6

Inay, A. Brunch Dining. [Online Image].
Retrieved December 20, 2016 from https://unsplash.com/@inayali?photo=y3aP9oo9Pjc licensed under CC0

Sikkema, K. Child grabbing strawberry. [Online Image].
Retrieved March 8, 2017 from https://unsplash.com/@kellysikkema?photo=PMxoh8zJNb0 licensed under CC0

Grab and Go 1

"germ". Dictionary.com Unabridged. Random House, Inc. 21 Dec. 2016. <Dictionary.com http://www.dictionary.com/browse/germ>.

Zeller, S. mannequin. [Online Image].
Retrieved December 21, 2016 from https://unsplash.com/@samuelzeller?photo=QJHzMkfrJpI licensed under CC0

Grab and Go 2

Rouse, A.D. Palace of Versailles, Versailles, France. Cheese and Bread. [Online Image].
Retrieved December 21, 2016 from https://unsplash.com/@alicekat?photo=9MzCd76xLGk licensed under CC0

Grab and Go 3

"Danger Zone" (40 °F - 140 °F)." Danger Zone. USDA, 27 June 2013. Web. 04 Jan. 2017.

"Keep School Lunches Safe." Keep School Lunches Safe | FoodSafety.gov. Foodsafety.gov, 7 Sept. 2010. Web. 04 Jan. 2017.

Links:

http://www.foodsafety.gov/blog/school_lunch.html
http://www.fsis.usda.gov/wps/portal/fsis/topics/food-safety-education/get-answers/food-safety-fact-sheets/safe-food-handling/danger-zone-40-f-140-f/ct_index
http://www.fsis.usda.gov/wps/wcm/connect/8b705ede-f4dc-4b31-a745-836e66eeb0f4/Danger_Zone.pdf?MOD=AJPERES

Lesson 5 Print Materials

NIAID. E. coli Bacteria [Online Image].
Retrieved December 14, 2016 from www.flickr.com licensed under CC BY 2.0

NIAID. Micrograph of Methicillin-Resistant Staphylococcus aureus (MRSA) [Online Image].
Retrieved December 14, 2016 from www.flickr.com licensed under CC BY 2.0

NIAID. Salmonella Bacteria [Online Image].
Retrieved December 14, 2016 from www.flickr.com licensed under CC BY 2.0

NIAID. Staphylococcus aureus Bacteria [Online Image].
Retrieved December 14, 2016 from www.flickr.com licensed under CC BY 2.0

General

Salmonellosis. (2009, November 16). Centers for Disease Control and Prevention.
Retrieved December 26, 2013, from http://www.cdc.gov/nczved/divisions/dfbmd/diseases/salmonellosis/

Wenner, M. (2007, November 30). Humans carry more bacterial cells than human ones. Scientific American.
Retrieved December 26, 2013, from http://www.scientificamerican.com/article.cfm?id=strange-but-true-humans-carry-more-bacterial-cells-than-human-ones

www.ingramcontent.com/pod-product-compliance
Lightning Source LLC
LaVergne TN
LVHW070909210926
848482LV00017B/1034
* 9 7 8 1 7 3 2 9 8 2 3 0 7 *